'The joy of Jason Burke's book is that his account of people and places caught up in complex and ferocious struggles is based on long personal experience . . . Burke's account is by far the best to appear on the intertwined battles sparked off by 9/11'
Patrick Cockburn, *Mail on Sunday*

'Insightful, thorough, and at times fascinating . . . leaves the reader more informed, though often appalled by policymakers' ignorance and furious when well-intentioned policies backfire' Daniel Byman, *Foreign Policy*

'At a time when more books than ever have been published about terrorism, *The 9/11 Wars* must certainly be considered one of the best' al-Sharq al-Awsat

'For the sheer pleasure of reading top-notch journalism, this is the one book about the last decade you can't fail to read' Arun J Nair, *Hindustan Times*

'Burke's book may never be bettered as a holistic account of what followed from the 9/11 attacks' Whit Mason, *The Australian*

'His is a history from below, not of the kind written by court historians, academics or parachuted journalists who make episodic visits to the war zone. He has been, and remains, a reporter who has spent a great deal of time the field, and it tells in the work' Manoj Joshi, *Mail Today*, India

## ABOUT THE AUTHOR

Jason Burke is the South Asia correspondent for the *Guardian*. He has reported around the world for both the *Guardian* and the *Observer*. He is the author of two other widely praised books, both published by Penguin: *Al-Qaeda* and *On the Road to Kandahar*. He lives in New Delhi.

# JASON BURKE

# The 9/11 Wars

PENGUIN BOOKS

PENGUIN BOOKS

Published by the Penguin Group
Penguin Books Ltd, 80 Strand, London WC2R ORL, England
Penguin Group (USA), Inc., 375 Hudson Street, New York, New York 10014, USA
Penguin Group (Canada), 90 Eglinton Avenue East, Suite 700, Toronto, Ontario, Canada M4P 2Y3
(a division of Pearson Penguin Canada Inc.)
Penguin Ireland, 25 St Stephen's Green, Dublin 2, Ireland (a division of Penguin Books Ltd)
Penguin Group (Australia), 250 Camberwell Road, Camberwell, Victoria 3124, Australia
(a division of Pearson Australia Group Pty Ltd)
Penguin Books India Pvt Ltd, 11 Community Centre, Panchsheel Park, New Delhi – 110 017, India
Penguin Group (NZ), 67 Apollo Drive, Rosedale, Auckland 0632, New Zealand
(a division of Pearson New Zealand Ltd)
Penguin Books (South Africa) (Pty) Ltd, Block D, Rosebank Office Park,
181 Jan Smuts Avenue, Parktown North, Gauteng 2193, South Africa

Penguin Books Ltd, Registered Offices: 80 Strand, London WC2R ORL, England

www.penguin.com

First published by Allen Lane 2011
Published in Penguin Books 2012
001

Copyright © Jason Burke, 2011

The moral right of the author has been asserted

Typeset by Jouve (UK), Milton Keynes
Printed in Great Britain by Clays Ltd, St Ives plc

A CIP catalogue record for this book is available from the British Library

ISBN: 978-0-141-04459-0

www.greenpenguin.co.uk

MIX
Paper from
responsible sources
FSC™ C018179
www.fsc.org

Penguin Books is committed to a sustainable
future for our business, our readers and our planet.
This book is made from Forest Stewardship
Council™ certified paper.

ALWAYS LEARNING

**PEARSON**

*To Anne-Sophie and to Victor*

# Contents

PART FIVE
## Afghanistan, Pakistan and Al-Qaeda: 2008

PART SIX
## Endgames: 2009–11

# List of Illustrations

# Acknowledgements

A long book means a long list of people to thank. First of all, there are all my various editors who, over the last fifteen years of foreign reporting, have sent me around the world on assignments that have been sometimes testing, always fascinating and often hugely enjoyable. Roger Alton, Paul Webster and John Mulholland at the *Observer* and Harriet Sherwood at the *Guardian* all funded trips, found me space and, equally important, gave me time to travel, to talk, to listen and to write.

Years of reporting means years of accumulated favours owed. There are many hundreds of fellow journalists, translators, fixers, drivers, experts, soldiers, bureaucrats, diplomats and others, too many to mention individually, to whom I am genuinely indebted for their generosity, company, learning, advice and assistance.

As for the writing of *The 9/11 Wars* itself, I would like particularly to thank Paul Harris and Marc Thibodeau for their helpful criticism of early drafts. I am particularly grateful to Iain King for his careful reading and to Toby Dodge, Owen Bennett-Jones, John Boone and Alexander Evans for agreeing to look over drafts. Owen's comments, astute and informed as ever, were of particular help.

Nadja Korinth, Aashish Jethra and Kailash Prasad all helped enthusiastically and competently with research and fact checking. A series of major events in 2011 meant scant time for final verifications. All errors are, of course, my own.

As ever, without the advice, inspiration, competence, drive and perspicacity of Toby Eady, my agent, and Simon Winder, my editor, this book would never have come to be. My thanks to them and all who work with them, especially David Watson for his fine work on the text.

My thanks too to my parents-in-law for their hospitality during long weeks at Lancieux and, of course, to my own parents, brothers and sisters for their forbearance and support for a stressed son or sibling.

But most of all my thanks to my wife, Anne-Sophie, for her love, understanding and encouragement and to Victor for his laugh.

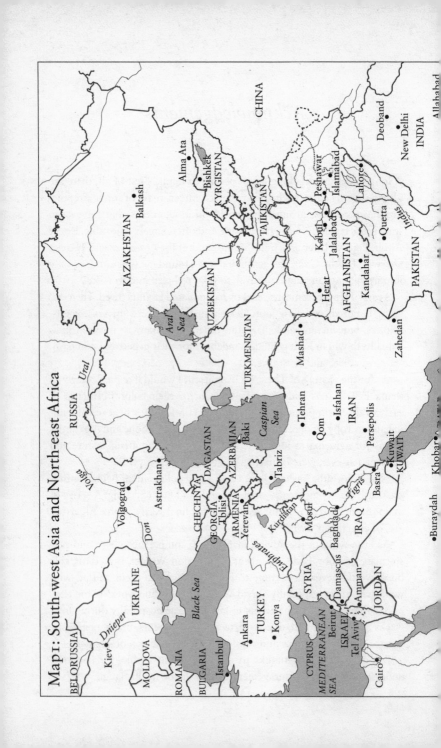

Map 1: South-west Asia and North-east Africa

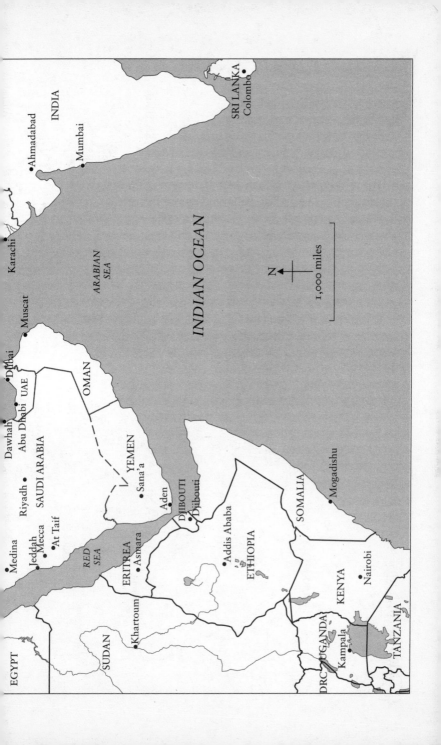

Map 2: Afghanistan and Pakistan

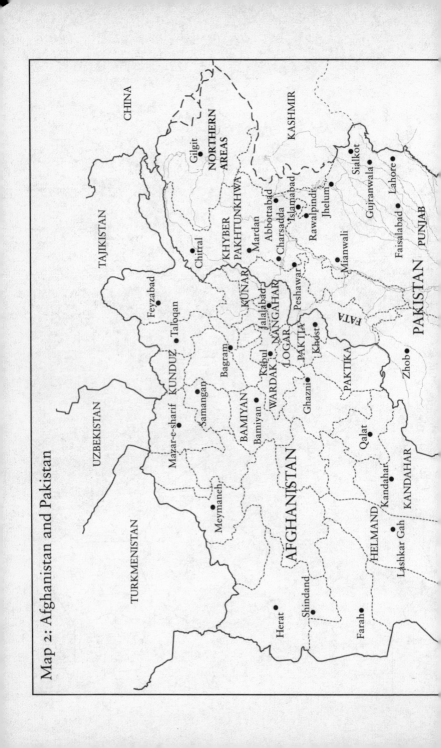

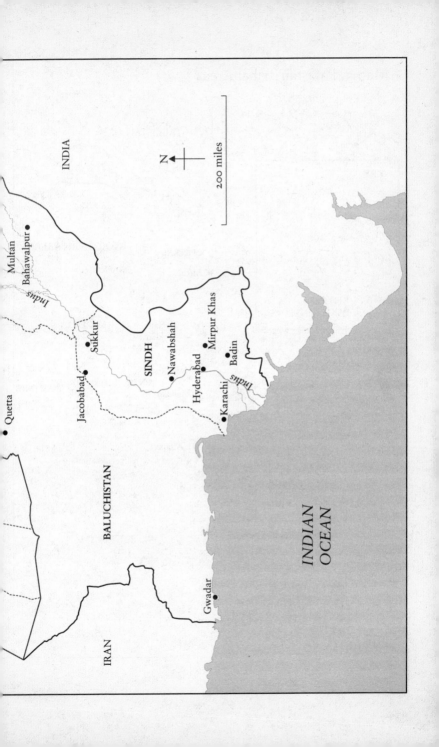

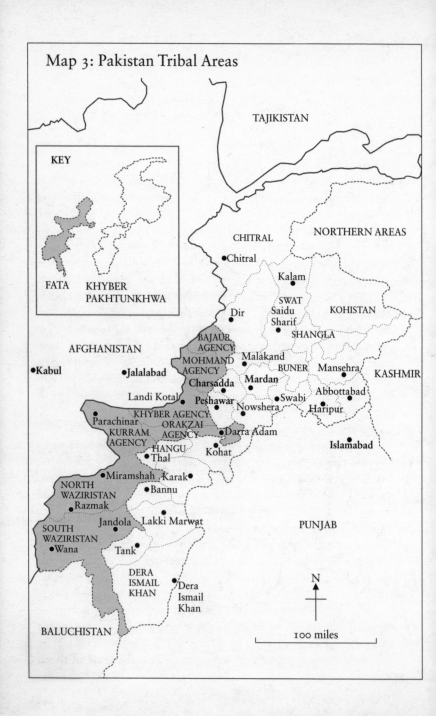

# Introduction

If you had looked down through binoculars on to the battered runway of Bagram in the summer of 1998 from frontline Taliban positions on the heights overlooking the Shomali plains, 30 miles north of Kabul, you would have seen little that indicated the role the old Soviet-built airbase could possibly play over the coming years. Through the dust and haze, you would have made out a cluster of ruined buildings surrounded by broad zones of overgrown land strewn with rusting metal stakes, a single battered jeep and no actual aircraft at all on the scarred strip of concrete shimmering in the Afghan sun. The group of scruffy Taliban fighters in filthy clothes who manned the makeshift trenches on the heights would probably have served grapes and tea to you as they did to the rare reporters who wandered up to the frontline in the dead years when no one was interested very much in an intractable and incomprehensible civil war in a far-off land. Occasionally, the fighters fired a rusty artillery piece in the general direction of the airstrip and of their enemies, usually hitting neither.

If you had come back four years later, say in the spring of 2002, you would have seen a startling difference. With the Taliban apparently defeated and dispersed, a bright new era for Afghanistan seemed to be dawning. The once-ruined airstrip down on the plains had become the fulcrum of a build-up of American and other international forces in the country that would continue inexorably over the next years. The bulldozers, the tents going up in the sand and the jets and helicopters lined up in serried ranks on the newly surfaced runway gave a sense that something extraordinary was happening, something of genuine historical importance. The only problem was that the exact nature of its importance was still very unclear. Now, many years on, though much inevitably remains obscured by the immediacy of events, something of that nature has become clearer. The form and the flow of events are beginning to emerge from the chaos of war. This book is an attempt to describe them and through describing them to make sense of them.

Bagram is now a small town of around 10,000 people, with its own shopping centres, gyms, evening classes, pizza parlour, Burger King, multi-denominational places of worship and mess halls all protected by treble rows of razor wire and electrified fences. The Taliban are in the hills around, though not yet back in their former positions from where they fired their poorly aimed shells and shared their tea and grapes.

As this book is rooted in many years of ground reporting, it has a different perspective from many of the works written about the events of the years since the attacks of September 11, 2001. Its focus is not the decisions taken in Western capitals but the effects of those decisions. Its aim is to suggest a grubby view from below, rather than a lofty view from above. It is primarily about people rather than about power, particularly people for whom life has changed in ways that no one could have predicted a decade ago. Occasionally these changes have been for the better; sometimes it is still too early to tell what they will bring; often these changes have been, savagely and brutally, for the worse. Sometimes these individuals and communities are passive victims. Often they are actors. Either way, they are not those whose decisions and motivations dominate many accounts. It is out of this intricate web of individuals, communities and events, however, that the story of the conflicts which we have watched, been touched by, even participated in directly or indirectly, is inevitably woven.

This account does not pretend to be objective. Though one aim of the book is to provide a historical record, it does not pretend to be comprehensive either. Such a work, even if practically realizable, would probably be unreadable. Too much has happened in too many places to too many people in too complex a way for it to be compressed and explained even in some 500 pages. The path this narrative takes is thus not necessarily the most direct or the most obvious. The places it visits are not always the most central. In journalism, analysis and academia there is a natural trend to the general, the global and the aggregated. The complex and often messy reality of history as it happens is reduced to single explanations or overarching theories. Though without synthesis nothing is comprehensible, there is a risk that, in reducing the complexity to find an answer, that answer is wrong. The devil is very often in the detail. Much of this book is devoted to exploring this detail.

The dangers of relying on broad generalizations or analyses that ignore the specificities of place, history, personality, culture and identity is very evident in the pages that follow. One early and costly error was a fundamental failure to properly understand the phenomenon of 'al-Qaeda'. This took years to right. A broader mistake which also proved tragically expensive in lives and resources was the insistence that the violence suddenly sweeping two, even three, continents was the product of a single, unitary conflict pitting good against evil, the West against Islam, the modern against the retrograde. For the last decade has not seen one conflict but many. Inevitably, a multi-polar, multifaceted, chaotic world without overarching ideological narratives generates conflicts in its own image. The events described in this book can only be understood as part of a matrix of ongoing, overlaid, interlinked and overlapping conflicts, some of which ended during the ten years since 9/11 and some of which started; some of which worsened and some of which died away; some of which have roots going back decades if not centuries and some of which are relatively recent in origin.

This is not a unique characteristic of the current crisis but is certainly one of its essential distinguishing qualities.[1] The wars that make up this most recent conflict span the globe geographically – from Indonesia in the east to the Atlantic-Mediterranean coastline in the west, from southwest China to south-west Spain, from small-town America to small-town Pakistan – as well as culturally, politically and ideologically. With no obvious starting point and no obvious end, with no sense of what might constitute victory or defeat, their chronological span is impossible to determine. No soldiers at the battle of Castillon in 1453 knew they were fighting in the last major engagement of the Hundred Years War. No one fighting at Waterloo could have known they were taking part in what turned out to be the ultimate confrontation of the Napoleonic Wars. The First World War was the Great War until the Second World War came along. Inevitably perhaps, this present conflict is currently without a name. In decades or centuries to come historians will no doubt find one – or several, as is usually the case. In the interim, given the one event that, in the Western public consciousness at least, saw hostilities commence, 'the 9/11 Wars' seems an apt working title for a conflict in progress.

Another major theme running through this work is inevitably that of religious extremism. What motivates the militants? How are they radicalized and mobilized? Why do they and how can they commit such terrible acts? The answer, as this narrative seeks to make clear, does not appear to lie in poverty, insanity or innate evil. Nor does it lie in Islam, though Islam, like all great religions, has a wide range of resources within it that can be deployed for a variety of functions including encouraging or legitimizing violence. The problem is not Islam but a particularly complex fusion of the secular and the religious that is extremely difficult to counter. The critical question is why this ideology, itself continually evolving, appeals to any given individual or community at a given moment. The answer, as one would expect, varies hugely over time and space. All ideologies are rooted in a context, and radical Islamic militancy is no different. These contexts inevitably change, and charting those shifts is one of the aims of this book.

Looking at violence leads into other major themes. It is now a commonplace to say that recent years have seen a hardening of identities based around ethnic, faith or other communities in response to the supposed 'flattening' of local difference by a process of globalization based in a heavily European or American market capitalist system. This is undoubtedly the case and has been consistently underestimated by policy-makers in London and Washington, who remain convinced of the universal attraction of the liberal democratic, liberal economic model in spite of much evidence to the contrary. But a key element missed by many analyses is the degree to which radical Islam is in itself as hostile to local specificity as anything that has come out of the West. One major current running through the pages that follow is the constant tug of war between 'the global' and 'the local', the general and the particular, the ideological and the individual. It is this tension that has defined much of the form and the course of the 9/11 Wars. The conflict was launched in the name of global ideologies. It was the rejection of global ideologies by key Muslim populations in the middle years of the decade that changed the course of the conflict. Ironically after years of vaunting the merits of the global, the West's greatest ally at a critical moment was its opposite: bloody-minded local particularism. The same force was also to work in less favourable ways elsewhere however.

This book ends with an account of the more recent phases of the conflict, where, even if cause for great concern still exists, the more apocalyptic predictions of a decade or so ago remain unfulfilled. This relative stabilization of the situation is precarious, however. Only a close examination of the previous course of 'the 9/11 Wars' and their antecedents can tell us whether what we are currently witnessing is simply a pause before a new cycle of violence or the uncertain early days of a definitive and positive trend towards something that resembles peace.

This book remains, however, primarily a work of journalism and not of history. It aims, in the long tradition of reportage, to reveal and communicate something about the world and about key events through the voices and views of those who participate in them and are affected by them. Its main aim is to provoke and inform discussion of vital questions rather than confidently lay out certitudes. As new material becomes available, others will improve the accounts of many of the events contained in the pages that follow. Overall I have tried to catch something of the nature of the conflict that has gripped and affected billions of people in recent years. Watching the aerial bombing of Tora Bora in the mountains of eastern Afghanistan in December 2001, with vapour trails from B-52s slicing across the pale sky above the snowy peaks and row upon row of rocky ridges successively lit by the slanting rising sun, a fellow journalist commented as a scene of untold horror and violence and extraordinary aesthetic beauty unfolded before us that only a vast novel really could make sense of what was happening. He was probably right.

# PART ONE

# Afghanistan, America, Al-Qaeda: 2001–3

# I

# The Buddhas

## ALI SHAH

The winter had been hard, and in March 2001 the snow still lay thick on the passes. The only road open into the valley was a thin trace of black meltwater and icy mud. The small Afghan town of Bamiyan was virtually deserted. Men of working or fighting age had either fled or been forced out by the fighters who now walked down the single street of the bazaar, squatted by their pick-up trucks or sat on the grubby, threadbare carpets of the *chaikhana*.[1] The sky was an icy blue overhead, and it was still very cold.[2] To the south of the town, in a shallow river valley, almond orchards and slender silver-leaved poplars lay below low hills covered in cemeteries and fields desiccated as much by the freezing winter nights as by the summer heat. Behind, stretching to the horizon, were the higher mountains of Afghanistan's central highlands banded in different shades of brown, ochre and sand like a beach at low tide and ending in snow. Through the slats of a stable door beside one small mud-brick and wood home in a stand of trees near the river, a young man, sixteen years old, carefully watched the fighters walking through the streets.

Ali Shah had left with his parents, two sisters and two brothers when the Taliban had first arrived in Bamiyan weeks earlier but had returned to check on the family home. He had slipped back, easily evading sentries on the paths through the hills. Years of guarding sheep on the hills around had given the teenager a deep knowledge of the remote tracks that crossed the apparently barren peaks. He watched through the slatted doors of the stables beside the locked house and waited.[3]

The town of Bamiyan lies at the intersection of four roads, 9,200 feet

3

up on an outlying spur of the Himalayan mountains. One leads west across the snowy peaks and ridges of Afghanistan's central highlands to the city of Herat and on to the Iranian frontier. A second leads southeast, across a high pass and through a narrow valley studded with small fortified villages and ribbed by terraced fields of wheat before dropping down to a shallow and fertile plain, where it joins the main road that runs from the Afghan capital Kabul down to Kandahar, the southern city that was the cultural and administrative centre of the Taliban. As this road drops off the high plateau of Bamiyan, it crosses the religious, ethnic, cultural and linguistic divide between the lands of the Shia Muslim Hazara, of central Asian ancestry, and the southern and eastern regions, where the ethnic Pashtuns, almost all Sunni Muslims, dominate.[4] The third road that leads out of Bamiyan runs north to the grassy steppes and eventually to the Amu Darya river and the frontier with the former Soviet Republics of Uzbekistan and Tajikistan. The fourth and final road leads east over yet another pass and down through a deep gorge to the fertile Shomali plains and the frontlines across which the fighters of the Taliban confronted the ragged troops of the Northern Alliance, the last remaining opposition to their rule over Afghanistan, firing desultory shells at Bagram airport and serving tea to the occasional visiting reporter.

Though in one of the poorest and most isolated provinces of Afghanistan, Bamiyan had once been a thriving and prosperous centre of trade and religion. In the fourth century, two huge Buddhas, one 175 feet high, the other 120, had been built into cavities hewn from the sandstone of the cliffs just to the north of the present-day town of Bamiyan. The statues themselves were not carved directly from the rock face but made of successive layers of mud and straw and finally painted plaster laid over a rock core. Beyond their religious purpose, they served too as giant landmarks for travellers on one of Asia's great trade routes.[5] With the vast statues, a monastery had been constructed, a mixture of wooden scaffolding built against the cliff face and caves. The Buddhist monks and believers who had once lived and studied there had long gone, as had the wooden passageways and façades, but even in 2001 the caves were still inhabited. The families who lived there were mainly destitute refugees who survived on thin earnings as shepherds and day labourers and ate stale bread scraps left over by the inhabitants of the town below their barely accessible and uncomfortable homes. The frescoes and murals on the inside of the monastic cells and pilgrims' accommodation had long since been defaced in waves of iconoclasm or simply obscured by the soot from decades of cooking fires. It was these giant Buddhas that the Taliban had come to destroy. Ali Shah waited until nightfall and slipped away.


## THE TALIBAN

In successive campaigns the Taliban had brought 80 per cent of Afghanistan under their nominal rule. The movement had its origins in a vigilante group founded by a mullah, the equivalent of a country priest or parson in clerical terms, near Kandahar in September 1994. The very fact that it was the mullahs, traditionally lowly figures in Afghan society, who were in charge signalled the revolutionary nature of the new movement. The new group's innovatory style of fighting, which involved night combat and highly mobile 'charges' on the back of pick-up trucks, was another radical change.[6] Though often described as 'medieval', the Taliban were thus profoundly contemporary. Ideologically they were radical too and 'revolutionary' in the sense of the word that would have been understood by rebels seeking a return to an imagined earlier era of social justice across the ages. A worldview and language heavily informed by a utopian vision of an idealized past hid the fact that they actually sought to create something that had never existed: an Afghan state and society that resembled in culture, government and religious practice the idea they had of a perfect Pashtun village. That idea may have been a myth, but it was very real to them, and so was the political project of creating it.

At the beginning the Taliban's aim had simply been to end the anarchy and civil war into which Afghanistan had been plunged at the end of the decade-long Soviet intervention in 1989.[7] But the movement very rapidly acquired a variety of different and sometimes contradictory agendas, each representing one of the myriad fracture lines of an Afghan society fragmented by decades of war and uneven development. Ethnic splits, cultural divides, resentments nurtured through a conflict in which the bulk of the fighting had pitted Afghans against other Afghans, as well as a host of external interests came rapidly into play. The name Taliban, an Arabo-Persian word which means seekers of knowledge or religious students, reflected the origins, leadership and project of the new movement.[8] Initially welcomed in many parts by a population tired of war and insecurity, the Taliban had advanced rapidly, aided by their opponents' lack of unity, by local traditions which encouraged rather than stigmatized changing sides at the right moment and, at critical moments, by logistic and technical aid from the main Pakistani military intelligence service, the Inter-Services Intelligence Directorate (ISI).[9] Skilfully exploiting all the fracture lines of Afghan society, Taliban leaders ignored urban areas and institutions and instigated an extremely effective rural grass-roots outreach programme.[10] Using networks of association built up through family or tribal connections, in the refugee camps of Pakistan or among fellow veterans of the Soviet war, they approached tribal leaders, militia commanders, anyone who they felt could be co-opted, offering security, moral certainty, a restoration of social justice and order and personal advancement.[11] Their uncompromising message was nonetheless carefully tailored to fit local needs and identities. Those Taliban leaders with particular knowledge of a specific district's customs, history and dialects were sent there. Where a little encouragement was still needed, intimidation and selective violence usually sufficed.

Yet not only were the Taliban unable to turn their vision into reality but they proved incapable even of beginning to tackle the myriad problems of the country. In September 1996 the Taliban had captured Kabul, where their conception of an ideal Afghanistan and their literal reading of the Islamic holy texts was very alien to the better-educated urbanites of the city, many of whom had lived well under the Soviets.[12] The latter, at least for the better-off and better-educated, had been modern and liberal rulers who cleared slums, built schools and polytechnics and offered employment in a new, sprawling bureaucracy and military. Though the depredations of the post-Soviet period when the various *mujahideen* factions had fought over the capital meant that the Taliban seizure of the city was welcomed by some Kabulis, the five years that followed had seen increasing repression, haphazard government, growing violence against opponents and dissidents, and, apart from the booming drugs industry, a moribund economy. It had also seen the failure of the Taliban's early attempts to distance themselves from the rest of the world. Partly this was due to their own need for weapons, manpower and instruction, much of which came from across the border in Pakistan. Partly this was due to the fact that, as had been the case through the nineteenth century and before, Afghanistan was a ground across which the rivalries of bigger powers played out.

Some of these powers were formal states recognized by international law. The security establishment and successive governments of Pakistan had seen the Taliban as the perfect vehicle to project their own interests in Afghanistan and funnelled money, fuel, food, advice and ammunition to these new actors on the Afghan scene.[13] Very significant numbers of young fighters came from the religious schools of Pakistan's north-west frontier, where many Afghans, refugees or otherwise, were educated. Others sent over from the religious schools in Pakistan's eastern province of the Punjab were easily recognizable. The author found squads of them doing star jumps on the frontline north of Kabul in 1999. Other overseas allies were non-state actors, though powerful nonetheless. Much of the movement's money came through donations from clerical networks in Pakistan and further afield. Rich donors in the Gulf, devout and deeply conservative Muslim businessmen or royalty, contributed significant funds, happy to help to further the spread of the rigorous strands of Sunni Islam that they themselves followed.

If the web of alliances, funding streams and ideological strands drawn together in the Taliban was complicated so too were the networks that centred on the various factions opposed to their rule. Limited to the north and north-east of the country, denuded of material and men, each broadly representing a different ethnic minority, these groups were dependent on different regional sponsors for money and weapons and connected to different drugs or smuggling networks. The Hazara minority, for example, made up between 10 and 15 per cent of the overall Afghan population, and their factions were backed by the Iranians. This created a Shia axis that was a counterpart to the informal Taliban–Pakistani Sunni alliance on Afghanistan's other flank. The Uzbeks constituted 5 to 15 per cent, and their militia were supported by Uzbekistan. The Tajiks, who made up around 20 or 25 per cent, got funding and weapons from Tajikistan and from India.[14]

Amidst all these frames of geopolitical and regional alignment, the enormous majority of Afghans simply tried to survive. A measure of the plight of the Afghan people was that in 2001 nobody knew how many of them there were as there had been no census since 1979. Around 5 million were estimated to be living outside the country, largely in refugee camps in Iran and Pakistan, and perhaps 15 million remained in

Afghanistan. The population of Kabul was around half a million and, though it was by far the biggest Afghan city, its streets were empty, bazaars were bare, fuel was scarce and electricity rarer still. The only entertainments were executions and occasional football matches in the city's sports stadium, woefully ill-equipped gyms and boxing clubs, which provided an outlet for jobless teenagers, and a motorcyclist who set up a 'wall of death' in the central Ariana Square. That most of the spectators at the executions the author attended were there simply because there was nothing else to do was ample testament to the desperation and meanness of their lives. Many hours each day were devoted to procuring enough fuel in the winter and clean water in the summer. Ministers with little more than a basic religious education sat in the corner of decrepit offices warmed by Chinese-made bar heaters. A handful of students walked through the derelict halls of the university and the polytechnic was too heavily mined to be used. On the wall of the offices of the religious police, who were largely composed of young men armed with sticks or lengths of rubber hose who harassed women whom they deemed immodestly dressed or men whose beards were under the regulation length of the width of a fist, a scrawled slogan read: 'Throw reason to the dogs, it stinks of corruption.' The rural areas were worse. In the north-eastern Badakshan province, communities stockpiled animal fodder for human consumption. Life expectancy was around forty-two years (one year more than it had been in 1990), literacy rates were no more than 30 per cent, and 18 in every thousand women who gave birth died, the highest rate in the world. The word that featured most frequently in conversation with ordinary Afghans in the years before 9/11 was *mushkil*, difficult. This was the backdrop against which the first encounters of the 9/11 Wars were fought.[15]


## BAMIYAN


The way into Bamiyan for the Taliban had been opened when a local commander had swapped sides in the classic Afghan fashion to allow his erstwhile enemies across the northern passes into the valley. Desultory fighting had continued for some months, however, and finally a specially constituted Taliban 'taskforce' was dispatched in January 2001 with the aim of subduing the central highlands and the Hazaras once and for all. Its young commander was Mullah Dadaullah Akhund, who had already acquired a reputation for brutality, atrocity and violence.[16] Charged with establishing full Taliban control in Bamiyan, Dadaullah set to work with terrible efficiency. In two days alone, his troops, reinforced by international militants and hundreds of teenagers from religious schools in Pakistan, used bulldozers, explosives and their bare hands to destroy villages, schools, mosques, clinics and orchards, effectively replicating what the Soviets had done to much of the Afghan countryside in the 1980s. Around two-thirds of the local population fled. The family of Ali Shah, the young shepherd, was among them.[17]

With Bamiyan now securely in Taliban hands, the question of the future of the Buddhas was raised. A meeting of senior ministers was convened to decide their fate.[18] It was not the first time that demolishing the great Buddhas of Bamiyan had been envisaged. The 'destruction of icons' in Afghanistan had been discussed for many decades in the conservative Islamic circles from which the Taliban drew their religious inspiration and had always provoked fierce debate. Early on the Taliban had seemed to value the cultural heritage of Afghanistan, allowing themselves to be convinced that they should protect the Buddhas and other remnants of Afghanistan's pre-Islamic past just as Egypt had worked to preserve the pyramids, and when Dadaullah's request reached the Taliban ministers in Kabul many argued that the Buddhas should be left as they were as 'cultural monuments'.[19] But such voices had powerful opponents.[20] There had long been bitter arguments between moderates and conservatives within the Taliban over a variety of issues: tactics of ethnic cleansing, the education of girls, engagement with the international community, the ban on opium that had been successfully implemented in 2000.[21] This time the hardliners outmanoeuvred their opponents by the simple expedient of making sure the question of the Buddhas was referred to their supreme leader, Mullah Mohammed Omar.

In the spring of 2001 Mullah Omar was forty-two years old. Tall, dark-skinned, reclusive, of limited literacy, relatively inarticulate, he had recently swapped the cheap mass-produced Pakistani-made *shalwar kameez* he had worn previously for a higher-quality local version with traditional embroidery. His eye-patch had been replaced by a foreign-made glass eye.[22] Yet these small concessions to comfort barely countered the overall impression of asceticism. Omar rarely appeared in public and gave few interviews but did not need to be seen or heard to keep command. The authority of the Taliban leader depended instead on his reputation for fierce probity, his war record from the days the Soviet occupation and his subsequent success at leading the movement to control much of his country.[23] Whether receiving visitors sitting on a cheap prayer rug in the mud mosque of his village home or in the run-down residence of the governor in Kandahar, Omar, despite his modest appearance, remained unpredictable and independent-minded. The self-styled *amir-ul momineen*, leader of the faithful, was a charismatic and instinctive leader with a natural talent for spectacular symbolic gestures such as publicly wrapping himself in the cloak of the Prophet Mohammed, a relic kept for more than 200 years in Kandahar and rarely shown in public.[24] Even after several years in power, as the Taliban more generally had begun to lose the support of many of their key constituencies in the east and south of the country, Mullah Omar himself retained significant personal authority.[25]

Presented with the demand from Mullah Dadaullah for permission to destroy the Buddhas, Omar requested a judgement from the Afghan Supreme Court, which comprised senior religious scholars, or *ulema*. Courts were perhaps the only functioning institution in Afghanistan. They applied, with relative honesty, efficiency and speed, a rigorous and literalist interpretation of the Shariat, the body of law based on the Koran, the sayings and deeds of the prophets and centuries of interpretation, exegesis and precedent. The clerics of the Supreme Court, all extreme conservatives and all appointed by Omar, unsurprisingly ruled that the destruction of the Buddhas was not only in accordance with the teachings of Islam but also strongly recommended. On February 24 Omar personally radioed Dadaullah in Bamiyan with the news and personally gave his instructions for the statues to be levelled.[26]

Many different strands – from the cosmic to the brutally practical, from the parochial to the international – determined the decision. On one level, the destruction of the Buddhas was a carefully weighed and calculated political act which to many of Mullah Omar's followers at the time seemed a logical response to the strategic and tactical challenges facing them. From this perspective, it was fanatical, perhaps, but far from irrational.[27] Omar had many very mundane reasons to destroy the Buddhas. The first was rooted in the internal dynamics of the Taliban. In the months before the demolition, Omar had increasingly found himself under pressure from a faction of committed extremists among the senior ranks and the younger generation of extremely violent new leaders rising through middle ranks best represented by Mullah Dadaullah. Destroying the Buddhas was thus a useful way for Omar to marginalize any moderate challengers while rallying the hardliners behind him. Equally, with a new fighting season about to start and complete victory still distant even after nearly seven years of gruelling warfare, the destruction of the Buddhas would energize and radicalize a movement which was losing momentum in the face of growing discontent with their rule, even among constituencies which had previously supported them.[28] Also, the demolition of the Buddhas was an act of communication in a predominantly illiterate land used to such public spectacles of violence. Successive rulers in Afghanistan recognized the importance of such gestures. The Mughals in the sixteenth century had built 'pyramids of skulls' of their enemies and made sure that potential opponents were kept well informed of the extreme violence they risked if they resisted. Abdur Rahman, known as the Iron Emir and widely credited with building the basis of Afghanistan as a nation state in the late nineteenth century, had publicized rather than hidden the excesses associated with his repeated campaigns of ethnic cleansing.[29] The Taliban had always understood and exploited the symbolic and the ritual. Their public hanging of a corrupt, child-abusing warlord-cum-bandit in 1994 near Kandahar and subsequent dismantling of the 'chains', the roadblocks where armed groups extorted money and abused local traders and travellers, had been the foundational acts of the movement. With their delivery of justice haphazard, the Taliban relied on the visibility and violence of punishment rather than its inevitability to discourage crime. To have the desired deterrent effect, that violence had to be seen or, as very few Afghans had access to televisions, at least imagined.

Then there was a more mystic element. The destruction of the Buddhas was part of a continued violent campaign prosecuted by the Taliban to extirpate all that they saw as counter to their vision of the authentically 'Afghan' Afghanistan, whether that involved pre-Islamic artefacts, the presence of Shia Muslims such as the population in Bamiyan or on the Shomali plains, heresy and 'modern' or Western influences. The destruction of the Buddhas was also an act by which they would be doing God's work. The order to demolish, Mullah Omar told some interlocutors, had come to him in a dream.[30] 'If on Judgement Day I stand before Allah, I'll see those two statues floating before me, and I know that Allah will ask me why, when I had the power, I did not destroy them,' he told one visitor.[31]

Finally, there was the influence of the various international extremists who were based in Afghanistan in the late 1990s. The most prominent among them was the al-Qaeda group led by Osama bin Laden, who had arrived in Afghanistan in 1996 after being forced out of Sudan and who had, as the years had passed, become increasingly close to Omar.

Bin Laden's relationship with Omar and other senior Taliban has been the subject of much debate. Often described as close, in fact it appears to have been characterized more by ambivalence and tension than complicity.[32] The Taliban were constantly torn. On the one hand they admired the Saudi-born extremist's apparent grasp of global politics, respected his piety and needed the money he could bring them through his contacts in the Gulf as well as the fighters he could supply. But they nonetheless remained irritated by the lack of respect this foreigner frequently showed them, their people and, despite his occasional praise, their country. Continually concerned about the damage that his ambitions might do to their own campaigns, senior Taliban figures repeatedly described bin Laden, whose arrival in Afghanistan had been the result of an invitation extended by a group of warlords who had been their opponents, as 'a problem inherited from the days of the civil war'.[33] The tensions were rooted too in the mutual wariness between the Afghans and the largely Arab international militants of al-Qaeda – predominantly Egyptian, Yemeni, Saudi or Algerian – and exacerbated by profound differences of outlook, worldview, religious practice and strategy.[34] Bin Laden's enemy was different from that of the Taliban, who were focused on conquering the pockets of resistance to their rule in Afghanistan. Bin Laden and his associate, the veteran Egyptian militant Ayman al-Zawahiri, saw their primary targets as the regimes of the Middle East, particularly those ruling in their native lands, or, as they announced in a series of public statements, America. Few among the Taliban knew or cared much about the USA or were particularly preoccupied by the political situation in Egypt or Saudi Arabia.[35] A second difference was theological. The Taliban had been raised in the hierarchical Deobandi school of conservative Islam, a discrete south-west Asian strand of Islamic thinking and practices very different in crucial aspects from the Gulf-based schools of the international militants. One reason Omar had turned to the judges for a decision on the Bamiyan Buddhas was that, in the fiercely hierarchical tradition of Deobandism, a mere mullah such as the Taliban leader was simply not qualified to pass judgement on such a question. He and other senior Taliban figures were thus shocked and angered to see bin Laden giving interviews on television, which was banned in Afghanistan, and issuing *fatawa*, scholastic opinions which they believed should only be given by senior religious scholars, not autodidacts who had trained as civil engineers.[36]

Nonetheless the international extremists did have an influence. From late 1998 onwards, there is much evidence of a more internationalized outlook among the Taliban leadership. For the first time, their propaganda began to refer to Zionist spies and American Crusaders, phrases borrowed directly from men like bin Laden. If Mullah Omar had his own reasons, cosmic and mundane, for assenting to Dadaullah's request to destroy the Buddhas he was at the very least encouraged by the foreign extremists who increasingly determined his perception of the world beyond the borders of his homeland.

## THE WORLD TO THE RESCUE

The news of Omar's decision broke rapidly, and, one after another, a whole range of international actors set out to dissuade the Taliban. The first to fail were the Americans. Though to start with Washington welcomed the Taliban as a potential stabilizing force, that initial positive sentiment towards the movement was rapidly dissipated. First, there was increasing concern over human rights abuses. Then came the double bombing in 1998 of two US embassies in east Africa by al-Qaeda teams sent from Afghanistan and the subsequent refusal of the Taliban to withdraw their protection of bin Laden. The attack and the shelter offered to the perpetrators had provoked unilateral American sanctions in 1999 and a series of acrimonious exchanges through 2000. The affable Taliban ambassador in Islamabad, the capital of neighbouring Pakistan, continued to be received at the embassy – 'No one recognizes us but everyone recognizes me,' he explained – but apart from frequent demands made by State Department officials that bin Laden be handed over and occasional conversations it was a dialogue of the deaf.[37]

With no leverage on the Taliban the Americans were forced to rely on the Pakistanis. Islamabad sent both formal and informal deputations to

Kandahar and Kabul. Yet, though diplomatic as well as military assistance continued, Pakistan's leverage over the Taliban was less than was often thought, particularly following al-Qaeda's bombing of the embassies in east Africa and the messy battles around Mazar-e-Sharif in 1998 and 1999, during which widespread atrocities by both sides were widely reported.[38] A series of incidents – such as the beating of the Pakistani youth football team, who had made the mistake of wearing shorts to play in Kandahar, by the Taliban's religious police – had reinforced the impression that Islamabad was losing any grip it had once had on the movement.

By 2000, many in Pakistan's foreign ministry were expressing grave concerns about the diplomatic damage being done by their country's support for their increasingly unpredictable and extreme allies.[39] The Pakistani efforts to convince the Taliban to leave the Buddhas intact met with no success. Neither the interior minister nor retired senior Pakistani soldiers who had personally contributed to the movement's early victories were able to influence their former students to change their mind.

Relations with the Saudi Arabians had also soured long before. Along with Pakistan and the United Arab Emirates, Saudi Arabia had recognized the Taliban as the legitimate rulers of Afghanistan by 1997, seeing the movement as one of many vehicles for the propagation of the kingdom's brand of rigorous Sunni Islam across the Islamic world that merited financial and diplomatic support. This early enthusiasm had quickly evaporated, however. Again it was the presence of bin Laden and other militants that most angered Riyadh. After a particularly ill-tempered exchange following the bombings of 1998, official support for the Taliban ceased, though of course private Saudi Arabian supporters of the movement and their project remained numerous.[40] Unsurprisingly, Riyadh's efforts to influence the Taliban when news of the decision to destroy the Buddhas broke met with no success either. Given the propensity of the Saudi religious establishment for iconoclasm within the kingdom, that such efforts were relatively feeble surprised few.

For a time, there was hope that where the Pakistanis and Saudis could not or would not succeed the United Nations might. The UN had been present in Afghanistan for many years, and the Taliban, recognizing that the humanitarian work done by the organization at the very least spared them the trouble and expense of trying to feed and house hundreds of thousands of urban and rural poor, had initially cooperated relatively well with senior international officials. But the United Nations' values had often been difficult to reconcile with the Taliban's vision of Afghanistan. The idea that the organization represented some kind of benign 'international community' had little currency in a country where, at least in living memory, almost everything from abroad, and particularly from beyond the Islamic world, represented a threat. Senior Taliban figures, unsurprisingly given the widespread view among them that the UN was a Trojan horse for moral corruption and an assault on 'traditional' Afghan and Islamic values, had always showed profound hostility to UN staff, and relations only deteriorated further as time passed.[41] There continued to be contacts between the special United Nations envoy, veteran Spanish diplomat Francesc Vendrell, and high-ranking Taliban moderates with a more worldly outlook, but none of Vendrell's interlocutors had any real influence on Mullah Omar or on the direction the movement was taking. One of the last attempts to win a reprieve for the Buddhas saw an extraordinary meeting, organized by Vendrell, between Wakil Ahmed Muttawakel, the Taliban foreign minister, and Kofi Annan, the UN secretary general. It took place in the five-star Marriott Hotel in Islamabad. Few encounters better encapsulate the gulf between the Taliban and the developed, Westernized world than this between the urbane New-York-based Ghanaian diplomat and the envoy from Kabul. The meeting was polite, indeed relatively convivial. But even as Muttawakel pledged on behalf of his government that no harm would befall the Buddhas, preparations for their destruction were underway.[42]

The final attempt to save the Buddhas came from within the mainstream conservative Muslim community, in the person of the senior Qatar-based Egyptian cleric Yusuf al-Qaradawi. This could perhaps have been expected to stand a greater chance of success. Known throughout much of the Islamic world for his extremely popular and influential television programme in which he drew on his deep religious knowledge to issue instant *fatawa* in answer to viewers' queries about the correct Islamic response to topics as varied as oral sex and the plight of the Palestinians, al-Qaradawi travelled to Kandahar with a group of very senior conservative clerics intending to convince Mullah Omar to spare the Buddhas through a careful argument based on key Islamic texts, quotations and precedents. Classic diplomatic means involving bilateral relations and multilateral organizations had failed and this was an attempt founded in a long tradition in the Islamic world of debate and argument. However, not only were al-Qaradawi's ideological roots very different from the neo-traditional revivalism of the Taliban's religious culture but he was also seen as having 'sold out' to 'apostate' governments in the Arab world, not only by the international extremist clerics but also by their local Deobandi counterparts, to whom Omar was prone to listen for spiritual guidance. In many ways, al-Qaradawi's world, that of the major Islamic universities, of televised religious advice with audiences of millions, of the core Arab Middle East, was as alien to the Taliban as that of Kofi Annan. From the start the visit went badly with the eminent cleric's party ordered out of the cars bringing them from Kandahar airport and forced to pray in the sand by the side of the road by excited young Taliban fighters. Omar showed little interest in al-Qaradawi's sophisticated, learned and utterly pragmatic argument that, though the Taliban were justified in their belief that the Buddhas should be destroyed, there was an equally strong argument that the act, though undoubtedly legitimate, should be postponed until a more favourable conjuncture of political circumstances. Al-Qaradawi and his delegation left empty-handed, vocally complaining about their hosts' political immaturity.[43]

However, despite his apparent parochialism and mysticism, Omar sensed what effect the destruction of the Buddhas would have on the international community. Steps were taken to make sure that the audience overseas understood what was being said. His edict announcing the demolition was distributed to international journalists, the act itself was filmed by a cameraman, and its aftermath was later proudly shown to the international press.[44] To underline the message, Taliban spokesmen briefed reporters, claiming that the rest of the world had no right to complain. 'They give us nothing ... Why should we listen to them?' one senior Taliban official in Islamabad said. 'They care more about old statues than Afghans starving.'

The destruction of the Buddhas started at dawn on March 1 and took at least ten days. The practical difficulties of demolishing such enormous objects, built on to a cliff face, had been grossly underestimated. Tank shells and rockets fired had little effect, simply sending showers of splinters into the air. The Taliban, who had originally thought they could destroy the statues in a few hours, were forced to resort to other means, eventually stacking shells and loose explosives found in the stocks held by the warlords they had defeated or co-opted in the valley around the base of the statues. This too failed, however. On the morning of the third day, Taliban fighters and coerced local men were lowered on ropes from the galleries around the sculptures and, dangling above the void, drilled holes into the now rock-hard ancient clay and straw mix into which they introduced explosives prised out of mines. This had more effect, and repeated blasts over the next twenty-four hours slowly reduced the two giant edifices to piles of yellow rubble. Footage showed huge explosions blasting dust out of the cavities housing the Buddhas high into the air as turbaned Taliban fighters cheered with shouts of 'Allahu akbar' (God is great). Two great plumes of yellow dust and black smoke hung in the clear blue sky for many hours after the statues had ceased to exist.[45]

## THE BAMIYAN BUDDHAS
## AND THE 9/11 WARS

The episode had given an early glimpse of a multitude of key strands that would mark the future course of the 9/11 Wars. First of all, there was the complexity of the environment, a thick matrix of overlaid and interwoven legacies of scores of conflicts over previous decades and indeed centuries, meshing the local, national and geopolitical with the tribal, ethnic and individual. It showed too the variety and division within entities often seen from the outside as relatively monolithic, whether that be the Taliban or even 'Islam'. The episode had revealed at least five different tendencies within Muslim practice – the Taliban's Deobandi neo-traditionalism, Gulf-style Wahhabism, the radically contemporary fusion of political Islam with ultra-conservatism of al-Qaeda, the internationalized orthodoxy of al-Qaradawi, the more moderate folksy traditions of the Hazara in Afghanistan – all competing for ideological and often physical space. All these elements, apart from the last, could be termed 'Salafi', in that they sought inspiration from the earliest generations, the *salaf*, of Islam and were part of a project to reproduce today the (imagined) society of the first Muslims on earth.[46] But as the destruction of the Buddhas showed, their internal differences of practice and outlook were vast. The episode had demonstrated how Islam is no more a 'religion of peace' than any other faith but a repository of resources which can be creative and destructive, positive and negative, depending on how they are instrumentalized. The episode had also shown the uses of spectacular violence, something else that was to mark the course of the conflict to come. The Taliban's iconoclasm was 'shock and awe' in a pure and raw form. It was a form of intimidation and of communication too, of 'propaganda by deed'. It was effectively an act of terrorism, though directed at inanimate if valued objects, not living people. Then there was the agency of key actors. Mullah Omar had not acted because he was mad, in thrall to someone else or simply reacting to the West but had made independent decisions based on his own perception of his best interests in the situation in which he found himself. And the episode had also shown the deficiencies of the West in understanding, shaping and genuinely seeing what was happening elsewhere. The response to the destruction of the Buddhas also revealed something else that would be frequently apparent over the coming years: the international community's chronic inability to focus on any one problem for a significant period. For after a week of well-ventilated shock and anger, attention drifted. Very quickly political leaders, reporters and editors turned to other stories, and politicians looked to other issues. There were suicide bombings in Israel and a riot in Bosnia-Herzegovina, Tony Blair won a second term as prime minister in the UK and in the US President George W. Bush, who had taken office in January after a contentious election, saw his package of massive tax cuts signed into law. A G8 summit in Genoa, Italy, was marred by violence, and the United Nations sanctions imposed on Iraq in the wake of the 1991 Gulf War were extended amid acrimonious debates. Afghanistan was no longer news.

In April Ahmed Shah Massood, the Afghan opposition leader famous for his long and effective guerrilla war against the Soviets and resistance to the Taliban, travelled to France to raise funds and his profile but had little success with either goal. Others who made the trip to Europe included Hamid Karzai, a young Afghan exile whose father, leader of the southern Pashtun Popalzai tribe, had been murdered by the Taliban in 1999. Karzai visited London with two older experienced Pashtun leaders from the days of 'the jihad' against the Soviets but received a relatively frosty reception from senior officials at MI6, Britain's foreign security service, who, though concerned about the situation in Afghanistan, were unconvinced of the need for urgent action.[47] Another visitor to MI6 was Mahmud Ahmed, director of the Pakistani ISI spy agency, who made repeated attempts to convince both Richard Dearlove, head of MI6, and his deputy, Nigel Inkster, to help get British diplomatic recognition for the Taliban despite the recent 'fuss' over the destruction of the Buddhas. Over dinner one evening Ahmed insisted that Dearlove should travel to Afghanistan to meet Mullah Omar, whom he described as 'a political visionary'. Dearlove declined.[48]

# 9/11

As the Taliban had been preparing to destroy the Buddhas, a thirty-one-year-old Yemeni called Ali al-Bahlul was putting the finishing touches to a video. Watching it on a laptop computer in a house in Kandahar, he was proud of his handiwork. Carefully edited on a laptop computer with pirated software, the images flowed smoothly one after the other. In the longest sequence, a young, bespectacled, bearded man, with a red and white *keffiyeh* scarf around his shoulders vivid against a backdrop of dusty southern Afghan hills, poured bile on the West, Israel, Saudi Arabia and the 'apostate regimes' of the Islamic world, occasionally waving his finger at the viewer.[49] The video had been specially commissioned, and though al-Bahlul had made many videos in the previous eighteen months none had been like this. He knew the young man on the screen personally as they had shared a house in Kandahar for many months the year before. Al-Bahlul did not know exactly what the video was for, though he was aware it was the last statement of someone who had been chosen to die for the cause. Al-Bahlul had left his home in the Yemeni region of the Hadramawt two years earlier, making his way to Afghanistan via Pakistan. It was his second trip to Afghanistan. On his first, like many such volunteers, his intention had simply been to find and fight for the Taliban. This time, inspired by the bombings in east Africa the year before, he wanted to find Osama bin Laden and, if possible, join al-Qaeda.[50]

Al-Qaeda had been founded by bin Laden and fourteen associates in a series of long meetings at a rented house in a western suburb of the noisy, dusty Pakistani frontier city of Peshawar in August 1988.[51] The meetings had stretched into the small hours as discussions ranged over the aims of the group, its composition and hierarchy. The 'organized Islamic faction' that was eventually created was not big – of its fifteen members, nine sat on the leading council – but it had grand ambitions.[52] Little thought appears to have been given to the name the founders chose for their group, but it was an appropriate and useful one nonetheless. 'Al-Qaeda' is a commonly used word in Arabic and, though often simply translated as 'the base', in fact has a range of other meanings too. This variety and consequent flexibility, itself a departure from the style of names adopted previously by militant groups, was to prove key in the coming years.

Bin Laden was thirty-one in the summer of 1988 and had spent the preceding years shuttling between his native Saudi Arabia and Pakistan, raising funds and organizing everything from medical care to earth-moving equipment for the Afghan *mujahideen*. In around 1987 he had actually seen combat in a series of skirmishes, later vastly mythologized, around the village of Jaji in Afghanistan. The legend of bin Laden's warrior prowess is linked to another myth: that the war against Soviets was fought and won by men like him who were backed – even 'created' – by the CIA. In fact, with tens of thousands of Afghans in the field at any one time and only a few hundred Arabs, the contribution of the latter, especially as they were largely inexperienced and untrained, was negligible. As for the support, the CIA did not enter Afghanistan nor instruct any Arab fighters nor disburse funds or weapons to them. Any US contact with *mujahideen* of any background was indirect, as the Pakistani ISI acted as intermediaries for all assistance, deciding which of the seven Afghan factions would receive what proportion of aid. Techniques taught by the ISI on the basis of US manuals and instruction from the CIA did bleed into the world of the Arab volunteers, but no direct contact took place. Indeed, the foundation of al-Qaeda was not the consequence of American intervention in any way but of bin Laden's frustration with the deep parochialism, national chauvinism, jealousy and feuding that marked relations between different Arab – as well as Afghan – factions during the war against the Soviets.

For what marked Al-Qaeda out among the multitude of other militant groups active across the Islamic world at the time was its avowed internationalism. Its founders' aim was to unite the disparate groups of militants who had fought in the war in Afghanistan to focus their collective energies on new targets. The fragmented factions that composed the world of radical Islamic activism would not restrict their activities to 'liberating' their respective homelands from 'despotic, hypocrite, apostate rulers' but would fight together, directed, coordinated and assisted by al-Qaeda. Their campaign would take two main forms: irregular warfare waged against the 'enemies of Islam' on 'open fronts of conflict', effectively guerrilla wars like that that had defeated the Soviets, and a series of spectacular and violent actions which would radicalize and mobilize all those who had hitherto shunned the call to arms, eventually provoking a mass uprising that would lead to a new era for the world's Muslims. The two strategies would be mutually reinforcing.

Though focused on the contemporary 'plight' of the world's Muslim community, the founders of al-Qaeda were drawing heavily on a long chain of militant scholars and strategists. Each had attempted to formulate a response adapted to his time. They included key Middle Eastern thinkers from the colonial period as well as strategists from the 1960s and 70s such as the Egyptians Syed Qutb and Abdelsalam al-Farraj. However, the most significant was Abdullah Azzam, the Palestinan ideologue, organizer and propagandist who had become the key point of reference for international radicals drawn to the war in Afghanistan during the 1980s. Azzam had not just theorized the duty of each individual Muslim to wage jihad, in this context defined as a violent effort to defend Muslims under attack, but had also been able to practically put it into effect too. As Soviet troops prepared to pull out of Afghanistan, Azzam had called for 'a vanguard that gives everything it possesses in order to achieve victory . . . [and] constitutes the solid base [*al-qaeda al-sulbah*] for the expected society'.[53] The founders of al-Qaeda aimed to be that vanguard and that base.

When al-Bahlul arrived in Afghanistan in 1999 al-Qaeda was reaching the peak of its capabilities. The eleven years since its foundation had not been without trouble. In 1990, with the war in Afghanistan descending into chaos, bin Laden, like the vast bulk of the foreign militants who had been fighting there, had gone home, returning to the city of Jeddah, where he had passed a comfortable youth as the seventeenth son of an immensely wealthy construction magnate. His welcome there was chilly, however, and, after a personal offer to the Saudi royal family to raise an international militant army to defend the kingdom from invasion by Saddam Hussein had been peremptorily rejected, it became clear that if he was to stay he would have to abandon his radical activities.[54] Bin Laden headed for Sudan, where the Islamist regime of Hassan ul-Turabi was in power. Khartoum was the destination of choice for those Arab veterans of the Afghan war who were increasingly unwelcome in Pakistan or in their native lands. Re-creating the atmosphere of Peshawar during the 1980s, Algerian, Libyan, Tunisian, Lebanese, Palestinian, Yemeni and other groups all co-existed in a constant stew of petty jealousies, temporary alliances and noisy boasting. Few among the groups and activists in Sudan at the time had heard of bin Laden, even fewer of al-Qaeda. Their attention was captured by developments elsewhere: the 1993 attack on the World Trade Center orchestrated by Pakistani-born militant Ramzi Yousef, the 'Black Hawk Down' episode in Somalia, which saw the effective defeat of US forces sent to secure the delivery of humanitarian assistance in the country, the terrible violence of the campaign by local militants against authorities in Algeria, the fighting in Bosnia-Herzegovina, Chechnya, the Philippines and in Egypt.[55]

In 1996, bin Laden had been expelled from Sudan when the regime decided that offering a haven to international militants was doing them more harm than good and had fled to Afghanistan. The next years finally saw al-Qaeda, already the vanguard, finally become the 'base' or 'foundation' too, as originally envisaged. Working with a growing group of experienced collaborators, bin Laden and al-Zawahiri set up or appropriated dozens of training camps, guesthouses and other facilities which provided them with a pool of ready volunteers for various ongoing projects. At the same time they launched a sophisticated outreach programme, sending emissaries to groups throughout the Islamic world offering cash and technical help in return for a degree of fealty. Such bids were often unsuccessful, with groups in Algeria, Indonesia, Chechnya, Uzbekistan and elsewhere jealously guarding their independence, but they were accepted frequently enough for a 'network of networks' to begin to emerge. The basic strategy remained the same: a series of spectacular violent actions to radicalize and mobilize potential recruits, to weaken the enemy economically and morally and to eventually provoke a mass uprising that would lead to a new era for the world's Muslims.

The idea for the September 11 attacks originally came from Khaled Sheikh Mohammed, an experienced and capable Kuwait-born Pakistani militant who travelled to seek out bin Laden shortly after the latter's arrival in Afghanistan.[56] Building on schemes he had tried to implement in the Far East, Mohammed's ambitious plans for hijacking dozens of aircraft to strike American targets was initially rejected by bin Laden, but then dusted off, revised and finally accepted after a series of heated meetings of al-Qaeda's senior leadership in the spring of 1999.[57]

The volunteers for the plan could be found simply by scouring the various training camps, either those offering basic training for foreigners arriving to fight with the Taliban or those where more advanced candidates were being trained by al-Qaeda instructors in techniques of urban terrorism. Though most in the camps were there simply to gain combat skills for battles elsewhere in the Islamic world, senior al-Qaeda leaders had little difficulty in finding suitable candidates for a spectacular martyrdom mission. Many recruits were found in one particular camp – al-Farooq near Kandahar – where around 100 volunteers were undergoing basic and advanced training. Investigators later said that al-Farooq was where al-Qaeda sent its top operatives to be prepared for their missions, but for David Hicks, an Australian convert who spent time in the camp in 2001, it was where 'all the oddbods' who did not already belong to any particular group ended up and thus was full of more cosmopolitan, Westernized militants of diverse origins. The proof, he said, was the ease with which he found fellow English-speakers. It was in al-Farooq that a team of volunteers who would be able to evade detection in America was assembled and trained.[58] One of them, a highly committed Egyptian called Mohammed Atta, was designated the operational commander of the attack in the USA. The video that Ali al-Bahlul was so proud of was the 'will' of another team member, his former housemate Ziad Samir Jarrah.

The summer of 2001 passed in final preparations as the hijacking teams arrived in America. By the end of August Atta signalled that the attacks were planned for the second week of September. In his compound in Kandahar bin Laden warned his entourage to prepare to move as an operation was imminent and ordered the evacuation of al-Qaeda's training camps.[59]

One preparatory strike by al-Qaeda, repeatedly postponed, was finally carried out with only forty-eight hours left before the operation in America was due to be launched. On September 9, two Tunisians killed both themselves and Ahmed Shah Massood, the main military leader of the Afghan opposition, with a bomb hidden in a TV camera during an interview at the veteran guerrilla leader's headquarters in the northern town of Taloqan.[60] The delay had largely been due to the target's busy schedule.[61]

On the day of the assassination of Massood, bin Laden and a handful of trusted and well-armed followers left Kandahar in a convoy of four ordinary cars and headed north to Kabul. On the 11th, they left the Afghan capital early and headed east, towards the Pakistani border, and by three o'clock were high in the hills of Logar province, not far from the villages where bin Laden had fought the Soviets over a decade before. Ali al-Bahlul, now appointed bin Laden's personal media technician, was driving a beige Toyota minibus that he had converted into a mobile media centre, fitting it with a satellite receiver, a monitor, a Toshiba computer, a VCR and a video camera. By late afternoon, the van was parked with the other vehicles in the convoy in a remote complex of run-down houses and cement buildings in one of the less-well-known training camps.[62]

Before leaving Kabul, bin Laden had told al-Bahlul that 'it is very important to see the news today' and had asked if he could get US networks on the satellite receiver. In the hills of Logar, however, the mountainous terrain blocked the signal. Instead al-Bahlul tuned a short-wave radio to the BBC Arabic Service. The presenter finished a report and then broke off scheduled programming. A plane, he said, had just crashed into the World Trade Center in New York. Bin Laden's entourage erupted into cheers, some prostrating themselves on the ground. It was 8:48 a.m. New York time, 17.18 in Afghanistan. Bin Laden held up a hand to quiet them. Half an hour later came the news, broadcast immediately this time, that another plane had hit the second of the twin towers. Again bin Laden calmed those around, this time holding up three fingers. The men wept and prayed. Almost exactly an hour later came news of a third strike, this time on the Pentagon. Bin Laden held up four fingers.[63] The final attack never came. A fourth plane, aiming for Washington's Capitol Hill, had crashed into a field in Shanksville, Pennsylvania, after a desperate attempt by passengers to wrest back control. The final death toll from the attacks would be just under 3,000. By nightfall, bin Laden and his followers and al-Bahlul's media van were gone.[64]

# 2

# 9/11, Before and After

## THE REACTION TO 9/11

In the hours after the attacks world leaders received briefings from their security agencies about who might be responsible and what threats the perpetrators might still pose. The immediate fear was of a second or even third wave of strikes. Before the third plane had even hit the Pentagon, the White House 'counter-terrorism coordinator', Richard Clarke, had told Condoleezza Rice, the former academic who was national security adviser to the Bush administration, and Dick Cheney, the vice president, that America had been attacked by al-Qaeda. By early afternoon, individuals known to have links with bin Laden's organization had been identified on the passenger manifests of the hijacked planes.[1] In London, 'everyone seemed to think it was bin Laden'.[2] Blair was briefed by Stephen Lander, the head of MI5, the domestic intelligence service, and John Scarlett, the Chairman of the Joint Intelligence Committee, the government body tasked with aggregating the product of the British intelligence community for decision-makers. Both made it clear that bin Laden and al-Qaeda were the only people capable of such an attack. Scarlett pointed out that the strike was 'less about technology and more about skill and nerve'. Lander stressed that the US would be under enormous pressure to respond quickly and that Iran, Iraq and Libya were potential targets as well as Afghanistan. Both men told Blair that they ruled out 'the involvement of any other governments'.

Many TV networks had trained cameras on the Twin Towers after the impact of the first plane and thus captured both the arrival of the second plane and the eventual collapse of the entire complex. The strikes had been conceived to exploit the capabilities of new communications technology and in this had succeeded perfectly. The events and the live broadcasting of images of it were without historical parallel.

Though there were to be many more terrorist attacks over the coming decade – as there had been over previous centuries – none would come close to being as individually striking as the 9/11 attacks. Though over coming years terrorists would inflict many more casualties than the 2,977 victims who died in New York, Washington and Pennsylvania, no one incident would break so dramatically with previous examples of spectacular political or religious violence. The impact of the 9/11 attacks was inevitably magnified by their sheer unexpectedness. Many later accounts refer to the 'clear blue sky' from which the planes came, a metaphor for an imagined pre-war calm supposedly shattered by the strike. That the victims were in the middle of such mundane rituals as settling at a desk in the morning before a day's work, so well known to so many in the West, also amplified its effect, as did the extraordinary scale of the attack. There was the almost unimaginable sight of the collapse of two 110-floor towers but simultaneously there were the individuals caught up in the tragedy: the husbands ringing wives from their offices as the floors below burned, the 200 men and women forced to chose between fire or falling as a mode of death and who opted for the latter, the calls from the passengers before their ill-fated bid to retake control of the fourth hijacked plane, the firemen who continued to search empty floors in the doomed towers unaware because of faulty radios that orders had been given to evacuate the burning buildings and who perished as a result. The dead came from sixty different nations and represented almost every religion on the planet. Apart from fifty-five service men and women who died in the Pentagon, they were all civilians. They were bankers and postmen, short order chefs and stockbrokers, cleaners and artists, aspirant writers and out-of-work actors, senior counter-terrorism officials and tourists. Over 400 were emergency workers. The youngest victim was two-year-old Christine Hanson of Groton, Massachusetts, who was with her parents aboard the plane that crashed into the South Tower. The oldest was eighty-five-year-old Robert Grant Norton of Lubec, Maine, on the plane that struck the North Tower. 'Today is obviously one of the most difficult days in the history of the city,' Rudy Giuliani, the mayor of New York, told reporters at a hastily arranged press conference hours after the towers had collapsed, with the air still thick with ash and acrid smoke. 'The number of casualties will be more than any of us can bear ultimately.'[3]

Reactions around the world were instant and, as the attacks had been, were broadcast live. They naturally comprised, in those early instants of horror and shock, automatic, instinctive expressions of sympathy for the bereaved and solidarity with the American people. Early estimates of casualties ran higher than 15,000 – the number of people who were thought to be working in the World Trade Center at the time. 'We are all traumatized by this terrible tragedy,' Kofi Annan, the United Nations secretary general, said as the organization's headquarters building in New York was evacuated. In London, the national anthem at the Changing of the Guard was replaced by 'The Stars and Stripes'. Queen Elizabeth herself expressed 'growing disbelief and total shock' at the events. *Le Monde*, the French newspaper, declared, 'we are all Americans now'. The prime minister of New Zealand spoke of 'the sort of thing the worst movie scenario wouldn't dream up'. Many spoke of the 'barbarity' of those responsible. Gerhard Schroeder, the German chancellor, said the attacks were 'a declaration of war against the civilized world'. The European Union's external relations commissioner, Chris Patten, called the attacks 'the work of a madman'.

Within twenty-four hours NATO had unanimously invoked Article Five of the North Atlantic Treaty, which describes an attack on one member as an attack on all, and diplomats were calling for the United Nations Security Council to impose sanctions on any governments or groups found to be responsible. European foreign ministers scheduled a rare emergency meeting to discuss a joint response. Around the world, government installations and tall buildings were evacuated amid widespread fear of imminent further strikes. Information on supposed plots, on sleeper cells waiting to be activated poured in as intelligence services, stunned by their collective failure, scanned every last file for any hint of a potential danger. President Bush, who had spent much of the previous day in the air or in protected bunkers far from Washington, was told on the morning of the 12th that the CIA believed there were more 'al-Qaeda operatives' within the USA and that they wanted to attack with biological, chemical or nuclear weapons.[4] The ambient fear deepened and spread. Each public reaction provoked its own reaction, sparking a chain of accelerating, proliferating live commentary on an event the scale and significance of which no one knew quite how to gauge.

But even as their aides issued their statements of sympathy and grief, many world leaders saw immediately how the 9/11 attacks could be exploited to their own personal advantage and that of the nations they led. In public President Vladimir V. Putin publicly supported a tough response to the 'barbaric acts'. Privately, speaking to Blair on the afternoon of the attacks, the Russian premier lectured the British prime minister about how the world had long ignored his warnings about 'the threat of Islamic fundamentalism' and hoped that would now change.[5] Putin, who had been the first foreign head of state to call the White House on September 11 itself, repeated his message to Bush on the day after the disaster. For several years Putin had sought to cast the brutal war in the southern breakaway republic of Chechnya as a battle against Islamic radicalism rather than the latest manifestation in a centuries-old conflict between local irredentist tendencies and the Russian state. He had astutely sensed the shift that would now come in the perception of any conflict that could be said to involve Islamic militants. Ariel Sharon, the hawkish prime minister of Israel, was also equally quick to realize that the attacks, whatever the immediate calls by statesmen across the world for reconciliation and moderation, signalled a paradigm shift that would allow Israel greater freedom of action in combating Palestinian militant groups in Gaza and the West Bank and in consolidating the Israeli hold on the Occupied Territories.[6] Sharon immediately declared a national day of mourning in solidarity with the United States while urging the world to fight all terrorism. The coming weeks would see politicians ranging from David Trimble, the Northern Irish Unionist leader, to Robert Mugabe, the dictatorial ruler of Zimbabwe, all proclaiming that their long-term domestic or international enemies were in fact the equivalents of the terrorists who had struck the US.[7] Efforts to misrepresent domestic enemies or long-standing local conflicts as generated by or at the very least exacerbated by al-Qaeda were to become systematic over coming years, becoming a key element of the 9/11 Wars.

Across the Islamic world, there were effectively three different types of reaction: those of heads of state, those of the clergy and those of the general population. Figures like President Mubarak of Egypt and King Abdullah of Jordan, favoured allies of the USA and recipients of significant American aid, all expressed sympathy and offered cooperation with America, refraining, at least in the first instance, from any attempt to exploit the attacks. This was largely predictable. Whatever their views in private, such leaders understood how poorly a wounded America would view any disloyalty. More surprising was the strong condemnation of the attack by President Mohammad Khatami of Iran and Libya's Colonel Muammar Gaddafi. Khatami went as far as describing the strikes as 'terrorist', and Gaddafi offered aid to the American people. Only the Taliban and Saddam Hussein's Iraq broke ranks. Spokesmen in the former denied bin Laden was responsible. State television in the latter hailed the attacks as the 'operation of the century' which the United States deserved because of its 'crimes against humanity'.[8]

Clerics in the Islamic world had a more delicate path to tread. The fact that their influence depended not so much on any formal qualifications or positions but largely on the number of people who accepted and acted on their *fatawa* made them naturally more responsive to public opinion. A compromise needed to be found between the strongly pro-American position taken by rulers and the much more ambivalent sentiment of the street. Clergy close to or protected by governments, like Mohammed Tantawi, the Grand Mufti of the hugely prestigious al-Azhar university in Cairo, and Abdul Aziz Abdullah al-Sheikh in Saudi Arabia, could call the strikes 'stupid', 'forbidden' and underline that they constituted a 'grave sin' that would be 'punished on judgement day', but other religious figures needed to be more nuanced in their response.[9] So although Yusuf al-Qaradawi, the cleric who had attempted to dissuade the Taliban from destroying the Bamiyan Buddhas, denounced the attacks, particularly on those simply 'earning their daily bread', as a 'heinous crime' and urged Muslims to donate blood for the victims, he made a point of simultaneously stressing the United States' 'political bias towards Israel' as a reason for the strike and went as far as implicitly criticizing its perpetrators for mistaking their target. Instead, he said, Muslims should 'concentrate on facing the occupying enemy directly' inside Gaza and the West Bank.[10] This was to recur as a key argument – and a dynamic debate – in the decade that followed.

Beyond the clergy and the rulers came the genuine popular reaction. It was deeply conflicted. Horror, shock, genuine sympathy for individual victims was mixed in much of the Islamic world with a strong sense that the attacks were, if not legitimate in themselves, at least justified by the perceived misdeeds of America and Americans over recent decades. Bin Laden had previously been careful to pick targets that would have some popular resonance – the strike which had immediately preceded the

9/11 attacks was against a US warship anchored off the Yemeni port of Aden in October 2000 – and there can be no doubt that levels of anti-American sentiment in the Islamic world in the late summer of 2001 were high. Certainly this had been abundantly clear to anyone travelling in the Middle East, Pakistan or the Muslim majority countries of the Far East. The author spent the week before the September 11 attacks in Algeria, passing several evenings in the garden of one local human rights activist whose friends, most of whom would have been described as 'cultural' rather than practising Muslims, took American enmity towards the Islamic world as an indisputable given, barely worthy of discussion. The same had been the case in Jordan and in Morocco, as well as among many Muslims living in the West.[11] Yet such sentiments were far from straightforward. Few remained unmoved before the images of those forced to jump to their deaths.[12] Nor was the sense that the USA had somehow 'got what it deserved' limited to the Muslim world.

These various tensions were one of the reasons for the astonishing rapidity with which conspiracy theories sprang up, spread and became embedded in the public consciousness in the Islamic world and beyond. Within days of the attacks al-Manar, the satellite chain run by the Lebanese Hezbollah militant Islamist organization broadcasting from Beirut was reporting that 4,000 Jews 'remarkably did not show up in their jobs' on September 11, clearly implying that responsibility for them lay with some kind of global Jewish conspiracy rather than with the nineteen hijackers and their organizers.[13] Rooted in longstanding and widespread anti-Semitic stereotypes, some imported from Europe, such ideas, often strongly encouraged by governments and carefully fused with anti-Zionist rhetoric, had become a part of general daily discourse in much of the Middle East over previous decades. Others strands of conspiracy theory and denial, such as the idea that 'it must have been the Jews or the Americans' as it was impossible that Arabs could organize such a complicated operation, revealed a noxious mix of psychological evasion of the hard questions posed to Muslims by the 9/11 strikes and to a lesser extent the internalization of centuries of Western statements about the incapacity of Muslims or Arabs. Sitting at dinner with American Under Secretary of Defense Douglas Feith in Riyadh during a short tour of the Gulf and central Asia by Defense Secretary Donald Rumsfeld, Prince Saud al-Faisal, the Saudi foreign minister, wondered aloud who indeed was behind such a sophisticated operation given it was inconceivable that 'cave dwellers in Afghanistan' were responsible. As America was now at war with the Islamic world, al-Faisal mused, the answer surely would be found by seeking out who stood to benefit the most. After all, he continued, he had read press stories that Israel had warned Jews who worked in the Twin Towers not to go to the office on the day of the attacks.[14] Overall, one poll found, only 18 per cent in the Middle East as a whole, 4 per cent of Pakistanis and just one in ten Kuwaitis believed that Arabs were responsible for 9/11.[15] A poll in November 2001 showed that, while 81 per cent of British Muslims felt the 9/11 strikes were unjustified, 60 per cent felt that America was wrong to blame them on al-Qaeda.[16] Conspiracy theories also spread rapidly among non-Muslim populations, especially among the extreme left or in countries like France with a long history of anti-Americanism.

## A FAILURE OF INTELLIGENCE

Key to the speed at which the conspiracy theories spread was incredulity that Western security services could not have prevented the attacks. Much has now been written about this failure, one of the greatest of the many intelligence failures of recent decades. There is no space here to tell once again the long story of administrative squabbles, petty bureaucratic feuds and institutional failings that allowed the 9/11 hijackers to avoid the attention of American law-enforcement agencies despite the plethora of individual clues to their presence and plans that were uncovered through the spring and summer of 2001. In very simple terms, the 9/11 hijackers slipped through the gap between domestic security services looking for American citizens attacking in America and overseas security services, mainly the CIA, looking for foreign citizens attacking US interests overseas. Though it was understood that a third scenario – foreign citizens attacking in the US – was increasingly likely, the systems to deal with such an eventuality were not in place. The CIA picked up the trail of key individuals in the 9/11 plot in Malaysia but was unable to exploit the opportunity they were given to unravel the conspiracy. When the 9/11 teams did arrive in the US, a series of errors, avoidable delays and bad luck meant they evaded detection and capture. Finally no one had imagined terrorists ever using tactics like those that the hijackers were to adopt.

There is no space either to retell the story of the failure of various attempts to eliminate bin Laden in the late 1990s. What appears clear, however, is that, though American decision-makers undoubtedly recognized the threat bin Laden and his associates posed to US and other nations' interests, certainly from 1998 onwards, they simply did not have the mental, legal, technical and cultural equipment to formulate and execute an effective policy to counter that threat.[17] One reason for this was the lack of a legal framework to deal with an amorphous, dynamic and fragmented movement based more on personal relations and a shared worldview than on formal membership of an organization. So when in 2001 the perpetrators of the 1998 embassy bombings went on trial in New York, al-Qaeda was represented in the courtroom as a classic hierarchical terrorist group. Prosecutors and investigators were constrained both by their training and the legal tools at their disposal to fit this radically new phenomenon into a pre-existing schema, deploying laws designed to fight serious crime in order to obtain convictions. Equally, the nature of Islamic militant activism posed difficulties when it came to pre-emptive action to stop a plot. At what point and against whom, senior Clinton administration figures asked, could one intervene with military force before an attack took place? Was it justified to assassinate bin Laden when there was no direct evidence linking a conspiracy to him?[18] One result of this ongoing debate was a lack of concrete purpose. 'No one said kill him. The word used was "neutralized", which covers a multitude of sins,' remembered Jack Cloonan, who was a special agent for the FBI's Osama bin Laden unit from 1996 to 2002.[19]

A further problem was finding a way of using military force against these irregular fighters in a distant country who, despite their unconventional structure and behaviour, nonetheless threatened attacks that could incur levels of physical destruction and casualties which had previously been the monopoly of states. American defence spending in 2000 was budgeted at $267 billion, with intelligence agencies receiving significant resources too, but this did not mean the right tools had been developed for such a technically difficult task.[20] A project to mount missiles on the new unmanned surveillance drones being developed was being held up by squabbles between government departments and intelligence agencies over its funding. There were also problems with putting 'boots on the ground', i.e. combat troops into Afghanistan. The military, suited by habit, doctrine and equipment to fight single, strategically critical battles against conventional enemies, showed both an innate conservatism and an understandable reluctance to get involved with unorthodox plans often hatched by civilians whom they saw as dangerous amateurs.[21] The missile strikes on Afghanistan and in the Sudan following the 1998 east African bombings had been an embarrassing failure, missing all major targets, killing a few recruits from Pakistani-based militant organizations who had camps in Afghanistan that were independent of those of al-Qaeda, incinerating a few tents and destroying what appeared to be a factory for making veterinary antibiotics at a total cost of more than $50 million.

Through 1999 and 2000 many alternative plans for 'neutralizing' bin Laden were discussed and rejected. Complicating the situation was an absence of actionable intelligence. This was inevitable given the lack of cultural resources suffered by Western intelligence services and the weaknesses in the relations with their counterparts in the Islamic world. The CIA and counterparts elsewhere in the West, with the possible exception of the French DGSE, had a very limited number of Arabists, and almost no one who spoke the languages of Afghanistan or Pakistan with any proficiency. MI6 did not have a single Pashto-speaker on its staff in 2001.[22]

The consequences of this lack of both a ground presence and detailed understanding were exacerbated by an increasing reliance on high technology and communications intercepts in place of so-called HUMINT, intelligence gathered by live human beings on the ground. Then there were the tight restrictions under which the CIA in particular worked. Often living in diplomatic compounds, sometimes not even speaking local languages, hedged round by security restrictions, intelligence operatives found even the most banal of relations with their local counterparts difficult. Developing the kind of range of contacts they needed for a genuine understanding of any given society, culture, country or community and the various forms of militancy and extremism it could produce was almost impossible. Many stations had been shut down in the early 1990s, and often the US agencies simply had no permanent physical presence. In Tajikistan, marginal in global terms perhaps but crucial for Afghanistan, the level of lawlessness and street violence was deemed 'simply too great to allow CIA officers to visit there for more than a day or two at a time ... once a month'.[23] The CIA had few high-quality assets in Afghanistan, though they had developed a range of basic tribal contacts, and none within the senior ranks of the Taliban or circles close to bin Laden.

The degree of ignorance of local conditions was illustrated by a plan during the summer of 2001 to use Ahmed Shah Massood's northern troops to attack or capture bin Laden, despite the fact that their target spent most of his time hundreds of miles from the dwindling pocket of territory Massood and his allies held. Massood's men were predominantly Tajik and thus instantly recognizable outside parts of the north-east and Kabul. This posed an evident tactical problem. To show willing, Massood sent a detachment to fire some rockets into a training camp near Darunta when it was thought bin Laden might be in the vicinity.[24] Predictably the strike had no effect. In the capital, a series of attempts were made to find out where bin Laden stayed and when he would be there. These too came to nothing.[25] In the end it was al-Qaeda who, with lethal consequences, penetrated Massood's security, killing the best asset America had in the country.

Another major obstacle was poor intelligence passed on by those who did have a better handle on what was going on than their Western counterparts. Despite relatively close relations with the Americans, information flowing from services in countries such as Jordan, Egypt and Algeria was designed primarily to convince the US government of the bona fides, stability and competence of the organization and government supplying it, not to give the recipient a fair and accurate assessment of distinctly sensitive issues such as international extremism or their own problems with domestic radical Muslim activism. Equally, key potential allies like the Pakistanis or the Saudi Arabians simply could not be trusted. Though it was in fact a variety of factors (including a last-minute decision by a driver) that had saved bin Laden from the missiles fired at eastern Afghanistan by Clinton in the wake of the 1998 east African bombings, US intelligence officials were convinced that their target had been tipped off by Pakistani security services.[26] Following blasts targeting American troops in Saudi Arabia in the 1990s, Riyadh's security services had done as much to hinder American agencies' investigations as to aid them. As for Yemeni authorities supposedly assisting Americans tracking those behind the attack on the USS *Cole* in 2000 they were 'worse than a joke', according to US officials working on the file at the time.[27] Indian intelligence fed a steady stream of highly politicized 'findings' to American counterparts throughout this period. These were largely focused on proving Osama bin Laden's connection to, or even presence in, the disputed Himalayan territory of Kashmir.[28] A variety of Middle Eastern intelligence services insisted that the Saudi was seriously ill from a kidney disease, a falsehood that was to surface regularly over the following years.[29]

Despite the obstacles, an understanding of what was happening in Afghanistan did gradually emerge. The CIA had set up a special unit to track bin Laden in 1996, which, after a difficult start, had begun to formulate a more accurate vision of the man and his operations.[30] When it came to individual threats, formidable resources could be deployed. Following the 1998 east African attacks an extraordinary and very successful investigation led by the FBI saw the rapid detention of many of the key individuals involved. When it was feared that Islamic militants were planning a series of attacks on the eve of the new millennium, a vast worldwide operation of intelligence gathering, analysis and interdiction was launched. Hundreds of CIA officials worked round the clock through the last weeks of December 2000, checking every lead, trawling through vast banks of intercepted communications or reports received from overseas stations and foreign services. 'It was extremely intense. There were rows of people sitting in jeans and sweatshirts all day and all night, all through the weekends,' remembered Art Keller, a junior CIA official involved in the effort. 'There was a genuine sense of urgency and threat.'[31] But despite the growing body of knowledge about what was going on in Afghanistan, the true nature of the threat posed by al-Qaeda and Islamic militancy as it evolved in the last years of the twentieth century still seemed to escape many senior intelligence and counter-terrorist officials and, more importantly perhaps, their political masters. The shrill warnings from the CIA's bin Laden unit – Alec Station – earned its staff a reputation as fanatics who suffered from a lack of perspective.[32] Just a year or so before the September 11 attacks, researching the international militants in Pakistan was the job of the most junior member of the MI6 station in Islamabad.[33]

One key weakness was intelligence on exactly who was travelling to the camps in Afghanistan. In the years following the attacks counter-terrorist agencies would make massive efforts to fill this gap, working feverishly to understand the identity of those attracted in such numbers by the structures that al-Qaeda and a multitude of other groups had created there in the late 1990s. 'In retrospect, there was one question we simply never really tried hard enough to answer,' remembered one former MI6 officer. 'Who were the volunteers?'[34]

## THE VOLUNTEERS

Male, young, Muslim but otherwise very varied, those in the camps were the products of various broad trends affecting Islamic communities across a vast stretch of territory from Morocco to Malaysia, via Europe, the Balkans and central Asia.[35] Though some were from developed Western countries, often second-generation immigrants or converts, most came from Egypt, Saudi Arabia, the Yemen and Algeria.[36] There were, the Pakistani ambassador to Kabul at the time cabled home, also hundreds of central Asians, Bangladeshis and a hundred or so Uighurs.[37]

Three elements were immediately striking. The first was the age of the volunteers – eighteen to twenty-eight for the most part, which placed them firmly in the 'youth bulge' seen across the Islamic world in the late 1990s. They were the children of the economic boom in the Middle East fuelled by the oil price hikes that followed the 1973 Arab–Israeli war. Each stage of their relatively short lives had been marked by a new broad ideological development. Their first memories would have been of a time when the secular pan-Arab or nationalist ideas which had been dominant since the colonial powers left the region were being questioned in an unprecedented way following decades of economic mismanagement and graft. They had grown up during the 1980s, a decade which saw political Islamism come of age as a mass ideology in their countries of origin, particularly when left-wing ideologies were fatally undermined by the collapse of the Soviet Union. They were teenagers at precisely the time when political Islamism itself had began to lose momentum in the face of intransigent regimes and a failure to broaden its appeal beyond sections of the conservative urban middle and upper working class. And they reached adulthood at exactly the moment when the violent insurgencies of the early 1990s which had followed the failure of the Islamist project themselves began to run into difficulties as their indiscriminate brutality alienated potential supporters.

In their short lives, therefore, the young men who ended up in the camps in Afghanistan between 1998 and 2001 had seen the failure of the nationalism of the first mid-twentieth-century postcolonial regimes, the socialism or pan-Arabism of their largely incompetent successors, the moderate Islamism of the opposition groups in many of their home-lands and finally the violent extremism targeting local regimes. The new internationalist extremism of men like bin Laden was, at the very least, untried.[38]

The second macro-factor evident was that a very large number of the volunteers making their way to Afghanistan in the late 1990s were either immigrants themselves or the children of immigrants. This immi-gration might be international, in the case of Ziad Samir Jarrah, Atta and the rest of the 'Hamburg cell' who led the 9/11 hijackers, or internal, from rural areas to urban areas. The family of al-Bahlul, the young man who had struggled to set up the television for bin Laden to watch the 9/11 attacks live, had, like tens of millions of others in the Islamic world over previous decades, made the transition from the countryside to the town, in its case from a small village in the Yemen to Sana'a, the capital, before subsequently living in Saudi Arabia. Bin Laden's father had made a similar journey, leaving the Hadramawt region of Yemen for Saudi Arabia's most cosmopolitan city, Jeddah. Three of the 9/11 pilots had emigrated from their homeland to the West. There were myriad other examples. In every case, such displacement implied a significant change in terms of environment and of social codes and traditions and the necessity of finding a new set of values and modes of behaviour and of integration.

The third obvious macro-factor was the new wave of anti-Americanism that coursed through the Islamic world in the 1990s. There had been previous such waves, of course, but post-Cold-War American hegemony had focused resentment on the new 'hyper-power' in a new and urgent way, sharpening the two-centuries-old dilemma in the Islamic world of how to confront, deal with, profit from, learn from or indeed influence the West. This anti-Western sentiment, which had often provoked a var-iety of revivalist religious sentiments, was reinforced by the new media technology emerging in the 1990s which allowed someone like bin Laden to reach an audience directly without risking years of dangerous activism on the ground. It also accelerated a process, seen outside the

Islamic world too, of the construction and consolidation of new, often deeply conservative, communal and sectarian identities, in this case an unprecedented sense of solidarity with Muslims elsewhere in the world.

Al-Jazeera, the feisty satellite TV channel launched from the gas-rich Gulf emirate of Qatar in 1996, played a part in this, along with its many emulators. The channel pioneered a new, sharper style that broke with the stolid traditions of heavily censored state broadcasters in the Middle East and tried to represent the views and interests of ordinary people. This, however, meant that the channel's programming often reflected and reinforced prejudices rather than challenging them. News bulletins from Gaza, southern Lebanon, Chechnya, Kashmir or elsewhere played into a generalized narrative of victimhood. Simultaneously Western soap operas and documentaries, beamed directly into tens of millions of homes, raised expectations and aspirations as well as resentment at the economic success of the West and the Far East. The internet, which more than any other medium allows individuals to construct their own personal worlds of information without being challenged, also spread rapidly despite many governments' attempts to control its use. By 2001, even Saudi Arabia with its then restrictive media regulations had 100,000 net subscribers.[39]

Exacerbating this, of course, was Western policy. By omission as much as commission, successive American and European governments through the mid and late 1990s failed to engage with the tough core issues that had long troubled their relations with the multiple communities and countries that constitute the Islamic world. The Arab–Israeli peace process, so promising at the beginning of the decade, was allowed to fail, and longstanding strategies to secure the stable flow of strategic resources such as oil to world markets and key short-term domestic factors were allowed to continue to determine policy. European powers and Washington appeared to be, at the very least, insensitive to the plight of Muslim communities during the wars in the former Yugoslavia. A Cold War legacy of support for repressive regimes was continued with the new enemy becoming the Islamists rather than the Communists. The bulk of the volunteers flowing into Afghanistan came from countries – Saudi Arabia, Jordan, Egypt, Algeria – whose governments received significant support from the West. Even if the West was by no means at the root of all troubles, as often argued, the policies and language of Western countries did help militants 'frame' the world's problems and their own grievances within a simple and persuasive single narrative of Muslims suffering at the hands of a belligerent, rapacious America and, to a lesser extent, its allies. This may not have been true but was nonetheless convincing to many.

The volunteers making their way to Afghanistan were, however, a minority of a minority. Of a global population of around 1.2 billion Muslims and a population of perhaps 300 million in the Arab world, perhaps between 10,000 and 20,000 individuals travelled to Afghanistan through the 1990s and underwent some kind of militant training or experience of combat there.[40] One thing that is certain is that they were not mad, poverty-stricken or stupid. There is no evidence that levels of mental illness exceeded those of the population in general. Also, though volunteers from central Asia were often much less well off, the vast bulk of those from the Middle East, and indeed the handful from the West, were from families that were, if not wealthy, then far from poor.[41] Any link with poverty was thus indirect. As was to be seen again throughout the course of the 9/11 Wars, a lack of means was a poor predictor of radicalism. Equally, though some were of below-average education, particularly in terms of their theological knowledge, most were of a normal or often superior intellectual capacity. Those in the camps had travelled for a wide variety of reasons: political, religious and personal. Though some were motivated by a specific desire to meet Osama bin Laden, the main aim of most was to get training to fight in Kashmir (especially for those from the British Pakistani community), Chechnya (for Saudi Arabians, Algerians and Egyptians) or in Afghanistan itself against the Northern Alliance, who were seen as enemies of Islam.[42] Some were outraged at the second Chechen war of 1999 or events in Israel-Palestine. Some travelled for religious reasons stemming from genuine conviction: to fulfil a religious duty of jihad and potentially to achieve martyrdom without the political context being particularly important. Many were motivated by more personal factors: a genuine desire for adventure, to flee 'family problems' or to go in the footsteps of relatives or friends who had previously travelled. A relatively high number had suffered educational or business failures. Some came from jihadi families with numerous examples of volunteers. Fathers of others had fought in wars of independence against Western colonizers in Algeria, Libya or elsewhere.[43] Often motives were mixed within the groups who set off. There were even brothers who travelled together but for different reasons – one out of a genuine sense of religious duty, the other almost as a 'lifestyle choice'.[44] Those who facilitated the passage of the young men to Afghanistan tended to be older, part of the generation of militants formed during the 1980s. There is no evidence to suggest anyone was 'brainwashed', however. A few were genuinely 'groomed' to travel by recruiters who carefully targeted vulnerable and suggestible individuals and drew them into activities that they appear never to have fully understood. To the unskilled and jobless, jihad was presented as an alternative employment, an extension of the charity work at home that many were already involved in.[45] But the vast proportion actively sought out the networks which could help them fulfil a relatively mature ambition. Certainly few hid their destinations or ambitions from friends, families or even their governments. As during the war against the Soviets, videos of 'atrocities' and feats of arms were effective means of sensitizing, mobilizing and radicalizing individuals already rendered receptive by other factors.

In Afghanistan, separated from their home environment, their radicalization accelerated. A whole range of key concepts embodied in Islamic history and holy texts were deployed in the camps to reinforce the sense that the volunteers were engaged on a righteous, rational path. Often early weeks of instruction were dominated by lessons in theology. The idea of *hijra*, the flight from an unholy, ignorant and barbaric environment to a remote place where a true community of believers, the *jemaa islamiya*, could be constituted before returning to establish a new golden age convincingly reformulated the story of the Prophet Mohammed to better fit it to the 'reality' of the current situation of Muslims. The cosmic single narrative of the age-old war between good and evil, belief and unbelief could be further embedded, the 'enemy' could be dehumanized, fellow Muslims of insufficient piety deemed unworthy of the faith, an extreme and minority interpretation of jihad could be reinforced, and a powerful sentiment of belonging to an elite vanguard encouraged. The theological and psychological indoctrination was, of course, backed up by the practical excitement of weapons training and the team-building effect of physical hardship.[46]

The process was far from universally effective. Letters from volunteers and later testimony speaks of disappointment at the quality of teaching, at the lack of solidarity between groups of students (who were taught according to language or nationality) and at the food.[47] Around a quarter to a third of volunteers, few of whom had ever travelled before, suffered gastro-intestinal problems or other illnesses, and few camps had even rudimentary medical facilities.[48] But volunteers were never prevented from leaving, and many dropped out, returning home or simply hanging around in Jalalabad or Kabul, living in the many guesthouses established by the various groups or funded by the major Islamic NGOs or missionaries in Afghanistan at the time. 'I never at any moment felt I couldn't leave. It was all very casual. You could walk in and walk out,' David Hicks, the Australian convert who ended up in al-Farooq camp in 2001 after fighting in Kashmir, said.[49]

Nonetheless, as the 9/11 attacks revealed, the system, if more chaotic and ramshackle than often thought, worked. And not just for al-Qaeda either. By the late years of the decade, militant organizations ranging from the Islamic Movement of Uzbekistan through to fragmented groups such as the Jordanians who had established camps in the west of Afghanistan to the Algerians who had their guesthouses in Jalalabad were all receiving more recruits that ever before. There were so many that those trying to administrate the scores of guesthouses, camps and training centres in Afghanistan frequently complained of the sheer numbers.[50]

## LONDONISTAN

The final problem for those seeking to protect the West against the new threat that radical Islam posed was thus one of imagination: the failure of so many, particularly in America, to understand what globalization actually meant and what kind of new menace it could generate.[51]

This failure was not restricted to the US. It was certainly evident in the UK, where the true role of key individuals based in London through the late 1990s almost entirely escaped British security services.[52] The importance of the city as a secure base from which to organize fundraising, propaganda and recruitment for the international militant movement was consistently missed by officers from Special Branch and MI5, who were more used to dealing with Irish republican terrorism. Hundreds of militants wanted in their own countries for a range of activities had arrived in the UK in two broad waves between the end of the 1980s and the mid 1990s. Some were relatively harmless, relatively moderate political Islamists. But others posed a much more serious risk to Britain and its allies which was seriously underestimated.

Nothing shows the confusion of this period clearly more than the question of a 'Londonistan deal' by which militants were allegedly allowed to stay in the UK as long as they refrained from targeting British interests. For many militants, such a pact undoubtedly existed. Omar Mahmoud Othman, better known as Abu Qutada, a Jordanian Palestinian and radical scholar who was both a key ideological reference and a key organizer for al-Qaeda, had several meetings with MI5 soon after his arrival in the UK during which he offered to report on anyone harming *British* interests.[53] Other key militants in the UK at the time later spoke of how British security services had told them that they would be guaranteed the rights of the 'British constitution' as long as they refrained from fighting each other on UK soil, from targeting the UK itself or from using UK territory as a base from which to attack other countries.[54] A third militant activist later linked to the radicalization of perpetrators of terrorist attacks, a Syrian-born preacher based in north London called Omar Mohammed Bakri Fostok, frequently told prayer meetings that the Koran teaches that covenants exist between believers and non-Muslim authorities who give them shelter. He even on one occasion made the argument to British viewers of a middlebrow afternoon television show.[55] When Algerian militants in London passed a message to operational commanders waging a vicious war in their home country that their presence would be tolerated in the UK provided they did not break any laws, the then leader of the main militant group in Algeria, Djamel Zitouni of the Groupe Islamique Armée, responded by offering not to harm Britons anywhere.[56] British officials and politicians have always denied coming to any arrangement with any activists. 'They were told their rights and the legal position was explained, nothing more,' said one senior British police officer.[57] The likelihood is thus that the 'deal' was more a product of cultural misunderstanding than any conspiracy. The militants, coming from repressive states of the Middle East, naturally saw things differently from the British police, whose legalistic position – if you break no laws we can't touch you – would have seemed nonsensical unless part of a bargain. That the anti-terrorism laws in effect at the time in the UK did not cover conspiracies to attack overseas must also have escaped the comprehension of the new arrivals – as they escaped that even of close allies like the French.

Deal or no deal, what is certain is that British security agencies had difficulty tracking the shift in the orientation of militants in the UK over the decade. Whereas early arrivals had been largely focused on the 'near enemy', the regimes of their home countries, later on in the decade it was the 'far enemy' of the US and by extension its allies that had become the target for London-based militants. In this, of course, activists in the UK were following the broader trend across the Muslim world that had seen the 'internationalization' of Islamic radical activism over the decade. But such esoteric technicalities largely escaped those tasked with monitoring Britain's radical population and there was trouble quantifying quite who threatened whom. Another strand that went virtually ignored was what was to eventually come to be called 'home-grown militancy'. Throughout the 1990s, young British men of Pakistani origin made their way to Kashmir to fight with local groups there. Their activities were monitored by the security service but again were not seen as a potential threat to UK interests even when British citizens died in suicidal assaults on Indian troops or paramilitaries. Funds destined for Kashmiri groups, often collected in mosques in the Midlands or the north of the UK, were seized frequently, but logistic support networks were more or less tolerated.[58] In general, however, security services were too busy with other issues raised in the chaos of the collapse of Communism to think too much about the apparently fringe problem of radical Islamist activism. A third of the 1,800 staff of MI5 was focused on Irish republican violence. Turkish groups such as the PKK or Dev Sol, which ran rackets in north London and were actively involved in criminal activities, were a significant concern. One major problem was that the service had very few offices outside London and none at all in the areas where much of the British Muslim population was concentrated.[59] As relations with local police were often poor, this meant very limited visibility on the ground.

'[Islamic radicalism] was a concern but far from a real priority,' one senior MI6 official said later. 'We had a lot going on [and] had suffered significant cuts in resources in the search for a post-Cold-War peace dividend. But we were not approaching the problem in the right way or digging in the right places. We were looking but simply not seeing.'[60] Parliament's Intelligence and Security Committee later said that the British JIC had in fact warned Blair in its weekly intelligence assessment of July 16 that al-Qaeda – operating from bases in Afghanistan – was in the 'final stages' of preparing a terrorist attack on the West, probably targeting Israelis or Americans, though the details, timings and methods of attack were not known. The nature of the threat was not 'understood' at the time, the Committee noted, 'due to a failure of imagination'.[61]

## A GLOBAL WAR ON TERROR

In the eight months between taking power and the attacks of 9/11 the president, Condoleezza Rice, the national security adviser, and Colin Powell, the former general who had been appointed secretary of state, had shown little interest in the Middle East in general and in Islamic terrorism in particular, preferring to focus on more traditional sources of danger such as Russia and China or states with long records of hostility towards the US such as Iraq. One major preoccupation was the question of missile defence.

Rice later mounted a spirited rebuttal of the criticisms of the Bush team's record in the months before 9/11, saying that their priorities were in line with briefings by the outgoing administration which had emphasized North Korea, Iran and the Balkans. Rice claimed too that a major strategy aiming to deny sanctuary to al-Qaeda and its various offshoots and affiliates in Afghanistan and to freeze the assets of the group and those of its benefactors was being put into action by the late summer of 2001.[62] Much of the acrimonious argument after the 9/11 strikes revolved around a series of warnings received by the Bush administration during the summer of 2001. In his memoirs, Bush recalled that CIA intelligence before 9/11 had first pointed to an attack 'overseas' and that during the late spring security had been 'hardened' at embassies abroad, cooperation with foreign services increased and warnings issued to domestic American authorities about potential hijackings on internal flights. In early August Bush was briefed that bin Laden intended to strike in the US. Though the possibility of a hijack was raised, concrete details of what form that strike might take were thin.[63] A meeting of the top-ranking 'Principals Committee' to discuss the terrorist threat – repeatedly postponed through the Bush administration's first eight months in office – finally took place on September 4.[64] By the time it met, it was, of course, far too late to do anything. 'On 9/11 it was obvious the intelligence community had missed something big,' the president later wrote.[65] It is hard to escape the impression that, even if the warnings reaching him were vague, Bush, who had taken a vacation of record length through the summer, was at the very least guilty himself of a degree of slackness that bordered on the negligent.

Even more has been written since September 2001 on the internal workings of the Bush administration in the days and weeks following the September 11 attacks than on the failure to prevent the 9/11 plot. The immediate reactions to 9/11 on the part of key individuals in the Bush administration were clearly crucial in setting the broad lines along which US strategy would at least initially evolve and in 'framing' the conflict more generally for nearly 400 million Americans and many more people around the globe. The major long-term significance of the 9/11 attacks lay to a very large extent in the reactions they provoked.

Though privately the reaction of President Bush himself to the attacks was unequivocal – 'my blood was boiling. We were going to find out who did this and kick their ass' – his initial public response was hesitant.[66] It was only at his third attempt that he began to deliver the simple, reassuring and confident rhetoric that the hurt, frightened and angry US population expected, needed and appreciated. In his first major address, broadcast at 8.30 on the evening of the attacks, Bush said no American would ever forget 'this day', that 'our fellow citizens, our way of life, our very freedom' had come under attack, that America had been targeted because it was 'the brightest beacon for freedom and opportunity in the world'. He quoted Psalm 23: 'though I walk through the valley of death'. No distinction would be made between terrorists and those that harbour them, he said. The perpetrators of the attack would be hunted down and brought to justice.[67]

With each further speech, the narrative of righteous vengeance, of a new era dawning and of religiosity, became better defined. Bush's prose, terse and folksy as it may have been, was soaked in a sense of American exceptionalism, the 'manifest destiny', two centuries of American belief in its own role in the world as a beacon of enlightenment and progress, the sense of an existential battle between freedom and repression. 'This will be a monumental struggle of good versus evil. But good will prevail,' Bush told Americans on September 12.

The president's chosen strategy – the Global War on Terror – took around a week to be clearly formulated. Though often seen as a simple and instinctive product of a simple and instinctive view of the world, this is to underestimate its intellectual coherence and internal logic. The thinking among many in the American Department of Defense is revealed by the account of a lengthy debate among senior Pentagon political appointees on the day after the attacks. Related by Douglas Feith, the under secretary of defense for policy, the conversation involved General John Abizaid, who was to take command of US forces in the key theatres of the war on terror within two years and who would start to develop the American military's thinking on 'the 9/11 Wars'.[68] It took place on board a military transport plane bringing the Americans back to Washington from Moscow, where they had been discussing the abrogation of Cold-War-era missile control agreements.

The president had already told his most senior intelligence officials that their mission was now to 'disrupt attacks before they had happened' and stressed the need for deterrence.[69] Starting from the principle that their primary task was not to punish those responsible for 9/11 but to prevent such attacks happening again, the men on the plane talked for many hours about how best to target the shadowy and elusive group of individuals responsible. The answer lay in the nature of the enemy, which, Feith argued, comprised two main elements: a network of interlinked terrorist groups apparently including al-Qaeda, Hezbollah in Lebanon, Hamas in the Gaza Strip, the Indonesian Jemaa Islamiya and many others and the states which supported them. These latter included, *inter alia*, Pakistan, Iraq, Iran and Taliban Afghanistan. If America was to be protected in the future – especially from the threat of chemical, biological or nuclear weapons – then this network needed to be broken up and these states – and potentially others such as North Korea and Libya – needed to be made to cease their sponsorship of terrorists. It followed that any strike on Afghanistan could only therefore be a component of a much broader effort against multiple targets. One key element of any campaign would be the necessity to intimidate actual or potential sponsors of terror around the world.[70] Indeed, the operations in Afghanistan against al-Qaeda – part of the network – and the Taliban – the sponsoring regime – would have to be the first demonstration of the new strategy but far from the last. For if intimidation did not work, then forcing regime change needed to be considered too. America's future safety lay in the resolve with which this new policy of prevention by deterrence was prosecuted. There had to be a definitive end to the drift and indecision that had so gravely weakened the USA over previous years. Otherwise, the logic ran, there would be another September 11.[71]

Over the coming weeks, despite the protest of many other loud voices in the administration who favoured a much narrower 'law enforcement' approach focusing on the perpetrators of 9/11, this reasoning would prevail. The thinking of senior figures such as Cheney and Rumsfeld as well as the input of less important but nonetheless ideological influential figures such as Feith and Paul Wolfowitz, a brilliant career academic and diplomat who had been appointed deputy defense secretary, would be condensed into the Defense Department's strategic plan for what had become, after the idea of declaring 'a War on Radical Islam' or 'a War on Islamic Extremism' were both rejected, a 'Global War on Terror'. Five days after 9/11, Bush was promising to rid the world of 'evil doers'.[72] Before two weeks had passed, he promised that 'our war begins with al-Qaeda but it does not end there'. Instead, 'it will not end until every terrorist group of global reach has been found, stopped and defeated'.[73] All the major figures in the administration stressed repeatedly that this new conflict would last a long time.

## OPERATION ENDURING FREEDOM

By the end of September 2001 the US war plan for the first action of the Global War on Terror, the attack on Afghanistan, had been finalized. The aim of Operation Enduring Freedom was both to capture or otherwise eliminate al-Qaeda and to depose the Taliban.[74] Difficult negotiations with Uzbekistan to secure basing rights for American planes had been successfully concluded. More crucially, General Pervez Musharraf, the army general who had seized power in Pakistan in a bloodless coup in 1999, had agreed to a list of seven demands including full intelligence sharing, the use of two small airstrips and a halt to his nation's support for the Taliban.[75] The close, if tense and unstable, working relationship that successive Pakistani governments and the Pakistani security and military establishment had established with the USA through the Cold War had soured through the 1990s, and the relative ease with which Musharraf's acquiescence appeared to have been obtained through a mixture of cajolery and threat heartened the White

House. Offers of assistance or cooperation from more than seventy countries ranging from the Republic of the Congo to South Korea had been received and, on the whole, politely rejected. Congress had appropriated $40 billion for the coming campaign.[76]

The strategy for Afghanistan decided on by Bush, Rumsfeld, Cheney and the military was determined by a variety of considerations. One key element was the desire of the president to 'change the impression' he felt had been left by successive withdrawals in the face of threat over the previous twenty years. This had been an invitation to ever more brazen attacks. Only 'the most aggressive' of responses would suffice to deter the enemy.[77] That did not mean huge numbers of troops, however. Both Bush and Rumsfeld believed that modern wars could be won by forces 'defined less by size and more by mobility [and which] rely more heavily on stealth, precision weaponry and information technologies'.[78] They thus explicitly rejected the 'Powell Doctrine', named after the administration's secretary of state, who as an army general had commanded coalition forces in the First Gulf War. That doctrine had meant only going to war with massive and overwhelming numbers and was deemed outdated or, at the very least, unsuitable to Afghanistan. No one had any desire to end up where the Soviets had found themselves, and the key to this was seen as keeping a 'light footprint' to avoid becoming an army of occupation and sparking a generalized insurrection. There was also the wish, particularly of Wolfowitz, who had been heavily influenced by his direct experience of relatively successful processes of democratization in south-east Asia, to see 'the Afghans liberate themselves'.[79] Finally, there were longstanding American conservative suspicions, nurtured through the Clinton era, of the use of military forces for 'soft' liberal humanitarian-type tasks.

Equally, though Bush had said that the White House would 'rally the world', Afghanistan would be an American campaign. Tony Blair, who had immediately offered to supply any help the US required, was told that joining the coalition involved 'accepting the doctrine' and that though 'the wider the coalition the better, [we] are going to do this anyway'.[80] The Bush administration, and especially Rumsfeld, was determined to avoid any repetition of the 'war by committee' that had been seen during the Kosovo campaign of 1999 and, they felt, had severely hampered the use of US military power. When NATO invoked Article Five of its charter, summoning all members to the aid of one who had been attacked, the gesture went unacknowledged by the White House. Building a coalition, Rumsfeld insisted, should not become an end in itself as conditions posed by participants risked 'limiting the ability of the president ... to protect the United States'. The coalition should not be allowed to define the mission, he told subordinates and wrote in the *New York Times*.[81]

Once it had been decided to avoid the use of large numbers of American troops on the ground, the question of the military capacities of the Northern Alliance, the rough coalition of the various militia which made up the opposition to the Taliban in Afghanistan, became critical. The CIA's poor view of their competence and reliability was shared by General Tommy Franks, the commander of the US military operation, and was only reinforced as more was learned about General Mohammed Fahim, the late Massood's uninspiring and uncharismatic successor. The State Department also had serious concerns about the consequences for a post-war Afghanistan if the opposition groups ended up with too much power. The Pakistanis had made their own reservations about the disparate factions of the anti-Taliban opposition taking power abundantly clear to the Americans, enlisting the Saudis in a fairly unsubtle lobbying campaign, and important voices within the CIA were 'sensitive to Islamabad's concerns'.[82] This led to a natural tendency in the intelligence community to favour the strategy of undermining the Taliban's hold on the south and the east of Afghanistan by exploiting tribal splits and discontents rather than throwing American military and diplomatic weight entirely behind the rag-tag anti-Taliban forces in the north. The senior leadership at the Department of Defense disagreed, and the result was a compromise. Though the first option remained the 'southern strategy' of provoking a rebellion among the Pashtun populations who provided the bedrock support for the Taliban, measures were taken to prepare a 'northern strategy' if it proved necessary. Teams of CIA operatives were thus airdropped into the north of Afghanistan to link up with the Northern Alliance.

The first American boots arrived on the ground in Afghanistan at about the time when, after convincing the army high command that his decision to offer full cooperation to the US was the only viable option, President Musharraf went on Pakistani state television to explain that he had acted in his nation's interests by accepting American demands. In Washington the reaction to his announcement was watched warily, as it was clear from secret polling that support in Pakistan for Mullah Omar's regime had actually hardened after 9/11.[83] There was, however, little real opposition to Musharraf's decision. Religious parties organized a few relatively small rallies around the country. In Peshawar police baton-charged students from the religious schools around the city, but the anger seemed half-hearted. At most rallies the police exercised restraint. A pair of fingers that the author saw lying in the road had been severed from the hand of a demonstrator by a simple tear gas canister. Other protests, however, degenerated, and authorities, fearful of a wider breakdown of law and order, ordered the use of live rounds. Inevitably, a handful of demonstrators were shot and killed. They became the first victims of the 9/11 Wars outside America.[84]

# 3

# War in Afghanistan

## FIRST STRIKES

On the eve of war Mullah Omar addressed his followers. He told them that they were facing an extremely powerful enemy and that defeat and death were probable – though the forces of Islam would eventually prevail over the very long term. He admitted his own very human fear at the prospect of losing his family, his friends, position, privileges and, quite probably, his life. However, his reasons for fighting were clear. Omar said he 'did not want to become a friend of the non-Muslims for [they] are against all my beliefs and my religion' and was thus 'ready to lose everything'. He would trust, he told his troops, only 'in Islam' and his own 'Afghan bravery'.[1] There was no reason to doubt the sincerity of the Taliban leader's words. The chances that Mullah Omar would even discuss agreeing to US demands and handing over the Saudi-born militant who was theoretically his guest, however poor relations often were between Afghans and the Arabs living in their country, were always extremely slim. However, beyond the rhetoric and the genuine emotion was another purely rational calculation. If Omar had surrendered bin Laden even to a 'third country', his credibility and thus authority within the Taliban would have been destroyed, and the movement would have most likely disintegrated. If he refused to hand over bin Laden, however, the Taliban would probably be defeated but not necessarily decisively. Certainly the movement's ideological credentials would remain untarnished, as would Mullah Omar's own moral authority. His refusal of the American ultimatum and of Pakistani attempts to mediate some kind of deal was thus predictable.[2] 'Try as we did we could not persuade Mullah Omar to let go of bin Laden in the window available before the deadline imposed by President Bush,' General Musharraf later recalled. With the cursory diplomacy over, the war could start.[3] The bombing began on October 7.

To start with, there was little in the way of 'shock and awe', as Rumsfeld had originally wanted. Sorties were flown against fifty-three targets in the first twenty-four hours and continued through the following days at the same relatively low intensity.[4] To the frustration of the defense secretary, the strikes were steered deliberately away from frontline positions by General Tommy Franks, the military commander in charge of the campaign, to allow the CIA's 'southern strategy' to develop. Bob Grenier, the CIA chief in Pakistan, had twice met one of the Taliban's most senior military commanders in the luxurious surroundings of the Serena hotel in the western Pakistani city of Quetta, only 110 miles from Kandahar itself, first to reiterate the American offer of negotiations if bin Laden was handed over and, at the second meeting, to suggest a possibility of an internal coup against Mullah Omar.[5] Elsewhere, the CIA and to a lesser extent MI6 were handing out dozens of satellite phones accompanied by packets of $10,000 to warlords and tribal chiefs within Afghanistan and approaching scores more.[6] Many took the cash and handed the telephone to the Taliban. Others simply rejected the CIA's offer. The Taliban themselves had a rudimentary but effective intelligence system and made scores of arrests in Jalalabad, in Kabul and in the eastern city of Khost, where, at least before the US-led air strikes started, local tribes had looked to be wavering.[7] The bombing continued, largely ineffectually, with Taliban commanders mocking the American efforts, for a second week and then a third. Early bombing had been directed at the sort of rear area targets that would have been useful when fighting a more conventional enemy – supplies depots, vehicle parks – but anyone who knew Afghanistan at the time knew that talk in Pentagon press conferences of 'degrading command and control systems' and suppressing anti-aircraft defences was nonsense. The local version of the former was a man sitting on a rug with a radio, of the latter Soviet-era heavy machine guns that needed to be manually sighted. 'We are not running out of targets ... Afghanistan is,' General Richard Myers, chairman of America's joint chiefs of staff, said.[8] But this was a problem. With no sign of any significant movement against the Taliban among the tribes in the south and the east, frustration in Washington and among the teams of American operatives in the north mounted. The latter sent back cables pleading for more resources. The Islamabad CIA station insisted their strategy would work if given sufficient time.[9]

## ABDUL HAQ

The coming war did not just pose challenges to states and their security services, however.

A few days after September 11 a portly forty-three-year-old Afghan flew into Peshawar from Dubai. His name was Abdul Rauf Humayun Arsala, but everyone called him Abdul Haq. His life had been profoundly intertwined with the conflicts that had racked south-west Asia over previous decades, and his death would be too. Though a very minor player in the great scheme of what was happening in late September 2001, Haq's story was a useful reminder of the reality on the ground in the places where the 9/11 Wars were to be fought over the coming months and years. For in places like Peshawar or Jalalabad and for men like Haq the grand rhetoric of a 'global war on terrorism' meant very little.

A Pashtun from a landowning family from the eastern Afghan province of Nangahar with a long history of serving their country's monarchs, Abdul Haq and his two elder brothers had been among the first to start fighting the Afghan Communists who had seized power in 1973, ending the thirty-year-long rule of King Zahir Shah. His brothers, Abdul Qadir and Din Mohammed, had both been influenced by new Islamist doctrines coming from the Middle East, and Abdul Haq, a rebel by temperament, quickly found himself involved in active violence.[10] Haq's entry into the world of violent political dissidence showed many of the factors that would prove later so common among militants of a different stamp: the example of respected peers or family members; a temperamental disposition to adventure or practical action; generalized support among his community for the cause in the name of which he was acting; a particular incident which triggered the transition from talk to execution – in Haq's case a public reprimand from a detested Communist teacher at school.[11]

Across Afghanistan at the time there were thousands of other local leaders launching similar attacks by similar bands of rebels against efforts of the committed Marxists of the People's Democratic Party of Afghanistan to forcibly haul their country out of its 'feudal torpor' and into the bright new era of revolutionary Socialism.[12] By 1978 the tiny clique of hardline Communists in Kabul had lost control of vast swathes of the Afghan countryside, and Moscow began to contemplate a 'temporary' armed intervention. When the Soviets invaded to bolster the tottering regime in December 1979, aiming to stay only for a few months, Haq and his brothers found themselves fighting a new enemy.

Haq had a good war. Active in the faction of the Hezb-e-Islami party loyal to the senior cleric Younis Khalis, boisterous, charismatic, energetic, with moderate political views, good English and, at least early on in the conflict, a relatively impressive combat record, he got on well with representatives of Western intelligence agencies and journalists.[13] He got on less well, however, with the ISI, who favoured hardliners such as Gulbuddin Hekmatyar, an Islamist former engineering student with whom they had had an ongoing relationship since the early 1970s and who now headed the main Hezb-e-Islami, or Abdul Rasul Sayyaf, whose group was mainly bankrolled by the Saudi Arabians. By 1992, with the Soviets gone, the regime they had left deposed, the various *mujahideen* factions in Kabul and the country plunging towards a vicious civil war, Haq had left for exile in Dubai, where he had contented himself with a series of minor business ventures in the United Arab Emirates. His taste for political manoeuvring had never left him, however. He kept up contacts with British intelligence developed during the war against the Soviets and had been one of the Afghans who had walked through the twin gates and airlock doors of the headquarters of MI6 in London's Vauxhall with the much younger Hamid Karzai in the months before the 9/11 attacks.[14] For Haq the 9/11 attacks, which he watched on a television screen in the internet café he ran in Dubai, were not an 'attack on freedom', as President Bush described them, nor was the reaction to them 'the new Jewish crusade campaign on the soil of Pakistan and Afghanistan', as bin Laden described it in his first public communication after 9/11.[15] Instead, they signified the latest phase in the ever-shifting matrix of Afghan politics and, crucially, an opportunity to return to his native land and, potentially, to wealth and possibly power. Haq, however, had underestimated the complexity of the game currently being played out by the Pakistanis, their intelligence services, the CIA, those directing the war from Washington and a variety of local actors in Afghanistan.[16]

This time, Haq was not backed by Western intelligence services. The CIA did not believe that he was a credible candidate to raise the eastern tribes and had offered him only derisory help.[17] Nor did the Pakistani security establishment have any intention of seeing one of their former enemies, a moderate with excellent connections in the West who was close to the viscerally anti-Pakistani exiled Afghan king in Italy, at the head of a broad-based revolt that might place a new leader in Kabul. So, though Haq's men had found themselves hindered and even attacked by local tribesmen when buying weapons, they found the road to the border mysteriously clear of checkpoints when they finally headed into Afghanistan to lead what they hoped would become the revolt that would overthrow the Taliban.[18] Haq's operational security had been lamentable, with the whole of Peshawar aware that he had ordered leaflets and paper flags from local printers in preparation for an expedition across the border. The Taliban, who had their own spies moving throughout the frontier region, were naturally waiting for him. Within days of entering Afghanistan, Haq was in trouble, tracked by superior forces across the scruffy hills south-west of Jalalabad. Though the area was his tribal homeland, the communities Haq had hoped to raise remained uncommitted. Frantic calls by his backers in the US alerted the CIA and the Pentagon to his plight, but missiles launched from a CIA Predator drone – now finally operational – did little to hold back the Taliban fighters closing on his small band. Out of ammunition, outnumbered and cut off, cornered in a dry gorge that had once been one of the *mujahideen*'s favourite spots for ambushing Soviets, pinned down for most of a day, Haq eventually had no choice but to surrender. Within hours, Din Mohammed, Haq's brother, received a call in Peshawar. It came from the satellite phone his brother had taken into Afghanistan three days earlier. The Taliban were on the line. They had captured his brother alive. Within twenty-four hours Haq's mutilated corpse was hanging from a makeshift gibbet in Jalalabad bazaar.[19]

## THE NORTHERN STRATEGY WINS OUT, THE FIRST VICTORIES AND THE RACE IN THE EAST

In Washington, Haq's death did not help the protagonists of the 'southern strategy'. By the end of October the senior members of the administration were beginning to worry about the approach of the brutal Afghan winter, the growing anger in the Islamic world sparked by a number of recent incidents involving civilian casualties killed by US bombs and the increasingly negative domestic press coverage. Much to the irritation of Bush, some pundits spoke of a 'quagmire' and even invoked the dreaded 'Vietnam'.[20] An attempted raid on a deserted air-base in the southern Afghan deserts had descended into farce, with special forces troops wounding themselves with their own demolition blasts. Bin Laden had not only succeeded in having a pre-recorded video broadcast by al-Jazeera within hours of the first raids on October 7, in which he made a series of points about the 'humiliation' the Islamic world had suffered for decades at the hands of the West, that resonated widely but also successfully met journalists subsequently. At home, the US population remained febrile, frightened, hurt and angry. Sales of flags soared. People stockpiled food. On October 17, a detector at the White House apparently found traces of a biological toxin known as botulinum. For twenty-four hours, the president and his top officials awaited the results of tests on mice that, if positive, could mean their own imminent deaths. The results were negative. Robert Mueller, the director of the FBI, told Bush that there were 331 potential al-Qaeda operatives inside the United States.[21] Successive scares of new attacks, misinformed and exaggerated reporting (as it later proved) of al-Qaeda's destructive potential and the appearance of fatal anthrax-filled letters believed erroneously to have been sent by Islamic militants or even Saddam Hussein's intelligence services to congressmen and media organizations all combined to increase the pressure.[22]

The emphasis thus began to shift. There was no sudden rejection of the 'southern strategy', but, once the Northern Alliance had promised the president himself not to enter Kabul, Rumsfeld asked General Franks to step up bombing of the Taliban frontlines in the north. Concerns about the consequences for the long-term stability of Afghanistan were brushed aside.[23] Within a week 90 to 120 sorties a day were being flown, of which the vast proportion were in direct support of the opposition troops. Now guided in by small groups of American special forces oper-atives who, after being delayed by poor weather, had reached the northern end of the Shomali plains 40 miles from Kabul and the rolling steppe around Mazar-e-Sharif, the strikes quickly brought more impres-sive results.[24]

On November 10, Northern Alliance forces, who used some of the tens of millions of crisp new dollar bills given to them by the CIA to buy off key commanders around the northern city of Mazar-e-Sharif and open a way through its defences, took the city after air strikes which saw B-52s using some of the heaviest arms in the American sub-nuclear arsenal on Taliban trenches. The next day, massive strikes broke the resistance of the Taliban troops defending Kabul, allowing opposition troops to surge across the battered villages, derelict orchards and mine-strewn fields of the Shomali plains. Though everyone along the decision-making chain from the Shomali to the White House was aware that theoretically it would be better to stop the Northern Alliance short of Kabul, the plans carefully drawn up to balance Pakistani and Afghan Pashtun sensibilities with those of the factions now advancing towards the capital were rapidly forgotten in the excitement and relief. The senior CIA man on the ground had raised no objections when told of their allies' plans to advance into the city, and by the evening of November 13, the Northern Alliance was in possession of Kabul. A few Arabs were shot around the city, but the major force of foreign *mujahideen* which some feared would defend the city simply did not exist. Their putative commander, a senior Libyan militant known as Abu Laith, had spent the previous weeks arguing with the al-Qaeda senior commanders for more troops. First he had been promised 200 men, then told to make do with only fifty. When even these did not arrive, Abu Laith complained again, only to be told there were now no spare troops as the bulk of the Arab fighters were already heading east towards the Pakistani border.[25] There was no resistance from the Taliban either. The vast bulk of the movement's forces withdrew from Kabul the evening before the arrival of the Northern Alliance in long convoys of their trademark pick-up trucks. 'We left at night like frightened women. It was a disgrace. We left in small groups and in any vehicle we could find. We did not know where we were going and we were scared of the missiles,' remembered later one young Pakistani volunteer with the Taliban at the time.[26]

The Northern Alliance commanders would argue that, as they could not have left Kabul without any government whatsoever, there was no alternative but to move in. Their case had a certain logic – at least the capital was temporarily secure – but their seizure of the city was to cause major problems later on.[27] The primary casualties of the war so far had been those civilians who had been unable to flee. Stray missiles and bombs in the capital had killed somewhere between 50 and 150 people. The family of Ali Shah, the young shepherd who had watched the preparation of the destruction of the Buddhas, had had a narrow escape. They had fled to Kabul and were lucky enough to find a room in a home of wealthier relatives. In one of the early strikes on the capital, bombs fell only a 100 metres or so away, hitting an old warehouse near by, where a small detachment of Taliban was based. The Taliban were killed, but so were a dozen refugees sheltering alongside them.

The most immediate effect of the fall of Kabul was to deprive Afghanistan of any kind of formal authority. The Taliban regime had been ramshackle but had provided a degree of overall government. Even if traditional tribal structures now filled the breach in many areas, the situation was fluid and chaotic. In the south fighting was continuing around Kandahar. In the centre, Hamid Karzai, the young exile who had travelled into Afghanistan with the CIA's blessing early in the campaign and was protected by American special forces, was steadily overcoming the initial reluctance of local tribes in Oruzgan province to commit to a rebellion against the Taliban. But though he was gaining support, Karzai controlled no ground, and his position was tenuous.[28] Towards the Pakistani border, in provinces such as Paktia, there was a confused struggle between former warlords and tribal leaders. In the north-east, Taliban and foreign fighters from various groups which had been based in Afghanistan prior to 9/11 – al-Qaeda, the Pakistani Harkat-ul-Mujahideen, the Islamic Movement of Uzbekistan and others – were still fighting hard but were cut off from supplies and surrounded. In the west, Ismail Khan, one of the best-known veterans of the war against the Soviets and the subsequent civil conflict, was back in the city of Herat. Bamiyan had reverted to the Hazaran militias. All around the country, American airpower was now simply hitting any target of opportunity that presented itself. When accurate, their strikes were of devastating power and lethality, killing hundreds of Taliban fighters in hours.

In the east, three different forces were racing for Jalalabad. The main contenders in the race were Hazrat Ali, an illiterate and brutish minor warlord known for his involvement in the drugs trade and a brief alliance with the Taliban who had recently joined the Northern Alliance, and Haji Zaman Gamsharik, a Pashtun who had been expelled from a comfortable and lucrative position in eastern Afghanistan by the Taliban and forced into exile in France. Like Abdul Haq, he too had returned to try his luck after September 11. The only things Hazrat Ali and

Gamsharik had in common were that they were both veterans of the jihad against the Soviets and were both receiving weapons, cash and logistic assistance from the Pakistani ISI, which was trying desperately to salvage something from the wreckage of its Afghan policy. Having lost both Mazar-e-Sharif and Kabul to the Northern Alliance, the Pakistanis were now determined not to lose influence over Jalalabad. As ever, local competition for power and resources became overlaid with multiple regional – and in this instance global – dimensions.

The third contender in the race, Abdul Qadir, was the outsider. He was the late Abdul Haq's second brother, and for him the new turn of events in Afghanistan represented an opportunity to return to power, wealth and influence. He too had fled the Taliban, to Germany, and was unwilling to travel to Pakistan and place himself under the dubious protection of the ISI. Instead he had entrusted his twenty-seven-year-old son, known as Haji Zaheer, with the task of spearheading his re-entry into the rude game of Afghan politics. Haji Zaheer, already a hardened veteran of the vagaries of Afghan politics and well aware of the price of failure even before the death of his uncle, was on a plane to Zahedan, the south-eastern Iranian desert city, within hours of his receiving his father's orders.

Zahedan is one of the great smuggling centres of the Middle East and Asia, a key hub for the passage of narcotics to Europe. Zaheer knew that the ISI would be looking for him and was unwilling to risk the conventional border crossing. Instead he had himself smuggled over the Iranian border into the south-western corner of Afghanistan before cutting back into Pakistan across the unguarded desert. Keeping to remote back roads running across the arid mountain wastes of the Pakistani province of Baluchistan, he headed east and then swung north, following much of the length of the 1,600-mile-long frontier and finally reaching Peshawar, at the foot of the Khyber Pass and just 25 miles from the Afghan border and 120 miles from his destination, Jalalabad, after three days of solid travelling. The already substantial population of Afghan refugees, parked for a decade or more in sprawling refugee camps on the outskirts of the city, had been swollen by new arrivals fleeing the American bombing, but otherwise little had changed since Zaheer had last been in the city five years before.

Zaheer's father was one of the best-known and respected of all the local warlords, and his son was thus able to rapidly rally a makeshift force. Each local commander brought in a dozen or so men who themselves could answer for another score or so. Equally important, Zaheer was able to arm them too. Each commander, of whatever power and influence, knew that at some stage in the future his loyalty would be rewarded with cash, in drugs, a lucrative official post or in some other way. Each of their men expected the same: a few thousand rupees, a weapon, further employment.

One of the legacies of the Khyber region's role in the 1980s as a rear area for the Afghan *mujahideen* were the numerous arms factories and dealers. When Zaheer cited his father's name to one merchant in the town of Landi Kotal, high in the Khyber Pass, the man simply opened his warehouse doors and handed over 450 Kalashnikovs, rocket-propelled grenade launchers, light machine guns and ammunition. After receiving an admonitory call from his father, Zaheer led his men at night across a smugglers' track from the top of the Khyber Pass and on to the main road leading from the official border crossing to Jalalabad, 10 miles inside Afghanistan. The march took until dawn. When the fighters reached the main road to the city, they easily routed a unit of fifty Taliban, teenagers mostly, still cleaning their teeth with neem sticks and making tea for breakfast when Zaheer's men found them. The Taliban in Jalalabad itself had already melted away and Zaheer took control of the city. His father, having travelled from Germany on planes, helicopters and finally in a jeep, arrived at dawn. The other contenders in the race, Hazrat Ali and Gamsharik, drove in twelve hours later, each accompanied by thousands more fighters. Under pressure from the ISI and with significant amounts of Western cash on the table, the three commanders came to an uneasy power-sharing agreement, though the city rang with undisciplined gunfire for forty-eight hours.[29] Jalalabad too had now fallen. Only Kandahar remained in Taliban hands.

Lying in a crook in the Kabul river and surrounded by glades of palm trees, well-irrigated fields, with busy bazaars and a famous university, Jalalabad had always been one of the most cultured and wealthy cities of Afghanistan. Yet the fall of the Taliban – or rather the arrival of the various militia forces from Pakistan – brought mixed reactions that surprised many of the Western, especially American, reporters who drove in from Pakistan and gave an early indication that reality on the ground might be more complex than the simple narrative of liberation repeated in Western capitals suggested. 'I am sick when I see what is happening.

There is no discipline here. There is no police, no army, no government. Everyone has a Kalashnikov,' said Rehmat Ali Khan, a spice trader in the once busy bazaar, eyeing the militia men who had flooded the city. 'Thank you, Britain and America, for allowing these men [Gamsharik, Hazrat Ali and Qadir] to come back and rob and beat us again,' another man shouted. Others worried loudly about the presence of Northern Alliance troops. 'We are Pashtuns,' one man said. 'The Tajiks have never been good to us.' At the filthy and battered local hospital where more than 300 civilian victims of the bombing raids had been treated in the last two months, Waly Yad, a twenty-four-year-old doctor, was unafraid to voice his support for the Taliban. 'They followed Islamic law, and that is the only way to resist America's tyranny . . . Osama is a very good Muslim. This is all wrong now.'[30]

## 'THE BASE' DISINTEGRATES AND TORA BORA

Bin Laden himself had spent the first weeks of the war moving between Kandahar, Kabul and Khost, where he took time to meet local villagers and hand out cash.[31] Though constantly mobile, he had nonetheless found time to receive a veteran Saudi Arabian militant cleric. Though bin Laden had given at least two major interviews during the war and issued two communiqués, he had hitherto avoided claiming direct responsibility for the attacks, possibly wanting to see what the reaction in the Muslim world to them would be before admitting or boasting that they were his work. Sitting in what appeared to be the guestroom of an ostensibly ordinary Afghan middle-class home with his visitor, however, he happily described how he had always been convinced that the impact of planes loaded with fuel would bring down the Twin Towers. A video of their conversation later found by the CIA and released by the White House furnished the first indisputable proof of bin Laden's responsibility for the 9/11 attacks.[32]

On November 8, bin Laden and al-Zawahiri were in Kabul, where they attended a memorial service for the Uzbek militant leader Juma Khan Namangani, who had been killed in a US air strike a day or so before, and met a Pakistani journalist.[33] The next day the pair set out for Jalalabad, where bin Laden had lived on his arrival in Afghanistan from the Sudan five years before. Four days later, Jalalabad itself was to fall to the forces led by Haji Zaheer and his rivals but with Kabul clearly on the point of being lost, must have nonetheless seemed relatively safe to the al-Qaeda leaders. Their small convoy shunned the direct route from the capital to the eastern city, itself a bone-shaking five-hour drive, and instead took smaller, even worse roads further south, where sympathetic local tribes provided greater security. After a night spent near Jagdallak, the al-Qaeda senior commanders had arrived at their destination on November 10.[34] There was rout in the air, and Jalalabad's streets were full of refugees and demoralized Taliban fighters. The city had been home to a large population of older international militants and workers with Islamic NGOs, who now choked the streets as they loaded their families into buses or pick-up trucks heading for supposed safety to the east. Large contingents from Pakistani militant groups or the tribal militias raised by radical Pakistani clerics slept on the floors of mosques or in the gardens of the run-down governor's residence, resting briefly on their way back to their home villages across the border. On the evening of November 11, local tribal leaders and Taliban notables from the area gathered in an Islamic centre in the city to hear bin Laden make a rousing speech about resistance.[35] The al-Qaeda leader handed out $100,000 and then left the next day in a small group of vehicles, crossing over the old metal bridge that marks Jalalabad's southern limits, climbing the short, steep slope off the river plain and heading due south towards the mountains lining the horizon 30 miles away.[36]

The convoy drove up the increasingly poor roads and on towards the small village of Ghani Khel, a cluster of mud-walled homes, a couple of mulberry trees and a small run-down concrete mosque, tucked in among the foothills of the ranges behind. Arriving at the village in the late evening, the occupants then left their vehicles and walked higher still towards Tora Bora, the name given by local people to the shelf of wooded hills below the final high snowy ridges of the White Mountains that mark the border with Pakistan.[37] A day after bin Laden's flight, a second convoy left Jalalabad. It too headed south, carrying the local Taliban leadership and several hundred fighters, and also passed by Ghani Khel before working its way up the slopes above the village and then stopping where four or five cars were drawn up in a heavily guarded clearing. The Taliban sent fighters to learn what was happening. They returned angry. Bin Laden was there, recently returned from a brief reconnaissance of the rocky slopes above, and his guards had warned them away. Mullah Jan Mohammed, the private secretary of the governor of Taliban Nangahar, remembered his irritation. 'It was our country. How could they tell us where to go?' he said. Overhead, B-52s were already leaving their distinctive traces in the sky.[38]

The two convoys in mid-November were only a minute part of a vast exodus which saw tens of thousands of people moving across Afghanistan's western frontier by foot, motorbike, in SUVs, buses and trucks in the last six weeks of 2001. Some fugitives even travelled by plane. The most northern element of this chaotic retreat was the flight of several thousand militant fighters from combat zones around Mazar-e-Sharif, Kunduz and Taloqan, many hundred of whom were transported in an extraordinary airlift organized by the Pakistani secret services. Others, including Mullah Dadaullah Akhund, the brutal Taliban leader who had overseen the destruction of the Bamiyan Buddhas, slipped into north-western Pakistan after paying off local Northern Alliance commanders.[39] Further south, either side of Jalalabad, scores of tracks and dirt roads along a long stretch of frontier saw heavy traffic of fugitives from mid-November onwards. Malik Habib Gul, a tribal elder, described how he arranged mule trains for over 600 militants in the first two weeks of December, charging between 5,000 and 50,000 Pakistani rupees to lead them out, not over the high mountain ridge behind Tora Bora itself but by longer but more practicable routes to the east and north.[40] One local smuggler on the Pakistani side of the mountains described leading 100 fighters to safety across these passes in five separate trips through late November.[41] Rehmat Ali, a farmer from Ghani Khel, spoke of accompanying 'sixty or seventy foreigners' over the same period.[42] Other fighters slipped out by crossing the Kabul river and then heading east into Pakistan through the deforested hills and steep valleys of Kunar province along tracks that had been used by Alexander the Great's army as it fought its way down to the Indus more than two millennia before. There, a single local commander helped up to seventy-five to escape – after relieving them of vehicles and valuables.[43] Finally there was the exodus along the roads around the Afghan city of Khost and across the long unguarded frontier running down to the official border post at Chaman. Most of those who had left Kabul on the eve of its fall had driven across eastern Afghanistan and crossed without difficulty into Pakistan. The foreigners in Afghanistan had a tougher time than the locals. The Pakistanis arrested somewhere between 600 and 700 of them.[44] They included Ali al-Bahlul, the al-Qaeda media specialist who had listened to the news of the 9/11 attacks with bin Laden, who was detained at the frontier near Khost on December 15. Bin Laden's three current wives and dozen or so children, however, crossed the border without incident.[45]

Reports of the fighting at Tora Bora gave the impression of a pitched battle, the Americans and the Afghans below, bin Laden and his men on the high ridges above. But the accounts that have emerged over recent years point to something much more chaotic and much more dispersed. The fighting at Tora Bora was scrappy in the extreme. Though there was a hardcore of militants determined to seek martyrdom, many of those who filled the defences scraped in the mountainsides stayed only for a couple of days, sometimes even a few hours, before once more moving on through the wooded peaks on their way out of Afghanistan. One was Mohammed Umr, a young Afghan-born militant who had been raised in Saudi Arabia and who, despite a budding career as a professional foot-baller, had left his home in the Saudi city of Medina to get training in the militant camps in Afghanistan.[46] When the 9/11 attacks took place, Umr had left his camp when warned about likely bombing and had crossed the country on buses, passing through Kabul a day or so before its fall and arriving in Jalalabad just a few days after bin Laden had left. After hearing that 'the sheikh' was in the mountains to the south of the city, he too had got a lift to Ghani Khel and then walked on up into the hills, finally finding a small group of other Saudis who were fortifying an old stone shepherd's shelter built around a shallow cave. All over the hillsides around the small band Umr had joined were other groups, a random selection from the various extremist groups which had been present in Afghanistan under the Taliban. All were building up positions as best they could to resist the assault they knew was coming. 'The trenches were all hand-dug, not linked and poorly defended,' one twenty-two-year-old Algerian who shared a foxhole with four others later recalled.[47] Arms and ammunition had been brought in on donkeys but were still in short supply. 'There were sixteen Kalashnikovs for two hundred people,' said another survivor of the battle. 'There was no one in charge.'[48]

According to the official American military history of the campaign, analysts within both the CIA and US Central Command (CentCom) had been speculating for several weeks that bin Laden would make a stand along the northern peaks of the Spin Ghar mountains at a place they called 'Tora Gora'.[49] It took some time, however, for a significant force to be deployed, with the first special forces units arriving in Jalalabad on December 2.[50] Eventually, around ninety American special forces troops supplemented by a handful of their British and Australian counterparts had taken up positions on the lower slopes. As auxiliaries they had recruited several thousand Afghan fighters under the command of Hazrat Ali, Zaman Gamsharik and Haji Zaheer, the three commanders who had raced for Jalalabad three weeks earlier and who were now being paid by the CIA. The plan was for the Afghans to act as beaters moving up the northern slopes of the Spin Ghar mountains while other Afghans blocked the escape routes to the east and west. As the opposing militants revealed their positions to the special forces accompanying the lightly armed irregulars, air strikes would then be called in with the laser guiding technology used over previous weeks. After some debate, the idea of using American troops – 1,000 Marines had recently arrived in the south of Afghanistan – to block the southern escape routes over the back of the mountain range behind Tora Bora was rejected by the White House and Tommy Franks, the commanding general directing the operation from the headquarters of CentCom in Florida. So too were suggestions from the field to parachute in special forces. The task fell to the Pakistanis instead.[51] The assault was launched on December 8.

After just forty-eight hours of fighting, American special forces commanders were confident they were closing in on their target. Though they had had great difficulty getting the local forces to close with the enemy – or indeed preventing them from returning to their bases below the mountain when dusk fell – the air strikes were beginning to tell on the militants high on the mountain. On the 12th a communication was heard by the American troops indicating that bin Laden was joining one of the groups of fugitives that continued to pour over or around the mountain range.[52] On December 14, bin Laden appears to have completed his last will and testament on a laptop computer. 'Allah bears witness that the love of jihad and death in the cause of Allah has dominated my life,' the al-Qaeda leader wrote, adding that 'if it were not for treachery, the situation would not be what it is now'.[53] Around December 15, bin Laden's voice was heard over the radio, giving permission for a general withdrawal to his troops.[54] By the 16th or 17th, more than a month after they had passed through Jalalabad and thirteen days since the start of the battle, bin Laden and al-Zawahiri were gone, leaving subordinates to lead any remaining fighters to safety. Their departure was precipitate and inglorious. [Bin Laden] even 'left his bodyguards in Tora Bora', one captured militant later told interrogators. '[He] suddenly departed Tora Bora with a few individuals [he] selected,' another remembered. A third said bin Laden left owing one local commander $7,000, a debt only paid ten months later. Though many Taliban fugitives, including the convoy of leaders that had been irritated by being warned off by the al-Qaeda leadership's guards at Ghani Khel, headed south from Tora Bora into the narrow salient of Pakistani land that extends into Afghanistan, bin Laden and al-Zawahiri appear to have headed in the other direction, north and away from the Pakistani border, slipping through the lines of the special forces and their Afghan auxiliaries, lying low in the house of an Afghan sympathizer near Jalalabad for a few days before heading on into the rough and remote Kunar on little-known trails, probably on horseback. Then, deep in the mountains, they disappeared.[55]

The battle at Tora Bora was declared over on December 16, when the three Afghan commanders hired by the CIA paraded an unimpressive bunch of fifty-seven shell-shocked and half-starved Afghan and Arab prisoners before local journalists. Equally unimpressive were the famous 'cave complexes'. These had been repeatedly described in Western media as vast bunkers with floor after floor of armoured gun positions, bedrooms, offices and ammunition stores all equipped with electrics and computer systems, sanitation and even power plants. There was not just one but many of these constructions, Donald Rumsfeld told a television interviewer, after being shown an astonishing graphic featuring a hollowed-out mountain fortress in the London *Sunday Times*.[56] The reality was more mundane. Only simple caves existed. They offered some protection, however. 'I remember the Afghans below and the American planes above,' Mohammed Umr said later. 'We got used to the bombing even when it was near us. Sometimes we got bombed when we were cooking so we had to keep moving the pot all the time. But otherwise it was OK.' However, the total absence of interconnecting passages between the caves naturally cast some doubt on the lurid accounts of Western soldiers clearing cavern after cavern in vicious hand-to-hand fights as they advanced deeper and deeper into bin Laden's lair in a real-life video game. Nor were there any extensive catering or medical facilities. 'There was no normal food,' said Abdullah al-Batarfi, a doctor who ended up at Tora Bora during the fighting. 'I did a hand amputation with a knife ... a finger amputation with scissors.'[57] After the battle, reporters searching the caves found little more than basic field dressings, some petrol camping stoves and tin after tin of baby food and jam.[58]

The total number of militants actually killed at Tora Bora is unknown. Some estimates run into the low hundreds.[59] 'Dalton Fury', the leader of the American special forces during the fighting, says that 220 militants were killed and 52 fighters captured.[60] Few bodies were found, however, though several dozen dead militants appear to have been buried in rapid makeshift graves during the battle by local tribesmen or their comrades. Some survivors spoke of dozens more being buried alive in caves by bombs.[61] A few score died on the high passes on the way into Pakistan. One, Djamel Loiseau, had made his way to Afghanistan from Paris' eleventh arrondissement and died of hypothermia high amid the ice and snow of the frontier ridge after volunteering to wait on the summit to guide groups of fugitives still making their way up the mountain in the dark.[62] Several of the columns of fighters organized by the subordinate al-Qaeda leaders were badly shot up.[63] But most of those defending Tora Bora escaped alive. Bin Laden himself claimed that only sixteen of a force of 300 had been killed.[64] The truth probably lies somewhere between this claim and those of the US-led coalition. Either way the numbers of fighters who actually resisted the oncoming Afghan and American forces would appear to be substantially lower than often imagined. So too is the number who died.

Mohammed Umr was one of the last to leave. Around December 17, probably after the departure of bin Laden, Umr was told by the senior al-Qaeda commanders 'to go to Pakistan', make his way home to Saudi Arabia and wait to be contacted. For Umr, the only option for escape was to follow the most risky of the many routes that fugitives had taken the previous month. With around 100 others, most of the remainder of fighters then at Tora Bora, he walked for a night and most of a day through pine forests and then through snow fields at between 10,000 and 14,000 feet, before crossing into Pakistan. The group was found and then betrayed by local tribesmen, who revealed their location to the Pakistani army. Umr was eventually handed over to the Americans.[65]

Soon after the end of the fighting, recriminations over the failure to capture bin Laden began. If it had been hard to read rapidly evolving events – senior British intelligence officials later spoke of 'a fast-moving and confused situation' on which 'it was very difficult to get a real handle' without the satellite surveillance capabilities that would later become almost banal – there was little excuse for the decision to believe that local auxiliaries could do as effective a job at Tora Bora as they had done around Mazar-e-Sharif or on the Shomali plains. Western troops and their commanders clearly had enormous trouble simply grasping the nature of the war they were fighting, of their allies and of their enemies. For the Americans, this was a just war of righteous vengeance to eliminate a group of evil men opposed to all that was good in the world, summed up rhetorically as 'freedom'. To the Afghan commanders, this was another round in a continual contest for power, influence and resources pitting individuals who had been competing for decades and communities that had been competing for centuries against one another. The Americans were new actors in this game, undoubtedly the richest and the best-armed to date, but, everyone suspected, unlikely to be playing too long.

The commander of the US special forces at Tora Bora later complained that all his Afghan allies would do was 'go up, get into a skirmish, lose a guy or two, maybe kill an al-Qaeda guy or two and then leave', adding that 'it was almost like it was an agreement or an understanding between the two forces [to] put on a good show and then leave'. Unwittingly 'Fury' had nicely summed up the traditional style of Afghan combat. In a society where reaching adulthood was already an achievement and where communities were unwilling to waste precious lives, war was more often a negotiating tool in the perpetual bargaining for scarce resources rather than a means of annihilating opponents. The 1980s had taught the Afghans a bitter lesson about fully industrialized warfare and at Tora Bora they had logically reverted to older customs designed to preserve life more than take it. Most of the Afghan troops were neither professionals nor ideologically motivated. One fighter, returning to his makeshift camp at the end of the day, described the day's fighting to the author as 'work', using the Pashto word for repetitive agricultural labour. Being a soldier was just a better-paid and more dangerous alternative to farming. And if there were other opportunities for further self-enrichment, all the better. The sub-commander designated to cut off one key escape route, paid $10,000 to do so, was simply paid more by escaping Arabs. Though a principal ally of the Americans, Hazrat Ali himself was overheard by reporters in the Spin Ghar hotel in Jalalabad negotiating the safe passage of senior militants.[66] Some of his men appear to have attempted to levy money at checkpoints from the American special forces themselves.[67] Such men were certainly unlikely, as one US officer angrily exhorted them, to 'destroy, destroy, destroy', not least because they were the ones who would have to live with the consequences of any destruction.[68]

The Pakistanis also had their own interests. Contrary to what is often said, the Pakistanis did in fact move large numbers of troops, both regular and paramilitary, up to the border behind Tora Bora and even ferried Bob Grenier, the Islamabad CIA station chief, up to the frontier to review them on two occasions.[69] But coordination had been poor, and the senior Pakistani civilian and military leadership claim to have been unaware of what was happening at Tora Bora until very late. Maleeha Lodhi, the Pakistani ambassador in Washington at the time, remembers that the precise timing of American actions on the other side of the mountains was never communicated to the Pakistanis. General Ali Mohammed Jan Orakzai, the officer who commanded the deployment of the two Pakistani brigades to the frontier behind Tora Bora, claims to have learned of the December 8 offensive from CNN.[70] Even once their troops were mobilized, Pakistani commanders had to negotiate access to the high valleys behind the Tora Bora massif with the local tribal elders, or the troops would have been attacked themselves. The result was that the Pakistani troops took up their positions several days after the American special forces and their Afghan auxiliaries had started pushing up the slopes of the mountains from the northern side. Even when they were in position, Afghan members of the Taliban were allowed to pass through their positions. President Musharraf had already made his position clear to Wendy Chamberlain, the US ambassador in Islamabad, telling her days after 9/11 that 'we will hand over AQ but handle Pakistanis and other locals ourselves'.[71] The troops who deployed behind Tora Bora were accompanied by ISI officers, who made sure that it was international militants who were detained while potentially useful proxies who might help the Pakistanis rebuild their Afghan strategy in the future were allowed to go free.[72] In any case, the senior Pakistani generals and President Musharraf were, true to the historic prioritization of threats by Pakistani strategists, much more concerned by the reaction of India to a spectacular and bloody attack on the national assembly in New Delhi launched on December 13 by a group based in Pakistan than what was happening on their western borders.

Like the destruction of the Bamiyan Buddhas, Tora Bora was one of those episodes which, though misunderstood at the time, gave a very clear indication of what kind of conflict was coming. The fighting there had revealed how combat in the 9/11 Wars was going to be. Hugely complex, it involved at least five different forces all fighting for different reasons. Often referred to as a battle, it was in fact more of a long-drawn-out sequence of inconclusive skirmishes than a climactic strategic event. Difficult to define in terms of time or space, simplified and mythologized in the popular imagination, Tora Bora was about small groups of militants scattered across a very large area of very broken terrain fighting a series of disjointed and chaotic actions of varying intensity with Western troops and their local auxiliaries, who had enormous difficulty bringing their massively superior firepower to bear. It was thus less the final engagement of the 2001 Afghan war and more the first major action of the conflict to come. Equally, the highest casualties may well have been among civilians. Within two days of bin Laden's convoy passing through, the village of Ghani Khel had been virtually flattened by a massive bombing raid which, though it had killed at least forty Arabs, had also left an equal number of non-combatants, including the children of several of the elders of the village, dead. A second air strike days later on the nearby village of Pacheer Agam missed its intended target – a reported intermediary between al-Qaeda and local Afghans – and killed around seventy civilians.[73] Other similar incidents went unreported, but the 300 civilians that doctors at Jalalabad's hospital said they had treated indicated they were numerous.

While Tora Bora had been unfolding, the Taliban's last redoubts had fallen. In the south Mullah Omar had been tracked by American special forces to a valley in the province of Helmand, west of Kandahar but predictably escaped an operation to capture him that, as at Tora Bora, relied on the use of local forces as auxiliaries to secure the village where he was believed to be hiding. The Taliban leader was last seen heading towards the southern Dasht-e-Margo, the Desert of Death, on a motorbike.[74] On December 7, Kandahar was secured by American special forces soldiers, who had as much trouble with skirmishes between rival 'liberating' groups as they did with the remnants of the Taliban and international militants. On December 11, Hamid Karzai, who had emerged as a consensus candidate among the various Afghan factions collected by the Americans under the auspices of the United Nations at a hotel near Bonn in Germany, received the news that he was to be the new leader of his country. Eleven days later, he was sworn in as chairman of the Interim Government in Afghanistan. The White House was careful to steer away from any triumphalism, but the new 'coalition information centers' that had been set up in London, Washington and Islamabad, where hundreds of journalists had gathered, issued a rousing pamphlet entitled 'The Global War on Terrorism: The First 100 Days', which boasted of how fewer than 3,000 troops had brought 'broad military success'.[75] The campaign had been cheap, short and apparently successful, a 'bargain' in the words of President Bush.[76] In all, beyond the massive airpower deployed, the US commitment to overthrow the Taliban on the ground had been about 110 CIA officers and 316 special forces personnel.[77] The former had distributed $70 million.[78] Though eleven reporters had died, the military had not suffered a single combat fatality. When a soldier had been shot in the arm on December 4 it was front-page news.[79] It had almost been too easy.

There were, however, various worrying postscripts to the war other than the escape of the al-Qaeda leadership from Tora Bora and Mullah Omar from Kandahar. The first was the secret airlift that had brought hundreds of Pakistani militants who had been fighting alongside the Taliban in Kunduz back home. With the carefully leaked news that the ISI had continued supplying arms and ammunition to the Taliban after the bombing had started on October 7 and the blind eye turned to the arrival of Taliban fugitives on their soil, this indicated that the Pakistanis' reversal of their previous policy in Afghanistan clearly had limits.[80]

The second worrying postscript involved reports of further air strikes that had caused significant civilian casualties. One incident saw a party of tribal elders on their way to Kabul for the inauguration of the new president methodically annihilated by US navy jets and gunships. Fifty were killed in their vehicles on the road, and more died as the survivors tried to find refuge in two nearby villages. American authorities first denied that the attack had taken place and then claimed the dead were Taliban. In fact the strike had been based on information that had come from Bacha Khan Zadran, a Pashtun anti-Taliban warlord who had exploited the anarchy following the fall of the Taliban regime to claim effective rule over a chunk of eastern Afghanistan after being recruited as part of the CIA's 'southern strategy'. Zadran, having learned that the elders travelling in the convoy opposed his claim to rule three provinces, had cynically exploited American ignorance of local conditions to eliminate his personal political opponents by telling the CIA that they were hostile to the coalition.[81] The final incident saw a village in Paktia province destroyed and ten men, seventeen women and twenty-seven children killed. The Americans claimed this time that the village was a weapons depot. Again, the information was out of date. The Taliban were long gone. These were the incidents that were sufficiently egregious to come to the notice of reporters or NGOs. There were many other deaths that went unreported. Near Gardez a father who had lost three daughters to an American bomb showed the author their shredded clothes, hung on a line to dry when the missiles had struck. 'The Taliban were in the town but they left days ago,' he told the author. 'Why do they bomb us?'

In retrospect another worrying postscript could be added. Within twenty-four hours of the September 11 attacks, senior officials in Washington had suggested that Saddam Hussein was involved. On the orders of the president, Franks and his Centcom staff had begun planning for a potential invasion of Iraq shortly after the fall of Kabul in the fourth week of November.[82] On December 20, little noticed among the chaos of Tora Bora's aftermath and the inauguration of Karzai, the *New York Times* published an article by Judith Miller, a reporter at the paper. 'An Iraqi defector who described himself as a civil engineer said he personally worked on renovations of secret facilities for biological, chemical and nuclear weapons,' it began.[83] The broader aims of the Global War on Terror remained unchanged. Less than a month after Tora Bora, President Bush had used his State of the Union speech to further flesh out his doctrine of pre-emptive intervention against entities posing an actual or potential threat to the USA and had named three – Iran, Iraq and North Korea – as comprising an 'Axis of Evil'. The next phase of the 9/11 Wars was already underway.

# 4

# The Calm before the Storm

## THE PHONEY WAR

Looking back, the fifteen months following Tora Bora, seem, given the sudden and extreme violence that preceded them and the escalation that followed them, like a moment of relative calm. This calm was tempered by profound anxiety but was coloured too by a suspicion that perhaps, despite the extraordinary events unfolding across the planet and the enduring trauma of 9/11, the world had not changed quite as much as many had thought on that day in early autumn 2001 when the planes had arrived from the clear blue sky in New York and Washington. As the first phase of the 9/11 Wars – the immediate aftermath of 9/11 – shaded into the second phase of the conflict, it appeared more and more likely that the apocalypse that many had thought imminent a few months previously had at the very least been postponed. The institutions of Western and Middle Eastern societies appeared stronger than many had thought. Those seeking to undermine them seemed weaker. And the critical middle ground – the hundreds of millions in the Islamic world whom bin Laden had hoped to radicalize and mobilize – remained at the very least uncommitted.

Certainly the war in Afghanistan had not provoked the violence across the Islamic world that some had predicted. Operations there appeared to be going relatively well, and Pakistan, where General Musharraf successfully managed elections to keep hold of power partly by co-opting local Islamist parties and partly by ensuring that the country's most prominent democratic political leaders stayed in exile, remained more or less calm. Musharraf himself remained relatively popular domestically, and his speeches announcing a policy of 'enlightened moderation' in religion and neoliberal economic reforms reassured much of the international community. Tensions in Europe between Muslim communities and the broader population remained negligible. Counter-terrorist authorities in the UK and elsewhere were still directing the bulk of their efforts at rounding up foreigners rather than focusing on the far more worrying threat that their own citizens might pose. The attacks that did occur – though spectacular and bloody and though often targeting Westerners – were in places that appeared very distant from Europe or the USA.

Equally, the hunt for bin Laden, though there were no definitive leads on its principal target, appeared to be making progress. Many of those foreign volunteers and militants who had fled Afghanistan in November and December 2001 had first sought security in cities in Pakistan, exploiting the relationships with local groups they had made over previous years. But urban centres had proved far from safe, and with cooperation between American agencies and the Pakistani ISI better than it had ever been before – senior CIA officers in Islamabad met their ISI counterparts almost daily to exchange information and plan operations – a series of raids rounded up many of the most senior or at least most notorious al-Qaeda figures.[1] Ramzi bin al-Shibh, a young Yemeni who had been a key planner and aspirant hijacker in the 9/11 conspiracy, was detained in Karachi, and Khaled Sheikh Mohammed, the overall mastermind of the plot, was found in Rawalpindi. 'There was a sense we were closing in,' remembered Bruce Riedel, a senior CIA analyst at the time.[2]

Though large numbers of fugitive militants were concentrating in and around towns like Shakai in the tribal agency of South Waziristan or further north in Miram Shah and Mir Ali in North Waziristan, their arrival had gone largely unnoticed and thus did little to mar the overall impression of progress.[3] Elsewhere, the seizure of a theatre in Moscow by Chechen groups was a spectacular and horrifying reminder of the variety and dynamism of terrorism but had little broader impact, and though the stand-off between a nuclear-armed India and Pakistan sparked by the Islamic militant attack on the Indian parliament in December 2001 was worrying, the tension it provoked was hardly something new in the region. Violence in Gaza and the West Bank, especially an alleged massacre at Jenin during the summer, continued to rouse passions across the Islamic world, further sensitizing potential audiences to extremist messages, and a spate of suicide bombs hit Israel in an all too familiar way, but if or how such events played into the bigger picture of modern Islamic militancy in the post-9/11 era was unclear.[4]

In the shadows, the CIA was already well engaged on an extensive programme of kidnapping suspects overseas, illegal detention, collusion and direct participation in torture, but little had yet become public, and little was yet known about abuse at bases in Afghanistan. The extension of electronic surveillance in America without warrants remained secret, and the passing of the Uniting and Strengthening America by Providing Appropriate Tools to Intercept and Obstruct Terrorism, or USA PATRIOT Act, which, among other provisions, gave new powers of surveillance to investigators, was achieved with minimal opposition. A new 'Department for Homeland Security' was also created. Most of the public outrage was directed at the establishment of a detention centre for supposed high-level 'enemy combatants' on the 45 acre site of a former coaling station leased from Cuba under a treaty from 1903 and known as Guantanamo Bay. For some time in the autumn of 2001, detainees had been held on navy ships in the Arabian Sea, but transferring them to American territory could mean they would receive protection under the US constitution. The right to silence they would then be able to invoke particularly worried Bush administration officials. Guantanamo Bay – or 'Gitmo' as the centre became known – was the 'least worst choice' available for holding such men, they claimed.[5] That there was not a greater outcry was a mark of quite how exceptional the atmosphere in the immediate aftermath of the 9/11 attacks was. As so often in the 9/11 Wars it was an image – of the first inmates wearing orange jump suits, ear defenders, blindfolds and wrist and ankle shackles kneeling in fenced-off pens shortly after arriving at the camp – which provoked the greatest reaction.

And at least through most of 2002, until the press campaigns to crank up support for the Iraq war started in earnest and the overall temperature began to rise, levels of enthusiasm for bin Laden in the Islamic world or negative Western feelings about Muslims barely changed.[6] Indeed polls in the months following the strikes and the Afghan campaign in fact showed remarkably positive views of Islam among many Americans and Europeans. One revealed that Americans saw Muslim neighbours more favourably than they did before the September 11 terrorist attacks, a trend analysts attributed to the average American's increased familiarity with the religion over the previous three months.[7] A study of discussions of terrorism in US newspapers revealed that early coverage tended in general to be relatively generous towards 'Islam'.[8] Teenagers in the US even felt confident enough to appropriate the vocabulary of the new conflict, describing a messy bedroom as 'ground zero', something out of date as 'so September 10th' and using 'terrorist', 'fundamentalist' and 'Osama' as terms of abuse.[9] In the Islamic world, though broad views of the USA had gone from bad to worse, a relatively low 28 per cent, 35 per cent and 33 per cent of respondents in Pakistan, Turkey and Indonesia respectively told pollsters that the West posed a general threat to Islam.[10] Nearly 80 per cent of Pakistanis saw terrorism as a major problem.[11] Surveys such as Zogby International's 'Arab nations' impressions of America' poll or the Pew Research Centre's 'How global publics view their lives, their country, the world' showed that a profound belief in values seen as typically American (elected government, personal liberty, educational opportunity and economic choice) co-existed with visceral anti-Americanism. Work by the University of Michigan's Institute for Social Research found that the most positive attitudes to American culture in the Arab world were found among young adults, regardless of their religious feeling.[12] The sharpening in rhetoric and radicalism on both sides was to come later, particularly in the months before the war on Iraq and when that campaign began to go badly wrong.

Nonetheless, many elements that would come to define the 9/11 Wars had in fact begun to reveal themselves. It was just too early to know how characteristic of the conflict – and its many sub-conflicts – they were to be.

The polyvalence of the 9/11 Wars has already been mentioned. But that the conflict has many dimensions is self-evident. Already we have seen how for different people – Abdul Haq, Zaheer Arsala, Mohammed Umr, Dalton Fury – the war sparked by the 9/11 attacks meant different things. Most major conflicts are complex affairs, subsuming many sub-conflicts, and it would be surprising if, despite attempts by many to minimize this vast diversity, the 9/11 Wars somehow were an exception. Yet even the most multidimensional of conflicts have distinctive qualities which give them a particular character and significance that mean they are more than simply the sum of their various parts. As the Wars continued, the common elements naturally became more pronounced. Cross-fertilization of tactics among all the protagonists, the simple movement of individuals from one theatre to another, public discussion and communication all helped stitch together the mesh which made up the conflict. At Tora Bora something of its chaotic nature had become clear. Through 2002 and into the early months of 2003, a variety of other elements also emerged. All evolved over the years that followed and all were important in defining the nature of the 9/11 Wars. This chapter examines two of those characteristics, both in evidence during the campaign in Afghanistan in 2001. One was the odd mix of ideology, blithe optimism and lack of judgement which characterized the approach of Western governments to extremely difficult and delicate interventions in foreign lands, at least for the first five years of the conflict. The second is the problems Western militaries, and in particular the American army, had in understanding the challenges the fighting posed and in evolving effective responses to it.

## IDEALISM, IDEOLOGY AND HARD CASH: HAPPY EARLY DAYS IN AFGHANISTAN

In Afghanistan, by the spring of 2002, the fighting of a few months previously and the 'quiet of the grave' under the Taliban was a distant memory. Under the trees in a dusty courtyard in the southern suburbs of Jalalabad, slates on their knees, books shared between three, latecomers searching for their friends among the rows of blue headscarves before the blackboards, the 800 girls of a newly reopened school were starting a new year. Pupils of all ages sat together in classes, the cheerful, flustered headmistress said, because many had missed several years of schooling under the Taliban. Now thousands sought to make up the time they had lost.

In Jalalabad itself the bazaars were lively, the restaurants full. Saif Shezad, a businessman who had spent eighteen years in Pakistan, said he was 'very happy' with how things had turned out. He ran Jalalabad's biggest music and video shop. All his music, let alone the Indian 'Bollywood' movies that were his clients' favourites, had been banned by the Taliban, and now Shezad sold 200 videos each week. Next door was a pharmacy run by Sikhs. They too were content. Not just because, as one of Afghanistan's religious minorities, they had faced discrimination under the previous regime but, Gurmut Singh said, because now they could play billiards and computer games at an arcade near by.[13] Near the former militant training camp of Darunta, there were rows of new cars waiting to be sold. Every day scores of taxis bounced along the road west, too dangerous to travel without a heavily armed escort just six months previously, weaving among the over-laden lorries ferrying goods to and from the Afghan capital.

Kabul too was transformed with hundreds of new businesses and restaurants now open. There was an internet café and a mobile phone network in a city where a single satellite phone at the general post office once provided the only public international phone connection. There were even traffic jams. A huge fruit market had opened on the city's out-skirts, and a new hotel or guesthouse appeared every week. One or two of the most daring and most liberal-minded women had substituted a headscarf for the *burqa* when they left home.[14]

It is easy to forget the heady days in Afghanistan in the wake of the Taliban's fall from power, especially given the violence and disillusion that came later. Yet through 2002 the worry among the vast proportion of Afghans, including much of the deeply conservative south and east where the Pashtun ethnic tribes dominated, was not that foreign troops would stay too long in their country but that they might prematurely leave. Many spoke of the country's collective experience after the Soviet war to justify their anxiety. Polls said that 80 to 90 per cent of Afghans supported the presence of the ISAF troops.[15] This may have been an exaggeration, but everywhere one travelled – and for around eighteen months it was possible to travel anywhere without concern for anything other than the appalling state of the roads – one found the expectation that a new era of security, stability and prosperity was dawning. The failure to manage these expectations was arguably the first major non-military strategic error made by the international community.

But few at the time thought expectations even needed to be managed. The soldiers of the newly formed International Security Assistance Force, led to start with by the British and then the Turks, were popular in Kabul and successfully achieved their limited aims of ensuring secur-ity in the city and protecting the new government and the thousands of Westerners who had arrived there to assist with the nation's reconstruc-tion. An emergency *loya jirga* (grand assembly or council) involving 1,501 indirectly elected delegates including 160 women was held, the president inaugurated with a two-year term, a constitution and eventual 'free, fair and representative' elections prepared. At Tokyo in January 2002 the international community had pledged $4.5 billion of redevelopment funds which, though about half of what the World Bank said was necessary, was seen at the time as a sufficient sum.

By the end of the year a substantial proportion of the 4.5 million Afghans living as refugees in Pakistan and Iran had returned to their homeland under the auspices of international agencies working through the newly created United Nations Assistance Mission in Afghanistan (UNAMA) in what was one of the biggest peaceful voluntary transfers of populations in recent history. A significant number of educated and capable Afghans from the US and Europe had returned too. A single and stable currency was created, banks and banking systems were set up, ministries were created, equipped and staffed (albeit fairly rudimentarily compared to the resources available to the new offices of the international organizations or the UN), and a British team collated, compiled and revised the nation's maps. After President Bush personally resolved a year-long internal stand-off between the American government development agency USAID, who wanted to prioritize rural development, and those in the administration who favoured using the money to hire (foreign) contractors to start road-building projects, work finally began on resurfacing the Kabul–Kandahar highway.[16] Tens of thousands of weapons were collected in a rolling programme to disarm militias. Many of the arms were old, and huge stocks remained, but it was a start nonetheless. Corruption, astonishingly, was actually reduced, with Afghanistan improving its rating by Transparency International, the international NGO that monitors the problem.[17] Private investment flowed in – from the Gulf, from the Afghan diaspora, from China. A media sector of great energy and very variable quality sprung up almost overnight. Foreign reporters working in Afghanistan split into those who were seeing the country for the first time and were surprised by its poverty and the apparent lack of progress and those who had known Kabul and other cities under the Taliban and for whom the change was dramatic. There was much talk of 'the international community'.

For the 'international community' had certainly arrived in Afghanistan – or in Kabul at least. Journalists filled the coffee-shop-cum-bar at the Mustafa Hotel in Shar-e-Nau, watching DVDs of Russell Crowe in *Gladiator* on a new flat-screen brought over from Dubai, and held impromptu parties on the roof that provoked complaints about late-night noise from the newly refurbished Interior Ministry. NGOs poured in international staff, many coming direct from the Balkans, Africa or Pakistan. Thousands of often young, usually highly educated, largely white Western people arrived. Many were serious, experienced and highly qualified experts in their fields; others were not. There were ex-British army engineers, wide-eyed American college graduates, Italian jurists, Californian water specialists, polylingual veterans of a dozen anti-narcotics campaigns from everywhere between central Asia and Latin America. One new 'adviser' cheerfully confessed to having been hired on a Tuesday and arriving in Afghanistan, a country he had never visited before, the following Sunday. Hundreds of brand new luxury four-wheel-drive vehicles jammed the streets – white for the United Nations and the diplomats, black for the private security companies also arriving en masse, khaki for the militaries. Inevitably, an infrastructure sprang up to serve this large and wealthy new population – courier companies, fixers, translators, workmen, drivers, cleaners and bars such as 'L'Atmosphère', where steaks, imported bottles of French wine, a swimming pool and the thrill of being in a supposed conflict-zone encouraged a holiday atmosphere. Visiting dignitaries haggled over carpets and 'genuine' Gandharan relics made in sweatshops in Pakistan. Rents rose five- or tenfold in desirable parts of the city such as Wazir Akbar Khan, the upmarket northern suburb undamaged during the civil war of the early 1990s. One evening in 2002, as off-duty Italian soldiers, Dutch and French NGO workers, British anti-narcotics experts, American journalists and a gaggle of recently hired consultants to the newly created ministries drank and danced, the author was offered ecstasy by a development specialist who had flown in that day from Frankfurt.

These were not the first representatives of the developed West to arrive in Afghanistan in recent decades, of course. Apart from isolated travellers or academics, the first wave had been the hippies during the 1960s. But these visitors were few and minimal in terms of their social impact. There had also been the limited number of American development experts and contractors who had arrived to oversee the spending of the aid that both superpowers used in a proxy competition for influence in Afghanistan. The Soviet military intervention had seen another kind of foreign presence, of course. In the 1990s, Afghanistan had been a backwater. This latest influx was thus unprecedented.

Quite when the intervention in Afghanistan was expanded from a pure security operation aimed at dismantling Osama bin Laden's terrorist infrastructure first to a relatively limited nation-building project and finally to an extremely ambitious bid to reconstruct and develop Afghanistan in the image of a liberal, democratic and pluralistic Western state is unclear. Certainly many of the more hard-working and sensible development workers or consultants were as surprised and concerned by it as anyone else. As with so many such phenomena, it was the result of a range of different factors, each unremarkable in itself but together almost irresistible.

One was the background. The intervention in Afghanistan came at the end of a long run of other 'peace' or 'nation-building' operations in Somalia, the Balkans, East Timor, Sierra Leone and elsewhere. It was thus a culmination of the forward momentum these had generated, in terms of action both on the ground and the new philosophies – moral, legal and political – that informed them. A second factor was the dynamic generated by those arriving in Kabul themselves. Usually Western or Westernized in outlook, they were, whatever their personal politics, representatives of a new and powerful industry of humanitarian assistance and activism that had grown enormously through the 1990s. Though total financial assistance to the developing world had diminished in quantitative terms since the end of the Cold War, with governments ceasing to fund massive politically inspired infrastructural projects such as those seen in Afghanistan or across much of the Middle East in the 1960s and 1970s, the numbers of people engaged in the 'third sector' of non-governmental aid had increased exponentially. Along with the military and national foreign services they had become a major player deeply engaged in post-conflict environments, a diverse but nonetheless clearly identifiable institution with its own norms, interests, lobbying, capacity and desire for resources, funding, exposure and employment. Finally, there was public consciousness in the West. Since the 1980s, a new awareness among citizens of their ability to 'aid' the miserable and suffering, encouraged by a series of international landmark legal agreements such as those banning the use of landmines and reinforced by unprecedented levels of individual activism, had created a new and potent global force recognized and reinforced by politicians and the media. Every new intervention or emergency operation through the 1990s had intensified this new sense of empowerment and zeal. Rebuilding Afghanistan, however, was a very different prospect from a famine-relief operation, separating rival groups in the Balkans or protecting breakaway republics.

One key element that had become rapidly woven into the post-war project for Afghanistan was the issue of women and women's rights. This continued the dialogue initiated during the autumn when the repression of Afghan women under Taliban rule had been an important part of the political rhetoric of leaders in America and in Europe to the point of almost becoming a *casus belli* in itself. Laura Bush, the president's wife, had bluntly stated that the 'fight against terrorism is also a fight for the rights and dignity of women', and in the days after the fall of Kabul, Blair, watching television in Downing Street, had pointed to images of women without *burqas* in the streets of the capital as a vindication of the war and how it had been conducted.[18] The fact that the *burqa* was worn by Afghan women long before the Taliban came to power and owed as much to the detribalization and urbanization of Afghan society than reactionary rule in itself was ignored.[19]

The 'liberation of women' thus became a key element of the new enlarged project for Afghanistan's future too.[20] Quite what this would entail or how it would be achieved was never fully defined. Bianca Jagger, the human rights campaigner, flew in to Kabul for an International Women's Day organized by the United Nations and spoke of the 'passive resistance of Afghan women' over decades.[21] Such an event would have been 'unthinkable under the oppressive Taliban regime', said a British Ministry of Defence press release. One difficult and revealing moment came when a young Afghan woman, Vida Samadzai, who had been living in the USA since 1996, controversially took part in the Miss World beauty pageant. Habiba Surabi, the minister for women, told reporters that Samadzai 'is not representing Afghanistan's women ... and appearing naked before a camera or television to entertain men is not women's freedom'. When the twenty-three-year-old, the first Afghan in three decades to take part in a beauty contest, confessed her own unease during the beachwear round of the contest and then failed to make the semi-finals, the judges announced that, for the first time, they were giving her a new 'beauty for a cause' prize for 'representing the victory of women's rights and various social, personal and religious struggles'.[22]

Such sentiments betrayed at the very least a certain naivety. With the vast bulk of the international community rarely travelling beyond Kabul and certainly having little contact with rural communities, the deep conservatism of much of Afghan society, which the Taliban in part represented, was obscured. Instead, with their interlocutors selected from educated and highly Westernized returning exiles or exceptional women such as the unique (and much-interviewed) former TV news presenter, the vision of the visiting dignitaries who flew in for a short period or of some journalists of Afghanistan as a country ripe for 'modernization' and Westernization, the two being increasingly projected as synonymous, went largely unchallenged.[23] Even if the core issue remained development, the concentration on the rights of women had the effect of establishing the '*burqa* ratio', as one senior European diplomat in Kabul cynically put it, as a key metric for success in Afghanistan with domestic public opinion in the West. History, however, argued that any effort to radically change Afghanistan needed very careful thought. Change was not impossible, but if any measure came to be seen as alien or imposed efforts could badly backfire. As early as the late nineteenth century, bids to change by force the customary relations of rural Afghan communities had provoked violent revolts. Efforts by King Amanullah during the 1920s to follow the example of Kemal Ataturk in Turkey and force Western-style modernity on reactionary rural populations had provoked a rebellion that eventually led to his deposition. Along with the imposition of secular curricula in schools, the primacy of state law and the reduction of the autonomy of the clergy, it was the issue of female education that had been a particular flashpoint. The same issues led to revolts in the late 1950s and, particularly when allied to land reform, to the protacted and extensive violence in the 1970s which had seen men like Abdul Haq take up arms and had so weakened the Marxist regime of the 1970s that Moscow had felt obliged to intervene.[24]

Many Westerners in Afghanistan at the time knew this and were wary of the expanded project for the country and the values with which it was loaded. Some of the better constructed aid programmes were designed to encourage a slow change in mentalities through empowering women by obliging men to allow them take part in the decision-making process that might trigger the delivery of funds to the village and in the management of the money.[25] These projects encouraged basic economic activity – and thus often literacy – among women and were very successful. But such schemes were all too rare. Though Lakhdar Brahimi, the UN special envoy, had recruited many of the most informed people, often long-term residents who spoke local languages, as political officers, they were sidelined relatively rapidly by the new arrivals. So too were many of the more capable and aware local Afghan operators. The project in Afghanistan could have benefited from their deep knowledge and pragmatism. Instead, often following mission statements drafted in distant Western capitals, everything began to take a strongly ideological turn.

As so often, tensions became condensed in individual figures. One had been the aspirant Miss World, Vida Samadzai. Another was Malalai Kakar, one of Afghanistan's rare female police officers. Small, active, sharp-featured, Kakar was undoubtedly both impressive and brave. She looked after the Kandahar Department of Crimes against Women, a tough and valuable job in an extremely dangerous environment.[26] Her work, she explained, usually involved 'family clashes' or 'boy and girl friendships where they run away'. Her days were spent trying to stop young women being killed by relatives for having 'shamed' their families by exercising a small degree of independent choice. Few such elopements ended in a sexual relationship. Many, however, ended in death. Kakar spoke about her work but was not interested in answering questions about the 1980s, when, having been inducted into the police in the footsteps of her father, she had served the Communist government. 'I was a police officer before the Taliban came and I joined again to serve the people,' she said drily, standing in the courtyard of Kandahar's main prison with a mobile phone in one hand and a *burqa* thrown over her arm. Seen with some justification as a courageous campaigner for women's rights in the West, Malalai Kakar was viewed rather differently locally. In her person, many local fault lines were reunited: urban and educated versus rural and illiterate, 'modernizing' and Westernized versus what was locally perceived to be authentically 'Afghan' or 'Pashtun', secular versus religious. For many around Kandahar, perhaps the most conservative part of the country and a zone where the Soviet war had seen huge destruction, displacement and loss of life in rural areas, Kakar represented memories of an earlier experience of a reforming project under the auspices of the 'international community' and of those who had collaborated with it. They hated her as a result.

## THE 'GREEN MACHINE'

Major Hilferty took as long a view of the conflict as anyone. Throughout most of 2002 the American reservist officer started every day by giving reporters a reminder of why they, he and around 4,000 other soldiers from a dozen or so countries were at Bagram airbase. 'Today is the two hundred and thirty-third day since al-Qaeda terrorists murdered three thousand innocent people when they attacked the World Trade Center in New York,' he said at 9 a.m. one morning in early May as he briefed journalists. He then read out another short obituary of one of the victims of the 9/11 attacks culled from the *New York Times*. On one morning it was 'Robert McCarthy, thirty-three, a trader with Cantor Fitzgerald who gave his wife six dozen roses on their anniversary. Five for each year they had been married and a dozen for her colleagues. Every time she looks into the eyes of her son Shane she sees her husband.' The next it was 'Ricardo Quinn, forty, a paramedic who loved to make life-size sand sculptures on Jones Beach, where he loved to go with his family.' Hilferty used the same formula – the time elapsed since 9/11, the obituary – every day. He ended every briefing with: 'The hunt goes on. The war on terrorism in Afghanistan continues.'

By May 2002, nearly 13,000 foreign troops had been deployed in Afghanistan, including 8,000 Americans involved in the ongoing Operation Enduring Freedom (OEF) and 4,650 of the newly established International Security Assistance Force (ISAF). The aims of the OEF troops were, as Hilferty said, to find and kill or capture American enemies in Afghanistan now usually labelled 'AQT', or 'Al-Qaeda-Taliban'. Their task thus differed dramatically from that of ISAF, which, as the name suggested, was to ensure basic security in the zones where it was deployed and thus to assist stabilization operations and eventual reconstruction. Bagram was the main OEF base, and the specific task of the troops there was to be ready to be airlifted to wherever they might be needed as reinforcements for the special forces soldiers who were out in the hills trying to physically catch the fugitives. The one major engagement in previous months had been a bloody fiasco with eight dead American soldiers after planners had grossly underestimated the strength of a force of international militants and former Taliban fighters who had taken them on amid the mountains of Shah-e-Kot in the east of the country. Since then, the 'Green Machine', as its soldiers called the US military, was having trouble finding anyone to fight, and conventional military activities had largely been restricted to what Colonel Patrick Fetterman, commanding officer of the 187th Battalion of the 101st Airborne, called 'clean and sweep' operations.

Fetterman, a small, wiry forty-year-old, described the one contact his unit had had with the enemy in the last ten weeks. Four Afghan men had been killed after they opened fire on an Australian special forces patrol who had then called in support. Two hundred men from the 187th were airlifted in when the shooting started: 'We landed on a hard LZ [landing zone] in very steep terrain above a village. We moved down into it and found blood traces and three large caches of ammunition. We had overwhelming force and, though some villagers were not very happy about it, we asked them to unlock their doors and we went through the village. Sometimes we had to break down doors, and that was hard for my guys, who are going from strong sunlight into interiors that could be hostile. Any AQT elements would not have been able to flee because we had air [support].' His men had fired just one shot, to kill a dog that had attacked a soldier. 'It was a pity, but better than one of my guys getting rabies,' the colonel told the author.[27]

Fetterman's statement encapsulated the flaws of the American military effort in Afghanistan at the time. The colonel, an intelligent graduate from West Point, was operating at battalion level, but the failures of the tactics he was employing were reproduced all the way up to the very highest levels of military and civilian leadership. The fundamental problem was that the American army, an extraordinary force of 1.8 million men and women funded by a defence budget in 2002 of $328 billion, had misconceived its mission.[28] Instead of framing its operations as counter-insurgency, with a consequent emphasis on protecting the population from the enemy and on creating an environment propitious to the development of security and progressively stronger governance, the American army, from the top of the Pentagon to the lowest footsoldier, saw its job as 'killing bad guys, not protecting good guys'.[29] US commanders and the CIA were under orders not to refer to their task as fighting insurgents but as counter-terrorism.[30] If villagers were upset by their operations, so be it.

Not that US troops would be around to see the consequences of the offence they caused. Strategy and doctrine called for the amount of time troops spent among Afghans to be minimized. Troops launched rapid raids from heavily fortified bases before returning as soon as possible to their Cheesy Nachos, beef jerky teriyaki, Pop-Tarts and bibles in tactical camouflage covers. Until the summer of 2002, food for the troops in Bagram was cooked at US bases in Ramstein, Germany, then flown 4,000 miles, reheated and served. The isolation meant, as conversations with US soldiers made absolutely clear, the environment 'outside the wire' was seen as populated by people who were at best picturesque, at worst evil. This created an inevitable vicious circle, making any contact with local communities much less likely, leading in turn to the reinforcement of the isolation. One soldier said that he liked going on patrol because it was like 'being on safari'. Within weeks local trucks were known by the soldiers as 'jinglies', a reference to their jangling metallic decorations, and local people were called 'habibis' or, more disrespectfully, 'hajis'.[31] Both the latter terms were, of course, Arabic in origin and had come, like the military's taste for huge walled-off bases with all home comforts, from earlier deployments in the Gulf and the tedious task of flying enforcement missions over Iraq through the 1990s.

The consequences of this mix of physical and cultural isolation and ill-adapted tactics were exacerbated by the low number of troops committed to Afghanistan. At the end of 2002 the twin operations of ISAF and the American Operation Enduring Freedom, the former still restricted to the capital Kabul and 'peacekeeping' while the latter hunted for AQT targets, still only totalled around 14,000, which worked out at well under one soldier per thousand inhabitants. This compared unfavourably with the ration of 9.8 per thousand inhabitants in East Timor, 19.3 in Kosovo, 17.5 in Bosnia, 20 in Northern Ireland and a massive 89.3 per thousand in Germany after the Second World War.[32]

For political leaders such as Rumsfeld, who were committed to a continuing and broader Global War on Terror, it made sense to hold back as many resources as possible, partly to have more for further operations but also to enhance the deterrent effect that operations in Afghanistan were designed to have on others who might sponsor terrorism. The lesser the fraction of total available resources America deployed, the more impressive the operation would be. There was also the continuing desire to avoid the fate of the Soviets and not get bogged down in a country with such a long history of resisting outside interventions. A large army was not only slow, unwieldy and hugely expensive, but its presence would almost inevitably spark a national uprising, men like Wolfowitz and Feith still argued.[33] Strong pressure from allies such as Tony Blair and from within the State Department to increase the size and extend the remit of ISAF to allow a physical permanent presence of up to 25,000 'peacekeeping' troops across much of Afghanistan was therefore stubbornly resisted by Rumsfeld and the Pentagon.[34]

Senior British military officers also resisted proposals by British diplomats to station the country's first 'Provincial Reconstruction Team', a joint base of soldiers and development and aid specialists, in Kandahar, arguing that the area was 'too large and dangerous'.[35] This meant that large parts of the country, such as the strategically critical south and south-west, remained without anything but the smallest presence of foreign troops throughout 2002 and 2003, frontiers went unsecured and the use of local proxies was continued and indeed expanded despite the problems experienced at Tora Bora and elsewhere.[36] It was not just the return to prominent positions of warlords such as Rashid Dostum, Mohammed Fahim and Gul Agha Sherzai (the veteran and broadly feared commander who had won the race for Kandahar the previous autumn with the help of US special forces) that shocked many Afghans. They were also horrified by the emergence as local powerbrokers of a multitude of less high-profile figures. Around two-thirds of provincial governors appointed in 2002 led armed groups, and the sight of such men – especially when physically protected by American soldiers or clearly benefiting financially from a relationship with international powers – undermined the fledgling Afghan government's attempts to re-establish some kind of central authority. Even down at district level, the best-armed and the best-connected were able to capture key elements of local government. The most sought-after posts were naturally those which commanded considerable opportunities for corruption, such as chief of police. Entire militias, often tribal in organization, were inducted into local security forces. Not only did this damage the credibility of the Western intervention but it also fuelled the usual Afghan competition between powerbrokers at every level from province to village across the entire country.[37]

## PRISONER ABUSE STARTS

Alongside the 'ideological turn', the mistaken tactics and the 'light foot-print' approach, another element that emerged very rapidly and then subsequently flowed on to other theatres was the abuse of captives. This occurred early in the conflict and continued in a systematic way through-out almost all of it. Of course, atrocities are a feature of most wars, and there seems no reason why this one should be any different. But the par-ticular quality of the abuse, its odd uniformity across theatres and protagonists, is nonetheless striking. It is also significant that, though the mistreatment of prisoners in American-run facilities was to climax in 2004 and 2005, it was already widespread even before senior White House officials met to construct a legal framework that would officially determine procedure for prisoners captured during 'the Global War on Terror'. This suggests the abuse was thus both a 'ground-up' and a 'top-down' phenomenon and thus deeply representative in a profoundly worrying way of the essence of the broader conflict. Along with images from live executions of detainees by militants, the abuse of prisoners by US troops would produce many of the starkest and most memorable visual images of the 9/11 Wars.

The precursor to the abuse in American facilities was the inaction of American special forces and CIA personnel who witnessed, or were made aware of, torture, abuse and mass executions without trial during or following the collapse of the Taliban. This was particularly wide-spread in the north of Afghanistan, where several thousand prisoners, a mixed bag of Pakistanis, Afghans and international volunteers, had been taken by General Dostum, alongside whom American military and CIA operatives had been fighting for several weeks in and around Kun-duz. Many hundreds, if not thousands, were murdered, some apparently buried alive, others driven long distances loaded into container trucks from which, one of the drivers recalled, the bodies 'spilled out like fish' when they were later opened.[38] US special forces at the very least knew this was happening even if they may not have been directly involved.

The most famous detainee in the north was John Walker Lindh, a young American who, after a long journey from California through radical Yemeni and Pakistani religious schools, had ended up fighting with the Taliban. Captured, he was refused medical treatment, was blindfolded with a rag with 'shithead' scrawled on it by soldiers, who, in another precursor of what was to come much later, then posed around him for a photograph.[39] In Pakistan, American personnel were visiting prisons and holding centres established to handle the fugitives caught crossing the border and taking part in interrogations where their Pakistani counterparts beat detainees badly, denied them sleep or placed them in stress positions for many hours at a stretch.[40] By December, CIA personnel in Bagram were forcing captives to stand for hours on end and wear spray-painted goggles with the deliberate aim of inflicting severe sensory deprivation to facilitate interrogation. By January, concerned British intelligence officers on the ground in Afghanistan were reporting mistreatment to their superiors, and assaults that would incur lengthy prison sentences in most nations were becoming widespread.[41] In February President Bush made public his decision that captured al-Qaeda or Taliban suspects would be treated as non-combatants rather than prisoners of war and denied the protection of the Geneva Convention and thus subjected to an arbitrary regime that would allow the US military to hold and interrogate them for as long as was desired. This breached almost every broadly established standard of international law. What by most standards would be defined as cruel and unnatural was now enshrined as official policy.[42] Bush's announcement undoubtedly had an aggravating effect – one interrogator who served in Afghanistan told the *New York Times* that 'giving [detainees] the [status] of soldier would have changed our attitudes toward them' – but also simply legitimized something that was already happening.[43]

Kandahar prison, established at the airport 10 miles east of the city, had opened in early December and received its first major batch of detainees just as the fighting in Tora Bora was winding up and a few days before the inauguration of Hamid Karzai. For the next three months it would be the main holding centre for prisoners in Afghanistan. The interrogators at Kandahar had three tasks: to obtain 'actionable intelligence' to be passed to the special forces units and the CIA to initiate immediate operations in Afghanistan or elsewhere; to elicit information that would fill the vast gaps in the American understanding of the enemy they faced; and to ascertain whether detainees were the high-level al-Qaeda and Taliban figures they were believed to be and thus worthy of transfer to the new facility being constructed at Guantanamo Bay. The pressure to get information was very high, especially as it was believed that some of the detainees probably knew about forthcoming or planned terrorist attacks.

Kandahar was brutal from the start. On planes to the prison in December, detainees were locked down in painful positions, hit with rifle butts and verbally abused. On arrival they were, according to one military interrogator, 'bound together in long chains', marched down a ramp, screamed at by military policemen shouting 'commands and obscenities audible even over the roar of the plane' and 'hurled' to the ground. Screaming and struggling, anticipating rape or execution, the detainees then had their clothes, often soiled with excrement or urine during the flight, cut away. Naked, hooded and still in chains they then underwent a full intrusive medical examination, were interrogated rapidly to establish a provisional identity and then locked, twenty-five at a time, into tents equipped with a single toilet bucket and little else. Ringed with barbed wire, open sided, the tents were unprotected from the fierce cold of a southern Afghan desert winter night. If the detainees tried to communicate with each other, they were beaten.[44]

The early 'rough treatment' soon escalated. Detainees later claimed that guards and interrogators at Kandahar had assaulted them, made death threats, deprived them of sleep, urinated on them, burned them with cigarettes, inserted sticks or poured petrol into their anuses and, again in ways that would become all too familiar later, 'took photographs of [them] completely naked' and 'stripped and piled [them] naked on each other while soldiers in full uniform took pictures and laughed'. One military translator complained to his hierarchy that special forces soldiers had used some kind of 'electric device' on one detainee. As the vast bulk of detainees were neither senior al-Qaeda nor senior Taliban and sometimes totally innocent of any involvement in violence, their interrogators inevitably failed to obtain any useful intelligence from them. Increasingly frustrated, they intensified their efforts to 'get a result'.[45]

What was happening on the ground in Afghanistan was happening elsewhere. Through late 2001 and 2002 the CIA set up a system of secret prisons across the Middle East and Asia – with some facilities in Europe or on board ships in international waters too. Within this and the parallel military detention system practices flowed from one prison to another, from one theatre to another, sometimes passing through the White House or the Pentagon, where senior administration figures effectively signed off on what was already happening, sometimes simply transferring horizontally among those involved in the interrogations at a lower level.[46]

The treatment of Zayn al-Abidin Mohammed Hussein, a thirty-year-old Saudi-Arabian-born Palestinian better known as Abu Zubaydah and alleged to be a key militant, illustrates the steady intensification of violence in this period and the way, as each new level of abuse was reached in one location, it affected behaviour elsewhere. Detained in a joint local and American operation in Faisalabad, the sprawling eastern Pakistani industrial city in March 28, 2002, Abu Zubaydah was first transferred to a secret prison in Thailand and then passed through a series of facilities in eastern Europe before finally arriving in Guantanamo Bay. As such he was one of the first few dozen detainees in the 9/11 Wars to be subject to a 'rendition', a covert transfer to third countries or into US custody by the CIA of an individual seized overseas and one of the first to be shipped around the world through the new networks being established at the time. These saw planes flying suspects from Egypt to Azerbaijan, from Thailand to Libya, from Italy to Germany via Egypt, from Tanzania to Djibouti, from Zimbabwe to the Sudan.[47] Abu Zubaydah's itinerary was relatively mundane by comparison. The treatment he received was not, however. Though his interrogation was initially handled by the FBI, it was taken over by the CIA, who were convinced that more robust measures were needed to get significant information out of their prisoner. One problem may well have been that Abu Zubaydah was simply nowhere near as knowledgeable of al-Qaeda's inner workings as he was believed to be. Over the next months he would be subjected to the full range of interrogation techniques seen in Afghanistan in previous months including dousing with freezing water, sensory and sleep deprivation, forced nudity and stress positions and the rediscovered practice of 'waterboarding', the repeated near drowning of a subject of interrogation by placing a cloth over the face and pouring water into the mouth.[48] The introduction of waterboarding has been attributed to specialist private consultants who had researched Soviet, Chinese, Korean and Vietnamese techniques and who were hired by the CIA to direct Abu Zubaydah's questioning.[49] Despite claims to the contrary such practices and thinking may have been relatively widespread. At least one former detainee in Afghanistan told the author he had undergone waterboarding – or a form of waterboarding – while in

American detention shortly after being arrested near Jalalabad in October 2002.[50]

Once abuse had reached the level of nearly killing prisoners, it did not take long before the inevitable next stage of escalation was reached, and by late December 2002 detainees had begun to die. In Afghanistan, the first was Mullah Habibullah, a big, confident man wrongly accused of links to a Taliban commander from Oruzgan who died in his cell at Bagram after six days of violent beatings. The second fatal casualty was a taxi driver called Dilawar, detained with three other men on information from Bacha Khan Zadran, the warlord who had provided the false information which had led to the bombing of the convoy of elders near Gardez a year before, who, though he had been dumped as a political ally, was still being used as an intelligence source. Dilawar, a small, frail man innocent of any involvement in violence, was subjected to a series of assaults of extreme brutality. In the last sessions, as his legs were already so damaged, he was thrown against a wall. Dilawar too died in his cell.[51] It is almost certain that there were other deaths that went unrecorded. Omar Deghayes, a Libyan NGO worker detained in Pakistan who ended up in Bagram in late 2002, claimed to have witnessed at least one murder, saying he saw 'a prisoner shot dead after he had gone to the aid of an inmate who was being beaten and kicked by the guards' and another 'beaten until [he] heard no sound of him after the screaming'. Deghayes said the incident was followed by 'panic in prison and the guards running about in fear saying to each other "the Arab has died"'.[52]

Such events were but a way point on a continuing descent. In addition to Bagram and Kandahar and the various unofficial prisons on various smaller bases across the country, there was the network of secret detention centres in Afghanistan run by the CIA. Details of two are now known: the 'Salt Pit' and the 'Dark Prison', both apparently operational early in 2002 and both key facilities of the international system of 'ghost' prisons that the CIA had established across the world. Conditions in these were even worse than in Bagram. Cells measuring 2 by 3 metres contained ten men. Prisoners were kept for months in pitch-black cells, fed once a day. The use of extreme cold or heat to 'prepare' a subject for interrogation was routine.[53] At least one, possibly half a dozen, detainees died in these two prisons. At least three others were killed elsewhere in Afghanistan at different forward operating bases in Gardez, in Kunar and in Gereshk in Helmand. In Gardez, the victim was an eighteen-year-old Afghan army recruit who died after being beaten with hoses and cables, immersed in cold water and subjected to electric shocks. In Kunar, it was a twenty-eight-year-old who approached American troops with information after a rocket attack and was beaten to death over a two-day period by a private contractor using 'his hands and feet and a large flashlight'.[54]

The spiral of escalation and abuse throughout the global network being established by the CIA was to continue over coming years. Much would slowly become public, provoking horror and anger even among allies. Senior officials at MI6 later described, disingenuously given that British intelligence officers were happy to receive information from some of the 'more muscular' interrogations and indeed may have facilitated a number of them, being 'as shocked as anybody'.[55]

In Afghanistan the detention, humiliation and abuse of thousands of often respected men was to have predictable consequences. Many of those rounded up in raids like those of Colonel Fetterman, by special forces or delivered by warlords' militia to the CIA were innocent; some were allies who were playing key roles in stabilizing the country smeared by rivals in complex local Afghan politics; all were linked into extended familial and tribal networks which meant that violence against one was seen as violence against scores or even hundreds.[56] One interrogator at Bagram said he felt he was on the receiving end of an invisible war, with barely identified individuals brought to him from out 'beyond the wire' by special forces teams and CIA operatives fighting a shadowy conflict that he knew little about. The same, however, could be said of the men out on the raids themselves, who appear to have had almost no understanding of who and what they were looking for. The three locations that had seen fatal beatings – Gardez, Asadabad and Gereshk – were among the first where violence against the coalition would start to surge. One village elder from near Kandahar who was accused wrongly of being a senior Taliban commander told his jailers shortly before his release after two years in Guantanamo Bay: 'This is just me you brought [here] but I have six sons [and] ten uncles who will be against you . . . I don't care about myself but have 300 male members of my family there in my country . . . If you want to build Afghanistan you can't build it this way . . . I will tell anybody who asks me this is *zulm* [arbitrary rule or tyranny].'[57]

# PART TWO

# Escalation: 2003–4

# 5

## The War in Iraq I: Threats, Falsehoods and Dead Men

The fifteen months between January 2002 and March 2003, if something of a phoney war, had seen a series of visual elements emerging that would come to represent the 9/11 Wars. All conflicts have their iconic images. These are often based on newly introduced technology or newly evolved tactics. The helicopter in Vietnam is one example. The trenches of the First World War is another. The tank or possibly the nuclear bomb are icons of the Second World War. If the characteristic tactic of the 9/11 Wars was the suicide bomb, it was the defences erected to defend against such strikes which became the marker of this new conflict. Before 9/11, few had ever seen the inverted Ts of concrete from which the newly necessary blast walls were constructed. By the end of 2002, placed in long lines to form instant walls of astonishing ugliness, it was increasingly difficult to escape them.

After that first period of relative calm, the 9/11 Wars would escalate massively. That escalation was to bring many new elements to them as well as embedding, magnifying, amplifying and extending existing characteristics. Not only did the war in Iraq flow naturally out of the campaign in Afghanistan – the ease with which that conflict appeared to have been won bred a confidence in the White House and a more general sense of opportunity in America that greatly informed the decision to press ahead – but much of what had been seen in the earlier fighting would be repeated in this new theatre. There was the same chaotic, indefinite new form of warfare seen at Tora Bora, the lack of genuine comprehension on the part of Western militaries of the tactics necessary to successfully fulfil the tasks they had been assigned and their vision of the population as a battlefield across which the shadowy insurgents were to be fought. There was also the violence dealt to civilians by all parties, the brutalization of prisoners, the continuing importance of the image and of spectacular violence broadcast to as large an audience as possible, the critical interplay between the local identities and global narratives and ideologies, and the systematic use of misinformation. All have been seen in previous chapters and were to feature, often on a far greater scale, in Iraq.

## 'TWO IRAQIS, THREE SECTS'

One key quality that the Iraq conflict shared with that in Afghanistan was the long roots of the various sub-conflicts of which it was composed. Few states, even in the rough neighbourhood of the central Middle East, could claim as turbulent and brutal a history, recent or otherwise, as Iraq. From its early origins as three frontier provinces established by the Ottoman Turks on the rich lands along the Tigris and Euphrates rivers on their frontier with Persia, through its forced birth as a nation under the British, through the turbulent years that followed the end of the Hashemite monarchy in 1958 and on through the early years of Ba'athist rule and the dictatorship of Saddam Hussein and the Iran–Iraq war of the 1980s, Iraq had been racked by violence, competition and instability. It had also, however, been relatively wealthy – in the 1970s Iraq was one of the most developed of all Arab states – and the drastic retreat from affluence was arguably more damaging to social fabric and attitudes than poverty alone ever could have been. There had also been the quarter of a million casualties in the war against Iran,[1] the huge financial cost of that conflict and then the economic and military catastrophe that had followed the invasion of Kuwait in 1990. The Iraq that Western forces and civilians found in the aftermath of the invasion of 2003 was thus bitter, disillusioned and brutalized. A national identity that was stronger than many believed bred a sense of wounded pride and a xenophobia that complemented rather than countered strong sectarian or ethnic identities.

The 1990s had seen a low-intensity war between Saddam Hussein and the West and a higher-intensity if unwitting war between the West and the Iraqi people in the shape of the United Nations sanctions imposed in 1991. These brutally punished ordinary Iraqis without harming the regime. In Baghdad expensive restaurants were full while over half the country's children were malnourished, many critically.[2] The wounds of the country were hidden, not least because no one risked speaking frankly to reporters. Almost everyone in Iraq lived in fear.

The country was divided into three. In the mountainous north were the 4 million Kurds, semi-autonomous under the umbrella of the northern no-fly zone patrolled by US and British aircraft since 1991 and set on defending their precarious liberty not just from Baghdad but from Ankara too. Below Mosul and the contested, mixed city of Kirkuk with its surrounding oil fields, the majority of the population across the central belt of the country was Sunni Arab. These were the four provinces that had remained loyal to Saddam during the bloodily suppressed revolts that had followed the Gulf War. Overall the Sunnis made up another 4 or 5 million. Then came the Shia south, scarred by war, violent repression and deep poverty.

Two roads led south from Baghdad to the southern port city of Basra. One took you down the Tigris, through rough towns like Amarah, across the old battlefields of the Iran–Iraq war and past the famous marshes that Saddam had drained to deny shelter to insurgent bands fighting his rule. The other followed the Euphrates past the shrine cities of Najaf and Karbala, the holiest sites in Shia Islam, and through seething cities like Nasariyah. Both skirted the vast oil fields and entered Basra through slums composed of row after row of decrepit single-storey brick and concrete homes with scant electricity, limited sanitation and borderline starvation. Largely purged from the Ba'ath Party, particularly after Saddam Hussein and his fellow Tikritis took power in 1979, one element that all Iraqi Shia shared was a desire to see the end of centuries of Sunni monopoly of central power.[3]

These apparently homogeneous communities – Kurd, Shia Arab and Sunni Arab – were, however, internally deeply divided. Though the northern zone was increasingly prosperous and stable, the Kurds had ended a vicious civil war only a few years previously. The Sunni community itself was split between those who benefited from a direct collaboration with the regime – these, of course, included Saddam's own tribesmen from his hometown of Tikrit but other major tribes too as well as others co-opted into the state military, security or bureaucratic establishments – and those who did not. The Sunnis were also split along class lines between urban and rural populations and between the educated middle class that had seen their wealth and status destroyed by war and sanctions and the newly enriched businessmen who had made money from smuggling. The Shia majority – 65 per cent of the population by some estimates – were far from a homogeneous body either. They too were fragmented along tribal lines, culturally between urban and rural or previously rural communities and divided religiously too. Baghdad itself condensed all these various fractures.[4]

Iraq also lay at the centre of an extraordinarily complex regional picture. Around its borders lay six states – Turkey, Iran, Saudi Arabia, Jordan, Kuwait and Syria – which each had its own distinctive governmental system, popular culture, worldview and history and which each had its own interests to pursue in Iraq. To the old local proverb 'two Iraqis, three sects' could be added four classes, five regional backers and six different strands of religious observance. The author, working in Iraq from 1999 to 2002, found as in Afghanistan, the sense of a multiplicity of interwoven, overlaid conflicts almost overwhelming.

## THE USE AND ABUSE OF INFORMATION BEFORE THE WAR

The process of preparing public opinion for the conflict which had started with the selective leaks of raw intelligence to newspapers such as the *New York Times* towards the end of 2001 reached its climax with the United Nations presentation made in February 2003 by Colin Powell. The only member of the Bush administration to have sufficient broad credibility to convince those doubtful of the White House's case for war, Powell, who had spent days closeted at CIA headquarters before his speech going over the intelligence, claimed that Saddam Hussein's regime was trying to acquire nuclear weapons capability and that there was 'no doubt' that Iraq both possessed and was prepared to use biological and chemical weapons of mass destruction (WMD).[5] None of these statements proved correct.[6] David Kay, the man charged by the Bush administration with running the Iraq Survey Group to find the evidence of WMD after the invasion, later said bluntly: 'We were almost all wrong.' Kay's successor, Charles Duelfer, concurred. The resulting ISG report said 'with high confidence' that there were no chemical weapons on Iraq soil.[7] None has ever been found, and President Bush himself has admitted that this failure gives him 'a sickening feeling' whenever he thinks about it.[8]

The key problem for any analyst was that, particularly following the departure of United Nations inspectors from Iraq in December 1998, reliable information was very thin on the ground. In the absence of any alternative sources, the reports of the United Nations Special Commission (UNSCOM) had provided the basis for almost all intelligence estimations of Saddam's capacity and intentions. But their data were swiftly out of date. In 1999 the CIA had acknowledged it was receiving very little that was new and was forced to hedge its bets over whether Iraqi stocks of components for WMD had been reconstituted from the enormous WMD programme developed by Saddam before the first Gulf War. This lack of certainty continued through 2000 and 2001, with American agencies raising the possibility that some 'non-weaponized' components for weapons might exist but admitting that there was no real evidence that this was the case.[9]

By late 2002, however, the qualifications had disappeared. In the USA, and in virtually every Western nation, intelligence agencies, undoubtedly aware of the importance of avoiding another grotesque failure such as that which had resulted in 9/11 and unwilling to risk a damaging row with political masters, began to issue much more alarming analyses of the potential threat that Saddam posed. What had been speculation rapidly became fact, buttressed by a stream of falsehoods transmitted by defectors close to the Iraqi exiles lobbying for the invasion. Material that had once been discarded as unreliable was re-examined and, often after have been laundered through a series of different agencies across the world, became the basis for new and more aggressive threat assessments. Not only was information from the Iraqi National Congress (INC), the opposition group led by Iraqi dissident and former banker Ahmed Chalabi, the source for over 100 individual news stories in major publications ranging from *Vanity Fair* to *The Sunday Times* (and subsequently syndicated to, or reproduced in, thousands more) but it was also fed directly to senior officials at the Department of Defense and in the office of the vice president.[10] Beyond recounting Saddam's debauchery, many of these stories reported that Iraq had mobile biological warfare facilities disguised as yogurt and milk trucks or hid banned weapons production and storage facilities beneath hospitals, fake lead-lined wells and Saddam's palaces. Others revealed that Iraq had the capacity to launch toxin-armed Scud missiles at Israel. Several such tales, often embellished with convincing detail, came from an Iraqi refugee in Germany codenamed Curveball, who later confessed to trying 'to fabricate something to topple the regime'.[11] The truth, however, appears to have been that, though he may well have still harboured a strong desire to possess such arms, Saddam had halted production and destroyed almost all WMD stocks in stages between 1991 and 1999. In a fatal miscalculation, he continued to obfuscate out of fear of being seen as vulnerable by regional enemies, in particular Iran. His failure to fully cooperate with the returning United Nations inspectors as the war drew closer was therefore due to a misreading of where the true threat to his regime lay. The last weeks before the Iraq war thus saw a miasma of untruth, myth and miscalculation on all sides.[12]

Further sources for the erroneous claims about Iraq's WMD was testimony from detainees. These included Abu Zubaydah, the detainee who had been waterboarded after capture in Pakistan, and Ibn al-Shaykh al-Libi, another senior al-Qaeda detainee who in early 2002 was tortured in Egypt at the CIA's request.[13] These two men appeared to corroborate the INC's defectors' allegations that al-Qaeda had received assistance for a WMD programme from Saddam Hussein's regime. Information also came from a smuggler imprisoned in a Kurdish jail who told interrogators (and journalists) stories of phials of chemicals being transferred from Baghdad to Kandahar. However, the smuggler, whose claims were widely disseminated in the American press, was a fantasist, unable to even accurately describe Kandahar to the author when interviewed in northern Iraq in August 2002 and al-Libi later retracted his own statement as having been procured under duress.[14]

Such claims naturally played into the question of far broader links between bin Laden's organization and Saddam Hussein's regime. In his speech to the United Nations Powell had described a close and long-standing relationship between al-Qaeda and Saddam Hussein. His claims were conservative in comparison with many of those made by senior White House figures who had repeatedly suggested that the 9/11 attacks had depended on Iraqi assistance or even been an Iraqi plan from the beginning. These ideas were based on a highly selective mix of unverified, false or misinterpreted intelligence stripped of all context.[15]

The picture built up from these various scraps of information was only convincing if, either through genuine 'cognitive dissonance' or deliberate mendacity, any contradictory evidence or contextual analysis was screened out. So when Powell told the UN that there had been contacts between representatives of bin Laden and Iraqi intelligence agents, he was not actually lying. There had indeed been around a dozen such meetings, and though most dated largely from the early and mid 1990s, when bin Laden had been based in Sudan, at least one had occurred more recently, in 1998 in Afghanistan.[16] But, as classified CIA assessments in June 2002 had already concluded, none of these meetings had succeeded in doing anything other than confirming the profound differences between the two parties concerned. This crucial qualification did not feature in the secretary of state's speech.[17]

The same was the case with the idea that al-Qaeda fugitives making their way to Iraq were being sheltered and co-opted by Saddam. Again Powell was right in saying that militants had reached Iraq from Afghanistan. However, he failed to make clear that almost all were heading for the Kurdish zones outside the control of Saddam Hussein at the time. This was not just misleading but revealed once again the fundamental misunderstanding of the real nature of Islamic militancy that had crippled the American response to the threat revealed by the 9/11 attacks hitherto. The whole concept of a link between Saddam and bin Laden was underpinned by the belief that radical Muslim activism could (a) only exist with the support of an individual state or of a shadowy coalition of states and (b) was largely the result of the activities of bin Laden himself or those around him. Yet the situation in northern Iraq in 2002 clearly demonstrated how badly wrong both those presumptions were. Though some militants did make their way to Baghdad, they did not do so at the invitation of Saddam, nor were they welcomed by the Iraqi regime. Indeed, a letter found after the invasion revealed that Saddam was not aware of the arrival of the militants in the Iraqi capital nor particularly happy about it when he did finally learn of their presence. Concerned about the potential threat the new arrivals posed, his intelligence chiefs had in August 2002 been ordered to comb the city to find them as a 'top priority'.[18] Equally, militancy in northern Iraq dated back to the early 1990s and, like almost all such activism at the time, had developed entirely independently of any contact with bin Laden or his associates. Its roots lay in factors as diverse as the civil war between secular Kurdish factions in the middle of the decade, the rejection of radicals at elections in the Kurdish enclave in northern Iraq in the early 1990s and a long tradition of political Islamism in cities such as Mosul and Arbil.[19] Contact between the various groups operating in northern Iraq and bin Laden had come very much later.

In 2000 two of the three largest groups based in the enclave they had been able to create north of the town of Halabjah had sent emissaries to bin Laden in Afghanistan to solicit logistical aid and training. Bin Laden had provided some meagre resources but exploited the opportunity to first establish relations with the third group and then finally, months before September 11, seal a union between the three factions. The group created was called Ansar ul Islam but could in no sense be considered a creation of bin Laden comprising as it did local militants already active in some cases for decades.[20] Powell also claimed that the group had constructed a chemical and biological weapons facility in the mountains of north-eastern Iraq, where they had carved out an enclave. Again, when the author was able to visit the site in April 2003, there was little evidence to back up the statement. An exhaustive investigation by American intelligence agencies found indications that experiments with poison such as cyanide had taken place but nothing to support any claim of any link with al-Qaeda.[21]

A final element that had fed the claim that al-Qaeda and Saddam had cooperated was a report filed by the CIA on September 17, 2001, noting that 'a foreign intelligence service' – in fact the Czechs – had reported that the leader of the 9/11 hijackers, Mohammed Atta, had met 'the local Iraqi intelligence service chief' in Prague in April 2001. Subsequently, this too was contradicted by both the FBI and the CIA after analysis of Atta's cell and bank card records in the USA during the relevant period.

The British MI6 had remained consistently sceptical of efforts to link al-Qaeda and Saddam throughout the run-up to war and their stance was reflected in the public positions taken by UK politicians. Even Blair avoided any direct claims of an actual current relationship, though he did raise on a number of occasions the possibility that one could be formed in the future.[22] The British government issued a series of dossiers, first to MPs and then to a larger audience, in which a mix of intelligence material and public information was presented to argue that the Iraqi leader and his regime represented a clear and urgent danger to global security in general, to the West and to the UK in particular. They focused on the supposed threat posed by WMD. Such dossiers had long been a favoured means by which Downing Street influenced public opinion and had been presented to parliamentarians and journalists during the NATO intervention in Kosovo in 1999 and more recently to set out the case that bin Laden had been responsible for 9/11. Increasingly controversial, they were discontinued after the third prepared during the run-up to the Iraq war was revealed to be largely based not on secret intelligence at all but on hastily cut and pasted information from an out-of-date doctoral thesis found on the internet.[23]

One point worth stressing is that the debate about the potential threat from Iraq took place in a context where abuses of information had become almost banal. Reports of allied and civilian casualties in Afghanistan had been systematically proved to be inaccurate. The British government dossier on bin Laden issued in the autumn of 2001 had included a reference to al-Qaeda's involvement in the narcotics trade, which was known by British officials at the time to be at the very least doubtful.[24] (The 9/11 Commission was later to conclude there was 'no reliable evidence that bin Ladin [*sic*] was involved [in] or made money through drug trafficking'.[25]) More broadly there was the flagrant abuse of the patchy public understanding of what al-Qaeda was and what threat it posed. By early 2003, the list of governments seeking to exploit the atmosphere of fear inspired by the 9/11 attacks was long. States from Uzbekistan to the Philippines had claimed – without real challenge – that local Islamic militant movements owed their existence to the agency of Osama bin Laden rather than their own repressive, self-serving and incompetent policies. India, Russia and China labelled longstanding local separatist conflicts with roots dating back decades if not centuries as 'al-Qaeda-led' or at the very least 'al-Qaeda-linked'.[26] In Macedonia, senior elected officials went as far as staging a shoot-out with supposed al-Qaeda fighters set on attacking embassies 'to impress the international community'. The victims were in fact entirely innocent Pakistani economic migrants whose bodies had been dressed in combat uniforms by officials before being displayed to the press.[27]

In the UK, as in the USA and many other nations, legislation granting radically enhanced powers to police and security services had been passed in an atmosphere of profound anxiety exacerbated by a series of high-profile arrests of terrorist suspects and a stream of sensationally reported alleged threats from terrorists, ranging from plots to release gas on the London Underground to schemes to plant a series of bombs at Old Trafford football ground, the home of Manchester United.[28] Many turned out to be hugely inflated if not downright fantasy. Though police announced that ricin, a poison made from pounded castor beans, had been found in a raid in which a group of alleged Algerian militants had been arrested in a flat in north London, specialist scientists from Porton Down, the British government biological weapons centre, found that none had actually been manufactured. This did not stop the non-existent ricin being cited in Powell's United Nations speech as a potential link between al-Qaeda, Iraq and Europe.[29] The alleged plot to attack Old Trafford ran across front pages and led bulletins in Britain for two days but turned out to have been entirely based on the discovery by investigating policemen of a couple of ticket stubs and a scarf in the homes of one of the accused, who, ironically, were Iraqi Kurdish refugees who had fled Saddam Hussein's regime.[30] When in August 2002 a man was arrested in Stockholm's Västerås airport with a gun in his toilet bag the mere fact that he had been travelling on a plane with a group of Muslims who were on their way to a conference on the Salafi strand of Islam in the British city of Birmingham was enough for UK newspapers to splash a 'bin Laden link' on their front pages. Prosecutors found no such connection or indeed any terrorist intent at all.[31]

In America, there was much talk of 'dirty bombs', devices laced with sub-explosive radioactive material, largely based on the interrogation under torture of Abu Zubaydah and of an American Hispanic former gang member and convert detained in 2002.[32] One major scare, which led to flights to the USA from Britain and France being cancelled and warnings from officials of a looming 'spectacular attack' to rival 9/11, was based on an elaborate confidence trick by a compulsive gambler who claimed to have developed software that allowed him to decrypt messages to al-Qaeda sleeper cells buried deep in America hidden in al-Jazeera broadcasts.[33] Official statements, such as the leaked intelligence estimates that there were as many as 5,000 'al-Qaeda terrorists and supporters' and warnings by FBI director Robert Mueller of a 'support infrastructure' in America 'which would allow the network to mount another attack on US soil', stoked further fears.[34] The strand of extremist ideology that bin Laden had propagated over previous years had indeed penetrated some American communities – a group of young men of Yemeni origin from the nondescript New York state town of Lacka-wanna who had travelled to an Afghan training camp before 9/11 were arrested amid massive publicity – but its purchase was extremely limited. The impression that a few deliberately fuelled the fear of many to build support for a deeply divisive policy is strong.

For though Bush's memoirs and other similar accounts emphasize the supposed threat posed by Saddam's weapons of mass destruction, the idea that Iraq posed a clear and present danger to the United States or more broadly to world security was only one of the reasons for going to war. It was the most prominent in the run-up to the conflict because, as Paul Wolfowitz later admitted, 'it was the one reason everyone could agree on'.[35] There was never a single instant when a categoric decision was taken to militarily depose Saddam Hussein but rather a growing consensus within the inner circle of the Bush administration that built on the original impulses of key individuals like Cheney and Rumsfeld in the immediate aftermath of 9/11 and made conflict inevitable.

This consensus comprised many strands. There was the original logic of the Global War on Terror: that only through aggressive, forceful and pre-emptive action by the US could potential aggressors be dissuaded and future terrorist attacks averted. There was also a strong sense that, after what was now felt to be aimless drift and weakness under Bill Clinton, a moment had come to radically change the status quo in the Middle East region in America's favour. Here both ideological visions of an invasion of Iraq triggering a wave of liberal-democratic and free-market capitalist reform in the region, forever draining the 'terrorist swamp', and more realist views based on securing the long-term future of Israel, implanting American power in the Middle East region more fully and assuring that key strategic resources such as oil flowed freely on to the world market for the foreseeable future came together.[36] Iraq, after all, had the second-largest oil reserves in the world. The human rights record of Saddam Hussein played a role too, though very much a secondary one, in the collective thinking at senior levels of the Bush administration, as did the Iraqi dictator's earlier attempt to kill Presi-dent Bush's father. A desire to eliminate or at least severely weaken a perceived threat to Israel, carefully focused and reinforced by senior Israeli politicians and army officers in repeated interactions with admin-istration officials, also contributed. One element that was notable in all these calculations was the degree to which they were 'driven by theory – general ideas about what might or could happen'.[37] Like the intelligence about whether Saddam Hussein had WMD or a relationship with bin Laden or the strength of the regime's popular support, few of these theses could be tested in a definitive fashion other than, as historian Lawrence Freedman pointed out, by the supreme empirical test of a war and, more importantly, whatever would follow it.[38] This apparent unwillingness to consider or analyse potential negative outcomes and their consequences when so much was at stake was rooted in a deliberate attempt to deal with risk at a strategic level in a radically new way. 'We don't exactly deal in "expectations" ... and ... we're not comfortable with predictions. It is one of the big strategic premises of the work that we do,' Douglas Feith at the Department of Defense explained.[39] Historical precedents were thus dismissed as irrelevant. So instead of viewing the war in Vietnam as an example of the limits of American power, the earlier conflict was seen instead as a warning that policymakers had to have enormous determination and dedication to a given policy to achieve victory. Nor was the example of British rule in Iraq – or Western rule more generally in the region in the first half of the twentieth century – considered worthwhile of study. Doubt was seen as likely to lead to self-fulfilling failure.[40]

Much of the post-invasion criticism focused on this blithe optimism. Several members of the Bush administration have defended their record, saying that they in fact spent a significant amount of time pondering possible outcomes post-invasion and planning for them. President Bush himself has said that he spent 'hours' talking over a possible humanitarian crisis.[41] However, it is clear that any planning that did occur was based on assumptions about the post-invasion situation that were entirely wrong. The Pentagon, charged by the president with managing the post-war phase, worked on the basis that following the deposition of Saddam Hussein there would be large numbers of Iraqi security personnel willing and able to support the occupation, that 'significant support' from the 'other nations, international organizations and non-governmental organizations' would be forthcoming and that an Iraqi government would rapidly emerge, allowing a 'quick hand off to [an] Iraqi interim administration with [a] UN mandate'.[42] The latter would, it was imagined by officials such as Feith and Wolfowitz, be largely composed of the Iraqi exiles who had spent the last decade or so in the

UK, US and elsewhere. These central assumptions were shared by more in the vast apparatus of the US government than was later admitted.[43]

Another key principle was that the invaders would be greeted broadly as liberators. Senior administration figures quoted American professor Fouad Ajami, who foresaw that the streets of Baghdad and Basra were 'sure to erupt in joy in the same way the throngs in Kabul greeted the Americans'.[44] Dick Cheney, the vice president, explained that there was 'no question' but that the Iraqi people would see the United States as 'liberators'.[45] Such views were echoed by many exiles too. Kanan Makiya, author of the much-read and harrowing denunciation of Saddam's regime *The Republic of Fear*, spoke of a welcome with 'flowers and sweets'.[46]

## THE WAR AND EARLY DRIFT

The war of March and April 2003 was over quickly and, as journalist Thomas Ricks has astutely commented, is now chiefly of interest for the problems it bequeathed. It had started earlier than had been planned as last-minute intelligence suggested that Saddam Hussein was at a compound on the outskirts of Baghdad. A hastily programmed missile strike missed him, however. The next day the 145,000 troops massed in Kuwait over previous months crossed the border prepared for a campaign of three months.[47] A British armoured division advanced to secure the crucial oil infrastructure on the Fao Peninsula and to surround Basra while the American forces pushed rapidly north. Resistance did not come from conventional Iraqi army forces – even from the 70,000 elite Republican Guard and the 20,000 strong Special Republican Guard – but was offered in key cities on the invasion route by swarms of irregular *fedayeen*. One of the first American soldiers to die was Platoon Sergeant Anthony Broomhead, riding in a tank in the vanguard of the advancing 3rd Infantry Division. When he waved at a group of Iraqis as his troop drove towards a bridge over the Tigris 60 miles from the city of Nasariyah they did not wave back but launched RPGs instead. 'For the first but not the last time well-armed paramilitary forces, indistinguishable except by their weapons from civilians, attacked,' the army's official history of the invasion said.[48] The idea that the attackers might in fact have been civilians does not seem to have occurred to the author.

Notwithstanding sandstorms and logistical hold-ups, Baghdad was reached relatively easily, and the city's defences, such as they were, col-lapsed after two American armoured columns pulled off daring raids into the heart of the city and to the airport.[49] A supposed 100-day cam-paign had lasted just over three weeks and had cost the coalition 133 US and 32 British soldiers. Between 3,000 and 11,000 Iraqi soldiers and between 4,000 and 7,000 Iraqi civilians are thought to have lost their lives.[50] One element that would be important later was the extremely graphic images of the fighting, casualties and destruction broadcast by Arabic-language satellite channels and to a very much lesser extent their Western counterparts. As Saddam's regime had crumbled, satellite dishes had proliferated throughout Iraq, and so much of the population was able to watch the invasion of their own country effectively live on TV, a probable historic first.[51]

For a few weeks after the collapse of the regime, most of Iraq was rela-tively quiet. Once the spasm of looting, conducted in front of American troops who had no orders to intervene, had subsided Baghdad and other cities were left tense but calm. The expected humanitarian crisis had not occurred, but then nor was there any functioning government. Even if anyone had wanted to try to run the country, most of the ministries were now gutted shells. The Office of Reconstruction and Humanitarian Assistance (ORHA), set up under a retired general to oversee transition to a new Iraqi government and deal with millions of refugees, thus found itself largely redundant. Most of the population, as had been the case in Afghanistan in the immediate aftermath of the deposition of the Taliban, fell back on local social mechanisms, particularly tribal or clerical systems of authority, justice and distribution of resources. The occupier was, for the moment, largely ignored.[52]

The late spring and early summer months also saw febrile political activity. A whole range of groups had emerged to manoeuvre for power. Many had existed in exile in the UK, the US or Iran for decades. There were the revolutionary Iraqi nationalist Islamists of Dawa, the more pro-Iran Islamists of the Supreme Council for Islamic Revolution in Iraq (SCIRI), the relatively secular Iraqi National Congress of the smooth Ahmed Chalabi with his Pentagon connections and the dissi-dent Ba'athists of Ayad Allawi's Iraqi National Alliance (INA), who had been based in London. Once in 'liberated' Baghdad, the various groups jostled and argued, appropriating houses, villas, archives and offices, largely isolated from their own communities and the concerns of the moment. That they would clash with the 'indigeneous' groups that had emerged during the 1990s inside Iraq and which profoundly resented the arrival and presumption of the returning exiles was inevitable. One of the earliest such confrontations saw the moderate cleric Sayid Majid al-Khoie killed in Najaf by a mob of supporters of a young and relatively unknown militant cleric called Muqtada al-Sadr who were apparently incensed by al-Khoie's presence in the city's main shrine in company of a well-known local official seen as a collaborator with the regime.[53]

Yet, despite the sudden and largely spontaneous outbreaks of extreme violence, the general atmosphere across most of Iraq in the immediate aftermath of the invasion was not of bloody chaos but of drift and uncertainty mixed with a degree of jubilation that the largely hated regime had gone. In the capital, the restaurants were open in the upmarket neighbourhood of al-Mansour, shops selling satellite dishes and air-conditioners did excellent business in the middle-class Karada, and the famous fish cafés along Abu Nawas street on the banks of the Tigris were full all through the balmy evenings and late into the night. American soldiers lounged on their tanks or patrolled in their armoured Bradley fighting vehicles leaving a trail of empty Gatorade sports drink bottles in the dust and potholes behind them. With electricity very limited – the acute pre-war lack of power had been exacerbated by the disruption and destruction of the fighting – millions of people simply spent much of their time trying to avoid the searing heat of the Iraqi summer. No power meant not just no fans or fridges in temperatures above 45 centigrade but often no sanitation or irrigation pumps either. The temperatures were a significant disincentive to any activity, insurgency included. Basra and the south were also relatively quiet. An apparently impressive number of wanted members of the old regime were being found and arrested. Saddam's sons Qusay and Uday had been killed in the northern city of Mosul. As in Afghanistan, something of a honeymoon period had followed the actual invasion. In Iraq, however, it was to be very short.[54]

## THE COALITION PROVISIONAL AUTHORITY

The summer and autumn of 2003 are seen as the time when the White House, having won a short war in Iraq, then lost the peace. It is certainly the case that, if the Bush administration's project in Iraq had ever been realizable, the errors made in the space of a few short, hot months ended any chance of success. When it became clear that no new government was going to emerge to replace the state that had disintegrated with the deposition of Saddam, the White House decided to replace the ineffective Office for Reconstruction and Humanitarian Assistance (ORHA) with a much more powerful Coalition Provisional Authority (CPA). They thus, with their allies in the 'coalition of the willing', effectively accepted the role of occupying power, a situation recognized by the United Nations Security Council in mid May.[55]

After four other candidates refused the post, a retired diplomat and businessman with no prior experience of Iraq or the region, Paul Bremer, was appointed as the CPA's head vested with extraordinary plenipotentiary power.[56] Bremer swiftly implemented three measures which together made what was already going to be a very hard job almost impossible. The first was the disbanding of the 385,000-strong Iraqi army along with a wide range of other state entities including large chunks of the Ministry of the Interior. The second was a radical 'de-Ba'athification' decree designed to make the rupture with the previous regime both irreversible and evident. The third was the postponement of elections until an undefined date in the future. Quite why these measures were taken with such alacrity has been long debated, but one answer may be that senior CPA officials were taking what they believed had worked in post-1945 Germany as a useful template. This was so much the case that a twelve-page draft of orders to be presented to Bremer for signature included the phrase 'the only currencies that will be used shall be dollars and Reichsmarks'.[57] A second reason may have been the simple necessity to be seen to be taking charge of a country already sliding into anarchy. A third was that the true impact of these policies was not fully understood. Officials from CPA said that they expected 70 per cent of soldiers from the old army would join the new army – when it was set up.[58] Equally the aim was only to remove the elite – the senior four levels – of the 600,000-strong Ba'ath Party. Officials were therefore surprised when, largely due to the zeal with which de-Ba'athification was pursued by the US allies entrusted with executing the policy, many more were expelled from positions than they had anticipated.[59] The problem was exacerbated by Saddam having devalued rank in the party in recent years to bolster support. Bremer later claimed that he had been told by Douglas Feith, the acutely ideological under-secretary at the Pentagon, that de-Ba'athification should be completed 'even if it causes administrative inconvenience'.[60] The British deputy ambassador in Baghdad described the de-Ba'athification decree as prompted by popular opinion after 'an intense period of listening to Iraqis'.[61] Quite whom they had listened to was unclear.

Together, the dissolution of the army and the aggressive de-Ba'athification programme denied jobs, pensions and what remained of an often already very battered sense of personal dignity to several hundred thousand soldiers, policemen and bureaucrats.[62] They also eradicated the only institutions that provided a genuine unifying structure to the country and stripped those that remained of their entire management. Even headmasters and senior doctors found themselves unemployed.[63] A third of the staff of the Health Ministry simply gave up work.[64] The secondary effects of such mass enforced redundancy – the loss of revenue for the main breadwinner in a household for example – affected many millions of people. In writing in a memo that he wanted his arrival in Iraq 'to be marked by clear, public and decisive steps' which would 'reassure Iraqis' that Saddamism would be eradicated, Bremer was falling into the classic trap of so many senior figures in the 9/11 Wars.[65] He could not see the situation in Iraq through any other eyes than his own or those, in very general terms, of his compatriots.

Then there was the decision to postpone elections indefinitely, effectively to allow a suitably pro-American, moderate, pro-free-market, relatively secular Iraqi political class some time to emerge.[66] Rumsfeld had already warned that the United States would not allow Iraq to become like Iran, confusing the idea of including *sharia* in Iraq's new constitution with creating a theocracy.[67] A CPA spokesman justified the postponement by the lack of a census and the fact that 'rejectionist and religious parties' were the most organized.[68] However, delaying the polls simply confirmed the worst suspicions of millions. One of the points missed in the West was the degree to which the nearly forty-year-old Israeli occupation of the West Bank and Gaza influenced views in Iraq of the length of time it was believed the Americans might remain there. 'Why if the US just want to leave have they cancelled the elections? This is a kind of tyranny,' said Haider Abdul Numin, a money-changer in

Najaf.[69] A weak 'Iraqi Governing Council' was created, packed with pro-American exiles and then largely ignored.

## AN INSURGENCY GETS UNDERWAY

As the spring had passed and the long, hot summer months went on, violence began to rise steadily. Much of it remained the work of unco-ordinated groups who took direction, if at all, from local clerics or from former senior regime members. These groups were bands of friends or former colleagues, men who prayed at the same mosque, went to the same café or even, in the case of one group of insurgents the author interviewed in Baghdad, half a dozen fathers whose children went to the same school.[70] Some were former professional soldiers, almost all knew how to handle weapons though not usually place bombs or fire mortars. They were professors, businessmen, civil servants, mechanics and the unemployed.[71]

They included men like 'Abu Mujahed', as he called himself, a thirty-year-old bureaucrat. A Sunni from the big Baghdad neighbourhood of Adhamiyah, Abu Mujahed had never been a member of the Ba'ath Party and said he had been 'very happy' to hear that the Americans were coming to 'liberate Iraq'. American culture had symbolized freedom, meritocracy and opportunity and Bon Jovi, the stadium rock band, he remembered. The process of disillusionment was rapid, however. First came the images of civilian casualties broadcast by Arabic-language satellite channels and watched on an illicit dish during the war itself. Then there was the sight of Americans troops doing nothing to stop the looting of Baghdad. The latter, Abu Mujahed said, had convinced him that the Americans were not here to help the Iraqis but 'to destroy them'. This was not enough in itself to push Abu Mujahed into violent militancy. Over several months other factors each furthered his progression towards taking up arms. One significant moment, he remembered, came when the Americans started 'killing and arresting' his 'own people'. Another was when he realized that, with food prices rising rapidly since the invasion, his pay as a minor government functionary was no longer sufficient to feed his family decently. 'I could no longer afford a chicken to put on the table in the evening,' he said. In addition, he said, none of the advantages he had hoped for from the invasion had come to pass.

There was no democracy, he claimed, especially for Iraq's Sunni Muslim minority, and no electricity or proper sanitation either.

It would have been difficult to describe Abu Mujahed as an 'Islamic militant'. Certainly his beliefs and values had little in common with those of a reactionary cleric or an autodidact extremist organizer and propagandist like bin Laden. He only went to mosque on a Friday and rarely prayed five times a day except during Ramadan. However, religion clearly played a significant part in his worldview and was particularly important in unifying his group and, crucially, legitimizing its actions. 'Always we discuss what we are going to do in religious terms so we can say we are fighting for the sake of religion,' he said. 'We have formed our group to fight for religion, and the main thing for our group is religion.' Abu Mujahed said that above all he felt 'humiliated'.

Over a period of weeks a group of six or seven like-minded men came together. There was no major effort at recruitment, certainly no direction from above or outside, just a band of people sharing a fairly indistinct goal and similar sentiments. The group contained, Abu Mujahed said, 'one man fighting for his nation, another fighting for a principle', as well as someone who was 'very religious'. He was the leader but not through any formal mechanism. More because 'someone has to organize things a bit', he said. Nor was the process by which his group sourced the various basic elements that all militants and terrorists require – weapons, expertise and somewhere to train and rest and hide – any less amateurish or haphazard. Careful if casual inquiries established that there was an underground network of arms suppliers already in existence. Saddam had distributed vast numbers of weapons, and the locations of dumps – often left untouched and unsecured by American troops for fear of lethal chemical or biological weapons – were known to many. Finding people who had the specialized knowledge that the group needed to use the arms that were available took longer, but step by step Abu Mujahed and his friends were able to locate experts in weapons, concealment and communications among demobilized members of the Iraqi army. 'They would help us out as a favour and did things like show us how to use a mortar in the front room of someone's house,' he said. 'Bit by bit, we learned what we needed to know.' One former army officer joined the group.

Abu Mujahed and his friends soon began establishing contacts with other similar groups, all of which paid nominal allegiance to a single tribal sheikh. There were no specific commands as such but merely broad direction from more senior tribal leaders. Over the next months the group tried various tactics: sniping at Americans, learning about remote-controlled bombs, laying mines where they knew patrols would pass and using mortars.

In every way, Abu Mujahed's operations were typical of those of such men in Iraq and in many other theatres of the 9/11 Wars. His motivations or those of the others in his group – a mixture of disappointed expectations, wounded pride, concepts of tribal and national honour, socio-economic hardship and a desire to avenge killed, injured or humiliated loved ones or associates, the smooth fusion of global Islamic narratives with local nationalist or sectarian ones – were broadly representative. The emergence and instrumentalization of religion was classic too as Islam, as we have seen in early chapters, has consistently played a role as a rallying flag and a discourse to concentrate, express and unify diverse grievances. The deteriorating economic situation of the last years of Saddam Hussein's regime had also seen a strengthening of kinship and tribal ties. These tribal and family associations sometimes clashed with more nationalist and religious identities but were often easily combined – as in the case of Abu Mujahed's band.

However, the activities of men like Abu Mujahed were still of little strategic significance in the summer of 2003. There were others who were much more organized and who targeted their efforts much more carefully. Before the war, defence officials in London and Washington had briefed reporters on the new form of warfare that the conflict in Iraq would demonstrate. The intention was to reinforce domestic support for the war while simultaneously undermining morale in Iraq. One aide to the British secretary of state for defence explained to the author over lunch off Trafalgar Square how 'networkcentric' warfare would incapacitate the key internal communications systems of an opposing force, effectively ending its ability to respond to orders, manoeuvre and fight. A key element of networkcentric warfare, he said, involved getting inside the enemy's 'decision loop' or more technically 'Observation-Orientation-Decision-Action time' (OODA), effectively acting repeatedly before the opponent had had time to react and thus, like a boxer with a winning combination, landing a flurry of blows of such power and rapidity that the total collapse of all opposition was assured. In the event, it was the insurgents who successfully got inside the OODA of the coalition forces and seized the tactical and strategic initiative. They were to hold it for at least three, arguably four, years.

Within only a few weeks of the invasion powerful bombs began to go off. The attacks, largely massive suicide blasts, could have directly targeted the Americans. Instead, they were focused on all other actors whose presence in Iraq could render the occupation of Iraq more legitimate in the eyes of locals and the international community. The massive bomb that destroyed much of the United Nations' Canal Road headquarters and killed twenty-three, including Sergio Viera de Mello, the UN's well-liked and competent special envoy to Iraq, on August 19 was just the most spectacular of the series. The target was justified in the eyes of many Iraqis as the UN's role in administering the sanctions that limited medicine and other essentials all the while keeping Saddam in power (and providing good jobs to hundreds of foreigners) during the 1990s meant that it was widely disliked. One poll in 2003 revealed that 69 per cent of Iraqis thought the UN would hurt rather than help Iraq over the next five years.[72] Senior UN staff were blissfully unaware of this, and the bombing effectively removed any major United Nations presence from Iraq and prompted other major multilateral entities like the World Bank and the International Monetary Fund to leave too.[73] A series of attacks on NGOs such as the Red Cross and Save the Children had a similar effect.

Ayatollah Mohammed Baqr al-Hakim – head of SCIRI and the most senior Iraqi political figure to publicly back the occupation – died in a massive blast that sent a very clear message about what was likely to happen to anyone contemplating taking a similar stance. Other attacks hit diplomatic representations – such as those of the Turks and the Jordanians – whose presence might too have been seen to legitimize the occupiers' presence in the Arab or Muslim worlds. American coalition allies, such as the Italians, were also targeted. The tactic was an old one, familiar to Saddam's intelligence services. Rather than directly attack an individual, particularly one who might still have some residual ability to cause harm, Saddam's intelligence services would pick off those around him, threatening, abducting, raping, beating family members and associates, leaving their real target more and more exposed and weaker and weaker until finally little effort was needed to finish him off. Though the background hum of violence might have been the work of men like Abu Mujahed, the string of major 'headline' attacks throughout the summer of 2003 was the work of senior and middle-ranking officials from within the security establishment of the former regime. They used both Iraqi and foreign volunteers as suicide bombers to deliver the bombs, an example of the 'odd couples' the 9/11 Wars sometimes threw together. The bombs progressively isolated the Americans as all those around them who could lend legitimacy and capacity to their rule fell away.

As autumn approached, a second series of targets began to be developed too: the Shia community and anything that could possibly provide any nascent government with an effective security infrastructure. Shia targets and security targets often coincided as few Sunni policemen had remained at their posts. Those standing for hours in the unprotected recruitment queues were almost all Shia too. When the Red Cross had been attacked, three police stations were hit with it. And when SCIRI leader al-Hakim died so did nearly 100 others, all Shia, in Najaf, the holy city. That those behind the attacks knew exactly what they were doing was evident. Their identity, however, was still a mystery to the coalition.

## SIX DEAD MEN

If Afghanistan was a war of far hills and valleys, Iraq was going to be a war of scruffy streets in hard-scrabble towns. Their names would become depressingly familiar over the coming years. One such place was Majjar al-Kabir, a chaos of cement-and-brick tenements, houses and slums by the Tigris 100 miles north of Basra and 250 miles south-east of Baghdad, which was the site of a short and brutal engagement in late June 2003 typical of much of the fighting that was to come.[74] As such, it is worth looking at in some detail.

Majjar al-Kabir, home to around 35,000, had been one of the many places in Iraq to liberate itself during the invasion. When American troops had arrived in the town they had found it already under the control of former anti-Saddam fighters. The US units had none too diplomatically sidelined the locals and had then handed over to the British troops moving up from the south. By June, it was a senior soldier, a British Parachute Regiment colonel, who was, despite the presence of the newly created Coalition Provisional Authority and a variety of now fairly disgruntled local actors, the de facto authority in the town.

The British decided that the priority needed to be establishing a 'secure' environment and that this aim could not be achieved without disarming the local population. Every rural household in Iraq has at least one small arm and many have heavier weapons too. Majjar al-Kabir had been close to the battle fronts of the Iran–Iraq war, had seen an anti-Saddam insurgency as well as decades of internecine tribal warfare, widespread banditry and smuggling and as a result was heavily armed even by local standards. As the population was not going to hand in their weapons voluntarily, the troops had to search for them. This they did in the same way as they had done in Afghanistan and with similar results. It did not take long for locals to make their anger at the disarmament operations very clear. At the small village of Abu Ala, a collection of breeze-block homesteads ringed with thorn bushes, thin-ribbed sheep and filthy children on the outskirts of Majjar al-Kabir, there were scuffles as locals reacted angrily to British troops entering women's quarters and using dogs, seen as unclean in many Islamic societies. 'They came into our houses with no respect,' Mohammed Ayub, a forty-five-year-old farmer, told the author.[75]

The incensed villagers organized a demonstration in the main town which degenerated into a small riot ending with British troops, pelted with stones, firing into the air. To calm tempers, a long meeting was held between British officers and local representatives, mainly elders and clerics, and an agreement drawn up. The locals would hand in their heavy weapons within a month, and the British would stop the searches. In the meantime, there would be no British presence in the town.[76]

The problem lay in differing interpretations of the latter phrase. The British took it to mean *permanent* presence, locals thought it meant *any* presence. When the British sent a patrol through Majjar al-Kabir the day after the agreement it encountered no trouble. When twenty-four hours later another patrol set out it quickly found itself hemmed in by an angry, rock-throwing crowd. The troops fired rubber bullets and then, when they had no more non-lethal ammunition, fired live rounds into the air. The crowd withdrew a little, allowing the British soldiers to reach the town's marketplace, at which point someone opened fire from a top-floor window of a nearby building. The gunman was shot dead, but two others started shooting from another direction. These too were hit, but soon, in the laconic description of the official report into the events, 'numerous members of the crowd were firing on the patrol'. For the next hour there was a chaotic street battle as more and more locals joined the fight, and the cornered British troops tried to defend themselves.[77] A Chinook helicopter carrying reinforcements was badly shot up as it flew over the town and, with half a dozen of the troops it was carrying seriously wounded, had to return to the British forces' base at Amarah 'pissing blood and oil', in the words of Lieutenant Colonel Stuart Tootal, in the operations room at the main base of the British force outside the town of Amarah, 15 miles away. 'We looked at each other. We thought the wheels were coming off, that this was our Blackhawk Down,' Tootal remembered.

Eventually reinforcements from Amarah arrived and brought sufficient firepower to bear on the gunmen – now hundreds strong – to allow the British troops to be extricated. It was only then that it was realized that the paratroopers' patrol had not been the only British military presence in Majjar al-Kabir. At 10 a.m., half an hour after the patrol had reached the town, six military policemen, or 'Redcaps', assigned to the rather thankless task of trying to rebuild and reform the town's police force had also arrived to talk to the newly appointed police chief about renovating the local station – a 'reconstruction' mission typical of those assigned to thousands of British soldiers at the time.

The men were under the command of Sergeant Simon Hamilton-Jewell from Thames Ditton in southern England. A mechanic and judo black belt, he had first joined the army as a reservist in 1979 aged twenty-eight, before enlisting in the regular forces. Hamilton-Jewell had served with British special forces for six years before joining the Royal Military Police and still described himself as 'sixteen stone of romping, stomping airborne fury'.[78] Respected and liked by the much younger men in his detachment, 'HJ' was known as a competent, experienced and motivated soldier.

It had taken nearly an hour for the group to drive slowly in two open-top landrovers from the base at Amarah to Majjar al-Kabir. Forty-five minutes after the six soldiers arrived at their destination – the battered single-storey police station 100 metres or so down a turn-off from the main road out of town – they heard gunfire from the town centre. They had no idea that the Parachute Regiment patrol was there, let alone that it had come under attack. Very soon, groups of armed Iraqis started appearing in the streets around them.

Newspaper reports in Britain later spoke of a 'last stand', as if Hamilton-Jewell and his men were cornered imperial soldiers resisting the onslaught of natives.[79] In fact, events were messier than the image suggested. The gunmen surging out of Majjar al-Kabir following the retreating paratroopers moved into buildings around the police station and started firing on the Redcaps, quickly wounding two. The soldiers abandoned their positions around their vehicles in front of the police station and moved indoors, taking up positions at windows and around the small internal courtyard, levelling their SA80 automatic rifles at the oncoming attackers.[80] With their only radios on their now burning Land Rovers, Hamilton-Jewell turned to one of the policemen who had remained in the station and asked if he had any means of communication. He did not and implored the Redcaps to flee through a window at the rear of the building.[81] It was, however, too late. The station was surrounded. After another brief exchange of fire, a local elder forced his way through the crowd around the station and convinced the gunmen outside to let him negotiate. Entering the station, he found one British soldier apparently dying and three others propped wounded against the walls of one of the storerooms. But the crowd had followed him in. The elder was pulled out of the way, Hamilton-Jewell shot and then the other soldiers, though they held out pictures of their children and wives and pleaded for their lives, executed.[82]

The violence at Majjar al-Kabir appeared to defy explanation. The men who fought the British in the town were not 'foreign fighters' nor 'regime dead-enders' but from the southern Shia populations who had suffered most under the regime and were rightly thought most likely to support the invasion and deposition of Saddam. 'We all hated the dictator and his terrorists,' Talal Abid Ahmed Zubaida, a local tribal chief and militia leader said the day after the killings of the Redcaps.[83] The local power was Karim Mahoud aka Abu Hatem, aka 'the Lord of the Marshes', a charismatic, brave, effective, ruthless and unscrupulous former guerrilla leader, who had taken charge locally after the invasion until forced to bow before the new powers in the land, but he had no immediate interest in provoking a confrontation.[84] The economy, the provision of jobs or the supply of electricity were not major factors as most locals understood that any economic improvements would take months to be seen. Indeed, electricity provision to Abu Ala, the village where the trouble had started, had actually improved in previous weeks as power that was once reserved for Baghdad was more equitably distributed.[85] The impact of the dissolution of the army and the purging of the bureaucracy of all supposed regime loyalists had also been limited in a rural, poor, relatively remote Shia area. Even the struggle for power between militia loyal to the (very) relatively secular and moderate Abu Hatem and networks loyal to the young militant cleric Muqtada al-Sadr was at an embryonic phase, and though the local supporters of the latter had an interest in disrupting the city, later arrests of the presumed murderers revealed that they were not behind the killings of the Redcaps.

There is, however, one explanation for the violence that was barely cited in the weeks that followed the fighting in Majjar al-Kabir. Two months after the killings there a senior aide to the British minister of defence told the author that, unlike the Americans, 'the British are not intrinsically viewed as an occupying force in Iraq'.[86] He was wrong. Many have spoken of the 'antibody' theory by which any foreign troops are inevitably attacked, particularly in Arab or Islamic lands. Such generalizations are of little use, however. As subsequent events in Iraq and elsewhere were to show, all depends on the role foreign troops are expected to play, their actions and the context. In Majjar al-Kabbir foreign troops were attacked because of a fundamental problem of legitimacy which fed a visceral emotional reaction. The fact that the people of both the town and the city of Amarah had liberated themselves during the campaign in March, pre-empting the arrival of coalition troops, made the perceived humiliation of the weapons searches, itself symbolic of the broader humiliation of occupation, even sharper.[87] There was a practical issue too. With the elections postponed indefinitely, local people believed the British wanted the arms to ensure there could be no serious resistance to their long-term projects for 'occupying Iraq and stealing its oil'. 'During Saddam's time, people reacted in the same way when they searched for weapons,' said Hamid Shagambi, one of the local elders sitting on the town's council.

Some of those who had opened fire in the marketplace had been waiting to do so. But they were few. Once the fighting had started, scores, if not hundreds, fetched their weapons. Mohammed Nasr Amari was one. In Baghdad fourteen months after the events in Majjar al-Kabir, he explained to the author: 'Some people started fighting the soldiers when they were there in the town. Perhaps they had organized it like some kind of ambush, I don't know, but when it started we all went and got our guns. Of course everyone joined in. Who would want to be without honour? Who would want to be the one who did not take up his gun? If they hadn't been there we wouldn't have shot at them.'[88] Majjar al-Kabir would remain effectively outside the control of the coalition forces and successive Iraqi governments for years to come.[89]

Hamilton-Jewell had written a letter to his mother to be opened in the event of his death:

Dear Mum, If you receive this, then I have been killed in the conflict. Don't be sad for me because I died doing the job I enjoy. I have had a good life and that was thanks to my upbringing. I valued right from wrong and I believe what I was doing was for the purpose of good and my life is a small price to pay for peace. Just because I didn't always show that I cared doesn't mean that was the case. I always cared and appreciated you and how you were always there for me. It is just that I am not always good at showing my emotions. I hope you are proud of me and realise that there is nothing to regret in my passing, because my life has been good and my ambitions fulfilled. I don't really know what else to say other than I love you and I don't want you to be sad because I did my duty and loved life. There are a lot of people in the world who have not been blessed with the great life I have had. Love, Simon. Army number 2447779.[90]

# 6

# War in Iraq II: Losing It

## THE SUNNIS AND THE FIRST BATTLE OF FALLUJA

Saddam Hussein was pulled from a small underground hiding place in the village of al-Auda on December 14, 2003 and definitively identified by the tribal tattoo of three dots on his wrist.[1] 'We got him,' a triumphant Paul Bremer announced at a hastily arranged press conference a few hours later. He and others pronounced themselves confident that any resistance to the occupation would wither away. Instead it intensified, and the year of 2004 would be one in which it all went very badly wrong in Iraq. Why did the insurgency not die when Saddam had been captured? The answers to the question lay, as so often in the 9/11 Wars, in the deep-rooted historical factors that determined the context.

One major factor was demographic. The March 2003 war plan had been focused on decapitating Saddam's regime. Its targets were Baghdad and the senior ranks of the Ba'ath Party or Saddam's own clique. The areas that in many ways were much more critical – the western provinces, the fertile belt of farmland surrounding Baghdad and stretching away up the Euphrates valley towards Syria and the string of tough towns along the highways radiating out from the capital – were largely ignored. These areas, however, were the heartland of Iraq's Sunnis, who for five centuries had been the ruling caste and received the largest share of resources. Saddam had not broken with this tradition. Travellers driving down from the northern Iraqi city of Mosul in the late 1990s knew when they had reached Tikrit, the dictator's home town, because the road widened, and rows of brand new strip lights appeared along either side interspersed with giant, very well-watered trees. But the hard demographic logic of Iraq was clear to all. If the country was to be a democracy – as the Americans and their coalition partners repeatedly proclaimed – then the Sunnis would be the losers. The dissolution of the army, the de-Ba'athification campaign and a range of other measures made it very clear very early what being a loser looked like. If the 22 per cent of Iraqis who were Sunnis were going to keep at least some of their privileges they were going to have to fight.[2]

Secondly, both modern and traditional strands of Islam were much stronger than many outside the region – indeed outside the country – thought. The modernity of Iraq during the 1970s, the image projected both by the secular leadership and allies such as America during the war against the 'fanatics' of Iran and the difficulties involved in reporting the true sentiments of Iraqis during the 1990s had combined to embed the sense that Islam played a less important role in the culture and politics of the country than elsewhere. Nothing could be further from the truth. Though not as overtly politically religious as Iran nor as religiously political as Saudi Arabia, faith remained as deeply ingrained in the lives and worldviews of most Iraqis, particularly the poorer and rural communities, as it did in other countries across the region. Nor had Iraq been immune to the broad ideological shifts affecting other nations in the region over previous decades. In every other Arab nation, the opposition to the kind of discredited Socialist, nationalist or pan-Arab ideologies that many regimes had originally espoused had been Islamist since the mid 1980s at the very latest. In Iraq too the same conditions existed that had led to the popularization of Islamism elsewhere and also to the growth of Salafi tendencies. Throughout the 1990s, Saddam himself had tried to co-opt this tendency by launching his own 'Islamification' drive. Bars and clubs had been shut down, a once-thriving gay scene repressed, hundreds of mosques built and a new Islamic slogan placed on the national flag. Saddam was pictured at prayer on many of his newer portraits, readings of the Koran were introduced on state television, and the construction of a vast mosque was started which was to house a Koran supposedly written in the blood of the nation's 'Great Uncle' or 'Anointed Leader', as he called himself.[3] But Saddam's new-found piety was far from credible. As he was broadcasting his spurious religious credentials, clandestine preachers from the Gulf were moving through his country, funded by private donors and wealthy foundations in Saudi Arabia, Kuwait and elsewhere.

Local Iraqi activists of the Muslim Brotherhood were also at work. Both they and the Salafis focused on the same social and geographic terrain. Avoiding the cities where Saddam's security services would have easily discovered their activities and the remote rural areas where there was insufficient population for their purposes, they concentrated their efforts on the proud, independent-minded Sunni communities of the agricultural or semi-urban hinterland of the capital, towns like Baqubah, Ramadi, Muhammadiya, Balad and Samarra, where they found a welcome in once-thriving farming communities for whom Ba'athist nationalism had meant war and repression and for whom the West meant support for Israel and sanctions.[4] The radical, austere but coherent message spread by the travelling clerics and activists fell on fertile ground. It was not surprising that one of first bits of graffiti the author encountered on the road running south-west from the central city of Kirkuk into the Sunni-Arab-dominated zones days after the fall of Saddam was the slogan of the Brotherhood: 'Islam is the solution'.[5] Nor was it surprising that the bomber who had killed himself destroying the United Nations headquarters and mission in August 2003 had been a young man who had been both a Ba'ath Party member enrolled in Saddam's *fedayeen* militia and a member of radical Islamic circles in his small home town just south of Baghdad.[6]

A third major factor was the simple conservatism and xenophobia of the Sunni communities beyond the elite circles from amongst whom the majority of Western interlocutors were drawn. Falluja, a city of 400,000 at a strategic crossing point on the Euphrates surrounded by rich farmland which was to become the centre of the Sunni insurgency during 2004, had always been one of the most conservative communities in Iraq. Unlike somewhere like Tikrit, where the tribes were relatively urbanized, the tribes of Falluja were concentrated in the rural areas surrounding the city and were still heavily influenced by decades or centuries-old tribal traditions and customs.[7] Like so many towns, Falluja had also liberated itself, with local sheikhs and clerics establishing a series of management councils largely based in the many mosques in the city after the fall of the regime. These had successfully prevented any looting and made sure that if anyone was going to raid traffic on the major highways leading west which passed the city it was locals.[8] 'We all know one another here, there were no problems,' said shopkeeper Abdul Kadeer.[9] Falluja was thus another one of those cities like

Majjar al-Kabir whose inhabitants did not consider themselves to have been defeated and who believed that they had a right to govern themselves according to their own customs. Powerful and well-armed local tribes with their own wealth from agriculture and smuggling such as the al-Dulaimi had been treated warily by Saddam Hussein even as they remained one of his most important bases of support.[10] Though some experts made efforts to point out these crucial elements to key individuals in the Pentagon or the White House itself – some featured in the vast multi-volume work produced by the State Department before the invasion – their warnings were largely dismissed. American strategic thinking was conventional. Objectives were seen in terms of individuals – particularly those with political power such as Saddam and his clique – or geography – crucial terrain features or facilities such as airports or roads. As had been the case in Afghanistan, there was no concept of populations like the Sunnis of the western provinces or the Baghdad hinterland as objectives in their own right. Such communities nonetheless constituted 'terrain' of the highest strategic importance.

This inevitably contributed to a final factor: the counter-productive behaviour of the occupiers. It was not just the well-reported civilian casualties or the looting of the invasion itself. Within weeks of the invasion, there had been a series of incidents in or around Falluja in which American troops had killed significant numbers of local people. American commanders denied frequent accusations that they were trigger-happy, but anyone accompanying their troops on raids could see the impact their tactics had on local populations. When men from the 3rd Armoured Cavalry Regiment in Falluja and its nearby smaller twin Ramadi set out on an operation to round up suspected insurgents in June 2003 they blasted the doors of the suspects' homes off their hinges with explosives, ransacked rooms and forced scores of men to squat with bags over their heads for hours in the sun waiting to be 'processed'. Returning to their base in a commandeered palace outside Ramadi, troops played gangster rap at high volume through speakers mounted on their armoured vehicles. 'It's good for morale,' Lieutenant Colonel Hector Mirabile explained to the author. On patrol at night the soldiers, mainly reservists from Florida, came under sniper and mortar fire while locals made mock howling noises in the dark and shouted that the 'amriki' would 'die like dogs'. The soldiers replied with insults they had picked from interpreters. On the streets that had been raided the anger was palpable. Few hid their sentiments. 'I am not sorry for the US dead. They cross the ocean to come here to plunder our wealth not to help us,' said Jamal Nawaf, a sixty-year-old shopkeeper. 'They don't respect old people. I can't sleep because of the helicopters. If even the kids throw stones they shoot. They have taken my Kalashnikov, they have taken money from my house, they have taken my pride.'[11]

Yet it would be a mistake to see the growing insurgency in Iraq as either homogeneous or particularly organized. General John Abizaid, appointed commander of US Central Command in the aftermath of the campaign of 2003, described the conflict in Iraq his troops were engaged on in Iraq as a 'classical guerrilla-type campaign'.[12] In fact, the opposite was true. As Professor Bruce Hoffman pointed out after a visit to Iraq, what the US and their allies were facing there was anything but classical. Hoffman observed that the Iraq insurgency had no center of gravity, no clear leader or leadership, made no attempt to seize and actually hold territory, had no single, defined, or unifying ideology or identifiable organization. Iraq, Hoffman argued, was a 'loose, ambiguous, and constantly shifting environment, [where] constellations of cells or collections of individuals gravitate toward one another to carry out armed attacks, exchange intelligence, trade weapons, or engage in joint training and then disperse at times never to operate together again.'[13]

What this structure, or lack of structure, brought the insurgents was a formidable ability to adapt and evolve. Networks of fighters were not only able to form but to change their tactics, adapting to unpredictable events and unforeseen opportunities with extraordinary rapidity. Their evolution was more the result of fragmentary connections between semi-autonomous parts or 'localized tinkering' than hierarchical command and control or intelligent design and was thus much better suited to fast-changing local circumstances than the ponderous and structured organizations, whether military or other, trying to eliminate them.[14] The insurgency was adaptive, social, informal and dynamic. It was perfectly suited to and a perfect product of the first decade of the twenty-first century. Nothing illustrated this better than the rapid adoption of Improvised Explosive Devices (IEDs) as a weapon of choice. That the IEDs became the preferred arm of the insurgents was, unless one believed the rhetoric about 'loving death more than you love life', hardly surprising. Insurgents soon worked out that IEDs, though once disdained as somehow unmanly, gave them a much better chance of causing casualties and of escaping unscathed than taking on heavily armed allied soldiers conventionally. The tactic thus combined the two qualities sought by all those who use political violence: capability, in that they were effective, and resilience, in that they did not expose those using them to excessive risk.[15] But no one commander in chief took a decision to adopt the use of IEDs as a primary tactic. The process by which cells came together to build and place IEDs was chaotic and haphazard. This was one reason it was so hard to counter. If the militants themselves did not know where they were to meet or when an attack was to take place, it was inevitably impossible for those hunting them to focus the undoubted firepower they had at their disposal. During 2003 an average of less than a dozen US troops had been killed by roadside or other bombs detonated from a distance each month. In 2004 every single month saw at least twenty killed by such devices with significant spikes in such attacks (and resultant casualties) whenever a major conventional operation was underway.[16]

In Falluja particularly, any vision of a broader, united, strategically directed movement broke down entirely. The growing insurgency against the occupiers developed in tandem with growing civil conflict in which the Americans had only a background role. The city was rent by the firefights and score-settling that went with the ferocious and fast-moving manoeuvring for power between sheikhs and a variety of tribal and political factions all looking to exploit the collapse of Saddam's regime. Among the contenders were the Association of Muslim Clerics, who represented the extremist neo-traditionalist 'Salafist' tendency closest to al-Qaeda's or the Taliban's style of Islam, and the Iraqi Islamic Party, who were the local branch of the Islamist Muslim Brotherhood. These two tendencies clashed repeatedly. What Hoffman had seen among insurgents attacking American forces was equally true of groups of Iraqis attacking one another. Tribal groups formed, launched an attack against their rivals and then dispersed with bewildering rapidity. Some tribes showed themselves more amenable to the occupiers, often looking for lucrative contracts for reconstruction work. Others shot, kidnapped or threatened anyone cooperating with the Americans or their allies. It was difficult to tell exactly who was in charge in Falluja, though it was evident that it was not the CPA or the American army. As it became obvious that Saddam's capture had not ended the insurgency, Falluja began to shift to the forefront of American strategic thinking about Iraq. Dealing with Falluja, it was reasoned by Abizaid and others, would definitively end the resistance in the country. Months before the first battle for the city it was clear a major confrontation was inevitable.

The American commanders were not, however, able to choose the moment of that confrontation. A division of US Marines, better trained for lighter, faster expeditionary and irregular warfare than their regular army counterparts, had taken over responsibility for Anbar, the western province that was becoming the heart of the insurgency, in March 2004, and their commander on the ground, Major General James Mattis, a loud-talking but deep-thinking bachelor with a passion for military history, had drawn up a careful and long-term strategy based on sound counter-insurgency theory that he hoped would allow him to win over the city and its hinterland through a careful mixture of big, 'kinetic' stick and financial and developmental carrot.[17] The strategy required a long period of preparation and a slow and steady approach once launched. Mattis' plan was overtaken by events when, on March 31, 2004, four private contractors working for an American security company were ambushed in Falluja, lynched, and their bodies dragged through the streets, mutilated and then torched amid scenes of celebration. The ambush had been the work of insurgents, the lynching was a spontaneous reaction by locals led by day labourers waiting with their tools in the central marketplace to be hired.[18]

In previous conflicts, perhaps, the violent deaths of four civilians would have had little effect. But the ritualized violence in Falluja was filmed and uploaded on to the internet, and images of the unrecognizable remains of the contractors swinging from a bridge were broadcast by almost all major media outlets within hours. 'The moment we saw it we knew this was going to be a problem. Everyone from the president down were all shouting "sort this out",' Andrew Rathmell, a senior British diplomat attached to the CPA in Baghdad, remembered. Bremer, the British and the CPA's political officers were all initially against any precipitate action, Rathmell said, some arguing that they had 'interlocutors' in the city, others simply pushing for Falluja to be 'isolated'.[19] But no one in the US military, the Pentagon and the White House was interested in 'half-measures'. Early plans that involved 'more or less carpet-bombing Falluja' were shelved after strenuous protests from Downing Street, the British Foreign Office and senior British officers in Baghdad – as well as some American officers on the ground in Iraq – and instead Mattis and his Marines were ordered to move immediately into the city, re-establish order, hunt down the culprits of the killing and expel the insurgents.[20] It was a tall order. The Marines had 'little idea how well organized, armed and determined the insurgents were', and though they had set out with the intention of avoiding reducing the city to rubble they were eventually forced to call in intensive artillery bombardment of civilian neighbourhoods.[21] The fighting was dirty, tough and extremely dangerous work, involving close-quarter combat of a rarely seen intensity. The insurgents, not unreasonably, concluded that the battle was 'of great importance because the Americans wanted to make an exemplary punishment of all cities', according to one senior leader, and resisted with determination.[22] The Marines, surprised by the sophistication and defences of the 1,000 or so combatants who faced them, took significant casualties as they advanced very gradually into the city. After three weeks of inconclusive urban fighting the Marines were ordered to halt their advance. The American troops had suffered 26 killed and 90 wounded, an estimated 200 insurgents had died. So too had as many as 600 civilians, including at least 300 women and children.[23] Though deeply unpopular with troops on the ground, the ceasefire appears to have been agreed by senior military commanders in Iraq, Bremer and the White House.[24] Control of the city was ceded to a hastily created 'Falluja Brigade' commanded by a former general of Saddam's Republican Guard, and the Marines pulled out, having failed to fulfil any of their original objectives. This was described by coalition spokesmen as 'handing over to Iraqi partners'. The 'Falluja Brigade' disintegrated a few weeks later, its 800 US-issued AK-47s soon in the hands of the insurgents.

Whatever the spin placed on the outcome, Falluja I was a victory for the insurgents.[25] It had been a pitched battle, one of the very few that took place during the 9/11 Wars, and in strategic terms a major check for the occupying authorities. It inspired insurgents all over Iraq, provoking what one officer called 'a jihad wildfire, spreading mosque to mosque from the Syrian border to Baghdad'.[26] Hastily produced DVDs of the fighting, edited to mournful music and melodramatic soundtracks, flooded local markets. With saturation coverage of the fighting across the Islamic world, Falluja had become a household name, a byword for successful Arab and Islamic resistance against the 'neo-imperialist crusading Americans and their Jewish manipulators'.[27] It was equally clear to all parties that a second battle for the city was inevitable. Until that moment, Falluja was left more or less to its own devices, an unofficial 'free capital' of the growing Sunni insurgency.

## ABU GHRAIB

The need to gather intelligence on the networks responsible for the increasingly lethal and increasingly numerous IED attacks was stressed by a number of high-level US army reviews during 2004.[28] But the American intelligence operation in Iraq, as in Afghanistan, was hobbled by a lack of local knowledge and cultural understanding and an over-reliance on 'SIGINT' or technical communications intercepts.[29]. The response of ground commanders – with one or two notable exceptions – was to fall back on the same tactics as were being employed in Afghanistan: 'cordon and sweep' operations designed to hoover up potential insurgents. Through early 2004, the tempo of such raids had accelerated. They were indiscriminate and resulted in huge numbers of suspects being sent into the American military-run prison system. On one raid the author joined in Tikrit shortly after the fighting had ended in Falluja, troops first knocked down the door of the wrong home and then detained a suspected financier on the basis that, as a professed taxi driver, he could not afford the china on display in his dining room. The suspect affected a studied insouciance, sniffing a flower from his garden, which prompted Captain Eric Coombs, thirty and in charge of the operation, to comment disgustedly, 'It's like he's French or something,' and take him into custody.[30] Back at Coombs' base, a solitary tank fired shells at irregular intervals into a patch of open ground a mile or so away from which mortar attacks were occasionally launched. There was no evidence of any insurgent movement at the site, which was taken as proof that the 'terrain-denial' operation was working. 'No one is going to shoot anything at us from that bit of Iraq,' said the tank's gunner. A day later, news of what had been happening at Abu Ghraib prison west of Baghdad broke.

In the short term the scandal at Abu Ghraib resulted from the huge flow of detainees from units on the ground like that of Coombs or Hector Mirabile in Ramadi conducting their vast dragnets. These sent tens of thousands of detainees into the creaking system set up by the coalition. As there was never meant to be an occupation let alone an insurgency, no one had thought about what might need to be done with captured Iraqis and hastily created facilities, chronically undermanned and under-resourced, were quickly swamped.

Abu Ghraib itself, one of the most notorious jails under Saddam Hussein and a symbol of the violence of the past regime, had been reopened by the Americans in August 2003 as a holding centre for captured former regime figures and common criminals, the two mixed together in contravention of the Geneva Conventions. Looting after the invasion had not just gutted the ministries but had rendered most of Iraq's extensive prison system unusable too. Some 75,000 secure prison places were needed, experts estimated. A few thousand were available.[31] By the end of the year, however, Abu Ghraib alone had a population of 7,000. Poorly defended, situated between the hardline Sunni suburbs of western Baghdad and the rough towns of Falluja and Ramadi, the complex was an obvious target and was soon being regularly mortared. The servicemen posted there had little training for running a detention facility and lived among decomposing rubbish, ate monotonous and unhealthy combat rations and showered under drums of cold water. The prisoners and 'security detainees', the new term usefully blurring their exact legal status, lived in abject squalor, many exposed to the elements, to insects, rabid dogs and the fire of the insurgents. Others, in the rehabilitated Saddam-era concrete cell blocks, had marginally better physical conditions but were exposed to the worst of the mistreatment perpetrated by the gaolers. There were frequent power and water cuts. Unsurprisingly, there were also riots, some of which were put down with live ammunition. The commanding officer, a reservist brigadier general, tried to raise these issues with her higher command but without success.[32]

However, if the abuse occurred for a variety of specifically local reasons the forms it took were those that had evolved so early in the conflict in Afghanistan. Many American interrogators and prison guards in Iraq had served in facilities like Kandahar or Bagram, where interrogators had faced the same circumstances and similar pressures for results. Indeed some of those now in Iraq had already been implicated in serious abuse. One, Captain Carolyn Wood of the 519th Military Intelligence Battalion, considered herself 'very knowledgeable of interrogation techniques'. At Bagram, Wood had issued a list of recommended techniques – from sensory deprivation to the use of dogs – without precedent in American army history and it was under her command that the three deaths detailed in chapter 3 had occurred. Decorated for her service in Afghanistan, she was appointed head of interrogations at Abu Ghraib in August 2003 and immediately issued a new list of techniques more appropriate for 'the Arab mind-set'.[33] When American military interrogators across Iraq were told by superiors that 'the gloves were coming off regarding ... detainees ... we want these individuals broken', the suggestions as to how this might be done revealed how extensive the influence of the first major campaign after 9/11 had been.[34] One soldier answered the memo outlining the new, tougher approach, saying he had 'spent several months ... interrogating the Taliban and al-Qaeda' and as a result recommended 'open-handed facial slaps from a distance of ... about two feet and back handed blows to the mid-section from ... about 18 inches' as well as exploiting 'fear of dogs and snakes'. Another respondent to the memo recommended using closed fists and 'low voltage electrocution', also practised in Kandahar.[35] Indeed, almost all the abuses in Abu Ghraib – stripping prisoners naked, low-voltage shocks, humiliating sexual practices, stress positions, cold and heat, chaining to bars or walls, beatings and the compulsive photographing or filming of such acts – had already been seen in Afghanistan.

A second influence was the example of practices in the broader network of US prison facilities that had been constructed over the previous two years. The idea of exploiting the psychological fears of those under interrogation had been suggested with Abu Zubaydah, the supposed al-Qaeda senior leader detained the previous year in Pakistan and subsequently waterboarded. In August 2003, General Geoffrey Miller, who as commander of detainee operations at the Guantanamo Bay prison camp had introduced a much harsher regime there, visited Iraq as part of a review of intelligence-gathering operations and recommended charging prison guards with preparing, i.e. softening up, detainees for questioning.[36] This new definition of the role of the guards in American prisons in Iraq undoubtedly exacerbated the deterioration in conditions at Abu Ghraib. Staff Sergeant Ivan L. Frederick II, a member of the 372nd Military Police Company and a central figure in the Abu Ghraib scandal, wrote home describing how he had 'questioned some of the things' that he had seen such as leaving inmates in their cell naked or dressed in female underwear, handcuffing them to the cell door, isolating them with no clothes, toilet facilities, ventilation or running water for up to three days but had been told that 'this is how military intelligence (MI) wants it done'.[37]

As in Afghanistan an interesting question is whether the abuse was driven from the bottom or from the top. Did it evolve endogeneously or as a result of directives from the most senior levels of political and military leadership?[38] Certainly in Abu Ghraib – as well as in the prison at Camp Bucca in the south and countless smaller facilities – detainees were often seen as terrorists responsible for 9/11 and treated as such. An example of how language percolated through all those involved in a mission was the memo referred to above which used words – 'the gloves coming off' – borrowed directly from the Bush administration's 'point man' on counter-terrorism, Cofer Black.[39] Also, the connections between theatres, units, individuals and policies make it hard to argue either that the handful of low-ranking soldiers disciplined for the Abu Ghraib abuse were simply the proverbial bad apples or, as Pentagon undersecretary Douglas Feith claimed, that their actions were 'a matter of personal sadism by a small number of individuals'.[40]

Abuse was of course far from universal – the American soldiers the author was with when the scandal broke were horrified – but it had become an integral part of the American military and counter-terrorist effort. For example, interrogators at Camp Nama at Baghdad International Airport had also systematically stripped prisoners, employed stress positions and sleep deprivation, had punched and kicked them and, according to one report, added a new technique of shooting them with paintballs.[41] Nor was such behaviour restricted merely to the Americans. Abuse by the British in Basra and other parts of the province was astonishingly similar to that practised elsewhere. Though smaller in scale, abuse by British troops too featured ritualized sexual humiliation, beatings, exposure to heat, thirst, stress positions and it too saw soldiers, some eventually implicated in the deaths of a series of detainees between 2003 and 2004, film or photograph their actions with careful attention to the *mise en scène*.[42] The conclusion must be that such behaviour was at the very least a phenomenon that had both a 'top-down' and 'bottom-up' element. The Bush administration encouraged and aggravated problems that had, from the very earliest days of the war, been evident. In Abu Ghraib itself, the role that interrogators from Military Intelligence played in driving the abuse was paradoxically underplayed by the photographs that eventually emerged which showed only low-ranking military police personnel.[43] Whether directed from above or the result of the independent actions of hundreds, if not thousands, of individuals, the result was the same. The abuse of prisoners by all sides rapidly became one of the defining characteristics of the 9/11 Wars, somehow integral to the very nature of the conflict. Certainly the images that depicted the abuse at Abu Ghraib – the hooded man, the leashed man, the slavering dog inches from the face of a terrified detainee – became some of the Wars' most recognizable and enduring icons.[44]

One of the most worrying elements of the Abu Ghraib scandal was the lack of reaction it provoked in Iraq. Among those waiting outside the prison the day after the scandal broke was Zacaria Falah, from the northern city of Mosul, who had spent seventy days in Abu Ghraib. His older brother was still imprisoned. Both had been accused of helping 'the resistance' – a charge they denied. Falah said he had been taken from his home, which was ransacked during the raid, in the middle of the night and transported to a base in the northern city of Mosul known as 'Camp Disco' to Iraqis because of the habit of the guards of putting on loud music and making the detainees 'dance' for hours on end. From there he was taken to Abu Ghraib, where he was housed in a tent, sleeping on the floor with thirty-four other men. 'Of course, everything that you are now talking about was happening,' he said. 'That is what the Americans are like. We have known for years. We have always been angry. Why be more angry now?'[45]

## THE GREEN ZONE

Saddam had walled off a city within a city along the Tigris in the centre of Baghdad, where he had built a vast palace, rows of villas for members of his extended clan and senior officials, guardhouses, even hospitals and schools. It was here that the Coalition Provisional Authority was based. This was the Green Zone, named after the shading on Coalition security maps, where red marked danger and green its opposite. At night, with much of the city plunged into steaming darkness due to power cuts, the Baghdadis sleeping on their roofs to avoid the heat could see the ten hectares of the Green Zone 'lit up like a wedding in an Indian musical', as Bashem Jaffar, a hairdresser in the upmarket Karada area, put it. Joining the CPA in its heavily defended enclave was most of the diplomatic community. As had happened in Kabul eighteen months earlier, the British had reopened their colonial-era embassy, realized it was indefensible and then, as the security situation deteriorated, been forced to leave the garden and the colonnade and retreat to a new complex behind the blastwalls.[46] Elsewhere in the capital, long lines of concrete T-blocks were beginning to block off streets, bridges, a view of the sky.

Like the huge military bases going up around the country (and in Afghanistan) the Green Zone was profoundly isolated. The food in the vast mess hall was all imported and included an extraordinarily high proportion of pork products.[47] A variety of bars, licit or otherwise, provided often hard-working and stressed CPA officials the chance to blow off steam. Women went jogging in singlets and shorts. The scene in the ballroom nightclub of the al-Rashid hotel in the centre of the Green Zone was surreal – a frenetic decadence fuelled by cheap whiskey and recent broken marriages. Identical SUVs, Humvees and shuttle buses ferried people around. Most staff were on short-term contracts, and very few spoke any Arabic.[48] Visiting the Green Zone involved crossing at least three checkpoints manned variously by American troops, a range of coalition allies and private security guards. Reporters had to do this often – it regularly took an hour or more – if they wanted to attend the press briefings held at the convention centre opposite the al-Rashid hotel. At the briefings they would be told about the latest initiatives taken by the CPA, and occasionally there would be some details of military operations. There was a café and a board on which press releases detailing events such as 'ribbon-cutting ceremony al-Nathana bridge, 9am saturday' were posted alongside the latest casualties, increasingly from IED attacks. 'Every single one haunts us but we are not wavering,' said the American military spokesman. Another notice announced that 'several planned reconstruction projects have been suspended due to the non-permissive environment posed by terrorists'. In one briefing an Iraqi reporter asked what he should tell his frightened children woken by the sound of low-flying military helicopters. 'Tell them that is the sound of freedom,' came the response. General Ricardo Sanchez, the US commander in Iraq, told assembled reporters that he was 'very optimistic' and was sure that he had the 'combat forces' to prevail. A banner hung above the new Iraqi Business Development Center: 'Peace and best wishes from the children of America to the children of Iraq'.[49]

Bremer and the most senior CPA officials had their offices in the giant palace, which was still adorned with vast busts of the former dictator. Between 1,000 and 1,500 – the CPA was permanently understaffed – people worked there. Supposedly international, the operation was '99 per cent American, half a per cent British, half a per cent the rest,' remembered Andy Bearpark, the CPA's director of operations.[50] They were an odd bunch. Some were grizzled veterans of nation-building efforts hired by the CPA who had come direct from Afghanistan or, like Bearpark, from Kosovo. The rest were either drawn from America's best and brightest or knew someone in the Republican Party or both. They were often extremely young. The mixture of jaded pragmatism, can-do naivety and starry-eyed ideology was striking. 'The CPA is having to invent this day by day,' said Mark Kennon, the authority's coordinator for Salahuddin province. Contacts with the local population were limited. When people did travel they ended up 'looking at Iraq through armoured glass surrounded by guns,' in the words of Rory Stewart, deputy governer in Maysan province and then in Nasariyah.[51] In the provinces, moving three CPA engineers involved a convoy of seven Humvees, two with .50 calibre machine guns and seven squad-level weapons. The atmosphere was rendered even more surreal by two enormous disconnects: between official language and reality 'beyond the wire' and between what was expected of the CPA and what it could deliver. One reporter turned his mobile back on after sitting through a long briefing on how security was excellent around the country to find messages reporting a series of car bombs.[52] As in Afghanistan, 'there was a crisis of expectations', according to Bearpark. Tom Parker, a Briton who headed the CPA's Crimes against Humanity Investigation Unit, was blunter. 'First impressions count, and the first three months were a disaster,' he said.[53]

If talking to the Iraqis was tough, so was talking to other CPA officials. Links with the offices in the various provinces, set up several months into the CPA's rule, were haphazard at best.[54] Emails from distant governorates went unanswered or unreceived. Cash was distributed in thick wads of plastic-wrapped new dollar bills.[55] With nearly $10 billion owed to Iraq under the Oil for Food programme that had been languishing in United Nations accounts, money was not short, but finding a sensible and productive way to spend it was complicated.[56] With the twin hierarchies of civilian and military command meeting only in Washington at stratospherically high levels, coordination of effort was almost impossible. Enormous amounts were lost through corruption or simply accounting incompetence. The consequences were evident to anyone travelling around the country.[57] Before the overthrow of Saddam, 95 per cent of urban Iraqis and 75 per cent of those living in rural zones had access to clean drinking water, according to needs assessments by the United Nations. By 2003, these levels had declined to 60 per cent and 50 per cent respectively. By the end of 2005, the figure had dropped to 32 per cent.[58] When the CPA was criticized for missing the target of generating 4,400 Kw of power in July 2003, the target was then achieved two months later by the simple expedient of switching on all the facilities in the country for twenty-four hours. Many were then shut down for 'maintenance' and remained closed. In much of Baghdad water supply was down to three hours per day by the end of the year. Though hospitals were receiving a better supply of basics such as insulin or antibiotics, often provided by independent NGOs such as the Red Cross or Médecins Sans Frontières, there were no drugs for any more advanced treatments.[59]

It was not the cultural inappropriateness nor the dysfunctional administrative systems – which many of the bright, experienced and hardworking officials eventually got to work – nor even the isolation of most of those who lived, ate, drank and breathed only in the Green Zone that crippled the CPA. It was what it was trying to do. The mission statement of the CPA appeared relatively uncontroversial. The aim was to reach an endstate defined as 'a durable peace for a united and stable, democratic Iraq that provides effective and representative government for and by the Iraqi people; is underpinned by new and protected freedoms and a growing market economy; and no longer poses a threat to its neighbours or international security and is able to defend itself.'[60] Yet the ideological roots of the project were obvious. When a year after the 9/11 attacks the Bush administration had published a National Security Strategy, its first page had included the pledge: 'We will actively work to bring the hope of democracy, development, free markets and free trade to every corner of the world.'[61] Across most of the globe, the obstacles to fulfilling this were manifest. However, post-invasion Iraq, both for those with little interest in the history of the local communities or for those who were well-informed but ideologically committed, appeared to be the perfect place to realize that promise. The mission statement of the CPA was a wish-list drawn up by people who were absolutely certain that their values and models were applicable and attractive to other societies and cultures *whatever the circumstances*. The latter qualification is of critical importance as it traces a path between essentialist arguments that 'Muslims' or 'Arabs' cannot ever be receptive to 'Western' ideas of democracy, free-market capitalism, human rights and so forth and the equally problematic argument, favoured by so many within the Bush administration, that such ideas were a universally applicable panacea. In fact, as the 9/11 Wars were to demonstrate again and again, any culture, taken to mean the totality of values, norms, learned behaviours and worldviews of any community, is infinitely flexible and dynamic all while evolving within inherited boundaries set over time. Unlike in Afghanistan, where the security project had seen an ideological component grafted on to it, the project in Iraq had been ideological from the start. It was not rooted in a continuing, sensitive and informed appraisal of the measures best suited to bring security, stability and prosperity to Iraq in 2003 or early 2004 but in a utopian, universalizing vision which, as the National Security Strategy had made clear, served American interests. It suffered enormously as a result.

For the primary obstacle to the American plan to re-create Iraq rapidly became the paradox of many such attempts by one community to change the behaviour and nature of another: the values that the powerful foreigners hoped to encourage, support or, if they had to, impose were fatally tarnished by the indelible fact that they were those of the occupiers or at least those the occupiers preferred. Though a significant minority of Iraqis still saw a Westernized future for their nation as preferable, vast swathes of the population had come to see such values as foreign. When asked if 'democracy can work well in Iraq', 51 per cent said, 'No, it is a Western way of doing things and will not work here.' All that was conservative, religious and nationalistic was thus naturally vested with a new sense of being 'Iraqi' and acquired a powerful legitimacy as culturally authentic. Whether or not this had been the case before the invasion was immaterial.[62] The invasion and the subsequent acts of the CPA had triggered vast change. Any predictions based on anything other than the finest knowledge of pre-war conditions were now unreliable at best. Often they were entirely redundant.

By the spring of 2004, as the CPA began to prepare for an eventual handover to restore sovereignty to Iraq and to transfer its responsibilities to a nominally independent government, it had long become clear to most observers that the 'endstate' originally envisaged in Washington and elsewhere was a long way off. This was made very evident when Bremer had postponed elections and hinted strongly he envisaged a process of undetermined length, possibly up to two years according to one British diplomat, to design a constitution.[63] Eventually, in June 2004, the CPA handed over to an interim government led by Ayad Allawi, an exile, a moderate Shia and former Ba'athist dissident with good Western intelligence connections who, though he had a narrow support base within Iraq limited to educated secularists, was seen as at least relatively pro-American. Three elections were scheduled: in January 2005 for a new transitional assembly which would elect itself a new prime minister, a referendum to ratify a constitution and finally, at the end of the year, for a government that would sit for a four-year term. There was no public leaving ceremony for Bremer, and the CPA was dissolved in some disorder. On June 28, Condoleezza Rice scribbled a note which Donald Rumsfeld then passed to President Bush at the NATO summit in Turkey, informing him that Iraq was sovereign. 'Let freedom reign,' the president wrote across it and turned to shake hands with the man on his right, Tony Blair.[64]

## THE ROAD TO NAJAF

The new Iraqi government's first real test came in August 2004 with a fresh round of fighting between American and allied military forces and the al-Mahdi Army militia of the young cleric Muqtada al-Sadr.[65] This second strand to the insurgency in Iraq had emerged in the spring. Very different in its origins, structure and aims from the Sunni insurgency, being far closer to an organized religious, cultural and political movement like the Taliban in Afghanistan in the 1990s, Hezbollah in Lebanon or Hamas in the Gaza Strip, it nonetheless shared some qualities of other insurgents in Iraq. There was the same pattern of recruitment through association, the same often chaotic reliance on self-forming communities, the same capability to rapidly adapt to changing contexts and challenges. There was also the same rapid development of a capability to cause serious harm and to pose a significant threat to the stability of Iraq.

Muqtada al-Sadr and the al-Mahdi Army were the product of the intersection of the major historical trends which have already marked much of this narrative: demography, Islamism, nationalism and cultural revivalism. The demographic element had two elements, both with significant political consequences. Firstly, the Shia, a minority in Iraq when it had been ruled by the Sunni Ottomans, had been a majority since the southern desert tribes had converted in the eighteenth and nineteenth centuries and thus collectively felt that Saddam's deposition would inevitably lead to their domination of any subsequent political set-up. Secondly, Saddam's Iraq had seen the same explosive population growth rates as the rest of the Middle East in the 1970s and 1980s. This meant a huge number of potentially troublesome young men by the first decade of the twenty-first century. Naturally, then, in the aftermath of the invasion, it was likely that Shia male youth would be a source of trouble.

Like the young men who had made their way to the Afghan camps, their counterparts in the slums of Basra, Nasariyah or Baghdad had also seen a series of different ideologies fail in their short lives. Pan-Arab secular Socialist nationalism was clearly associated with their oppressor, Saddam Hussein, and brutal Sunni repression and discrimination; their only real experience of Western liberal democracy had been the betrayal of the Iraqi Shias in the aftermath of the 1991 war, when hundreds of thousands who had revolted against the government were butchered without any Western intervention, and then the punishing sanctions that had followed; the fall of Communism had discredited left-wing thought and Saddam's highly effective purges had destroyed any left-wing activism. All that was left was religion in its various politicized and non-politicized forms.

Here Muqtada al-Sadr had a unique advantage: the two great dissident Islamist leaders in recent decades in Iraq had been his father, Ayatollah Mohammed Sadeq al-Sadr, and his father-in-law, Ayatollah Mohammed Baqr al-Sadr.[66] Both had been killed by Saddam Hussein and were popularly venerated as martyrs. They were known as al-Sadr I and al-Sadr II. The first had been one of the key thinkers of the wave of new radical ideology that emerged in the 1960s among Shia Muslims. This matched strains of Sunni political Islamism being developed elsewhere and found its most obvious expression in the 1979 Iranian revolution. Men like al-Sadr I and his contemporary Ayatollah Ruhollah

Khomeini in Iran developed the radical new concept of *wilayat al faqih* or 'the guardianship of the jurist' and challenged the long-established Shia tradition that the clergy should remain aloof from 'corrupting' secular politics.[67] Both saw mass activism as the only way to realize their respective theocratic visions.[68] Despite their assassinations and the ruthless repression of activists both older al-Sadrs had retained a following that was still extensive in Saddam's final years.[69]

The young Muqtada al-Sadr was careful, however, to combine the appeal of this activist Islamism with an appeal to Iraqi nationalism. Like their religious identity, the national identity of the Iraqi Shia had always been stronger than many, especially relatively Westernized exiles, had given them credit for. Their perpetual grievance was that they had been deprived of a fair share of power in the Iraqi state – not that the state itself was somehow illegitimate. It was their senior clerics who had hoisted the banner of jihad in the great Iraqi revolt against the British in 1920, and when the question of national allegiance had been posed sharply during the Iran–Iraq war of 1980 to 1988 the Iraqi Shia troops who made up the bulk of the rank and file fought, often bravely.[70] The posters pasted to walls all over the slum suburb of Baghdad once called Saddam City and now universally known as Sadr City showed Muqtada al-Sadr's chubby, acned face in the foreground, his respected forebears and the Iraqi national flag behind.

Another element that al-Sadr was able to exploit was a resurgent revivalist Shia identity which overlapped both with Islamism and nationalism, reinforcing and amplifying both to create a potent vision of a conservative, Islamist, Shia-dominated Iraq. Though part of the broader surge in such identities through the 1990s across much of the Islamic (and indeed non-Islamic) world, the new piety and identification of the Shia in Iraq can be explained also by the way in which long Shia traditions of martyrdom and suffering, of passive resistance to tyranny and of internal spiritual renewal and questioning were perfectly adapted to the poverty, frustration, anger and brutal repression experienced by the community under Saddam Hussein. The strong social revolutionary strand within Shia thought, traditionally if somewhat simplistically seen as a faith of the underdogs and of the poor, also lent longstanding religious and historic myths an immediate relevance that they might not otherwise have had. By the late 1990s, in homes across Iraq, the garish pictures of Ali, the son-in-law of the Prophet Mohammed assassinated

in AD 661, and his son Hussein, killed in battle fighting against overwhelming odds by forces loyal to the dictatorial caliph Yazid, went back
up on the walls of Shia households. Immediately after the invasion, millions took part in ritual pilgrimages that had been banned for many
decades.[71]

Finally there was a very specific social and economic dynamic too.
Muqtada al-Sadr was not able to garner support among the broad
masses of Shia society – most people remained loyal to the revered
Grand Ayatollah Ali al-Sistani and the college of clerics, the *hawza*, that
he led – but was able to make significant inroads among the young
unemployed urban working-class men from the seething slums of cities
like Baghdad, Basra, Nasariyah, Kut and others. Beyond the broad
structural trends, such men joined the movement for a typical range of
more immediate factors. It was here where there was some overlap with
the young men flowing into the networks of Sunni insurgents. Years of
anti-Western propaganda, the lived experience of the consequences
of United-Nations-sponsored and American-backed sanctions and the
rhetoric both of resurgent Islamic extremism and of the mainstream
Arabic-language media, all encouraged a profound antipathy to the
invaders and made the idea of taking up arms more attractive too. The
Shia community too was affected by the looting that followed the invasion or the insecurity that it brought. Though initially many services
improved for Iraq's Shias as Saddam's discriminatory policies were
reversed by the new rulers, they soon deteriorated. So the continuing
failure to provide power, sanitation, medical services and jobs also
fuelled discontent.

Nor was the fact that these young men, often only a decade younger
than Muqtada al-Sadr himself, were also joining a revolt against the
traditional Shia authorities, the *hawza*, insignificant. If they rejected the
automatic authority accorded to Grand Ayatollah Ali al-Sistani, it was
not just in a spirit of adolescent rebellion but also because his quietist
message matched neither their aspirations nor their instincts. Angry
young men in desperate times demanded desperate and angry measures.
That said, most joined not for ideological or religious reasons but
through personal associations, because in the microcommunities that
structured life in the overcrowded slums where most lived, joining the
al-Mahdi Army was encouraged or was simply what most of their peers
were doing. The al-Mahdi Army offered adventure, comradeship, social

mobility and a clear, certain, lucid dogma that made sense of a world turned upside down. Most of the young activists of the al-Mahdi Army had nothing else to do and understandably preferred carrying weapons, enforcing local order or simply contributing to the various social activities that Muqtada al-Sadr's office sponsored to hanging around on street corners watching American patrols go by.

Muqtada al-Sadr, thirty years old in 2003, was also helped by the way in which coalition leaders, political advisers and military intelligence officers consistently underestimated him in the way that they underestimated so many opponents in the early years of the 9/11 Wars.[72] Few in the West had ever heard of al-Sadr before the invasion – he did not feature in any of the cursory briefings received by Hilary Synnott, the British diplomat sent to Basra to be the CPA representative in the south, before leaving the UK in July 2003 – and no one anticipated his extraordinarily rapid rise from unknown junior cleric to major power-broker.[73] Though he admitted that the self-styled 'Sadr III' represented a genuine popular constituency, David Richmond, the British special representative in Iraq, professed 'reasonable confidence' in March 2004 that al-Sadr would be 'wound down and put back in his box' without too much trouble.[74] For Brigadier Kimmitt, chief US military spokesman, al-Sadr led an 'illegal mob'. One US intelligence officer described the cleric to the author in March 2004 as 'a fucking punk, an opportunistic little bastard'.[75] A week later the al-Mahdi Army launched an armed insurrection against occupation forces which plunged much of Iraq into chaos and would take six months to suppress.

The spring fighting saw the ragged and untrained teenagers of the al-Mahdi Army fighting coalition troops, attacking CPA offices and attempting to eliminate rivals within the Shia community. Many of the major routes to the capital – such as the huge supply lines the Americans had constructed across the desert or through remote villages and farmland so they could avoid the main arteries – were rapidly rendered unusable. Others were made extremely dangerous by the breakdown in law and order that was a consequence of the fighting. Driving to Karbala to cover the fighting, a car carrying other journalists only a few minutes ahead of the author's own vehicle was ambushed and its occupants shot dead, their corpses spread in the dirt by the side of the road. Civilian traffic from Jordan and Kuwait was cut off. The CPA even started drawing up plans for rationing in Baghdad's Green Zone. Across a swathe of southern Iraq, in towns such as Amarah, Kut and Nasari-yah, the half-trained teenagers from urban slums brushed aside Western troops whose political leaders and generals had never anticipated their soldiers participating in real fighting. In Nasariyah an Italian contingent lost control of the city, refusing to engage the mortars set up by the al-Mahdi Army that were bombarding the CPA's offices. In Kut, the Ukrainians, who had a reputation locally for taking bribes at their checkpoints, tried to run away.[76] In Najaf, Spanish troops refused to leave their base.

Al-Sadr's initial success did not last, however, and as more American troops entered the fight, it had rapidly become clear that the al-Mahdi Army's undoubted zeal was no match for a modern professional mili-tary, especially one with the firepower the US army could muster. In Sadr City, support for the militia had remained relatively solid. But the com-mercial and educated classes of the Shia community were contemptuous and fearful of al-Sadr's predominantly working-class fighters, and any backing outside the tougher suburbs of Baghdad or the southern cities rapidly fell away as the fighting continued. In the holy city of Najaf, leaflets had denounced the al-Mahdi Army as 'thieves, robbers and per-verts under the command of a one-eyed charlatan'.[77] Nor had al-Sadr himself mapped out a broader political strategy to take advantage of his military gains. By the end of May, much of the south had been retaken by coalition troops, and the *hawza* had made their disapproval of al-Sadr very clear. Al-Sadr called off the fight, the CPA dropped demands for the dissolution of his militia and, like the Sunnis in Falluja, everyone began to prepare for round two. Al-Sadr had much to show for his efforts, however. He had emerged as a player in the new post-invasion Iraqi politics – aided in no little way by the largely uncritical saturation coverage he had received from al-Jazeera and other Arabic-language sat-ellite channels. Polls showed the impact the fighting had had on al-Sadr's profile. When asked in February 2004, 'Which national leader do you trust the most?' only 1.5 per cent of respondents had mentioned al-Sadr's name. Four months later that figure was 7.4 per cent, still low in overall terms but the highest jump in popularity for any Iraqi political figure.[78]

Over the summer, as the political situation more generally in the country evolved rapidly, al-Sadr embedded his organization still further in his bastion of Baghdad's Sadr City. There his office set up judges, unofficial police forces, organized food distribution – in short did everything that the government could not or would not do. The social movement began to evolve into a genuine social force as al-Sadr attempted to organize and discipline his followers. There is also some evidence of contacts at this point with elements within the Iranian government. The Iranians may have supplied weapons or at least training and technical advice to parts of the still fairly fragmented al-Mahdi Army, but their aid was probably less substantial than alleged by many at the time.[79] The militia's leaders had learned from experience, and by August, when al-Sadr moved again to take control of Najaf and the vast wealth its pilgrim trade generated, the force was more than the collection of carloads of young gunmen that it had been earlier in the year and easily occupied the key religious sites there and in nearby Kerbala, once again forcing government forces and those loyal to the traditional clerical authorities into flight or hiding. A force of newly arrived US Marines decided to deal immediately and aggressively with the new threat and attacked.

Again the fighting was intense, particularly in Najaf. Over ten days the American troops forced the militia back through the vast cemeteries around the city to positions around the main shrine itself. The scene in Najaf's centre was one of devastation. Whole blocks of homes, shops, hotels and restaurants had been reduced to a mass of rubble, twisted iron and hanging wires. Helicopters circled overhead, air strikes were called in, tanks inched their way down the narrow lanes with infantry crouching in the dust behind. American snipers had ringed the city and picked off anyone bringing supplies in to the centre, shooting the donkeys that carried them. Al-Sadr's men had turned their office in the city into a torture centre, and its courtyard was filled with dozens of rotting bodies, opponents who had been executed over previous weeks. The wounded were dragged in sheets to a makeshift dressing station inside the shrine, where scores of young men from Baghdad, Nasariyah, Basra and elsewhere lay moaning on tiling slick with blood. 'We are here to defend our leader, our country and Islam against the invaders,' Haider Abbas, an unemployed nineteen-year-old from Sadr City who had been in Najaf for months, told the author. 'Our weapon is faith. They have tried to kill us with everything but not succeeded,' said Khalid Hada, twenty-three, who had been a soldier in Saddam's army until it was demobilized. The young men spoke of death, of angels, of how the bodies of martyrs smelt of musk, all images and ideas common to their counterparts in Pakistan,

Afghanistan and elsewhere. With the militia entrenched in the houses around the main shrine, difficult to dislodge, the Americans were unwilling to risk an all-out attack. Iraqi troops were neither sufficiently well armed nor trained nor motivated to fight their way in alone, and there appeared no obvious way of rapidly ending the violence. Al-Sadr remained defiant. Those local people who had stayed were resigned to the destruction of their town and livelihood. Salah Alawi Jassm, fifty-eight, had remained in his home for fear of looters. Down a side street strewn with debris, paper, spent ammunition, wire, dead dogs and all the other detritus of battle, the house had largely escaped damage. Over the hammering of automatic weapons a few hundred metres away and the screech of shells he told the author that the people of Najaf had two enemies: 'the Americans and the Mahdi militia'. At the city's main hospital, tired doctors did what they could for children suffering from dehydration or diarrhoea. In lulls in the fighting, civilians picked their way through the rubble and the rubbish to get water. The scenes that had so gripped Iraq and the Islamic world more generally five months earlier in Falluja were being repeated.

Eventually it was not the Marines but Grand Ayatollah Ali al-Sistani who broke the deadlock by telling his followers to march peacefully on Najaf and reclaim the shrine. It was a powerful demonstration of his continuing authority over Iraq's 14 million Shias. With elections now looming in January, the *hawza* did not want their political strategy derailed by the young radical al-Sadr though they recognized his new appeal as a figurehead for resistance for significant parts of their community. For his part, al-Sadr could not confront al-Sistani, even if some of his followers rejected the authority of the ageing scholar and even if the wealth of Najaf was at stake. At dawn on a Friday morning, with the low sun glinting off the golden dome of the shrine, the pilgrims marched along the pocked roads through the ruined city centre and to the shrine. Al-Sadr's men loaded their weapons on to carts and slipped away.[80] In the vast cemetery where much of the fiercest fighting had taken place over previous weeks, exhausted US soldiers, their uniforms stained with sweat, hollow-eyed and pale with fatigue, sat or lay in the shade of the tombs with their weapons beside them. Many were sleeping for the first time in days, one officer said. A sergeant questioned passing journalists on events elsewhere. He was pleased to hear that the country was now mostly quiet. 'Do you think we are going to have to do this all over again?' he asked.

Al-Sadr was not to appear again in public for many months and was never again to directly engage coalition troops on such a scale. Recognizing that at the very least al-Sistani's policy of conditional cooperation with the occupation authorities was leading to polls which would inevitably imply a vast shift of power to the Shia, al-Sadr made a strategic choice. 'The Sadrist movement first resorted to peaceful resistance, then to armed resistance and finally to political resistance. This does not present a problem: every situation requires its own response,' he told one interviewer.[81] For the national assembly elections in January 2005 al-Sadr joined the United Iraqi Alliance (UIA), a grand coalition of Shia parties supported by al-Sistani. The ayatollah told his millions of followers: 'Voting is a religious duty like prayers and fasting and your abstention constitutes disobedience of God Almighty.' An aged Iran-born senior cleric who had always refused to meet any representatives of the occupying powers and had simply insisted on nothing more than a rapid move to polls had become American's greatest helper in the effort to bring democracy to Iraq.[82] Al-Sistani's assistance was far from unconditional however. His message to Bremer had been simple, acutely pertinent and unanswerable in its logic: 'You are an American, I am Iranian. Why not let the Iraqi people decide?'

The Shia UIA coalition won 48 per cent of the vote and 140 of the 275 seats available. A total of 23 were won by candidates linked to Muqtada al-Sadr, who, as a self-styled senior cleric, distanced himself from active involvement in electioneering.[83] The respectable moderates of incumbent prime minister Ayad Allawi received 14 per cent of ballots cast. The turn-out was higher than expected even if scores of polling stations were attacked, and the pictures of patient Iraqis standing in long lines protected by local security forces provided a welcome morale boost for increasingly concerned Western populations and politicians. But Iraq's Sunnis had largely boycotted the vote. In Anbar, less than 2 per cent of those eligible participated. Whether this was from fear or from a genuine disaffection with a process which many Sunnis felt was dominated by their ethnic rivals was unclear. The newly elected body now had to form a government and draft a constitution in an increasingly divided country that continued to slide towards yet worse chaos and violence.

# 7

# Al-Qaeda and the 9/11 Wars

## THE 9/11 WARS EXPAND

The invasion of Iraq saw the extension of the 9/11 Wars to an entirely new theatre that previously, if not at peace, certainly had not been an integral part of the conflict. It resulted too in a higher level of overall daily violence, conventional or otherwise, than had yet been seen anywhere or at any time since September 11, 2001. By the end of 2004 more people were dying every month in Iraq than had been killed in any of the bloodiest terrorist attacks of the period excepting those of 9/11 itself.[1] But the war in Iraq saw more than simply the expansion of the 9/11 Wars in geographic terms to include both south-west Asia and a major state in the core of the Middle East. It provoked a wave of radicalization and mobilization in the Middle East not seen since the Arab–Israeli conflicts of 1967 and 1973. This wave of heightened political consciousness, anger and frustration did not just affect the countries close to Iraq but extended throughout almost the entire Islamic world, exacerbating many of the trends which had contributed to the surge of militancy through the 1990s and the broadening radicalization seen since the 9/11 attacks. It also reinforced the credibility of the extremists' key message that a belligerent West led by America was set on the subordination, exploitation and humiliation of Muslim lands and it boosted further the image of the extremists as the legitimate defender of a beleaguered community. The images of American tanks in front of mosques in Baghdad, the seat of the caliphate for half a millennium and the scene of some of the most glorious chapters in Islamic history, had enormous emotional impact.[2] According to the Pew Global Attitudes survey, in Pakistan the proportion of Muslims seeing Islam as threatened – often by the West – more than doubled in twelve months to reach a level of 64 per cent in March 2003, in Indonesia the proportion went from 33 to 59 per cent, in Turkey from 35 to 50 per cent. The same poll found that 77 per cent of Moroccans said they felt 'more solidarity with other Muslims these days' and 49 per cent said they had confidence in bin Laden to 'do the right thing in world affairs'.[3]

Yet if this new anger was welcome to the senior leadership of al-Qaeda, the situation emerging in the aftermath of the loss of their haven in Afghanistan and the invasion of Iraq posed serious challenges as well as opportunities. Militant thinkers and leaders, like Western policy-makers and strategists, found themselves struggling desperately to grasp the contours and dynamics of the complex and chaotic new circumstances. The 9/11 attacks had been controversial among extremists, with many within al-Qaeda itself concerned that, by risking the safe haven the group had secured in Afghanistan, they could prove counterproductive. Outside al-Qaeda, the strikes had been by no means universally welcomed, with many long-term militants deeply concerned that the attacks might jeopardize any gains that the extremist movement had made over previous years. When in the aftermath of the Afghan campaign the fractious community of foreign militants in Afghanistan had dispersed they had divided often along ideological lines. A febrile debate was already underway by the summer of 2002 over how best to deal with the coming invasion of Iraq – a development that no extremist ideologue, strategist or propagandist had actually predicted. Though the arrival of large numbers of Western troops to fight a war in the core of the Middle East, particularly in a part of the region with as long and resonant a history as Iraq, was a chance for many radicals to realize long-held strategic aims, the new situation was not without its potential pitfalls. Equally, the new radicalization provoked by the war needed to be successfully managed if it was to benefit the jihadis. In these changed circumstances the thinking that had evolved during the 1990s was clearly no longer relevant. The period of 2002 to 2004 was thus one of particular intellectual activity within militant circles as major ideologues and strategists tried to formulate and impose different responses to the rapidly evolving situation.

The most obvious tension among them pitted once again the global against the local. Two broad schools of thought developed among radicals, with bin Laden and Ayman al-Zawahiri, faithful to their vision of al-Qaeda as an overarching, unifying and directing structure for disparate groups and strands, trying to find middle ground and struggling continually to overcome personality clashes, deep ideological divisions, reluctance among many to accept their leadership and the very real practical problems posed even by communicating with other major figures and thinkers in the world of Islamic militancy. The most prominent advocate of the 'global' approach, which rejected attempts to carve out actual chunks of 'liberated' territory in favour of launching the ultimate decentralized campaign based on individuals and self-radicalizing and self-organizing cells, was the Syrian Mustafa Setmariam Nasar, better known as Abu Musab al-Suri. Those who held true to a more 'local' strategy which sought to find, fight for, clear and hold physical bases for jihad and eventually for a new caliphate, were best represented by Jordanian-born Ahmad Fadeel al-Nazal al-Khalayleh, who was to become infamous across the globe under the *nom de guerre* of Abu Musab al-Zarqawi.[4] Both men had been among those who had escaped Afghanistan at the end of 2001, and the ideological contest between them was to be critical in shaping the form of Islamic militancy and thus of the 9/11 Wars over the coming years.

## ABU MUSAB AL-SURI

As the bombs had fallen on Tora Bora, al-Suri, forty-three in 2001, had headed west into Iran before looping back to reach the dry mountains and valleys north of the Pakistani city of Quetta by the end of the year.[5] Al-Suri appears to have been convinced he was likely to be either captured or killed in the imminent future and thus spent much of his time in an unspecified 'mountainous retreat' finishing a huge volume distilling decades of strategic criticism, historical analysis and theory that he hoped would be a template for a new form of structure for the radical Islamic militant movement. The work, *The Call for Global Islamic Resistance*, was finally published on extremist websites in late 2004. It was only then that al-Suri's significance as one of the primary strategists of contemporary Islamic militancy was genuinely understood in the West.

Al-Suri never fitted the standard stereotype of the extremist, though his route into radicalism was relatively typical of his generation. His long career took him through many of the most significant locations of late twentieth-century Islamic extremism. Born in Aleppo, Syria, in 1958 to a well-off, socially conservative and religious family whose economic and social status as well as cultural values were threatened by the new modernizing nationalist, secular Ba'athist regime, al-Suri became involved in underground 'Islamic resistance' groups when young.[6] Trained as an engineer like so many militants at the time, he escaped the bloody crushing of Syrian Islamists in 1982 and fled first to France and then to Spain, where he married a convert and had three children. By 1988, he was in Peshawar, where, he later claimed, he became involved in the foundation of al-Qaeda and worked as a trainer in camps for the 'Arab Afghan' *mujahideen*.[7] Even at this early stage, his relations with bin Laden were cool. Al-Suri did not like leaders of any type, and his own intellectual curiosity and contrarian spirit contrasted strongly with bin Laden's carefully cultivated asceticism and dogmatic rigour. After four years spent instructing militants in explosives and urban guerrilla warfare techniques, he left for Spain, where he spent three years in the southern city of Granada before finally arriving in London in 1995.[8] In the British capital, he collaborated with Algerian militants and the Jordanian-born radical scholar Abu Qutada, running propaganda operations for the Groupe Islamique Armée (GIA), whose battle against Algerian security forces was reaching a climax.[9] Al-Suri, however, broke with GIA leaders over their policy of sowing terror through indiscriminate massacres and started working for other groups active at the time, including al-Qaeda. The decision appears to have been based as much on personal pique as anything else.[10] By 1998, after a brief incarceration by British police when his involvement with senior active militants including bin Laden was revealed, al-Suri moved with his family to Afghanistan, which he described as 'the best example of a Muslim state on earth today'.[11] There, he appears to have become close to Mullah Omar. Confident of his own understanding of the West after fifteen years living in Europe and of his standing among fellow militants, al-Suri established his own training camp, prepared propaganda tracts for the Taliban, ran a rudimentary think-tank in Kabul and 'wrote thousands of pages in ideology, political, military and martial science and sharia studies'.[12] He kept away from bin Laden and, he claimed, was unaware of the 9/11 plot. This distance from al-Qaeda was not due to any moderation. In his lectures in Afghanistan he told listeners: 'Kill wherever and don't make a distinction between men, women and children.'[13] One of the many criticisms he subsequently levelled at the 9/11 attacks was that, if they were going to be done at all, they should have been done properly, i.e. with weapons of mass destruction.[14] Neither a gifted organizer nor an orator nor a particularly experienced fighter, al-Suri theorized the evolution of al-Qaeda post-9/11 into something much more contemporary, much less conventional and much more effective. 'Al-Qaeda is not an organization, it is not a group, nor do we want it to be,' he wrote in his 1,600-page final magnum opus. 'It is a call, a reference, a methodology.'

As mentioned briefly in Chapter 1, al-Qaeda had always been in part a 'methodology'. The word al-Qaeda itself comes from the Arabic root *qaf-ayn-dal* and, though it can mean 'a base', as in a camp or a home, a military installation, a foundation such as that beneath a house or a pedestal that supports a column, it has a range of other meanings as well.[15] It can, for example, be used to indicate the revolutionary vanguard envisaged by early thinkers and activists – the *al-qaeda al-sulbah* – and, crucially, can also mean a precept, rule, principle, maxim, model or even pattern.[16] The al-Qaeda phenomenon had always incorporated these three elements, a physical base, the vanguard or leadership element and a free-floating worldview and ideology. These elements had interacted with each other in a dynamic way, each becoming more dominant depending on the circumstances, each influencing the others' evolution. In the 1988–96 period, without a base or a coherent ideology, al-Qaeda had largely meant its senior leadership, the vanguard. From the return to Afghanistan until the end of 2001, as al-Qaeda acquired a geographical base, this latter physical element came to acquire much greater significance. Through this period too the ideology of al-Qaeda was honed and then disseminated, first through press conferences, tapes and press releases and then increasingly through acts of spectacular violence such as the strikes against American embassies in east Africa, on the USS *Cole* and finally in America in September 2001. In 2002, 2003 and 2004, with the physical structures of the group overrun and the leadership scattered, it was logical that the ideological component of al-Qaeda would take its turn as dominant. Al-Suri's thinking not only shaped the evolution of al-Qaeda or international violent Islamic extremism in the early years of the twenty-first century but described it too.

Al-Suri's argument was radically modern and relatively simple. His motto was '*nizam la tanzim*' or 'system not organization', and his vision was of a broad, self-organizing popular uprising that would have no leaders, no organizations but simply like-minded highly motivated activists 'swarming' together for specific attacks.[17] These would be on targets which, after having consulted his own writings, everybody understood to be legitimate and which would cumulatively, particularly through their propaganda value, advance the overall cause. One of al-Suri's sources for this vision was his own largely inaccurate reading of the second Palestinian Intifada, still ongoing as he worked on early drafts of his work and receiving easily as much coverage on Arab-language satellite television as anything al-Qaeda was doing. He understood the Intifada to be the sort of 'strategic phenomenon', a bottom-up spontaneous mass participation leaderless revolt, which he wanted to see across 'all corners of the Islamic world'.[18] But al-Suri was also a realist. He saw the Islamic militant movement as on the defensive, with huge and potent forces ranged against it. One advantage of al-Suri's strategy would thus be the increased resilience it would give militant networks, albeit at the cost of their capacity to organize major strikes against distant targets.[19] At his Afghan camp, al-Suri had advised his protégés to form no cells bigger than ten members for, 'if you are caught, they are all caught'.[20] Logistics would be dealt with locally and communications kept to a minimum. Autonomous local units would be empowered to act along broad strategic guidelines without seeking further authority, and there would be no oath of allegiance to an *emir*.[21]

In addition to boosting security, al-Suri hoped to end the 'disunity' or *fitna* that he, like bin Laden, saw as the greatest threat to the movement by dissolving all difference in a single, 'flat' ideology that took no account of local specificity. There would be an end to the previously incessant arguments about which country would be the base of the new caliphate because no country would be. His book, accessible to everyone via the internet, would provide the guidance formerly provided by a central leadership. Al-Suri's vision thus combined the local – individuals doing what they could where they could – with the global – a common goal and style of all the combined efforts. Like the 9/11 Wars themselves, al-Suri's jihad would be composed of an infinitely complex matrix of sub-conflicts the sum of which would be greater than the parts. One thing for al-Suri was certain: open confrontation with superior 'Crusader-Zionist forces' must be avoided unless victory was absolutely assured. The 9/11 attacks had been a catastrophic strategic error, he felt, casting 'jihadists into the fiery furnace ... a hellfire which consumed most of their leaders, fighters and bases, leaving only a very few to escape either capture or death'.[22]

Through 2003 and 2004 more and more evidence began to emerge that something approaching al-Suri's vision of individual militants acting individually according to a universal template was actually already happening. One area was in the Far East, specifically in Indonesia, where a series of new networks evolved in the immediate aftermath of the war in Afghanistan and the invasion of Iraq. These successfully launched a series of attacks on Western targets, particularly Australian interests, and on local people or groups associated with the West.[23] The most shocking and ruthless was the strike on nightclubs in the resort town of Kuta beach in Bali in October 2002 in which more than 200 people, including many tourists, lost their lives. In August 2003, the Marriott hotel was attacked in Jakarta, and just over a year later it was the turn of the Australian embassy in the Indonesian capital.

As ever, the violence in Indonesia had long roots, stretching back to resistance by revivalist Islamic groups to Dutch colonizers and then the various governments that had followed them.[24] Local Salafis had also received large amounts of Saudi Arabian money in the 1980s.[25] Sectarian unrest in the 1990s and in 2000 had fuelled the growth of radical Islamic ideologies, and by the turn of the millennium Indonesia had developed a thriving and relatively large and heavily politicized extremist Islamist movement, Jemaa Islamiya (JI), which was rooted in an extensive network of religious schools across the country. As elsewhere, the Indonesian government went to some lengths to stress the international connections of many of JI's senior members and ignored the longer and much darker purely national history that lay behind its emergence.[26]

The JI organization became the focus of attention following the Bali attacks and their successors. It had certainly provided the organizers of the strikes with a reservoir of manpower for the recruitment of many of those involved. Yet organizationally it was not linked to al-Qaeda. The leading players in the Bali plot had been in Pakistan in the late 1980s and early 1990s and had attended what were effectively terrorist training camps, but the facilities where they had learned about bombing, counter-surveillance and so on had been run by Abdul Rasul Sayyaf, an Afghan cleric with strong Saudi connections who led his own '*muja-hideen* faction' and who was a rival of bin Laden rather than an associate. Ten of the score or so individuals closely involved with the Bali bombing were alumni of Sayyaf's Sadda camp near Peshawar.[27] There were a handful of key individuals, often operating outside the structure of JI, who acted as go betweens with al-Qaeda at the time of the Bali plot. They exploited personal relationships with al-Qaeda leaders established before 9/11 during the period when the group was fully established and operational in Afghanistan to source some assistance for their campaign. But their role was less than has often been said. The test came following the arrest of Riduan Isamuddin, aka Hambali, in Thailand in August 2003, the man said to be key link between al-Qaeda and operational groups in south-east Asia, who had, according to local and American intelligence, brought cash from bin Laden as one-off funding for the Bali attack.[28] Despite his removal from the scene, the bombs continued. The man behind them, Noordin Top, had never travelled to Afghanistan and was not in contact with the al-Qaeda leadership – though he nonetheless called his group Tanzim Qaidat ul Jihad. He also translated documents from al-Qaeda's online magazines and took the *nom de guerre* of 'Ayman', almost certainly after Ayman al-Zawahiri, whom he had never met. Top, an extremely effective, ruthless and dedicated operator who would continue to launch a series of attacks throughout much of the decade, was an example of how al-Suri's vision was already being realized by the time the Syrian strategist was putting pen to paper in his mountain hide-out.[29]

Other attacks provided further apparent proof. Many occurred on the other side of the world, testament itself to the apparently global relevance of al-Suri's strategy. Three in particular – in Casablanca, Morocco, in March 2003, in Istanbul eight months later and in Madrid in March 2004 – showed this very clearly. The Casablanca attacks, which killed twenty-nine people, were organized by two men who had recently been in training camps in Afghanistan but were carried out by fourteen suicide bombers recruited locally. All were young men, all aged between twenty and twenty-four, from the sprawling Casablanca slum of Sidi Moumin. For several years radical preachers in these slums, often educated in, or influenced by, Saudi Arabian religious schools and foundations, had been attracting a growing following among the offspring of immigrants who had arrived from poor rural communities over the previous three decades.[30] Such groups tapped into similar local conditions to those that were leading to the growth of al-Sadr's militia in Iraq and, like the al-Mahdi Army, provided a coherent set of values, aspirations, explanations and an identity to young men growing up in communities largely marginalized from mainstream social, cultural and political life in Morocco, including from the officially sanctioned Islamist parties.[31] Also like in Iraq, they formed semi-criminal gangs, enforcing their own law and even carrying out scores, possibly hundreds, of executions. Almost all those who killed themselves in the Casablanca bombing were unmarried, unemployed, poorly educated and so unworldly that their failure to find the targets they were aiming for in the centre of the city revealed not just their amateurism but the fact that many had barely travelled further than the edge of the violent slum that was home. Only one, a substitute teacher, had graduated from high school and been to college. None were previously known to the authorities, none had any previous known involvement in Islamic activism, and all were recruited during the four months it took one or two senior activists to plan the attack. The attacks came two months after the invasion of Iraq, an event cited as critical in almost all the interrogations of the survivors of the cell once they were rounded up by Moroccan security services. They had no connection to anyone among the senior leaders of al-Qaeda.[32]

The bombings in Istanbul in November 2003 came against a similarly febrile background. In few places was the radicalization and the concomitant aggravation of anti-Americanism caused by the Iraq war more evident than in Turkey, a majority Muslim nation but a secular, historically pro-Western state. Though bin Laden remained deeply unpopular, not least because he was an Arab, as many as 31 per cent of Turks nonetheless said that suicide attacks against Americans and other Westerners in Iraq were justified, a sentiment that undoubtedly encouraged domestic militants to see bombing campaigns as likely to be approved by a significant proportion of their own community.[33] In spring of 2003, the Americans had made huge efforts to negotiate passage for 15,000 crucial troops across the territory of their NATO ally into northern Iraq for the invasion of Iraq, sending Zalmay Khalilzad, the urbane Afghan-born special emissary of the White House, to spend days in Ankara negotiating with Recep Tayyip Erdogan, leader of the moderate Islamist Justice and Development Party (AKP). Erdogan, who had just been appointed prime minister after clearing legal hardles following a landslide victory in 2002, got the consent of his cabinet to a deal worth $6 billion in grants and $20 billion in credit guarantees but ultimately failed to convince parliament.[34] The rejection of the American offer was acclaimed almost unanimously by a Turkish public which polls said was 94 per cent against the US invasion plan.[35]

Of a very similar nature to those in Casablanca, the Istanbul bombings too revealed both the impact of the new diaspora of Afghan veterans and the ease with which they recruited new volunteers for the cause. One of bin Laden's last acts before 9/11 had been to receive a deputation of Turkish militants and approve their request for $10,000 to fund operations in their homeland.[36] The attacks, which targeted two synagogues, a British-owned bank and the British consulate, left fifty-eight people dead, generated worldwide media coverage and were considered a success. Though two of the most senior militants involved escaped to Iraq, most of those they had recruited were rounded up. One explained his vision of the group's activity to Turkish police. 'We are different from al-Qaeda in terms of structure,' said Yusuf Polat, who admitted serving as a lookout for the bombers. 'But our views and our actions are in harmony.' The quote summed up al-Suri's vision of militant activism perfectly. The passive acquiescence of the 400 people who investigators calculated knew something about the planned strike but had said nothing indicated the degree to which, by the end of 2003, many of the precepts underpinning the extremists' worldview were taking hold on a much wider population.[37]

That the violence was going to spill over into mainland Europe was probably always inevitable, though few anticipated quite how spectacular the first attacks on European soil would be. They came on March 11, 2004 between 7.38 and 7.43 in the morning when eleven bombs detonated almost simultaneously on commuter trains pulling into Madrid's Atocha station and two suburban stations. The death toll eventually reached 191 and one of the most appalling scenes of the 9/11 Wars must be the shattered trains with, as rescue workers fought to free casualties and corpses, the constant ringing of mobile phones called by anxious relatives who had heard the news of the blasts and whose loved ones would never answer. About a third of the dead were immigrants from eleven different countries.[38] Once again these attacks seemed to show that al-Suri's vision of a genuine popular uprising spearheaded by self-radicalizing militants was being realized.

The Madrid strikes were very different from many previous such actions. The bombers did not die in the attack itself, thus failing to demonstrate the supposed faith of those behind the attack as the attacks over previous years had so often sought to do. Martyrdom or *shahadhah*, as the etymology of the word in both English and in Arabic implies, involves the act of bearing witness by one's voluntary death before a real or imagined audience, and this, contrary to standard al-Qaeda practice, the Madrid bombers did not do.[39] Neither, on the whole, had previous strikes been conducted in such a way as to kill and maim hundreds of ordinary people without even the pretence of attacking a military, administrative, political or commercial target. The targets in Casablanca – a restaurant frequented by tourists and the elite, a Jewish-owned hotel, a synagogue – had been at least representative of the standard enemies of radical Islamists. The same was true of the bombings in Istanbul. Bin Laden, al-Suri and others understood that they needed to justify civilian deaths as part of a broader defensive effort against a bigger target, such as Israel or America. Even tourists could, at a push, be portrayed as 'ambassadors of depravity, corruption, immorality and decadence', in al-Suri's words. But killing crowds of ordinary commuters on their way to work was far harder to 'sell' to potential sympathizers and thus risked delegitimizing the cause as a whole.

The reasons for this series of ideological and tactical differences became clear as investigations into the attacks in Madrid progressed. The attackers were not experienced al-Qaeda operatives parachuted in from overseas as initially suspected but were first-generation Moroccan and Tunisian immigrants who had been living in Spain for some time.[40] Neither was it directed by some kind of shadowy al-Qaeda 'head of operations' from afar. The group had largely formed in 2001 and 2002, drawing on a base established largely by Syrian activists fleeing persecution in their own country who had arrived in the mid-1990s. It had, however, evolved fast as new members were drawn into or left the overlapping networks of friends, family and associates that it comprised. No one recruited its members or brought them deliberately together with the aim of creating a terror cell. They formed like any unorganized social group. A police informer, the cleric at one of the mosques they frequented, described the men meeting at apartments to chant jihadi songs and watch videos of jihadi preaching 'clandestinely, with no regularity or fixed place, by oral agreement and without any schedule, though usually on Fridays'.[41] Soon, most had 'reached the conclusion that they had to undertake jihad'. If there was a leader it was Abd al-Majid al-Fakhet, an intelligent thirty-five-year-old Tunisian-born economist with Spanish citizenship. His key associate was an energetic and violent BMW-driving drug dealer of Moroccan origin, Jamal Ahmidan, who was known as 'the Chinaman' on account of his large oval eyes and diminutive stature. The latter, whose commitment to radical Islam had come after addiction to alcohol and crack, was still involved in the heroin trade, though no longer a user himself, and provided the bulk of €55,000 needed for the attacks. Most of the rest of those in the various sets of social networks – 'childhood friends, teenage buddies, neighborhood pals, prison cellmates, siblings, cousins' – that formed the group were poor, ill-educated and marginalized.[42] Only one marginal member of the group had ever travelled to Afghanistan, and though the web of connections around the group was vastly complex, touching the UK, Morocco and Italy, no clear direct connection to the al-Qaeda senior leadership has ever emerged. After several years of investigation, Spanish intelligence and police investigators concluded that the bombers were acting largely on their own. There were, officials said, 'no phone calls to al-Qaeda and no money transfers' nor any solid evidence of any direction from bin Laden other than the portraits of him some of the bombers had on the screens of their mobile phones.[43]

One much-debated question has been whether or not the Madrid attacks were timed to achieve the specific short-term political gain of swinging the imminent Spanish election to ensure the withdrawal of Spanish troops from Iraq. According to Spanish court documents, the intentions and plans of its leaders only began to become concrete following the invasion of Iraq.[44] The earliest ambitions of the group, discussed at length in various apartments or on picnics by the banks of the Navalcarnero river outside Madrid in between games of soccer and while children ran around and wives prepared food, had been to travel to Afghanistan to fight.[45] However, by late 2002, a new member of the group, an Egyptian called Rabei Ousmane Sayed, suggested that instead of travelling all the way to Afghanistan or Chechnya they should focus their efforts closer to home. According to the police informer, Sayed told the others: 'We need martyrs who are ready where they are. If one lives in France, then he's prepared for France; if one lives in Spain, then he's prepared for Spain.' Sayed then asked who was 'prepared' for martyrdom. 'Everybody raised their hand,' the informer said.[46]

Yet there was still no focus on who or what to attack or the timing of any strike. In late December 2003, a document entitled 'Iraqi Jihad, Hopes and Risks' was circulated on the internet. Of uncertain origin, it nonetheless summed up contemporary thinking in extremist circles about how to force the retreat of Western troops from Iraq by attacking 'weak links' in the US-led coalition.[47] Spain, where 90 per cent of the population were opposed to the conservative government's decision to dispatch Spanish troops to Iraq, was designated as vulnerable. The tract gave the key figures in the Madrid group – 'the Chinaman' and the Tunisian al-Fakhet – the idea of launching an attack before general elections due in Spain in March 2004. The plot itself was largely organized from a farmhouse outside Madrid that belonged to a relative of one of the group. Explosives were sourced through a Spanish ex-convict working in a quarry whom the Chinaman knew through criminal contacts. The bombs were prepared, placed in bags and dropped off on the trains. If the Atocha train had not been running late, the devices hidden aboard would have exploded in the station itself, killing at least several hundred more.

The influence of Iraq rapidly became very clear. On the day of the bombing, with the government still insisting the attack was the work of ETA, the Basque separatist organization, a Madrid television station received an anonymous statement from a man speaking Arabic with a Moroccan accent who said the attacks were revenge for Spain's 'collaboration with the criminal Bush and his allies'. More attacks would follow if the injustices did not end, the man, later identified as the Chinaman, said. 'You want life and we want death,' he added, echoing a phrase bin Laden and other radical propagandists had used repeatedly.[48] One key element that the invasion of Iraq provided in the eyes of the extremists was a justification for such an attack on ordinary commuters. The support of the Spanish administration for the invasion had strengthened the Islamic militant argument that the group's proposed victims were not mere civilians but, because they had voted at elections for those who had dispatched the Spanish troops, complicit in military attacks on Muslims. The war in Iraq, like the broader 'War on Terror', also allowed the militants to imagine themselves as glorious defenders of the Islamic faith, tapping into the powerful psychological resources of a highly selective and martial version of Islamic history. One of the videos found in the ruins of the apartment in a suburb of Madrid where seven of the group blew themselves up when surrounded by police three weeks after the attacks refers to 'the Spanish Crusade against the Muslims . . . the expulsion [of the Muslims] from Andalusia and the tribunals of the Inquisition'.[49] Such arguments, though theologically weak and morally repugnant, were emotionally very powerful and by the spring of 2004 attractive not just to a handful of young alienated immigrants in a run-down inner-city district of Madrid but to many other young men among Muslim communities elsewhere in Europe and elsewhere in the Islamic world. As every month passed and 24 million Iraqis, through little fault of their own, lurched further away from the path towards stability, prosperity and democracy that the White House had hoped they would pursue and further towards a grim future on what was now dubbed 'the central front of the War on Terror', they grew that much more convincing.[50] If there was no sign yet of a generalized 'Intifada' across the entire Islamic world and among European Muslims as al-Suri had hoped, the appalling events in Madrid showed the trend was very clearly towards greater radicalization, a greater degree of autonomy on the part of individual militants, greater resilience of terrorist networks and, almost inevitably, a greater extent of violence as a consequence.

## AL-ZARQAWI AND ANOTHER VIEW OF VIOLENCE

Of course, al-Suri was not formulating his theories in a vacuum. He was attempting to explain and guide fast-moving events on the ground. He was doing so from some distance. Others were much closer to the gritty reality of 'the struggle' and held rather different views. So when, ten days before the first battle of Falluja in April 2004, a group of senior militants had met in the western Iraqi city 'to review the situation', they had little time for any strategy of 'leaderless jihad' as advocated by al-Suri. Their priorities and interests were much more concrete. Settling down to 'study recent accomplishments', their conclusions were far from edifying, recorded Abu Anas al-Shami, a Jordanian Palestinian cleric who was the group's religious adviser and a fighter and present at the meeting. 'We realized that after a year of jihad we still had achieved nothing on the ground,' Abu Anas wrote in a diary published on the internet a few months later. 'None of us had even a palm-sized lot of earth on which to reside, no place to find a refuge at home in peace amongst his own . . . We had all abandoned our homes, our families, to become wanderers.'[51] The outlook, the militant leaders unanimously agreed, was bleak. All felt they had 'failed resoundingly' and that a change of plan was needed. The new approach would involve a reaffir-mation of a familiar strategy. What was needed was territory, fortifications, bunkers, a physical front; in short, a base that would be a home, a haven and, of course, a springboard for further expansion once the immediate defensive phase of fighting, so like the early trials faced by the Prophet himself with his small band of followers, was over. 'So we decided to make Falluja a safe and impregnable refuge for Muslims and an inviolable and dangerous territory for the Americans, which they would enter in fear and leave in shock, burdened by their dead and wounded,' Abu Anas wrote.[52]

If Falluja came to be the city which embodied the insurgency, then the individual who became the face of the violence in Iraq in 2004 and on into 2005 was Abu Musab al-Zarqawi. Born, as his *nisbah* suggested, in the rough industrial city of Zarqa in Jordan in 1966, al-Zarqawi had grown up in relative poverty. A violent petty criminal as a youth, he travelled to Afghanistan around 1989, probably influenced by propa-ganda videos and stories of glorious battles retold in his local mosque. He had, however, at least according to some reports, arrived too late for the fighting against the Soviets and became a reporter for a Pakistan-based radical newspaper instead.[53] On his return to Jordan, al-Zarqawi became involved in a militant plot, was arrested, imprisoned and then released in an amnesty in 1999. Free again, he returned to Pakistan and then crossed into Afghanistan, where he established his own very basic training camp in the west of the country near to Herat. Despite his lack of facilities and funds, al-Zarqawi rejected the patronage of bin Laden after a meeting with the Saudi in mid 2000. Like al-Suri he was unaware of the September 11 attacks before they occurred but nonetheless was able to successfully evacuate his camp and the families of his followers to Iran in their aftermath, a feat which, though he still remained little known outside certain tight circles of Jordanian militants, undoubtedly added to his status.[54] It is likely that al-Zarqawi reached northern Iraq towards the end of 2002, probably passing through Iran clandestinely, and established himself in an enclave in the hills of the north-east corner of the Kurdish-ruled autonomous parts of northern Iraq held at the time by Ansar ul Islam, the group of local and international militants who had succeeded over the previous decade in securing themselves a chunk of mountainous territory and who had developed some links with al-Qaeda itself in the year or so before the 9/11 attacks.[55] Al-Zarqawi's entry into the lists of top wanted militants came a month before the 2003 invasion, when he played a starring role in US Secretary of State Colin Powell's speech to the United Nations setting out the American case for attacking Iraq. In the speech al-Zarqawi was described as an 'associated collaborator' of bin Laden and blamed for a range of attacks – including the supposed 'ricin' plots in the UK. This was simply untrue. Like al-Suri, al-Zarqawi saw himself as a rival of bin Laden and had never made any formal alliance with bin Laden or any of his close associates.[56] Obviously, Powell also failed to make clear that al-Zarqawi, if present in Iraq at all, was one of those militants based in a zone outside Baghdad's control, telling the Security Council simply that Iraq 'harbours a deadly terrorist network' that al-Zarqawi 'headed', which may have been a factually accurate statement but was grossly misleading.[57] Claims that al-Zarqawi had visited Baghdad for medical treatment after losing a leg fighting in Afghanistan were also tendentious in the extreme, as was amply demonstrated when he eventually surfaced with both lower limbs very much intact.[58]

As the American tank columns advanced from Kuwait in the south, US special forces and Kurdish *peshmerga* irregulars had flushed out the Ansar al Islam fighters from their bases in eastern Iraqi Kurdistan. The militants had then dispersed.[59] Some had headed into Iran, others set off south. Having escaped the bombing and the dragnet, al-Zarqawi worked his way down into the heartlands of the Sunni insurgency. Over the months to come he was joined there by hundreds of other fighters. Some were fleeing the north like him, others were fugitives direct from Afghanistan, many were from core Middle Eastern countries and had come to Iraq to fight as *fedayeen* irregulars during the fighting in the spring and had stayed on. Renaming his group Tawhid wal Jihad (Unity and Jihad), al-Zarqawi showed both extreme brutality – himself executing by knife several hostages – and a talent for media manipulation – rapidly and effectively ensuring the broadcast of the atrocious images of the executions by internet and video. Some of these videos were produced in terrible makeshift studios-cum-torture chambers in Falluja and elsewhere and were thick with instinctively but adeptly chosen symbolic touches such as dressing prisoners in orange overalls like those worn by detainees in Guantanamo Bay.[60] They were viewed by extraordinary numbers of people across the Middle East and the world – the video showing the beheading of the kidnapped American contractor Nicholas Berg was downloaded half a million times in the first twenty-four hours it was online – and together with the continuing bomb attacks he was able to launch both against American troops and Iraqi government forces rapidly made him by far the best-known foreign Islamic militant fighting in Iraq.[61] It was also al-Zarqawi who had been responsible for many of the attacks on Shia in the summer and autumn of 2003. At the time the identity of those behind the growing carnage among the Iraqi Shia population had been unclear. Al-Zarqawi, however, had made little secret of his hatred for those he called 'snakes', and the attacks escalated through the early months of 2004, becoming a new bloody strand of the violence seizing Iraq.[62] Another reason for the extraordinary profile that al-Zarqawi enjoyed as the first anniversary of the invasion approached was the concerted effort by the American military to focus media attention on him in the hope that projecting the Jordanian extremist as the leader of 'the resistance' would provoke a xenophobic reaction from Iraqis, splitting the insurgents. In weekly briefings for reporters in Baghdad, US spokesmen regularly displayed slides showing his face, generals mentioned him as often as possible in public, and a variety of steps were taken to 'boost the Zarqawi factor' in local coverage of any violence whether directed against American or local forces. This effort was, one of its instigators was later reported to have said, extremely effective.[63]

Al-Zarqawi's strategic thinking – inasmuch as there was any – differed profoundly from that of al-Suri. The two had very different personalities and very different experiences of militancy too, and this showed in their vision of how 'the jihad' should be fought. Al-Suri's formative experience was the destruction of his fellow Syrian Islamists after their revolt against the Syrian regime in 1982. President Hafz al-Assad had acted without pity, razing much of the city of Hama, their base, and giving al-Suri an early and profound lesson in what too great an attachment to controlling physical territory might bring. Al-Zarqawi's formative experiences were the opposite. He had ended up in prison because he had had no base and nowhere to hide when the Jordanian security services came looking for him in the early 1990s. He thus saw the establishment of physical enclaves as the key goal of any militant movement. This was a more traditional vision of guerrilla warfare, involving the creation of secure havens where insurgents could plot, train and rule, preparing for the major conflicts to come but also drawing on a whole range of theological resources such as the concept of the pure 'Islamic community', living as an isolated example in a sea of barbaric ignorance, jahiliya, that was recurrent in both recent radical Islamic thought, such as the works of thinkers such as Syed Qutb, and in its antecedents stretching back to the righteous community of the Prophet Mohammed himself. This perfect imagined Islamic community could be realized both metaphysically – in terms of a personal spiritual withdrawal – and physically – as militants had done in Egypt in the 1970s. A related concept was that of takfir.[64] Being a takfiri meant assuming the right to designate others who called themselves Muslims as kufr, or non-believers, and was an integral and controversial part of the ideology of al-Zarqawi, his associates and their spiritual mentors. So, for example, Abu Anas al-Shami, the militant Falluja-based cleric, said in a radio message in July 2004, that anyone collaborating with the coalition in Iraq was an unbeliever and it was permitted, indeed encouraged, to kill them.[65] But takfir also implied a separation from the corrupt, the hypocritical and the apostate which true believers should attempt to realize in real concrete terms. It was not enough merely to try to engineer a righteous community, but territory needed to be defined, seized, sacralized, Islamicized and purged.

The last decades had seen attempts to do this at all levels within the Islamic militant movement. The history of the 9/11 plot itself was replete with examples. From the Hamburg flat of the hijacker pilots to the Islamic centres where they met and the prayer rooms they established in the universities they attended through to the training camps in Afghanistan and finally the Islamicized Taliban Emirate, purged of impure objects and influences such as the Bamiyan Buddhas, the concept of finding, controlling, defining and occupying space had been key. The aim of al-Zarqawi and his followers was to re-create the Taliban's Afghanistan in Iraq.[66] The 'home' that they had said they missed so much, the patch of land where they could unfurl their prayer mats, had to be rigorously policed if it was going to be held against the huge forces ranged against them. So in Falluja, the men of al-Zarqawi's group spent much of the summer and early autumn of 2004 trying to eradicate everything in the city that contravened this radical vision. In the run-up to the battle of November 2004 the effort they made to enforce a strict code of personal behaviour on local populations who did not share their rigorous interpretation of Islam – in part by subjecting them to the sight (or experience) of spectacular public violence involving torture, beatings and videoed humiliation – was at least as great as the energy they dedicated to constructing bunkers to resist American troops. Al-Shami, head of al-Zarqawi's *fatwa* committee, declared both equally valid and necessary ways of preparing the defence of the city.

## FROM SAUDI TO IRAQ, THE FOREIGNERS ARRIVE

In the early autumn of 2004, as the fighters in Falluja dug in physically and spiritually, Hizam al-Ghatani, a softly spoken twenty-six-year-old shopkeeper from the south-eastern Saudi Arabian port town of Jizan, left his home, his wife and small son and set out for Iraq. No one told him to do so, no one 'brainwashed him', he was not 'recruited' in the conventional sense of the word. A thin, bespectacled orphan with poor educational qualifications who had scrabbled to support his family, al-Ghatani found his own way into militancy, overcoming significant obstacles to reach his destination. He did not expect any material rewards. Indeed, he was not even sure of what he expected at all. But he travelled willingly, even if anxiously.[67]

Al-Ghatani was not alone. Many hundreds – possibly many thousands – of volunteers were arriving in Iraq through the late spring, summer and autumn of 2004. Their numbers were often exaggerated as was their importance in what remained a predominantly local insurgency. But that they came is beyond doubt. An analysis in early 2005 of fatal casualties among such *mujahideen* recorded on Arabic-language extremist websites over the previous six months found mentions of 154 non-Iraqi Arabs killed in the country.[68] Very few had any combat experience at all.

There was nothing inevitable about al-Ghatani's transition from shopkeeper to *mujahed*. He had been shocked and upset by the 9/11 attacks. 'I was not happy because all those people were civilians,' he remembered, admitting that he 'was not clear about al-Qaeda or their ideology'. He had also been horrified by the violence in his own country, where returning Afghan veterans had built networks, recruited volunteers and eventually launched a series of increasingly bloody attacks from May 2003. But for al-Ghatani, as for most Saudis, Iraq was different. 'I saw the TV, al-Jazeera, the internet news websites and I was angry at the aggression against civilians, the children being killed, the air attacks . . . I wanted to be of service . . . They were at war, I was at peace. I wanted to do something to help them,' he said. 'I knew nothing about the criteria for a jihad. I just thought it was simple: you fought unfair aggression.'

In Mecca in mid 2004, the young man met a band of Iraqis who described the situation in their homeland in graphic terms. Al-Ghatani needed no further convincing. The group put him in touch with a smuggler in Kuwait. He paid the man $1,000, and together they walked and drove across the shifting rock and sand of the desert frontier with Iraq before another car picked him up and drove him to Baghdad.[69] The Iraqis he had met in Mecca were waiting for him in a house in the city's al-Doura district, a stronghold of the insurgency. 'I was thinking more of being a stretcher bearer or a medic, but they convinced me to become a fighter,' al-Ghatani said. The young man was told he was going to Falluja. He had never used a gun before and was apprehensive.

The highest proportion of foreign militants in Iraq – up to two-thirds by some estimates – came from Saudi Arabia, and most had reached Iraq not via Kuwait like al-Ghatani but through Syria. This Syria–Saudi nexus was not foreseen by Western pre-war planners but, admittedly with hindsight, seems eminently logical. It evolved organically and rapidly, because it suited ground realities as well as the interests of the individuals and states involved. It is a perfect example of the sort of secondary effects the confident and ambitious American project in Iraq could generate in such a complex region and of the kind of transient phenomenon that characterized much of the continually evolving internal dynamics of the 9/11 Wars.

That a number of Saudi citizens – a small fraction of the Kingdom's 23 million perhaps but significant nonetheless – would be motivated to fight in Iraq was always probable. Even in 2003 and 2004 the power and legitimacy of the ruling Saudi royal family still rested on two pillars: the pact established with the kingdom's religious establishment at the foundation of the state more than seventy years before and the generous disbursement of the country's vast oil revenue via jobs and welfare. Both of those pillars were unsteady. The pact – by which the descendants of Ibn Saud would exercise temporal power and be permitted to appropriate a very large proportion of the kingdom's immense wealth in return for allowing the clergy control over education, enormous financial resources themselves and relative autonomy – had been strained by the nation's continuing alliance with the United States and by elements within the royal family's continued attempts to gradually lead a profoundly conservative society in a more Westernized, less rigorous direction. Simultaneously the buying of social peace was threatened by a whole series of parlous economic indicators: per capita oil revenue was lower than it was in the 1980s, unemployment was up to 20 per cent.[70] None of this necessarily guaranteed a flow of militants to Iraq, but against the background of decades of the intense propagation of a particularly conservative strand of Islam and coming on top of almost all the factors seen elsewhere – such as massive rural–urban drift, a huge youth bulge and a powerful narrative of Muslim solidarity in the face of a supposedly belligerent and anti-Islamic West – it did make it much more likely.[71] One significant factor which undoubtedly encouraged many to travel to Iraq was the strong support of local clerics. Again, though, along with the macro-factors there were the micro-factors: low-level, 'flat' social networks played an important role too, with most volunteers making their way to war in groups of friends, neighbours or worshippers at the same mosque.[72] Significantly, the networks through which volunteers came together and then travelled were entirely distinct from those of al-Qaeda in Saudi Arabia. The rapid rise and abrupt fall of 'Al-Qaeda in the Arabian Peninsula' (AQAP) is explored further in later chapters. For the moment, it is simply worth stressing that, however much their ideology and rhetoric may have seemed superficially similar, AQAP remained operationally and organizationally distinct from the much broader movement of volunteers from the kingdom to Iraq.

The Syrian connection owed more to the longstanding poor relations between Damascus and Washington. A brief period of optimism following the accession of Bashar al-Assad as president in July 2000 had been rapidly followed by a new nadir in relations as the Syrian security establishment reasserted its grip on power and continued its support for Hezbollah in Lebanon and other Islamic militants across the region.

A complicating factor in an already complex situation was that, though they watched over a predominantly Sunni country, the Syrian security establishment was dominated by Shia from the tiny Allawite sect, including the ruling family. Tolerating, if not actively assisting, the passage of volunteers across their territory served several of the Syrian intelligence services' interests: it fuelled the insurgency in Iraq and therefore made a US intervention against Damascus less likely, it provided a useful card to play in any potential negotiations with Western states or even Israel and, as Saudis and other foreigners paid considerable sums to smugglers and to border tribes who often had connections with the security services, it made them money too. Finally it also diverted the attention of anyone who might otherwise be tempted to take up arms against the Syrian regime, which, as secular Ba'athist and in large part Shia, represented two of contemporary Sunni militancy's priority targets. The necessity for such a safety valve was shown, not only by the rising number of incidents within Syria, but also by statistics on the origins of the volunteers arriving in Iraq. Up to a fifth were Syrian, their homeland naturally no more immune to the broad currents of radicalization coursing through the Islamic world than anywhere else in the region.[73]

The journey was not always simple. Mohammed al-Fawzan, a thirty-five-year-old from the wealthy al-Shifa neighbourhood of Riyadh, was an example not just of how any inevitable link between poverty and violent activism is difficult to construct but also of the obstacles those who set out for Iraq had to overcome to reach their goal. Al-Fawzan too blamed al-Jazeera and 'the TV' for his decision to try to become a *mujahed*. A self-confessed partygoer more interested in football than religion, al-Fawzan, sixth of nine sons of a rich businessman, said that neither the al-Aqsa Intifada nor the war in Afghanistan had 'meant much' to him, but the images from Abu Ghraib in particular and from Iraq more generally, as they had done with al-Ghatani, created 'a kind of mental shock'. 'When I saw those pictures, it came into my mind that I had to do something,' he recalled. Al-Fawzan, who had a secure and relatively well-paid government job in the Transport Ministry, sought out a relative in Mecca who was already sending volunteers to Iraq and was despatched, after some basic training in the Yemen, to Damascus, where he was hidden by a 'coordinator', a fellow Saudi, in an apartment and furnished with false ID papers. After a month, however, with no sign of an imminent departure and unable to leave the safehouse, al-Fawzan lost patience, decided to try another way to reach Iraq, returned to Saudi Arabia and was arrested.[74] Others, such as Abu Thar, a Yemeni taxi driver and religious student who also said he had left his home after seeing the images from Abu Ghraib, were more determined. Abu Thar described spending weeks moving between cheap hotel rooms, mosques, rooms above religious schools in Damascus, Aleppo and elsewhere as he waited to cross into Iraq from Syria. In each, he said, he found another dozen young volunteers.[75] Finally, he was taken to a village on the Syrian side of the border close to a checkpoint where the police had been bribed and, after a frightening trek through the desert, was led into Iraq and to Falluja.[76]

Al-Ghatani the shopkeeper had arrived in Baghdad in October, dropped off in a safehouse in the rough Sunni-dominated al-Doura neighbourhood of the city. There he had handed over more cash to another group of militants-cum-criminals – documents later seized by US troops confirmed that $1,000 was more or less what the smugglers to whom insurgents tended to subcontract the task of bringing in recruits charged Saudis – who drove him to the outskirts of Falluja and left him by the roadside.[77] Al-Ghatani, who had travelled without any introduction from any known figure in Saudi Arabia, failed to convince the *mujahideen* in the city of his bona fides. He was not discouraged, however, and instead spent the next four months fighting with 'the tribes', as he called them, along the short stretch of road between Falluja, Ramadi and Baghdad. 'They taught me to use an AK-47. I shot at the Americans when they attacked us,' al-Ghatani said. 'They would use planes, and I saw old women and children killed, and I buried them myself and I let the anger out by shooting and fighting.'


## FALLUJA TWO

The long-awaited American offensive into Falluja started on November 7, 2004. There had been sustained fighting across the Sunni Triangle through most of the summer and early autumn. Weeks of raids, firefights and occasional air strikes were punctuated by more conventional engagements. Several took place around Abu Ghraib, as al-Zarqawi's fighters from Falluja and local tribes mounted sustained attacks on American positions. 'I've got to tell you, we've killed a lot of people carrying weapons this week . . . I'm talking hundreds,' Brigadier General Hertling, deputy commander of the 1st US Armoured Division, had told reporters in Baghdad in late September. Among them was Abu Anas al-Shami, the *takfiri* cleric, head of al-Zarqawi's *fatwa* committee and occasional diarist.[78]

For the second battle of Falluja, General Mattis deployed 9,000 troops, four times as many as in the first battle seven months before. They included 2,000 Iraqis. In the spring the vast bulk of local troops and police deployed in Falluja had deserted or refused to fight, so this new engagement would be a key test of the US strategy of building up local security forces.[79] Eleven million rounds of ammunition had been stockpiled and efforts made to close the Syrian border to halt the flow of foreign militant volunteers.[80] The city's defenders were estimated to number around 2,000, of whom perhaps a quarter were foreign nationals.

This time the American troops pushed right through the city. After ten days of fighting, several hundred insurgents, fifty-four Americans and eight Iraqi soldiers had been killed. The latter had performed marginally better than before, though they were still far from being able to operate independently. The fighting was possibly the most intense seen by American troops in recent decades, a succession of vicious house-to-house fights with tanks firing from a few metres away into buildings, protracted artillery bombardment and air strikes. It was the apogee of the kind of 'kinetic' warfare the Marines had originally hoped to avoid. In a sense it was the climactic battle that the initial campaign of March 2003 had lacked.

Though the 'international' or 'foreign' fighters were outnumbered at least three to one by Iraqi fighters in the opening stages of the battle, many of the latter slipped away as combat intensified, returning to their homes in the farmland around the city or going to ground elsewhere in the country and leaving a higher and higher concentration of foreigners in the city. By the final stages of the battle, American troops fought a heterogeneous force of militants from outside Iraq in the ruins of an Iraqi city largely deserted by the Iraqis themselves.

A month before the battle came, al-Zarqawi had finally pledged allegiance to bin Laden and accepted his role as an 'al-Qaeda affiliate', the local representative of the global brand. In so doing he made the second battle of Falluja the only conventional confrontation on such a scale between a force at the very least nominally loyal to al-Qaeda and troops fielded by the US or their allies in the whole of the 9/11 Wars.[81] What was supposed to be a battle for territory – for the safe haven and few square metres of ground that the militants had said they so desired – had become invested with a new significance. For many of the combatants Falluja – and by extension Iraq – had been reduced simply to a stage on which a titanic struggle between the forces of good and evil, belief and non-belief, would take place. 'We are not here to liberate Iraq, we're here to fight the infidels,' Abu Osama, a Tunisian, told one reporter bluntly days before the fighting began.[82] The people of Falluja – few of whom took part in the actual fighting in the city – had little role in this great imagined drama of cosmic conflict between faiths, cultures and civilizations.

## BIN LADEN REDUX

Shortly after the end of the fighting in Falluja, four days before the American presidential elections, a video was released by bin Laden, his first for eighteen months. It directly addressed the 'People of America', advising them on 'how to prevent another [9/11]'.[83] There was little new in bin Laden's rhetoric, though the careful *mise en scène* – a lectern, no weapon, the robe of a respected statesman and scholar – indicated that the leader of al-Qaeda sought to project a more nuanced image than had hitherto been the case. In the tape, bin Laden suggested that it was what America did, not what it was, that provoked the attacks against it, pointing out that al-Qaeda did not target Sweden.[84] Bin Laden almost certainly sought to influence the American poll – or at least exploit the opportunity for further publicity it provided. It is less clear that the forty-seven-year-old fugitive wanted Bush to win, however. In the event, the incumbent was re-elected with ease.

The video dominated headlines and news bulletins on the eve of the elections, a powerful reminder of bin Laden's ability to project himself globally and of who, after all the interest in al-Zarqawi and others, still remained the pre-eminent leader of the global jihad. It was also a reminder of the very obvious failure of the most expensive manhunt in history to make any evident progress. Since the al-Qaeda senior leadership had disappeared after Tora Bora, Western intelligence services had been unable to obtain any solid lead as to where they might be.[85]

Most of the militants who had fled Afghanistan had ended up in South Waziristan, the most southerly of Pakistan's Federally Administered Tribal Areas (FATA), so the working theory among Western intelligence that bin Laden was there too was, though little more than informed speculation, reasonable. Mahmood Shah, the chief civilian administrator of the FATA from 2001 to 2005, remembered that the foreigners had begun arriving in Shakai, an impoverished area of pine forests, mountains and valleys close to the border, in early 2002.[86] Secret American intelligence reports later used in the compilation of dossiers on detainees at Guantanamo Bay contained repeated references to meetings of the al-Qaeda leadership in Shakai in late 2003 and 2004. One report even implied that, after the capture of Khaled Sheikh Mohammed in Rawalpindi, al-Zawahiri himself had moved to the area from an unspecified urban area.

But it was not actually clear if 'high value target one', as the al-Qaeda leader was known to the teams tracking him in Pakistan, Afghanistan and from America, was even in the frontier zone at all. With little fresh human or technical intelligence coming in, the hunters adopted some unusual methods of analysis. In 2003 it was rock types in the background of one video that featured the al-Qaeda leaders that were scrutinized closely. A year later trees pictured in another video led investigators to believe bin Laden might be in the valleys of Chitral, hundreds of miles or more north of Shakai and South Waziristan. But if his references to current events and people showed the fugitive leader had access to some kind of news media, there was little else to go on. Hundreds of leads were being developed by the CIA. There was a particular interest in finding and tracking the couriers bin Laden was known to use. His extensive close family – three current wives, a dozen or more children – was a possible weakness. But beyond that, there was nothing.

Yet, despite the problems of their pursuers, the situation of any senior militants in Pakistan remained precarious. Once the presence of hundreds, possibly thousands, of international militants in South Waziristan had been detected by Western intelligence services, pressure had been put on President Musharraf to launch a series of military offensives to deny al-Qaeda any secure base there.[87] A first effort in 2003 had concentrated on a 30 square mile area in South Waziristan under the control of local Pakistani militants suspected of harbouring 'foreign terrorists', and, even if this was a bloody fiasco as local and foreign militants ambushed ill-prepared troops and inflicted heavy losses, other offensives had followed.

These made clear that, though the senior al-Qaeda leadership had seen their ideology propagated across the world through spectacular violent acts such as 9/11 or the various strikes it had subsequently inspired, they were still a long way from finding a replacement for the secure base they had once enjoyed in Afghanistan.[88] If the attractions of a strategy based on a decentralized 'global, leaderless jihad' were strong, the late 1990s had amply proven how useful a genuine safe haven could be. As a result, bin Laden had carefully followed a middle road in strategic terms in his statements over the previous eighteen months, seeing his role as being 'inciter-in-chief' along lines closer to the thinking of al-Suri without entirely renouncing al-Zarqawi's strategy of creating a physical base from which to launch the great campaign to build the new Islamic caliphate.[89]

If the testing ground for al-Zarqawi's ideas was to be the campaign in Iraq, the testing ground for al-Suri's strategy of incitement of a decentralized, leaderless jihad would not be in the traditional lands where Islam has been the dominant religion for centuries, the *dar ul Islam*, the land of peace, however. Instead, it would be in a new zone of conflict: in the *dar ul kufr*, the land of unbelief, and more specifically in Europe, where 20 million Muslims living in the heart of the unbelievers' societies constituted an immense potential strategic asset for the global militant movement.[90]

# PART THREE

# Europe, the Darkest Days:
# 2005–6

# 8

# The 9/11 Wars Reach Europe

## A MURDER IN HOLLAND

Sitting on a sofa upstairs in an open-plan office off a quiet street in an unfashionable part of Amsterdam, Gijs van de Westelaken was talking about his dead friend and business associate, the film-maker and professional controversialist Theo van Gogh. 'He was provocative but never just for the sake of provocation. He wanted to know what made people tick,' de Westelaken said. 'He always said he would go on saying what he wanted to say whatever the threats.'[1] A few yards away, two tall blonde Dutch women in long denim skirts stood sipping warm white wine out of plastic cups and spoke in low voices. Some children played under desks, between architects' design tables and coiled cables of state-of-the-art computers. This was van Gogh's wake. A day earlier, on November 2, 2004, the forty-seven-year-old director had been cycling along Linnaeus Straat a few miles away from where de Westelaken was talking when he was stopped by a young man in a hooded sweater. A brief altercation followed, shots rang out, van Gogh collapsed, his attacker bent over his body, cutting, stabbing, then running. Panicked passers-by crowded round the corpse, a note pinned to its chest by a knife. Van Gogh's last words were: 'Surely we can talk about this?'[2]

The death of van Gogh, notwithstanding the bombings in Madrid seven months earlier, revealed to a shocked public in Holland, Germany, France, the UK and elsewhere that the 9/11 Wars had reached Europe. The strike in Spain had involved first-generation immigrants, most still barely integrated, many of whom elected to speak Arabic in court as their Spanish was too limited. Mohammed Bouyeri was very different. The 2,000-word note he had left was written in good Dutch, which was unsurprising as its twenty-six-year-old author had been born, raised and educated only a few miles away and at least in legal terms was as Dutch as his victim. It was in fact addressed not to Van Gogh but to Ayaan Hirsi Ali, a Somali-born refugee and member of the Dutch parliament with whom the director had been working on a film about Islam and domestic violence called *Submission*, which featured lines from the Koran projected over a semi-naked woman. The letter was in part a screed of incoherent apocalyptic poetry and in part a distillation of the familiar radical Islamic worldview. Hirsi Ali, who had made a series of controversial and uncompromising public statements criticizing Islam as a backward religion that encouraged violence to women, was an apostate, it said, working for hidden Jewish masters who ran Dutch and global politics. Those to blame for the terrible current situation of the world's Muslims were all those supposed believers who failed to act in the face of such clear provocation. Bouyeri's origins, act and views, especially as it became clear that he was connected to a much wider circle of radicalized young Dutch Muslims, thus apparently signalled that the scenario most feared by the counter-terrorist community, policy-makers and the general population – the radicalization and mobilization of the Muslims of Europe – was being realized. For major countries with large Muslim communities such as France, Germany and the UK, the killing of van Gogh meant that the war they had found themselves caught up in since 2001 no longer solely involved battles or bombs in far-off, dusty, hot countries but had reached them, their homes, their places of work, their friends and family.

For ordinary people in London, Amsterdam, Copenhagen, Rome, Stuttgart or any number of smaller cities and towns across Europe, the coming years would be marked by anxiety, anger and deep pessimism. Every day brought news of further attacks. The world seemed launched on an ineluctable course towards a dark and violent future. The 'Clash of Civilizations' appeared not just to be inevitable but a reality. Nor were such impressions entirely without foundation. Iraq continued to slide deeper into chaos, public debate globally became increasingly bitter and polarized, relations deteriorated between Western countries and a series of Muslim majority states, polls recorded more and more extreme positions becoming increasingly widespread among huge swathes of populations who had often previously shown themselves largely uninterested in politics or activism. There was a deep, and possibly well-founded, fear that the world would soon become divided into two warring camps. These years, from 2004 to 2007, saw the 9/11 Wars reach a new level of intensity, touching, irrevocably altering, indeed sometimes destroying, the lives of hundreds of millions of people across the entire planet. It was in this period that the 9/11 Wars came closest to being a genuine global conflict.

In this new and violent phase, Europe was crucial. The wars had expanded from south-west Asia to Iraq and had inflamed much of the Middle East. As al-Suri and bin Laden had both recognized, what happened in Europe would determine whether the wars would continue to broaden and deepen as a conflict or whether its hitherto apparently inexorable expansion would falter, opening up the possibility that the slide towards a deeper and broader chaos could be slowed, possibly halted and even, perhaps, reversed.

## EUROPE AND ITS MUSLIMS

The problem with even the most cursory overview of relations between 'Europe' and 'the Islamic world' is that defining either entity is difficult and sketching a single history impossible. If Europe has a geographic unity, encompassing more or less the tract of land bordered by the Atlantic, the Mediterranean and an imaginary line somewhere between the Vistula river and the Ural mountains, there exists no consensus among its infinitely diverse communities as to what being a 'European' actually entails. Equally, though the 'Islamic world' is supposedly defined by faith, the definition of 'Islamic' varies so dramatically as to almost invalidate the very concept of a global community of Muslims. This, as the previous chapters have explored, was the fundamental problem for al-Qaeda from the outset. It is unsurprising that it poses challenges for historians too. It is thus also inevitable that readings of the last 1,300 years of relations between these two already poorly defined and largely imaginary blocs are so often highly subjective and politicized.

So while some readings emphasize the rich cultural exchange between, for example, Muslim Moorish Spain and more northern Christian interlocutors in the early medieval period, others emphasize the violence that occurred at the same time. While some prefer to emphasize how the eleventh and thirteenth centuries saw European crusaders fighting and sacking their way across the Holy Land with an extraordinary and often indiscriminate brutality, others stress how trading contacts thrived despite the hostilities and underline the constant flow of words, ideas, tastes and practices from the Islamic world – algebra, admiral, coffee, guitar – into Europe and vice versa. Some see the first battle of Poitiers in 732 as the moment when a united Christendom successfully repelled a concerted attempt by Islamic armies to subdue and colonize northern Europe, others portray it as nothing more than the heading-off of a raid by Moorish armies set on gathering gold rather than spreading the faith.[3] Some prefer to emphasize the long centuries of strife between a newly potent Ottoman Empire and 'European' Christian powers following the 1453 fall of Constantinople, while others point out that Francis I of France allied with Sultan Suleiman the Magnificent to fight his rival, the Holy Roman Emperor Charles V, and that Queen Elizabeth I of England asked one of Suleiman's successors for naval assistance to defeat the Spanish Armada.[4]

What is certain is that the view that Europeans have had of the Moor, Saracen, Turk or Mohammedan has often been determined by the potential threat the latter have been thought to pose.[5] With Muslim armies advancing on Constantinople and Ottoman navies surging into the Mediterranean, commentators and writers such as Nicetas Byzantios or Dante Alighieri reserved the worst of their bile for 'the bad and noxious' religion of Islam with Mohammed 'the Antichrist' at its head. With the Ottomans on the defensive after the failed siege of Vienna in 1683, the Turk was seen instead as exotic and eccentric but not necessarily dangerous.[6] The Crimean War of 1853 to 1856 saw Anglican Christian Britain and Roman Catholic France allied with the Ottomans to defend Constantinople against a Russian (Orthodox) Empire demonized by Western European clergy as 'impure, demoralising and intolerant'.[7] As European colonial armies pushed deeper into the Islamic world – the French into what was to become Algeria, the Spanish into Morocco, the British into the Asian subcontinent and the Dutch into what was to become Indonesia – Muslims, Turks or Moors became decadent, sensual, poetic, representative of the supposed simplicity, honesty and 'honour' that an industrializing West was leaving behind.[8] When the 'Oriental' was depicted as violent, the violence was usually directed at others of his type through exotic punishments, duels, incomprehensible tribal wars. In all cases, the Western viewer could rest assured that these heroic warriors' picturesque *jezzail* muskets and long curved *yatagans* were no match for well-drilled troops with contemporary Western armaments. The superb duelling Arab or Berber horsemen painted by Eugène Delacroix to the acclaim of Parisians through the middle of the nineteenth century were being wiped out by modern armies armed with modern weapons even as the artist's canvases dried.[9] When a threat surfaced, however, so did the old stereotypes. So during the Indian Mutiny or War of Independence of 1857 'proud, vengeful and fanatical ... cunning and cruel' Muslims were blamed in Britain for the trouble even though 90 per cent of the mutineers were Hindu.[10] A decade or so later, when the immediate scare had passed, a less negative vision of 'the Mohammedan' returned to dominate literature, popular journalism and art.

The myths woven through this vexed and complex history of representation and misrepresentation have permanently marked imaginations and identities. Few of the clichés bear much relation to reality. Early Islamic armies fought on foot with spears, not waving scimitars from Arab stallions as popularly imagined, not least because they tended to be composed of poor desert tribesmen who could not afford a mount.[11] The great Christian knight Roland, the paragon of medieval chivalry, died fighting Basque bandits who had lain in ambush in a Pyrenean mountain pass, not 'the Moors' as recounted in later literature. The sensuality of the East so dear to nineteenth-century travelling (or indeed sedentary) French poets revealed more about the conservative contemporary mores of their homeland than about the Levant. More recently a series of commentators and analysts have opposed 'Oriental' and 'Western' styles of warfare, unconsciously reproducing the old stereotypes of the wily, highly mobile Saracen with the sharp scimitar trying to outwit the manly, slightly plodding but fundamentally honest and upstanding Western warrior with his heavy broadsword that featured in primary school history books even in the 1970s.[12]

But if there is Orientalism, a false and romanticized vision of 'the East' informed as much by the prejudices and complexes of 'the West', there has also been Occidentalism, the equally distorted vision of 'the West' in the Muslim world (and elsewhere) too.[13] Many of the prejudices so tediously trotted out by radical Islamic militants such as Bouyeri have roots as deep as any of those of 'European' visions of Muslims. They too have been embedded by successive decades of representation in literature and films. The vision of the European in much of the Islamic world has been as heavily mythologized as any representation of the sensual or violent Moor in Europe and has also depended to a considerable degree on the degree of perceived threat posed by the West at a given time. The resilience of such stereotypes is striking too. During the eleventh and twelfth centuries Muslims 'regarded the Franks . . . as little better than animals in manners of sexual propriety' and Crusaders were, like American troops today, seen as dirty, polluting, indelicate and bestial.[14] 'All those who were well informed about the Franks saw them as animals who are superior in strength and aggression,' said Usama ibn Munqidh in 1095. And Saladin himself is meant to have commented on the 'obstinacy' with which the 'Franks . . . fight for religion'.[15] In the eighteenth century, the famous Ottoman scholar Naima compared contemporary European states to those of the Crusaders and concluded that they were so backward and barbaric as to not be 'worthy of his attention'.[16] Concepts of infection or corruption by a decadent and depraved West go back to anti-colonial rhetoric from the first half of the last century and well beyond. There are the key texts of radical Islamic militancy such as those of Sayyid Qutb, who, after a short voyage in America in the late 1940s, dismissed Western civilization as lascivious, materialist and base, citing it as the modern version of pre-Islamic ignorance and barbarism, *jahiliya*.[17] Another solidly rooted generalization is that Westerners in general and Western soldiers in particular are cowards, afraid to fight man to man but who rely instead on their technological superiority. Interrogations of aides of the dictator revealed that the latter presumption was one reason why Saddam Hussein – who distributed videos of the film *Blackhawk Down* to his generals – failed to avail himself of the various possible options that might conceivably have averted the war of 2003.[18] It was also one reason why bin Laden took the enormous strategic gamble of 9/11, though better informed associates warned the US would react like 'a wounded bear'. Such ideas have bled into mainstream political, public and private conversation in much of the Islamic world, which is often marked by a depressing level of ignorance and prejudice.

Another important part of Occidentalism has long been a crude anti-Semitism. As the writings of Qutb show, negative images of the Jew have long been associated with urbanity and thus a 'decadent' modernity.

Hatred of Jews in many Muslim countries, despite some historic examples of peaceful and fruitful coexistence, was extremely widespread even before the foundation of Israel. Since the establishment of the Jewish state, the fusion of the political and the religious has given rise to an anti-Semitism that is impressive in its vitriol. 'Read history,' Sheikh Abdur-Rahman al-Sudais, the imam of the Grand mosque in Mecca and a controversial figure who has also been seen by some as a proponent of moderation, preached in 2004, 'and you will understand that the Jews of yesterday are the evil fathers of the Jews of today, who are evil offspring, infidels ... calf-worshippers, prophet-murderers, prophecy-deniers ... the scum of the human race whom Allah cursed and turned into apes and pigs ... These are the Jews, a continuous lineage of meanness, cunning, obstinacy, tyranny, licentiousness, evil, and corruption.'[19] A favourite theme of soap operas in Egypt, Jordan, Turkey and elsewhere is the shadowy Zionist-Semitic conspiracy and its brutal American accomplices.[20] *The Protocols of the Elders of Zion*, a tract first published in 1903 supposedly outlining a Jewish conspiracy to take over the world and exposed many years ago as a fake by the Tsarist secret police, has long been on sale throughout the Middle East and beyond.[21] The tract's claims, which featured prominently in the foundational literature of groups such as Hamas that were increasingly popular with European Muslims and others from the 1990s onwards, were seen as entirely uncontroversial by many hundreds of millions of people in the Islamic world and in Muslim communities in Western Europe by the end of the twentieth century.[22]

Such stereotypes – the Frank, the Moor, the Saracen, the European colonizer, the American neo-imperialist – had rarely survived contact with reality. Until very recently, the distance that allowed them to persist unchallenged remained. But in Europe in the last forty years that distance has vanished. Communities that were once free to imagine the worst of one another without such preconceptions being challenged – or having direct effects on everyday life – live intermingled. New and difficult questions of integration and assimilation are being posed that a thousand years' worth of myths and misrepresentations aggravate rather than resolve. As it was meant to do, the Islamic extremist violence of the middle years of the decade revealed the tensions this new proximity has generated in a cruel and effective way.

# THE MECHANICS OF IMMIGRATION

As the American conservative commentator Christopher Caldwell has usefully pointed out, Europe acquired a large immigrant population of which a substantial proportion define themselves as Muslim 'in a fit of absence of mind'. Though a provocative formulation, Caldwell's phrase nicely encapsulates the lack of foresight, management or even recognition of large-scale immigration through the latter half of the last century.[23] Few had ever predicted that Europe would become home to tens of millions of Muslims in less than fifty years, and therefore little forward planning was ever done to deal with an eventuality that many could neither envisage nor countenance.[24] That influx has naturally created a number of difficult issues specific to the continent.

Immigration to Europe from colonies had grown steadily, especially towards the end of the nineteenth century as European nations began to industrialize. That increase was minimal, however, compared with that which came after the Second World War when, denuded of manpower and money by the conflict, Western nations looked to their former overseas possessions, many still in the process of gaining their independence, for cheap labour. For the French this was mainly Algeria, theoretically part of France until 1962; for the British it was the Caribbean, India, Pakistan (particularly rural areas in the north-eastern lowland regions adjacent to Kashmir which had long supplied recruits to the Merchant Navy) and from the Sylhet region of Bangladesh which also had a long tradition of providing labour. Where former colonial links did not suffice, other sources were found. Germany and Holland, as well as several Scandinavian countries, looked to Turkey. The Dutch brought in substantial numbers of Moroccan workers.

At first, it was intended that such workers would spend only a couple of years in their new host nations, living in relatively isolated communities often on the outskirts or in run-down central neighbourhoods of cities, before returning home. Most did just that. However, not least because employers preferred to avoid the complicated and expensive process of refreshing their diligent, cheap and compliant labour force every couple of years, many ended up staying. Wives and other family members were allowed to join them and communities became, often literally, more concrete as local authorities recognized that having tens of thousands living in shantytowns was a hazard both to public order and to health and replaced makeshift accommodation with more permanent structures. This was done with little genuine planning and as cheaply as possible.

The sites where the earliest workers were more or less dumped had been chosen to maximize ease of access to the heavy industries where most of them worked and minimize their impact on 'native' communities. However, it did not take long before there was a strong reaction from local populations, who felt their jobs and, to a lesser extent, lifestyles threatened. By the 1960s governments were beginning to limit entry to family members of existing settled migrants and a relatively small number of asylum-seekers. These restrictions were progressively tightened, particularly as the post-war economic boom gave way to the downturn of the 1970s and mass unemployment. Yet such efforts to restrict the new migration came late.[25] By the later 1990s, the population referred to or declaring itself as Muslim in the UK numbered 1.6 million (out of a total of around 60 million), in France around 5 to 6 million (8 to 9.5 per cent), in Germany 4 million and in Holland around 800,000 (5 and 6 per cent of total populations respectively). In all, if the centuries-old 6-million-strong Muslim communities in the Balkans were included, it was thus thought that at the time of the 9/11 attacks just over 20 million Muslims lived in Europe.[26]

All these communities had three things in common. Firstly, in every country, an increasing proportion of the so-called immigrant population, Muslim or otherwise, had been born locally.[27] Secondly, though their conditions varied, almost all the communities designated Muslim in Western Europe scored significantly lower on most social and economic indicators than their 'host communities' and many non-Muslim immigrant communities. So, in Holland, at the time of the murder of van Gogh, 27 per cent of Dutch Moroccans and 21 per cent of Dutch Turks were unemployed in contrast to a rate of only 9 per cent among 'native' Dutch.[28] In the UK, the 2001 census found that Muslims had the poorest health and lowest educational qualifications of all British communities. In 2003 and 2004, British Muslims also suffered the highest unemployment rate, topping 14 per cent, around three times the national average, and young Muslims from sixteen to twenty-four had the highest unemployment rates of anyone at 22 per cent, twice as high as their non-Muslim counterparts.[29] In Germany and France, where data are not broken down according to religion, extrapolating from existing statistics indicated that a similar situation prevailed. According to the 2005 data from the National Institute for Statistics and Economic Studies (INSEE), unemployment among people of French origin was 9.2 per cent while for those of foreign backgrounds, the rate was 14 per cent. More importantly perhaps, in comparison to a 5 per cent overall employment rate for people of French origin, 26.5 per cent of university graduates with North African backgrounds were unemployed.[30] Thirdly, the communities themselves were immensely varied and often remained separated internally between Moroccan Berbers and Arabs, Pakistani Punjabis, Mirpuris and Pashtuns, between the various Kurds who speak the mutually unintelligible Kermanji and Sohrani dialects, and so on. Marriages between immigrants and 'native-born' French, German, Danish, Dutch or British men and women often outnumbered those between members of communities portrayed as homogeneous monoliths by outsiders.[31]

As the profile of such communities evolved, so models developed or discussed by policy-makers to deal with issues of integration and assimilation – the two being far from the same thing – did so too. These also predictably varied enormously between European countries. In the UK, policies were largely based on a strong belief that different cultures could coexist in relative harmony without imposed overarching narratives of national identity as long as the bedrock principles of British society was observed. Given the rather grand name of multiculturalism, seen as irresponsible and naive laissez faire by its critics and as a tolerant celebration of an economically and culturally enriching diversity by its supporters, this model had been under significant strain since the late 1980s. The controversy following the publication of Salman Rushdie's *Satanic Verses* in 1988 had revealed deep tensions. Subsequent rows over faith schooling, scares over the number of *medressas* and clashes over arranged marriages continued to expose and exacerbate them. One of the problems was that no one was very clear about exactly what the British model actually implied. Did it involve a 'pure multiculturalism', in which no single culture was seen as more valid or more 'native' than any other, or a softer version, where minorities were allowed very considerable autonomy within a dominant culture? One interpretation, rooted in a rejection of assimilation in the 1960s and heavily influenced by left-wing thinking from the 1980s that had been particularly dominant among those running many of Britain's inner-city municipal councils, was based on a complicated argument that as citizens had 'differing needs' equal treatment meant taking 'full account ... of their differences' and that 'equality' needed therefore to be defined in a culturally sensitive way that was 'discriminating' but not 'discriminatory'.[32] Others, such as Trevor Phillips, the head of the Commission for Racial Equality and a former television executive and presenter, demanded the opposite: that there should be more 'Britishness'. But what was Britishness? For Phillips, it was 'an inclusive culture which allows you to be all sorts of strange and eccentric things as long as the core values are accepted'.[33] Others defined Britishness very differently, appealing to ideas of island nations, green and pleasant lands, warm beer and even, in the title of one book, the 'Warrior Race' that the British apparently constituted.[34] In fact, the most British quality of the concept of Britishness appeared to be not only that it was so undefined but that most people were happy for that to be the case. British multiculturalism as a model tended in practice to be a compromise of the sort only acceptable in a country where there is no perceived need for either a fully codified law or a constitution.[35]

The French model of *laïcité*, an imposed theoretical equality before the law and before a rigorously secular state, had deeper ideological roots than the British model and a more coherent intellectual structure and came in for less criticism within France through the middle years of the decade, though it was often attacked externally. Different models had developed in Germany, Spain, Italy and the Scandinavian countries. In Holland, the system was known as the 'pillars' and was based on a denominational segregation where each community had its own schools, trade unions, social associations, even hospitals. Though the system, originally designed to manage the nation's numerous churches, had largely broken down by the time of van Gogh's murder, it still allowed, indeed encouraged, Muslim communities to live with a significant degree of separation from the rest of Dutch society and culture. 'We've had a tolerant tradition since the seventeenth century ... but a lot of difficult issues here were never discussed. The dark side of multiculturalism has been taboo,' said van de Westelaken, the late van Gogh's friend.

Equally, the immigrants themselves developed their own models of integration or assimilation. Often seen as the passive subject of policies or attitudes in their host countries, in fact immigrant communities dynamically developed their own ways of dealing with the situations that they found themselves in. The encounter with the West had been one of the primary drivers for reflection and for religious and political activism throughout the Muslim world from the nineteenth century onwards, and life in late twentieth-century Europe provoked a similar range of responses among immigrant communities. As they had done in countries from Morocco to Indonesia over the previous two centuries, these responses included outright rejection, an attempt to appropriate certain elements deemed compatible with a given vision of culture and belief, wholesale and enthusiastic acceptance and pretty much every possible shade in between. One important determining factor was, of course, conditions in the countries of origin. Turkish immigrants in Germany who came from developed Western Anatolian cities had advantages that arrivals in the UK from poor rural Pakistani villages did not. The difference between the opportunities open to savvy Moroccan townsmen and Berbers from the Rif mountains was huge. So too was the difference in social outlook. Immigrants from Pashtun communities on the northwest frontier of Pakistan were much more conservative as a general rule than those from much more literate and broad-minded Kurdish villages of northern Iraq, for example.

Also significant, despite the heterogeneity of the various immigrant communities, was the political evolution of their countries of origin. Complexes and conflicts from 'the old country' were often imported, and new emerging problems in states many thousands of miles away could have a significant effect in Bradford, Rotterdam, Hamburg or elsewhere. With most Dutch Muslim communities coming from relatively stable states such as Turkey and Morocco, Holland was spared some of the backwash of radicalism that troubled other nations. However, parts of the French immigrant population were deeply affected by the savage civil war in Algeria during the 1990s.[36] In Britain, in a much less evident way, the radicalization of the Kashmir conflict in the same period led to thousands of young men from communities in the west and north of England travelling to Pakistan not just, as many hundreds of thousands did every year, for family visits but to actively participate in a violent insurgency led by increasingly extremist groups. Another important example of this transfer between immigrants' countries of origin and the West was the composition of the various organizations that sprang up through the late 1980s and 1990s as representatives of newly vocal communities. Some British groups were close to Saudi Arabia, others to

Iran.[37] The Muslim Council of Britain which was founded in 1997 and would become the privileged interlocutor of the Labour government elected in that year had strong links to Pakistani Islamist organizations.[38] National and ethnic splits riddled the various representative bodies in France. Already in the 1990s European Muslims had become a prize in the internal battle for influence, power and worshippers between the various opposed strands of religious practice seen in the Islamic world with Gulf states, notably Saudi Arabia, pouring funds into bursaries, mosque construction, preaching and public meetings to further the reach of their own rigorously conservative brand of Islam. The contest between various strands of Islamic observance within Europe in the key period of 2004 to 2007 must thus be seen as an extension of both an ongoing struggle within the Islamic world more broadly and the longstanding competition between Muslim states for the loyalty of European Muslim communities. As ever, the 9/11 Wars played out within a framework of older conflicts. As ever, they involved the subtle interplay of a huge range of global and local factors and trends.

Many of these global trends have already been explored earlier, when discussing the flow of young volunteers from the Middle East to the militant training camps set up in Afghanistan by bin Laden, al-Zarqawi, al-Suri and others for example. They included a 'youth bulge' and immigration from the countryside to the cities or internationally. There was the discrediting of left-wing, nationalist or other ideologies and the subsequent wave of religious revivalism that had swept the Middle East in the 1980s. There was the surge of politics based on religious or sectarian identities around the globe in the 1990s and the construction of a new more global Islamic identity and narrative infused with a strong anti-American or anti-Western sentiment. Looking back, it is clear that Britain and Europe were far from immune to these broad historical trends affecting the Islamic world more generally.[39] There was also the impact of events such as the war in the former Yugoslavia, the conflict in Chechnya and the Second Palestinian Intifada. All of these episodes – especially the war in the Balkans – could be portrayed as evidence that Christian Europe did not care about Muslims.

Many felt the tensions coursing underneath. There were clues to what was happening. French authorities began recording a rise in anti-Semitic attacks – after years of decline – that were largely perpetrated by young men from Muslim immigrant communities.[40] In the UK, violent riots in

Bradford in 2001 had revealed deep social problems. Whereas once young 'British-Pakistanis' had experienced outrage at 'racism', seeing themselves as 'black', many now saw themselves as victims of Islamo-phobia, defining themselves as Muslims.[41] The success of radical Islamist groups such as Hezb-ut-Tahrir and of other similar organizations on university campuses showed how easily such ideologies could attract sig-nificant numbers of young people. In October 2001, two young Britons from families of Pakistani origin who had joined the Taliban in Afghani-stan were killed in Kabul in a missile strike.[42] Two months later, a young British convert tried to blow himself up on a transatlantic jet. In April 2003, two Britons tried to bomb a Tel Aviv nightclub 'for the sake of Allah and to get revenge against the Jews and Crusaders', according to a videoed will in a rare example of the 9/11 Wars suddenly surging into the otherwise largely autonomous conflict in Israel-Palestine. One of the pair detonated his device outside the club, killing three and wounding more than fifty.[43] The other, whose bomb failed to detonate, turned up dead on a beach ten days later.[44] In Holland, 'a different political wind [had been] blowing since the 9/11 attacks', Mohammed al-Aissati, of the Dutch Association of Moroccan Immigrants, told the author on the day after van Gogh's death.[45] 'We all had a good feeling about how we were doing here in terms of tolerance but 9/11 changed all that. This murder could not have come at a worse time.'

## EUROPEAN INTELLIGENCE SERVICES ON THE BACK FOOT

In the early years of the 9/11 Wars, with a poor understanding of the nature of the problem, creaking structures better adapted to Cold War enemies or more traditional terrorist groups and limited resources, intelligence services in Europe rapidly found themselves on the back foot. By early 2004, though it was clear that the conflict would almost inevitably come to the continent, few had grasped the nature or scale of the threat. A series of meetings the author had with senior British secur-ity officials at the time was salutary. The officials privately expressed their concern at the lack of 'handle' they had on the problem and wor-ried about the possibility both of a major attack and of lower-level violence by 'self-radicalizing' freelance militants. They frankly admitted that their knowledge of processes of radicalization and of the workings of modern Islamic militancy was superficial and worried that the terms with which they described their 'clients' – their analysis was based on groups, cells, operatives – did not adequately capture the nature of the phenomenon they were trying to grasp. Though some of the discussion was about so-called 'cleanskins' – 'It is not the ones we know about who worry us but the ones we don't,' the head of the militant Islam desk of the Metropolitan Police's Special Branch said over a drink in one of the pubs around Scotland Yard – the focus was more on 'sleeper cells' implanted by al-Qaeda over previous years which could be activated when needed. According to Stella Rimington, former head of MI5, these were 'networks of individuals ... that blend into society ... who live normal, routine lives until called upon for specific tasks by another part of the network.' One of the lessons learned from other modern terrorist conflicts, Rimington explained, was that terrorists aimed 'to hide in plain sight, to be seen but not noticed and to all intents and purposes to live a law-abiding existence'. One of the key targets of her service's efforts, she said, were people who might offer logistic help from the UK to overseas militants to strike abroad. In this Rimington revealed quite how far from fully comprehending the nature of the threat she and her service were.[46] The biggest danger, as events would shortly reveal, was in fact posed by militants who were very much British *receiving* aid from overseas to strike *locally*. The individuals involved in radical Islamic militancy 'blended into society' and 'lived normal, routine lives' for the very simple reason that they *were* normal members of society.

This, of course, meant that a preventive strategy based on the idea that it was possible to find potentially dangerous individuals through 'profiling', i.e. seeking those whose qualities might indicate a vulnerability or a tendency towards violent militancy, was unlikely to meet with much success. It was swiftly clear that being young, male, Muslim, anti-Semitic, pro-Palestinian, anti-American, of immigrant background, with conflicted identity issues and poor relations with one's parents in, say, late 2003 was not particularly useful as a predictor of any terrorist activity. The sheer number of those sharing some or all of those qualities was in the hundreds of thousands in Britain alone. A government report later found that during 2004, MI5, though one of the better resourced European intelligence services, was unable to watch even the fifty-two suspects classed as 'essential targets' and could only provide 'reasonable' surveillance coverage of about one in twenty terror suspects.[47] Outgoing Metropolitan Police commissioner Sir John Stevens spoke of 2,000 'al-Qaeda-trained' militants stalking British streets only a few months after the killing in Amsterdam, clumsily ratcheting tensions higher for little obvious purpose.[48] In Germany, local services found 31,000 individuals who they believed posed a significant security risk.[49] One potential solution suggested in the UK was the introduction of identity cards. That classic visual symbol of the 9/11 Wars – the concrete barrier – began to appear outside key London sites such as the Houses of Parliament and the American embassy like outriders of the coming storm.

In Holland, local authorities had been wrestling with the same issues. In late 2001 and early 2002 Dutch security services had begun monitoring Salafist mosques and prayer halls suspected of acting as centres of recruitment and logistics hubs for young Muslims hoping to travel to a variety of 'theatres of jihad'. One criterion for focusing their efforts was whether a given institution had financial links to Saudi religious foundations such as al-Haramain International, which had been blacklisted for its links to militant Islam. This led them to the al-Tauheed mosque in the north of Eindhoven, where they identified a group of young Dutch Muslims, largely the children of immigrants of Moroccan origin, who had gathered around a Syrian-born cleric. One, a seventeen-year-old still at school, set off for Chechnya in January 2003. He was arrested. Another travelled to Spain to seek out a radical cleric tangentially connected to the Casablanca bombings which had occurred a few months before.[50] Two or three others actually made it to Pakistan. Another had discussed jihad and training with al-Qaeda sympathizers on the internet. A fifth is believed to have been in the process of making multiple plans for terrorist attacks in Holland. But the Dutch services had failed to pay any serious attention to the group's self-appointed 'media coordinator', apparently only a peripheral member who after the 9/11 attacks had been making public pleas for intercultural dialogue and tolerance.[51] He was deemed to be relatively harmless. This was Mohammed Bouyeri, the killer of van Gogh.

## THE PROCESS

The various factors described above are important but can only be a part of any explanation of what lay behind Islamic militancy in Europe or indeed elsewhere in this period. One problem with the classic approach employed by security services in the early years of the conflict was that it was based on seeing radicalization as a consequence of an accumulation of the right elements at the right time. In fact, it is also possible to see radicalization as a process which itself often generated the conditions or qualities that led an individual to extremism and eventually violence. The key was not necessarily in the 'who' – essential character traits or profile of an individual – nor even in the 'why' – the sense of injustice or the attraction of a cause – but was to be found very often in the 'how'. It is this dynamic, complex and often chaotic interplay of environment and agency that, through the stories of a range of British militants of varying extremism who were active in the UK between the 9/11 attacks and the 7/7 bombings of 2005, the rest of this chapter sets out to explore.

If the process started anywhere it started not in the backroom of a radical-run mosque but in the frontroom of a family home. Ed Husain, who once held a senior position in Hezb-ut-Tahrir, the international Islamist organization that aims to overturn the alleged Western dominance of Muslims by forming Islamic states in what are seen as historically Muslim countries and is banned in many countries, remembered how as a teenager, despite years spent intensively studying with a traditional Pakistani Islamic spiritual leader, he had become increasingly distant from his conservative family.[52] They were steeped in the religious and social customs of Pakistan, which no longer interested him. A self-confessed 'misfit' at school, Husain soon found himself at the centre of the tension between the old systems of religious observance imported by first-generation migrants, which saw politics as something to be shunned, and newer styles of worship, often heavily influenced by Saudi Arabia and other Gulf countries, which adopted an aggressively political stance and were boosted by a massive, well-funded propaganda campaign. The latter had a strong appeal for Husain. 'What they [Hezb-ut-Tahrir] were saying seemed more relevant, more contemporary,' he said. 'They answered my questions.'[53]

Other catalysts for a shift towards involvement in radical organizations or towards an interest in more extreme strands of Islam were arguments over choices of sexual or marital partner, going out late at night, drinking, using soft drugs. Most of these would be familiar to many teenagers but were exacerbated in the context of the British

Pakistani community by a deep cultural generation gap which extended to almost all aspects of social relations within Britain's Muslim communities, from education to employment. The *biraderi* social system of north-eastern Pakistan, by which the interests of the individual are always subordinated to those of the extended family and broader social group or tribe, was difficult to reconcile with Western and urban values of individualism and personal empowerment. Under the system, communities were informally run by elders whose authority could not be challenged without risking total ostracism.[54] One response to this was radical secularism and rejection, another extreme religiosity.[55]

But the paths into radicalization were as many and varied as the responses to such tensions. Minor events such as incidents of racism or petty humiliations played a role. Major events could create the critical 'cognitive opening' that could lead to a radical change of direction. Shiraz Maher, then a history student at Leeds University, had never been attracted to any kind of activism before 9/11. His family had never been observant, he drank, smoked and 'was a normal first-year student'. And though in the summer of 2001 Maher had started seeing a more observant Muslim girl who had encouraged him to go to mosque more often and chided him for his lack of religious rigour, he was still far from any form of extremism. The 9/11 attacks, however, 'forced a choice', Maher said.[56] 'The rules of the game were clearly changing. You had to decide where you stood. I suddenly started asking questions that I had never asked before about Islam, about my identity, about the world.' A few days after the attacks in New York and Washington, outside the mosque where he prayed, Maher was approached by a Hezb-ut-Tahrir activist. The man, an Arabic and politics graduate from Maher's own university, was just a few years older, knew the Koran by heart but wore a suit and was clean-shaven. He 'seemed to have the answers' to the questions that Maher was now asking and was convincing too. 'I thought, here is someone who is successful and who talks my language,' Maher said. Within months Maher was meeting his mentor two or three times a week. The older man suggested ideas, leading rather than dragging his target in a certain direction. 'I felt he understood me,' said Maher. 'When I said, "I've been clubbing, I've smoked some weed," he was cool. At a traditional mosque in the Pakistani community [in Britain] they would have told me I was going to Hell, but he just said, "If it wasn't fun people wouldn't do it," and suggested that there were more rewarding and important things in life.' None of the conversations between Maher and his recruiter took place in mosques, which after 9/11 were under close scrutiny either by the security services or by local communities. This was typical. Apart from during the earliest years after 9/11, recruitment and the subsequent activism in the UK took place in independent Islamic centres, in private homes, in cafés, not in obvious locations such as the infamous mosque at Finsbury Park in north London. All the major terrorist plots in the UK in this period took shape in zones that are outside traditional established authority, religious or secular. Typically too, Maher was profoundly ignorant of Islam at the time of his recruitment. In this he was similar to the bombers in Madrid and to Bouyeri, all of whom had relatively poor and superficial understandings of the faith's teachings and doctrines. Maher went on to spend four years in the Hezb-ut-Tahrir group, rising up the ranks and recruiting scores of new activists himself.[57] Maher and Husain's respective routes into radical activism show many common elements found elsewhere but were atypical in one important aspect: both men were, at least in part, radicalized within a large organization. Most militants in the UK – or for that matter France, Holland, Germany or elsewhere – had never been part of any other group but were 'self-starters'.

## THE SELF-STARTERS

As security services in the UK began to make significant efforts to analyse militants and their behaviour they informally grouped them into various categories.[58] There were the 'followers' – people who were vulnerable to the right approach from the right person at the right moment, particularly if they were already partly radicalized by a particular event that made them question their identity or their own cultural background for the first time. Then there were the 'seekers', those who actively went looking for people with authority, knowledge and the crucial contacts who could help them get to where they wanted to go and often used the internet if there was no other option. One example in 2006 was an eighteen-year-old school boy who became attracted to radical Islam – he was known as 'the terrorist' at school because of his frequent statements of support for terrorists and his avowed anti-Semitism – and then got in touch via the internet with a group of students at Bradford university who were themselves planning trips to training camps in Pakistan. He was arrested after his mother called the police after finding a suicide note, a library of extremist videos and a desktop icon that played a song about martyrdom on his computer.[59]

Another category, however, were the self-starters, the natural leaders, those who were motivated and active and wanted, through their own actions, to change things. Again, many such figures have featured in previous pages: Ali al-Bahlul, for example, the Yemeni who sought out bin Laden and became his media secretary; Abu Thar, who left his family to fight in Iraq was another; Al-Fakhet, the Tunisian-born Spanish immigrant who led the Madrid bombers, was a third; Mohammed Bouyeri, deeply involved in local community work and profoundly frustrated and bitter when his projects did not receive government funding, had the same profile. A classic 'self-starter' was Hanif Qadir, a successful British small businessman in his forties who became involved in radical activism in 2002 and who spoke to the author shortly after deciding to end his involvement. Never particularly bothered by politics previously, Qadir had, however, followed the typical path from practising the traditional Barelvi Islam of his Pakistani-born parents to the Saudi-style Salafi rigorous conservatism which had spread from Pakistan into many of Britain's Pakistani-origin communities in the 1990s.[60] As with so many others, the 9/11 attacks were critical in focusing his growing new political and religious consciousness. Qadir began fundraising 'for the jihad', as he described it, in 2002.[61] 'I had always been involved in charity work, in helping out in the community, in doing stuff, and for me it was just an extension of that,' he said. 'It was like stepping in to help someone out who is being beaten up. There was no question in my mind that I was on the right side. I watched the news, saw what was happening over there [in Afghanistan] and got going.' Qadir started off simply asking friends, relatives and clients for donations for 'the jihad'. He made little effort to hide what he was doing. The money was passed to an Afghan refugee in London, who sent it via Pakistan to be used to buy weapons and equipment for the Taliban. On one occasion Qadir's contact presented him with a letter that was said to come from Mullah Omar, the leader of the Taliban, thanking him for his support. 'I was blown away. I was on cloud nine. I saw what I was doing as my duty, as the only thing I could do in the circumstances, but that was a true reward,' Qadir said. 'The fact that I was funding people who were killing British soldiers did not bother me at all.' Finally, after raising tens of thousands of pounds to help others to fight, Qadir decided to see action himself. Using his fundraising contacts, he travelled to Pakistan and to Peshawar with the aim of joining the Taliban. There, after briefly being vetted, the London-based businessman was packed into a bus with dozens of other volunteers for the journey into Afghanistan. Qadir never reached the frontline. After seeing wounded men coming back from the fighting and experiencing the way local fighters treated the international volunteers as 'cannon fodder', Qadir turned back. Many others did not.[62]

## OPERATION CREVICE

On October 22, 2003, a nineteen-year-old British student called Jawad Akbar was talking with an old school friend, a twenty-one-year-old college drop-out called Omar Khyam, at Akbar's small flat in a university hall of residence in Uxbridge, a nondescript commuter town west of London. The conversation was recorded by MI5 and subsequently produced as evidence in court. 'You're thinking airports, yeah, [but] what about easy stuff where you don't need no experience,' Akbar said. 'You could get a job like, for example, [in] the biggest nightclub in central London, where now no one can even turn around and say "Oh, they were innocent, those slags dancing around" ... then you will really get the public talking ... if you went for where every Tom, Dick and Harry goes on a Saturday night then that would be crazy.'

'If you got a job in a bar or club, say the Ministry of Sound,' said Khyam. 'What are you planning to do then?'

'Blow the whole thing up,' said Akbar. 'The best thing you can do is put terror in their hearts. There is no doubt, that is the best thing, there is nothing better than that.'[63]

The conversation could have been dismissed as youthful bravado were it not for the fact that the men had recently spent time in a training camp in Pakistan, at least one of the pair had met senior militants of al-Qaeda, and both were involved in the purchase of 600 kg of ingredients for rudimentary if powerful explosives less than a month after their talk about potential targets.[64] In April 2004, Akbar and Khyam were both arrested along with five other men aged between nineteen and thirty-five from south and west London and charged with being the ringleaders of the so-called 'Operation Crevice' plot, one of the biggest terrorist conspiracies uncovered in the UK in the years following 9/11. Named after the law-enforcement operation which foiled it, the plot involved a complex network of dozens of individuals, many of whom were dedicated to committing a string of violent attacks in the UK. Their trial revealed an enormous amount about the way those involved in the plot were drawn into violent extremism and how they changed from angry young men into potential mass murderers.

The five men eventually convicted for their roles in the plot were as representative as anyone else of the young men who were becoming radicalized in the UK at the time. Four were of Pakistani origin, either first- or second-generation immigrants, one was born in Algeria but raised in Britain. The average age of those in the group when they were sentenced was 28.4, almost the exact average of British militants.[65] The sprawling nature of the cell, with its multiple links and indistinct hierarchy, was also typical. A chart drawn of the links between the terrorists was an astonishingly complex maze of common connections – a far cry from the clear organogrammes traditionally used to depict the structure of militant groups and movements. In more general terms, 'Operation Crevice' also revealed the degree to which, even by 2003, Western Muslim populations had begun to produce violent radicals whose major drawback, much to the authorities' relief, was their glaring lack of technical skill and inexperience, not a lack of commitment.

Those involved had met each other at school or socially: through mutual friends, through relatives, at Luton mosque, at an Islamic fair at the University of East London or at religious discussion groups. These 'horizontal' patterns of recruitment have often featured in previous chapters – in the bombings in Madrid and Casablanca, to take just two examples. The backgrounds of the men were entirely familiar too. A couple came from broken homes. Some came from observant families, the others were raised in homes where the family Koran literally gathered dust on a shelf. Few were religiously observant as teenagers. None came from genuinely deprived backgrounds, most had got GCSEs or 'A' levels. Though at least one was an academic high-achiever, several were college drop-outs, and at least two could be described as disappointments to families with high aspirations. Some enjoyed sport, others preferred nightclubbing. The 'Crevice' plotters also showed evidence of profound identity issues, with surveillance tapes revealing them insulting Pakistan and 'Pakis' and referring appreciatively to 'the good old

British police' while simultaneously talking about blowing up a British Airways jet or a shopping centre. One of the defendants, the Algerian-born Anthony Garcia, had anglicized his real name, Rahman Benouis, to give it a 'better ring' in the modelling business where he hoped to make money, some of which he planned to use to finance 'the jihad'. None showed any evidence of mental illness. As with so many militants, none had anything but the most superficial knowledge of Islamic theology or, for that matter, of world politics.[66] The men were recorded arguing over whether Chad and the Sudan were Muslim-majority countries. They decided they were not. They are.

The paths taken to radicalization by the dozens of men involved in the Crevice plot had been typically varied too. For some, the process took years, for others just months. In some instances, videos – including one of attacks on Muslims in India and others of Taliban or Kashmiri fighters in action – played a key part. For others, the court heard, it was taped sermons by extremist clerics or television images of 'Muslims suffering' that had played an important role. At least two involved had had contact with an extremist breakaway faction of Hezb-ut-Tahrir. One senior policeman described them as 'a pretty fair broad cross-section of young British working-class Muslim males', adding that 'there was nothing particularly noteworthy about any of them'.[67]

The first stage of almost all the plots featured in the previous chapters had involved a loose group of individuals with a strong interest in becoming involved in jihad coalescing around an individual with a degree of authority and leadership capacity, a 'self-starter'. Khyam had credibility because in 2000 he had travelled to Pakistan to train in a militant camp in Kashmir and had made a second journey, this time into Afghanistan, a year later. By the time the group began coming together in Luton, Uxbridge and south-west London he had spent many years fundraising for fighters both in Kashmir and in Afghanistan and thus had connections and kudos. The next stage, once a group has formed, is the hardening of the bonds that bind together its members and the focusing of their resolve to act. Social workers in east London pointed out the parallels between local radical extremists and criminal or teenage gangs they saw on a daily basis.[68] The clusters the militants formed often showed the same structure as gangs, the social workers said, with a leader, his close circle, the one who does the finance, the 'one who makes them all laugh, the hangers-on who don't really know what to do or why they are there'. Then there are rituals and coded jargon. Ed Husain recalled how the first Islamist organization he had joined – the Young Muslim Organization based at the East London Mosque – had a reputation of being 'tougher than the toughest gangsters . . . They were as bad and cool as the other street gangs, just without the drugs, drinking and womanizing.'[69] The Crevice defendants spoke to each other of 'the cause' or 'the thing', meaning militant Islam, of Israel as 'Yahudi land', using the Arabic for Jews, and of non-believers as 'kuffs', short for *kufr*, or unbelief. They also revealed deep rivalry between different groups of militants, who referred to each other as 'crews', as do British gangs. Members of both gangs and militant Islamic organizations and groups referred to each other as 'brother' too. A fairly well-defined sartorial code became current for young 'Islamic militants', a mixture of military-style Western gear, Pakistani traditional clothing and 'streetwear'.[70] 'Jihad' had also become a relatively glamorous alternative lifestyle choice for some young men, symbolizing adventure, rebellion, clandestinity, and this was reflected in their 'jihadic chic'.[71] Several militants in this period indiscreetly boasted of their exploits to women they were seeking to impress, in one instance an undercover female police officer. Others recorded raps. But gangs, groups and even families need to be tightly bonded together and, as any army drill sergeant knows, the best way to develop solidarity is through shared pain, adventure, fear and fun.

## SUMMER CAMP

Three months before the conversation about potential targets that had been recorded by MI5, a small minivan had pulled out from in front of the Avari hotel in the centre of the eastern Pakistani city of Lahore and headed off into the choking traffic. In it were all the key Crevice plotters – Omar Khyam, Jawad Akbar, Anthony Garcia – and a handful of others. Posing as tourists, they broke up the seventeen-hour drive into the mountains along Pakistan's frontier with Afghanistan with stops to photograph each other. Instead of heading into the rugged tribal areas south of Peshawar, where Osama bin Laden was hiding and where al-Qaeda fugitives had been able to set up makeshift training camps since fleeing Afghanistan just over eighteen months earlier, the group turned north as they approached the Afghan frontier, heading up into the picturesque Swat valley, a jumble of high valleys and pine forests which was then still a major tourist destination for wealthy Pakistanis and an area renowned for its natural beauty. Khyam had organized the trip after raising £3,500 through collections among sympathizers in the UK. Most of the money was to pay a local tribal leader and businessman to run a training camp for him and his band of friends. Khyam's aim was not to teach Akbar, Garcia and the others how to make bombs but to draw them together as a unit. The minivan dropped them at Kalam, a trekking and trout-fishing resort at the northern end of the valley.[72]

Kalam is surrounded by high mountains, difficult terrain where government authority is virtually non-existent. The only roads are dirt tracks. After resting in a cheap hotel, the group of Britons, equipped with only rudimentary hiking gear, set off towards the camp. It was tough going, and, unused to the exercise, the group went so slowly that they had to spend a night in the open. With the altitude and the heat, at least one collapsed. When they reached the camp, it was not quite what they had expected. 'I was thinking about something with ranges and assault courses, like I'd seen on TV,' one of the group said later. 'But it wasn't that at all.' Instead, the cash raised by Khyam had bought them two tents – one for the local men who ran the camp and the other for everyone else – and a field. The group had to dig a hole for their own latrine. The first day was spent doing physical exercises, then, on day two, the local men brought out some AK-47s, a light machine gun and a rocket launcher, and the young men, 'scared but excited' according to later testimony, took turns to fire the weapons. 'It was wicked,' one recalled. Eight days later, the men walked back down to the valley, drove back to Lahore and, apart from Khyam, who remained to continue practising his bomb-making skills in the back garden of a house in the city, flew back to the UK. Though makeshift, the camp was effective. Junaid Babar, one of the group, later told the FBI, 'After attending the camp ... the guys were much more serious. [Before] they were joking around and using slang. After the camp the guys were talking jihad, praying and quoting the Koran. They would say, "One day of jihad is better than eighty days of praying." By the end of the camp they were saying, "Let's go kill the non-believer." '[73]

Such episodes were common to almost all plots in the UK at this time. Some went hiking in the Lake District, others went white-water canoeing. As one MI5 analyst commented: 'The moment when someone put himself in danger for another member of the group or took on an additional burden, when he reached out of a canoe or picked up someone else's rucksack to help them over the last few miles, was worth more than years of propaganda.'[74] But it was not just the new solidarity within a terrorist cell that was important. It was also the way the group began to see others. Ed Husain and Shiraz Maher, the two former members of Hezb-ut-Tahrir, both described how they had been very quickly sucked into a world that was entirely closed off from the rest of society. 'Almost all my social contacts were within the movement,' said Maher. For some, Husain said, the group provided 'an entire existence': food, lodging, employment and company, even wives or husbands. This phase of 'isolation' appears to have been critical. Hardline Islamic websites consulted by British militants in this period were dominated by advice given to those asking about 'true Muslim practice' in any given situation. Often the sites quoted the Koran or senior clerics to reinforce the idea of a separation from society more generally, a version of the *takfiri* ideology of al-Zarqawi and his fellow international militants in Iraq. As the groups like the Crevice plotters became more and more bound together the outside world and those who lived in it retreated, merging as they did so into an undistinguishable mass devoid of the characteristics that mark them as living, talking, walking, feeling people. This process of 'dehumanizing' potential victims – an integral part of all genocides or massacres over the decades – was key to moving the group to the final stages of radicalization, where preparations for executing acts of extreme violence began. So the end of the Crevice plotters' summer training camp did not mean that Omar Khyam's work was finished. The ten-day trip in the Pakistani mountains had been useful to bind the group together, but there was more for its leader to do. A week after the rest of the group had flown home, Khyam set off from his Lahore base once again, this time to meet al-Qaeda.[75]

## AL-QAEDA

Khyam had met senior al-Qaeda figures before. When he had arrived in Pakistan in the spring of 2003, a few months before organizing the summer training camp, he had apparently hoped to join the Taliban to fight against allied troops in Afghanistan. He was not, his lawyers said later, planning attacks on the UK at that stage. However, when friends in

Lahore, part of the loose network of British militants linking Pakistan and the UK, put the twenty-one-year-old in touch with contacts in Pakistani extremist groups who themselves would lead him to the Taliban, his plans started to change. One of the 'British brothers' in Lahore had already established contact with Abdul Hadi al-Iraqi, al-Qaeda's 'number three' or 'director of external operations' at the time. Al-Iraqi's role was to do what bin Laden, al-Zawahiri and others had done in the late 1990s in Afghanistan: to receive the delegations from overseas coming to request logistical aid with a variety of projects as well as the young volunteers arriving in search of assistance or direction.[76] Despite the limited facilities available at the time – only the most makeshift of training camps could be set up, and many of the best instructors had been killed – the al-Qaeda senior leadership could still try to exploit the raw material that reached them. The primary attribute young Europeans had for the group was not their ardent if unfocused desire for 'action' in Afghanistan or any other theatre of jihad – a relatively mundane contribution to the cause – but their passports and lack of criminal records. These made them ideal candidates for much more valuable projects. When al-Iraqi met Khyam he apparently told the young Briton that, praiseworthy though his ambition to fight for the Taliban was, 'if he was serious', he should 'do something' back home.[77] This marked a turning point in the Crevice conspiracy. Rather than introduce Khyam to the Taliban, al-Iraqi arranged for him to spend a weekend in a house in the dusty western Pakistani town of Kohat learning more about bomb-making. The al-Qaeda militants' suggestion to strike at home had apparently fallen on fertile ground. One witness described how Khyam came back from the Kohat camp convinced that 'the UK should be hit because of its support for the US in Afghanistan and Iraq and because, [as] nothing has ever happened in the UK, the UK is unscathed'. Previously he had expressed the view that the coalition campaign in Afghanistan had been 'more or less' justified. Now his views had hardened considerably. 'Khyam said we need to do more, we should hit . . . pubs, trains and nightclubs,' the witness continued. '[Khyam said] targets in the UK are legitimate because British soldiers are killing Muslims and because military targets are too difficult to hit.'[78]

This was the critical contribution that, from the autumn of 2002 on, al-Qaeda was in a position to make. The hardcore leadership clustered around bin Laden in the zone along the Afghan–Pakistani frontier gave the volunteers who sought them out crucial direction, focusing their violent ambitions to fit in with the broader global strategy the al-Qaeda senior leadership were trying, not without some difficulty, to orchestrate. This was neither 'top-down' nor 'bottom-up' activism, neither vertical nor horizontal models of militancy. Instead it was hybrid, a mixture of both. Young men who had by themselves formed a group set on violence and who were convinced that they were to be soldiers in a global war in defence of Islam were taken a few vital steps further down that path by senior militants with prestige and authority. Men like Abdul Hadi al-Iraqi used a carefully honed message that exploited key elements in Islam – such as concepts of an enlightened and embattled elite, the idea of a world split into a domain of faith and peace and a domain of war and unbelief or a particular interpretation of jihad – to harden the resolve of the young volunteers. The 'who' and the 'why' were important in bringing them this far. The 'how' – the dynamics within the groups of extremists and the inputs from outside – was crucial in taking the next step.

There was another crucial dynamic at work. The recruits had come seeking to participate in the international jihad with their heads full of rhetoric about pan-Islamic solidarity. Their missions, however, were to be local, using their local knowledge, difference and cultural specificity as British or German or Belgian or other Muslims to successfully execute attacks that would take place at most a few hours' travelling from their homes or even where they were born. The global was fused with the local with devastating efficacy.

There were three other contributions – more practical – that al-Qaeda could make to a homegrown plot between 2002 and 2005. There was guidance on the nature of the strike: Khyam also apparently came back from that meeting saying that his instructions were to work towards 'multiple, simultaneous' attacks, an al-Qaeda hallmark.[79] There was technical assistance. And finally there was help in turning volunteers into the weapon so characteristic of the 9/11 Wars: suicide bombers.


# THE MARTYRS

Personal accounts from successful suicide bombers that go beyond banal propaganda are rare – for obvious reasons. Statements by failed suicide bombers elsewhere – such as in Israel or Afghanistan – are often highly unreliable. However, they do exist, and suicide bombers who at the last minute decided not to blow themselves up interviewed by the author in Iraq, Afghanistan and Pakistan give some indication of the state of mind of individuals on the point of killing themselves and dozens of others. The process of radicalization that most described was typically gradual. In the case of the Iraqi it started with prayer meetings at a mosque and then moved deeper into radical militancy. It took many months before the young man, aged nineteen, began contemplating a suicide attack.[80] He was a 'follower' rather than a 'self-starter', deeply admiring of a more confident and more radical friend, and was susceptible to suggestion. 'Martyrdom operations' were introduced as an idea after many months of discussion and only raised seriously when the young man had made his way to a remote training camp far from his hometown. There, along with the physical exercise and small-arms training, he was exposed to hours of videos showing Muslims as victims of violence in Afghanistan, Iraq, Kashmir or elsewhere and to lectures from senior clerics on the rewards of martyrdom in the afterlife and the fame and glory such a sacrifice would attract. The friend said he would conduct a similar attack simultaneously. A critical element, the young man said, was that he was absolutely convinced that his action would be seen as praiseworthy by his family, his peers and the community as a whole. So much so, that when his mother located him and came to get him at the camp, he turned her away in tears. What was most important, he stressed, was the gradual way in which he had been led down the path towards 'martyrdom'. 'Each step logically seemed to follow from the next one,' he said. 'I ended up somewhere I had no intention to go without really knowing how I had got there.' He also, he added, did not want to let his friend down. The Pakistani interviewees described similar experiences. One had been recruited through 'friends', another through the militant organization that he belonged to. Both had then been isolated for long months and exposed to long hours of heavily slanted religious instruction interspersed with emotive videos before finally being judged ready to carry out their tasks.[81]

Before the actual attack, the young Iraqi spoke of being 'calm', of 'thinking about nothing', and of 'not wanting to fail' by refusing to go through with the bombing. The youngest of the Pakistanis, twenty-one at the time of the attack, spoke of a 'numbness' as he drove his heavily loaded truck towards its target listening to Koranic chants on the stereo.

He gave himself up when he saw there were no Americans at the checkpoint he was supposed to attack. The Iraqi only decided not to detonate his device when, in the seconds before he flicked the switch around his belt, he heard his potential victims talking with the accent of his hometown. In that instant, those he was about to kill became human once again, he said, and he could go no further and surrendered. Again, however, though many chose not to make the ultimate gesture and chose another path, others continued, right to the bitter end.

# 9

# Bombs, Riots and Cartoons

## 7/7

At 8.24 on the morning of July 7, 2005, four men had said goodbye in front of the Boots chemist's shop at King's Cross station. They had huddled for a moment, hugged each other, and then, 'euphoric, as if they were celebrating something', had split up.[1] At 8.50 three set off simultaneous bombs, killing themselves and thirty-nine others, on the London Underground. At 9.27 the fourth, delayed by a defective battery on his bomb, had boarded a number 30 bus outside King's Cross station and taken a seat on the top deck. He sat there for twenty minutes as the bus edged its way through the chaotic London traffic, nervously fiddling with a rucksack at his feet.[2] Earlier he had called the phones of the three others, who he must have suspected were already dead, leaving the message 'I can't get on the Northern Line' and asking what he should do. It is unclear whether he meant that his resolve had failed – at the time of the call much of the Northern Line was in fact still open – or whether he was merely looking for last-minute instructions.[3] At 9.47, when the bus reached Tavistock Square, possibly because he mistook a traffic warden talking to the bus driver for a policeman, he set the fourth bomb off. It killed him and thirteen others and injured dozens more. The total dead in the 7/7 bombings eventually reached fifty-six, counting the bombers, with around 700 wounded. The four bombers were rapidly identified. They were: Mohammed Sidique Khan, a thirty-one-year-old former social worker who grew up in a suburb of the northern English city Leeds called Beeston; Shehzad Tanweer, also from Beeston, and the twenty-two-year-old son of a local businessman; Germaine Lindsay, a nineteen-year-old Jamaican-born convert raised by his mother in Huddersfield, another grim northern British town with deep social and economic problems and a large population of Pakistani immigrant origin;[4] and Hasib Hussain, the bomber on the bus, an eighteen-year-old from Leeds.

The respective journeys into violent radicalism of the four were, as ever, unique to each individual while nonetheless showing elements common to very many radicals in the UK, in the Middle East and elsewhere in areas affected by the 9/11 Wars. The route taken by Mohammed Sidique Khan, the 7/7 leader, showed almost all the factors that were explored in the previous chapter: he faced a variety of problems in his home town of Beeston, itself a community that was physically and culturally isolated from mainstream British social, political and economic life; the conservative, folksy Pakistani religious traditions of his parents were not, he felt, relevant to the present time; Khan had become alienated from his family when he refused a traditional arranged marriage, choosing instead a girl he had met and fallen in love with while studying at the vast Leeds Metropolitan University and turning to more modern and politicized Islamic ideologies at the same time.[5] However, Khan's biography reveals that many of the factors often cited as predictors of violent extremism are only at best indirectly responsible. Khan was not poor, and in no sense can poverty, relative or absolute, been seen as a motivation for his actions. Nor was he badly educated – he was a graduate – nor particularly well educated either – his business studies degree from a far from prestigious establishment was hardly a guarantee of a broad range of opportunities for a fulfilling and satisfying professional career.[6] Like so many other radicals too, Khan was a man of projects and action. A professional youth worker, he and other strongly religious individuals in Beeston had once formed a gang called the 'Mullah Boys', who took on drug dealers in their neighbourhood and forced addicts in the Pakistani community to go 'cold turkey'. He was thus in a good position to recruit others when the time came. One of the primary ways he did so was by offering to organize ceremonies for marriages that were outlawed by the traditional community. Married himself with a young child, he was a peer but a peer with standing and confidence.[7] He was very much a self-starter.

In the years after 9/11 – which he initially opposed as an unjustified attack on civilians – Khan had come to share the classic 'single-narrative' view of the world common to Islamic militants. In a video released after his death, he explained to the people of Britain that, just as their role in voting for governments who 'perpetuate atrocities against [his] people' made them 'directly responsible', he was 'directly responsible for protecting and avenging [his] Muslim brothers and sisters'.[8] The text, it was later realized, drew heavily on the published will of a young Briton killed at Tora Bora who came from a similar background to Khan.[9] Also in the video, in a section that was not broadcast by most mainstream media outlets, Khan criticized 'corrupt and incompetent' traditional Muslim clerics in Britain.[10] The tape, in a major innovation, had English-language subtitles which emphasized that its key audience was intended to be the UK, the USA and, to an extent, Europe.

As for the three younger men who joined Khan in his scheme to kill and maim hundreds in London, while their own backgrounds show once again the factors seen elsewhere, they equally demonstrate the sheer variety of paths into militancy. All four were young immigrants or the children of immigrants. Germaine Lindsay was a convert, an increasingly present subset of militants through the period. One came from a broken home, one was an under-achiever at school, two appear to have enjoyed happy and relatively stable backgrounds. Typically, too, they were not recruited in mosques but through personal contacts, people they happened to know or happened to meet. There was certainly little in the lives or characters of the 7/7 bombers that made them radically different from hundreds of thousands of young British or European men, Muslim or otherwise.

The four men followed the course of those involved in the Crevice plot, going whitewater rafting together to build solidarity, living in virtual isolation from the *kufr*, 'who they gradually came to see as less and less human'. Like Khyam, indeed probably with Khyam, Khan had travelled to the tribal areas of Pakistan to meet senior al-Qaeda figures who convinced him to launch attacks in the UK rather than fulfil his own ambition to fight alongside the Taliban.[11] The 7/7 plotters showed more professionalism than the Crevice group, however, making technically more complex devices and successfully hiding their preparations from the security services. On the morning of the attacks, they took a train from Luton station, where an image from a surveillance camera shows them walking through the ticket gates in jeans and jackets at 07.21 with the rucksacks containing their bombs, packed with nails, over their shoulders. Commuters on the 07.23 Luton to Brighton train, on which the bombers travelled to London, later described them as 'smiling, laughing and generally relaxed'.[12]

What is the significance of the 7/7 attacks in the 9/11 Wars? That the 7/7 attacks showed the polyvalence or multidimensionality so typical of the conflict was evident. They were the result of short-term factors such as the effects of the invasion of Iraq catalysing a whole range of broader trends which have frequently been seen in previous pages. As elsewhere too, the key question was how easily the ideology of contemporary international militancy would be grafted onto a pre-existing local situations of tension, if not open conflict. The project that al-Qaeda had proposed to Khan in the tribal areas of Pakistan had been another perfect example of thinking globally – i.e. in terms of a cosmic struggle between faiths, communities, good and evil – but acting locally. The 7/7 attacks also saw one of the defining tactics of the 9/11 Wars – suicide bombing – extended to an entirely new theatre. Finally, they, or at least their aftermath, provided another example of the politicization of intelligence and debate so characteristic of the conflict so far.[13] But the real significance of the 7/7 attacks was not the degree to which they were representative of the various established qualities of the 9/11 Wars but what they threatened for the future. Exactly two weeks after the bombings came another round of attempted attacks on London's public transport system. Though they were all young Muslim men, the profile of those responsible was different from that of the 7/7 attackers. They were first-generation immigrants of East African origin, most living marginal lives, poorly educated, inadequate, ill-equipped for making their way in London. Their leader, Muktar Said Ibrahim, was the twenty-seven-year-old Eritrean-born son of asylum-seekers with a police record for sexual assault and disorderly conduct. Ibrahim had swapped a life of petty crime for radical Islam while incarcerated in a young offenders institution and, a classic 'self-starter', actively sought out training and combat experience on his release. In December 2004, Special Branch officers stopped him at Heathrow and discovered thousands of pounds in cash, cold-weather camping gear, a military first-aid kit and a manual on ballistics in his baggage. Though he was questioned for three hours, Ibrahim had not committed any crime and was thus allowed to board a plane to Islamabad.[14] Ibrahim was in Pakistan at around the same time as Mohammed Sidique Khan and Omar Khyam of the Crevice plot and is thought to have received some training there. Indeed, it is possible all three trained together and that the '21/7 attacks' had been planned as a second wave by the al-Qaeda leadership themselves. However, whatever skills Ibrahim had learned were insufficient – another example of poor tradecraft among militants – and the bombs at three London Underground stations and on a bus all failed to explode. Nonetheless, the attempt created panic in the UK and provoked excited reactions from militant leaders and thinkers.

Taken together, the two attacks in London seemed to indicate that the strategy of Abu Musab al-Suri might be succeeding. Five years previously no one would have dreamed that a strike on the London Underground could be successful, let alone one followed up by a separate wave of attempted bombings. Now it appeared a fire had been lit in Western Europe that would be hard to extinguish. Al-Suri, whose name had been mentioned as a possible 'mastermind' of the London attack, posted a long statement on the internet immediately after the bombings in which he described how, 'when the attacks on the historic stronghold of oppression and darkness [London] took place', he had been among 'the hundreds of millions of Muslims who joyfully watched the events unfold'. Al-Suri denied any personal connection to the attacks and called 'upon the *mujahideen* in Europe . . . to act quickly and strike'. His strategy of provoking a global 'leaderless jihad' was bearing fruit, and victory, he clearly believed, was at hand. 'We are at the height of the war, and the enemy is on the verge of defeat, as many signs clearly indicate,' he boasted. 'Whoever stays asleep now might not be able to participate upon finally waking up.'[15] In the event, al-Suri's own participation was cut short not long after he posted his 'message to the British and the Europeans' when he was captured after a shoot-out with local security forces near the Pakistani city of Quetta.[16] But though al-Suri had been permanently removed from the scene – the Pakistanis had handed him over to the Americans by the end of 2005 – the fear that he had correctly read the broad strategic situation remained.


## THE AFTERMATH

On the afternoon of the 7/7 attacks, in the perfect summer sunshine, Londoners stood in long queues for telephone boxes because their mobile phones had been rendered useless by the overloaded networks, sat on the grass in parks, drank on benches outside pubs, waited to go back to their homes. 'What do you feel about those who did this?' one television reporter asked a wounded survivor. 'Contempt. No anger. Just contempt,' he replied. Down below, in the shattered wreck of the three tube trains, rescue teams worked among the twisted metal, charred corpses and body parts. The attack, said Ken Livingstone, the mayor of London, was 'not . . . against the mighty and the powerful', not 'aimed at presidents or prime ministers' but at 'ordinary, working-class Londoners, black and white, Muslim and Christian, Hindu and Jew, young and old'. Livingstone, himself a controversial figure criticized for talking a soft line with Islamists and accused of anti-Semitism, had caught the mood of the city. One blogger posted that, whatever Londoners might think of the government's policy in Iraq or elsewhere, as a community they had their own ways of dealing with things, and these did not include blowing people up. Livingstone said that the strikes were not 'just an indiscriminate attempt at mass murder'. Their objectives were instead 'to divide Londoners . . . to turn Londoners against each other'.[17]

In fact, the exact objectives of the 7/7 bombers have never been made entirely clear. The videoed testaments broadcast after the attack revealed why, in their own minds, Khan and Tanweer felt such an act was necessary and justified but not what they hoped to achieve by it. Nor has the targeting of the strikes ever been satisfactorily explained – though the timing was probably determined by a desire to coincide with the summit of the G8 nations – Canada, France, Germany, Italy, Japan, Russia, UK and the US – in Scotland. No one knew where Hasib Hussain, the bus bomber, was actually meant to detonate his device. All that was obvious was that the three locations hit had no evident political, military or broader symbolic importance. It may be that they were determined simply by timing, and the three bombers had set out in different directions from King's Cross itself to blow themselves up at exactly the same moment wherever they might have been. It may be that to search for overt symbolism in the targets would be wrong. For many such attackers it is after all simply their violent suicide that, as a statement of will and faith, is as important as any direct consequence of an attack. One quality that did link the sites of the explosions was that each one was strongly representative of the cosmopolitan nature of the UK's capital city. Tanweer detonated his bomb at Aldgate East, the historic heart of successive waves of immigration to the city including, most recently, Pakistani and Bangladeshi communities. Khan detonated his device at

Edgware Road, centre of one of London's major Middle Eastern Arab communities, and King's Cross itself, as the casualty lists showed, is one of the most cosmopolitan places in one of the most cosmopolitan cities on the planet. In 2005, a third of Londoners had been born outside the UK, and some 300 languages were regularly spoken in the city.[18] Those who died in the explosions included Ojara Ikeagwu, Shahara Islam, Anat Rosenberg, Karolina Gluck, Ciaran Cassidy, Rachelle Chung For Yuen and Benedetta Ciaccia, who, from a distinguished Italian family, had come to London to work as an au pair ten years before and, engaged to a Muslim, was preparing for a wedding ceremony in Rome which would have united Catholic and Islamic rites.[19] Even the upmarket Tavistock Square, where Hasib had detonated his device, is a neighbourhood given a distinctly international character by high numbers of foreign students and tourists. Consciously or otherwise, it seems likely that, as Livingstone suspected, the 7/7 bombings were an attack on the ideas of integration and assimilation as much as anything else. The last thing the bombers would have seen before exploding their devices would have been a crowded tube train or a bus full of scores of people of all races, colours and creeds coexisting in relative harmony as they started another day.

In addition to the role and nature of al-Qaeda and the effects of the Iraq war, the 7/7 attacks thus naturally focused attention on the British model of multiculturalism. Much of the debate picked up on themes broached following the murder of Theo van Gogh in Amsterdam nine months previously. This time the debate took place in an extremely polarized environment that left very little room for reasonable commentary. It was perhaps inevitable that during a period of intense violence – or at least fear of intense violence – the debate was dominated by aggressive and extreme voices and characterized by an astonishing disregard for facts. This was the case on all sides. Iqbal Sacranie, the general secretary of the Muslim Council of Great Britain, repeatedly claimed that '95 to 98 per cent of those stopped and searched under new anti-terror laws are Muslims', though the true total was around 15 per cent.[20] Others compared the situation of Muslims in Europe to that of the Jews in pre-Holocaust Germany, an ugly and insulting exaggeration. Diatribes of extraordinary vitriol, many soaked in a primary anti-Americanism or sophomoric analyses of American imperialism, were directed at President Bush and Blair. Conspiracy theories were rife.

In France a book by a Marxist polemicist called Thierry Meyssan which argued that 9/11 was set up by the American 'military-industrial complex' was a bestseller. Similarly, in the UK such views were not simply restricted to the 45 per cent of the British Muslims who thought that 9/11 was a conspiracy between the USA and Israel but bled inexorably into the mainstream.[21] Even usually relatively sensible newspapers like the centre-left *Guardian* printed a 2,000-word comment piece by Michael Meacher, a former government environment minister, which suggested that the Bush administration had, at the very least, allowed 9/11 to happen so as to be able to execute a new strategy of global domination formulated by American conservatives in the late 1990s. The US were not seriously pursuing bin Laden as he was too useful a pretext for their plans to seize key strategic resources across half the Middle East, Meacher argued, and implied that the response to the hijacking of the planes that would go on to strike the Twin Towers had been deliberately slowed to allow them to reach their targets.[22]

There was no shortage of extreme voices on the right either. For conservatives, attacks on multiculturalism blurred with criticism of welfarism and the general moral decadence of the West. If many left-wing voices lapsed into uninformed rhetoric about 'the Americans', the right reverted to the most basic essentialist vision of a monolithic and unchanging Islam and a weak and emasculated Europe. For many of these commentators, Arabs and Muslims were conflated into a single body of civilizational enemies whose millennium-old war against the West was an historical fact rejected only by those who were at best naive and at worst criminally negligent collaborators. In Italy Oriana Fallacci's *The Rage and the Pride*, replete with descriptions of Muslim immigrants as 'terrorists, thieves, rapists. Ex-convicts, prostitutes, beggars. Drug-dealers, contagiously ill' and of 'Arab men' as 'disgusting to women of good taste' sold over 1.5 million copies.[23] The oldest stereotypes of the Turk, Mohammedan, Saracen and Muslim were recycled and, as was usual in a time of perceived threat, it was the most negative representations that prevailed. Other popular works on similar themes included Bruce Bawer's *While Europe Slept: How Radical Islam Is Destroying the West from Within*, Mark Steyn's *America Alone* and Melanie Phillips' *Londonistan*.[24]

Much of the argument of these books, particularly those from American authors, was based on the idea of Europe being 'flooded' by Islamic populations. This idea had already been proposed at various moments of ethnic tension since the mid-1960s but had been focused most recently on Europe's Muslim communities by right-wing politicians such as Holland's Fritz Bolkestein and the populist maverick Pim Fortuyn. 'Current trends allow only one conclusion: the USA will remain the only superpower. China is becoming an economic giant. Europe is being Islamicized,' Bolkestein said in Leiden in September 2004.[25] Bernard Lewis, the highly respected conservative American historian of the Ottoman Empire and the Arab world, breezily told one audience a month or so later that within a few decades Europe would 'be part of the Arabic west, of the Maghreb'.[26] For one columnist in the neoconservative *Washington Times*, writing shortly after the 7/7 bombings, 'the threat of the radical Islamists taking over Europe is every bit as great to the United States as was the threat of the Nazis taking over Europe in the 1940s'. Europe, he wrote, would soon become pockmarked with 'little Fallujahs ... effectively ... impenetrable by anything much short of a U.S. Marine division'.[27] Nor was this kind of rhetoric limited to cranky or partisan publications. The prestigious *Foreign Affairs* spoke of 'distinctive, bitter and cohesive' European Muslims forming 'colonies' on the continent.[28] Charles Krauthammer wrote in *Time* of 'this civilizational struggle taking place in France'.[29] In the *New York Times*, Niall Ferguson, the conservative British historian, posed once more the great counterfactual questions asked by his Georgian predecessor Edward Gibbon: 'If the French had failed to defeat an invading Muslim army at the Battle of Poitiers in A.D. 732, would all of Western Europe have succumbed to Islam?' Back in 1788, Ferguson wrote, 'the idea could scarcely have seemed more fanciful ... Today, however, the idea seems somewhat less risible.'[30] Ferguson spoke of how 'a youthful Muslim society to the south and east of the Mediterranean is poised to colonize ... a senescent Europe'[31] and, along with conservative commentator Barbara Amiel, approvingly cited the Egyptian-born writer Bat Ye'or. Bat Ye'or's book *Eurabia: The Euro-Arab Axis*, published in 2005, had outlined an extraordinary conspiracy theory by which a secret organization known as 'The Euro-Arab Dialogue' at the heart of the European Union has 'engineered Europe's irreversible transformation through hidden channels' into 'a fundamentally anti-Christian, anti-Western and anti-Semitic ... cultural appendage of the Arab/Muslim world'.[32] That even the concept of 'Eurabia' could be taken seriously let alone seep into the mainstream conversation was a sign of the times. *The Economist* even devoted a cover story to exploring Bat Ye'or's propositions, though happily decided that her thesis was 'alarmist'.[33]

The al-Qaeda senior leadership, from the distant Pakistani tribal areas, exploited the febrile atmosphere as far as they could. The various communications released by al-Zawahiri and bin Laden at this time have a far more confident air than a year previously. Four weeks after the July 7 London bombing and two weeks after the so-called 21/7 abortive attacks that had followed them, al-Zawahiri, on a videotape broadcast on al-Jazeera, explained that the 'volcanoes of wrath' were the consequence of Britain rejecting an earlier offer of a truce from bin Laden that was conditional on the withdrawal of its troops from Iraq. 'Blair's policies will bring more destruction to Britons after the London explosions, God willing,' he promised.[34]

## A RIOT OF MY OWN

Four months after the London bombings, a banal incident in the outer suburbs of Paris sparked rioting, predominantly involving French immigrants of 'Arab or African origin' and of nominally Muslim denomination, which continued for three weeks. The disturbances were of a violence and extent unprecedented in recent decades and seemed to support all the most alarming predictions of the conservative commentators, Ayman al-Zawahiri and Abu Musab al-Suri alike.

Late in the afternoon of October 27, 2005, three teenagers were coming home from a game of football in the run-down, overcrowded town of Clichy-sous-Bois, 10 miles north-east of Paris, when they heard police sirens and saw other youths running. Worried about being late home for the *iftar* dinner which breaks the fast of Ramadan and because they did not have their identity papers on them as French law requires, the teenagers ran too and then decided to hide. Scaling the gates of a local electricity transformer, they waited thirty minutes, hearing the voices of police officers, barking dogs and more sirens outside. In trying to climb back out, they received massive electric shocks. Two, fifteen-year-old Zyed Benna and seventeen-year-old Bouna Traoré, whose parents came from Tunisia and Mauritania respectively, were killed. The third, also

1. Bamiyan, Afghanistan. The Taliban's destruction of the ancient statues of Buddha in March 2001 was not simple fanaticism but a carefully judged act of spectacular violence designed to send a message to various local and international audiences and thus a sign of what was to come.

2. The folksy language and faith of George W. Bush connected with Middle America – whatever people thought overseas. The forty-third US president remained committed to a radical and ideological foreign policy throughout his time in office. In his memoirs, he said history would vindicate his decisions.

3. The key aim of Saudi Arabian-born Osama bin Laden was to radicalize the world's 1.2 billion Muslims and thus mobilize them to revive their faith and fight 'injustice', tyranny and the West. But his ideology – a selective mix of politics, religion and myth – showed little respect for local cultural differences or identities and eventually failed to attract mass support.

(*opposite*) 4. The ruins of the World Trade Center. Nearly 3,000 died in the September 11 attacks on New York and Washington. Rooted in a strategy of 'propaganda by deed', viewed by hundreds of millions of people, their significance would be defined as much by the reaction to the strategy as by the number of people it killed or the economic damage it caused.

5. The fighting at Tora Bora in eastern Afghanistan in December 2001 was less the last stand portrayed by Western media than a chaotic fighting retreat by international militants. With its lack of clear frontlines, blurring of civilians and soldiers and the conflicting agendas even of allies, it presaged much of the combat in the 9/11 Wars.

6. The aftermath of the Bali bombing. Through 2002, veterans of the al-Qaeda training camps in Afghanistan and existing militant networks around the Islamic world launched attacks from Morocco to Indonesia. Some strikes could be directly attributed to bin Laden or associates; others were the work of independent groups. The blasts in Bali killed more than 200 and were the bloodiest.

7. Anti-war march, London. The invasion of Iraq – at least without a specific United Nations resolution – was opposed by the vast majority of Europeans and many Americans too. It took the 9/11 Wars into new territory, bringing an extension and an intensification of the violence as well as sparking a wave of anger in the Muslim world not seen since the 1970s.

8. The Iraq War. The invasion campaign was supposed to last 100 days. In the end Saddam Hussein's detested and brutal regime collapsed much more quickly. But errors made in the spring and summer of 2003 – most rooted in a grave lack of preparedness and huge overconfidence – soon saw the situation in the country deteriorating very quickly.

9. The Iraq War. Heavy-handed coalition tactics, indiscriminate raids such as this one in search of an elusive enemy and deep ignorance of Iraqi society all helped fuel an insurgency. Within months, it was the fast-adapting networks of irregular Iraqi fighters that had seized the initiative from the slow-moving American army.

10. After the invasion, the Iraqi Shia population experienced a potent cultural revival. For young, unemployed, uneducated urban men, the attraction of populist revolutionary Islamism was strong. Here, followers of the young cleric Moqtada al-Sadr carry his picture and chant under a banner of his father-in-law and father, both murdered by Saddam Hussein's regime. Tens of thousands joined his al-Mahdi Army.

11. Murals on a Tehran street. The abuse of Iraqi prisoners by US soldiers at Abu Ghraib prison in western Baghdad revealed in March 2004 was cited by militants everywhere as a key in convincing them to participate in the 'jihad'. Though there was much abuse elsewhere, the image of a hooded prisoner threatened with a mock electrocution became an icon of the 9/11 Wars.

12. Jordanian-born Abu Musab al-Zarqawi was a former petty criminal and veteran militant who only reluctantly joined al-Qaeda in late 2004. A believer in seizing territory as a base for 'jihad', his taste for extreme and indiscriminate violence as well as his lack of respect for local Iraqi tribal leaders eventually alienated local and international supporters.

13. The aftermath of the Madrid train bombing. In March 2004 a series of bombs exploded on commuter trains in Madrid, Spain. Planted by a group of recent immigrants with no links to al-Qaeda who had been living in Spain for some time, it signalled the arrival of the 9/11 Wars in Europe and was a step towards 'home-grown' terrorism.

14. 7/7. On July 7, 2005, three suicide bombers exploded devices on tube trains and one on a bus in London. They had been born or had grown up in Britain. Key to the attack was the combination of the UK's links with Pakistan, where al-Qaeda had reconstituted a basic infrastructure, and the radicalization of some parts of the country's immigrant population.

seventeen, was badly injured but managed to call for help. For decades in the *cités* – as the vast complexes of public housing built around urban edges in the 1950s and 1960s are known in France – such incidents have been followed by riots. Usually disturbances follow a fairly well-worn pattern. Cars are burned, there may be some minor looting and arson and, though warm weather may prolong the fairly ritualized confrontation longer, everything is over after three days and two nights.[35] At first, it seemed like the riots – *émeutes* in French – sparked by the deaths of Benna and Traoré would follow the normal course. On the first weekend after the deaths a silent march was organized through Clichy-sous-Bois, and the following night was relatively calm. But then the rioting started again, shifting up a gear in intensity after a tear-gas canister fired by the police landed in the forecourt of a mosque in the town during prayers, and spread over subsequent nights across much of the Seine et Saint-Denis department, an area north-east of Paris with a population of nearly 1.5 million packed into 95 square miles. It then flared in Yvelines, 40 miles to the south-west, an area with broadly similar social and economic characteristics, and then spread out across much of the Ile de France region, home to around 15 to 20 million people and of course the economic, cultural and political centre of France. Soon hundreds of vehicles were being burned every night, and there were long and violent clashes with the police as well as attacks on public transport and firemen. The centre of Paris itself – with a largely wealthy population of 2 million – was almost untouched with a very small amount of violence in the relatively poor and mixed eighteenth, nineteenth and twentieth arrondissements in the north and east of the city. But as the rioting died away in the belt of *cités* around the capital it flared up elsewhere, starting during the night of November 3 and 4 in Lyon, in the western cities of Rouen and Rennes and in the northern former mining and steel towns along the Belgian border. The peak of the rioting came three days later, when 1,500 cars were burned in a single night in around 300 cities and towns.[36] For the first time in the contemporary history of France, a riot in one town had sparked similar events hundreds of miles away.[37] Only Marseille, where one in four of the population was born outside France and which has a huge Muslim population living in vast expanses of tough public housing projects, remained calm. No one appeared entirely certain why.

The *émeutes* provoked two totally different debates inside France and overseas. Domestically, the argument was about whether or not the rioters were '70 to 80 per cent' hardened criminals fomenting trouble the better to protect the 'no go areas' which they needed to continue their cocaine and cannabis businesses as Nicolas Sarkozy, the then minister of the interior, claimed.[38] The row continued for a week or two but died down when Sarkozy modified his language as it became clear that his denigration of the rioters as criminals had an immediate inflammatory effect and after judges told the press that in fact the vast majority of those the police brought before them were first offenders.[39] In fact, later detailed studies revealed a complex picture of three types of rioters: a hardcore with criminal records (though not for serious offences) who took the initiative, then a larger number of youths mainly without records who refrained from active involvement in the more spectacular criminal acts such as arson but did join in when it came to attacking the police, and a third group, by far the most numerous, who simply enjoyed 'le spectacle', running when the police charged, taunting them from afar but not actually engaging in any confrontation or destructive acts.[40]

Outside the country, the debate was framed very differently. It revolved, fairly predictably given the febrile atmosphere at the time, around religion. That it was France that appeared to have a problem with its Muslim minority – the largest such minority in Europe – provoked an extraordinary outpouring of bile from right-wing commentators who immediately linked the rioting with French opposition to war in Iraq, theorizing that France had tried to block the conflict to avoid angering its Muslim minority. Thrown into the mix was further criticism of French welfarism, which was now seen as a way of buying off a truculent and violent Muslim population, and a series of reheated and long-established stereotypes of French decadence, double-dealing, laziness and lack of virility. The end result was a perfect morality fable of the 'cheese-eating surrender monkeys' facing at home the very threat against which they had actively impeded the Americans fighting abroad.[41] That the riots were indeed 'Islamic' in origin and nature was taken as a given. That they were part of a broader uprising or potential rebellion by Europe's Muslim population was apparently evident. 'What we are seeing is, in effect, a French intifada: an uprising by French Muslims against the state,' said Melanie Phillips in the Daily Mail.[42] 'The Eurabian civil war appears to have started some years ahead of schedule,' Mark Steyn told readers of the *Chicago Sun Times*.[43] Some terrorism experts even argued that the rioting was 'jihad' by other means.[44]

One reason for the violence of the reaction to the *émeutes* overseas was the very real and important question they posed. If the French riots of November 2005 had indeed been motivated by radical Islamic ideologies, organized by extremists or justified by an appeal to a global Islamic identity, they would have indicated not just that al-Qaeda had succeeded in mobilizing and radicalizing an entirely new population in the heart of Europe far beyond its usual constituency but equally that the ideas and the violence that the group had set out to popularize more than fifteen years previously were no longer restricted to an extremist fringe prepared to use terrorist violence but had for the first time sparked a genuine popular mass uprising. This would have taken the 9/11 Wars into entirely new territory and marked a critical turning for the worst. Previously the conflict had not seen the emergence of a single genuinely popular Islamist movement or at least not one that involved more than a fraction of a nation's population. Even the Sunni militancy in Iraq had comprised a minority of a minority. The followers of Muqtada al-Sadr were a few hundred thousand strong at best. Jemaa Islamiyya in Indonesia was minuscule compared to the major local Islamist parties. Even Pakistani extremists, despite their visibility, were still small in number, though their social roots ran deep. The same went for Morocco and Turkey, where those who had been responsible for bomb attacks, even if they had benefited from the tacit support of many, were still shunned even by mainstream Islamist parties. The Madrid bombings had been perpetrated by a dozen or so individuals linked to networks which, at an absolute maximum, had a membership in the low hundreds. In none of these societies, nor in any other, had the increased political consciousness, popular anger, ambient anti-Americanism, radicalism and mobilization of the late 1990s and the years since 2001 yet been translated into a mass popular movement. Only in the specific circumstances of the Lebanon and the Gaza Strip did groups such as Hezbollah and Hamas – both bitter enemies of al-Qaeda – have a mass following. But if tens if not hundreds of thousands of young Frenchmen – and most of the rioters were indeed born in France – were now taking to the streets, then that signalled an intensification and aggravation of violence which went well beyond anything seen before. This would mean that mobilizing

European Muslim populations had been relatively easy for al-Qaeda and that, instead of offering resistance to its expansion to the Atlantic or beyond, Europe's 20 million Muslims would have acted to accelerate the process of the broadening and deepening the conflict. And if it happened in France, it could happen in Germany, the UK, Holland and eventually, despite the differences in background and socio-economic achievement of American Muslims, even in the USA. If this was indeed occurring, as al-Suri, the al-Qaeda senior leadership and the right-wing commentators apparently all believed, then the Madrid attacks, 7/7, even 9/11 would be rapidly forgotten in a civil war of appalling violence which would tear apart half the planet. Pinpointing the exact reasons for the rioting in France in November 2005 and the real motivations of those involved, obscured beneath the layers of heated rhetoric at the time, was thus critical.

The first clues as to how the immediate and most worrying reading of the *émeutes* might not have been entirely justified were clear, as is so often the case, to anyone who witnessed them at first hand. Firstly, there was little in the 'uprising of Europe's Muslims' which actually indicated that the disturbances were in any way more 'religious' than any other that Europe had seen over previous decades. In three weeks of reporting the rioting, the author heard no slogans, saw no grafitti and read no demands that were in any way related to faith. The firing of a tear-gas canister into a mosque in Clichy-sous-Bois may – though this is disputed – have led to shouts of 'Allahu akbar' (God is great), but otherwise there was nothing. In all the ground reporting of the riots, by foreign or French journalists, religious imagery, vocabulary or ideas had a negligible presence. References to Iraq or Palestine or any expression indicating that the rioters were acting or saw themselves as acting out of some kind of solidarity with Muslims elsewhere in the world were extremely rare – though one *émeutier* did confess to wanting to create 'a bit of Baghdad'.[45] Rioters mentioned a range of grievances when interviewed, but these were almost all restricted to immediate issues touching their daily lives, particularly alleged racial discrimination. All displayed a profound animosity towards the French state and its various manifestations. The most dominant theme was that hardy perennial of urban violence: Fuck the police, *nique la police*.[46] A large proportion were still in school, which may in part explain why the primary targets of arson and vandalism were educational establishments which were, with the police, the strongest state presence in their lives. 'Me, what I wanted to do during the rioting was burn the high school, because they are the ones that fucked my future,' said one nineteen-year-old small-time cannabis dealer.

What was also notable by its absence from the *émeutes* was anti-Semitic violence.[47] Anti-Semitism in immigrant communities in France was undoubtedly a serious and growing problem. Until 2004 the spikes in anti-Semitic violence had largely come at times of increased tension in Israel-Palestine and the Middle East more broadly, such as during the Second Intifada of October 2000, the 'battle of Jenin' in the West Bank in April 2002 and during the 2003 invasion of Iraq. However, from 2004 the correlation had broken down as what appeared to be a structurally greater level of anti-Semitic violence became the norm.[48] In 2004, nearly 1,000 attacks on French Jews took place, with, as previously mentioned, the proportion of the perpetrators from 'Muslim' immigrant communities much larger than previously seen. The total number of attacks dropped significantly the following year but remained high.[49] The abduction, torture and murder of a young Jewish salesman, targeted by a gang of young immigrants of mixed backgrounds led by a self-confessed 'Salafist', in January 2006, was thus part of a broad trend.[50] However, alarming though these tendencies undoubtedly were, there was no suggestion that Jewish or Israeli targets were targeted in France during the *émeutes*. Indeed, all religious sites were largely ignored. The targets of the rioters, like their language, were non-sectarian.

A second element of importance was the identity, in both senses of the word, of the rioters. Not all the rioters were 'Muslims', however defined.[51] A number were of non-immigrant background or, as their Spanish, Italian or Portuguese names indicated, from earlier waves of immigration. A larger number were relatively recent arrivals from sub-Saharan African countries, especially the Democratic Republic of the Congo, Cameroon, Equatorial Guinea and Cape Verde. These largely non-Muslim populations were among the most active in the riots according to later studies.[52] One acquaintance of the author was typical: a twenty-seven-year-old aspirant rapper from the twentieth arrondissement of Paris whose Congolese parents worked double shifts as cleaners to support four children and went to church every Sunday. Certainly French authorities did not frame the troubles in a religious narrative. According to a leaked confidential report by the Direction

Centrale of the Renseignements Généraux, the intelligence service of the French police, the *émeutes* were 'a form of unorganized urban insurrection', a 'popular revolt of the *cités*, without leaders or demands' led by youths 'full of a sense of identity based not only on their ethnic or geographic origin but on the condition of social exclusion from French society'.[53]

That identity was in fact the opposite of the globalized Islamic one, being extremely local. French expert Olivier Roy later referred to it as 'le nationalisme du quartier' (neighbourhood nationalism). Others spoke of the ambivalent relationship of pride and resentment rioters displayed for where they lived.[54] Rioters talked of their 'shitty neighbourhoods' all the while boasting how they had vied with other nearby housing projects for the highest number of cars burned – even though the cars belonged to their neighbours. 'I just wanted to get on the evening news like them in Montfermeil,' said Rabat Sifaoui, fifteen, mentioning a well-known *cité* 7 miles away from his home on the fifth floor of a run-down block in Bobigny. One rioter from the rough northern part of the town of Aulnay-sous-Bois spoke of how seeing the slightly less rough eastern part on TV had motivated him and his friends to go out on the streets to defend their own neighbourhood's long-established reputation for confronting the forces of order.[55] As ever, even this local identity had multiple layers. At the most specific or particular it was based on individual housing estates. When asked where they 'came from', most rioters named the projects – 'Cité des 4000' at La Courneuve; 'La Madeleine' at Evreux; 'Val Fourré' at Mantes-la-Jolie; 'Les Minguettes' at Vénissieux, near Lyon – where they lived. At its most general level the young rioters' identity was merely that of coming from a département. The most infamous of these was Seine et Saint-Denis, which was known colloquially by its number, ninety-three, though given as 'Neuf Trois', not *quatre-vingt-treize*, as it should be in correct French. 'Neuf Trois' was known throughout France for being the toughest of all departments and thus had a name to live up to. 'When I say us, I mean the kids from round here, from Aulnay, from Neuf Trois,' twenty-two-year-old Mehdi in Aulnay-sous-Bois told one interviewer.[56] There was no evidence of any broader national, international, ethnic or religious identities. There was no tension between the global and the local as so often seen elsewhere in the 9/11 Wars for the simple reason that the global was not present.

Another problem for the 'Intifada' thesis of either al-Suri or the right-wing commentators was that no Islamists, al-Qaeda-type militants or members of France's community of rigorous Islamic conservatives from quietist traditions were involved in the violence. This was despite a substantial population of all three. Islamic militant violence in France, with a few specificities of its own such as a tradition of cooperation between armed robbers and Islamic militants and the origins of its Muslim immigrant populations largely in the Maghreb rather than south Asia, had its roots in the same causes and catalysts as did violence in the UK.[57] Though French radicals lacked the ease of access to Pakistan and thus to the al-Qaeda senior leadership that their British counterparts enjoyed, patterns of radicalization in France had been broadly the same as across the Channel with, at least in the 2001–5 period, recruits drawn from the same social strata of the marginally better-off, better-educated, relatively well-integrated working classes. There was also the same pattern of family tensions and generational difficulties and recruitment by peers, brothers and friends rather than older clerics. This occurred, as in the UK, around rather than in mosques or in Islamic centres, in homes and in prison, where in some French institutions upwards of 60 per cent of detainees were self-declared Muslims, even if few were particularly observant.[58] The same processes of the evolution and radicalization of cells were also evident: the outward-bound trips, the bonding sessions, the same role for images – especially of the abuse in Abu Ghraib – and the internet.[59] At least four Frenchmen had died in or around Falluja in 2004, and several dozen others were said to have travelled to Iraq.[60] One issue that concerned French security agencies, as it did their British counterparts, was the constant flow of young men to Riyadh, Cairo or radical religious schools in Pakistan for instruction in extremely conservative if pacific broadly 'Salafi' strands of Islam. Significant subsidies from the Saudi government facilitated the trips and between 2004 and 2005 around 250 travelled, not enough to be a mass phenomenon, as one French intelligence officer commented, but enough to be worrying.[61]

Salafi movements such as the Jamaat Tabligh, a vast network dedicated to preaching and good works that professes to shun violence, had recruited tens of thousands from all walks of life in France as in the UK. French intelligence services had been watching such groups as well as freelance preachers often sponsored by Gulf-based religious organizations for many years. But, instead of causing trouble themselves during the *émeutes*, senior French Salafis suspected of involvement in militant activities were heard by eavesdropping security operatives complaining that the rioting caused problems for their recruiting by attracting unwelcome police attention. The neighbourhoods where the Salafis (both those suspected of involvement in radicalism and those known to be law-abiding) had the most influence remained quiet.[62] Of the 3,000 rioters arrested in the Paris region, not one was previously known to the French security services. Instead surveillance revealed genuine violent extremists going to ground, suspending efforts to send new volunteers to Iraq or leaving areas for fear of major security operations.[63] There was certainly no evidence of any involvement by anyone associated with al-Qaeda in the rioting. Nor was there any surge in recruitment to radical Muslim groups or networks either, security agencies found.[64] Instead, the weeks after the *émeutes*, due to a high-profile campaign led by figures respected locally such as the rapper Joey Starr, saw a significant surge in registrations to vote in the forthcoming 2007 presidential elections in the *cités*.[65]

Finally, and more fundamentally, describing the revolt as 'Muslim' or by Muslims was misleading because it reduced the nature of religious identity to a 'one size fits all' that took no account of the range of what it meant to be 'Muslim' in France – or elsewhere for that matter – in the autumn 2005. This went beyond a simple challenge of describing the vast diversity of the Muslim community – Arab, non-Arab, black African, practising, non-practising, 'cultural Muslims', 'street Muslims', theological Muslims, political Muslims and so on – and to the heart of a difficult problem of terminology that caused grave problems for all discussions of the issue at the time. Identity is not only multiple – age, educational background, marital status, gender, life course, ethnic or geographic origin, interests, profession, aspirations, tastes – all furnishing a potential identity or elements of an identity but profoundly dynamic as well. 'I am French one day, of "Algerian origin" the next, a Muslim the third,' one demonstrator protesting the lack of public recognition of the deaths of scores of Algerians in Paris at the hands of French police in the 1960s told the author in late 2005. 'It depends who I am talking to.'[66] The particular element that is dominant at any one time depends on the situation and, crucially, the interlocutor. Identity is thus a conversation, a dialectic and never static. Defining the *émeutes* as 'Muslim revolts' was not only factually misleading and counterproductive but hindered a balanced, more nuanced and more accurate analysis. This is not to say that religion does not play a role in the *banlieues* – often a troubled one – and is not sometimes deeply important to young men like those who rioted in France in November 2005, but it was not the reason that they went out and threw stones and petrol bombs at policemen. So what were the reasons?

The *cités* where the rioters lived and where the riots took place were – if not true ghettos – a 'ghetto phenomenon' with a rare combination of severe social and economic problems.[67] Many were extremely physically isolated, built on the edges of cities with little public transport where the heavy industry that had once required their presence was long gone. Around Paris, the *cités* were separated from the twenty arrondissements of the city itself by a strong symbolic and administrative frontier that ran along the line once traced by the nineteenth-century city defences that was now the route of the six-lane orbital highway known as *le périphérique*.[68] The physical environment of the *cités* was often severely degraded. In the famous Neuf Trois – the département of Seine et Saint-Denis – over a third of the population were foreign-born and 18 per cent lived below the poverty line.[69] Nearly 20 per cent had no hot water, and a quarter of housing units had no indoor shower or bathroom.[70] Then there was unemployment – rising through the 1990s to reach levels of over 40 per cent for young unqualified men nationally.[71] Jobs that were available were often of extremely low quality, partly due to some genuine discrimination based on colour, name or religion, but also partly due to the strong negative image associated with the *banlieusard*, an image which the subject consciously or unconsciously reinforced through immediately recognizable speech patterns, clothing and so on. Often the perceived deficiencies in social skills, language competence and so forth were real. Schools were under-funded and staffed by often young teachers ill equipped to deal with the range of social problems with which they were confronted.[72] Two in five male pupils from north African backgrounds left school without any qualification at all.[73]

Though such areas were far from being zones of '*non-droit*' or 'no-go areas', as so often claimed, they were places where the presence and authority of the République Française was undoubtedly contested and weak. A report by domestic intelligence services a year before the *émeutes* spoke of hundreds of 'sensitive neighbourhoods' where 'populations conserve cultural traditions and ways of life and parallel institutions for social regulation and conflict'.[74] Political representation was almost non-existent. There were no Muslim members of parliament, very few of first-generation immigrant origin and a minimal representation in mainstream parties. The Communist Party's hold on the working-class population of towns in the north, the east or the Paris region had disappeared along with the heavy industry, and the weak French Socialists, whose senior and middle ranks showed even less ethnic and religious diversity than their right-wing opponents, had no real support among a largely depoliticized immigrant population. The main presence of the state in the *cités* was a police force whose philosophy of law enforcement has always favoured the coercive over the consensual and was heavily resistant to ideas of community or neighbourhood policing.[75] Policing of the *cités* was thus extremely confrontational, with almost exclusively white officers in riot gear patrolling or mounting raids from heavily protected individual bases. None of the local police were from the places they patrolled, and banter with local youth was limited and often abusive.[76]

Along with the political and the physical exclusion went cultural exclusion. The vision of France promoted by the elite internally and largely accepted externally is of a country of fine wine, good cheeses, *saucisson*, stunning mountains, the beaches of St Tropez, an immensely rich literary and intellectual heritage, fashion, elegance and history. Little of any of this is to be found in the *cités*. Faiza Guène, a young and popular author from a *cité* on the northern rim of Paris, explained how the France in which she had grown up was very different. Her mother, born in Morocco, had only ever seen the Eiffel Tower once and would not normally have been able to afford her own daughter's highly successful, ironic book on life in the *banlieues*, she said. The French Republic – one, indivisible and secular according to the constitution – accepted new arrivals often with a singular generosity but on its own terms. One reason for the success of Guène's book, *Kiffe Kiffe Demain*, was an ending in which republican France triumphed, largely resolving the problems faced by the characters in the *cité* as they accepted its values, myths and institutions.[77] Anis Bouabsa, a baker in Paris' twentieth arrondissement appointed to supply the daily bread for the president's table, was also seen as an example of successful integration. But Bouabsa, whose parents had been born in Tunisia, had earned the contract by being more classically French than any Frenchman, winning an award for Paris' finest baguette.[78] Chefs of Moroccan cuisine, though their dishes were enormously popular, did not win any of the myriad prizes for *gastronomie* awarded every year. One problem was the very high goals the French Republic set for itself. More often than sometimes thought overseas, the system did assure a measure of *liberté*, some *égalité* and, to a lesser extent, *fraternité*. But not in Aulnay, Clichy, Sevran, La Courneuve and so on.[79] The *émeutes* saw non-sectarian political violence involving a ritualized and low-casualty confrontation with the forces of order which was in fact one of the few quintessentially French activities, generally accepted and approved of, in which the young men who comprised the rioters could actually participate.[80] The riots were a demand for more integration, not a rejection of integration.

Within weeks of the riots, the profile of the *émeutier* was thus fairly clear. He was a minority of a minority of a minority. Aged between twelve and twenty-five, a first- or second-generation immigrant, interested more in Air Max and 'le polo Lacoste' or mobile phones than religion or politics, bored, alienated, resentful, full of complex identity issues, desperate to 'get on TV' to get some attention, however fleeting. If asked, he might have called himself a Muslim, though not in the sense meant either by conservative commentators or by Abu Musab al-Suri. Within days of the end of the violence, the people who had rioted could be seen again, either in their neighbourhoods or in specific favoured zones within Paris such as the shopping mall at the Gare du Nord or Les Halles, chatting up girls, comparing phones, arguing with the police. Such young men were a problem certainly, potentially a very serious one. But they were not part of a global radical Islamic militant network. If European Muslims were on the brink of an uprising, it had still to come.

## THE CARTOONS

Hardly had the French *émeutes* died away, however, when a new confrontation blew up, international rather than local this time, which again, not least through the striking images it generated, forced all the same issues raised by the rioting back on to the front pages of the world's newspapers and into the lead of global television bulletins.

Its origin lay in the publication by a little-known Danish newspaper,

*Jyllands-Posten*, of some not particularly amusing cartoons of the Prophet Mohammed. One showed him with a bomb tucked in a fold of his turban; in another he was greeting suicide bombers in heaven, saying, 'Stop, Stop! We have run out of virgins!' An accompanying text, written by the newspaper's forty-six-year-old culture editor, Flemming Rose, shortly before the crucial pages went to press explained: 'Some Muslims reject modern, secular society. They demand a special position, insisting on special consideration of their own religious feelings. It is incompatible with secular democracy and freedom of expression, where one has to be ready to put up with scorn, mockery and ridicule.' The cartoons were published on September 30, 2005. The 'crisis' they caused occurred almost five months later. The intervening months had been filled by the concerted efforts of individual clerics seeking personal advancement and of states to manufacture a confrontation.

The cartoons crisis had its origin in a story reported in Denmark about the difficulties faced by an author who wanted to find an illustrator for his children's book on the life of the Prophet Mohammed which had struck editors at *Jyllands-Posten*. The author concerned had found that potential illustrators systematically refused the commission, and the only one who accepted insisted on anonymity. The story tied in with a series of other incidents in Denmark, Sweden and elsewhere in Europe which appeared to reveal a widespread trend of artists, museum directors or creators avoiding controversial subjects or withdrawing works from exhibition to pre-empt any threat of violence from Muslim extremists. Searching for a way to follow up the story with empirical evidence that such self-censorship was widespread, the *Jyllands-Posten* editors hit upon the idea of asking several dozen Danish cartoonists to send in images depicting the Prophet 'as they saw him' for publication to see how many would accept. A dozen did so, and their work was published. Several of the images mocked the *Jyllands-Posten* itself. These, however, were ignored in the controversy that was to follow, and it was the three depicting Mohammed negatively that were to receive all the attention. 'It never occurred to me that there could be a problem. We were not focused on Muslim reaction but on the problem of self-censorship within the artistic community in Denmark,' Rose recalled.[81] Two of the cartoons' authors were to receive anonymous death threats within a fortnight.

The initial public reaction to the publication of the cartoons had been muted, though editors at the *Jyllands-Posten* were aware that they had created a stir. On the day the cartoons came out, Rose received a telephone call from an irate vendor in Copenhagen who said he would never sell the newspaper again. But there was little anger expressed publicly, and journalists of the *Jyllands-Posten* were forced eventually to contact a number of local clerics for their response to the cartoons to get a follow-up story.[82] Among them was a former mechanical engineer turned cleric called Ahmad Abu Laban, who had come to Denmark in 1984 after being expelled from Egypt and the United Arab Emirates. He had already become something of a 'rent-a-quote' for Danish journalists, having called bin Laden a 'businessman and freedom fighter'. Once alerted to the cartoons' publication, Laban saw a clear opportunity to boost his profile and garner support, donations and influence. Hitherto, the group of Islamists he led had numbered only a few thousand despite inflated claims of a much greater strength.[83] Abu Laban and other Muslim religious leaders in Denmark therefore called loudly for the *Jyllands-Posten* to make an apology and, when none was forthcoming, organized a demonstration in Copenhagen that was attended by between 3,000 and 5,000 people. There was some further local anger when the Danish government refused to intervene.[84] Then the affair appeared to die away. Even when the cartoons were reprinted in an Egyptian newspaper alongside an incendiary editorial, no one took to the streets either in the Middle East or in Europe. There the matter might have rested.

Abu Laban did not give up, however. He and a group of other Danish clerics put together a dossier including the cartoons published by the *Jyllands-Posten*, three far more offensive images of Mohammed from an unidentified source, clippings and hate-mail allegedly sent to Muslims in Denmark and travelled to the meeting of the Organization of the Islamic Conference (OIC) that was being held in Mecca. The clerics then passed around their file, calling for action. With no alternative, the OIC issued a condemnation and demanded United Nations action against Denmark. Still not satisfied, a new delegation of Danish clerics then set off around Middle Eastern capitals, presenting their dossier to religious and political leaders, claiming, as they had done before, that all the cartoons it contained had been published repeatedly in the Western press. On January 10, 2006, a Christian publication in Norway reprinted the three original images, allowing the clerics to claim a concerted campaign in the West to slight Islam. With this new publication, Abu Laban and his associates began finally to make some progress. Saudi Arabia recalled its ambassador from Denmark and declared a consumer boycott. On January 30, the Danish prime minister and the *Jyllands-Posten* tried to defuse the growing row by expressing their regret at any offence caused to Muslims. Their carefully worded semi-apology – 'we learned that in Arabic "regret" isn't very easily understood, so we made a semantic change, but nothing changed in substance because we could not apologize for something we did not believe was wrong,' said Rose – triggered a backlash in Europe, and a number of newspapers in France, Spain, Germany, Holland and Italy republished the images.[85] The cycle of escalation soon developed a momentum of its own, helped by reporting of the story in the Middle East in particular that was often inflammatory and inaccurate.

Within a few days, there were riots in Pakistan, Afghanistan, Lebanon, Syria, Libya, Nigeria and elsewhere. In the West, the row was once more cited as evidence of a clash of civilizations and an augur of violence on the streets of Europe. In the Muslim world, it was seen as further proof that a belligerent and aggressive West was incapable of 'respecting' Islamic faith and culture. Once more, however, there were deeper forces at work. A close look at the demonstrations organized around the world and at the origins of the more inflammatory statements that fuelled the cycle of escalation reveals that those hurling stones, burning flags and chanting slogans may have been less representative of entire communities than they might have looked at the time. For, as had been the case during the Rushdie affair seventeen years before, different Middle Eastern governments, religious leaders and movements all sought to exploit events, seeking to outdo each other in indignation and to use the opportunity offered by the crisis to reinforce their otherwise often shaky religious credentials. After the local Danish clerics, it was the turn of the major international religious figures. Following relatively moderate early statements, the immensely influential Egyptian university of al-Azhar issued a statement signed by its Grand Sheikh, Mohammed Tantawi, which said the cartoons showed 'contempt [for] the religious beliefs of more than one billion Muslims around the world'. Yusuf al-Qaradawi, the conservative Islamist scholar who had tried to dissuade the Taliban from destroying the Buddhas almost exactly five years earlier and who had a following of tens of millions, used his programme on al-Jazeera to call for secular rulers to keep on stoking 'the awakening of the Muslim nation' after various rivals used their own broadcasts to voice more extreme statements.[86] Clerics in Saudi Arabia, particularly aware of the importance of not letting the government take the lead in the campaign against the cartoons, told their congregations to 'rise up . . . grab swords . . . they have trampled on the Prophet'.[87]

If there was competition between clerics, it was nothing in comparison to that between states. The Rushdie affair had been played out in a context of vicious rivalry between Saudi Arabia and Iran for the symbolic leadership of Islam. Nearly twenty years later, that rivalry still existed along, of course, with many others. Few states in the Middle East or further afield could allow themselves to be seen as soft on those who insulted the Prophet. In Syria, where any unauthorized political demonstration would have faced violent repression, 'spontaneous' crowds sacked the Danish and Norwegian embassies in Damascus. Denmark's embassy in Tehran was attacked by another 'spontaneous' crowd hours after the Iranian government announced a suspension of trade links with Denmark. Kuwait and Egypt organized a consumer boycott and allowed demonstrations of a violence that would normally have brought a crushing police response. In the Palestinian Occupied Territories elements of the more secular Fatah, fresh from a heavy defeat in elections in January 2006, made statements far more inflammatory than those of their victorious electoral opponents, the Islamists of Hamas.[88] In Lebanon, as ever, a more complicated agenda fuelled events. In Beirut, Christian shops were sacked and the Danish consulate attacked by a crowd containing significant numbers of Syrian citizens, prompting observers to point out how Damascus had an interest in destabilizing the incumbent Lebanese prime minister.[89] The cycle continued for several weeks until well over 100 people had been killed (mainly by police firing on crowds), the al-Qaeda senior leadership had issued a statement threatening reprisals against Denmark, and, according to polls in the West, several tens of millions more Europeans and Americans had been convinced that Islam was either a threat or incompatible with democracy or both.[90] The issues raised by the cartoons affair – of free speech in largely secular societies, of the place of Muslims within European nations – were important and difficult ones. They were also unlikely to find an easy resolution in the near future. 'We found ourselves involved in a story where people had to make tough choices about what they believed was right and take the consequences,'

Flemming Rose told the author. Abu Laban, the man who had fuelled the furore in the first place, explained that 'though these riots were not on our agenda . . . it might be good for the West to know what happens when you insult Mohammed.'[91]

## TOUCHING THE BOTTOM

If you had marked with a red spot every violent incident justifiably linked to radical Islam on a map of the world in 2001, most would have been clustered on Afghanistan with a sprinkling elsewhere and four key markers on the east cost of the USA. In 2003, the affected areas would have been much greater. Though there would have been nothing in America, a thick red line would have stretched across North Africa, broadening into a bloody smear across Iraq and the Arabian peninsula, before arcing across south-west Asia and on into the Far East. The map would have shown a noticeable and worrying increase on 2001. Yet this increase would be nothing compared to what was coming. By late summer 2006, as the fifth anniversary of 9/11 approached, whole swathes of the globe would have been covered in red: red across parts of the UK; red across parts of western Europe; red across the Maghreb, where counter-terrorism services and newly re-energized radical movements in Morocco, Libya and Algeria played a deadly game of survival, torture, conspiracy and killing; red across Lebanon, where hopes of a democratic revolution had rapidly faded to be replaced by a vicious and hard-fought short war between Hezbollah and Israel; red across Gaza, where Hamas was increasingly powerful; red across Saudi Arabia, where authorities continued to round up militants responsible for a series of bloody attacks and from where hundreds continued to head for jihad in an Iraq that itself was apparently plunging deeper and deeper into a terrible savage violence; red across the Yemen, where senior militants planned attacks on oil refineries and Western interests; red across Pakistan and Afghanistan and into India, where for the first time in recent decades there were indications of problems of extremism among the nation's 150-million-strong Muslim minority. More than 200 had died in bombings in Mumbai, the country's commercial centre, organized by Pakistani-based groups and the local Students Islamic Movement of India working together. There was red too in Africa, where in the dust and gravel of the great empty wastes of the central Sahara troops from Mauritania and Niger backed by American special forces fought a running battle with a growing number of semi-criminal militants and where, in Somalia, Islamic militias in part inspired by the Taliban fleetingly seized Mogadishu before being forced out by Ethiopian troops. As for the Far East, in Thailand a long-running insurgency pitting Muslims of Malay ethnic stock against an often brutal and exploitative government seen as representing only the interests of the Buddhist majority population had flared back into life with radical Islam now replacing revolutionary Marxism as the dominant discourse. And in Indonesia, the world's largest Muslim-majority state, Jemaa Islamiya, though weakened, was still dangerous, and violence continued. Australian security services were extremely nervous and there were even reports – ludicrously overblown as it turned out – of activity in South America. It was a picture grimmer than had been seen for many decades, and little augured well for the future.

There had, of course, been a few glimmers of something more positive – or at least less negative. Actually quantifying the menace al-Qaeda posed was very hard, and the numbers involved in radical activism remained a minuscule fraction of Muslim communities, particularly in the West, and of the world's Muslim population. In the USA, despite a few isolated influences, the better-integrated, -educated and -accepted Muslim community posed no obvious problem for the moment despite the febrile atmosphere. As more became known about the real reasons for the French riots of the autumn before and about the machinations of clerics and Middle Eastern regimes during the cartoons crisis, more measured analyses of what the two episodes meant for Europe began to roll back some of the hysteria. After all, the riots had led to only two deaths, and in Europe the cartoon crisis had seen nothing but largely legal protests through traditional channels.[92] But the bad outweighed the good. The French riots may not have seen the worst predictions fulfilled, but community relations across much of Europe had nonetheless reached a long-term low, with evidence of a growing and potent trend of the consolidation of sectarian and ethnic identities. The cartoon crisis had shown the power of crowd violence and crowd psychology, how hysterical populism could resonate among anxious and insecure populations and the ease with which rumours and myths could become the received wisdom for millions. A major initiative launched by the Bush administration in 2004 to promote democracy in an overconfident bid to 'drain the swamp' of support for terrorism in the 'Greater Middle East' had foundered on the entrenched interests of local regimes and those who benefited from them and on the gap between what the Americans were promising and what was being delivered in Iraq, Afghanistan and elsewhere. In Cairo in June 2005, Condoleezza Rice, now secretary of state, had pledged a new era in relations with the Muslim world. For too long, Rice told her audience, the United States had pursued 'stability at the expense of democracy in the Middle East'. In the future, she said, 'supporting the democratic aspirations of all people would be the touchstone of the administration's policies in the region'.[93] However, exactly what had been happening in Guantanamo, Bagram, Kandahar and in secret 'black prisons' was increasingly clear as was the true extent of the CIA's rendition programme, and when it came to a genuine choice between supporting a long-favoured ally such as Hosni Mubarak or backing a nascent reform movement, it was fairly clear where the White House's priorities lay. Polls showed that around 7 per cent of the global Muslim population – 100 million or so people – believed the 9/11 attacks were '*completely justified*'.[94] Security authorities appeared at best nervous, at worst trigger-happy and paranoid. A young Brazilian called Jean Charles de Menezes had been shot dead by British anti-terror police at a tube station in London the day after the abortive 21/7 attacks – they mistook him for a fugitive bomber – and hundreds of innocent citizens continued to be caught in massive dragnets in the US and in Europe. And all the while the steady background drumbeat of increased and more extreme violence, horrific videos of executions viewed by hundreds of thousands and communiqués from the senior al-Qaeda leadership continued.[95] As 2006 ground on, the 9/11 Wars seemed to be showing no signs of doing anything other than broadening to new parts of the globe, deepening further in terms of their intensity and intractability and causing more pain, destruction and hate all while inflicting long-term scars that would take decades to heal if they were to heal at all. As autumn turned to winter and the end of 2006 approached, there was one faint light just visible in the gloom. It shone from a very unlikely direction: Iraq.

# PART FOUR

# Iraq and the Turning:
## 2005–7

# 10

# The Awakening

## A BAD YEAR, A BOMB IN A SHRINE . . . AND CIVIL WAR

On the night of February 21, 2006, six men wearing police uniforms entered the huge al-Askariya shrine in the town of Samarra, 70 miles north of Baghdad.[1] The leader of the group was a local Islamic extremist called Hathim al-Badri. With him were four Saudis and a Tunisian. The men rapidly overpowered the policemen guarding the complex, tied them up and then set about wiring several large bombs underneath its gilded main dome.[2]

The next morning two American infantry officers embedded with a force of new Iraqi 'special police commandos' in Samarra left their base at around 6.30 a.m. to set up a cordon and search operation in the neighbourhood adjacent to the mosque. It was the third such operation in three days. Though they had received no intelligence that the shrine might be attacked, they had been repeatedly told ammunition and explosives were being stored inside the rambling complex of buildings around the edifice of the main mosque. It was not clear, however, who was storing what, and as regulations prevented them searching religious sites without solid evidence the Americans had started combing the surrounding districts instead.[3] The two operations the previous mornings had turned up nothing. This time, even before the search could begin, there was an explosion. Then came silence and then a second blast, much bigger than the first. 'You blink and shudder and hunch down. You're thinking: "What the heck happened there?"' Major Jeremy Lewis, one of the two US officers at the scene, later recalled. 'My gunner says, "Sir, it's fucking gone! It's gone." I'm like, "No it's not gone, it's not gone." But then the wind carried the plume of smoke away.'[4] The entire main dome of the shrine had indeed disappeared.

The Shia police commandos, Lewis remembered, were 'very, very upset ... like when one of them had died'. The al-Askariya mosque complex contained a shrine to the twelfth 'hidden' imam, 'Muhammed al-Mahdi', the ultimate saviour of human kind, kept from the world by God until the day of his return. It also contained the tombs of the tenth and eleventh of the Shia imams, the ultimate Mahdi's immediate predecessors. A site of immense importance for all Shias, though particularly for those of the 'Twelver' strand, the Samarra shrine had been carefully chosen as a target to provoke a violent sectarian response. For a short period, almost as if people did not want to accept the implications of the act, the attack was blamed on the 'Jews' and 'Americans'. But the bombing came at the end of a long series of similar strikes directed at the Shia by extremists in networks run by Abu Musab al-Zarqawi which had killed hundreds of people over previous months and wounded thousands more.[5] Only six weeks earlier around sixty had died when suicide bombers had hit a shrine in Karbala, and the culprits of this latest attack were fairly obvious even before the yellow dust of the ninth-century mosque had settled.[6] Within hours, carloads of gunmen from the al-Mahdi Army were pouring out of Sadr City, the huge Shia slum in east Baghdad, and shooting up Sunni parts of the city. Across the country thirty Sunni mosques were rocketed, sprayed with automatic fire or incinerated. The next day, just to stoke the fires further, Sunni militants in police uniforms set up false roadblocks a few miles south of Sadr City and executed forty-five Shias.[7] Similar incidents were occurring wherever Shia and Sunni communities lived close to one another, each designed to accelerate the plunge into all-out sectarian warfare. Over the next weeks, the pace of such killings picked up. 'The day [the Samarra shrine] blew up every last one of us said it was the beginning of the civil war in Iraq,' Major Lewis remembered in his post-tour interview.[8]

The signs of the impending civil war had been plain for some time. The conflict was partly a result of the longstanding tensions within Iraq and partly due to the total failure of the coalition's military and political strategies from the second Falluja battle of November 2004 through to the summer of 2006. On the political front, the three national polls held during the period which had been supposed to provide the political architecture that would lead Iraq into a new era of democratic progress, multi-ethnic harmony and non-sectarian stability had instead exacerbated rather than healed the divisions between Iraq's main communities. Largely boycotted by the Sunnis, they had resulted in successive victories for Iraq's Shia. The big electoral gains of the United Iraqi Alliance, which broadly reflected the popular will and culture of the religiously and socially conservative Shia masses, meant control of most of the government apparatus was in Shia hands, and with the Sunni stranglehold on political power broken for ever, many in the Shia community felt there was no longer any need for the restraint once counselled by conservative religious leaders such as Grand Ayatollah Ali al-Sistani. If anything, they believed, Shia dominance needed to be reinforced to ensure that there was no chance of the beaten Sunnis returning to power. Many simply sought power and money. Ibrahim Jafaari, the weak and incompetent compromise candidate eventually chosen as prime minister after months of negotiation, proved both unable and unwilling to rein in the growing excesses of either those loyal to Muqtada al-Sadr, whose representatives had done well enough in the polls to be rewarded with effective control of the Ministry of Health, or the hardline Islamists of the Iran-linked SCIRI, who had got the Ministry of the Interior, from which they ousted all Sunnis before turning the police into an armed Shia militia that collaborated in sectarian killings. With no effective administration or law enforcement and a legacy of graft from the days of the Coalition Provisional Authority, corruption had flourished on an astonishing scale. Inevitably the meagre services that had been restored or maintained in 2004 had collapsed across much of the country, though Sunni areas suffered worse as resources were diverted to Shia communities by the now largely Shia-run central government. If, towards the end of the year, the flow of refugees from Iraq eased up, it was only because all those who could leave had already done so.[9]

Militarily, too, the situation had deteriorated. The American generals, driven by an administration whose policy was to make the Iraqis 'stand up', so American troops could 'stand down' and leave, were caught in vicious circle.[10] Aiming to weaken the insurgents sufficiently to allow a handover to the still under-equipped, poorly trained, demoralized and politicized Iraqi security forces, they launched successive efforts with names like Operation Dagger, Sword, Spear, Quick Strike, Iron Fist and Steel Curtain in a bid to clear the crucial Anbar province.

But the gruelling and resource-intensive battles fought along the Euphrates valley towards the Syrian border merely fuelled the insurgency. In 2004 the Americans had lost 848 dead and 7,989 wounded. In 2005 their casualties remained as high.[11] Iraqi security forces lost many more, and at the end of the year were no nearer acquiring the capabilities to take over from the Americans than at the beginning. The US strategy was fundamentally flawed. It was based on handing over to a government that could both militarily defeat the insurgents and work towards national reconciliation. However, not only were the Iraqi government and its forces incapable of defeating anyone, but, certainly after the elections of 2005, their collective sectarian bias was probably the primary obstacle to any national unity.

Worse, in preparation for an eventual handover and departure, US troops were pulled back from city centres into huge Forward Operating Bases (FOBs) with massive defences behind which soldiers could sleep in air-conditioned barrack blocks, eat imported steaks and lobster tails in the vast dining facilities, buy DVDs, phone home and go to the gym. Relations with the local population for the bulk of the 140,000-odd American troops in Iraq were limited to relatively hostile encounters while on patrol. The US military existed in Iraq like some kind of hermetic circulatory system within the body of the country. Servicemen flew from the US, arrived in Iraq from Kuwait in army planes, drove in armoured vehicles, lived and ate behind triple blast walls in bases supplied by huge convoys that arrived from Kuwait or Turkey, carrying even water and salad. Flying over the truck parks of the huge logistic base at Balad, effectively the beating heart of the American military effort in Iraq, was the only way to appreciate the size of the undertaking and the degree to which it was self-sufficient. Hundreds and hundreds of vehicles needed to ferry the supplies consumed by the vast apparatus of the army formed queues for miles around the base, ready to be emptied or refilled. Returning to the base from a twelve-hour patrol with one unit, the author witnessed a grimly amusing argument between infantrymen and the military traffic policeman who tried to book them for speeding. The only Iraqis were menial staff, a few advisers, a handful of translators and an unknown number of detainees. The special forces units, who were supposed to show a degree of cultural sensitivity that was not expected from the average infantryman, were paradoxically among the most isolated as they were charged with picking up 'high-value targets' on night raids, an activity unlikely to engender any relations at all, let alone cordial ones, with local people. One special forces officer commented that he had never met an Iraqi who was not in handcuffs.[12]

Bases like that at Balad were the result of various factors. First was the weight of decades of previous practice. Back in Bagram in Afghanistan in 2002 there had never been any questions over what sort of base was going to be built there. It was always going to be a small corner of America transplanted to a foreign field. One influence, as mentioned earlier, was the example of the bases constructed in the Middle East for operations over Iraq in the 1990s. In Saudi Arabia, due to the sensitivity of the American presence in the Land of the Two Holy Places, all troops had effectively been confined to their bases even if, given the cultural gulf between most American servicemen and women and the societies around them, there had been limited reasons why any of the 10,000 or so who were stationed in the region would mix at all with locals.[13] A second influence was the autonomy that had so marked American military communities based overseas in Europe or east Asia through much of the Cold War. The historic isolation of American forces deployed abroad thus had long roots. It reached, however, an entirely new scale with the deployments of the 9/11 Wars.

A second logic was that of General John P. Abizaid and other senior officers and officials in the US government. Abizaid, the commander of the US Central Command from 2003 to 2007 and one of the most intellectually able and aware of the American higher military command, had a Lebanese Christian Arab father and had learned Arabic and this, rightly or wrongly, gave his opinions significantly more weight than they might otherwise have had. Abizaid's 'antibody theory' held that societies, especially Muslim and Arab societies, inevitably reject the foreign. The profile of American soldiers in Iraqi towns – as in Afghan towns – should thus be as low as possible. Their presence on the streets and amid the people should be minimized to avoid provoking automatic rejection due to wounded personal pride, a sense of national, religious or ethnic identity or simple misunderstanding. This had influenced strategic thinking in Afghanistan and, by 2005, coincided perfectly with the desire of the increasingly troubled Bush administration to limit casualties and its avowed belief that, when it comes to democracy, too much care can kill the patient. Again and again, the mantra 'we will stand down as they stand up' was repeated and the American military withdrew further, out of towns and major cities, into their huge bases, sending ever more optimistic assessments up their chain of command.

But the reality of war in Ramadi, Tal Afar, Kut and hundreds of other Iraqi towns and cities was very different, and the seemingly aimless and endless combat, the mounting casualties and of course the isolation inevitably took their toll on morale and discipline. While the second Falluja battle had been winding down, a unit of American marines in the upper Euphrates town of Haditha had shot dead twenty-four Iraqis in the aftermath of an IED attack that had killed a well-liked twenty-year-old corporal. At least fifteen of the casualties were unarmed Iraqis killed in their homes, including seven women and three children. 'I couldn't see their faces very well – only their guns sticking into the doorway. I watched them shoot my grandfather, first in the chest and then in the head. Then they killed my granny,' Eman Waleed, a nine-year-old child, told Tim McGirk of *Time* magazine.[14] An old man in a wheelchair had been shot nine times.[15] As bad as the incident itself was the profound lack of interest of the Marines' senior officers. The killings, which provoked uproar in the USA when they were revealed, were indicative of a much broader malaise. A US army survey at the time showed 40 per cent of soldiers disliked the Iraqis and 38 per cent believed they did not have to treat them with respect.[16] About two-thirds of Marines and about half of army troops said they would not report a team member for mistreating a civilian and 10 per cent admitted they had personally been involved in abuse.[17] In the south, British confidence in their 'softer' touch, cultural sensitivity and discipline had long looked somewhat misplaced. The cheery 'salaamaleikums' and waves from the back of open-top Land Rovers of 2003 were a distant memory. Through 2005 British troops progressively withdrew into fortified bases in Basra and other southern cities which, if less luxurious than their American counterparts, were every bit as cut off from local populations. Their positions came under constant rocket and mortar fire, the local police were almost entirely infiltrated by various Shia Islamist groups and gangs fighting each other and foreign troops and central government control was nominal. Graffiti seen by the author on the inside of a bunker on one British post was telling: 'I am in a world of shit,' it read, a quote from Stanley Kubrick's 1987 Vietnam war film *Full Metal Jacket*. The isolation of the troops had predictable consequences. These were compounded by the farcical idea that British forces somehow understood their environment better than their American counterparts. In September 2005 two British special forces soldiers were taken captive as they attempted to drive around Basra 'undercover' on a mission to build up a 'pattern of life picture'.[18] Astonishingly, the soldiers had believed that darkening their skins, wearing cheap local shirts and driving a local car would allow them to 'blend in'. They were naturally as obvious as a group of Iraqi special forces trying to do something similar in a major British city would have been and were swiftly spotted and detained by Iraqi police. It took a full-scale armoured assault to free them.[19] Over the next two years, the British troops would gradually leave Basra entirely, ending up cantoned out in a big base at the airport, from where they launched occasional raids into the city but otherwise did little.

So 2005 thus ended as it had begun. In Washington and London, politicians continued to insist that progress was being made. That Iraqis voted 'yes' in the referendum on the constitution in October and had gone to the polls, again relatively peacefully, to elect a new full-term government in December was cited as evidence of political maturity and nascent stability. However, Sunnis had voted overwhelmingly against the constitution, which they believed would deny them a fair share of central political power and the immense oil wealth that went with it.[20] Many, both inside and outside Iraq, felt an explosion of violence was imminent. One senior British diplomat, speaking off the record shortly after returning from a long posting in Baghdad, dully summed up his time in Iraq in the first weeks of 2006. 'I think we will look back and say that 2005 was a bad year,' he said. 'I hope to God that the next one brings us something better.' In Baghdad's upmarket Karada, the barber Jaffar, who had grumbled about the Green Zone being lit up 'like in an Indian musical' two years previously had other things to worry about. No one came now to have their hair cut. Half the neighbourhood was deserted. Robberies were common. Bodies were turning up in the streets. Most were Shia, killed by Sunnis. Some were Sunnis, killed by Shia. At his local bakery, the young men sweating over the dough kept AK-47s close by. Most bakers were Shia and thus, like the queues of police recruits, easy and identifiable targets. 'I spend a lot of time praying,' Jaffar said. [21] Less than a month later came the al-Askariya mosque explosion and a further slide into terrible violence became inevitable.

## AL-QAEDA IN MESOPOTAMIA
## AND THE 9/11 WARS

When, in October 2004, Abu Musab al-Zarqawi had finally overcome his reluctance to enter into a close relationship with al-Qaeda and had sworn allegiance to Osama bin Laden, the name he chose for his network was 'Tanzim Qaedat al-Jihad fi Bilad al Rafidayn', usually translated as 'the Al-Qaeda Jihad Organization in the Land of the Two Rivers' or 'Al-Qaeda in Mesopotamia' or, becoming progressively more distant from the original, 'al-Qaeda in Iraq', or 'AQI'.[22] The problem with the repeated reduction of the admittedly long-winded original title to the snappier 'AQI' was that it obscured the group's independent origins, the nature of its project, its fragmented nature and its place within the broader 'jihadi' movement. For though al-Zarqawi was now nominally loyal to bin Laden, the name he had taken for his organization was in fact a clear statement that his 'territorialist' philosophy and local strategy remained very much intact. Firstly, there was his use of the word *tanzim*, which meant organization or armed militia in the context of an insurgency. This showed the difference between al-Zarqawi's approach, based on the establishment of a coherent and organized armed group, and that of strategists such as Abu Musab al-Suri. The latter's very motto was '*nizam, la tanzim*', 'system not organization'.[23] Secondly, there was the reference to a real, physical, identifiable place, the patch of ground that the militants meeting in Falluja had yearned for. This place, for al-Zarqawi, was 'the land of the two rivers', i.e. the fertile strip watered by the Tigris and the Euphrates, the cradle of human civilization. By using such an archaic name, al-Zarqawi avoided recognition of the existence of a nation state known as Iraq and, by extension, the 'unIslamic' concept of any nation other than the *ummah*, the community or nation of all believers. The insistence on place indicated too al-Zarqawi's practical attachment to the establishment of a physical geographic base for the radical Islamic movement from which a broader campaign to bring the rest of the Middle East and potentially the Islamic world within the boundaries of a new caliphate could be waged. The problem for al-Zarqawi was, of course, that he was not Iraqi and was thus attempting to appropriate territory to which he had no evident right and a war that was not his own.

This was not an unfamiliar problem for leaders of international Islamic extremist groups. Indeed the original *raison d'être* of al-Qaeda back in the late 1980s had been to draw together various different national strands of Islamic militant activity under a single umbrella, co-opting local campaigns with limited local objectives into one global strategy with global objectives. The foundation of the group had been one of the consequences of the bitter debate between thinkers who favoured a return to a fight against the 'near enemy', Israel and the 'hypocrite, apostate' Middle Eastern regimes governing at the time, and others who saw the defeat of the Soviet Union as showing the way forward. For the latter, the time had come for a global battle in which a key foe and target would be the 'far enemy' of the West and more specifically the USA. It was American support, they argued, that propped up regimes in Egypt and in Saudi Arabia (as well as Israel), and the only way to bring down President Mubarak or the House of Saud would be through attacks on the USA, which would force Washington to abandon its allies in the region. Through the 1990s, Al-Qaeda offered local groups resources and tried to draw together a web of networked militant movements. However, alliance with al-Qaeda was something of a Faustian pact, requiring the surrender of varying degrees of autonomy and an internationalization of what had usually only been seen as a local battle hitherto. By entering into a relationship with al-Qaeda with its globalized message and objectives local groups thus risked support in their own communities, where there may have been a desire for change in people's immediate circumstances but there was often much less enthusiasm for a war against the much more abstract 'Crusader-Zionist' alliance.

The 1990s had shown quite how resistant local communities often were to attempts to mobilize them for a greater cause. Despite the violence of the fighting on the ground, broadly moderate local Muslim populations in the Balkans and the Caucasus had unequivocally rejected pan-Islamic global 'jihadi' ideologies.[24] Initial attempts by Osama bin Laden in the early 1990s to co-opt the Groupe Islamique Armée in Algeria into his nascent global network had been angrily rebuffed.[25] Attempts a few years later to build links with Indonesian organizations such as the Lashkar Jihad involved primarily in local sectarian violence had also failed. An effort in the Philippines to co-opt the Abu Sayyaf group had had only very limited success. When radicals had succeeded in making inroads, their successes were more due to political manoeuvring among the local groups or the states (or even superpowers) that were backing them than any significant support among local people. By the end of the decade, the huge resources amassed by al-Qaeda were certainly proving attractive – leaders of Iraqi Kurdish groups had after all sought out bin Laden to ask for funds and training as did a range of other militants – but none of those making the trip to Afghanistan in the hope of obtaining financial or other aid had anything like a mass popular constituency. Even the relationship between the Taliban in Afghanistan and their foreign guests remained extremely complex, and support for the project of bin Laden and his associates among ordinary Afghans, where memories of the extremism and lack of respect to local cultures showed by largely Arab international fighters during the war of the 1980s remained fresh, was negligible.[26]

Bin Laden, al-Zawahiri and others were, of course, aware of this. After all, the whole point of the 9/11 attacks had been to broaden the support base of both al-Qaeda and its affiliates by sparking a wave of radicalization and mobilization across the Islamic world. In this, al-Qaeda had, as previous chapters have shown, met with some success. The question was whether in the extraordinary circumstances that existed by 2005, created as much by the actions of America and its allies as by al-Qaeda's various initiatives, this success would be consolidated and expanded. Would the resistance offered by broad populations to global radical ideologies through the 1990s be finally overcome? Or would the global ideology and culture of contemporary militant Islam, stripped as it was of much of its local specificity and context, once again have great difficulty in convincing local communities that their best hopes of salvation, however defined, lay in extremism? After four years of conflict, the most obvious test case was Iraq, where these exact questions were being posed at a local level in a very immediate way. If the battle in Europe would determine how far radical Islam would be allowed to spread in geographic terms across the world, the battle in Iraq would indicate how deep into societies extremism could penetrate. If al-Qaeda's brand of militant activism and ideology failed to attract mass support in Iraq, given the chaos, the violence and the American-led occupation, it was unlikely to do so elsewhere.

In retrospect there had been many early signs indicating what turn events in Iraq were likely to take. The foreign volunteers who arrived through 2003 and early 2004 had been neither universally nor unconditionally welcomed. In some instances the more nationalist, more secular insurgents steeped in Ba'athist pan-Arab ideologies called the newcomers *irhabeen*, or terrorists, and either avoided them or tried simply to exploit their willingness to participate in suicide operations. And though the first battle of Falluja in April 2004 had seen locals and foreigners fighting alongside one another, strains had emerged relatively soon both among the different elements within the insurgents and between local people and the foreign militants.[27] This was lost in the chaos, confusion and hyperbole surrounding events at the time and received little attention. But it was there nonetheless. Many points of difference were cultural. Though the footsoldiers of the new al-Qaeda-affiliated groups were often young local men, the leaders were largely foreigners who enforced a form of ultra-rigorous Salafi orthodoxy entirely stripped of any local cultural context. Militants connected to one group in Falluja stopped locals smoking, for example, though getting through a packet of cigarettes a day was almost as much a part of being an adult Iraqi male as being able to use an AK-47 or liking Egyptian soap operas (which were also now banned). Others attempted to force women to wear the full head-to-toe coverings traditional in the Gulf but alien even in conservative Anbar.[28] Other tensions were social. As had been the case with Arab volunteers in Afghanistan during the 1980s and in Bosnia in the 1990s, newcomers wanted relationships with local women. In part this was a deliberate strategy to build connections among local tribes and communities but also a simple consequence of the inevitable desires of young men at war. One aspect in which traditional society in Anbar resembles that in much of Afghanistan is the degree to which the honour of a man, a family or a community is vested in its women and so the demands of the newcomers, often backed by force, caused immediate clashes, often fatal. Again as in Afghanistan during the war against the Soviets, there were arguments over styles of prayer and worshipping at tombs, seen as polytheism or *shirq* by many raised in strict Gulf Salafi traditions. One Falluja resident was reported to have shot dead a Kuwaiti who told him he could not pray at the grave of his ancestors.[29] Then there were political divergences, particularly over the future or indeed concept of any Iraqi nation. Local fighters identified themselves both as defenders of Islam and of 'Iraq'. As the name of al-Zarqawi's group indicated with its reference to ancient Mesopotamia, the land of the two rivers, the foreigners saw the concept of the nation state as unIslamic. They were there to 'kill infidels' not liberate Iraq, as the young Yemeni fighter Abu Thar had said in Falluja in late 2004.[30] Then there were tensions over more mundane issues of basic local politics. The new leaders of the Islamic militants, whether foreign or Iraqi, were competing with the traditional local tribal sheikhs for power and resources. The new groups were unwitting social revolutionaries, attracting elements who previously had little status in traditional Iraqi rural society. One of the most notorious leaders of the militant groups which emerged in Falluja in the summer of 2004 was a former Baghdad electrician.[31] Then, there were economic reasons for tensions. Much of the local tribes' wealth was based on smuggling. By mid-2005, many of the more lucrative routes were in the hands of militants who, Iraqi or otherwise, diverted the funds away from local communities and their traditional leaders, denying the latter what was usually their most important source of patronage. Finally, there were simple military reasons for the growing disaffection. Though full of zeal, the foreign militants, as in Afghanistan in the 1980s, were untrained and unpredictable.[32] Though their operations often grabbed the headlines, the vast proportion of the IEDs and ambushes directed at coalition troops were the work of Iraqis for whom the insurgency remained first a local war against a foreign occupying force before being a global religious jihad.

By spring of 2005, armed clashes were being reported between tribesmen and foreign militants across Anbar province and elsewhere.[33] These intensified as the year went on. To make up for their loss of genuine popular support, militants of groups such as al-Zarqawi's were forced to rely increasingly on simple murder and intimidation. This violence, which was often deliberately public, took more and more baroque forms such as tying people to burning tyres, boiling them alive or killing them by drilling holes through their limbs.[34] Even by the tough standards of Anbar and Saddam Hussein's Iraq the brutality was shocking.[35] In Anbar, every such act sparked a new series of blood feuds, setting militants against families and tribes, leading to further alienation of local people and thus to even more killings and intimidation. One important moment was reached when a significant number of Sunni leaders in Iraq recognized that two and a half years of fighting had gained them very little, that the demographic superiority and consequent political dominance of the Shia was now an established fact and that they needed to participate in elections if they were going to have a chance of retaining any stake in central government. Such thinking naturally led to a direct clash between their local aims and the global, universal ideologies of the foreigners, who had no interest whatsoever in any accommodation with the new authorities in Iraq let alone their American allies.

The result was that when some Sunni communities in Anbar had decided to vote in the December 2005 national assembly elections they found themselves shot at and bombed on polling day by the militant groups who eighteen months earlier they had welcomed, albeit warily, as protectors. Their assailants justified the killings on the basis that participating in democratic elections was a challenge to the unique authority of God and therefore polytheism and therefore *takfir*. Old ladies voting were thus excommunicable and as apostates were legitimate targets.[36] This kind of uncompromising extremism and the sophistic arguments which purported to provide its intellectual underpinning were spectacularly ill-suited to running an insurgent campaign. A key moment came when, during the polls, nationalist insurgent Iraqi groups ended up fighting to protect Sunni voters alongside, though not in formal alliance with, American troops engaged in the same task.

This was a breakthrough. A second came in January of 2006, only a month before the bombing of the al-Askariya mosque in Samarra, when the tribes of Ramadi, the city where Colonel Hector Mirabile's men had blasted gansta rap on dawn raids in 2003, sent their sons to enlist in the police force to start a drive to force out al-Qaeda. Seventy were killed by a suicide bomber, and the leaders of the initiative were systematically assassinated over subsequent weeks. Despite the ongoing carnage, however, the balance was shifting.[37] The sheiks in Ramadi announced that they were 'withdrawing protection' from foreign extremists and those who fought alongside them. Clashes between tribal fighters and radical Islamic militants broke out in Falluja, Samarra and in the anarchic towns of Latifiya and Mahmoudiya on the main highway south-west of Baghdad.[38] Casualties among foreign militants mounted.

More experienced extremist strategists had tried to warn al-Zarqawi of how a loss of popular support could jeopardize his project in Iraq. Through 2005 and early 2006 the extremist leader had received a stream of communications from senior al-Qaeda militants in Pakistan and other senior figures in the jihadi movement. One, from al-Zawahiri, had thanked al-Zarqawi for 'his efforts and sacrifices' but reminded the younger man that 'popular support would be a decisive factor between victory and defeat'. Telling al-Zarqawi to be mindful that 'the mujahed movement must avoid any action that the masses do not understand or approve', the Egyptian explained that 'in a race for the hearts and minds of our Ummah ... more than half of this battle is taking place in the battlefield of the media'.[39] Significantly, the letter had pointed to the rout of the Algerian extremists in the 1990s as an example of what happens if popular support and legitimacy are lost.[40] A second admonishment, also citing Algeria, came from Atiyah Abd al-Rahman, a senior Libyan militant based in Pakistan who had watched events there at first hand having been sent to the Maghreb as an envoy of bin Laden in the late 1990s. Atiyah, as he signed himself, reminded al-Zarqawi of how 'at the height of their power and capabilities' the Algerian militants had 'destroyed themselves with their own hands by their alienation of the population with their lack of reason ... oppression, deviance and ruthlessness' and called on him to avoid 'things that are perilous and ruinous' such as killing tribal leaders or religious scholars. 'Their enemy did not defeat them,' Atiyah had said of the extremists in Algeria, stressing his credentials as an eyewitness. 'They defeated themselves, were consumed and fell.'[41]

In June, five months after the al-Askariya attack and as Iraq's slide into the Shia–Sunni civil war accelerated, al-Zarqawi was killed by two 500 lb bombs dropped by American aircraft on a farmhouse north-east of Baghdad in Diyala province, where he had apparently been hiding for six weeks.

## A TURNING

The beginning of the end for the leader of al-Qaeda in Iraq (AQI) can be dated to a night the previous November when suicide bombers blew themselves up in three luxury hotels in Amman, the Jordanian capital, killing sixty people, including thirty-eight members of a wedding party.[42] The attacks had been organized by al-Zarqawi, who claimed responsibility.

Almost all the victims were Jordanian, and the images of the bloodied and torn bodies of the revellers, broadcast continually for days by local TV channels, provoked an outcry locally with scores of well-attended and genuinely spontaneous demonstrations against such violence taking place over the days after the attacks. The extended family of al-Zarqawi took out advertisements in Jordan's three main newspapers to announce that 'the sons of the al-Khalayleh tribe' would 'sever links' with their kinsman 'until doomsday'.[43]

Subsequent polls revealed that the effect the November hotel bombings had on Jordanian public opinion. The kingdom had always been in a delicate position with its moderate religious and cultural tradition, frequently pro-American foreign policy and Westernized elite coexisting uneasily with a deep and popular Islamist sentiment. With its proximity to Israel and very substantial population of Palestinian refugees, Jordan had also always played a pivotal role in the core Middle East and for a long time support for Osama bin Laden and for suicide bombing had been higher there than elsewhere. This phenomenon was no doubt due in part to the sensitivity of the Palestinian issue in the kingdom and to the distinction between suicide attacks in Israel and elsewhere made by most local clerics and many local people. Support for the Iraqi insurgents had been even greater. From 2002 to 2005 support in Jordan for violence against civilians in 'the defense of Islam' had increased from 43 per cent to 57 per cent according to successive polls by the American Pew Centre. Another survey conducted by the Center for Strategic Studies at the University of Jordan in the second half of 2005 indicated that 70 per cent of the Jordanian public considered al-Qaeda an 'armed resistance organization' and not a 'terrorist group'. A further secret study by the Jordanian authorities confirmed the results.[44] Yet the November 9 bombings totally changed the dynamic. A public opinion poll conducted by Ipsos Stat for the Jordan-based *al-Ghad* newspaper in the aftermath of the attack revealed that 64 per cent of the respondents now had a negative view of bin Laden's group and only 2.1 per cent a positive view. When asked, 'Do you think al-Qaeda is a terrorist organization?' nearly 90 per cent answered 'yes'.[45] Polling by Pew six months after the attacks confirmed that the change was not simply a knee-jerk response: support for violence against civilians in Jordan had halved to 29 per cent. Confidence in bin Laden 'to do the right thing in world affairs', 64 per cent in 2005, had dropped to 24 per cent in 2006.[46]

The shift in public sentiment had an immediate tactical impact. Al-Zarqawi's networks in Iraq had a long logistical tail stretching back to hundreds of radical activists and extremist clerics in his native land who had promoted him as a true believer and *mujahed* and supplied significant practical, theological and financial support throughout 2004 and 2005. These had proved resistant to attempts by intelligence services to penetrate them.[47] Yet in the aftermath of the Amman bombings, new sources of information began to open up. In May 2006, an official serving on the western border was arrested by the Jordanian police. A key figure in the transfer of weapons, money and material to al-Zarqawi's fighters in Iraq from Jordan, he had been betrayed by associates who had been disgusted by the hotel attacks.[48] The details his interrogation furnished were fed through to the American teams in Iraq running the hunt for the fugitive leader of al-Qaeda in Mesopotamia. Clever and patient questioning – far removed from the atrocities of Abu Ghraib – by US interrogators of an ever-lengthening list of close associates through the spring and summer of 2006 and information volunteered by senior figures, many still active in the insurgency, within major Anbar tribes, meant that the identities of most of those in al-Zarqawi's inner circle were now known.[49]

By the early summer of 2006, the animosity towards al-Zarqawi and his foreign militants in Anbar meant the province was no longer safe for the AQI leader. Effectively on the run, moving from safehouse to safehouse, the forty-year-old traversed the semi-rural belt to the north of Baghdad and ended up in a small village in Diyala province, not far from the tough mixed Sunni and Shia town of Baqubah. When a former associate of al-Zarqawi, 'turned' by Jordanian security forces after being betrayed by a suspicious hotel owner and arrested early in the year, provided a key telephone number, this lead, together with the work of the interrogators in Iraq, allowed al-Zarqawi's spiritual adviser, Sheikh Rahman, to be physically located and put under surveillance. A Predator drone then followed the cleric to the farmhouse where al-Zarqawi himself was believed to be staying. The two men and two or three women and children also staying in the building died almost immediately in the ensuing strike.[50] In addition to the new sophistication of American methods, key to the capture of the militant leader were thus two critical phenomena: the alienation of the tribes from the foreign extremists within Iraq, forcing al-Zarqawi to leave Anbar, and the changing attitude of ordinary people in Jordan towards a man whom many had once seen as a heroic resistance fighter which had led to crucial leads reaching the Jordanian intelligence services. But the real significance of the plunging support for radical Islamic violence and senior militant leaders in Jordan had ramifications much more wide-ranging than the death of a single militant, albeit one of the notoriety of al-Zarqawi. If the same phenomenon was reproduced elsewhere then it was clear that it would signal a genuine strategic shift in the evolution of the 9/11 Wars.

It had been obvious for a long time to anyone working or living in Muslim-majority countries that support for bin Laden or for radical Islamic militants was far from universal and that, by the middle of the decade, more and more people were beginning to question al-Qaeda's means and message. In a barber shop in the Sabra and Shatila refugee camp in Beirut, the site of the infamous massacres of 1982 and as likely a location for support for radical Islam as one could hope to find in the region, three brothers gave three different answers – 'Yes, it is justified', 'No it is never justified', 'It depends on the circumstances' – when questioned by the author about suicide bombings and executions of civilians in Iraq in late 2005. Similar responses were heard in living rooms, shops and restaurants in Indonesia, Pakistan and Qatar, in Morocco in January 2006 and among British, French, German and Dutch Muslims. Along with the indication of the beginning of a reaction against extremist violence came a clue as to why and where this emerging trend might be strongest. There was good evidence, though at that time still only anecdotal, of a strong correlation between the proximity of any violence and the degree of support for the perpetrators of violence.

By the spring of 2006, however, starting with the surveys in Jordan, a wealth of polling had begun to put flesh on the anecdotal bones. In Indonesia support for radical violence had dropped in the wake of the first Bali bombing in 2002 from the already low level of 26 per cent to 20 per cent and then continued to drop further to 11 per cent after a further round of bombings in 2005.[51] The most dramatic drop in support for terrorism had been seen in Morocco, where fully 79 per cent of those surveyed said that support for suicide bombing and violence against civilians was never justified – more than double the percentage (38 per cent) who had expressed this view in 2004.[52] In Turkey, despite the growing chaos in Iraq, confidence in bin Laden to 'do the right thing in world affairs' dropped from 15 per cent before the Istanbul bombing of 2002 to 7 per cent a year after it and to 3 per cent by 2005.[53] In

Egypt, the attacks, in the holiday town of Taba in the autumn of 2004, Cairo in April 2005 and then in the Red Sea resort of Sharm-el-Sheikh in July of that year contributed to 68 per cent of people remaining 'very or somewhat concerned' about the rise of Islamic extremism in 2006.[54] One of the key reasons for the collapse of support for the militants of Islamic Jihad and Gamaa al-Islamiyya in Egypt in the 1990s had been the combination of local casualties and the economic damage done, especially to the crucial tourist trade, which had particularly hit the middle class, and the 2005 strikes in the country appeared to have a similar effect, with a decline in support for suicide bombing from 28 per cent to 8 per cent in 2007.[55]

In Saudi Arabia high levels of support for bin Laden and his violent tactics and for suicide bombing in general had plunged the instant that the first bombs had exploded on Saudi streets and the reality of what such attacks meant became clear. Though the shift in public sentiment was reinforced by the deliberate dissemination of graphic images by the Saudi authorities and statements against violence made by clerics once known for their radical stance, the reaction against the extremists was a genuine and deep one. 'When we hear bin Laden railing against the West, pointing out the corruption and incompetence of the Arab governments and the suffering of the Palestinians, it is like being transported to a dream, [but] when we see the images of innocent people murdered for this ideology, it's as if we've entered a nightmare,' one poll subject in a conservative southern Saudi town explained.[56] When violence remained abstract, something that happened over there to those people, it could be supported. But when it was local men, women and children who were blown apart, and local economies that suffered, and local governments who were undermined, the response was very different. Only one conclusion could be drawn: the moment communities started seeing close up what radical Islamic militancy genuinely meant, they turned against it. What had happened on a small scale in Anbar Province in Iraq was indeed happening on a much wider scale across the Islamic world.

This drop in support did not indicate lower levels of animosity towards 'the West', America, Bush, Israel and Jews, or lower levels of belief in conspiracy theories attributing the September 11 attacks to Mossad or the CIA. Large majorities in the Muslim world remained convinced that there was a widespread lack of respect for Islam in the

West and that any American rhetoric about spreading democracy was, like the 'Global War on Terror', simply a cover for a neo-imperialist strategy to divide and exploit.[57] But the polls did apparently show that, even as the apparently unstoppable wave of violence had broken across the Middle East and Europe over previous years, there had been a counter-current, a riptide, that had been difficult to see for what it was but was now finally making itself felt. The picture was messy. There was certainly little uniformity; visibility on a whole range of issues was very poor and a counter-example could be found for every more positive sign.

There was certainly much evidence that very serious problems remained. In August of 2006. a new plot had been uncovered in the UK centred on a group of young British Pakistanis in Walthamstow, east London. Very similar to the conspiracies that had preceded it except in its ambition, it would have seen suicide attackers mix liquid components to form explosives inside a series of airborne transatlantic jets, potentially caus- ing the deaths of as many as had died in the 9/11 attacks.[58] Shortly afterwards had come another wave of global controversy sparked by a speech made by the newly elected conservative Pope Benedict XVI, who unhelpfully quoted a fourteenth-century Byzantine Emperor, saying that the Prophet Mohammed had brought 'things only evil and inhuman such as his command to spread by the sword the faith he preached'.[59] Muslim leaders, clerics and activists responded as they had before, demanding once again why the West was set on the humiliation and subordination of Islam and calling again on 'the faithful' to show their anger. But as 2006 wore on, it became clear that for the first time since 9/11 not all the dials had their needles deep in the red zone. There were even grounds for, if not optimism, then at least a nuancing of the previ- ous deep pessimism.

Two months after the death of al-Zarqawi, in August 2006, militants linked to 'al-Qaeda in Iraq' assassinated a senior sheikh in Ramadi and dumped his body in undergrowth rather than return it for immediate burial as tribal and Muslim custom demanded. The incident provoked a young middle-ranking local sheikh called Abdul Sattar Buzaigh Albu Risha to organize a meeting to proclaim the formation of the Sahwa or 'Awakening' Council and to publicly call on the tribes to rise up against al-Qaeda. Sattar, who had had several relatives killed by the extremists, contacted the press in Baghdad to announce he had the support of twenty-five of the thirty-one tribes in Anbar and a strength of 30,000 armed men. It was a ludicrously inflated claim but that wasn't the point. One significant difference to previous such initiatives was that Sattar, who made up for what he lacked in genuine tribal status with charisma and drive, had secured a promise of support and, most importantly, protection from a far-sighted local American commander.[60] Over the following months, the tribes and the US forces began working closely together in Ramadi, gradually clearing the city of foreigners and extremists. Thousands of tribesmen were enrolled in the police or, if illiterate, into a range of auxiliary forces. As the US forces went from block to block, forcing out insurgents, these new reinforcements secured the areas they cleared. The rapid flow of large sums of cash disbursed by the local US senior officers for immediate reconstruction and development projects helped further consolidate the hold the new combined US and Iraqi regular and irregular forces had on any given neighbourhood and provided space for more durable political and administrative structures to be set up.

The motivations of Sattar and the tribes may not have been as altruistic or traditional as sometimes said. The murdered relatives for which Sattar sought vengeance had been executed after negotiating with coalition authorities for a slice of the vast reconstruction budgets available to local contractors. One reason for the Albu Risha, the clan to which Abdul Sattar belonged, turning against the foreign militants was that the latter had appropriated many of the lucrative smuggling, theft and extortion rackets focused around the main Baghdad–Amman highway which had provided much of the tribe's income for several decades.[61] But the exact motives of those picking up their AK-47s to fight beside the US and Iraqi government troops was not important. As the winter of 2006 came on, similar initiatives to that of the Albu Risha, all a result of a combination of similar micro-factors, had gained momentum in the town of Khalidiyah, where an al-Qaeda group had irritated local sheikhs by taking charge of the local distribution of smuggled petrol, in Haditha, scene of the massacre perpetrated by US Marines a year previously, and in a dozen other small towns across western Iraq.[62] Given the still generalized mayhem in Iraq, where levels of violence were as high as they had ever been across the entire country and there was an unprecedented degree of political chaos, it was not surprising that the apparently very minor bits of good news were missed. A change in the evolution of a phenomenon as complex and as diverse as either the war in Iraq or the 9/11 Wars more generally would not come from a single event, a single new trend, a single development but from the accumulated effect of scores of different factors which together would alter its path. But out in the scruffy, battered towns and the fields and date orchards of the upper Euphrates valley, as much as in the bazaars, cafés, living rooms and mosques of Jordan, Egypt, Turkey and elsewhere, another of the elements that together would begin a new evolution of the local conflict and the broader global one had fallen into place.

## 'THE LONG WAR'

If this key turn looked in any way possible it was in spite of, rather than because of, anything Washington was doing. In February 2006, a couple of weeks before the Samarra bombing, the Pentagon had published a 'Strategic Defense Review', its third such comprehensive assessment of how best to shape America's military forces to cope with the challenges that would face them over the coming two decades. The previous review, completed before the 9/11 attacks and published after them, had been largely obsolete by the time it had come out. The new version started with the unequivocal words: 'The United States is a nation engaged in what will be a long war.'[63] It went further than the simple reiteration of a fact that was clear to everyone, however. The document's first chapter was entitled 'Fighting the Long War' and set about defining a conflict that, it said, saw 350,000 American servicemen and women engaged in 130 different countries.

The term 'the Long War' had emerged in military circles at least two years before it made its public debut. The man credited with first using it to describe the ensemble of ongoing operations undertaken by the US army was General Abizaid. He had spoken of the Long War 'to underscore the long-term challenge posed by al Qaeda and other Islamic extremist groups' and had had his staff prepare presentations on 'The Long War 2006 to 2016'.[64] At the time his thinking was a radical departure from the vision that had previously dominated. Though only days after 9/11 Bush had warned America to expect a different kind of conflict, there was in fact more continuity than change. America's wars were still expected to be rapid and relatively cheap. The 'full spectrum dominance' which the US military believed it had attained, its huge technological advance on the rest of the planet and its energy, 'warrior spirit' and will were perceived as largely invincible. By 2005, mired in a hideous war of attrition for which they were neither trained nor equipped, senior American commanders were thus left groping for new conceptual tools to allow them to construct an appropriate strategic framework. The idea of the Long War, as evolved by Abizaid, with its implication of generational struggle, marathon effort and the interdependency of the various theatres in which the US military was engaged, appeared to explain the conflict in a new and potentially useful way.[65]

But there was another strand of thinking which had also sought to define the ongoing struggle and also used the term 'the Long War'. Developed by senior officials in the Bush administration and in intellectual circles close to them, it was more controversial. For the politicians and several highly influential conservative thinkers the phrase 'the Long War' became, in part, a replacement for the increasingly discredited concept of a 'Global War on Terrorism'.[66] More broadly, it framed the various contemporary conflicts as the successors to those fought by the West through the twentieth century against Nazism and Fascism and then Communism.[67] The National Strategy for Combating Terrorism of September 2006 clearly stated that al-Qaeda's 'ideology of oppression, violence and hate' was a 'form of totalitarianism following in the path of Fascism and Nazism'.[68] Such a view undoubtedly reflected the collective historical vision of the senior Bush administration and their view of the current conflict – indeed it reiterated almost word for word phrases used in the president's first address to Congress and the American nation nine days after 9/11. It also had clear political utility.[69] By extending the timescale in which results could be expected in this new conflict, the vision of 'the Long War' explained the apparent failure to achieve rapid victory in Afghanistan and Iraq, justified the continued commitment of very significant resources to what was perceived as a fight for the survival of the American nation and of American values – 'freedom' – and provided a rationale for the continuation of extraordinary legal measures and presidential powers for the foreseeable future.

Thinkers such as Samuel Huntingdon, author of *The Clash of Civilizations*, and Bernard Lewis, the scholar of Islam and the Middle East, were both widely cited to provide intellectual ballast. Underlying such analyses was the perception of the Long War as being a single conflict against a single, united and uniform foe. In an editorial called 'The Long War: the radical Islamists are on the offensive. Will we defeat them?' in the *Weekly Standard* journal in March 2006 William Kristol, one of the most prominent American neo-conservatives, posed a simple question: 'Does [the Bush administration] have the will ... to lead the nation toward victory in the long war against radical Islamism.' In this 'Long War' the enemy was aggregated. If it was not 'Islam' itself, as some argued, it was 'Islamism' or 'Islamofascism' or 'jihadism'. As the emphasis on states as sponsors of terrorism lessened so a new stress on the uniformity and unity of the non-state groups who constituted the enemy emerged. The bombing of the al-Askariya shrine, to take one example, was thus described as 'another indication of the worldwide jihadist offensive against the West', an odd description of an attack on a Muslim holy place by other Muslims.[70]

The problem with this highly ideological vision of the Long War was that it perpetuated one of the fundamental attribution errors that had underpinned the conceptualization and execution of the entire 'Global War on Terrorism'. Men like Abizaid within the military may have instinctively sensed that for their soldiers facing complex situations involving militancy on the ground such generalized responses were inadequate. But the development of any new strategies that might take local context into account or attempt to mitigate the violent reaction that efforts to impose wide-ranging political, social and customary changes on societies appeared often to provoke was politically very difficult. So though the Pentagon's review argued that there was no 'one size fits all' approach and that solutions needed to be 'tailored to local conditions and differentiated worldwide', the conflict was still compared directly to the Cold War. Though the review was careful to explain that victory would be elusive and would depend 'on information, perception, and how and what we communicate as much as application of kinetic effects', i.e. firepower, the enemy was described as 'global non-state terrorist networks'. Finally, though the review called for a new brand of warriors with deep cultural knowledge of the societies in which they operated. American soldiers were described bluntly as 'a force for good' and the enemy as opposing 'globalization and the expansion of freedom it brings'.[71] This tension ran through almost all American strategic thinking at the time. In his last press conference as chairman of the American Joint Chiefs of Staff in September 2005, General Richard Myers had picked up on a variety of semantic changes introduced by Abizaid – such as referring to 'violent extremists' rather than 'terrorists' – but nonetheless described the conflict as 'the long war against terrorism'. A seminar organized by the Pentagon on 'Defining the Long War' shortly after the publication of the review failed to come up with a satisfactory formula to describe and define the conflict.

Taken together this meant that, in the spring of 2006, little looked likely to change on the ground in Iraq or elsewhere in the near future. For authors of the Pentagon review the aims in Iraq remained those of 2003, 'a democratic [nation] that will be able to defend itself, that will not be a safe haven for terrorists, that will not be a threat to its neighbours, and that can serve as a model of freedom for the Middle East'. The means of achieving that goal were also unaltered. Having been successful in 'defeating the Iraqi military and liberating the Iraqi people', the effort remained focused on 'building up Iraqi security forces and local institutions and transitioning responsibility for security to the Iraqis'.[72] If anything was going to change in Iraq and if the more positive developments there and elsewhere were to be exploited strategically, the thinking that would allow that to happen was clearly not going to come from the White House or the upper levels of the Pentagon. As had so often been the case in the course of the 9/11 Wars, the crucial shifts occurred much lower down, much closer to the dusty and bloody ground, where some soldiers and specialists were realizing that real communities have histories, aspirations, resentments, myths, views, hopes and hates which cannot be reduced to simple single-sentence slogans.

# 11

# The Turning

## FIELD MANUAL 3-24

On the day of the bombing of the al-Askariya shrine in Samarra, an eclectic group of soldiers, experts, intelligence specialists, civilian analysts, human rights campaigners, anthropologists, historians and journalists were sitting around tables and half-empty cups of coffee in a nondescript meeting room in the American army staff college of Leavenworth, Kansas.[1] They were a very long way from Iraq, but the conflict was very much present.[2]

The meeting had been convened by General David Petraeus, the fifty-four-year-old senior officer in charge of the college who after serving in Iraq had seized the opportunity offered by his new tenure to formally reshape the American military's understanding of how to fight non-conventional operations. The various experts were there to discuss the draft of a new US military field manual on fighting counter-insurgency warfare. Politically adept, ambitious and driven, Petraeus had served as commander of the 101st Airborne Division during and after the 2003 invasion, where he had employed classic counter-insurgency doctrine to achieve a reasonable level of calm and stability in the difficult northern city of Mosul, a Sunni and Ba'athist bastion. A second tour in charge of training Iraqi security forces had been less successful but had nonetheless reinforced the reputation Petraeus had acquired for combining intellectual acumen and curiosity with practical effectiveness. A series of glowing media reports boosted his public profile and sparked some jealousy among the notoriously competitive senior ranks of the US military. Known to have been sceptical of the American involvement in Iraq from the beginning, famously asking 'how does this end?' during the invasion,

Petraeus represented a maverick minority strand of thinkers that had been largely marginalized within the American armed forces over the four years since 2003.[3] Within ten months of the Samarra bombing and the Leavenworth meeting, this minority would be determining US strategy in Iraq.

The writing of the manual, the sessions in Leavenworth, the debate sparked by successive drafts of the manual amounted to a huge and public self-criticism session for the American military. First, the flaws in the strategy and tactics implemented in Afghanistan in 2002 and 2003 were unpicked. The failure to secure borders, the raiding from big, heavily defended bases, the isolation from local people, the counterproductive emphasis on force protection, the cultural insensitivity, the chronic inability to understand local dynamics, the lack of sufficient troops to provide the security that could allow stability and economic development, the abuse and violence meted out to detainees were all discussed and analysed. The sessions were, as Petraeus had intended, lively and stimulating. The range of contributors, many from outside the US military, ensured a range of different inputs. One was David Kilcullen, an Australian former army officer with a doctorate in political anthropology, who matched experience from his country's deployment in East Timor in 1999 with that gained as a US state department consultant in 2006 in Afghanistan. Kilcullen fitted what had been happening in Iraq into a broader theory. When al-Qaeda activists established themselves in a lawless area and successfully provoked an outside intervention by local government forces or international actors, Kilcullen argued, local populations were radicalized and then fought alongside the extremists. These local warriors were not dedicated ideologically committed fighters, he said, but simply 'accidental guerrillas'. The right tactics and strategy could reverse the process by which they had come to take up arms.[4] Other contributors included British officers such as Brigadier Nigel Aylwin-Foster, who had served in Iraq himself and who, in a widely read article published in the Leavenworth College review, accused the US army of a lack of cultural knowledge and sensitivity that amounted to unwitting 'institutional racism'.[5] Aylwin-Foster also attacked American 'moral righteousness', 'damaging optimism' and 'focus on conventional warfare of a particularly swift and violent kind'. His article included statistics revealing that most American operations had been 'reactive to insurgent activity', i.e. effectively initiated by the enemy, and 'only 6 per cent had been aimed at securing a safe environment for the population'. This latter goal was at the heart of many contributors' thinking.[6] Lecturing from the British who, after all, had hardly been hugely successful in Basra, was resented by many American officers, but coming from the only ally who had significant numbers of troops deployed, the criticisms had a certain weight.[7]

Further input came from cultural anthropologists controversially hired by the Pentagon in a new initiative launched between mid 2005 and mid 2006. The doyenne among them was the flamboyant Montgomery McFate, who drew on close observation on the ground in Iraq – albeit under conditions that could hardly be described as academically ideal – to make a range of observations: that the frequent killings of civilians by US troops at roadblocks were in part due to the gestures indicating 'stop' and 'welcome' being reversed in American and Iraqi cultures; that coffee shops (forbidden to US troops on force protection grounds) were the natural conduit for information flow in Iraq, not broadcast media as assumed in the West; that confusion over the black flags Shia households traditionally flew from their homes caused needless casualties as Marines conditioned to think a white flag meant surrender assumed a black flag indicated the opposite. McFate did not pull her punches when it came to criticizing her nation's forces, attacking the 'ethnocentrism, biased assumptions, and mirror-imaging' she saw as endemic among American troops. 'Understanding one's enemy requires more than a satellite photo of an arms dump,' she wrote in one military journal. 'Rather, it requires an understanding of their interests, habits, intentions, beliefs, social organizations and political symbols – in other words, their culture.'[8] Eventually Field Manual 3-24, the result of the work at Leavenworth, mentioned 'culture' on fifty of its 282 pages.

For a technical military publication, Field Manual 3-24, was a work of extraordinary influence, discussed on television and in newspapers and bought in quantities normally reserved for airport thrillers. Its basic points were simple. Instead of prioritizing the finding and killing of insurgents, troops needed to make protecting local people from the militants the main focus of their efforts. Instead of trying to isolate Americans from local populations to both reduce casualties and to avoid provoking an 'allergic reaction' if foreign troops mixed with local people, soldiers needed to eat, sleep and, most importantly, walk among those they were now supposed to protect. The US military's overwhelming firepower needed to be used judiciously and with consideration of all the possible consequences. Often it was better not to open fire. If a single insurgent was killed and five of his brothers took up arms as a result, that was a net loss not a gain. Humiliating, injuring or killing civilians and damaging their property helped insurgents, whereas 'using force precisely and discriminately strengthens the rule of law that needs to be established'. The manual also reaffirmed the obligations imposed by Common Article 3 of the Geneva Conventions and called abuse of prisoners 'immoral, illegal, and unprofessional'.[9]

This latter injunction was not the only element that was politically controversial. A key theme, returned to again and again, was the importance of recognizing and respecting the cultural specificity of a given population. 'Cultural awareness is a force multiplier,' Petraeus had said in an article published in January 2006.[10] The manual itself went further, arguing that 'American ideas of what is "normal" or "rational" were not universal' but instead 'members of other societies often have different notions of rationality, appropriate behaviour, levels of religious devotion and norms concerning gender. Thus, what may appear abnormal or strange to an external observer may appear as self-evidently normal to a group member.' For this reason, the manual insisted, it was vitally important 'to avoid imposing' American ideas of the normal and the rational on other people. Culture, it said, was 'arbitrary, meaning that Soldiers and Marines should make no assumptions regarding what a society considers right and wrong, good and bad'.[11] This was not what most American conservatives – indeed most Americans – believed. It was certainly far from the thinking of the president, of many of his top officials or of the large number of evangelical Christians within the US armed forces.

Petraeus' manual was effectively recommending a culturally relativist approach which ran diametrically opposite to the 'moral clarity', the belief in American exceptionalism and the confidence in the universal application of American values that had hitherto been such a principal element of the Bush administration's post-9/11 security strategy.

Equally, the new approach ran counter to another key ideological component of the worldview of the White House. Back in 2002 the Bush administration had pledged 'to work to bring democracy, development, free markets and free trade to every corner of the world'.[12] In this approach, as British academic and Iraq expert Toby Dodge has noted, it was analytic categories derived from, or at the very least shared with, neoliberal economics that were dominant: the individual, the market, democracy and the threat of an overbearing state.[13] In Afghanistan and in Iraq, the Bush administration's emphasis on minimal levels of troops, 'a light footprint' and allowing local populations to 'stand up' owed as much to this as it did to fears of repeating the Soviets' mistakes or to General Abizaid's 'antibody theory'. But the counter-insurgency theories being elaborated by Petraeus and his team placed the state at the centre of any successful strategy. 'COIN [counter insurgency operations] ... involves the application of national power in the political, military, economic, social, information and infrastructure fields and disciplines,' the manual stated unequivocally on its second page.[14] The new manual drew heavily on the writing of David Galula, a French soldier who had used his experience as an officer in the Algerian war of 1954 to 1962 to write one of the fundamental texts of modern strategic thinking on counter-insurgency. In his work *Counter-insurgency Warfare: Theory and Practice*, which was repeatedly referenced in the new manual, Galula stated bluntly that the state, was 'the machine for the control of the population' and stressed that only 'four instruments of control count in a revolutionary war situation: the political structure, the administrative bureaucracy, the police, the armed forces'.[15] Again, the manual's emphasis the centrality of the state was in sharp contrast to cherished principles of the Bush administration and many of those who had voted for them.

Criticism from the right was however muted. On the left, several objections to the new doctrines rapidly surfaced. Some pointed out that this was not the first time armies at a loss to deal with a particular enemy had turned to 'culture' in a bid to find new arms or strategies and that doing so was no guarantee of success. There had been similar efforts during (or after) the Indian Mutiny or War of Independence in 1857, in the Pacific Theatre during the Second World War and in Vietnam.[16] Many detected the influence of a long tradition of Western 'Orientalism' in the text of the manual. Though it avoided some of the more classic prejudices, there was evidence, at least in the discussion of Iraq during the editing of the manual, of a typical European vision of 'the Arab', timeless and exotic, inscrutable or wily.[17] Some criticized the frequent citing of T. E. Lawrence, Lawrence of Arabia, the British soldier and romantic hero who had written nearly a century ago and whose best-known work, *The Seven Pillars of Wisdom*, was dismissed by some respected scholars as 'a fine piece of prose but almost worthless for studying the history or society of the Arab world'.[18] Others worried that the new doctrines were falsely reassuring, with the 'new and nicer' way of fighting they outlined considerably more compatible with the US's self-image as a source of universal good and universal values than the tactics previously employed and thus a useful way to convince an increasingly disillusioned American public to accept their soldiers continuing to kill large numbers of people in distant countries.[19] But the real problem was less academic. When the final draft of the manual was being prepared in June of 2006, there was little indication that anyone was seriously considering the wholesale practical application of what it recommended in Iraq or elsewhere in the near future.

## THE SURGE

Nearly 3,000 Iraqis were killed in December 2006, at least two-thirds in sectarian violence.[20] Jaffar, the Karada barber, remembered the last days of 2006 as 'the waiting room of Hell'. 'Everyday I heard of a relative dying. I never left my home,' he said.[21]

Lieutenant General Ray Odierno, returning to Iraq for the first time in over two years, was stunned by how badly the situation had deteriorated. 'Corpses were being found in trash heaps and along Baghdad's side streets by the day,' he recalled. Saddam Hussein, whose trial had been supposed to be a expiatory healing exercise for a brutalized country, had been handed over to Iraqi custody and was eventually hanged, days after Odierno's arrival in Baghdad, to the sound of triumphant shouts of 'Muqtadr, Muqtadr' from Shia officials at the execution. Images of this brutal and chaotic travesty of judicial process captured on a mobile phone were posted on the internet and widely circulated. Chaos apparently reigned.

An unusual soldier, Odierno's sheer physical size and billiard-ball bald scalp belied an acute intelligence. His first tour in Iraq as commander of the 4th Infantry Division had been tarnished by allegations of brutality by his troops – which he denied. However, it was Odierno too who had laid the basis for the capture of Saddam Hussein through charting the Iraqi tribal and kinship networks around the former dictator.[22] Given the unenviable task of breaking the apparently downward spiral in Iraq by his direct superior General George Casey, Odierno rapidly became convinced that the only way to do so was in fact to reverse the strategy of handing over to the incapable Iraqi security forces and instead to deploy further American troops to 'secure' the population.

Though Odierno's credentials were impeccable, his new thinking would have gone nowhere just a few months earlier. However, the November 2006 mid-term elections in America had seen, in the words of the president, a 'thumping' for the Republicans as the Democrats took both the Senate and the House of Representatives. Days after the polls, Bush had replaced Defense Secretary Donald Rumsfeld, who was stubbornly committed to the policy of drawing down troops from Iraq, with Robert Gates, a methodical and calm former career intelligence officer with a reputation for pragmatism. Rumsfeld had already told the president that he felt that 'fresh eyes' might be needed, and his departure completed an overhaul of senior Pentagon appointments that had already seen many of the most ideological members of the Bush administration sidelined.[23] Paul Wolfowitz, the deputy defense secretary and one of the keenest and most optimistic advocates of the original invasion of Iraq, had been moved sideways to the World Bank eighteen months earlier. Douglas Feith, the controversial under-secretary at the Pentagon blamed by many for circumventing normal procedures to 'stovepipe' raw and erroneous intelligence on Saddam's supposed weapons of mass destruction or links with al-Qaeda to senior decision-makers, had long since left the administration for academe. A new, colder and more realistic wind was blowing in Washington. Once the mid-term elections were over a franker debate within the White House and among Republicans about what was actually going on in Iraq became possible. The news from returning experts and fact-finding missions had been uniformly grim. A series of official internal reviews within the army, at least one well-known and respected former general and a range of Washington civilian defence experts were recommending similar changes to those sought by Odierno.

Rapidly, the new thinking in Washington began to crystallize around the general's demand for the despatch of up to 30,000 – or five brigades – of reinforcements who would move out into neighbourhoods in and around Baghdad, where 80 per cent of the violence in Iraq was taking place. Despite the vast effort involved, the peak troop strength would only be achieved for a short period between April and September 2007.[24] If only regular troops were deployed – and no one wanted to even contemplate a major mobilization of reservists – the surge was not sustainable beyond that date. Nor did anyone expect that the influx of new troops would resolve all Iraq's problems by itself. The aim was more modest. The new offensive would buy time to allow the Iraqi forces to finally become strong enough to start taking responsibility for their nation's security. It would also allow political actors a moment of relative calm in which they could make progress towards some kind of national reconciliation. The most important element was to break the vicious cycle that seemed to be leading Iraq towards greater and greater chaos and America towards a crushing strategic defeat. Critical to that was the implementation of all the new thinking that had gone into the new field manual produced by Petraeus at Leavenworth. American troops would live, sleep and fight among the people. They would try to bring security to communities, physically interposing themselves between the Shia death squads and Sunnis, between al-Qaeda and the Shias. Sensitive to the culture of both, they would go out of their way to do things 'the Iraqi way', however counterintuitive that might be for them. This would necessarily imply an initial spike in casualties, but, if the strategy worked, the number of dead and wounded would drop rapidly.

The National Security Council and Vice President Dick Cheney became rapidly convinced of the merits of the new plan, however militarily and politically risky it might be.[25] Bush too was persuaded that it needed to be tried and agreed to the proposals. There were to be no half-measures, no brigades dripped in over a period of months. American officials in Iraq had, through intercepted communications, learned that media reporting in the USA of the potential size and deployment of the new troops was already having a direct effect on the morale and strategic thinking of local insurgents and set about stoking the speculation among journalists further with selected leaks.[26] The final decision came fast. Odierno would get almost all the extra forces he had asked for. Petraeus would replace Casey as his immediate superior. It was, even many of his detractors admitted, a brave call for the president to make.[27]

In January 2007 Bush explained to the American nation that mistakes had been made in Iraq over previous years, that the situation there was 'unacceptable' and that a change of strategy was called for. The first new troops of what had been dubbed 'the Surge' started arriving within weeks. Even before they had arrived, US troops were moving out of their big bases and establishing combat outposts and 'joint security stations' with Iraqi forces in areas that were being contested by Shia militia and al-Qaeda-affiliated or other Sunni insurgent groups. Too few to cover a city of between 5 and 7 million inhabitants, they had been concentrated on the areas where sectarian violence had been worst.[28] A string of offensive operations were mounted against al-Qaeda and insurgent strongholds in Baghdad, in the vital villages and towns in the countryside around the capital and in cities to the north and south.[29] Petraeus arrived in Baghdad as commander of the war in Iraq and announced one of the new tactics he was planning to implement: walling off any vulnerable neighbourhoods with long rows of concrete blast walls.[30]

## THE SURGE WORKS

The 'Surge' was a success, at least in the sense that, by the end of 2007, after six months during which the new American troops had been deployed in and around Baghdad and had implemented the strategy developed by Petraeus and Odierno, violence in Iraq was falling. At Congressional hearings in September 2007 Petraeus was able to show slides of statistics showing a steep drop in attacks on American troops. Though casualty figures in the summer had spiked to the highest levels since the two battles for Falluja three years before, by the onset of winter fewer US soldiers were being killed than at any other time since the invasion of 2003. In May and June 2007, 227 had died; only 23 were killed in December. Civilian deaths too were much lower. From nearly 3,000 killed in December 2006, the total had dropped to under 1,000 twelve months later. Areas of Baghdad which had been almost devoid of life were now beginning to show signs of some economic activity.[31] There was even a trickle of refugees coming back from overseas. 'After spending more than a year in Syria, one day my father called me saying: "You can now return, and do not worry. Everything is fine now,"' said Mohammed Hussain, an office administrator from a mixed Baghdad middle-class neigbourhood. 'I reached [home] at 6 a.m.'[32] All things were relative, however, and the more triumphant commentaries on the Surge of 2007 failed to mention that it had succeeded only in reducing violence to the levels of 2005.[33] Petraeus himself stuck to describing progress as 'fragile' or 'tenuous'. 'Nobody is saying anything about turning a corner, seeing lights at the end of tunnels, any of those phrases,' he told reporters at the end of the year. 'There's nobody in uniform who is doing victory dances in the end zone.'[34]

What had happened? How had the Surge worked? Most recent accounts often give the overall impression of a battered American army snatching victory from the jaws of defeat with an audacious and brave last-minute strategic gamble. One reason for the successes seen over 2007 was undoubtedly the courage and competence of American soldiers, who fought long and hard in difficult conditions on the ground in gritty Baghdad neighbourhoods like al-Doura, Khazamiyah, Sadr City and elsewhere. But the Americans were only part of the broader picture. In mid 2006, US planners had distinguished nine 'different fights' in the country, ranging from skirmishes prompted by Kurdish expansionism in the north to 'Shia on Shia' violence provoked by political manoeuvring between increasingly fragmented Islamist groups in the south.[35] By 2007, the situation was even more complicated. One element stood out, however: only a minority of these 'different fights' actually directly involved Westerners. What determined the success or failure of the Surge was the particular conjunction of these various ongoing sub-conflicts at a given time. If the Surge had been tried six months earlier, it probably would not have worked. Four main factors, all largely beyond the control of even Petraeus and President Bush, meant that it did.

The first and most obvious factor was that the battle for the Iraqi capital was largely over by the time Odierno had arrived at the end of 2006 and begun to formulate his new strategy. The apparent climax of the sectarian violence in the late spring of 2007 was in fact a final spasm in a process of atrocious killing which had been going on for at least eighteen months. 'I left [in December 2006] after I passed a different dead body at the same crossroads near my house five days in a row,' Bashir al-Bassm, a Sunni taxi driver, told the author. 'The choice was either flee or die.'[36] Various dynamics had been at work, driving violence to progressively higher and higher levels. There had been the inexorable logic of revenge and sectarian vendetta set in motion deliberately by al-Zarqawi and continued by his followers after their leader's death.

Militants linked to al-Zarqawi's networks killed dozens, on occasion hundreds, of Shia, knowing that the Shia gangs would then retaliate with their own wave of shootings and assassinations of Sunnis. Sunni communities would then form their own defence groups or rally behind the Islamic militants responsible for the original attacks as the only viable way of protecting themselves. These latter would then set out on a new killing spree, thus triggering a new cycle of violence. Repeated across Baghdad, the civil war had been inexorably ratcheted up another notch by each round of murders all through 2006. Fear became the militias' greatest asset, driving even secular Iraqis to support or even join them. A related dynamic accelerating and intensifying the violence had nothing to do with the provocations of al-Zarqawi or his networks. From the middle of 2006, Shia politicians and militia leaders, the two often being coterminous, had set about methodically emptying Baghdad of Sunnis. Working from block to block in carefully picked neighbourhoods, death squads focused first on community leaders, clerics, merchants and businessmen but went on to kill indiscriminately, continuing the murderous violence until the refugees started flowing and the districts emptied. Gruesome methods – some, such as drilling or burning, inspired by those being employed out in Anbar province – were used to increase the level of terror and speed the exodus. [37] The incentive for those initiating the violence was partly political, partly financial. There was the power that accrued to the leaders of the gangs. And then there were the assets once belonging to the Sunnis such as houses and shops, that militia members, usually the same young working-class men who had fought in Najaf, Karbala and in the slums of Sadr City in 2004, were able to seize.[38] A glance at a map of Baghdad in the spring of 2007 showed how, though the Sunnis had successfully managed to take over the odd neighbourhood that had previously been mixed, it was the Shia who had effectively won the battle for the city.[39] Whole swathes of what had been Sunni or mixed communities had been purged. Neighbourhoods like Amel, once home to around 20,000 Sunni families with close links to the Ba'athist regime, were now predominantly Shia. By the time the main American reinforcements began to flow in, most of the communal fighting in Baghdad was over.

The second major factor behind the success of the Surge was, paradoxically, the success of the Shia militias over the period immediately before the new strategy had been implemented. Al-Sadr, the young cleric dismissed as a 'punk' back in 2003, had through adept tactical man-oeuvring and populist appeal become a major player in the Iraqi political scene. He had played a careful game since being militarily and politic-ally beaten in the fighting of 2004, skilfully juggling participation in democratic politics with harder-nosed demagoguery and real and threat-ened violence. His representatives had done well in successive elections, partly due to their organization and partly their continuing appeal in poor urban Shia neighbourhoods. Their influence on central govern-ment was enhanced by the fact that they, in contrast to many legislators, did not spend much of their time outside Iraq.[40] In Basra, al-Sadr had been able to exploit continuing British ineptitude and lack of resources to secure a hold over much of the city.[41]

Yet success and consequent expansion had brought grave structural problems. Since mid 2006 discipline in al-Sadr's movement had begun to break down. By the summer of 2007 half a dozen different militias were operating as part of his al-Mahdi Army as well as scores of splinter groups.[42] Their leaders often fought amongst themselves and many appeared more interested in money or local power than piety. Control of petrol distribution networks generated very significant sums, and racketeering became increasingly common, with Shia communities suf-fering as much as anyone else. Militia men were taking more than $10,000 per day from the four largest petrol stations in Sadr City alone as well as extorting substantial sums from private minibus services, electricity sub-stations, food and clothing markets, ice factories. Many even collected rent from squatters in houses whose Sunni owners had fled.[43] Some groups aligned themselves closely with Iran – receiving large amounts of cash and weaponry (and some training) and increas-ingly rejecting al-Sadr's leadership. The evidence for Iranian involvement in payments for attacks on coalition forces was irrefutable, though exactly which element of the sprawling and fragmented Iranian security estab-lishment was responsible remained unclear.[44] This naturally damaged the nationalist credentials that had always been important to the Sadrist movement. Also, the social and economic activism that had been an equal part of al-Sadr's appeal – the street sweeping, the clinics, the dis-tribution of food or water – became increasingly less apparent as the killing continued. With the Americans and the blast walls now between them and their Sunni enemies and with limited room for further expan-sion after the victories of the previous months, the strengths of the al-Mahdi Army became weaknesses, and the movement found itself overextended both geographically and financially. As their popularity plunged, discipline began to break down further, and, caught in a destructive logic familiar to many other such groups in Iraq and elsewhere, al-Sadr's fighters found themselves increasingly forced to coerce the local communities which had once voluntarily offered their support.[45] 'At the beginning, coming from a Shia family, I respected the al-Mahdi Army, because they stood up to protect us,' said Amal Kamel, a twenty-year-old economy and administration student at Baghdad University. 'But then I discovered they were savages and barbarians. They killed women for not wearing the veil or just for a simple reason such as their wearing make-up. They killed Sunnis like the three sons of my neighbours [in the predominantly Shia al-Hurriya neighbourhood] and forced them to flee.' For Kamel, al-Sadr and his followers had plunged Baghdad into 'a nightmare coloured by the blood of Iraqis'.[46]

There was more urgent pressure on the leadership of the movement too. Early in 2007 a change in the local political dynamics had diminished top-level government support for al-Sadr. This had allowed Petraeus to add the upper tier of al-Mahdi Army leaders to the list of Sunni and al-Qaeda insurgents that the increasingly numerous American (and some British) special forces were hunting.[47] Through the late spring and summer, hundreds of senior al-Mahdi Army militia leaders were thus killed or captured, both in Baghdad and increasingly in small rural villages where they sought safety. This had two main consequences. One was political: al-Sadr and his key remaining lieutenants were all eminently rational tacticians who had little desire for death or detention, and, with the assassination campaign dramatically increasing and with it the potential personal cost of continuing to use violence against other Iraqis or against coalition forces, alternative strategies became more attractive to them. The second was primarily organizational, though it had major political consequences. As the more senior al-Mahdi Army leaders were killed or arrested, they were replaced by younger, inexperienced militants who were less bothered about retaining popular legitimacy or the 'name' of the movement and whose indiscriminate violence exacerbated even further the problem of retaining popular support.[48] This too worried the leadership of the movement. So when al-Sadr finally declared a unilateral six-month ceasefire in August 2007, it was to save the lives of his close associates, to bolster the diminishing popular support and, last but not least, to restore some discipline and order among the rank and file by flushing out those who no longer recognized his authority. His decision had an important and immediate effect. In July, 73 per cent of American fatalities and injuries in Baghdad in July had been caused by Shiite fighters. Odierno later estimated that the truce brought an immediate drop of 20 per cent in the level of attacks on US troops in and around the city.[49] Sadr himself then left for Iran to further his religious education.

The Shia militias were not, of course, the only Iraqi force to have alienated their own erstwhile supporters. The third major factor behind the success of the Surge was the continuing success of the Sunni Awakening or *Sahwa* that had flowed into the capital from Anbar down the same tribal, kinship and clerical channels as the nascent insurgency had flowed in the other direction four years previously. It was co-opted by Petraeus, who enrolled the armed gangs of Sunnis keen on taking on their former allies among the al-Qaeda-affiliated networks into 'Concerned Local Citizens' groups'. These went by various names including the 'Sons of Iraq' in Anbar or the 'Amiriyah Freedom Fighters' in the eponymous Baghdad neighbourhood and were very effective. By the end of the year, even the tough Sunni neighbourhood of al-Doura was back under government authority. It was the presence of these *Sahwa* fighters that had convinced Mohammed Hussain, the office administrator who had returned from self-imposed exile in Damascus, that he could stay in Baghdad. Very often the splits within the Sunni community ran along tribal lines, especially in the vital belts of mixed agricultural land and urban settlements around Baghdad. When the Zobai tribe, who provided many of the insurgents in the resilient and effective '1920 Revolution Brigades', turned against al-Qaeda affiliated networks, largely from other rival tribes, the Americans needed simply to stand back and supply the Zobai with what they needed to eliminate their rivals. Eventually there were 100,000 or more of these Awakening auxiliaries receiving $300 a month from the American taxpayer and effectively securing their neighbourhoods, with US army and Iraqi security forces' help, against the religious militants.[50]

A fourth element in the success of the Surge was the actions of regional powers. The growing chaos in Iraq, the risk of domestic militant 'blowback' and international pressure forced the Syrians to at least restrict the flow of militant volunteers and to close down many of the logistic networks that provided support to the insurgents. The actions of Damascus were self-serving, unpredictable and inconsistent but were, in some cases anyway, helpful nonetheless. As noted above, Jordanian intelligence was increasingly effective and motivated following the Amman attacks. The Saudi Arabians had at last recognized that hundreds of their citizens travelling to fight in Iraq was probably not a particularly positive development for their own domestic security, given that most then returned to homes in Jeddah, Medina, Riyadh or wherever, and finally had taken steps to limit their travel.[51] Most significantly, support from Iran to various elements among the Shia militias and to their political masters remained carefully calibrated, partly as a result of the complex manoeuvres within the Iranian regime and partly as a result of the general perception that Iran's interests would not be best served by Iraq collapsing into total chaos. No groups within Iraq thus received the kind of high-power weaponry provided by Tehran to the Lebanese Hezbollah, for example. It is also possible that Iran, after having infiltrated various al-Mahdi Army offshoots and splinter groups, had encouraged al-Sadr's decision to call a ceasefire.

What Petraeus and Odierno were able to do with admirable acumen, imagination and courage was to exploit the strategic opportunities these trends represented. There had been the well-publicized decision to enrol the Sunni *Sahwa* forces. There were the 'capture or kill' operations launched against senior al-Mahdi figures. Then there was the vast secret effort against the remaining Sunni insurgents, al-Qaeda in Iraq and the other radical Islamic groups. By mid 2007, Joint Special Operations Command under the experienced and focused Lieutenant General Stanley McChrystal comprised more than 5,000 special forces troops with enormous logistic and technical support. Key innovations over the previous years were paying fruit. Most Iraqis now had mobile phones and many of the leads that were fed to the special forces teams on the ground came from new network analysis, in part developed to track senior al-Qaeda figures in Pakistan, of call patterns. The American National Security Agency had access to the details – if not the content – of every call made in the country.[52] Combined with innovative ways of patching together different streams of intelligence, of using local partners and of targeting the middle ranks of an organization rather than just 'HVTs' (high value targets), the pressure on the insurgents was immense. The famously ascetic McChrystal, who was said to eat a single meal a day, pushed his forces to maintain a relentless 'operational tempo'. Joint

Special Ops Command had estimated that by the end of 2006 they had killed 2,000 members of the Sunni jihadist groups as well as detaining many more over the previous two years.[53] The count was higher in 2007.

Major decisions such as co-opting the Awakening Councils in and around Baghdad or targeting the al-Mahdi Army were clearly significant but so too were small changes. On the advice of David Kilcullen, Petraeus had his troops patrol on foot. Worried about leaving the safety of their 'up-armoured' Humvees, the troops were told to stay in pairs, separated by sufficient distances to avoid offering too great a single target. After early teething problems, the system worked well, allowing a much greater contact with local people and giving soldiers a much deeper understanding of their immediate 'combat environment'. Other changes saw more culturally appropriate procedures for difficult and sensitive tasks such as paying compensation for damage or a civilian death for which US troops were responsible. Instead of handing cash directly to bereaved relatives, American officers began using tribal leaders as intermediaries, for example.[54] The broad approach of Petraeus and Odierno meant varied reforms in discrete areas had a powerful cumulative effect. The prisons were one example. Despite the Abu Ghraib scandal, the detention system had remained a problem throughout 2005 and 2006. Petraeus appointed a Marine reservist, General Douglas Stone, to overhaul how insurgents were arrested, held, interrogated and released.

Stone's starting point was that prisons allowed extremists immediate access to, and control over, large captive populations and thus opportunities for recruitment and radicalization. The same strategies that were applied in the suburbs of Baghdad thus needed to be applied in Abu Ghraib, Camp Bucca and in the other detention facilities that the US military ran. A counter-insurgency campaign was needed within the prisons themselves, Stone decided.[55]

One of Stone's first acts was to establish exactly who the 24,000 detainees in the American military prison system in Iraq actually were. Comprehensive interviews found that prisoners had an average age of twenty-nine, making them exactly as old as British-based violent extremists were and providing further evidence that it was not simply impressionable teenagers who were a problem. Less than 1 per cent were 'third country nationals' from outside Iraq, not even a tenth could be considered 'al-Qaeda-affiliated', even fewer were from the al-Mahdi Army, more than two-thirds were illiterate and 78 per cent claimed that their involvement with violence against the government or American or other foreign troops had been motivated by the prospect of financial gain. The latter statistic was probably vastly exaggerated by detainees giving interviewers the answer that they felt was most acceptable to their questioners, but in general the men in the prison camps largely seemed to be Kilcullen's 'accidental guerrillas'. The factors that had led them into violence, said Stone, were 'a sense of humiliation or lack of respect, the view their families might have of them, a sense of worthlessness, sexual frustration as well as the guidance offered by community, tribal and religious leaders'. Radical Islamic ideologies, as Pan-Arabism and revolutionary Socialism once had done, offered a sense of empowerment, a legitimacy, fellowship, respect, cash employment, upward social mobility, support for families and, in some cases, 'the promise of the ultimate fulfilment of martyrdom', he explained.[56] Stone's solution was a comprehensive programme involving the identification and segregation of extremists within prisons, the creation of teams of psychiatrists and psychologists to work with inmates as well as visiting clerics who organized religious discussion sessions in which detainees would be instructed in the basics of local more moderate and tolerant traditional strands of Islam. The latter started not with the relatively complex discussions about when jihad might or might not be justified but with the basics of prayer, ablutions and the fundamental tenets of belief. Visits from the International Confederation of the Red Cross were welcomed, a system of basic literacy classes introduced, family visits allowed, brick factories set up in which inmates could work to earn small amounts of money. On release, Iraqi judges sought pledges of good behaviour from detainees. In the first eight months of the programme, from June 2007 to February 2008, 7,000 men were released, of whom only five returned to jail. The only problematic prisoners were hardcore committed al-Qaeda-affiliated militants who, Stone said, feared just two things: that their families might be harassed or that they might be transferred to an Iraqi-run prison. This apparently small exception was later to be significant.

By the end of 2007, however, it was clear that some vague – and very relative – stability had thus been – at least temporarily – achieved in Iraq.[57] It might have been fragile, as General Petraeus continued to insist, but it was undeniable. Through winter, the Surge was rolled out through the belt around Baghdad and even finally into restive and violent Diyala province to the north-east of the capital, where al-Zarqawi had once sought refuge and where now hundreds of local Sunnis joined the militias paid for by the Americans or the police. Support for the insurgents bled away rapidly. 'There were almost 600 fighters in our sector before the tribes changed course ... Many of our fighters quit and some of them joined the deserters ... As a result of that the number of fighters dropped down to twenty or less,' one leader of a largely Iraqi hardline 'al-Qaeda-ist' group near Balad, north of Baghdad, complained in late 2007.[58] In Baghdad and elsewhere several thousand Shia too had signed up to Awakening-type militia by the end of 2007, partly for the cash, partly to fight the al-Mahdi Army.

The gravest problem, of course, remained central government, which was as corrupt, dysfunctional and deeply partisan as it had ever been. The whole aim of the Surge had been to buy time for the Iraqi security forces to develop – which was slowly happening – and also for Iraqi politicians to take steps towards a national reconciliation of sorts – of which there appeared to be little prospect. The political situation had benefited from the replacement as ambassador of the flamboyant Zalmay Khalilzad, an American-Afghan of Sunni ancestry of whom Iraqi Shia leaders were suspicious, by veteran diplomat Ryan Croker, who was able to build a stronger relationship with key political players and worked better with the US military than his predecessor. But Nouri al-Maliki, the fifty-seven-year-old senior figure in the Shia Islamist Dawa organization, who had become prime minister in May 2006, and the other Shia leaders who dominated the government seemed little inclined to make any concessions to the defeated Sunni minority. It was with only great difficulty that they could be persuaded to agree to 35,000 of those on the American payroll in the Sunni militias joining the new Iraqi security forces. Allying with the Kurds, they could also block any moves towards a genuinely equitable distribution of national resources, particularly the vast cash flows that oil production, which began rising again towards the end of 2007, was generating.

In the end no one seemed inclined to push the issue of reconciliation too far. The days of grand ideological projects in Iraq seemed well over, and few regretted their passing. It had tacitly been recognized at the highest levels in Washington that the lofty goals of 2003 were not just impossible to achieve but that continuing to strive towards them would be profoundly counterproductive. If the new counter-insurgency field manual referred repeatedly to the importance of respecting cultural difference at a tactical level, there needed clearly to be a parallel doctrine at a strategic level too. In January 2008, the de-Ba'athification laws passed nearly five years previously over the fateful summer of 2003 were reversed. When Petraeus returned before Congress in April 2008 to brief America's political representatives once again on the situation in Iraq, he was questioned on the long-term aims of the US project in Iraq by a forty-seven-year-old Democrat Senator representing Illinois. 'If the definition of success is . . . no traces of al-Qaeda, no possibility of reconstitution [of al-Qaeda], a highly effective Iraqi government, a democratic multiethnic, multi-sectarian, functioning democracy, no Iranian influence, at least not the kind that we don't like, then that portends the possibility of us staying for twenty or thirty years,' Barack Obama said. If, on the contrary, the aim was a 'messy, sloppy status quo but there's not, you know, huge outbreaks of violence, there's still corruption, but the country's struggling along, but it's not a threat to its neighbours and it's not an al-Qaeda base, that seems to me an achievable goal within a measurable time frame'.[59] Such aims had broad bipartisan support, despite being considerably more modest than those announced with such bombast in 2003 and repeatedly reaffirmed since. That they could still be considered relatively ambitious was an indication of how badly wrong Operation Iraqi Freedom had gone.

## THE SURGE AND THE 9/11 WARS

What had the Surge shown in the context of the 9/11 Wars?

The year 2007 in Iraq had shown the supremacy of local specificity. First it had been the global ideology proposed by the Americans and their allies that had been rejected. Not in its entirety, certainly, but in sufficient degree for it to become necessary for the original package of liberal democracy and free-market economics to have to be significantly altered for it to overcome the fundamental stain of being 'foreign' and get any purchase whatsoever. 'The Americans failed in Iraq because they did not understand how to treat Iraqis, and Iraqis became their enemies,' was the simple explanation of Thuryia Ismael, a sixty-year-old housewife in

Baghdad's Amariya neighbourhood. 'The political process in Iraq was built on wrong policies, and that effected everything: economy, health, education and security.'[60] Happily, the globalized ideology of al-Qaeda, as stripped of local context as anything Washington had ever tried to impose, had also been rejected. The fact that the aims, values and methods of al-Zarqawi and his like were ostensibly based on a version or reading of 'Islam' was not enough to compensate for the multitude of ways in which they failed to represent the aims, cultures, needs, aspirations, self-image and desires of the communities whose support – or at least fearful acquiescence – they wanted. The international militants or internationally affiliated networks in Iraq had made massive efforts to resolve the strategic problem their international dimension gave them. Al-Qaeda in Iraq had been dissolved and its various networks incorporated into the broader and more neutrally named Majlis Shura al-Mujahideen (Mujahideen Consultative Council) in the aftermath of the hotel bombings in Jordan. In October 2006, the formation of 'the Islamic State of Iraq' (ISI) was announced. Communiqués from its leadership stressed that the organization 'contained only 200 foreign fighters'. A cabinet was constituted with ministers for education and agriculture and statements disseminated on the internet called for volunteers to fight the 'Persians', i.e. Iranians and their Iraqi Shia proxies. But it was all to no avail. By the summer of 2007, the gap between even the 'al-Qaeda-ist' militants and the Sunni tribes was greater than ever and the divisions between the various elements of the insurgency – the ISI, the Islamic Army of Iraq, Hamas-Iraq, the 1920 Brigades, the Mujahideen Reform Front – were deeper than they had ever been.[61] Successive communities in Iraq in 2006 and 2007 had made their choices. Sunnis in Haditha or al-Doura, Shias in Nasariyah or Amarah had all turned away from global ideologies, whether they arrived on the back of an American tank, were spouted by a neighbourhood preacher or were imported by a foreign petty criminal turned militant leader like al-Zarqawi.

A second lesson, reinforcing that of earlier episodes in the 9/11 Wars, was thus that, in addition to being largely local, identities are dynamic. How Sunni populations in Anbar saw themselves and their duties as men, Iraqis, al-Dulaimi or Zobai, Arabs or Muslims differed between 2003 and 2007. It changed even over the year of the Surge. What had been acceptable to local populations once was no longer acceptable a short time later. One key question posed by the events of 2007 in Iraq was what would fill the gap left by the rejection by millions of people of both the Western universalizing package of liberal democracy and market capitalism and, at least in the short term, radical Islamic ideologies? What system would appear to be sufficiently authentic to local communities to bring a measure of stability? What set of ideas, norms and worldviews, in short what 'culture', would they generate themselves? The answers would undoubtedly have a major influence on the coming years of the conflict.

If anything was clear from the events of 2007 it was that any solution to Iraq's problems – and to those posed by the 9/11 Wars more generally – was going to evolve at a grass-roots level and work its way up rather than being imposed from above. Developments over the period in Iraq had reinforced again the degree to which events in the conflict were driven by what was happening on the ground. The thinking that led to the Surge had its origins with colonels out in Iraq's Anbar or Nimrud or Salahuddin provinces and had flowed back up the chain of command. The Surge had succeeded because of what had been going on in Sadr City and Ramadi well before even the decision to send extra troops had been taken in Washington. By the end of 2007, bin Laden and other members of the al-Qaeda senior leadership appeared as limited in their ability to project authority and power in Iraq as any Western general or political leader. Bin Laden had been sufficiently concerned by the situation there to dispatch a key aide, Abdul Hadi al-Iraqi, the associate who had steered the young Briton Omar Khyam and thus the other Crevice plotters towards targets in the UK, to try and bring some semblance of order. But al-Iraqi was arrested crossing from Iran into the north of Iraq not far from his native city of Mosul and disappeared into the CIA's prison system.[62] His capture underlined the obstacles bin Laden and the al-Qaeda hardcore were now facing. One consequence of al-Iraqi's detention was that, instead of a local man taking over the al-Qaeda operation in 'the land of the two rivers', the leader of those nominally affiliated with bin Laden's organization remained a foreigner of unclear origin, Abu Hamza al-Mohajir. Grotesque attacks by the militants continued but dropped from 300 bombings and more than 1,500 deaths in 2007 to 28 incidents and 125 civilian deaths reported in the first six months of 2008.[63] The flow of recruits on their way to Iraq began to slow considerably too, dropping, according to American officials, from around 120 to between 40 and 50 each month.[64]

The days when Amman, Damascus or Kuwaiti border villages were full of foreign volunteers seeking jihad were long gone.[65]

## THE OTHER SURGE

In the summer of 2007 Saudi authorities had opened a new facility just outside the small village of al-Thamama, a half-hour drive down an immaculate asphalt road across scrubby sand and rock desert outside Riyadh. Few of the locals knew what went on behind the iron gates of the small and heavily guarded complex of low modern buildings, but around the world there were many who were closely observing developments there.

For al-Thamama was a pioneering centre for deradicalization. Staffed by psychologists, sociologists and clerics who referred to their charges as 'students', its primary aim was to avoid problems of recidivism when Saudi veterans of the fighting in Iraq left prison. In his sumptuous marbled office, which two senior American security officials had just left, Prince Mohammed bin Nayef bin Abdul Aziz al-Saud, the deputy interior minister responsible for counter-terrorism, explained that the problems of social reinsertion of returning militants from Afghanistan in 2002 had been one of primary reasons for recruitment to extremist organizations responsible for the blasts and killings across Saudi Arabia between 2003 and 2005. The fear was that the thousands of young Saudis who had either fought in Iraq or tried to reach Iraq before being detained would follow a similar course, he said.[66] The details of how the 'deradicalization' would be carried out had been finalized by a team of highly qualified Ministry of the Interior social scientists. They relied on weeks of religious instruction and group discussions to convince the 'students' that the religious reasoning which had justified their decision to travel to Iraq had been erroneous. Any 'personal issues' which might also have been responsible were tackled with psychological counselling, team sport and even art therapy. Otayan al-Turki, a Swansea-educated psychologist working at the centre, was struck by how many of the prisoners had very poor reasoning capacity and poor communication skills. 'Most are young, many come from large families,' he said. 'Many come from a non-Islamic background. Some have led sinful lives and were looking for a shortcut to paradise.' The art therapy was aimed at stopping the young men 'reacting in such an immediate way to images they see on the television or internet by giving them different visual languages', he said.[67] To ensure that all those released remained 'well integrated into the mainstream' the government provided jobs, money, cars, even wives on occasion. 'To deradicalize them we need to gain their trust and we need to help them restart their lives,' said Dr Abdulrahman al-Hadlaq, a Ministry of the Interior criminologist working on the programme. 'This is not a reward. It is a necessary policy of containment.' The programme had so far proved to be extremely successful, he claimed, pointing out that the centre was yet to see one of their former charges relapse into violence or militant activism.[68]

Among the young men in the centre in the spring of 2008 was Hizam al-Ghatani, the thin, bespectacled former shopkeeper who had fought alongside the insurgents around Falluja in late 2004. Though motivated to keep fighting by scenes of carnage he had witnessed, al-Ghatani, who had originally only wanted to be a medic not a fighter, had been deeply disappointed by the growing internecine violence among the tribes and militants of Anbar and had returned to his home in Saudi Arabia in the spring of 2005, naively imagining that he would be received as a hero. Arrested immediately, al-Ghatani had been in prison since. Now on the brink of completing his time in detention, the former shopkeeper insisted he had been reformed. 'I am a very emotional man and I did not have a good understanding of Islam,' he said. 'Now I realize the wrong I did to my country and my family.'[69] Mohammed al-Fawzan, another volunteer who had tried to reach Iraq through Syria but had eventually been arrested, had recently returned to his family home in the middle-class al-Shifa neighbourhood in west Riyadh after serving his prison sentence. He was now back in his old job in the Ministry of Transport. He had also been given a car and had been found a wife – with the dowry paid by the government. 'I know now that I did not understand Islam and jihad,' he told the author. 'Now I still care about what happens in the world, but I understand that political things are the responsibility of the government, and I should not get involved. I am a soldier of the government. I should obey their orders and those of their representatives, even the traffic police.'[70]

The Saudi programme, which had started in mid 2007, was part of a wide range of similar strategies in countries as diverse as Indonesia, Egypt and Yemen.[71] General Stone's programmes with Iraqi detainees had in part been based on what the Saudis were beginning to do with their own imprisoned militants.[72] Though few such initiatives were on the scale or had the resources of the multi-million-dollar effort showcased at the al-Thamama centre, all were part of a range of new approaches by governments and intelligence agencies to extremist violence that were beginning to show results by around 2007 and 2008. No one was claiming they were a panacea to the problem of extremist violence – while committed to the reintegration of some, Saudi authorities were also building a series of purpose-built prisons with capacity for 6,400 militants who they believed too dangerous to release under any circumstances – but such strategies were nonetheless evidence that governments were willing to try new approaches and security services were looking at the problem in new ways. Nothing demonstrated this more than a secret conference of intelligence services including the British MI6, French DST and DGSE, German BKA, the Australians, the major American 'three-letter' agencies, the Saudis, Algerian and Egyptian *mukhabarat* and even the Pakistani ISI. They met in March 2008 in a Middle Eastern capital to spend three days discussing radicalization and to compare the research programmes many of them had launched to understand the phenomenon of Islamic militancy following the intensification of the 9/11 Wars between 2003 and 2005. One after another senior officers stood to give presentations in which, instead of talking about 'al-Qaeda', they focused on the process by which individuals became extremists. The British discussed the relationship between employment and educational level – overqualified people doing menial jobs was one risk factor – and spoke of 'vulnerable institutions' such as prisons or schools. The French emphasized second-generation identity crises. The Egyptians blamed the internet. The Australians underlined how internal competition for credibility and kudos within radical groups led to 'serial splitting' with more and more extreme sub-groups being formed as the process of radicalization advanced. The Saudis produced comprehensive research on those responsible for the wave of violence that the kingdom had suffered earlier in the decade showing how as time had passed the profile of militants had evolved with a clear decline in educational level and political and religious awareness and an increase in levels of previous involvement in violent crime. Early militants read commentaries on the Koran or histories of historical Islamic figures while later activists read thrillers if they read anything at all. The conference ended with a banquet and a show of local traditional dancing which saw the DGSE's *chef de délégation*, a colonel from the ISI and a long-haired German sociologist link arms amid sword-waving beturbanned locals, all watched by a wry, cigar-smoking senior FBI official.

Counter-terrorism was thus rapidly evolving too, undergoing its own version to the US military's 'cultural turn'. A broader 'surge' was underway, with extra manpower and resources being used in better, more effective, more intelligent ways in the fight against radical militancy. In 2002, only 2 per cent of British security agencies' budget had been devoted to prevention.[73] By 2007, MI5, the British domestic security service, flush with new funds released following the 7/7 bombings, had vastly expanded in all areas, but particularly in those dealing with countering processes of radicalization. From being principally focused on Irish terrorism, the organizsation had successfully reorientated itself to concentrate on an entirely new target and sections of British society and parts of the country that had previously been virtually unknown. Its understanding of the nature of the new threat had evolved rapidly too. Officials spoke of the 'paradigm shift' of moving from looking at a foreign-based to a 'homegrown' threat. The service's formal behavioural science unit had been enlarged too, giving the psychologists and social scientists who staffed it a more prominent role in planning of strategy and even of operations. MI5's analysts told the author in the summer of 2007 that activism in the UK was 'nothing to do with Islam' and 'everything to do with social movements . . . group think and social dynamics', which, whether true or not, at the very least marked a huge change from previous thinking.[74] As American soldiers had done in a rather different context in Iraq, MI5 also moved closer to the populations they viewed as critical, establishing regional offices across the UK, where intelligence operatives worked closely with local security forces – in this case, of course, the British police service, which is divided into local constabularies – who had the detailed low-level knowledge lacking at a national level.[75] Some old habits continued. Over previous years MI5 officers from the section responsible for running international terrorism-related 'agents' had systematically failed to intervene to prevent individuals of interest to them being tortured by local security services in Pakistan, Egypt and elsewhere and had been avid consumers of the 'product' of such 'robust' interrogations. The new approach complemented earlier strategies rather than supplanted them entirely.[76]

And though serious problems remained with the British government's new counter-radicalization strategy, known as 'PREVENT' and run by the Ministry of Local Government and Communities rather than the Home Office, it also signalled a new approach, one marrying 'hard' counter-terrorism with 'softer' counter-radicalization policies. One criticism was that PREVENT identified Muslims as a 'suspect community'. There were problems with both the generalized suspicion and the idea that Muslims constituted one community. Officials countered by pointing out that their target was not those actively involved in terrorism but 'the much larger group of people who feel a degree of negativity, if not hostility, towards the state, the country, the community, and who are, as it were, the pool in which terrorists will swim'.[77] One positive development was a new understanding of nuances of who actually ran the organizations that were supposed to be official representatives of the British Muslim community and had hitherto been treated as privileged interlocutors of the government. So, for example, the government moved steadily to find alternatives to the Muslim Council of Britain (MCB), a group which claimed to represent half the country's Muslims but whose leaders' views were often hardline and highly politicized.[78] The voices of the large numbers of Muslims in the UK who followed the more personal, mystic Sufi strands of practice or simply were not particularly interested in politics had barely been heard.[79] As the British government moved to distance itself from the MCB, new voices began to emerge from within the British Muslim population.[80] Again, the picture was mixed as any group receiving funds under the PREVENT intitiative risked being seen as tainted by their association with the government – the local version of the occupier's paradox that the Americans and their allies had faced in Iraq – but the series of former members of radical groups prepared to denounce their former associates were nonetheless useful in providing a 'counter-narrative' to the hitherto largely unchallenged language of global pan-Islamic solidarity, anti-Semitism, anti-Zionism and anti-Americanism.[81] The government's strategy for countering extremism consistently underestimated the role British foreign policy played in reinforcing the 'single narrative' propagated by extremists but, by 2007, moderate clerics who had often waged a lonely and misunderstood struggle against extremism – such as Musa Abu Bakr Admani, the Muslim chaplain of London Metropolitan University – began to feel more confident. 'When Muslim communities feel dislocated and uncertain, they have always gravitated towards utopian international ideas of Islam,' Admani, who had personally known several of those involved in the 2006 'airlines plot', told the author over tea and pasta in a café on north London's Holloway Road.[82] 'There is still a bumpy ride ahead, but values such as freedom, equality, human dignity and fairness, the well-embedded core of Britishness, are values which a lot of young Muslims identify with. They are Islamic as well as British values. Yes, we need to address the . . . hatred of the West; yes, we need to inculcate basic Islamic values such as compassion and respect. But people have woken up, and the debate on how to move forward has started.'

Admani's impressions appeared to be confirmed by events more broadly. Young British-born men continued to become involved in radical violence, and foreign militants continued to operate on UK soil, but general levels of radicalization remained apparently stable.[83] This was bad news in that a threat clearly remained – six plots were foiled in the two years following the 7/7 bombings, and the summer of 2007 saw a small group of highly educated young British Muslim doctors attempt a double bombing of a nightclub in London before two of them drove a vehicle loaded with petrol and gas canisters into the front of Glasgow airport – but it was good news in that at least things were not getting worse. London Muslims appeared as likely as the general public to condemn terrorist attacks on civilians and more likely than the population at large to find no moral justification for using violence in a 'noble cause'.[84] While 48 per cent thought it wrong that the security services should infiltrate Muslim groups, the same number thought it perfectly acceptable. Polls in Europe showed no great shifts in any direction either.[85] Converts continued to cause concern with a plot uncovered in western Germany in September 2007 involving two young local men who had become Muslims and who planned to blow up a 'disco full of American sluts' on an American base or a similar target. However, the danger posed by converts was not going to be enough to return European nations to the darker days of 2004 or 2005.[86] The growing general rejection of violent extremism seen in the Middle East appeared to be in the process of being reproduced among Muslim communities in Europe too.

A calmer atmosphere also allowed a more sensible general debate. Senior figures in the British police and the security services appeared less prone to terrifying doomsday predictions or to the systematic exaggeration of the threat posed by individual cells in the UK that had previously marked their statements. This was perhaps because by 2007 they now had the vast bulk of the increased powers that they had so vociferously demanded in the immediate post-9/11 years and were more confident that the legislation needed to secure convictions for a range of activities that previously might have escaped prosecution let alone significant custodial sentences was in place.[87] With populations now becoming habituated to repeated scares, claims of new threats were in any case greeted more sceptically and more phlegmatically than before. Few security officials would ever admit that the likelihood of a devastating attack had lessened – 'We'd be cutting our own budgets,' admitted one MI5 officer to the author in a moment of unwarranted frankness – but there was a realization that the public was much more critical of any claim of potential danger than had been the case before.[88]

One reason for this was the steady demolition of many of the tenacious if tendentious ideas about the capabilities of the enemy. Many of the claims of 2002 and 2003 had long been shown to be without foundation. The various investigations in Iraq had shown that Saddam had not possessed weapons of mass destruction, and some of the more fabulous inventions about the potential and nature of al-Qaeda had been effectively deconstructed as scholars, analysts and journalists picked over the voluminous material that had become available as years passed.[89] The debate over whether al-Qaeda was more ideology or more organization and whether bin Laden was 'inciter-in-chief' or of marginal importance or terrorist mastermind continued, as highly politicized and polarized as it had always been, but some broad areas of consensus had emerged. Around 1,000 English-language books with 'terrorism' in the title had existed in 1995. A decade later there were nearly eleven times as many, with most of the new additions focusing on Islamic militancy. Though the 'al-Qaeda industry' that had sprung up post-9/11 had attracted more than its fair share of frauds, fantasists and ideologues, it had nonetheless created a substantial body of research and a cohort of often very fine researchers whose conclusions filtered through both to policy-makers and to an increasingly well-informed public.[90]

In the US, 2007 too saw a broader reassessment of the more egregious excesses of the early years of the 9/11 Wars. This was in part enforced – the previous year had seen a landmark Supreme Court decision that prisoners in Guantanamo Bay were covered by the articles of the Geneva Conventions forbidding abusive or humiliating treatment of prisoners and that the military tribunals the detainees faced were illegal without explicit authorization from Congress – but was also due to a slow realization among some senior figures that at least some earlier policies had been counterproductive.[91] These changes sometimes occurred almost in spite of the ideological atmosphere. So, for example, as prosecutors and investigators received more resources and became more adept at framing charges, the law became a much more potent counter-terrorist weapon and much more attractive to the authorities as a consequence. Over the two years after the 9/11 attacks, only one in thirty American defendants described as 'terrorists' to the media when arrested were actually charged with terrorism offences. Only around a third of these were eventually convicted on terrorism charges. By 2006 and 2007, although the Bush administration's National Defense Strategy of 2005 had referred to the use of courts to pursue terrorists as part of a 'strategy of the weak', a range of improvements in training and organization as well as new legislative tools meant that nearly half of individuals labelled terrorists were charged as such and more than 80 per cent of these were convicted.[92] One major contributing factor was the success government prosecutors began to have in convincing defendants to cooperate. Another improvement, as in the UK, was an understanding of exactly what charge could be made to stick, particularly when it came to membership of a terrorist organization.[93] Almost by default, therefore, a much-derided 'legal approach' to counter-terrorism gained ground at the expense of hardline strategies which emphasized the extraordinary nature of the threat facing the USA and therefore justified deeply divisive 'extra-legal' responses to it.

Another important shift came within the American domestic intelligence community, and particularly the FBI, where Robert Mueller, the director, had set about changing the bureau's role from detection and law-enforcement to intelligence-gathering, more along the lines of the British MI5. Philip Mudd, formerly a senior official at the CIA with intimate knowledge of south Asia, the Middle East and Islamic militancy, was made deputy director of the agency tasked with consolidating and accelerating the changes. Mudd, an intense and scholarly analyst with a Masters in English literature, had very different views from his predecessor in the post, who had proudly declared that knowledge of subject matter was not essential for senior officials.[94] Though impressed by the FBI's information-gathering capabilities, he believed the bureau needed to focus less on problems 'that were known', i.e. law-enforcement, and more on what could be potential problems, i.e. security. Mudd and his boss, Director Robert Mueller, wanted their staff to be asking not 'Do we have a case open?' but 'Do we have a concern here worth investigating?'. By the end of 2006 the FBI had more than 2,000 intelligence analysts and, perhaps more importantly, nearly 1,400 linguists. The Americans also followed the Europeans in revising the vocabulary used to describe the conflict and their enemies. In late 2006, British cabinet ministers had been advised by the Foreign Office not to use the 'counterproductive' term 'War on Terror'.[95] The advice had had little effect until the June 2007 resignation of Tony Blair after ten years in power, when much of the more ideological charged rhetoric of the early years of the 9/11 Wars was immediately dropped. Blair's departure also allowed a frank discussion of the effects of the Iraq war on radicalization in the UK and elsewhere for the first time. Previously, ministers had tied themselves in rhetorical knots to avoid admitting that the invasion of Iraq had been a major factor in the intensification of the threat in Britain between 2003 and 2005, though in private they admitted that 'Iraq [was] a huge problem'.[96] For Jonathan Freeman, head of the British government's Combating Extremism Unit, the 'military language' used hitherto was 'just wrong'. 'You have to use language which does not alienate while not denying there are issues that have to be dealt with,' he said.[97] In January 2008, drawing heavily on the new British guidelines, a number of American federal agencies, including the State Department, the Department of Homeland Security and the National Counter Terrorism Center, advised staff not to describe Islamic extremists as 'jihadists' or '*mujahideen*', or to use terms such as 'Islamo-fascism'.[98] Such changes were easy to dismiss as superficial and it would certainly be wrong to exaggerate their impact. The 'cultural turn' naturally had its limits. A resumé of a US wargame, seminar and workshop exercise in late 2007 showed just how cultural sensitivity was often seen as a tactic rather than a principle and how 'winning hearts and minds' remained a matter of persuading others rather than having any kind of genuine conversation. 'The focus of effort in the persistent conflict environment must not be the opponents, but rather the people, the human terrain in which they operate,' the review said, citing word for word the new counter-insurgency doctrines being employed in Iraq. It then insisted, however, that 'the general population ... must be convinced of the correctness of Western values and ideas'.[99] But, as with so many elements of the 9/11 Wars, though individual measures may have had limited impact, cumulatively minor changes could have a significant effect, particularly when they acted to accelerate developments on the ground.

For the reaction against extremist violence in the Islamic world that had become evident in 2006 – though it had been underway in places like Saudi Arabia, Turkey, Morocco and elsewhere much earlier – continued to build and broaden. Successive polls reinforced the earlier indication that support for radicalism fell away rapidly whenever violence was experienced locally. In Lebanon, Bangladesh, Jordan and Indonesia, the proportion of Muslims supporting suicide bombing had dropped to levels that were half or less of those of five years before.[100] As ever, the picture was incomplete. In the deradicalization centres of Saudi Arabia 'students' were taught not that going to fight oppression of fellow Muslims in Iraq was necessarily wrong but that to do so *without the permission of the authorities* was wrong, a nuance that escaped most of the impressed Western politicians who were shown around the facilities. In Jordan, though 42 per cent said suicide bombing was never justified, 44 per cent continued to say it was sometimes or rarely justified. But overall it was difficult to argue that the same cycle of escalating chaos and violence seen during the earlier phases of the war was continuing unchanged. Support for Osama bin Laden declined further too, again most obviously in those countries which had suffered militant violence.[101] By 2007, only 15 per cent of Saudi Arabians had a favourable view of their former fellow citizen turned violent extremist and only one in ten held positive views about his group.[102] As if to emphasize the point, one of the original founders of al-Qaeda and a key ideological mentor of bin Laden and al-Zawahiri, Sayyid Imam al-Sharif, published a book from his Egyptian prison cell called *Rationalization of Jihad*, in which he argued that 'jihad had been blemished with grave Sharia violations during recent years ... Now there are those who kill hundreds, including women and children, Muslims and non-Muslims in the name of jihad.' Al-Sharif ruled that bombings in Egypt, Saudi Arabia and elsewhere were illegitimate and that terrorism against civilians in Western countries was wrong.[103] When they came from someone like al-Sharif, a respected senior figure within the movement who had been one of the first to elaborate the doctrine of *takfir*, such statements were an indication that an important shift was underway. Al-Sharif was not alone either. From mid 2007 onwards, scores of other well-known individuals also with impeccable extremist credentials began to make public statements denouncing al-Qaeda. One was Salman al-Auda, a Saudi scholar who had been a trenchant critic of the West and of Middle Eastern governments since the late 1980s and who had a cult following in Riyadh and east London alike. In September 2007, al-Auda had addressed bin Laden on a widely watched Arabic-language television network.[104] 'My brother Osama, how much blood has been spilt? How many innocent people, children, elderly and women have been killed . . . in the name of al-Qaeda? Will you be happy to meet God almighty carrying the burden of these hundreds of thousands or millions [of victims] on your back?'[105] The discovery of a plot to launch attacks in Saudi Arabia in Riyadh, Medina and even the holy city of Mecca during the pilgrimage period of Hajj in December of 2007 was important too. Whether or not the plot was genuine – Prince Mohammed bin Nayef, the deputy interior minister, insisted to the author that it was – the news that extremists were planning to target ordinary people performing one of the five fundamental duties of a Muslim had a powerful effect.[106] Bin Laden's communications were becoming increasingly defensive and increasingly frustrated. 'O Muslim youth of this generation! Why is there cowardice and frailty?' he asked angrily in a 'message to the Islamic nation' released in May 2008. 'Our lives are already ruled by harmful policies meant to discourage our beliefs. My brother! Jihad against the infidels is your duty. How can you fear death, when death is your paradise? The pillar of religion shall not become stronger by voting and elections. Anything but the sword shall be of no help, I swear.'[107]

By the late spring of 2008, it was thus possible to distinguish four broad phases of the 9/11 Wars to date. The first three had been obvious for some time. Act One had seen the initial explosion of violence and the Afghan war. Act Two had seen the lull, the phoney war of 2002, and Act Three, the intensification and escalation of violence of 2003 to 2006. A year or so later, however, this now appeared to have been the nadir. For the nature of Act Four was gradually becoming clearer. The new phase of the conflict had seen the slide into ever greater violence stopped, tensions dropping in relative terms, fewer major headline attacks, no riots, no collapse of any government and, though perhaps due in part to a normalization of a sustained and high level of threat, a relative sense of calm. If al-Zarqawi's strategy of 'local jihad' had failed in Iraq, al-Suri's strategy of 'global jihad' was meeting with equally little real success more generally in the Islamic world. Again, there had been no 'turning point', more a subtle shifting in the balance of tendencies that opened up the possibility that the future evolution the 9/11 Wars might be in a new, more positive direction. This small progress was undoubtedly easily reversible, as fragile an advance on the global scale as it had been on the local scale in the more limited environment of Iraq. There was no doubt that grave problems remained. Certainly, most of the underlying issues that had underpinned radicalization even before 9/11 had remained largely unaddressed, and a single major successful terrorist attack could, depending on the reaction, completely change the dynamic. So too could the emergence of another leader of similar charisma to bin Laden but with perhaps a subtly different message and style. And even if it was the case that al-Qaeda's global package had been rejected not just in Iraq but more broadly in the Islamic world, no one could predict what might fill the gap it left. But even if it was still very unclear what the next act of the conflict might bring, it was reasonable to hope that it would not be as grim as what had gone before.

One thing was certain. Despite their setbacks, radical Islamic militants in the spring of 2008 still retained the capacity to often think and move faster than those trying to kill or capture them. By late spring there were signs that well-known and capable individuals, some linked to the al-Qaeda senior leadership, were leaving Iraq and heading east.[108] For if the militants were having less success than they had hoped in the Middle East and in Europe, they were having more than they had ever expected in the first theatre of the 9/11 Wars: Afghanistan. The strategic centre of gravity of the conflict appeared to have shifted again. No longer Europe or the Middle East, it was, once again, south-west Asia.

# PART FIVE

# Afghanistan, Pakistan and Al-Qaeda: 2008

# 12

# Afghanistan Again

## KABUL, LATE SUMMER 2008

Even in the summer of 2008, even on a hot afternoon in mid-August at the height of the fighting season, there was little that indicated that Maidan Shar, a small town 30 miles south of Kabul, lay astride a frontline. The only signs of conflict were the wrecks of two trucks burned out in an ambush a few days earlier and dumped outside a scruffy row of mechanics' workshops and the Turkish armoured vehicles firing practice rounds into a hillside a mile or so away. A few ragged farmers sold small, bruised apples from battered barrows in the patch of dried mud that passed for a central marketplace. In the town's single restaurant a dozen men lay on grubby carpets spread on the flat concrete floor, sipped smeared glasses of tea amid clouds of flies and stared hard at strangers. The frontline, as ever in the 9/11 Wars, was poorly defined, invisible and intangible. But it was a frontline nonetheless.

The torpor was thus misleading. By 2008, much of Wardak, the province of which Maidan Shar was the capital, had slipped under the control of the insurgents. Though the Taliban did not control all of the 10,000 square miles of mixed mountain, desert and parched farmland that made up the province, only a fairly limited amount of territory could be said to be under the authority of President Hamid Karzai and his government either. Their power, weak at the best of times, was limited to the main roads, the district centres and Maidan Shar itself. 'Things are pretty safe round here,' the local governor, Halim Fedayi, said disingenuously in an interview in his heavily guarded office minutes before news came in that his deputy had narrowly escaped death in an ambush on the main road through the province – Highway 1 from Kabul to

Kandahar – a few miles away.[1] Outside, a crowd of tribal elders had gathered. They had been summoned to hear the governor, a former NGO worker and exile, speak about how the insurgents' interpretation of the Koran was erroneous. One, from a village only half an hour by motorbike away, summed up what many were thinking: 'What the governor says is very nice, but it's the Taliban who control my district, not him.' Sitting on a metal bed on a small hill a few miles north of Maidan Shar, Salim Ali, a twenty-year-old policeman, forced a thin smile. With three colleagues, for a pound a day, he guarded the narrow pass on the road to Kabul. 'There's less traffic these days,' he said. 'People are frightened.'

The Afghan capital in August 2008 was an anxious place. The situation in the city's immediate vicinity was unstable and fluid. It was very clear that insurgents were moving through surrounding villages, stockpiling weapons and establishing safehouses. Suburbs on the outskirts were unsafe and suicide bombers continued to hit targets within the city limits. Someone managed to fire an RPG – which has an effective range of a couple of hundred metres – at the new airport building. Even the streets of Shar-e-Nau, the centre of Kabul, saw a series of kidnappings. The road to Jalalabad was repeatedly cut by insurgent raids and roadblocks. Just north of the road in the valley of Uzbeen, ten French soldiers were killed in an ambush, pinned down amid rocks and on steep slopes as Afghan National Army soldiers fled in total disorder and NATO, which had around 25,000 heavily armed Western troops stationed within a hour's helicopter flight and jets permanently overhead, tried without success to bring its formidable airborne assets to bear. Though few believed the Taliban had any chance of actually capturing the capital, when traditional calls of 'Allahu akbar' resounded from rooftops on the first day of Ramadan, the Islamic holy month, local authorities thought the cries signalled an insurrection and ordered a major security alert. In a row of open-air workshops on the northern outskirts, labourers worked round the clock pouring concrete into battered metal moulds to meet the insatiable local demand for something barely seen in Afghanistan even five years before: the concrete blast wall. The big sections cost $550, the smaller a mere $300. A good team of workers could produce twenty a day. 'I sell them to foreigners mainly and make good money,' said Said Fahim, the owner of the biggest workshop. 'If Afghanistan was peaceful there would be no use for them. I'd prefer to be out of business.'

The ambient fear – as well as the blast walls – led many to make a comparison with Baghdad. Certainly, much in Kabul and in the country more generally in the summer of 2008 was familiar to those who had seen Iraq, particularly in 2004, 2005 or 2006. It was as if the great tide of radicalization and violence which had surged out of south-west Asia, across the Middle East and into Europe between 2001 and 2005 had carried back an accumulated load of detritus from these theatres as, on the ebb, it had returned to its source. The war in Afghanistan had even changed visually to resemble the conflict elsewhere. The vast bases on which most international troops lived – such as Bagram, Kandahar or Camp Warehouse outside Kabul – had been the prototypes for those in Iraq. Now the situation was reversed. The Afghan bases were now supplied by same contractors and thus had the same menus, facilities and even road signs as those in the Middle East. The military technology developed in Iraq – such as the 'up-armoured Humvees' – could now be seen on Afghan roads. Soon 'Mraps' – vehicles with V-shaped hulls to deflect IED blasts – would arrive. The same language – the acronyms, insults, slang and neologisms – could be heard. Naturally there were connections between the theatres in terms of personnel too. The new commander of ISAF appointed in June 2008, General David McKiernan, had played a key role in the 2003 Iraq invasion. General Stone, who had reformed the prison system in Iraq, had arrived to do the same in Afghanistan. A high proportion of the officers and men on the ground had experience on the streets of Ramadi, Kut, Mosul or Baghdad itself. The same went for many civilian employees, NGO workers and, perhaps more worryingly, the increasing number of security contractors arriving in Afghanistan. Many among the 50,000 strong private-sector mercenary army in Iraq had seen new opportunities opening up further east. 'Feels just like home,' laughed one South African employee of Blackwater, the most notorious of the private security contractors working in the Middle East, as he surveyed the scene of a suicide bombing on the Jalalabad Road a few days after flying in from the Gulf. He and his three colleagues were all wearing the beard, Oakley shades, T-shirt and combat trousers that had become the distinctive uniform of the mercenary in the 9/11 Wars. Though their company had recently been forced to leave Iraq after trigger-happy employees shot and killed at least fourteen civilians in unprovoked 'defensive' fire in Baghdad, there was plenty of demand for their services in Afghanistan.[2]

As the summer of 2008 passed and despite London politicians' insistence that the Taliban were being 'beaten back', a few British officials had begun to voice serious concerns at the direction Afghanistan had taken.[3] British intelligence analysts in Kabul privately described the Taliban as better armed and better organized than ever before and said that fighting in the coming months would be the toughest yet seen.[4] Many were deeply worried by the core weakness of the effort in Afghanistan: the incompetence, corruption, cynicism and effective paralysis of the central Kabul government. President Karzai, now in his seventh year in power, appeared incapacitated by a combination of extreme pragmatism and paranoia. The various 'GOA' (Government of Afghanistan) institutions such as the Afghan National Army and the Afghan National Police continued to suffer very serious structural problems ranging from huge ethnic imbalances in the under-resourced army to an almost total lack of capacity in the corrupt and violent police. The judiciary was a ruin, with many judges either fleeing their districts or simply handing over much of their caseload to clerics either linked to the Taliban or actively involved with the insurgents.[5] Privately, Sir Sherard Cowper-Coles, the British ambassador in Kabul, listed the intractable structural problems inside Afghanistan, in the region and further afield. One problem, he said, was the failure to get the Islamic world involved in the effort in Afghanistan. Turkey had contributed 860 troops, and the United Arab Emirates had a unit of special forces secretly engaged in the east, but otherwise Muslim-majority nations had almost no official military or civilian presence in the theatre. But this was only one of many things that needed to change if there was to be a hope of 'success'. There was also the lack of political will inside Afghanistan and of political focus in Europe. There was the drift in Washington as elections approached, the slumping support for the war among Western voters, the lack of regional diplomatic coordination and, perhaps most serious of all, the general lack of realism about what was now attainable in the short, medium and long term. 'We cannot win without a major shift in strategy,' Cowper-Coles said. 'And we may not win even then. Whatever winning means.'[6]

The obvious question was: how, with so many initial advantages compared to Iraq, had so much gone so badly wrong?

# THE TALIBAN RETURN, 2002–2006

The first thing the Taliban had done when crossing the border after fleeing Afghanistan in late 2001 and 2002 had been to make sure they had a secure base. Most returned to places that were well known to them: the religious schools or *medressas*, refugee camps and villages that had been home for many years and were still often home to relatives.[7] 'Kabul was falling; I drove with my family across the border. There was no problem at the checkpoint. I have a lot of land in Pakistan, and everyone knows me,' Maulvi Mohammed Arsala Rahmani, the former Taliban education minister, recalled.[8] The experience of the column of Taliban who had fled from Jalalabad over the Spin Ghar mountains in mid November as the fighting started in Tora Bora was typical. Several hundred strong, they had reached the high valleys in Pakistani territory before local troops had deployed. They then doubled back into Afghanistan and, after a further day and night of travel, had split up. At least a third of the group – young Pakistanis who had come from the religious schools of the North West Frontier Province and the tribal agencies – were each given 5,000 Pakistani rupees ($60/£40 at 2001 rates) and told to go home. A second group – several dozen senior Taliban officials – hired vehicles to drive further south into Paktika province before crossing into Pakistan by the remote Gumal pass and entering the tribal agency of South Waziristan, where they were hosted by relatives and supporters. A final group of twenty wounded fighters were sent directly across the border to hospitals in Peshawar with the cover story that they were villagers who had been injured by the American bombardment.[9] Thousands of other footsoldiers, hundreds of mid-level commanders and scores of senior figures – including almost the entire leadership of the Taliban – followed similar routes to escape from Afghanistan. By the middle of 2002, most had found new bases, either around Quetta, where a 'Quetta Shura' or leadership council under Mullah Omar was constituted, or Peshawar. Some found their way to more remote villages, and a very few ended up in Karachi.

If the secure bases they had across the border and the resources that flowed in from a network of supporters overseas in the Gulf and elsewhere were both key in sustaining the Taliban after their defeat and strategic retreat in 2001, it was nonetheless the particular combination of conditions within Afghanistan that created the vacuum and the griev-ances that allowed them to launch their campaign to return to power within a few short years and then build an insurgency of sufficient strength to cripple the Western project in the country. One crucial pre-condition for the Taliban re-establishing a presence within Afghanistan was the discontent of Pashtun populations in the south and east at what was felt to be an unjust post-war settlement. Pashtuns had ruled the Afghan state ever since it had been founded in 1747, with the only exceptions being chaotic interludes in 1929 and from 1992 to 1996, and though this narrative of Pashtun rule naturally glossed over the constant fighting between the great Pashtun tribal confederations of Durrani and Ghilzai, within tribes, between Pashtun *mujahideen* fac-tions during the war against the Soviets and between Pashtun Communists during the same period, between pro- or anti-Taliban factions in the 1990s and, of course, between communities every day over water, wood or decades-old perceived slights to honour, it still meant the Pashtun community was broadly convinced of its historic right to govern the country. Unlike the Iraqi Sunnis, who had lost demographic dominance around a century before losing their hold on power, the Afghan Pashtuns had remained the country's largest ethnicity – around 45 per cent, though no one really knew – and had retained a strong sense of entitlement.

In the aftermath of the fall of Kabul to the Northern Alliance, which had been broadly composed of Tajiks, Uzbeks and Hazaras, and the deposition of the largely Pashtun Taliban, many Pashtuns across Afghanistan were concerned that they would be the major losers in any new political set-up. The Bonn conference of December 2001, convened by the United Nations and managed jointly by UN and US diplomats to lay the basis for the future political set-up of Afghanistan, did little to reassure them. Karzai, the new 'chief executive' and president in waiting of the country, was a Pashtun but was highly Westernized, had returned from more than twenty years of exile and had little popular base beyond the following he had inherited from his father, a senior figure within the major southern Popalzai tribe.[10] Then there was the widespread and unchecked score-settling which targeted Pashtun minorities in the north of the country in the early months of 2002, the sidelining of the ageing (Pashtun) king and the appointment of Tajiks from the Panjshir valley to head the so-called 'power ministries' of Defence, the Interior and For-eign Affairs.[11]

These and other developments reinforced the sense of political marginalization among Afghanistan's Pashtuns, particularly in the rural areas or in the towns and cities of the south and east. This growing alienation was soon sharpened by a sense that the community was economically disadvantaged too. There were many areas of Afghanistan that benefited hugely in the years following the invasion. Kabul was transformed. So too were Jalalabad and Herat, with their links to Pakistan and Iran respectively. Even small towns like Pul-e-Khumri on the northern side of the critical Salang tunnel had bustling bazaars full of Chinese motorbikes, colourful blankets, inedible artificial jam that sold extraordinarily and inexplicably well, great piles of tin buckets and jerry cans of fuel. Bamiyan thrived, still poor and starved of development funds but stable and secure behind its mountain ramparts. But though the economy was booming, with growth rates of 8, 10 or even 14 per cent, the rural areas, particularly in the south, where the Pashtuns predominated, were missing out.[12] The 'primary beneficiaries of assistance were the urban elite,' the World Bank noted in a 2005 report, exactly the constituency whose loyalty to the Western project in Afghanistan had always been assured.[13] Kandahar itself might have changed – the governor's palace had been repainted, roads resurfaced, there were drugs in the hospital and scores of ornate villas in the style favoured by local drug barons – but even a few miles outside the city there was little sign of any physical improvement since the end of the Taliban's rule.

The reasons for this were simple: a lack of political attention, of funds, of security and of governance. Earlier chapters noted how Afghanistan received far less cash for reconstruction than almost all recent nation-building efforts.[14] According to aid agencies, only half of the $20 billion that the international community had pledged to Afghanistan over previous years had actually arrived, and around 40 per cent of what had turned up had been spent on corporate profits and consultancy fees. Of the $6 billion that was left, a third was wasted.[15] This meant that a fifth of what had been announced as given to Afghanistan actually reached Afghans.[16] Spending the money that did get through was not easy either. The failure to deploy sufficient numbers of troops to Afghanistan had meant a minimal military presence in what were among the most critical parts of the country in terms of potential for violence. There was a US base for 2,500 troops in Kandahar and a couple of forward operating bases manned by small detachments of special forces who spent their time hunting fugitives or protecting under-resourced 'Provincial Reconstruction Teams', but otherwise there was no significant military presence across the four southern provinces of Kandahar, Herat, Farah and Nimroz between 2002 and 2006. International forces failed to secure even the major towns and highways in the south let alone the long unguarded border.[17] In the four vital provinces further north – Oruzgan, Zabul, Ghazni and Paktika – Western troops were very thin on the ground too. As violence in the south began to increase from mid 2003, UN development agencies and Western and Afghan aid organizations were forced to first scale back their operations and then, by 2005, to virtually stop all work in what was the most strategically important part of Afghanistan after the capital.[18]

The consequences of the NGOs' absence were all the more grave given the vast problems of governance. In a rerun of what had happened further north around Jalalabad, two factions had raced for Kandahar as the Taliban's regime had collapsed in late 2001. Both were led by former warlords who had recently returned from exile. The winner was Gul Agha Sherzai, one of the most notorious of the commanders who had run the city and its surroundings in the early 1990s and whose depredations had prompted the foundation and permitted the early success of the Taliban. He owed his successful return to power in part to air strikes called in by American special forces and in part to the decision of two other major tribal leaders who had previously supported the Taliban to withdraw from the fight.[19] Men like Sherzai – similar figures were coming to power in many other provinces across the south and east – made little effort to hide their own involvement in narcotics, dealing openly with both major drugs traffickers and the insurgents on a daily basis.[20] They were neither interested in nor capable of dealing with the complex developmental challenges facing local communities at the time. These returning warlords had two layers of protection: the American special forces and intelligence agencies, for whom they acted as local proxies, and the Kabul government, for whom the sole criterion for resting in post was loyalty to President Karzai. For the majority of southern Pashtuns, these corrupt and brutal commanders, the administrations that such men led and the famously venal and violent police were the face of the new Afghanistan being built by the international powers.[21] Those communities and individuals who were denied a slice of the lucrative new economic opportunities opening up to anyone with power and influence from 2002 naturally looked for ways to preserve their own zones of influence, cash flows and, in the zero-sum world of Afghan micro-politics, worked to deny their immediate rivals any advantage.

None of this assured the return of the Taliban, but it did make it much easier. The 'strategic centre of gravity' of the Taliban's campaign lay in Afghanistan's 40,000-odd villages. For a long time, this had escaped their international adversaries, who, coming from highly urbanized societies, naturally concentrated their efforts on the country's cities and towns. Reinforcing this error was a failure to understand the Taliban's deep cultural and social roots and the nature of their rule in the 1990s. For though the Taliban had been an alien presence in much of the north and west of Afghanistan and in cosmopolitan cities such as Herat and Kabul, where Dari-speaking Tajik or Persian ethnic minorities dominated and levels of education were much higher, in most of the south and the east of the country the movement had often been an integral part of communities. Groups of 'Taliban', largely students, had fought, often independently of the increasingly discredited major *mujahideen* groups, against the Soviets.[22] As Mullah Omar's forces had advanced across Afghanistan between 1994 and 1996, they had attracted a variety of supporters. Sometimes these were sections of a community that had previously been marginalized, such as the lowly mullahs, landless families, those without connections to the central government or minor tribes who had historically been pushed around by bigger ones.[23] On other occasions those aligning themselves with the new force had been local 'commanders' or minor warlords forced out by rivals during the civil war and who thus grafted their own small cause on to the greater one of Mullah Omar's movement. Situations differed across the country, but in many areas the end of the Taliban rule in 2001 had not meant a liberation from a repressive and alien extremist state, as it was perceived to be so often in the West, but the defeat of one faction in a community and its replacement by another.[24] It was simply another turn in the long contest for power, particularly acute since the start of the civil war in the 1970s, which had been continuing in Afghanistan on and off for many decades. Sometimes, down at the most 'granular' level, the differences between pro- and anti-Taliban elements could be simply no greater than those imposed by a longstanding blood feud or a question of who had fought for whom when the Communists were in power. As in earlier conflicts, families very often had one brother or son with the Taliban, another with a different faction.[25] Language, ethnicity, culture and religious practice were thus broadly shared.[26]

It was these connections – both cultural and personal, general and very specific – that the Pakistan-based Taliban leadership exploited through late 2002 and on through 2003 and 2004. 'Our goal is to unify the country against the occupiers,' Maulvi Taj Mohammed had explained to the author six months after Tora Bora, adding that the movement aimed to 'move slowly' and to 'bring order' before launching 'military actions'.[27] As they set about rebuilding their strength in Afghanistan, often the Taliban used the same tactics employed almost a decade before, sending out emissaries to far-flung villages where local tribal and family connections guaranteed at least a hearing if not a welcome and running an extensive outreach programme to all those power-brokers, former warlords, commanders or elders who saw their rivals profiting from cooperating with the government or foreign forces. Efforts were made to reach all sections of the population – ordinary villagers as well as more powerful individuals. On occasion, loudspeakers were set up or even a portable FM radio used to broadcast the Taliban's message. Frequently violence was used to eliminate opposition.[28] Often generational tensions – familiar from other theatres in the 9/11 Wars including Europe – were exploited, with younger contenders for power and influence being turned against often more moderate and pragmatic elders. Many of the latter ended up dead or in exile. But the successful communication of the insurgents' discourse of Islam, nation and community, often relayed by the clerical network, depended as much on pre-existing xenophobia, the mistrust of Kabul, fear of bias towards ethnic rivals, anger at civilian casualties or intrusive searches by Western troops and, of course, a deep-rooted rural religious and social conservatism as on intimidation. When successful, the Taliban, or the local powerbrokers they had recruited into their ranks, were often able to take on a role as 'protectors' of a given community against local rivals, government officials and the few foreign troops who were ever seen. At the very least, given the vacuum in government authority in much of the country, they were simply able to establish some kind of rule of law where there was none. As it had been in the 1990s, the Taliban remained structured less as a militia or insurgent group and more as an 'adaptive social movement' in the words of political scientist Seth Jones or a 'caravan' in the more colourful phrase of the late Afghan expert Bernt Glatzer.[29]

To supplement the recruits brought in by their outreach programme in the villages the Taliban leaders, from their now secure base around Quetta and to a lesser extent Peshawar, drew on another tactic from the previous decade and mobilized the various resources of the cross-border ethnic and religious networks from which they had, in part, originally sprung. The most useful was the vast reservoir of combat-age manpower in the religious schools over the border in Pakistan. The young men who had sat in rows on the schools' concrete floors rote-learning the Koran had provided critical fighting strength in the early Taliban campaigns of the mid 1990s, and Taliban leaders naturally once more turned to the *medressas*. One recruit was nineteen-year-old Rahmatullah, who in mid 2003 had travelled to Pakistan to be a religious student and had returned to Afghanistan as an armed *mujahid*. He explained his recruitment in simple terms: 'I was in school, and my teachers told us that we should fight for my country and my religion against the unbelievers who had come to Afghanistan and the hypocrites in power. All my friends went, and I didn't want to be left behind.'[30] Older recruits were found in the large refugee camps in Pakistan, which were full of young men of Pashtun Afghan origins who had been raised on an ideological diet of radical conservative religion in communities stripped of the comforting traditional identities and hierarchies of tribe or village. Products of the extremely high fertility rates in the camps in the 1980s and early 1990s, jobless or chronically underemployed, they too, sometimes paid small sums, began to find their way across into the south-eastern provinces in increasing numbers by 2003 and 2004.[31]

The first areas to slip into Taliban control had been isolated districts on the eastern rim of the central mountainous core of the country as well as along the Pakistani border near the border point at Chaman.[32] By late 2003, raiding parties from bases in these areas had been regularly attacking the road from Kabul to Kandahar and government buildings in even major towns. The seductive images of voters queuing outside polling stations for successive elections of 2004 and 2005 had, as in Iraq at around the same time, obscured the growing strength of the insurgency.[33] By late 2005, significant parts of the environs of Kandahar, much of neighbouring Helmand province and large sections of the south-western desert were under de facto Taliban control, and groups of fighters loyal to networks allied to the Taliban, such as those run by former *mujahideen* leader and prime minister Gulbuddin Hekmatyar and Jalaluddin Haqqani, the commander and cleric who gained fame in the 1980s and had eventually become a key ally of the Taliban, were establishing their own authority over swathes of north-eastern and eastern border provinces.[34] The numbers of insurgents were still not great. If every fighter from tribal and village-level fellow travellers through to mercenary and criminal elements as well as contingents from the schools and the refugee camp populations had all been simultaneously mobilized, their number would not have exceeded several thousand.[35] But the numbers were not important. The fugitive Taliban leaders in Peshawar had outlined three phases of their campaign – establishing contact with potential allies, establishing permanent areas of influence and authority and only then moving to overt military action. One of the advantages of the strategy was that progress would only become obvious to the enemy when it was probably too late. 'By 2005 . . . we were looking carefully at a number of staff analyses that began to suggest the Taliban was exhibiting signs of defeat,' Lieutenant General David W. Barno, commander of US forces from 2003 to 2005, remembered.[36] General James Jones, then NATO's Supreme Allied Commander (Europe), announced bluntly in early 2006 that 'the Taliban and al-Qaeda are not in a position where they can restart an insurgency of any size and major scope'.[37] A much more pessimistic analysis from the head of the Afghan National Directorate of Intelligence, Amrullah Saleh, was brushed aside. Saleh recalled later being told the Taliban were 'irrelevant'. The Bush administration reduced its budgeted aid request to Congress for Afghanistan by 38 per cent to $3.1 billion.[38] As had been the case in Iraq, the initiative had been seized by the insurgents.

## THE AFGHAN FRONTS 2006–8

Shortly after Jones' statement, new Western troops began to arrive in Afghanistan in a major reinforcement of the international presence there. Given the prevailing wisdom that the Taliban were beaten, this would seem to indicate a serious divergence between public statements and private strategy-making on the part of Western politicians. In fact, it was more evidence of deep confusion among Western policy-makers and their very real failure to understand what was happening in Afghanistan at the time.

In theory the troops were the final part of a rolling extension through the country of ISAF, the International Security Assistance Force that had been created with a peace-keeping mission following the war of 2001.[39] The reinforcements arriving in 2006 would bring the total number of troops committed to Afghanistan to 46,000, still only a third of those in Iraq but an increase of 20,000 on the previous year.

Their aim remained largely the same as that of 2002. They were not coming to launch a new offensive to roll back the Taliban. They were coming to 'extend the authority of President Karzai's government, to protect those civilian agencies assisting them to build a democratic government and to enable security, stability and economic development throughout the country'. The resistance these troops, particularly the British, were to encounter thus came as a rude surprise. John Reid, the British defence secretary, had even raised the possibility of the soldiers not having to fight at all, speaking of his hope that the troops could withdraw in three or five years 'without firing a shot'.[40]

A secondary aim of the deployment had little to do with Afghanistan and much to do with global politics. European powers – particularly the British – had been concerned since 2003 that the increasingly unilateral approach of the Americans and the failure of other states to make any contribution to (or to stop) the war in Iraq would fatally undermine NATO, the keystone of the Western world's defence architecture. The expansion of ISAF into the south of Afghanistan, five years after it had originally been mooted, with all Afghan operations placed under NATO command except those American forces dedicated to hunting bin Laden along the eastern frontier, was a way of reinvigorating the alliance and proving its utility in the changed strategic environment of the first decade of the twenty-first century.[41] After some debate and argument, new Dutch, Canadian and British troops began arriving in Oruzgan, Kandahar and Helmand provinces respectively in the late spring of 2006. All spoke of winning 'hearts and minds'. 'We need to convince them that we are the winning team and once we do that – and we will – then they'll come over to us,' said Lieutenant Colonel Stuart Tootal, who deployed from Iraq via a stint in the UK to Helmand as part of the British 16th Air Assault Brigade. As he spoke, bulldozers lit by arc lights were shunting gravel into berms to protect Camp Bastion, the new British base in the province. Beyond the new ramparts, the desert stretched off into the night.[42]

Very rapidly, it became clear that potential resistance in Helmand and elsewhere had been grotesquely underestimated. Within weeks of arriving, the new troops across the country found themselves involved in heavy fighting. NATO officials in the headquarters compound in central Kabul, sitting in the garden of the coffee shop, attributed the increasingly extensive violence to international forces pushing into new areas and insisted that 70 per cent of the violence in Afghanistan was restricted to 10 per cent of the districts.[43] Both these statements were true but ignored the fact that the Taliban had met the arrival of the new troops with an offensive of their own. Attacks on international forces went from 300 in March 2006 to 600 per month at the year's end, traditionally a relatively quiet time.[44] By the end of 2006, after six months or so of renewed NATO activity, at least a third of the east and south of the country was shaded a vivid red for 'high risk' on the 'security charts' compiled by NGOs trying with greater and greater difficulty to work outside the main cities. At least in the short term, the arrival of the new forces did not appear to be making the environment more secure but considerably more dangerous. This, NATO officials in Kabul said, was 'the price of victory'.[45]

Each of the operational areas in Afghanistan had its own specificities. Kunduz and the north-east, where the Germans had been based from October 2003, had once been relatively quiet. Detractors of the Germans said this was because the legal restrictions under which the 2,700 German troops operated prevented them actively hunting any insurgents.[46] Supporters said their softly-softly approach had tipped few locals into insurgency. Either way, 2006 saw the Germans becoming involved in constant skirmishing and suffering increasing casualties. The eastern province of Kunar was the scene of serious fighting, with American troops engaging a series of different enemies ranging from angry timber smugglers to committed Salafi jihadists from local villages. Many insurgents crossed the frontier from Bajaur in Pakistan to fight and then returned to rest and reorganize.[47] Building steadily since 2003, violence there reached a new intensity, particularly in the Korengal valley. In the provinces of Loya Paktia in the east, a different dynamic again prevailed. Local tribes were historically equally distrustful of the government in Kabul and of the *mullahs* or tribal leaders of Kandahar and successive American units found themselves caught between a desire to pursue more classic conventional tactics aimed at inflicting heavy casualties on their elusive enemy and the 'hearts and minds' approach, which they hoped might bring them leads on the where-abouts of senior al-Qaeda figures. In the end, a mix of both strategies was adopted with predictably patchy results.[48] The proximity of the Pakistani frontier did little to ease the situation either. Then there were the various fronts around Kabul. There were dozens of towns like Maidan Shar around the capital and dozens of shifting, imprecise but nonetheless very real frontlines. Each province abutting the capital had its own specificity. In the Jalrez valley of upper Wardak, international forces were marginal to battles between local communities over land and grazing rights.[49] In Sorobi, out on the road to Nangahar, a single valley was the epicentre of violence as a result of a peculiarly noxious mix of local political micro-factors.[50] The variations extended across the country, giving the impression of a collection of individual campaigns rather than a single conflict. In this the war in Afghanistan was, like that in Iraq, a matrix of interlinked but often remarkably independent struggles evolving on a variety of different levels, from village to nation to region, with a degree of interdependence but significant autonomy too. In this it was, naturally, a microcosm of the 9/11 Wars more generally. Of the various operations undertaken in Afghanistan by Western forces from 2006 that in Helmand was perhaps the most challenging.

Helmand's strategic importance was due to its population of between 700,000 and 1.2 million, its status as the source of half the world's illegal heroin in 2007 and its position aside key national communica-tions corridors.[51] There was the critical ring road linking Kandahar with Herat, there was the Helmand river itself which swept south and then west in a long fertile arc before losing itself in the sands of the Dasht-e-Margo, the Desert of Death, and there were also the principal drug trafficking routes along which much of Afghanistan's narcotics export left the country.

The first force sent into Helmand by the British government was 3,300 strong, a ratio of one soldier for around every 300 local people. With too few troops to even patrol the major roads linking the half dozen main bases the British established, the only secure means of communication was helicopter. As the British only had a handful of aged Chinooks, this was a critical handicap. Beyond the lack of manpower and material, the actions of a resilient and effective enemy and the challenges posed by one of the most hostile physical environments in the world, a number of other factors, largely of the making of British politicians, bureaucrats and senior commanders, also combined to weaken the deployment's already slim chances of success.

The British were largely unprepared for the very tough fight they found themselves caught up in. In part this was due to the dearth of useful intelligence before the deployment of the British troops. Beyond the gross underestimation of the potential numbers of fighters that might oppose the new British intervention – General Chris Brown, the most senior British officer in Afghanistan, told the author in the summer of 2006 that there were around 1,000 Taliban active in the entire country, a ludicrously low estimate at odds with almost every other intelligence assessment at the time – there was also a severe lack of understanding of the nature of the enemy and the form resistance was likely to take.[52] Between 2002 and 2005, the south of Afghanistan had been without satellite coverage after surveillance assets were switched to Iraq.[53] Intelligence services were preoccupied with other theatres too. Though pre-deployment briefings for soldiers on their way to Afghanistan had improved since 2003, when troops had listened to veteran sergeant majors talk to them about how they had patrolled the streets of Belfast, the men of the 3rd Parachute Battalion were, a month or so before their deployment, yet to be briefed either on hazards such as the roadside bombs that would inevitably greet them or, far more seriously, on the combination of latent hostility and pragmatic neutrality which would characterize the response of the local population to their presence.[54] Ideas about the battlefield tactics of the Taliban were also extremely vague. A team from the SAS, MI6 and British defence intelligence had spent six months with American troops who had been in the Helmandi towns of Lashkar Gah and Gereshk but, not least because the Americans themselves had remained very constrained in their movements and had little to pass on, a remarkably small amount of useful knowledge had filtered back to the incoming force.[55] The vacuum allowed policy-makers and senior officers to conclude more or less what they wanted. A confidential report later commissioned on what was going wrong in Helmand spoke of how in the run-up to the deployment 'the Ministry of Defence was sanguine about security [in Helmand] and not disposed to negative messages'.[56]

With the aims of the mission unclear and no real grasp of the environment the troops were to be entering, British military planners themselves

turned not to the new thinking about counter-insurgency operations
that was coming through in the USA and elsewhere (and already in part
being implemented in places like Kunar or in the eastern Afghan provinces) but once again to the supposed counter-insurgency successes of
British colonial and postcolonial campaigns.[57] Most senior British officers continued to be convinced that, certainly compared to the Americans
and other Europeans, they were inheritors of a long tradition both of
'understanding' foreign societies and of successfully fighting counter-
insurgency wars.[58] This was a dubious claim that was based on an
anachronistic and distorted view of what had actually happened in
Kenya, Malaysia, Northern Ireland and elsewhere and, as it had done in
Iraq, once more led to a complacency that successive setbacks did little
to puncture. An example was the idea, derived from campaigns in south-
east Asia in the 1940s and 1950s, that 'inkspots' of security could be
established which would become attractive nodes of economic development and gradually spread across the blotting paper of Helmand's
myriad valleys, plains, deserts, towns and villages. In Afghanistan, these
inkspots, defended as they were by foreign troops, naturally found
themselves under attack from insurgents, thus forcing the exodus of the
very local people the forces had been sent to protect. 'The inskpots are
black because there are no lights on. Everyone has left,' bleakly joked
one local Afghan NGO worker.[59]

These various complex and interlinked problems were further exacerbated by the political necessity of reducing casualties in order to
maintain support for the war among domestic populations increasingly
sceptical of further expense of 'blood and treasure' after five years of
controversial and often inconclusive campaigns in various theatres. This
was a key consideration not just for politicians back home but among
senior officers in Afghanistan. When Brigadier Ed Butler, then the commanding officer of British forces in Afghanistan, spoke of the 'battle for
public opinion' in Kabul in July 2006 he was referring to that of his
compatriots in the UK, not Afghans.[60] The result was the dogmatic prioritization of 'force security'. This meant a very natural reliance on the
international troops' greatest advantage: their firepower. Between just
June and November of 2006 American airplanes and helicopters had
conducted 2,000 strikes, using an average of 98 large bombs and 14,000
bullets a month, three times the previous year's total.[61] One evening
at an outpost at the Kajaki dam hydroelectric plant, a key strategic

objective of the British deployment, the author witnessed troops respond to a couple of rounds fired into their positions from a compound a kilometre or so away with heavy machine-gun fire, a dozen or so mortar rounds, a Javelin heat-seeking missile and finally a 500 lb bomb dropped from a Harrier jet. The result, said the officer in charge, was two dead insurgents, although this was unconfirmed.[62]

Then there was the question of narcotics, a dominant factor in Helmand but important throughout most of the south and some of the east. The opium boom had begun in 2002, after a year in which farmers and traffickers waited to see what policy the new rulers of their country would adopt.[63] The factors lying behind the post-war boom in narcotics cultivation were manifold and included the destruction of irrigation systems over decades of war, patterns of debt and credit, the approbation or otherwise of the clergy, the size of landholdings and the price of wheat. One significant element in the vast increase in the area under opium – from 104,000 hectares in 2005 to 165,000 in 2006 alone and increasing year on year thereafter – was the deliberate and intensive drive by major actors in the local drugs industry.[64] In what must have constituted one of the most effective rural support programmes anywhere in Afghanistan at the time, traffickers had provided improved varieties of poppy seeds, fertilizer, technical advice on methods of cultivation and generous banking and loan facilities and paid for the temporary employment of hundreds of thousands during the poppy harvest.[65] The traffickers also developed close ties with the insurgents, who levied the customary 10 per cent tax on agricultural produce on the opium and thus generated tens, if not hundreds, of millions of dollars.[66] Documents seized from traffickers listed sizeable 'donations' – sometimes of several hundred thousand dollars – both to insurgents and to senior officials.[67] By 2007, it was calculated that the narcotics industry in Afghanistan was worth some $3 billion (out of a gross national product of $8 billion). Production in 2008 would top 7,700 tonnes of opium, twice the level of 2002, of which a substantial proportion was for the first time turned into high-value heroin locally rather than in laboratories in Iran, Turkey, Pakistan, the Balkans or central Asia. In the north-east, where security – and governance – was stronger, drug production had fallen away markedly. However, in the space of just six or seven years, southern Afghanistan had developed a complete and self-sustaining alternative economy based on narcotics.[68] The business had got so big that some senior Taliban figures even expressed misgivings over its size, worrying that the power and influence of the drugs industry could eventually surpass their own.[69]

As with the insurgency, Western officials systematically downplayed the drugs problem. British officials, particularly sensitive as the UK had been the 'lead nation' on counter-narcotics since 2002, stressed how only between 12 and 16 per cent of the farming population were involved in opium cultivation.[70] However, this missed the point. The problem was not necessarily the drugs – though Afghanistan was developing a problem with its own addicts of a scale never previously seen – but with the cash the drugs generated. Only a fifth remained with the hundreds of thousands of farmers, analysts from the United Nations Office on Drugs and Crime said.[71] The rest went to the traffickers. Naturally this mountain of money – perhaps $4 billion in 2008 – fuelled massive corruption among government officials with positions such as police chief in a potentially remunerative location costing applicants up to $300,000 in bribes.[72]

Interminable debates about the correct strategy to tackle the problem continued throughout 2006 and 2007, pitting Americans who favoured aggressive eradication against Europeans who preferred broader programmes with more carrot and less stick, and led to deep confusion over the coalition's policy on drugs. One result was that the British deployment in Helmand had no clear instructions about how to tackle the vast opium industry in the province.[73] To start with, soldiers who came across syringes, piles of chemicals or stacks of raw opium were simply told to leave them. 'Otherwise we'll have the whole place up in arms,' said Tootal. Six months later, there was a move towards limited programmes of eradication of the crops of 'the greedy not the needy', in the words of one British senior civil servant in Helmand, which would be undertaken by the Afghan government and contractors.[74] But the confusion brought the worst of both worlds. The drug traffickers who funded many of the hardest fighting insurgent factions in Helmand, particularly in the north, continued to earn huge sums of money, while the limited eradication allowed the Taliban to claim that the West was set on destroying the crops that many farmers depended on. In any case, the wealthy could simply bribe the police to leave their fields alone. A study in Kandahar revealed that poppy farmers were disproportionately represented in insurgent ranks. Many of the fighters interviewed by the researchers said they saw the Afghan government and its international allies as a threat to their livelihood. This was far from the only motive for taking up arms – others included the loss of family members in air strikes or crossfire, for example – but was a significant factor nonetheless.[75]

The problems for the British in Helmand were the same for other forces around the country. Then there were other huge structural failings that hobbled the NATO force. The lines of command for international forces were impossibly tangled, running through Kandahar, Kabul, London, Brussels and, for the special forces and other Operation Enduring Freedom troops, US Centcom in Florida. The British served six-month tours (while the Americans did twelve or even fifteen months), which were barely long enough for a unit to get established, learn a little about the terrain and launch a single major operation before it was time to pack up again. Each new commanding officer brought a different approach. So whereas the brigade commander in Helmand in the first half of 2007 spoke of wearing down the enemy through attrition, 'mowing the lawn' as he termed it, his successor had a diametrically opposite vision of counter-insurgency warfare, telling the author in January 2008 that victory in Afghanistan could not be achieved through military means.[76] Then there was the question of progress. How could it be measured? British government and United Nations officials all pointed to familiar markers: economic growth in the country as a whole, the number of girls in school, the explosion of the media sector, successful preparations for elections in 2009, minefields cleared, money spent, wheat distributed, the fact that most of the north, the west and the cities remained calm.[77] Seventy per cent of violent incidents still occurred within ten districts, as ISAF spokesmen continued to repeat. On the other hand, in 2008 there were a third more 'kinetic events' than the previous year and 50 per cent more kidnappings and assassinations.[78] Any private unease at the direction things were taking was kept very quiet. It was true that insurgents were being killed in large numbers. Though body counts were avoided – one commander spoke of them as a 'corrupt measure' – British senior officers nonetheless boasted of 'neutralizing' between 3,000 and 4,000 Taliban fighters in 2008 alone.[79] But keeping Western casualties to politically manageable levels was proving hard. Six British soldiers had died between the end of the 2001 campaign and the new deployments of 2006. More than ten times as many were to die in the following two years. Across the country as a whole, there were 416 coalition deaths between June 2006 and July 2008, more than had been killed in the previous four and half years.[80] Then there were the local casualties. Hundreds of government officials and nearly a thousand police died in 2007 alone. One was the courageous and effective female police chief in Kandahar, Malalai Kakar. 'We killed her,' a Taliban spokesman told AFP news agency. 'She was our target, and we successfully eliminated our target.'[81]

In the middle of it all were people like Roz Khan, a day labourer, and Gul Pari, a widowed farmer's wife. Both were villagers from the Sangin Valley, a crucial thoroughfare in the north of Helmand contested by British troops and insurgents. Forced to flee their homes, they described a grim daily routine of trying to reach their fields through air strikes and skirmishes, of pressure from the insurgents at night and of patrols by Western forces during the day. 'If it was just one or the other things would be better. But when there is a fight over your house you can't live in it,' said Roz Khan. Almost every family he knew had lost at least one member to stray bullets or Western bombing, either poorly targeted or attracted by insurgents who deliberately hid among the villagers. The husband of Pari, who had four young children, had been killed in a 'bombardment' but she was unsure which side to blame. 'When there was fighting, we did not know what was going on. But I think it was the fault of the Taliban because they were shooting and then there was an attack afterwards.'[82] Many tens of thousands had fled to Kandahar or Kabul, where they lived in squalor and destitution in makeshift refugee camps, ignored by the government and receiving only rudimentary assistance from overstretched aid agencies.[83] Pari tried to feed, clothe and house her family with the 50 Afghani [65p] that her eldest son earned from selling ice creams on the streets of the capital. She did not know how they would survive the winter.

With access to villages like those left by Roz Khan and Pari very difficult and their inhabitants very wary of speaking, piecing together an accurate picture of what communities genuinely felt about either the insurgents or the government and their Western allies was extremely difficult. But almost all the evidence confirmed that what most communities hoped most to avoid was rule neither by the Taliban nor the

'Amriki', as all international forces were known, but being caught between the two. The new fighting from 2006 on had suddenly placed hundreds of communities in an unenviable position between a Western rock and an insurgent hard place.[84] Certainly, for tribal elders trying to juggle the various pressures from different insurgent factions, the Afghan police, the Afghan army, drugs traffickers and various rivals ready to unseat them at the slightest misstep, the arrival of a well-meaning and heavily armed Western officer asking 'what he could do to help' was the last thing they needed. 'They keep asking us what we want. The answer is that they go away,' one told the author near Maiwand, outside Kandahar, in July 2006.[85] Such sentiments clearly posed a problem to a strategy based on convincing communities to 'join the winning side', as Tootal had described it.

That any elders tempted to cooperate with international forces or the government risked the wrath of the insurgents clearly did not help. This was especially evident during the successive operations to clear areas of Taliban. When the thinly spread international forces withdrew to commence another operation elsewhere, as they usually were forced to do, anyone who had cooperated locally was left very exposed. One of the more egregious examples occurred in Marjah, a rural district in central Helmand, which was cleared during an operation in 2007 and then turned over to 'local security forces'. The district was subsequently left unprotected, allowing the Taliban to move back in and kill scores of local notables. Watching a patrol of heavily armed UK soldiers plod down a back lane in Lashkar Gah, where the coalition force in Helmand had its headquarters, one elderly man told the author that the British were the twelfth fighting force he had seen from the gate of his compound in the last twenty years. (The others were, in reverse historical order, Americans, the Taliban, at least four warring *mujahideen* groups, Soviet troops and Afghan government soldiers from three different regimes.) 'They always arrive noisily saying they will win but leave much more quietly,' he added and shrugged. It was not as if the insurgents were very far away. In a small mechanics' workshop off the main bazaar in the town, only a few hundred yards past the gates of the NATO base, Fazl Rahman, forty years old, told the author bluntly: 'I am Taliban. Why should I be afraid? You British and Americans should leave this country. You are here for your own benefit, to destabilize our country, which is a castle of Islam, to destroy our religion. Soon you will run.'[86]

## THE END OF 2008: CHALLENGES AND OPPORTUNITIES FOR THE TALIBAN

No insurgency progresses in a linear fashion, steadily advancing across a map, increasing in a regular exponential manner until finally taking power or expelling the foreign occupiers. Expansion is always marked by a series of inflection points. These are critical moments when the future evolution of the revolt, rebellion, movement or whatever are determined. Such moments involve significant challenges that have to be successfully met by insurgent leaders – and often lower-level participants too – if progress towards any given goal is to be maintained. It was thus inevitable that Mullah Mohammed Omar and the senior Taliban leadership also faced a series of acute problems as a consequence of the movement's rapid resurgence between 2002 and 2008. These fell into three main categories: military, political and diplomatic.

The first and most pressing were the military challenges. The success of the Taliban had provoked a response from their enemies, belated but very real nonetheless, and the leadership needed to try to find a tactical and strategic answer to the successive NATO military efforts. One very costly experiment was a set-piece battle fought among the vineyards, villages and small mud-walled fields of Panjwai outside Kandahar in late 2006. Along with the district of Argandab to the north, the area had been a key battlefield during the war against the Soviets, and the Taliban leadership may have hoped either to definitively carve out a secure enclave from which to launch an assault on Kandahar itself – a sort of miniature 'al-Zarqawi' local strategy – or to inspire a more general insurrection across much of the country through seeking, and winning, a pitched confrontation in such a historically important location – the equivalent of al-Suri style 'global intifada', but on a national scale. Though the fighting was tough, with coalition forces close to running out of ammunition and suffering heavy casualties from both friendly and enemy fire, neither Taliban aim was achieved, and the insurgents were eventually forced to retreat in disorder across the desert to the south, where Western special forces killed hundreds.[87] Though such losses were swiftly made good with further recruiting drives in the *medressas*, refugee camps and villages across the border, no such operation was ever attempted again.

The 'caravan' of the Taliban movement was far from the sort of organized, hierarchical army that could formulate, institutionalize and execute doctrinal change with rapid efficiency and uniformity. The insurgency resembled more a swarm of wasps from different nests momentarily travelling together in a single, very broad direction. The impact of strategic direction from individuals such as Mullah Omar, Hekmatyar or Jalaluddin Haqqani (or increasingly his son, Sirajuddin) was always somewhat haphazard. Tactical innovation was thus the work of individual commanders and spread as 'best practice' through example, experimentation and word of mouth. As in Iraq, however, this meant a capacity to adapt very fast and very effectively. Improvements in manoeuvre and ambushes were soon noted by Western troops. So too was the steep increase in the number of IEDs. These inflicted a heavy toll with little risk and, as had been the case in Iraq, rapidly became a key weapon. The roadside bombings, booby traps and other similar devices did not replace the direct confrontations – the proportion of which in fact went from 47 per cent to 57 per cent of all insurgent attacks between 2006 and 2007 – but complemented them. Suicide bombs were particularly effective against softer targets such as Afghan government buildings or the police. However, the civilian casualties they often caused were problematic, and the tactic sparked a fierce debate within Taliban ranks.[88]

The second broad area in which expansion posed problems for the insurgent leadership was a familiar one: as the Taliban had grown, discipline had suffered. This in its turn imperilled the insurgents' hold on communities and thus the continued success of the movement. What the Taliban and the other insurgent groups needed to avoid was a cycle such as that which had so damaged al-Qaeda in Iraq and the al-Mahdi Army, whereby diminishing support necessitated greater measures of coercion, which exacerbated the original problem to the point where entire populations started shifting allegiance away from the militants. The steady attrition of experienced Taliban commanders such as Mullah Dadaullah Akhund – who had led the destruction of the Bamiyan Buddhas, had escaped coalition forces in 2001 and had gone on to become increasingly unpredictable, violent and powerful – posed a challenge that went beyond simply replacing capable individuals.[89] The 'degrading' of senior ranks led to a new cohort of younger leaders, many of whom had not been involved in the original Taliban movement of the 1990s, being appointed to run their own *mahaz*, or 'front'. As with the al-Mahdi Army in Iraq, these new commanders tended to be much less disciplined than their elders had been and their often violent and indiscriminate actions undermined much of the work done to secure the support of local communities by more experienced and more ideologically or politically mature figures. By 2007 there was significant unrest in Ghazni – where local commanders had beaten and tortured locals who refused to give them fuel for motorbikes – in Zabul, in parts of Helmand and elsewhere. The insurgents, well-informed analysts often said, had always depended on the active support of 10 per cent and the acquiescence of another 60 per cent of the population and in these places the behaviour of the 'new Taliban', as many locals called them, was threatening both.[90] Expansion also meant that the key tactic of providing honest and rapid justice, either through mobile courts or through local clerics acting with the authority of the movement, was being undermined because there were too few judges of sufficient calibre to fill all the posts in the new areas that came under Taliban control. Worse, a wide range of criminals had been passing themselves off as 'Taliban'. Some mixed actions commissioned by the real Taliban leadership with more freelance activities designed for pure personal gain, often at the expense of local communities. A few respected the orders coming down the satellite phone from Quetta or the tribal areas – at least two Western journalists avoided being put on trial as spies by local commanders after Taliban 'ministers' sitting on the leadership council in Pakistan were contacted – but many were not in the least bothered by any such sense of hierarchy and simply got on with looting and banditry.[91] A significant proportion of new commanders were too young to remember much of the pre-2001 Taliban rule.[92]

Much of 2007 and 2008 had thus been marked by repeated efforts of Mullah Omar to bring some order to his increasingly unruly troops. The 'shadow governors' appointed in key provinces were reshuffled – though not without resistance from some and resentment on the part of others.[93] A book of rules for combatants was issued, prohibiting (and thus implicitly admitting) practices such as temporary marriage to women, the ransoming of prisoners, theft, cigarettes, the summary execution of spies and, in a society where pederasty is common, the 'taking of young boys without beards to the battlefield or to homes'. Commanders were told that 'using the jihad for their own personal profit' was forbidden.[94] Simultaneously previously rigorous restrictions on music, television and such pastimes as kite-flying or dog fighting were loosened. Decisions over the vexed issue of women's education – many villagers wanted their daughters to be at least literate – were left to local commanders who were closest to individual communities and better placed to judge their preferences. In 2007, Mullah Omar himself said that implementing 'social edicts' was up to the discretion of local leaders. Often compromises were found with schools opening when elders approved by the Taliban were present to oversee teaching and strict segregation.[95]

Other issues where the military demands of running an insurgency conflicted with keeping the consent of local communities were harder to resolve. One was the difficult question of mobile phone coverage. Worried about spies reporting their whereabouts, many Taliban commanders had destroyed the masts necessary to relay signals, an act that was inevitably deeply unpopular with local people, for whom cheap telecommunications had often been one of the few tangible benefits seen since the invasion of 2001. The eventual deal reached in many places was that the masts would remain but the phone companies would switch them off at night, allowing any potential targets of coalition special forces to sleep without fear of a nocturnal tip-off and a 4 a.m. raid. The fact that the insurgents were able to extort significant sums as 'protection money' from the phone companies – as they did from businesses involved in the execution of coalition-funded development projects or even the transport of its military supplies – was also a factor. A good gauge of the extent of geographic influence of the insurgents at any given moment was the number of districts where there was twenty-four-hour mobile coverage. In the summer of 2008, only around half of all Afghanistan's provinces could promise all their inhabitants uninterrupted use of the now ubiquitous phones.[96]

The effects of these various measures were variable. The chaotic structure of the insurgency necessarily impeded their application, and there were significant limits to the compromises the Taliban leadership were prepared to make. The strategy of suicide bombing continued despite its unpopularity among locals and the arguments it generated within senior Taliban ranks. A careful information campaign designed to mitigate the negative publicity surrounding particularly bloody attacks and to justify the continued use of the tactics was launched with DVDs and radio broadcasts extolling the courage and honour of the bombers all while minimizing any reports of 'collateral damage'. The use of Pakistani rather than local Afghan suicide bombers was stepped up and the real PR disasters – attacks in which dozens of children were killed, for example – were simply disowned or blamed on the Americans.[97] There was no shying away either from coercion or intimidation when deemed necessary. The Taliban had learned that targeted assassinations of officials in places like Kandahar was an extremely effective way of preventing the government developing any real capacity on the ground. Such killings were also deeply unpopular but, like the suicide bombing, were apparently considered worth continuing for the overall strategic benefits they brought.

Overall, the insurgents seemed to have recognized that effectively fusing their military and information strategies could overcome many of the challenges posed by their growth and the initiatives taken by the coalition. Not only were atrocity stories – some barely exaggerated accounts of experiences in Bagram or Guantanamo Bay – circulated to build animosity against the international forces but stories of the supposed moral degradation of Kabul were disseminated too. Anything that could enhance the sense of the honest, suffering rural communities betrayed by the decadent, exploitative self-interested urbanites was emphasized. Explicit ethnicity was avoided in the messaging, which often took on a strongly nationalist tone.[98] Aware than their greatest advantage was perhaps the simple fact that they were Afghans and Muslims fighting largely white, Western, 'Christian' soldiers, the insurgents in their DVDs reinforced parallels with the 'jihad' against the Soviets, which was now portrayed as a rare victory against the international conspiracy of powers dedicated to destroying Islam and the Afghan 'nation'. Above all, violence was deployed to serve the purposes of the information campaign not vice versa. The continuing low-level fighting around the country was united into a single narrative of resistance – even if most of it was anarchic and opportunistic and related to local factors – while the more high-profile insurgent attacks were carefully designed for maximum impact. So the suicide bombing and raid on the five-star Serena Hotel in the centre of Kabul in January 2008 was worth the risk of collateral damage and disapproval of the tactics because the target – a luxury complex favoured by the Kabuli rich and foreigners – had such resonance.[99] The strike also showed the inability of the government – and ISAF – to protect even the centre of the capital. Equally, the spectacular Kandahar jailbreak of June 2008 was worth the risk of failure and high casualties. With hundreds freed for little loss and worldwide news coverage, it was a major success. A third example was the ambush of French troops in the valley of Uzbeen, north of Sorobi, in August 2008. Though the action itself was largely the result of a rivalry between three local armed groups all linked to Hekmatyar's Hezb-e-Islami, the ambush was rapidly and effectively exploited by the insurgents at a national level. Reporters in Kabul received text messages from Taliban spokesmen claiming exaggerated French losses even before the ISAF press office was apparently aware the fighting had taken place.[100] It appeared unlikely that the Uzbeen ambush had been commissioned by the insurgent leadership in the way that the attacks on the Serena – probably the work of Haqqani's group – and that in Kandahar had been. But it played firmly into a further new element of the insurgent strategy, which was to deliberately target public opinion in the West. Taliban media spokesmen boasted of closely monitoring Western press reports of both events in Afghanistan and the debate in the thirty-nine countries which had troops in the country. It was little surprise that news of the decision of President Sarkozy to fly to Kabul following the attack was posted on Taliban-linked websites, linked to translations of articles from French newspapers arguing for immediate withdrawal of the nation's troops from the conflict, within hours of it being announced. On occasion too the insurgents appeared happy to admit that they had sustained significant casualties, presumably aware that their ability to absorb continued losses demoralized their opponents and turned domestic opinion in the West further against the war.

The final challenge posed to the Afghan insurgents by their expansion – and their relative success in fighting the new Western forces to a stalemate – was perhaps the most serious. For many years, one subject had been taboo among Western diplomats, soldiers and politicians: the support offered by Pakistani intelligence services to the Taliban. Yet that the insurgents, whether from the core Taliban or from Haqqani's or Hekmatyar's groups, had been receiving assistance from within the neighbouring state had been an open secret for a long time. This was a delicate matter for the Pakistanis, who had no intention of abandoning the policy launched in 2002 of at least tacitly tolerating the presence of the Afghan insurgents on their soil so as to be better positioned for the West's inevitable eventual withdrawal from Afghanistan, but was potentially even more troublesome for the Taliban themselves. A misjudged local strike could therefore have damaging consequences that far outweighed any tactical advantage gained. So the bombing of the Indian embassy in Kabul in July 2008 may have been initially counted a tactical success but, after American intelligence reported monitoring conversations between ISI officers and the attackers in which the logistics for the strikes appeared to be discussed, it looked to be have been strategically counter-productive.[101] The bombing galvanized the White House into paying much closer attention to the apparent role Pakistani intelligence was playing in the continuing success of the insurgents and thus threatened the one thing the Taliban could not afford to jeopardize: their safe haven in Pakistan.[102] That the details of the overheard conversations were leaked at all was an indication of how concerned the American security establishment had become about Pakistan's role in Afghanistan.

The perpetrators of the attack on the Indian embassy died as they were meant to do, in a sudden moment of spectacular violence designed to frighten and impress as much as kill and destroy. This naturally rendered a full investigation of their identity and how they came to be in Kabul with suicide vests strapped to them difficult. However, as with such attackers elsewhere in the various theatres of the 9/11 Wars, an idea of the process which led them to blow themselves up on the streets of the capital can be reconstructed from the stories of others who did not travel quite to the very end of the same road. Abit, a slim, handsome twenty-one-year-old baker's son from Bahawalpur, in the south of the eastern Pakistani province of Punjab, had found himself strapped to a bomb in Afghanistan but had decided at the last minute not to die. He had been recruited by a friend who had, he said, suggested a 'tour' to a town close to the border with Afghanistan.[103] The 'tour' had in fact taken the pair directly to a compound run by local Taliban, where Abit's friend had swiftly disappeared, leaving him with a dozen other young men. Their days were spent reading the Koran, receiving specifically targeted religious instruction and viewing militant jihadi propaganda videos which had familiar themes.

'We watched films of bombardments and fighting in Iraq. They told me the whole infidel world was coming to Afghanistan to invade and repress Muslims and that it was the duty of all Muslims to resist. They told me about the rewards of martyrdom,' Abit said. Scared by tales of what might happen to him as an outsider if he went wandering in the local bazaar, he stayed within the compound's confines, entirely isolated from the outside world.

Abit, speaking in the offices of the Afghan national intelligence service in Kabul with the windows open and birdsong for once audible over the sound of the city, said the process was 'gradual' but that after several months he was prepared to 'sacrifice himself for Islam'. The men who ran the compound told him that everything was ready. The target – a US base on the frontier – had been selected.

'They told me there were just Americans there,' Abit said. 'They told me not to think about what would happen to my body because Allah ensures martyrs suffer no pain. They told me to remember that a martyr takes his relatives with him to paradise and that was as important for me as the infidels committing violence and tyranny.'

Abit was driven over the border to within a mile or so of the base, where a truck stuffed with explosives was waiting with a detonator button wired to the dashboard. 'I drove the truck towards the base,' he said. 'I was not thinking of anything. I just kept saying "Allahu akbar, Allahu akbar". I felt nothing.'

On reaching his target, however, Abit saw only Afghans. 'I could see no Americans,' he told the author. 'The soldiers told me to stop the truck, and I got down and I gave myself up. I am very sorry and I am glad no one was harmed.'[104]

# 13
# Pakistan

## 'THE MOST DANGEROUS COUNTRY ON EARTH'

Of all countries that became major theatres of conflict in the 9/11 Wars, Pakistan was perhaps the most important. It was certainly the biggest, with a population of around 177 million in 2007 and another 3 million being added every year, more than that of Egypt, Turkey and Iraq combined.[1] Pakistan was where al-Qaeda had been conceived and formed back in the late 1980s, where militant groups had proliferated through the 1990s with state support unparalleled anywhere in the Islamic world, where some of the most influential components of modern Islamist and Islamic militant ideology had been formulated and tested. It was where the Taliban leadership had found a safe haven following their fall from power in 2001 and where Osama bin Laden and other terrorist fugitives had been able to reconstitute a working terrorist operation the capacity of which had been amply made clear by successive bomb attacks in the region, in Europe and elsewhere, realized or thwarted. Pakistan was a nuclear power, with hostile relations with its neighbours that dated back decades and a range of social and economic problems that, though no means exceptional in the Islamic world or among developing nations generally, were nonetheless acute. In 2008, Pakistan was 141st out of 182 on the United Nations Human Development index.[2] Infant mortality rates were on a par with those in sub-Saharan Africa and much of the population did not have access to clean water let alone health care. If outright chronic malnutrition was rare, many millions of people ate poorly. Pakistan's size alone – often underestimated due to its proximity to giants India and China – and strategic position as a buffer state between the

Middle East and south Asia contributed too to a strategic importance that few other countries involved in the 9/11 Wars could rival. In this the country was very different from its western neighbour. Afghanistan was only considered crucial because it had been a launchpad for the 9/11 attacks and was seen as having the potential to become so again. Otherwise, a fractured state with a small population, negligible economic activity in global terms and limited resources other than some natural gas, minerals and metals, it had never been, nor was unlikely ever to become, a crucial piece of the geopolitical jigsaw. The ramifications of a collapse of Iraq would naturally have had very grave consequences on the Middle East and thus on the world's economy, spiking oil prices and releasing a wave of radicalism, but, appalling though such a prospect might be, the potential fall-out of such an eventuality would arguably be less than that of the catastrophic implosion of Pakistan. Reporting and analysis of Pakistan often reflected the deep fear on the part of Western policy-makers, analysts and strategists that the state's oft-predicted failure inspired. In late 2007 *Newsweek*, the American magazine, echoing the pronouncements of a range of Western, and particularly Washington-based, statesmen over the decade, bluntly told its readers that Pakistan was the 'most dangerous country on earth'.[3]

These often alarmist analyses seemed difficult to reconcile with the country's evident resilience. Created in 1947 in the blood and chaos of Britain's precipitate departure from the subcontinent, Pakistan had survived its traumatic birth, defeat in a series of wars, repeated internal insurrection, the loss of its eastern half, a series of military governments, brutal nationalization programmes in the 1970s, the consequences of the Afghan war against the Soviets in the 1980s, the turmoil of the end of the Cold War, sanctions and the chaotic and corrupt 'democracy' of the 1990s. The years immediately before 9/11 and through the first half decade of the wars had dealt the country blows that would have caused many others to fail: a coup (albeit bloodless) in 1999 which overturned an elected if deeply unpopular government, a lengthy military dictatorship, a series of rigged or semi-rigged elections, broad civil unrest, a scandal over the selling of its nuclear weapons secrets and a devastating earthquake. Somehow Pakistan managed not just to survive all this but, in some areas, to thrive. Pakistan was not so much a 'failed state' as a state which should by rights have failed long ago but had somehow successfully held on in the face of extreme adversity.

The greatest tests were yet to come. Though the country had played a very significant role in setting the scene for the conflict, the 9/11 Wars had largely avoided Pakistani soil in the years following the September 11 attacks. The waves of violence that had surged across Afghanistan, the Middle East, even parts of the Far East and Europe from 2001 on through the middle of the decade had barely touched the country. That began to change in the summer of 2007. In July, there was a pitched battle between Pakistani troops and Islamic militants who had fortified a mosque and *medressa* compound in the centre of Islamabad, the capital city. The late summer saw fierce fighting in the west of the country between Pakistani paramilitary forces and fighters from a whole set of new emerging radical factions who dubbed themselves the Pakistani Taliban. Then, after an unprecedented wave of blasts and shootings across much of the north and west of the country, Benazir Bhutto, former prime minister and self-dubbed 'Daughter of the East', returned to Pakistan from nine years of exile in Dubai. Landing in Karachi, Pakistan's southern port city, she was greeted by a huge bomb that killed 139 and injured several hundred. There is some suggestion that the bomb had been hidden in the crib of a small child.

## BHUTTO AND A CHANGING PAKISTAN

The idea of a separate nation for the Muslims of the subcontinent had sprung from a perception that to remain within a Hindu-dominated independent India after the British had left would mean risking discrimination, marginalization and the eventual extinction of any distinct south Asian Muslim culture and identity. Such fears were voiced by the unofficial posthumous poet laureate of the new nation, Mohammed Iqbal, the Indian philosopher and politician whose revivalist writings provided an eloquent literary and ideological underpinning to the idea of the Pakistani state and echoed sentiments present since the mid nineteenth century in much of the colonized Muslim world. Even if, as some historians hold, the concept of Pakistan was only ever a bargaining position on the part of the Indian Muslim League, the partition that was apparently so desired led to a bloodbath with somewhere between 500,000 and a million being killed as communities fled west or east to their new homes. The vast bulk of the capital, material wealth and infrastructure of the British Indian possessions remained in what became India. So too did almost all the major monuments and sites of the very south Asian Islamic culture the creation of the new state was meant to preserve. Pakistan was thus born with several major disadvantages: a bloody and frightening delivery, almost no resources, a clearly untenable geography with its eastern wing a thousand miles from the western part of the country and, perhaps most problematic of all, no clear idea of what the country was supposed to be.

Many analysts have noted the incoherence at the heart of the concept of the Pakistani state and the role of religion.[4] Though Pakistan was created as an Islamic homeland, indeed a refuge, its founder, Mohammed Ali Jinnah, the seventy-year-old Westernized lawyer who ran the Muslim League, had made clear that he saw the new nation's future as tolerant and pluralist with religion playing a major but not defining role in the country's political and legal structures and identity. Pakistan was not to be a theocracy. On August 11, 1947, in Karachi, Jinnah told the new nation's constituent assembly: 'You are free; you are free to go to your temples, you are free to go to your mosques or to any other place of worship ... We are starting in the days when there is no discrimination, no distinction between one community and another, no discrimination between one caste or creed and another. We are starting with this fundamental principle that we are all citizens and equal citizens of one state.' Jinnah died of lung cancer and tuberculosis only thirteen months after Pakistan's creation but, even if he had survived a little longer, it is unlikely that he would have been able to resolve the fundamental questions of identity the new country faced.

Born only six years after Pakistan's foundation, Benazir Bhutto's life had been intertwined with the troubled history of her country. By the time she was old enough to vote, she had already seen two military coups. The latter had brought General Ayub Khan to power in 1958. Like many other leaders in the Islamic and broader developing world at the time, Ayub Khan was a committed secular reformer who, influenced by Ataturk, promoted women's education and rights and made a genuine attempt at controlling population growth. He did not believe in democracy, or more precisely in politicians, and was forced from power in 1969, having failed to achieve most of his modernizing ambitions.[5] After a short interim, he was succeeded by Benazir Bhutto's father, Zulfiqar Ali Bhutto, a brilliant, charismatic and utterly unscrupulous minor hereditary landowner from the southern Sindh province. Z. A. Bhutto had cynically and skilfully exploited the aftermath of Pakistan's loss of its eastern, more populous wing following an uprising and a disastrous conflict with India in 1971 to force a situation where he had a chance of winning power. His strategy worked, and his newly formed Pakistan People's Party swept elections by campaigning on a platform of radical nationalist, socialist policies with the slogan 'Food, clothes and shelter'. His voters were to see precious little of any of the three, however, though Bhutto did implement a divisive and economically disastrous nationalization programme, expand the role of the intelligence services in domestic politics and ban alcohol in a bid to head off increasing discontent among the country's powerful and well-organized religious conservatives. His rule, first as president and then as prime minister, lasted six years until he was deposed in a military coup which occurred when the religious right wing, despite the concessions Bhutto had made to their demands, made Pakistan ungovernable. In the chaos, General Zia u'Haq, the chief of army staff, took power. He hanged Bhutto two years later, in April 1979. Benazir was one of the last to see her father alive. She spent much of the next decade under house arrest or overseas.

Zia had ruled, at least initially, with the support of Pakistan's numerous and well-organized Islamists, appointing many to political office, carefully directing funds to religious organizations, empowering the clergy and increasing the powers of the religious courts that had run alongside the previously largely secular legal system.[6] The biggest beneficiaries of this shift were naturally the members and supporters of Jamaat Islami, the vast and highly disciplined organization founded by the Indian autodidact cleric Abu Ala Maududi in 1941, who, despite the concept of the nation theoretically being an unislamic innovation, had, like Islamists elsewhere, nonetheless accepted the idea of the Islamic or Islamicized nation state, albeit preferring one that was run by religious leaders, to a Western-style democracy.[7] Maududi, who admitted that his vision owed much to revolutionary Communism and Fascism, was one of the most original thinkers of modern Islamic revivalism and a key influence on such major Middle Eastern figures such as Hassan al-Banna, Sayyid Qutb and the Ayatollah Khomeini, who translated his works into Farsi. It was Maududi, for example, who first began using the term *jahiliya*, which can roughly be translated as pagan ignorance, to describe almost all innovations since the time of the *salaf*, the early generations of Muslims, and who popularized the idea of the jihad as transcendental struggle, albeit a spiritual one.[8]

Zia was the son of a government clerk, and his animosity towards the Bhutto dynasty was, at least in part, based on class. Though his continued hold on power owed much to American support – the invasion of Afghanistan arrived at a particularly opportune moment – the courteous, pious and teetotal general also successfully played on the tensions between the old landed elite and the less privileged bureaucracy, the recently educated urban lower middle class and the conservative commercial classes to divide any opposition to him. Relations between the dictator and the Islamists steadily soured, but there was enough consonance between Zia's values and theirs for their agenda to be steadily advanced nonetheless. Though his death in a mysterious plane crash led to elections in 1988 which were, against all expectations, narrowly won by Bhutto and the PPP, the Islamists, though distanced from any formal power, retained a significant degree of informal influence, not least in the bureaucracy and the military.[9] Their organization also remained strong, particularly in the urban lower middle classes, the bedrock of political Islamism across the Muslim world.

This rough balance of forces led to alternate governments of Bhutto's PPP and the conservative Pakistan Muslim League (PML), now led by the unprepossessing Nawaz Sharif, through the 1990s. While Bhutto retained her power base in rural areas and in the south, Sharif, the son of an industrialist with solid Islamist connections, consolidated his own constituency in the relatively prosperous Punjab and among the urban population and reached out to Jamaat Islami.[10] Weakened by her second deposition in 1996 and the reputation of her husband, a former playboy from a third-rank landed family called Asif Ali Zardari, for corruption, Bhutto was unable to mobilize sufficient popular support to resist efforts to bring her to trial at the end of the decade. To avoid looming incarceration, she fled the country.

Sharif's triumph was short-lived, however. A combination of incompetence, graft and increasing authoritarianism rapidly alienated most of his erstwhile supporters, and when the army under General Musharraf moved in to depose him in 1999 the coup was largely welcomed as a result. Both Sharif and Bhutto had inherited vast problems from Zia but succeeded only in exacerbating them. Both had entered into a series of deals with religious parties to bolster their grip on power, allowing

Islamists and the conservative Deobandi clergy to develop a power base within the democratic political system. Both had allowed or encouraged the country's security services to aid the Taliban in Afghanistan and militant groups in Kashmir. Both, though ostensibly democratically elected and 'moderate', presided over a significant deterioration of relations with the USA. In 1990, the US imposed sanctions on Pakistan for pursuing its nuclear programme. In 1998, a new set of more sweeping restrictions was triggered by Pakistan's nuclear tests in May of that year.[11] Between them, Bhutto and Sharif left Pakistan's economy on life support from international agencies increasingly unwilling to lend, its political system riddled with graft, its society undermined by unprecedented levels of crime and its stability threatened by rising extremist violence.[12]

Once Bhutto had left the country and Musharraf had taken power, few in the West paid much attention to Pakistan. This was a mistake. Over the previous decades almost every one of the various factors that had contributed to the rise of radical violent Islamism elsewhere had been emerging. Like their Egyptian or Algerian counterparts in the late 1990s, for example, young Pakistanis in, say, 2002 could look back on the successive failures of secular modernizing dictatorships, populist nationalist Socialism, state Islamism and a debased form of democracy to solve the problems of their country. There was the vast 'youth bulge' seen elsewhere too. Between 2002 and 2007, when violence began to surge in a very serious way, the other key elements which had helped create the conditions for violence elsewhere also became evident. There was the growth of the middle class to a size where a new arrangement of power relations and a redistribution of economic wealth in the country became unavoidable if any semblance of stability was to be retained. There was the social change associated with rapid urbanization and economic growth, which boosted expectations without resolving the structural problems which made them almost impossible to fulfil. There was the exposure to new ideas of pan-Islamic solidarity and the supposed Western 'crusade' against Muslims. There were tensions between generations and a general breakdown in established social hierarchies. There was, particularly due to the growing influence of the Middle East, a new reaffirmation of a more defined and confident Islamic identity, one which promised a resolution to the fundamental historic incoherence at the heart of the nation. This was Pakistan, of course, not the countries of the Maghreb or the core Middle East, and therefore these factors played out in new and different ways. But some of the consequences – particularly in terms of violence – were the same.

## KARACHI

The problem, as ever, was not stasis or 'backwardness' but change. One place where the changes in Pakistan were very evident was Karachi. Two of the most significant developments in the time Bhutto was in exile were the economic boom during the period and the rapid growth of Pakistan's urban population. Both of these had fundamentally changed Karachi, as they had changed the nation as a whole.

To stand on a street corner in central Karachi in late 2007 and watch the traffic was as good a way as any to appreciate the rapid evolution of Pakistani society. The city was home to around 15 million inhabitants, composed of communities from all over the country.[13] It was dominated politically if not necessarily demographically by Mohajirs, the descendants of the refugees who had fled India in 1947. Yet the Mohajirs shared the city with around 4 million Pashtuns and large communities of Baluchis from the province to the west, Sindhis from the vast semi-desert interior province that dominates the south of Pakistan and a smaller number of Punjabis from the country's richest and most populous province in the north-east.[14] Each community had its own neighbourhoods, ran its own religious, cultural and social establishments and spoke its own mother tongue rather than, or at least in addition to, Urdu, the national language.[15]

The communities in Karachi had distinctive socio-economic profiles too. The Punjabis, small in number, were affluent; the Pashtuns were either wealthy and successful businessmen (particularly in the transport trade) or relatively poor immigrants; the Sindhis and the Baluchis, often recent arrivals from rural areas, were the poorest and lived in vast shantytowns. The Mohajirs constituted much of the mass in the middle: the petty tradesmen, the teachers, the pharmacists, the clerks, the minor officials, the small and middling businessmen, the doctors. On the whole the Mohajirs supported the disciplined, authoritarian, nominally secular (and on occasion extremely violent) Muttahida Quami Movement (MQM) party.[16] Some of the wealthy of Karachi, cantoned in the plush and leafy seaside suburbs like Clifton, had only recently become rich. Others were the heirs of the big proprietors created or co-opted by the British overlords during their conquest and occupation in the nineteenth century. It was there that the Bhuttos, quintessential feudals themselves, had their town home.[17]

Karachi had earned a reputation as a violent city in the 1980s and 1990s as political parties broadly representing the different ethnic groups fought bloody battles at elections and in the streets for control of the city. Thousands had died until the army had been deployed to restore order. Since then, the guns had largely fallen silent, though the city, caught nonetheless by some of the secondary effects of the 9/11 Wars, had still seen enough violence to reinforce its reputation for harbouring and nurturing extremism. There had been riots during the campaign in Afghanistan of 2001, and then in January 2002, Daniel Pearl, the American Jewish reporter for the *Wall Street Journal*, had been kidnapped in the city by a group of Islamic militants and then beheaded by al-Qaeda.[18] In the autumn of that year, it had been in an upmarket middle-class suburb of Karachi that Ramzi bin al-Shibh, one of the key 9/11 conspirators, had been captured. The city's many religious schools were a source for recruits not only to Pakistan's own many militant groups but for the Taliban in Afghanistan.[19] One, the famous Binoria, was draped in banners exhorting participation in 'the Afghan jihad' as late as 2006.[20] Most recently the lawless and deprived slums of Orangi in the west, split into Mohajir and Pashtun neighbourhoods, had seen riots and gunfights which had killed dozens over two days in May 2007. These were not, however, linked to any broader conflict, but due in part to ethnic tensions, in part to political manoeuvring between President Musharraf, his supporters and lawyers contesting his authority.

Yet Karachi, despite the crumbling infrastructure and the violence, remained the country's commercial powerhouse, alone generating 68 per cent of the government's revenue and 25 per cent of the nation's gross domestic product.[21] If the historic city of Lahore, 650 miles to the north, was Pakistan's cultural capital, and Islamabad, the new town created in the 1960s on a relatively cool plateau under the foothills of the Himalayas a two-hour flight away, was the administrative capital, then Karachi was the undisputed business and financial centre and continued to make money even in the worst of times. Off the main Ibrahim Ismail Chundrigar Road, the Karachi Stock Exchange had seen a 1,000 per cent rise between 1999 and 2007, making a small number of people extremely rich and a larger number significant amounts of money. According to the city's mayor in late 2008, Kamal Mustafa, the model for development for many in Karachi was not the West or even, more locally, 'Shining India', though Pakistanis were impressed by their neighbour's apparent rapid growth. Shanghai, Singapore and Dubai comprised 'the aspirational dream', he said. There were more flights to the United Arab Emirates, just two hours away across the Arabian Sea, than to Islamabad, Mustafa pointed out, and investment flows reinforced the sense of proximity as Middle Eastern cash poured into construction projects across the city.[22]

Standing on the corner, watching Karachi's traffic, you would see at first sight chaos, like anywhere in Pakistan. Donkey traps, trucks, multicoloured coaches, overloaded minibuses with dozens of schoolchildren hanging from the doors, hawkers pushing barrows, bicycles and cars of all sizes. The $1,000 motorbikes ceded passage to the tiny, tinny $5,000 five-seater Suzuki Mehrans, which gave way to the $15,000 saloons which in turn moved aside to allow the $60,000 SUVs favoured by major bureaucrats, senior businessmen, ministers and other wealthy and powerful figures to cruise past in air-conditioned comfort. To anyone who had seen Karachi in the 1990s the vastly increased amount of traffic choking the streets at the end of the following decade was striking. More than 500 new cars took to the road each day in 2007. There had been a total increase of 700,000 privately owned vehicles in five years.[23] Musharraf's finance minister, a smooth former banker, had pushed through reforms of the banking sector in 2001 and 2002 which had made credit easily available, and between 2001 and 2007 car ownership in the city had risen by roughly 40 per cent per year as a result.[24] Though unequally distributed, the new money had significant effects. Those who had once had a bicycle now had a motorbike; those who had had a motorbike now had their families loaded into an 800cc Mehran. Many of those once driving the tinny little Mehrans now had an imported saloon, and the number of SUVs had increased exponentially. According to pollster and economic analyst Ijaz Gilani, Karachi was 'an upwardly mobile place'.[25]

It was not just Karachi that had experienced such change during the years of Musharraf's rule. The combination of new neoliberal economic policies, the lifting of American sanctions, a massive flow of remittances from Pakistanis suddenly feeling precarious in post 9/11 USA or Europe, loan write-offs granted once Pakistani support for the 'War on Terror' was assured, the generous rescheduling of further debts as well as the effect of new technologies such as mobile phones had unleashed a comprehensive boom across much of the country.[26] Per capita revenues rose to over $1,000 for the first time.[27] Foreign Direct Investment in Pakistan had gone from $322 million in 2002 to $3.5 billion in 2006, and GDP had doubled between 1999 and 2007, with growth rates hitting 9 per cent. One consequence was soaring property prices, which themselves created a huge amount of new wealth, very visible in the deliberately conspicuous consumption on show at 'the society' functions favoured by the elite of the major cities.[28] The critical element in terms of political economy, however, was not that the rich got richer but that the economic growth also created a much bigger and better-connected middle class. Since independence, Pakistan had always lacked a middle class of the size and influence seen in much of the rest of the Islamic world. This was no longer the case, however. The World Bank estimated that 5 per cent of Pakistan's population – or roughly 9 million people – appeared to have moved from living in poverty to being part of the lower middle class between 2001 and 2004 alone.[29] These were the people who had swapped their family motorbike for a family car and who were now clogging the country's cities.

Another crucial shift was the acceleration of the already relatively rapid rate of urbanization in Pakistan. By 2008, well over a third of Pakistanis lived in cities, and the proportion was increasing by 3 per cent each year.[30] The rate of urbanization was one of the fastest in the world. With the population of the country itself continuing to grow rapidly, this meant the rapid creation of large urban masses. Karachi itself was adding more than half a million people a year to its population. Other cities – Nowsherah, Hyderabad, Faisalabad, Lahore, Rawalpindi – were growing equally fast. Why was the new wealth and the new urbanization important in the context of the 9/11 Wars? Because the urban middle classes were also the people who, from Morocco to Malaysia, had been absolutely key over previous decades in determining the political evolution of their societies. Above all, they had provided the principal constituency for political Islamism, underpinning the popularization of the ideology through the 1980s and, in many places, the 1990s too. There seemed little reason that Pakistan should be any different. One reason for the failure of Islamist parties in Pakistan in elections, apart from the deeply corrupt nature of the campaigning, was that there had been no substantial urban, particularly lower, middle class. By 2007, this was changing.

## FEUDALS, TELEVISIONS AND DEFERENCE

There were two further features of the decade that Bhutto had spent in exile that were particularly significant. The first was the impact of mass communications on Pakistani society. One of Musharraf's first acts had been to liberalize the country's telecoms sector, allowing hundreds of private satellite channels to start broadcasting alongside the stultifying state network. This was of added importance given the nature of the news that those television channels carried. The second was the steady weakening of traditional social hierarchies that the economic boom, the new media and increased literacy meant.

If, having stood on a street corner in Karachi for half an hour in that autumn of 2007, you had got into one of the overcharged, over-decorated buses coming past and, having changed at one of the vast and chaotic bus stations on the outskirts of the city, continued on one of the main highways north, crammed into your seat among the migrant workers, returning students, off-duty soldiers, pilgrims and chickens for five or six hours, you would have arrived at a nondescript, fly-blown country town called Moro. Taking a rickshaw for a further half-hour journey down country lanes between the sugar cane and wheat fields (the proportion of each crop depending on the time of year) would take you to the village of Jatoi, named after the local landowning family, one of the most powerful and wealthy in southern Pakistan. Here, even in this most rural of settings, you would have found evidence of these vital changes. The main division in the village was not between rich and poor, between those with their own cars or bikes or donkeys and those without, between those speaking the local language of Sindhi or the minority whose mother tongue was Soraiki, between Sunnis or Shias (10 per cent of Pakistan's population), or even between Muslims and the often persecuted local Christian community. It was not even between those who sided with the local barber and those who backed his wife in their interminable marital rows. It was between those who patronized the teashop of Ghulam Razzaq, who had installed a television a few weeks previously, and those who preferred the teashop of Hadyattullah, who had not.

By 2003, even before a second wave of deregulation, a third of Pakistanis were estimated to be regular watchers of TV.[31] By 2007, the proportion was even higher with some channels claiming national audiences of up to 70 million for some programmes. Tuned permanently to local Sindhi-language television, Ghulam Razzaq's television attracted a growing clientele who sat for hours, at least during the slack season when there was little work in the fields, before its soap operas, musical films and news bulletins and debates. The latter, vociferous, lively and often as ill informed as they were ill mannered, had become by far the most popular programmes on the major Urdu- and English-language channels such as Geo and Dawn TV, though their local-language equivalents also attracted huge numbers of viewers. Asked what difference the television had made to their lives, villagers were divided. Not much, said many. But all agreed they knew more now about 'world politics', which appeared largely to consist of the West oppressing Muslims in Afghanistan, Iraq or Pakistan, and about the venality and incompetence of their own rulers. As with al-Jazeera in the Arab world a few years earlier, the explosion of Pakistani media had not meant an informed and rational discussion of important issues but the broad dissemination and reinforcement of the outlook of the 'Pakistani street'. Al-Jazeera had broadcast graphic images of the second Palestinian intifada in 1999 and 2000 into the homes of tens of millions of people in the Middle East. The Pakistani channels had no shortage of such material. Launched at the beginning of the 9/11 Wars, they gave their viewers a gruesome and one-sided take on the war in Afghanistan, the invasion of Iraq and its aftermath, the problems in Europe, episodes such as the cartoon crisis and the continuing violence in Israel-Palestine. The news channels were flanked by scores of religious networks, devoted to twenty-four-hour readings from the Koran or sermons or lessons on Islamic jurisprudence which also attracted, cumulatively if not individually, a substantial audience.

The second change – though obscured by the timeless sight of peasants tilling crops by hand, of children scribbling on slates in open-air schools, of the shrines of local saints festooned with silver ribbons and offerings of sweetmeats and fruit – was less tangible but as profound. This was the rapid shift in attitudes and behaviours, particularly towards those to whom once the poor would have owed absolute obedience. Many of the peasants in the fields had worked in Karachi or even in Saudi Arabia or Dubai, where a boom in construction sites provided vastly expanded opportunities for relatively well-paid and steady work. The money they earned for their families meant a new freedom from the crushing physical work of farming and, often for the first time, disposable incomes. The spread of mobile phones meant teachers at the local schools kept in touch with relatives living elsewhere in the country with half-hour calls for a few rupees, further enlarging perspectives and encouraging a comparison between what was happening in different parts of the country.[32] Literacy had risen, albeit from the appallingly low level of 44 per cent in 1998 to 56 per cent ten years later.[33] If they weren't watching the television, people were reading the Urdu- or Sindhi-language papers or having them read to them if still incapable of deciphering the text themselves. Where the newspapers went so did conspiracy theories – that a picture of Mecca had been printed on footballs in international tournaments so it would be repeatedly kicked, that Indian troops had landed in Afghanistan, that Zionist spies were behind kidnappings in Karachi – and the same brand of angry, unbridled commentary as was carried by the new TV channels. Together, all the various developments worked to rapidly erode long-established customs, norms and, crucially, deference. It was not for nothing that landowning families in Sindh such as the Jatois were known as 'feudals'. They, like other local families including the Bhuttos, were benefactors, protectors, dispensers of justice and, often, of religious blessings too.[34] But Masroor Ahmed Jatoi, leaving the sprawling family home for a day on the stump as a provincial MP for the parliamentary elections scheduled for January 2008, said he no longer expected to win elections 'just because the village is named after my family'. Both Masroor and his younger brother Arif, a minister in the provincial government, had had to become, like all local politicians, masters of working the system to obtain maximum development grants to bring electricity, roads, sanitation and jobs to their constituents. Such work, which had become the basis of politics in Pakistan as across much of the region, still did not guarantee victory, however.

'[The people] have become highly politicized in their way,' Jatoi said. 'You can take nothing for granted.'[35]

## MILITANTS AND *MEDRESSAS*

Bahawalpur lay 500 miles to the north of Jatoi village, a ten-hour drive across dusty but fertile fields, along roads lined with mills, sugar refineries and dozens of scruffy small towns. A city of around 800,000 in 2007, Bahawalpur, along with nearby Rahim Yar Khan and the much bigger city of Multan further to the north, constituted one of the biggest single centres of radical Islamic militancy in the world and one of the least known.[36] The core of jihadi activism in Pakistan at the time was usually thought to be the zones along the frontier with Afghanistan, but the towns of southern Punjab were equally significant locally and regionally.[37] It was in these towns that many of the best-known and best-established Pakistani militant outfits were based and from these towns that Western and regional security services feared a new international threat might eventually evolve.

The Western interest in Pakistan in the 2002–7 period was largely and understandably focused on the large numbers of violent militant organizations based in the country. These had naturally attracted attention during the war of 2001, when they had launched the spectacular attack on the Indian parliament at the end of that year, as peace talks between India and Pakistan stumbled along through the middle of the decade and after each of the successive attempts to assassinate Musharraf himself. The interest spiked whenever Western concerns mounted over the policy of the Pakistani security establishment in Afghanistan and whenever such groups were found to be playing a role as intermediaries for Western – particularly British – Muslim extremists hoping to contact al-Qaeda. Many blamed the ISI and other Pakistani intelligence agencies for the groups' existence and apparent health.

The use of irregular proxies by the Pakistani military and civilian leaders was almost as old as Pakistan itself. Just months after gaining independence, the Pakistanis had sent a column of armed Pashtun tribesmen from high on the Afghan border towards Srinagar, the capital of the mountain state of Kashmir, to 'liberate' their coreligionists from their Hindu maharajah. The move prompted the maharajah to call for Indian military aid, and the months of scrappy fighting which followed only ended with a ceasefire brokered by the United Nations which left almost all the most important and most populous parts of Muslim-majority Kashmir, including the famously beautiful Vale or Valley, under Indian control. A second war was fought between India and Pakistan in 1965, again following the operations of Pakistani-backed irregulars. A third conflict with India occurred in 1971, prompted by political unrest in the then eastern wing of Pakistan. It ended too in a crushing Indian victory on two fronts and the creation of Bangladesh despite the horrific violence directed by local Islamists armed, organized and assisted by the Pakistani army against pro-independence activists and intellectuals.[38] These successive disasters paradoxically reinforced the use of proxies as a fundamental of Pakistani strategic thinking as it was broadly believed that only the use of such forces could offset the clear conventional superiority that the Indians had repeatedly demonstrated. The use of such forces was both defensive and offensive. Defensively, they constituted a 'strategic reserve', furnishing an irregular auxiliary force several hundred thousand strong in the event of an Indian attack and providing a harassing guerrilla capability if such an attack had been successful and a significant part of Pakistan occupied. Offensively, the militants could also be used in pursuit of key foreign policy objectives.[39] One strategy was to continually destabilize Kashmir to prevent the status quo of Indian control over most of the state hardening into an unchangeable geopolitical reality. A second was to secure a favourable government in Kabul, a long-term aim of Pakistani – and indeed Raj – diplomacy. For the Pakistanis this was in part because of a desire to secure rear areas west of the Indus river to have 'strategic depth' in the event of an Indian attack from the east but was also about projecting their national interests in what was, given the size of their other immediate neighbours, the only direction that it was feasible to do so. South-west Asia is, like the Middle East, a tough neighbourhood where the strong bully the weak and the weak bully the weaker. Pakistan, though one of the biggest countries in the world, is nonetheless dwarfed by India and China, and inevitably saw in Afghanistan an opportunity for strategic gain that was denied elsewhere.

The 1970s, 1980s and 1990s thus saw the systematic use of irregulars sponsored and often trained and funded by Pakistani security agencies, particularly in Afghanistan and Kashmir. The Pakistani role in Afghanistan is covered in more detail in the following chapter. The Pakistani involvement in Kashmir, which had a more direct importance for many of the Punjabi groups, was re-energized in 1989, as local Muslims in the state, in part inspired by events in eastern Europe, rose against the discriminatory and often brutal rule that had been imposed by New Delhi. Early armed Kashmiri groups were relatively moderate and favoured independence from both India and Pakistan but the ISI, looking to exploit the uprising to pressurize and weaken India, marginalized these and instead backed more compliant proxies. These organizations included one composed of fighters linked to the Islamists of the Kashmiri branch of Jamaat Islami, groups which had sprung up during the previous decade to fight the Soviets and were now at something of a loose end, and finally a new and extremely violent outfit called Lashkar-e-Toiba (LeT, The War Party of the Pure), which was based just south of Lahore but recruited heavily throughout the Punjab and provided the most fanatical and dedicated *mujahideen*.

Throughout the 1990s, these various organizations would send tens of thousands of young Kashmiri, Pashtun and increasingly Punjabi men (and even some Britons) to fight Indian security forces across the Line of Control (LoC), the ceasefire line agreed in Kashmir after the first Indo-Pakistani war.[40] By the mid 1990s, they dominated the insurgency in the disputed state. Progressively, the role of the Kashmiris themselves fell away. In 1999, it was militants from Pakistan-based groups including Lashkar-e-Toiba who, on the orders of senior army generals including Musharraf, had provided the bulk of the fighting force which occupied key heights across the LoC, thus provoking a limited conflict that, once again, was disastrous for Pakistan.[41] In the weeks after 9/11, with the acquiescence and often assistance of the ISI, thousands of fighters from these groups, including a newly formed organization called Jaish-e-Mohammed (JeM), travelled to Afghanistan to fight alongside the Taliban.[42] Such fighters had a new global perspective which was very different from the Kashmiri militants of a decade or so previously. They included young men like Asim, Jamal and 'Abu Turab', who, while waiting for transport into Afghanistan from Peshawar in October 2001, told the author: 'We were in India fighting the Indians. Now we are coming to Afghanistan. America, Israel and India are our enemies. Bush will die like a dog.' In the end it was such militants themselves who were killed in large numbers by coalition air strikes, special forces or the Northern Alliance.

The advent of the 9/11 Wars changed much for Pakistan's militants. Positive developments for groups such as Jaish-e-Mohammed and Lashkar-e-Toiba included the increase in the relative level of radicalization of much of the Pakistani population in the early years of the decade and a consequent surge in popular support, recruits and funds.[43] The downside of the conflict was that, under pressure from the international community, Musharraf banned dozens of extremist organizations. Though many in the Pakistani security establishment saw this as a betrayal of national interests, of national duty and of coreligionists in need, the crackdown, patchy though it might have been as a result, nonetheless had some effect.[44] The groups were not disbanded, but funds were restricted, recruitment cut back, propaganda operations forced underground and a proportion of the training facilities were shut. They continued to exist in a form which would allow them to be mobilized once again should need arise but were 'run down'. Successive attempts by different militant factions to kill Musharraf led to further repression and with thousands of young fighters idling in camps and with funds running short, many groups began to fragment, fusing with the sectarian groups long active in Karachi, the frontier and the Punjab and increasingly building connections with international militants. Before 2001, none of the groups active in Kashmir sought active involvement in the broader international jihad though they were aware – and often approved – of the pronouncements and views of men like bin Laden.[45] But the 9/11 Wars had seen the links between such groups and al-Qaeda figures active in Pakistan strengthen. The process had started as early as December 2001 with the abduction and killing of Daniel Pearl and then the capture of Abu Zubaydah, bin Laden's key logistics operator, three months later in a LeT safehouse. A year later, a pair of LeT militants had surfaced in Iraq. Then there was the growing role that individuals within Pakistani groups played as intermediaries for young British Muslims hoping to access al-Qaeda.[46] The burgeoning links with international activism were ad hoc and based on personal connections. One of the best examples of such links came with the exposure of the plot in the UK to bring down airliners flying across the Atlantic to the USA in 2006. A central figure in the conspiracy was a British citizen originally from the Midlands city of Birmingham called Rashid Rauf, who had been detained in Pakistan at the same time as the plot was rolled up in the UK and who was alleged to have played a key role in coordinating plotters in his native land and liaising with the al-Qaeda senior leadership.[47] Though family members and his lawyers denied it, Rauf was almost certainly a member of the Jaish-e-Mohammed group. Pakistani militant organizations were following, albeit with a lag of almost a decade, the trend towards a greater degree of globalization seen elsewhere in the Islamic world over previous years. This too was something that the Pakistani intelligence services believed they could manage.

In the West, in addition to being seen as sponsored by Pakistani security agencies, the activism of Rauf and people like him was often seen as linked to the existence and expansion of the network of religious schools in Pakistan. In October 2003, Donald Rumsfeld had asked in a note: 'Are we capturing, killing or deterring and dissuading more terrorists every day than the *medressas* and the radical clerics are recruiting, training and deploying against us?'[48] The then defense secretary was only reflecting a generally held view that the religious schools contained a huge reservoir of militants waiting to be unleashed. Rauf's connection to a radical *medressa* seemed further evidence that this was the case. The first problem with this analysis, as with so many others during the course of the 9/11 Wars, was not just that it was too simplistic but that, in simplifying, the genuinely worrying elements had been missed. First of all, there was considerable variety among the *medressas*. Three broad categories existed. The first included the village schools. They were often small, miserably poor, of the local folksy Barelvi School of Islam still dominant in rural communities. It was hard to argue that they posed much threat to anyone. The second category, which included the vast bulk of the *medressas* founded in recent decades, were Deobandi or Ahl-e-Hadith, the two most rigorous local strands of Islam, and were more problematic. Overall in Pakistan their numbers, though notoriously difficult to estimate, had gone from around 1,000 in 1967 to somewhere between 10,000 and 30,000 in forty years. Though many were located in the North West Frontier province, their numbers had increased exponentially in the Punjab too. In the town of Bahawalpur alone there had been only 278 religious schools in 1975 but approaching 1,000 by 2008, local officials said. But though these institutions propagated conservative values and an appallingly distorted vision of the world, there was little evidence to link them directly to violence.

Mohammed Chugti, who ran scores of *medressas* in Bahawalpur and was also a senior local politician with the Jamaat Ulema Islami (JUI), the political vehicle that had represented the interests of the Deobandi clergy and community in Pakistan for decades, told the author that students in the *medressas* he oversaw learned Arabic, Islamic law as well as English, science, Urdu, maths and 'arts subjects' and, though his charges were also, somewhat inevitably, taught that 'to fight in Afghanistan or Kashmir is a religious duty as part of the struggle with any forces that are against the religion of Islam' they were discouraged from actually doing so, at least until they had finished their education.[49] Chugti's *medressas* were not linked to local militant groups, he said, a claim backed up by local officials. It was a third category of *medressa* – those clearly associated with violent groups – that was the immediate problem. These were a minority but sufficiently numerous to be very worrying nonetheless. One high-profile example was the mosque and *medressa* complex in the centre of Islamabad that Pakistani security forces stormed in July 2007. The 'Red Mosque', as it was known, had been a centre of militancy for at least two decades, though after 9/11, following the more general evolution, it had shifted from activism focused almost exclusively on Kashmir to a more internationalized agenda. Maulana Abdul Aziz and his younger brother Abdur Rasheed Ghazi, the leaders of the group, saw Musharraf and all who supported him as complicit in the campaign of the West to divide, humiliate and dominate the world's Muslim community and exhorted their followers to fight against the 'hypocrite *jahiliya*' regime in power in Pakistan as a first step to liberating all Muslim lands.[50] The 'Red Mosque' was a particularly extreme example, but there were others. The alumni of the vast Binoria *medressa* in Karachi included many involved in local sectarian or other violence. Rashid Rauf had often been seen at the Dar-ul-Uloom Medina in Bahawalpur, a large complex that had been repeatedly extended over the forty years since its foundation as donations from the Gulf had flowed in. There a twenty-two-year-old student at the school told the author: 'Jihad is our religion. It is the order of God. When I finish here I will go to fight like many of my friends.'[51] According to local officials, the Jaish-e-Mohammed group not only ran the Dar-ul-Uloom Medina, where 700 teenagers and young adults lived and studied, but also a second, larger, semi-fortified complex in the centre of the city.[52] Though there was no 'production line', such institutions undoubtedly allowed militant groups to select likely recruits from among the students and then cultivate those receptive to their approach.[53] Such institutions evidently constituted a serious threat in the region and to the West but the idea that *medressas* were the root of the problem of militancy inside Pakistan was mistaken. For this was the second element that the reductivist analysis of Rumsfeld missed. The *medressas* did not exist in a vacuum.

The oft-heard argument that the *medressas* only thrived because they filled a vital gap left by the state by offering free education to the most miserable was only partially accurate. Statistics showed little correlation between the relative wealth of a family and the decision to send children to a *medressa*. This suggested that parents sent their children to *medressas* for reasons other than poverty.[54] Such a conclusion was further reinforced by research showing that around a quarter of religious students came from the richer families who could afford to send their children to any type of educational establishment they chose.[55] Equally, three-quarters of families with children in religious schools also sent other siblings to private or public schools. It was true that some families might only have sufficient funds to pay the albeit minimal school fees for one of their offspring but the figures nonetheless indicated fairly unequivocally that millions of parents across Pakistan simply sent their children to *medressas* because they wanted to have at least one child educated religiously and, crucially, because they agreed with what their offspring would be taught in a religious school about the world, about religion and about life.[56] This was of very great importance. For further statistical studies revealed that, even if levels of support for militancy or violence in the name of causes such as Kashmir or Palestine were higher among the students and teachers of religious schools, they were still at very significant levels in the supposedly non-religious educational establishments in which the overwhelming majority of Pakistani children were being educated.[57] One study found that graduates from state public schools, particularly Urdu-medium institutions, were only 'moderately more tolerant' than *medressa* graduates, with very significant numbers of the former favouring either open war or support for Islamic militant groups as means of 'liberating Kashmir', for example.[58] A study of the backgrounds of 517 Pakistani militants in 2003 found that most had relatively high levels of literacy and had been educated not in *medressas* but in government schools.[59] Similar studies five years later found that this had not changed.[60] Together, all these statistics reveal an unpleasant truth: that the gap between the broad political and religious culture of many of the religious schools and that of most Pakistanis, at least in late 2007, was much narrower than many in the West liked to think.[61]

## MIDDLE PAKISTAN

Nowhere was this more clear than in Multan, once simply a sleepy provincial town famous for its shrines but in November 2007 a city with a population swollen to nearly 1.5 million by migration from the poor rural zones around and still growing by an estimated 50,000 every year. On the outskirts, past the army garrison and the new hotels, shops and offices that were springing up along the potholed streets, past the occasional sports car and the crumbling public buildings, was the Bahauddin Zakariya University, founded in 1975 and one of scores of similar private institutions offering graduate-level further education to the children of Pakistan's new middle classes. It was here that the result of the various elements discussed above – the new wealth, the new urbanization, the impact of the new media, the new lack of deference, the consequences of decades of Islamist activism, the failure of successive alternative ideologies, the indirect impact of the 9/11 Wars – came together in a very obvious way.

On a late autumn morning, a few months after Bhutto had returned to Pakistan, some of the 14,000 students of the university were sitting on the grass in between the college's brick and concrete buildings, their books and files spread around them. A small queue had formed at the tiny kiosk selling small cups of sweet tea. A knot of young men inspected the motorbike one of them had recently bought. These young people were ordinary young Pakistanis, studying in a middle-ranking college, in a middling-sized town, in the geographic centre of the country. They were neither activists for secular parties nor Islamists. They were neither as Westernized as the elite youth of Lahore or Karachi, with their American college or exclusive English-medium local education, their cars and parties, nor as aggressively conservative as the Jamaat Islami members. Instead they were representative of a Pakistan that was rarely reported in the international media and had little place in conventional analysis of the country as a battleground between Westernized, democratic 'moderates' and fanatical 'fundamentalists'. They comprised the middle ground, what could be termed 'Middle Pakistan', a diverse yet definite body of people with a diverse yet definite worldview and value system who had been as active in building a coherent and authentic identity as any other group in the country. If not immediately, in a few years' time, they would be 'the Pakistani street', the people whose views and values would determine the country's course.

Visually, the scene at the Bahauddin Zakariya University revealed many of the essential elements of this new evolving identity. So, for example, the students sitting on the grass all maintained a strict and voluntary gender segregation. The girls were uniformly veiled – several wore a full Gulf-style *niqab* – and many of their male counterparts were bearded. Both veils and beards had been very rare a decade or so before, one teacher, a former student at the university himself, remembered.[62] The students' conservatism extended to more than where they sat or what they wore. The West's material conditions were undoubtedly attractive, many told the author during a long day of conversations and arguments, but there was no respect for women or the old in Europe or America and there was pornography, prostitution and AIDS too. Though they agreed that people should be able to chose whom they married and that women were, of course, the equal of men and could and should work – 70 per cent of the university's business studies students were female – women nonetheless had their roles in the home and a balance had to be kept. Though the students had a lucid view of their nation's problems, their patriotism was assertive and unabashed. Pakistan, a peace-seeking nation beset by Indian aggression and Western antipathy from its birth, was a great nation, a leader among Muslim states and deserved greater respect from the international community, they said, insisting too that Kashmir was illegally occupied and the Muslims there were 'as oppressed' as they were in Palestine. Abdul Qadeer Khan, the Pakistani atomic scientist who had first built his country a bomb and then, with successive governments' encouragement, sold its nuclear secrets to Iran, Libya, North Korea and a range of other clients, was 'a Pakistani patriot'. The blame for the problems in their country, they said, lay with corrupt politicians, self-seeking bureaucrats and religious leaders who were far from religious. Democracy, which they all supported as a concept, could only work when there was a political class of sufficient honesty and quality to lead. They were therefore less convinced that it could work – at least now – for Pakistan. The constant interventions of the army were a problem but comprehensible, though now it was time for Musharraf to move on. Above all, Pakistan's government should give way neither to terrorism – which they maintained was unIslamic, though suicide bombings in Israel were 'legitimate resistance' – nor to bullying by America. The students wanted to be doctors, lawyers, engineers, business people and journalists. Their parents, who paid their fees of between 48,000 and 60,000 rupees a year ($770 to $970, £340 to £550 at 2007 rates), were senior teachers, middling-ranking bureaucrats, pharmacists, farmers, traders. The family car was usually simply a Mehran (though some had recently traded up to a Corolla). For the students' questions about whether Pakistan was an Islamic state or not were almost nonsensical. Their nation was the Islamic Republic of Pakistan. They did not want their government to be composed of elderly clerics but they did want their leaders to reflect their identity, values and views.

That those young men and women were representative of Pakistan was beyond doubt. Firstly, they were young – and in 2008 the *median* age in Pakistan was twenty-one. Half the country's population were aged under twenty, with two-thirds still to reach their thirtieth birthday.[63] Secondly, as discussed above, they were from the urban middle class, the fastest-growing sector of Pakistani society. Thirdly, their views were distinctly uncontroversial for the vast proportion of Pakistanis. The students had called themselves 'moderates', and by local standards, if not for most in the West, they were. Their views on more or less every subject were exactly those which polls said, again and again, were shared by most of their compatriots. Their more overt religiosity was typical of much of the nation. Their views of the West too were representative of those of almost all Pakistanis in late 2007: overwhelmingly negative, coloured by conspiracy theories about the true perpetrators of the 9/11 attacks, by anti-Semitism and anti-Zionism, anti-Americanism and deep resentment. A survey by the independent think-tank Terror Free Tomorrow in 2007 found that around a half of Pakistanis viewed Osama bin Laden and militant groups fighting in Kashmir favourably, two-thirds were against the American military operating in Pakistan, and more than half blamed America for the violence in Pakistan at the time.[64] Other polls found that around three-quarters of Pakistanis wanted their country to be ruled by Islamic laws and that only 15 per cent of Pakistanis believed that 'Arabs' were responsible for 9/11. A further poll, on patriotism, asked: 'How proud do you feel to call yourself a Pakistani?' Nearly 80 per cent said they were 'very proud', particularly citing the country's nuclear capability.[65] Another found that 89 per cent of Pakistanis did not want their country to cooperate with the United States in the War on Terror, many more than in previous years. The overseas country that was most admired was Saudi Arabia.[66] Much of this had been anecdotally obvious to those visiting Pakistan regularly since 2001 and particularly to those who had known the country during the 1990s or before.

The new identity was built on long-developing trends that had gradually seen Pakistan shuck off the heritage of British rule and turn further and further towards the Middle East. It was not just investment flows or the ever-growing number of pilgrims travelling on Haj that increasingly linked Pakistan to the Gulf. Names of children had become more Islamic and more Arabicized from the turn of the millennium on. After 9/11, Osama had become popular; later in the decade it was Areeba, Malaika, Uzair, Emal which became widespread. Some 90 per cent of boys were named Mohammed following Middle Eastern practice.[67] Trends in clothes and language, crucial signifiers, were also revealing. The vast proportion of Pakistanis had kept their traditional *shalwar kameez*, leaving jeans and T-shirts to the Westernized elite.[68] Bollywood maintained its dominant position in terms of cinema and music, mitigating the bile directed at India in the mainstream media, but where dreamed-of holiday destinations had once been Europe or the USA, now they were Malaysia or the Gulf, partly out of a new sense of pan-Islamic solidarity, partly due to the difficulty of getting visas to visit the West and the suspicion that Pakistanis faced when they arrived there. A 'books section' in a new superstore in Karachi's wealthy Clifton area was entirely devoted to Islamic titles. In a Nike shop, speakers played recitations from the Koran. Mobile phone companies offered the call to prayer as a ring tone and Koranic recitations as free downloads. During the month of Ramadan international banks offered preferred clients boxes containing prayer beads, dates and miniature Korans.[69] When one Urdu-language columnist pointed out that there had never been a demonstration in Pakistan against 'Islamic terrorist' attacks in the West, he was vilified.[70]

This emerging identity was as politically conservative as it was socially and religiously conservative – which was one reason why revolution in Pakistan, Islamist or otherwise, did not seem likely in the immediate future. A factor in the failure of the violent radicalism of the militants or even their supporters among the Deobandi or Ahl-e-Hadith clerics to appeal to this emerging Middle Pakistan was because few, least of all junior bureaucrats, shopkeepers, teachers and doctors, wanted radical, sudden upheaval. If there was to be a revolution, it would be a gradual one that would not threaten too much disruption. That the identity of Middle Pakistan owed much to the influence of Jamaat Islami and the idea of its founder, Maududi, was undoubted. Despite the continued lack of electoral success of his organization over the decades, Maududi's ideas had eventually permeated whole sections of society. Now almost forty years after his death, what had once been seen as radically right-wing was now entirely normalized. This was often difficult for outsiders to see. The lawyers who received so much attention for resisting Musharraf's clumsy attempts at intimidation of the judiciary in this period, certainly beyond the upper layer of smoother English-speaking and UK-educated older leaders, shared many of the values and ideas described above, for example. So too did many of the millions who voted for the nominally secular MQM in Karachi. These vast constituencies were rarely counted in analyses of Pakistan overseas but were hugely important internally. The lessons of Maududi and other Islamists had become so internalized as to have become utterly unremarkable.

So instead of the oft-repeated analysis of Pakistan as a country with a fractured identity, as the first decade of the 9/11 Wars drew to its close, the opposite appeared to be increasingly nearer the truth. Though great ethnic, topographic, linguistic diversity remained, much of the ambiguity that had troubled the country about its identity since its foundation was being resolved, not exacerbated. Baluchis, Pashtuns, Punjabis, Sindhis might disagree on how fairly national resources were distributed and might discriminate or suffer discrimination, but few would disagree with the basic worldview and values articulated by the students of Multan. A fairly uniform, fairly coherent, Pakistani identity was emerging. This identity was broadly established across the country. To describe Pakistan as simply a battleground for extremists and their opposites was to deny the emerging mass of the middle ground – the 'Pakistani street' – its true importance. The direction in which they were taking Pakistan was not necessarily the one the West wanted the country to take.

## BHUTTO AND THE NEW PAKISTAN

The deal which had allowed Bhutto to return had been arranged with President Musharraf, then in his eighth year of power, in long negotiations over the spring and summer of 2007.[71] Corruption charges against the former prime minister and a treason conviction against her historic rival Nawaz Sharif, the fifty-eight-year-old leader of the Pakistan Muslim League party, had been set aside, and the two veteran politicians' exile ended. In return Bhutto and Sharif, who had been in Dubai and Riyadh respectively, promised to support Musharraf's bid to be re-elected by parliament as president for a further five-year term. Both British and American diplomats had acted as go-betweens, and it was fervently hoped in London and Washington that Bhutto would win the parliamentary elections scheduled for early 2008. With Bhutto as prime minister and Musharraf still president, though no longer chief of the army staff, Pakistan would have a pro-Western government which would retain, through the man President Bush had described as his 'buddy' only a year or so earlier, the support of the military.[72] This would, it was hoped, assure most Western strategic interests in the country while giving the Pakistani government the legitimacy of something at least resembling, however imperfectly, democracy. Musharraf detested both Bhutto and Sharif but was weak politically and had little choice but to accept the arrangement.[73] Despite the violence that had greeted her return, Bhutto, after a verbal broadside at the 'dark forces' that wanted her dead, threw herself into campaigning with energy undiminished by her lengthy exile. She would not comment on her chances of victory, simply saying the 'people of Pakistan' would decide.[74]

Recognizing that she needed to win over the undecided, Bhutto focused her efforts not on the heartland of her traditional support in the south but on the major population centres of the north, around the twin cities of Islamabad and Rawalpindi and further west, towards the Afghan frontier. Each day followed a similar routine with rallies, meetings, driving, more rallies, more meetings, more rallies. On December

17, 2007, for example, Bhutto left her home in Islamabad at around 9 a.m., was driven rapidly through the capital's wide, quiet streets in a white armoured landcruiser and then up the pristine six-lane highway which slices through the rural backcountry of the Punjab before crossing the Indus river and then swings in a broad arc through the fields and villages of the lowland areas of the North West Frontier province towards Peshawar. Since the highway had been opened exactly a year earlier, much of the fencing that lined it had been stolen to be resold as scrap, and the palm trees planted in the central reservation had died. But the surface remained good, and there was little traffic.[75] The convoy swept by villages where the mosque was the only concrete structure and dried cow dung the only fuel. Smoke from cooking fires rose straight into the still, chill morning air. Bullocks pulled carts down dirt roads which ran parallel to the motorway for a few hundred yards and then turned away across the fields, where small boys played cricket with sticks and goats wandered in search of weeds.

At Nowshera, a scruffy mid-sized town 30 miles from Peshawar, Bhutto had lunch with local candidates from her Pakistan People's Party (PPP) and then addressed a crowd. She spoke of the need for moderation, human rights, basics for the poor, an end to terrorism.[76] After the rally in Nowshera, Bhutto drove away, sufficiently exhilarated to stand up through the hatch cut in the roof of her vehicle and wave to bemused locals on the old Grand Trunk Road as she headed back towards the motorway and Islamabad. In the town of Pabbi, once a centre of militancy in the 1980s and early 1990s, she suddenly ordered her vehicle to stop and, to the consternation of the police escort, plunged almost alone into a roadside bazaar to buy oranges. Returning to the car, she told the author that, after such a long period out of her homeland, she needed to get to know her country again and that learning the price of fruit was an essential part of that process. 'I am out of touch, Mr Burke,' she said. 'I am out of touch, and that must be changed. I can now tell you what oranges cost.'

Bhutto was out of touch in ways that were more significant than simply not knowing the price of fruit. For it was apparent that the fifty-four-year-old politician had not taken full measure of the changes within Pakistan over the eight years of her exile. Weeks before returning to Pakistan, Bhutto had listed those whom she said she represented: 'the underprivileged, the peasants, women, minorities, all those who are neglected by elite government, the middle class'.[77] But it was exactly these constituencies that were changing the most rapidly, sucked into the cities, transformed by the rising incomes of the previous ten years, suddenly exposed to images from Palestine, Iraq or Afghanistan on the new satellite channels on their new televisions after years of turgid state broadcasting, dealing with the complex and conflicting streams of political and cultural thought flowing throughout the Muslim world during the 9/11 Wars. Equally, it was Bhutto's hardcore of supporters among the feudal aristocracy and the educated and moderate or even secular elite who were finding themselves increasingly challenged by the loud and numerous urban middle class or those who had once unquestioningly worked the fields and followed orders. In the new Pakistan, Bhutto's own Westernization, her backing from America or Europe, her ideas about opening up Pakistan's nuclear facilities to international inspectors, even her moderation on Kashmir, Afghanistan, Israel and other issues that had become touchstones in the new more international consciousness of many Pakistanis jarred with many more of her compatriots than would have been the case a decade previously. Potential allies – such as the new civil society groups that had emerged over previous years and were receiving so much international attention – were too few to fill the gap. An adept and perceptive politician, Bhutto clearly sensed the need to adapt to the broad shifts in her native land but was either unable or unwilling to do so in the short time she had.

Bhutto had also underestimated the capabilities and the intentions of Pakistan's militants. Bhutto was thinking in terms of the 1990s, with discrete groups pursuing discrete largely local agendas – sectarian, Kashmiri, criminal – and the independence of action of the vast proportion of militants heavily constrained by their dependence on the resources and protection of the state security establishment. In conversations with Bhutto over the months before her return, it was clear that the rapid evolution of Pakistani Islamic militancy over recent years, particularly in the pressure-cooker conditions of the 9/11 Wars, had escaped her.[78] Though, during the 100 or so days after her return from Pakistan she spoke often about her need for greater protection, the threat, she repeatedly said, came from her old enemies within the army, the ISI and the government. The source of the immediate danger was in fact very close to where she had stopped to buy her fruit: in the FATA and the broad zone along the frontier where new and potentially more dangerous actors had emerged while she had been in Dubai, Washington and London.

On December 27, 2007, as Bhutto was leaving a rally in Rawalpindi, waving to the crowd through the hatch of her vehicle, a fifteen-year-old boy fired three shots at her with a pistol before detonating a suicide bomb strapped to his waist.[79] In her last speech she had run through the same themes as throughout her campaign: the need for moderation, justice, food and shelter for the needy, an end to violence. In the seconds before the shots and the blast, the crowd shouted 'Bhutto de naray ... wajan ge' (the slogans of Bhutto ... will always be chanted).[80] She died in Rawalpindi general hospital of a wound probably caused by the blast of the explosion smashing her head into the metal handle of the hatch as she ducked to avoid the shots fired at her.[81] Bhutto became the single highest-profile casualty of the 9/11 Wars to date. Twenty-three less-high-profile casualties died in the same attack, and ninety-one were injured.[82]

## PAKISTAN POLITICS 2007–8

After the relative political stability of the six years after 9/11, the year following the death of Bhutto saw Pakistan plunged once more into political chaos reminiscent of that of the previous decade. President Musharraf was eventually forced to resign the presidency in August 2008, but five main political groupings – each representative of a broader constituency within Pakistan – had been battling for a share of power long before his final departure from power. The incumbent and his close allies within the military and among various key political powerbrokers whose interests had been well served over previous years constituted one faction in the mêlée. A second was composed of those within the army who had become frustrated with the president. Some had purely personal motivations, as Musharraf's long tenure had blocked the promotion of many senior officers; others were concerned by potential emerging threats to the material position of the military with its privileged lifestyle and commercial interests; still others were genuinely worried by the increasingly autocratic nature of Musharraf's rule. The power of these disaffected senior officers had been amply demonstrated when, following heavily managed presidential elections in October 2007, Musharraf was forced to rescind a state of emergency and resign as chief of army staff. A further show of strength came when the elections scheduled for January but postponed after the death of Bhutto were finally held in March 2008, and Musharraf's replacement at the head of the army, the dry, moderate and effective Ashfaq Kayani, made it very clear that he would resist any attempt by his predecessor to use the military or the various intelligence services to influence the vote. The elections, to most observers' surprise, were broadly seen as free and fair, something of a novelty for Pakistan.[83]

The third major group of players jockeying for power and influence were, of course, the extremists and religious conservatives. However, the Islamists of Jamaat Islami and the Deobandi clerics of the Jamaat Ulema Islami as well as the various religiously orientated splinter or smaller groups were largely absent from the democratic political process during this period, restricting their participation to large demonstrations 'in protest at the lack of true democracy in Pakistan', as Qazi Hussein Ahmed, the veteran leader of JI, put it over tea in the sprawling compound of offices, homes and schoolrooms that comprised the organization's national headquarters in Lahore.[84] In the North West Frontier province and in Baluchistan, provincial polls held simultaneously with national polls provided an unwelcome dose of 'true democracy' for the hardline religious alliance which had been in power or shared power in both provinces since 2002. The conservatives were unceremoniously dismissed from office by voters, who had had enough of government that was exceptionally incompetent even by low local standards, a useful reminder that appeals to religious or cultural identity do not always trump the basic human desire for a better quality of life.

The fourth of the factions contesting power in this turbulent period was Nawaz Sharif and the various lobbies he represented. Many Western analysts and policy-makers had difficulty understanding the appeal of the tubby, balding, middle-aged politician. Certainly his record of atrocious economic management, reputation for graft, poor English, lack of charisma, poor oratorical skills and total failure to articulate any kind of coherently formulated policies failed to impress successive Western interlocutors. Sharif's home was the Punjab, and it was to Lahore, or more specifically the family estates at Raiwind just outside the city, that Sharif had returned when his long exile in Saudi Arabia had ended. He had immediately mobilized his old power base – major

Punjabi industrialists, businessmen, conservative powerbrokers. To them Sharif was a known quantity. In his two previous stints in power in the 1990s, the main beneficiaries, beyond his own family, had been his supporters among the commercial classes of the Punjab who had been handed soft loans from banks, hugely profitable tariff arrangements and licences or development funds that they themselves could spend, on themselves or on those whose votes they wanted to secure as they saw fit. Many such people had rallied to Musharraf during Sharif's exile. Now, the political winds were changing, and their support was flowing back to the returning former prime minister.

But Sharif was also able to attract a new constituency. Though his wealth was inherited or earned during his years in power, he had the image of a self-made man, which appealed to the expanding lower middle classes. His taste for Punjabi home cooking was well known or at least well advertised, giving him an authentic image that may have been spurious but nonetheless convinced. His hesitancy in English reinforced his popular appeal. His nationalist rhetoric echoed the views of the Urdu-language papers and their tens of millions of readers.[85] Then there was the appeal of the image of Sharif as a social conservative and, at least ostensibly, a pious Muslim. Though not members of Jamaat Islami, the Sharifs were naturally close in culture and worldview to the Islamist party. In the second of his prime ministerial terms Sharif had attempted to force through a raft of legislation enhancing the weight of religious law in Pakistan and even tried to have himself named *amir-ul momineen*, leader of the faithful.[86] Even if in reality he was far from personally devout, such acts clearly had an impact. So too did the time Sharif had spent in Saudi Arabia and his apparent personal relationship with the kingdom's rulers.[87] 'The common man sees himself in Nawaz,' said Khwaja Asif, a major businessman and a senior PML figure.[88]

The final group lobbying for power was that connected to the Bhutto dynasty and the Pakistan People's Party. On her death, Bhutto's young son Bilawal, a student at Oxford University, had been dubbed heir to the family political fortune. However, it was her widely reviled husband, Asif Ali Zardari, who took charge of the political organization she had led. When Musharraf was forced out of office in August 2008 under the threat of impeachment, Bhutto's widower displayed political skill that few had suspected he possessed to secure the presidency. The former playboy, prisoner and consort inherited the presidential apartments in the palace at the foot of the Margalla hills and some of the most intractable problems faced by any leader in any theatre of the 9/11 Wars. Zardari was not known as an intellectual. This was not a problem, associates said, explaining: 'You don't necessarily need to be a bookworm type to be president of Pakistan.'[89]

# 14

# Another Country: FATA

## FATA

On the north-western border of Pakistan lies another country, not Afghanistan, but FATA, the seven 'Federally Administered Tribal Agencies'. With a total population of between 3 and 4 million and a landmass of 10,500 square miles, somewhere between the size of Belgium and Israel, the FATA is a land apart. In the summer of 2008, this land hosted five main armed groups, factions or coalitions: the Afghan Taliban, the Pakistani Taliban, al-Qaeda and various international militant groups, a range of tribal militia and the Pakistani army.

The roots of militancy in the FATA run back centuries. They had been created by the British in 1901 as a buffer zone along the western frontier of their south Asian dominions, adjacent to the border agreed with the Afghan monarch Abdur Rahman Khan eight years previously; the tribes there had long been known as reactionary, restive and independent. Indeed, the very establishment of such a zone was in part an admission by the British that, despite their superior weaponry and resources, continued campaigning against the Wazirs, the Mehsuds, the Afridis and the others was unlikely to definitively quell the repeated rebellions. Raj administrators agreed with local tribes that the legal reach of the authorities of India in the border zone would be limited to the towns and the roads (along with a strip of land 100 yards wide on either side) beyond which communities were allowed to police themselves, seek justice from their traditional assemblies, or *jirga*, and carry weapons. The British did, however, retain the right to mount punitive campaigns if, for example, the tribes raided the lowlands or otherwise disturbed the peace of the frontier. They were also careful to impose a system of officials known as political agents who, with their extensive powers of patronage and ability to call on significant military resources, were theoretically equipped with sufficient carrots and a big enough stick to keep order. Though the system broadly worked well, it occasionally broke down, necessitating large and lengthy deployments of troops to put down uprisings. Most of these were mobilized under the flag of revivalist Islam, even if the grievances which sparked them tended to be more banal. Often such revolts had motives that were strikingly similar to those cited by their counterparts a century or so later. Sometimes the local Pashtun tribes were simply pushing back against the authority of the Raj.[1] Sometimes the fighting was conceived of as a defence of culture and identity. 'The Turangzai Baba [local tribal leader and cleric] would say: "The donkeys [whites] are coming and we should stop them by force as he is destroying Islam and he is destroying our laws,"' remembered one elderly veteran of fighting in the 1930s.[2] Often the insurgents had projects of their own. In the 1920s, Deobandi clerics had led a group called the Jamaat-e-Mujahideen in a bid to establish a 'pure Islamic' state on the land between the Indus river and Kabul – exactly the same zone of conflict being fought over eighty years later.[3] Decades before the Afghan Taliban had created a religious police, tribes on the frontier had formed their own 'movement for the promotion of virtue and the prevention of vice'. Reformist Islamic ideas had begun to erode more 'folksy' Sufi-influenced forms of religious practice by the late nineteenth and early twentieth centuries.[4]

The British campaigns on the frontier spawned a body of literature and a set of romanticized myths in the West about the proud, honourable and warlike Pashtun, a worthy opponent for the Victorians and their successors, which proved to be both remarkably durable and remarkably inaccurate. Works of fiction, such as those of Kipling, and of questionable and highly politicized anthropology from the early twentieth century were still being quoted by Western analysts a century later despite the fact that society in the FATA, as anywhere else in the world, had changed enormously in the intervening period. This did not help those trying to formulate effective policy. As in Afghanistan and Pakistan more generally, the problem with the FATA was not that it was caught in some kind of time warp but the opposite.

How the FATA became the rear base for the Afghan *mujahideen* as well as a relatively small number of international, largely Arab volunteers is well known. However gripping the tale of spies, Saudi tycoons and Cold War manoeuvres may be, the story of the process of accelerated, violent and unmanaged social change in the FATA that was triggered by the instability of the 1970s and the wars of the 1980s and 1990s in neighbouring Afghanistan is of equal if not greater importance, though somewhat less picturesque. Traditional society on the frontier had been structured for many decades, if not centuries, by the major tribal groupings with their manifold subdivisions and by the carefully maintained balance between the religious scholars, or *ulema*, the major quasi-feudal landowners, or *khans*, and the senior tribal elders, or *maliks*, who often received substantial government patronage in return for representing the interests of the distant administration. Central too to order in the region was the harsh code of values and customs, the famous and often misunderstood *pashtunwali*, or 'way of the Pashtuns'. Together, these elements constituted a flexible, resilient and effective system of governance.[5] Each of the components of the system was, however, degraded severely during the 1970s and 1980s. Most obviously, there was the massive influx of Afghan refugees from the mid 1970s onwards who, having been forced out of traditional settlements and occupations and into packed camps where aid was the primary source of resources, rapidly lost their traditional identities, allegiances and hierarchies and thus became susceptible to the call of radical Islamist groups such as Hekmatyar's Hezb-e-Islami, which had previously struggled to recruit in Pashtun rural communities. Then there was the rapid expansion of rigorous neo-traditional Deobandi Islam, propagated by *medressas* built with donations from Middle Eastern countries now flush with oil money or with cash from General Zia's official religious funds discussed in the previous chapter.[6] Their teachings naturally reinforced conservative and revivalist forms of Islam that already existed in the FATA and gave the narrative of resistance to 'moral corruption', outsiders and 'unbelievers' that was a strong part of the local collective memory and identity a new and more contemporary dimension. In the north of the FATA it was the Ahl-e-Hadith or 'Wahhabi' strands, which became very powerful, again through the establishment of scores of *medressas* and an influx of foreign money. As in Afghanistan, the expansion of these more rigorous strands of Islam meant that the more tolerant and mystical Sufi-influenced strands were further weakened. This new radical conservatism inevitably threatened the position of many of the more traditional local clergy, who could not match the resources, spiritual or material, offered by their new competitors. It also consolidated the shared identity, clerical hierarchy, culture and world-view of the Pashtun population along the frontier zone, developing further a single common set of values, norms and worldview.

Then there was the new wealth flowing into the region. This had an equally destructive effect on local culture. With many Pashtuns working in the Gulf following the boom of the 1970s, unprecedented amounts of money had been reaching individual families in the FATA for some time. However, it was the 1980s, and the war against the Soviets, with the flow of massive aid funds and the opening up of extensive opportun-ities for illicit and lucrative activities such as manufacturing and trading weapons and growing, processing and trafficking opium, hashish and heroin, that saw the real collapse of the FATA's social system. If the rising power of rigorous and highly politicized forms of Islam was chal-lenging the power of traditional clerics, so new sources of wealth challenged the position of the *khans* and the *maliks*. Local hierarchies that had been based on patronage and resource distribution simply became redundant, with traditional landlords unable to compete with those who had access to the vast sums being generated through drugs, guns or Saudi, American and Pakistani aid. Nor, evidently, could they match their new competitors for firepower. The same was true for the political agents, the bureaucrats on whom the system for governing the FATA, barely changed since the days of the British, still depended. They too saw their powers of patronage eclipsed by new competitors and their powers of coercion rendered ineffectual against bands of heavily armed fighters or criminals.

Add a growing sectarian conflict which was in part a proxy war between major Sunni Muslim states in the Middle East and Iran, the broad rise of Islamist identities and ideologies across the Islamic world in the period and the continuing presence of hundreds of international militants in and around the FATA through the early 1990s and it is unsurprising that the region, as it had done so often over the previous decades at moments of crisis, saw the rise of a series of radical revivalist and reformist religious movements. Some were on a significant scale – such as that in Dir and Malakand to the north of Bajaur which campaigned, relatively successfully, for Shariat law in the mid 1990s. Others were more disorganized, such as the various bands responsible for what by 1998 or 1999 was being called the 'Talibanization' of the FATA. These groups often coalesced around veterans of the fighting in Afghanistan during the 1980s or early 1990s and led vigilante actions against DVD or music shops, hairdressers and other targets deemed responsible for the 'moral corruption' that local hardliners associated with 'Westernization'.[7] They also enforced a new version of traditional local honour codes and punishments just as the Afghan Taliban were doing on the other side of the porous border. As the decade ended, the radicalization had intensified. In 1998 or 1999 it was still possible for a Western journalist to travel in the FATA – the author even spent an afternoon at a *dastarbandi*, or graduation ceremony, at one *medressa* near Miram Shah, eating chicken cooked with oranges as successive diners arrived and stacked their Kalashnikovs in a corner – but such trips rapidly became risky. The 9/11 attacks thus came at a critical time. As was so often the case, the new conflict they triggered only aggravated and accelerated existing trends. In 2001, the memory of the earlier wars was certainly very present. In the Khyber Pass a month after the bombing of Afghanistan had started, young men from the local Afridi tribe were very clear about what the coming conflict meant for them. 'Our fathers, their fathers and their fathers' fathers fought jihad,' one said on a starry night in a compound a few miles short of the Afghan frontier. 'Now it is our turn. We will go to war.'[8]

## THE AFGHAN TALIBAN IN THE FATA

Within twenty-four hours of the 9/11 attacks, Maleeha Lodhi, the Pakistani ambassador in Washington, had been summoned to meet the American deputy secretary of state Richard Armitage to be asked if Pakistan was 'with or against America'. Lodhi was accompanied by Lieutenant General Mahmud Ahmed, the ISI chief who had tried to convince his MI6 counterpart only months before that the Taliban should be diplomatically recognized by Britain.[9] When Ahmed tried to tell Armitage that Pakistan had always been a friend of the USA, he was cut short and was told bluntly that it was what happened now and what was going to happen in the future that was important. 'History began today,' the American said.[10] Within a few weeks President Musharraf had purged the ISI of the most obvious sympathizers with extremism.

Ahmed was one of those forced out, and Western intelligence services took his departure as a sign that the 'bad old days' of Pakistan's sponsorship of violent proxies were over. Yet Musharraf had repeatedly made clear that he acted in what he felt were Pakistan's best interests, not for any greater international good. It was safe, therefore, to conclude that any backing for America's War on Terror was entirely pragmatic. Active support for the Taliban may indeed have been halted as the Americans had demanded, but that did not by any means signify that the Pakistanis would not aggressively pursue what were felt to be their national security priorities.[11] The ISI, which had initially resisted cutting off support to the Afghan Taliban, had been very active during the campaign of 2001. Sometimes the agency had worked with Western security services. Sometimes it had pursued its own agenda. But in either case, the ISI's institutional vision of Pakistan's strategic interests had always come first.

Richard Armitage had been right to talk to Lodhi and Ahmed about history but had been wrong to dismiss the past so lightly. Pakistani support for the Taliban had reached its peak in 1999 but had started in the early years of the movement. As stressed in previous chapters, the Taliban may have been an essentially Afghan movement with deep roots in elements of Afghan society, culture, history and politics, but assistance from the ISI was of great use at critical junctures. This support was not hidden from Pakistan's civilian leaders. Indeed, it was under Benazir Bhutto's second administration from 1993 to 1996 that the country's intelligence services had shifted their support from Hekmatyar to the Taliban. Diplomatic as well as military assistance continued under the administration of Nawaz Sharif from 1996 to 1999.[12] Such links became considerably more controversial after al-Qaeda's bombing of American embassies in east Africa, organized from Afghanistan, in 1998. Already soured by messy battles around Mazar-e-Sharif during which widespread atrocities by both sides were widely reported and a war with Iran was nearly provoked, relations deteriorated as the Taliban refused the demands of the Sharif government to hand over Pakistani sectarian militants responsible for widespread violence in the prime minister's native Punjab. Many in Pakistan's Foreign Ministry began to express grave concerns about the diplomatic damage being done by their country's support for their increasingly unpredictable and extreme supposed allies.[13] But though these tensions continued to grow through 2000 and

2001, particularly after Pakistan's failed bid to avert the destruction of the Bamiyan Buddhas, the Pakistan military as an institution continued to believe not only that they could manage a movement they saw as their protégés but also that, despite their faults, the Taliban remained the best available tool for the projection of Pakistani influence in Afghanistan.

In the changed circumstances following the 9/11 attacks, the strategic calculation of many within the Pakistani security establishment was thus relatively straightforward. Though Musharraf promised a clean break, both in private communications to the American administration and explicitly in public speeches such as his televised address of February 2002, a perception of his nation's strategic interests that had been reinforced over decades remained dominant. As seen in previous chapters, as the Taliban regime had collapsed, fighters and senior officials from the Taliban were thus allowed to cross into Pakistani territory and indeed were in some instances directed or even aided to locations where they would be safe. Only the foreign militants belonging to the international groups formerly based in Afghanistan were detained, imprisoned and turned over to American intelligence services in return for substantial payments.[14] By spring 2002, memos were crossing Musharraf's desk from senior officers attached to the ISI arguing that, as the West would inevitably be forced to withdraw their forces from Afghanistan, probably in between five and fifteen years, Pakistan needed to be positioned for the aftermath of the eventual pull-out.[15] The twin objectives of strategic depth and a pro-Islamabad government in Kabul, constant for three decades or more, remained unchanged. The parallel with the Soviet invasion was indeed explicit. As during the 1980s, the strategy was not so much to fight against 'foreign occupiers' as to make sure that Pakistan had proxies who would be well placed to take power once the foreigners had gone. During 2003, it became clear that most of the dominant players in Kabul and in many major cities were from factions or ethnic groups known for their animosity towards Pakistan. It also became clear that India was making a major effort to extend its influence through a substantial aid programme that involved high-profile projects such as the building of the new Afghan parliament and key roads often located in critically sensitive border regions. The Pakistani sense of encirclement was thus further reinforced, and the idea that the Taliban, or at least elements within them, should be allowed to regenerate sufficient capacity to serve Pakistani interests in Afghanistan in the future gained further momentum. The key, naturally, was not to get caught, nor to provoke too much attention by spectacular attacks, nor to cause a precipitous collapse of the Afghan government. As it had been in the 1980s, the aim was once more to 'make the water boil at the right temperature'.[16] There was one crucial difference from the early period, however: before, there had been, at least initially, no refugee camps in the FATA and fewer and lighter weapons, a smaller overall population, much weaker political vehicles for the religious lobbies, around a fifth as many *medressas* and, crucially, a much lower level of ambient animosity towards the West. Twenty years later, all that anyone hoping to maintain and manage elements within the Afghan insurgents needed to do was simply to allow them to exploit the huge support networks that were already in place and sentiments that were already running high. When, in late 2003, Yusuf Pashtun, the then governor of Kandahar, listed the training camps he said had been set up across the border and around Quetta, every single place he mentioned was the site of an already extant refugee settlement, many of which had been home to senior Taliban figures for three decades.[17] The new surge of anti-Western sentiment and religious fervour after 9/11, combined with cynical manipulation by the military government, meant too that, by 2002, the two provinces along the Afghan border and surrounding the FATA – the North West Frontier province and Baluchistan – were run wholly, in the case of the former, or partly, in the case of the latter, by the Deobandi hardliners of the Jamaat Ulema Islami party and the political Islamists of Jamaat Islami.[18] The new governments of the two provinces embarked on a project of radical Islamization, imposing *sharia* law, banning of music and 'obscene' advertising and firing hundreds of female bureaucrats and medical staff. These measures not only created an atmosphere that encouraged further extremism but were accompanied by rhetoric which was explicitly pro-Taliban. Ministers regularly attended the funerals for slain Taliban fighters held in or around Quetta and other cities.[19] Maulana Rahat Hussain, a senior cleric, JUI senator and junior minister in the NWFP provincial government, reeled off a list of his classmates at the Binoria *medressa* in Karachi who had all become senior figures among the insurgents. 'They were and are and will for ever be my brothers,' Hussain told the author. 'They are fighting an occupying force and *inshallah* they will be victorious.'[20]

The evidence of continued ISI support for the Afghan Taliban naturally posed a dilemma for Western policy-makers. Western officials on the ground pointed to the string of senior figures connected with the Taliban or Haqqani who somehow learned at the very last minute of impending raids and the presence of senior Taliban figures in or around cities such as Quetta or Peshawar and reported constant communication between Taliban figures and Pakistani military officials, some, but not all, retired.[21] One problem was diplomatic. Bush had repeatedly backed Musharraf as a key ally in the Global War on Terror and was unwilling to listen to criticism of a man in whom he had invested considerable political capital. Equally, even within intelligence services, no one was prepared to risk the continued and useful cooperation of the ISI in the hunt for senior al-Qaeda figures who posed a direct threat to the West. All were painfully aware that they were dependent on the Pakistani military and its intelligence services for any direct action against the international militants they were hunting. 'We had no illusions about what was happening but we had no capacity either. So we couldn't really be picky,' said one senior CIA official. 'The ISI was the only girl at the dance.'[22] A gap opened up between those operatives working in Pakistan on the hunt for senior al-Qaeda figures – who tended to maintain that only retired or lower- and middle-ranking serving Pakistani intelligence officers, possibly 'rogues' acting with no authorization, were involved with the Taliban – and those in Kabul, whose job consisted of fighting Afghan insurgents, who were much more critical of the ISI. Through 2004, 2005 and the spring of 2006, policy drifted. Over time, and not least because of the increasing difficulty in hunting al-Qaeda figures as they moved from the cities into the remote tribal zones, the attitude of Western intelligence services and politicians hardened. When, in the summer of 2006, coalition troops became involved in bruising combat with fighters who had often recently arrived from Pakistan, lost men to suicide bombers from towns in the Punjab, saw Pakistani paramilitaries engaging Afghan troops on the frontier or artillery fire being used to cover the passage of insurgents across the border, a major covert operation was launched by both MI6 and the CIA to secure solid information on the ISI's activities which could be used to confront Pakistani authorities.[23] The point of the effort, which lasted several months and at one point even temporarily drew resources focused on Iraq back to the region, was to establish if there was any direct involvement by Pakistani intelligence services in instigating or even organizing attacks on Western troops or their allies, as many were beginning to say openly.[24] But the intelligence obtained – much of which came from Afghan government sources with a clear agenda – was inconclusive, and no final report was ever compiled. It was left to individual commanders and institutions to try to influence public opinion and policy-makers. The split between those working within Pakistan, who needed to keep the ISI onside to continue operations against al-Qaeda, and those, inside and outside the intelligence community, in Afghanistan, who had no such concerns, widened. In early 2007, a frustrated General Sir David Richards, then the Commander of NATO-ISAF in Kabul, was openly saying that 'infiltration [of insurgents] from Pakistan was a very serious problem', and more junior NATO officers were explicit in their accusation that the ISI was aiding their enemy.[25] But intelligence officials in Pakistan were still conservative in their criticism of their local counterparts. In October of that year, American defence officials in Islamabad insisted to the author they were 'yet to see a smoking gun ... [or] any solid evidence at all' of ISI aid to the Taliban.[26] Their British counterparts restricted themselves to drily commenting that, while it was clear that the ISI, 'like any good intelligence service', was talking to the militants on Pakistani soil, 'no one really knew what they were saying to each other'.[27] Pakistani military officials readily admitted there were contacts. 'Of course we talk to them. That is what we should be doing. We need to learn about them and what they are doing,' one ISI colonel told the author in early 2008.[28] In presentations to the heads of foreign security services or governments, the ISI blamed their failure to move against the Taliban on the terrain, local animosity and, without fail, a lack of resources. The information provided by Western services about the location of senior Taliban figures on Pakistani soil was inaccurate, they said.[29]

Such arguments were rapidly becoming unsustainable, however. In the late spring of 2008, as Afghanistan plunged towards even greater depths of violence and chaos, a more aggressive and coherent Western position began to emerge. In January, Mike McConnell, the American director of national intelligence, sent an assessment to the White House in which he bluntly stated that 'the Pakistani government regularly gives weapons and support [to insurgents] to go into Afghanistan and attack Afghan and coalition forces'.[30] Key to McConnell's assessment was an intercept of a telephone conversation in which General Kayani, the new head of the Pakistani armed forces, was apparently heard speaking of Jalaluddin Haqqani, the Pakistan-based cross-frontier insurgent leader, as a 'strategic asset'.[31] In July there came the bombing of the Indian embassy in Kabul, and further intercepts apparently showing ISI officers giving instructions to Haqqani's men prior to the attack. American intelligence services, though they admitted the data were open to different interpretations, nonetheless saw them as clear proof of a new level of ISI involvement: the instigation and organization of strikes, not simply the manipulation or protection of insurgents on Pakistani soil. 'It was sort of this "aha" moment. There was a sense that there was finally direct proof,' one State Department official told the *New York Times*.[32] Shortly afterwards, classified documents compiled to guide interrogation teams at the Guantanamo Bay prison camp categorized the ISI as a terrorist organization, listing it alongside Hamas, Hezbollah, the Chechen Martyrs Battalion and al-Qaeda.[33] Publicly, British intelligence nonetheless went no further than saying that Pakistan was 'at the very least tacitly allowing Taliban activities on their soil'. Sir John Scarlett, the then director of MI6, stressed to the author that this was, however, something with which 'the UK' had a 'serious issue'. Scarlett described relationships with ISI counterparts as being 'awkward' and talked of 'undiplomatic' language used at 'the highest levels'.[34]

But still, even if senior spies and policy-makers were increasingly convinced that the ISI was playing what one official called 'a long double game', no one had yet evolved a policy to counter it. Western intelligence services remained still heavily dependent on the ISI for intelligence on al-Qaeda and were unable to operate in the FATA without the assistance of their Pakistani counterparts, who jealously restricted their allies' freedom of movement and operation within their country. Equally, it was still only the Pakistani military which could move against any 'safe havens' for the international militants. The ISI continued to show every sign of believing they could still manage the radical groups that they had protected for so long in the Punjab or sent into Kashmir. There was little reason to believe the ISI intelligence service would cease their efforts to manage the Taliban, Haqqani and Hekmatyar in the near future either, whatever the pressure put on them. Their support to the insurgents had always been predicated on the analysis that the

West's effort in Afghanistan would eventually fail. The deteriorating situation across the border thus appeared only to vindicate the Pakistanis' long-term strategy.

## ANOTHER FRONT IN ANOTHER WAR

The man who had been immediately blamed for killing Bhutto was Baitullah Mehsud, a thirty-four-year-old Pashtun tribesman and militant from the FATA. The evidence against him was circumstantial – a telephone conversation picked up by satellite surveillance in which he accepted the congratulations of a cleric and appeared to say that those who had committed the attack were part of the group of fighters he led – but was accepted as proof of what was largely already suspected by most security services and many analysts.[35] Mehsud, who led the rough coalition of groups known as the Tehrik-e-Taliban-Pakistan (Pakistan Taliban Union or TTP), publicly denied the killing but had already threatened to assassinate Bhutto.[36]

The various groups that made up the TTP – the coalition had formally been declared in the autumn of 2007 – had many qualities familiar from other parts of this narrative. Though numerous – the total force that could be mobilized at any one time was probably between 5,000 and 10,000 – it was still a tiny percentage of the overall population. The strong sense of cultural identity – reimagined, reconstituted and repackaged – was reminiscent of both the Afghan Taliban and the al-Mahdi Army in Iraq. The degree to which the groups found their broader rhetorical language in the debased global 'single narrative' popularized so widely in the Islamic world over the previous decade was also obvious. The economic growth enjoyed by Pakistan in the first years of the decade might have been largely confined to the eastern half of the country, but the new broadcast media certainly were accessible in the FATA. The way in which base manoeuvres for power, cash and influence were legitimized by appeal to a greater cause and the constant tensions between communities and militants seen in the FATA also had clear parallels elsewhere. So too had the nature of recruitment – flowing down lines of association, friendship, clan and family – rather than through any organized system. The conflict between the nation – it was after all the 'Pakistani' Taliban – and pan-Islamic identities was equally familiar. Two linked elements that were particularly clear in the character and internal dynamics of the Pakistani Taliban but were not often picked up in analysis at the time were the degree to which the militants drew much of their support from marginalized elements within their own societies and the way in which their rhetoric and ideology were informed by a socially revolutionary agenda. The striking fact about Mehsud and the men who he nominally led was not that they were 'pure products' of the traditions of the frontier but rather the effective collapse of such traditions in the new circumstances generated in part by the 9/11 Wars.

Mehsud, for example, came from elements within local Pashtun society which would never have had any power, influence or wealth only a decade or so before. Born near Bannu, a dusty town on the edge of the FATA, not a village in its heart, Mehsud came from a minor branch of a minor tribe, not a prestigious branch of a powerful or rich one.[37] His parents were not wealthy – his father was a low-ranking cleric – and Mehsud himself had been patchily educated, attending both a number of different religious schools and several different public institutions.[38] Though Mehsud liked to boast that he had fought with the Taliban, it appears he had in fact only spent a few months in the late 1990s guarding Kabul airport, so was denied even the prestige and social mobility that feats of arms might traditionally have afforded him. Even a hagiographic biography written by his deputy does not mention any combat role in the fighting during the fall of the Taliban regime, though it says that Mehsud assisted al-Qaeda fighters in escaping Afghanistan and finding secure havens across the border.[39] When, in 2004, Mehsud had succeeded in assuming the leadership of several hundred fighters in the strategically crucial agency of South Waziristan, he did so in a very modern way: the position was effectively vacant because the previous incumbent, the charismatic Nek Mohammed, had been killed by a missile fired by an American unmanned drone after he had given away his location by using a satellite phone in one of the first such assassinations in the region. Other militant leaders in the frontier zone in the autumn of 2007 and in the summer of 2008 also would have stood little chance of any leadership role, wealth or influence under the old traditional frontier systems.[40] Mangal Bagh, an independent militant leader in the Khyber Agency, was a former bus driver.[41] One of the rising figures in the northern agencies – Maulana Fazlullah – was a former mechanic who once maintained a miniature ski-lift for tourists visiting the scenic Swat valley. Muslim Khan, Fazlullah's close aide, was a secular-educated former PPP activist who had travelled widely in the Middle East and Europe as a merchant seaman, then spent years as a taxi driver in America before finally returning to his village shortly after the 9/11 attacks to open a drugstore.[42] Other militant leaders included barbers, butchers, itinerant salesmen, petrol pump attendants, criminals or, in a region where levels of unemployment touched somewhere between 60 and 80 per cent, were simply the semi-retired veterans of a variety of conflicts.[43] Leaders in Bajaur and in the valleys of Malakand and Swat made frequent promises to redistribute the often extensive properties of major landowners to those who had none, picking up historical local claims for land reform by agricultural day labourers going back to the 1970s and beyond.[44] The militants were not, by local standards, ignorant men. All but four of a dozen captured militants the author interviewed in Peshawar in November 2008 had travelled widely in Pakistan, two had worked in the Gulf and one had spent several years in east Africa and in the Middle East working and, he said, 'preaching'. Though their levels of religious knowledge and political understanding were relatively low, they were most definitely not farm boys who had picked up the family Kalashnikov. The militants fighting in the FATA were thus not the product of an ancient society resisting the modern but, like the Taliban across the frontier, a profoundly contemporary phenomenon.

As in Afghanistan and Iraq, the violence in the FATA resembled a matrix of multiple ongoing conflicts. The radicalization seen in the early years of the 9/11 Wars saw many of these conflicts, some of which stretched back decades, re-energized. So in the northernmost tribal agency, Bajaur, the three major local tribes had split very differently in terms of allegiance and ideology by 2002 or 2003 and, from 2006 onwards had been in open or semi-open warfare with each other or with the government. The largest and poorest tribe remained broadly neutral. A second tribe, the Salarzai, who were mainly relatively wealthy farmers, had rallied to the government. A third, the Mahmund, were the only local community that could truly be said to be integrated into the 'modern world', largely, it is true, through smuggling, the arms and drugs business, exposure to various strands of contemporary Islamist thought, pilgrimages to the Gulf, remittances from overseas and through hosting itinerant preachers (and occasionally al-Qaeda leaders). It was the Mahmund who were among the most enthusiastic supporters of the militants in FATA.[45] When not fighting the Pakistani military, the Mahmund fought either in Afghanistan or against the other two tribes of Bajaur.

The conflict in the FATA was thus, as in Afghanistan and in Iraq, in a large part a series of overlapping civil wars. Sometimes these took the form of an assault on traditional authority – hundreds, probably thousands, of traditional tribal elders were executed by militants between 2003 and 2008.[46] Sometimes, such as in Kurram agency, the conflicts had a more sectarian flavour, pitting Sunnis against Shia. In Waziristan, fighters under a rival commander from a rival tribe took on those of Baitullah Mehsud in a battle sparked initially by differing attitudes to the presence of Uzbek and other central Asian militants in local villages but which degenerated into a straight struggle for power and resources. In the Khyber Pass, three different factions, divided by sub-tribe and religious observance, patched together different alliances, fought each other and the government and engaged in kidnap and racketeering. The presence of fugitive al-Qaeda leadership elements, in Bajaur as elsewhere, also fuelled such local conflicts, not necessarily because of the radicalizing effect the propaganda of such individuals had but because of the competition for the very large rent payments they were prepared to pay to anyone prepared to take the risk of providing shelter.[47]

Like the Afghan Taliban, the Pakistani groups themselves faced a range of challenges, however. Their idea of government was largely inspired by that that their counterparts across the border had introduced during the late 1990s. But, though it was welcomed by some communities in the FATA for the same reasons that many in Afghanistan had supported the imposition of a rigorous and puritanical system there a decade earlier, the Pakistani militants were operating in a very different environment. Though old institutions such as the *jirga*, the consultative meeting of tribal elders, were breaking down in the FATA, most local people wanted them restored, not replaced by mediation by militant leaders or clerics.[48] Militant leaders like Mehsud claimed to bring justice and security, setting up courts to rapidly resolve disputes, creating vigilante police forces and building makeshift jails into which 'bandits' were thrown, exactly as the Taliban were doing in Afghanistan, but, though these were initially popular, attacks on symbols of government authority or so-called 'moral corruption' were less well viewed. Despite the profound conservatism of the local tribesmen – over 90 per cent said that women should remain in the home, more than two-thirds backed honour killings, and a vast majority favoured the imposition of strict *sharia* law – there was a broad desire for education. The systematic destruction of hundreds of schools and the murder of scores of teachers thus did little to endear the militants to the local communities.[49] Similarly the expulsion of all local and foreign NGOs from areas dominated by the radical groups was also unpopular. Successive surveys showed the local desire for the development such organizations could bring. Many of the local political figures targeted by the militants – often those linked to the Pashtun nationalist Awami National Party who did well in the NWFP and in the FATA in the 2008 elections – were popular and respected figures.

If the Pakistani Taliban had been a more cohesive phenomenon or had had aims that went beyond dominating a particular valley, road or racket, such issues might have caused serious problems. But such tensions, which themselves remained highly localized, were far from a strategic threat to militancy in an environment as radicalized as that of the Pakistani–Afghan frontier in late 2008.[50] One poll found that only 3 per cent of tribesmen saw the Taliban as terrorists. Equally, the clumsy tactics of the regular troops deployed to the periodic offensives in the FATA allowed, as had occurred in Iraq and Afghanistan, the militants to pose as protectors of local communities or at the very least to benefit ambivalent popular sentiments. Army officers, trained only for conventional operations against massed Indian armoured units on the eastern frontier, were utterly ignorant of counter-insurgency doctrine, old or new. Drawn from elsewhere in Pakistan and officered largely by Punjabis, who often needed interpreters to speak to local people, the military were often seen as an alien presence.[51] The army's successive 'cordon and sweep' operations between 2003 and 2007 involved either unwitting or deliberate destruction of the homes of very large numbers of locals as a collective punishment. In their major campaign in South Waziristan in 2004, the army had bulldozed over eighty houses, destroyed local irrigation works and wells and killed scores of civilians.[52] In January 2008, another major operation in the same area saw a further 4,000 houses reduced to ruins and bulldozers and explosives used to level one town's bazaar.[53]

The collateral damage inflicted by the rising number of air strikes from American unmanned drones in the FATA also drove communities towards the militants. Though undoubtedly an effective means of eliminating known militants and putting their associates under considerable pressure – men like Mehsud in the FATA in the summer of 2008 were sleeping outside to avoid being caught in a building and spent much of their time conducting purges against supposed informants – the drone strikes were a blunt instrument and killed many civilians. This was another reason for the Mahmund tribe of Bajaur taking arms against their fellow Bajauris and against the Pakistani government. Damadola, the Bajaur village which became the headquarters of local militants and was thought to have sheltered Ayman al-Zawahiri on a number of occasions, had been hit by a series of air strikes from 2005 onwards. Each time the cost of killing a handful of militants was the deaths of dozens of villagers.[54] In one strike an estimated eighty-three 'Taliban militants' were killed when a *medressa* was hit, though identifying who among the dead were militants and who were the sons of locals was hard. Another destroyed a series of compounds where al-Zawahiri was thought to be spending the night. 'They dropped bombs from planes, and we were in no position to stop them or tell them we were innocent . . . I don't know Zawahiri. He was not at my home. No foreigner was at my home at the time the planes came and dropped bombs,' said Shah Zaman, a jeweller from Damadola who lost a son and a daughter in the attack.[55]

## AL-QAEDA IN THE FATA

In June 2008, a strange and tense meeting had taken place in a compound high in the tribal area of South Waziristan. Six volunteers, two from France and four from Belgium, had decided to confront the man who was looking after their training as militants. He was a Syrian they knew as Driss, who they believed to be part of al-Qaeda. Before leaving their homes, they had watched al-Qaeda videos on the internet and seen images of massed battalions of *mujahideen* training on assault courses, exciting ambushes of American troops, tired but triumphant young fighters returning from battle and inspiring speeches by Osama bin Laden, they told him. But after five months in Pakistan's frontier zones they had done nothing more than some basic training on small arms, a day of shooting, spent an afternoon watching an instructor build a bomb and had many, many hours of religious instruction. Worse, they had had to spend hundreds of euros of their own money to buy their own weapons and equipment and to pay an extortionate weekly rent for the miserable accommodation offered by a local family.[56] They had been deceived, they boldly told the Syrian. The videos had lied.

The response was unsympathetic and unapologetic. Of course the videos were misleading, Driss told them, they were a 'trick . . . to intimidate enemies and to attract new recruits'.[57]

The exchange went right to the heart of one of the most controversial questions among analysts of al-Qaeda and the global Islamic militant movement of which it was a part in the seventh year of the 9/11 Wars. How close was the image of al-Qaeda projected through the internet and other media to the reality? What exactly was the capacity of the 'al-Qaeda hardcore'? What was life like for the leadership, for the more junior members or for the raw Western recruits who made their way to the tribal zones? And what were al-Qaeda's relations with other groups such as the Pakistani Taliban or the Afghan insurgent networks? These were questions Western and other security services had been trying for many years to answer – without a great deal of success.

Their difficulties were in part self-inflicted, in part a result of the extreme operating environment in the FATA and the surrounding regions. In 2008, at the time when Driss and the volunteers were having their talk, the last confirmed location of bin Laden and al-Zawahiri was still Tora Bora, nearly seven years before. Even in the days of relatively good CIA and ISI relations in the early years of the hunt for the fugitive leaders, ideas of their location were based on informed speculation rather than fact. Debates over whether the top two leaders were together, whether they were moving or 'hunkered down', whether they were in a Pakistani city or, as almost everyone thought, near the border, continued interminably. 'Anyone who says he knows is a liar,' one US Intelligence official told the author. Various hypotheses were advanced about the state of bin Laden's health including the idea, first circulated in the late 1990s, that the fugitive, fifty-one in 2008, might suffer from a serious kidney disorder. To the disappointment of many, it had become clear that, though bin Laden suffered from lower-back pain common in people of his height, which had meant occasional use of a walking cane and an end to his favourite pastime of horse-riding, there was no evidence of any other medical problem. For his part, al-Zawahiri, though approaching sixty, appeared in good health. Periodic breaks in communication sometimes raised hopes that one or other might be dead or seriously ill but always ended with a new video surfacing, often containing references to recent events that clearly indicated both men had been very much alive only weeks before. As late as 2006, the vast bulk of American intelligence came from the interviews of detainees – hardly the best method to obtain live and actionable information.[58] Excepting the interception of a courier suspected of having been recently in contact with one or other of the pair in the immediate aftermath of the capture of Khalid Sheikh Mohammed in 2003 and the information that had sparked the attempts to kill al-Zawahiri in Bajaur around 2006, there had been no 'strong lead' on the whereabouts of either man.[59] Tracking the senior al-Qaeda leadership was a dispiriting task, involving the verification and cross-referencing of thousands of leads on hundreds of individuals. The CIA teams assigned to the job were frequently changed to keep them motivated.

Nor were the resources being directed at the operation as significant as many outside the world of intelligence thought. The Iraq war had drained the effort to find bin Laden. 'By April, May 2002, we began losing people to the groups that were preparing for the Iraq war,' said Mike Scheuer, who, having headed the CIA's bin Laden unit from 1996 to 1999, went on to be chief adviser to his successor from 2001 to 2004. 'We were losing Arabic speakers. Very experienced people.' Bob Grenier, the then head of the Islamabad CIA station, remembered that 'a large number of the best and most experienced people were drawn off pretty early from Afghanistan and switched to Iraq, especially those with extensive counter-terrorism experience or regional specialists.'[60] The 5th Special Forces Group, which included the best linguists, was sent to the Gulf and replaced in Afghanistan by the 7th Special Forces Group, largely composed of Spanish-speakers with Latin American experience. Ron Nash, British ambassador in Afghanistan in the autumn of 2003, remembered later how the 'extremely useful' small groups of the UK's SAS and SBS who had been assuring security and gathering intelligence in far-flung Afghan provincial capitals in a low-key but effective way were all withdrawn by the end of the summer of 2002.[61] Art Keller, a CIA counter-terrorism and counter-proliferation specialist who himself volunteered for a tour in South Waziristan in 2006, described those operatives who ended up in Pakistan as 'the scrapings of the barrel'.[62]

Given one week to read up on the region before being dispatched, Keller spent six months as one of a small number of CIA officers, guarded by Pakistani special forces and chaperoned by the ISI, stationed in a Pakistani military base in Wana, the biggest town in South Waziristan in 2006. Life was not easy, either professionally or personally. The Americans, forbidden to leave the base, were supposed to generate the intelligence that would allow the Pakistanis to act. There were a number of problems with this arrangement, however. The first was the 'extreme reluctance' of the Pakistanis to mount operations, which Keller attributed to heavy casualties sustained on previous botched raids. The second was the cumbersome procedure for initiating any action. Target information – for example the location of a key al-Qaeda organizer – would be passed to the ISI in the Wana base for immediate action. It would then be sent up the ISI chain of command, who would ask for verification from their officers on the ground, before going to the Pakistani army, whose own intelligence service would verify again, before finally being sent to the Pakistani army's operations planning section. A successful raid, specialists say, needs intelligence on where a target *will* be in four hours, not where he was a couple of days before. This convoluted system also meant that drone strikes, which also had to be signed off by the ISI, remained a rarity. A third problem was simply logistics. As Keller was not allowed to venture out of the base in Wana, everything he did was through Pakistani liaison officers or via electronic means. 'I spent my days reading traffic from other stations and going through communications intercepts,' Keller remembered. 'Meeting sources was very hard.' Not that the information that did come in was particularly useful. Sightings of bin Laden were 'a dime a dozen' but in the end never checked out. Any halfway reliable lead was usually impossible to verify. Finally, there were the normal administrative fiascos that occur within any organization, even the CIA. When he was finally given a tip on a possible recent location for the al-Qaeda leader himself, Keller's emails got snarled up in a bureaucratic tangle when someone forgot to copy in the Islamabad CIA station and thus provoked an in-house political battle. 'If the American people really knew what the hunt for bin Laden actually meant, they would not be particularly impressed,' Keller said.[63]

In fact, al-Qaeda militants faced a difficult choice. True security meant finding a bolt hole and severing almost every link with the outside world. But this had enormous practical drawbacks, particularly for anyone involved in training, planning, recruitment, strategic liaison, communication or fundraising. For those whose tasks required at least a degree of exposure, whether people like Driss, the European volunteers' disappointing mentor, or more senior al-Qaeda militants, there was, however, another line of defence that mitigated the danger of working in the open. This was the sympathy of local communities. From its earliest days, al-Qaeda's success or failure had depended on its ability to reach out to local groups and leverage local conditions. An overwhelmingly Arab organization with the vast bulk of its members and supporters from Libya, Saudi Arabia and Egypt, it had always existed in 'foreign' territory. Even in 2008, there were no Pakistanis – or even Afghans – among al-Qaeda senior ranks, and though bin Laden, al-Zawahiri and other such international militants did have some residual connection with the NWFP and FATA from the 1980s and 1990s, including contacts with major powerbrokers such as Jalaluddin Haqqani, the frontier zone was still far from their natural environment.[64] In a good illustration of this, the meeting between Driss and his charges had seen a Syrian arguing in Arabic with two Frenchmen and four Belgians of north African origin in the middle of a Pashtun-dominated part of Pakistan. What al-Qaeda therefore undertook after drawing breath following their flight from Afghanistan in 2001 was a classic 'grafting operation' of the type that bin Laden had executed so well to secure himself a safe haven in Sudan during his time there in the early and mid 1990s and then again on arriving in Afghanistan immediately in 1996, when he had been able not just to convince the Taliban to give him shelter but to steadily gain greater and greater influence over the leadership and ideology of the movement. Even if he personally might be able to protect himself by withdrawing into some kind of sealed bunker, making sure that the FATA continued to be hospitable and thus secure for his followers was a vital task. Bin Laden applied the same tactics as had worked a half-decade before: a carefully orchestrated 'charm offensive' towards the local communities whom he needed to convince that their interests and those of his group coincided. The 'global' campaign of al-Qaeda needed to be superimposed or mapped on to local conditions without provoking the kind of backlash that had been seen in Iraq and various other theatres. Though it remained delicate, this task was rendered considerably easier by the dramatically raised levels of radicalization in the border zone at the time and, of course, by the previous local traditions of revivalist rebellions against various 'outside' authorities. Bin Laden's vision of al-Qaeda as a vanguard striving to defend true Islam thus meshed easily with the self-image of local communities who already saw themselves as guardians and repositories of an uncorrupted Islamic culture fighting to preserve their autonomy against the people of the plains and the cities, the Pakistani Army, the government, foreign imperialists, modernizers et al. Fusing Pashtun and global jihadi identity required only the relatively small step of adding the war against a 'global alliance of crusaders and Zionists' to the various foes aligned in an already deeply reactionary, intolerant worldview. As the al-Qaeda leadership had found over previous years, astute propaganda, careful outreach and very significant sums of money were, particularly in a conflict environment, an effective combination. One poll in 2008 suggested that 70 per cent of the 20 million people in the North West Frontier province and the FATA viewed bin Laden 'favourably'.[65]

As they had worked to assure a secure base for their organization, so too the al-Qaeda leadership had worked to rebuild something of the infrastructure they had lost when forced out of Afghanistan. This had taken some time, but, by 2005 and 2006, successive investigations of plots in the UK and elsewhere had revealed that al-Qaeda now had significant capacity. From 2007, the number of volunteers making their way to the FATA, particularly as the attraction of fighting in Iraq had waned, had increased sharply. Very few intelligence services had succeeded in penetrating the militants' security procedures and infiltrating agents into al-Qaeda ranks, so most of what was learned about the situation there was still thus received second hand – and therefore heavily filtered – from the Pakistanis or was patched together from surveillance intercepts or the interrogations of men like the disillusioned Europeans who were eventually arrested in December 2008, Bryant Vinas, a twenty-six-year-old American convert detained by the Pakistanis in Peshawar in October of that year and handed over to the US authorities, and the three Germans of the 'Sauerland cell' who had been arrested the year before in the northern Rhine region as they made final preparations for a bombing campaign. Slowly a more detailed picture emerged of al-Qaeda's exact set up in the FATA and its relations with many, many other groups based there.

One the most striking elements emerging from the testimony of such individuals was the sheer diversity of the international groups in the FATA in 2007 and 2008. Both Vinas and the Europeans of the 'Belgian cell' describe two major groups of central Asian militants, mainly Uzbek, each numbering over 1,000, various Arab groups, including al-Qaeda, each with a few hundred fighters, a Turkish group, a Uighur group and various mixed groups. On their arrival, the Belgian and French volunteers had asked to join the Arabs and had thus ended up with the Syrian Driss, they told their interrogators.[66] Vinas started off with a Pakistani group, probably Lashkar-e-Toiba, active in the northern FATA, from where he had joined attacks on American troops in Afghanistan's Kunar province before finding a contact who allowed him to approach al-Qaeda itself. The Germans had joined the smaller of the two Uzbek factions.[67] These groups were loosely organized but with significant degrees of internal bureaucracy. Al-Qaeda in particular appears to have been keen on new recruits filling out forms in triplicate with all their personal information, ambitions and opinions set down. One question was: 'What is your view of martyrdom operations? Would you participate in one?'[68] Swearing a formal oath of loyalty – a *bayat* – to bin Laden was not, however, essential.

A second element emerging from the testimonies was that conditions in the tribal areas were much tougher than they had been in Afghanistan in the late 1990s, when solidly constructed camps had provided accommodation for hundreds of trainees at a time. Volunteers in the FATA in 2008 fought and trained in small groups, living in dispersed compounds, with poor food and little medical care. When one of the Belgians fell ill with malaria he was 'left in a corner', according to a friend's testimony, and 'given a jab every few days by a kid who was the little brother of the local doctor'.[69] A reward for six months of good service was a trip to an internet café, from where an email could be sent home. The Belgians were allowed some chocolate to boost their flagging morale. All the different groups used the facilities of the towns of Miran Shah and Wana. 'This bazaar is bustling with Chechens, Uzbeks, Tajiks, Russians, Bosnians, some from EU countries and of course our Arab brothers,' one volunteer who visited the FATA around this time emailed an associate.[70] Many European recruits missed female company. Vinas was arrested while in Peshawar hoping to find a wife. Others were jealous of longer-established militants who had married local women. One German volunteer appealed for female partners to travel to the FATA so the *mujahideen* there could start families of young militants who would be 'entirely unknown to security services'.[71]

To participate – though not necessarily to die – in combat operations was the goal of almost all the volunteers making their way to the FATA. 'I saw myself as a soldier for Islam, fighting on the frontline, on raids and in combat and under bombardment,' one French volunteer later said.[72] Those who did see action were deeply marked by the experience. Aden Yilmaz, a member of the Sauerland cell, told a court that he 'savoured every moment' of the time he had spent fighting in Afghanistan.[73] When Western volunteers like Yilmaz, a Turkish national living in Germany, were deployed on terrorist operations in European countries, they often appeared to regret leaving the noise, chaos, danger and excitement of combat and the rude life on the frontlines. 'I would have liked to have stayed there,' Yilmaz recalled.[74]

Another question troubling analysts was the exact nature of the relations between al-Qaeda and the insurgent groups fighting in Afghanistan, particularly those directly loyal to Mullah Omar and the 'Quetta Shura', the council of senior Taliban leaders based in or around the western Pakistani city. Arab volunteers embedded in Afghan Taliban units continued to flow across the border – in the summer of 2008 up to 400 were estimated to be with Afghan insurgent units, especially those of Haqqani, bringing a new technological and tactical edge to combat, but the links between al-Qaeda and the Afghan insurgents still appeared to be loose.[75] A whole series of disparate but disorganized connections and liaisons combined into 'a working relationship based on individual personalities' rather than a formal alliance, according to British intelligence officials.[76] One key figure was bilingual Egyptian Mustafa Abu al-Yazid, who had developed a broad range of Taliban connections in the 1990s when head of al-Qaeda's finance committee and so was able to enhance otherwise fairly haphazard cooperation between his Arabic-speaking al-Qaeda associates and the Pashtun-speaking Afghan Taliban a decade or so later.[77] Al-Yazid liaised too with local Pakistani militant commanders like Baitullah Mehsud, who put their own considerable reserves of suicide bombers at al-Qaeda's disposal, in return for monetary or other assistance, as well as sending them into Afghanistan 'following the orders' of the senior Afghan Taliban leadership.[78] Al-Qaeda leaders also began establishing closer relations with the increasing number of individuals from Pakistani groups who were arriving in the FATA. Some had broken away from groups like Lashkar-e-Toiba which had remained focused on regional rather than global agendas. They had moved to the frontier both to evade security forces and to be able to pursue their vision of jihad unhindered. Others mixed outright criminality in Pakistan with sectarian violence and had some international involvement too when it suited them. Many retained networks in places like Bahawalpur or in Karachi. Several were suspected by Pakistani investigators of involvement in the first attempt to kill Bhutto on her return to Pakistan in October 2007. Others were thought to have provided safehouses in Rawalpindi for the successful bid to assassinate the former prime minister two months later. One key emerging figure was a veteran Pakistani militant known as Ilyas Kashmiri, who al-Yazid announced as the leader of the newly formed 'al-Qaeda in Kashmir'. This range of volatile and complex relations was not easy for any one individual, or indeed group, to manage. The FATA appeared perhaps to be less the Grand Central Station of international militancy, as one specialist from MI6 called it, than its Grand Bazaar.

And it was a bazaar that was under attack. The Belgian volunteers referred in their testimony to hearing 'frequent bombardments' and learning of the death of many 'brothers' in air strikes. Through 2007, with hard evidence of ISI support for insurgents growing, Bush had begun to lose patience with the Pakistanis' apparent foot-dragging and had moved to a markedly more unilateral use of drone attacks.[79] This may well have been exactly what the Pakistani senior command had wanted all along. By the summer of 2008, the Americans were launching strikes without consulting Islamabad if the target was on a list of two to three dozen senior figures agreed in advance with the new civilian Pakistani government and top generals.[80] The results of this shift had been seen as early as February 2008, when Abu Laith al-Liby, seen as al-Qaeda's director of external operations, was killed. Militants, the volunteers' testimony revealed, greatly feared some kind of computerized 'chips' which they believed were left by informers to guide missiles on to locations or individuals.[81] Over 300 'spies' died in repeated purges during the summer in part as a result, with over 100 being killed in only a couple of weeks following the death in July of Abu Khabab al-Masri, a fifty-five-year-old veteran who had run rudimentary chemical weapons tests at camps near Jalalabad prior to 9/11. Through the rest of the year such strikes intensified. The constant threat of a fiery death did not, however, dissuade some militants from enjoying the few distractions that life in the FATA offered. Vinas told his interrogators of long hikes in the company of one of the Belgian volunteers in the hills around the village where they were staying.[82] Others apparently rode horses.[83]

As 2008's long and violent summer turned to autumn, bin Laden, al-Zawahiri and the al-Qaeda senior leadership more generally thus continued to face a range of fairly familiar challenges. Though they had survived the loss of Afghanistan and had reconstituted a new base in Pakistan with some degree of success, the troubles they faced, on a tactical and a strategic level, were still very numerous. Chief amongst the strategic issues was their continuing failure to pull off a major attack. It had been more than three years since the bombings in London and Egypt, four since Madrid, five since Istanbul, Casablanca and the wave of violence in Saudi Arabia, six since Bali and, of course, seven years since 9/11 itself. Though the al-Qaeda senior leadership had always made it clear that they preferred rare and spectacular strikes to frequent and relatively minor ones and though 9/11 had set the bar extremely high, their apparent incapacity to fulfil their fundamental role of instigator and inciter of violence was a major problem. More broadly, bin Laden and al-Zawahiri risked slipping out of the mainstream of contemporary militancy, reduced to historic if iconic importance. Early 2008 had seen a sudden spate of videos clearly aimed at reinforcing the organization's credibility among veteran militant activists and, more importantly, among the new generation of younger activists too. For the latter, the 9/11 strikes were often a childhood memory, and, in the highly competitive world of Islamic militancy, al-Qaeda's senior leaders needed to continually reassert their primacy if they were not to be seen as belonging to an earlier time. The videos focused heavily on the Palestinian question, a subject to which bin Laden had returned repeatedly and which he knew had immediate and wide appeal.[84] Many of the new communications were also tailored to attract a younger audience, giving a starring role to Abu Yahya al-Libi, an experienced and charismatic militant, polemicist and propagandist in his early thirties known for his escape from the high-security detention centre in Bagram airbase in Afghanistan three years before.[85]

Other communications were clearly aimed at offsetting the criticism of bin Laden's leadership by the growing number of respected veteran militants. Al-Zawahiri had released a book called *The Exoneration* in March 2008, in which he inveighed at length against those who were 'now trying to serve Crusader Zionist interests' by 'dragging the *muja-hideen* away from the confrontation'.[86] The same month, Abu Yahya al-Libi weighed in with a video in which he claimed that the recent texts of Sayyid Imam al-Sharif, the Egyptian al-Qaeda founder who had renounced violence from his prison cell, were forgeries. In May, al-Zawahiri finally responded to questions he had invited on a radical web forum six months previously. Arguing that allegations that al-Qaeda had caused the deaths of 'Muslim innocents' were 'Crusader Zionist propaganda' or due to the use of civilians as 'human shields', he returned to the same themes he had covered in his book, pouring scorn on his critics, in particular the veteran Muslim Brotherhood cleric Yusuf al-Qaradawi, calling them faithless Western stooges, apostates and hypocrites. Like bin Laden, al-Zawahiri also focused on Gaza and Palestine, rebutting the charge that al-Qaeda had not done enough to help the Palestinians directly with the argument that the group had repeatedly struck the allies of Israel.

There was another key emerging theme in communications. The central al-Qaeda leadership had always tried to tread a careful path between the local strategy entirely focused on establishing individual 'fronts' aimed at securing slices of liberated territory, that of the late al-Zarqawi, and the global strategy focused on provoking a broad uprising of Muslims, favoured by the now incarcerated al-Suri. The 9/11 attacks had taken the organization, against the wishes of many of its members, towards the global strategy. Since, the local had progressively returned. Al-Zawahiri, with his direct experience of militancy in Egypt in the late 1970s, had always stressed the importance of securing a solid base from which to launch further operations. If bin Laden lacked his older associate's sense of the practicalities of clandestine violent extremism, never himself having ever been hunted through the streets of his hometown, he nonetheless recognized that the great campaign to liberate the Islamic world needed to be launched from somewhere. The question was: where? Al-Zawahiri's various writings made clear his long-cherished hope that his native land would be the centre of the new caliphate when it was restored. Bin Laden apparently hoped it would be Saudi Arabia. However, neither had been a practical prospect in the 1990s, and nor were they now. Hopes that Iraq might fulfil the role had been dashed, at least for the moment. Nor did Afghanistan look a likely candidate in the near future. But a new possibility, barely considered previously, now presented itself. A strife-torn, chaotic country of nearly 200 million Muslims, where bin Laden and his close associates had already established an ideological and physical foothold and where they were still more popular than almost anywhere else in the Islamic world: Pakistan.


## THE BATTLE FOR BAJAUR

In late November 2008, the Pakistani army fought its way into a small town called Loesam in Bajaur, the agency at the northernmost tip of the FATA which had been in part overrun by militants. Bajaur was used by al-Qaeda as an occasional haven, had been hit by repeated drone strikes and was a rear base for militants engaging US troops over the border in Afghanistan. By the time the troops had secured the town, there was not much of it left. To save it, they had destroyed it. The bazaar was a pile of rubble, almost every home had been reduced to its concrete foundations and the only building still upright was the mosque that stood in the corner of what once was the local petrol station. The population had fled, joining an estimated 200,000 refugees displaced by the fighting over previous months.[87]

If the scene was a desolate one, it was set in a landscape of striking natural beauty. A few hundred metres out of the ruined town men of the 25th Punjab regiment had dug trenches among stands of slim ash and birch trees. Heavy machine guns traded fire with militants who still clung to a few battered strongpoints concealed in the dry, sandy valleys that ran, half hidden, between the empty fields up into the hills beyond. Smoke from fires started in the dry grass and scattered patches of woodland by shelling drifted in long grey strands. On the horizon, distant but visible in the clear autumn air, was the long ridge that marked the Afghan frontier with a spur where Damadola, the village hit hardest by repeated air strikes over previous years and now the effective headquarters of the militants, lay. Tanks were being brought up to deal with the militants' mortars, which were still dropping shells just a few hundred metres from where Colonel Javed Baluch, the ground commander of the operation, sat by a pink plastic telephone and ordered tea, biscuits and artillery strikes with an equal nonchalance.[88]

Of all the armed groups in the FATA in 2008, the Pakistani army were clearly the biggest and the best-equipped force. They had been engaged in the frontier zone since late 2001, when troops had belatedly been sent to block the escape routes from Tora Bora. Over the intervening years dozens of operations the length and breadth of the FATA had cost over 1,000 Pakistani servicemen's lives. In late 2008, with Musharraf gone and a civilian government in place, a new series of offensives was launched. One reason was increasing American pressure on the Pakistani high command to justify the $2 billion annual subsidy from Washington for their counter-terrorist operations. Another was the international outcry after the death of Bhutto. A third, perhaps the most pertinent of all, was the unprecedented spate of attacks on the Pakistani military itself through the autumn of 2007 and on into 2008. Previously, the bombings that had killed so many elsewhere in the country had largely spared the army installations. This had changed. Of the fifty-six suicide bombings in Pakistan in 2007, thirty-six had struck military targets and in all nearly 900 Pakistani security forces and officials had died over the year. By June 2008, that total had already been exceeded.[89] A final factor was the realization by senior Pakistani military personnel of quite what sort of threat militancy now posed to the country. This had been reinforced when, in September 2008, hours after President Zardari's maiden address to parliament, a huge truck bomb exploded outside the Marriott hotel in central Islamabad, ripping away the entire façade of the building and killing fifty-four and injuring over 250. This attack, in the heart of the capital and only a few hundred metres from where the entire cabinet was dining, was a direct assault on the core of the Pakistani political and security establishment.[90] For once, rather than holding back the country's new political leadership, army commanders actively set out to build up their enthusiasm for a series of broad-ranging offensives, showing Zardari and senior politicians propaganda videos made by militants which showed adult 'spies' executed by recruits apparently only ten or eleven years old.[91]

The Bajaur operation was the first of the new offensives and was very carefully watched from overseas. The use of drones, it was widely recognized, was a tactical rather than a strategic solution to the threat to the West that emanated from the FATA, and any longer-term solution would have to come from the Pakistanis and in particular from the Pakistani army. The machinations of the ISI in Afghanistan had already shaken the faith of many in the West in the Pakistani military and security establishment, and Western powers were hoping for a show of competence and resolve in Bajaur followed by a swift extension of operations into every tribal agency along the whole border, starting with a push south through Mohmand, another into the Khyber and eventually an assault into North and South Waziristan to disrupt al-Qaeda and relieve the pressure in Afghanistan. The Pakistanis had a slower operational tempo in mind. 'Let's just say our agenda and that of our international friends don't always coincide,' said Major General Tariq Khan, who commanded the Bajaur campaign from the Frontier Corps headquarters behind the brick ramparts of the old Sikh- and British-built fort in the centre of Peshawar.

Though wary, Western observers were heartened by the apparent will shown by the Pakistanis. Fears of a repetition of the deal-making that had marked previous such operations appeared unfounded. By the time they had fought their way into Loesam, the Pakistani army had sustained hundreds of casualties in Bajaur and still seemed determined to continue fighting.[92] They appeared also to have inflicted heavy losses, not always a feature of previous campaigns. A pilot of one of the ageing but effective Cobra helicopter gunships recently supplied by the Americans and deployed in the operation described watching the militants running for cover or simply standing firing as he turned his Gatling guns on them. 'Often you can see their faces, and the first few dozen or so bothered me,' the thirty-eight-year-old told the author. 'But when you've killed hundreds, you stop worrying.'[93] Commanders on the ground said they had already killed around 1,000 militants so far.[94]

With the security of the West so intimately bound up with their actions and attitudes, it was natural that the Pakistani military as an institution would be the focus of much interest, frustration and bewilderment as the first decade of the 9/11 Wars had worn on. Early on, interest had mainly been in the political role played by the army, as was to be expected during a period of military rule. With Musharraf gone, the focus had become the capacity of the Pakistani army and in particular its ability and desire to implement the new counter-insurgency lessons from Iraq that were being introduced in Afghanistan. A slew of papers from Washington think-tanks and articles in specialized periodicals analysed the Pakistani army's multiple failings, most due to its orientation towards fighting conventional battles against India. Neither before nor after the departure of Musharraf was there much analysis of the Pakistani army and its relationship with Pakistani society as a whole. This was a mistake as the degree to which the military reflected other social, political, cultural and economic developments within the nation as a whole went a long way to providing an answer to many of the questions that Western strategists found themselves continually posing about the competence, will and worldview of their allies. This was certainly true of the ISI's Afghan strategy, as noted above. It was true too of the attitude of the military as a whole to operations in the tribal areas. The ISI did not exist in a vacuum. Staffed largely with officers drawn from the military on temporary attachment but with some civilian staff, it had, of course, developed its own institutional culture but represented that of the army more broadly too. The ISI's collective understanding of Pakistan's security interests did not diverge in any significant way from that of most Pakistani soldiers or indeed from most Pakistanis. The most obvious example was the glaring gap between how ordinary Pakistani officers who had nothing to do with the intelligence services viewed the enemy they were engaging in the FATA and how that enemy was viewed in the West.

Publicly, in Bajaur as elsewhere, officers and soldiers were careful to hide any misgivings about who they were fighting and why. 'I just need to think about what these guys do to prisoners, the decapitations and everything, and I am happy pressing the trigger,' said the helicopter pilot who had killed hundreds. For Colonel Javed Baluch, calling in the artillery fire in Loesam, the militants were 'enemies of my country and undermining our security'. Major General Tariq Khan insisted that, 'when our troops come into contact with the militants, they do not see them as Pakistanis or brother Muslims or whatever. They see them as the enemy.' Khan admitted that there were some who 'had doubts'. These, he said, were 'those who have not come into contact with the reality on the ground'. But the situation was complex and, whatever the rationalizations employed, so were the views and sentiments of many of those troops deployed into the FATA. Firstly, many of those engaged in Bajaur and elsewhere were paramilitaries from the Frontier Corps, recruited from the same tribes and often families as the militants and, as repeated incidents of desertion or disobedience to orders had shown, steeped in much of the same culture, ideology and worldview as their peers who had chosen a different way of getting paid, getting some prestige and getting to carry a gun. The attitude of regular soldiers too revealed a significant degree of sympathy for their enemy. All ranks routinely referred to the enemy as 'miscreants' – a far less loaded term than terrorists or even militants – and saw them as misguided rather than necessarily malevolent. 'They are our brothers who have been led astray and brainwashed,' said Colonel Mohammed Nauman Saeed, who ran the rear base of the Bajaur operation in the local administrative centre of Khar. 'But we have to fight them for the sake of our country as a whole.' Nauman would not be drawn on who was responsible for the brainwashing. Others, speaking privately, were more forthcoming. After giving a lecture on al-Qaeda at GHQ in Rawalpindi, the author was reprimanded by several officers of colonel and higher rank for repeating the 'lies of the Western establishment' about bin Laden's organization. Talking about the militants in Pakistan, their views were very clear. Those against whom their comrades were fighting in the FATA had been led astray by India, the CIA or 'the Jews', they said.

With no systematic surveys of the opinions of the half million men of Pakistan's fighting forces, there was little empirical evidence that could help gauge quite how widespread such views were. This had long been a problem. The stories about Western analysts counting the beards on group pictures of senior Pakistani army officers were sadly not apocryphal. 'It is simply very difficult to know,' admitted one Western intelligence officer.[95] Signs that a minority within the Pakistani military were increasingly drawn to radical Islamism had been there for many years. Not only had there been the relatively well-publicized involvement of military personnel in plots to kill Musharraf and a range of other violent acts, but there were also several much less well-known incidents of officers refusing to obey orders to fight militants, some as early as 2002.[96] Then there was the small but significant number of former military personnel, mainly NCOs and junior officers, who had joined violent outfits such as Lashkar-e-Toiba on leaving the military or, in some instances, had actually left the army in order to pursue 'the jihad'. Put together, these various elements often provoked claims that the entire Pakistani military was increasingly contaminated by extremism.

Yet, as with the broader analysis of the country as a whole, the focus on the most radical elements underplayed the impact of the much more significant general trends within Pakistani society – the growing mild Islamism, the social and political conservatism, the increased religiosity, the cultural turn towards the Middle East – on the army's institutional culture, worldview and understanding of Pakistan's interests. All militaries are institutions that are representative of the societies that produce them so it was inevitable that many if not all these elements would be present in the Pakistani army too. Indeed, various further factors meant that many of these trends were not simply represented within the army but *over-represented*.[97] One was historic: as the first decade of the twenty-first century passed, men who had joined the army during the Islamicization programmes introduced by General Zia when he had been in power during the 1980s had started reaching senior rank in significant numbers. Twenty-nine brigadiers appointed to general rank in January 2006 had been from 'the class of 1978 or 1979', and the proportion of officers who had served their early years and thrived sufficiently to climb the command hierarchy under Zia was rising with each passing wave of retirements.[98] A second factor was the long hiatus, due to American sanctions imposed in 1990 and lifted in 2001, in overseas training for Pakistani officers in the USA.[99] Many Pakistani officers serving in 2008 had simply never had any real contact with the West. Most had never travelled outside Pakistan. Nor, unlike in previous periods, were many likely to travel independently to Europe or America. This was partly because, like their civilian counterparts, most army officers appeared more likely to prefer, in the polarized and often hostile climate created by the 9/11 Wars, other destinations but also because they simply lacked the funds. A further factor in the over-representation of 'Middle Pakistan' in the army was that recruiting patterns had shifted over recent decades, and whereas, in the first decades after independence, army officers had been drawn almost exclusively from the wealthy landed elite, by the 1980s and 1990s they were increasingly drawn from the urban lower middle class. By 1998, 42 per cent of officers, an over-representation of at least a third, came from cities.[100] A decade later, the proportion was even higher. They were educated in government schools or on scholarships to the more elite educational institutions, and their fathers were bureaucrats, pharmacists, engineers, teachers or indeed lower-ranking servicemen. Several of the students on the grass in the Bahauddin Zakariya University in Multan had said they wanted to be army officers. This, of course, had consequences that were naturally broader than the determination of the choice of a few hundred officers' holiday destinations. The origins of this new mass of officers were in the 'emerging urban centres', which were, as the historian of the Pakistani army Shuja Nawaz has noted, 'the traditional strongholds of the growing Islamist parties and conservatism associated with the petit bourgeoisie'.[101] This meant that when one colonel, at the end of a diatribe against Bush, Blair, Israel, the Indians and the West in general, said, 'We are the army of the nation,' it was a statement that was more accurate than many in Europe and America cared to think.

## A SAVAGE INTENSITY

In late 2007, Mohammed Ajmal Amir, a former labourer with minimal education from a small town just north of Multan, approached a Lashkar-e-Toiba recruiter at a market stall in the city of Rawalpindi. His primary aim was far from religious. A petty criminal with ambitions to pursue a career as a robber, he wanted to learn how to use automatic and other weapons and thought the militant group would teach him the requisite skills.[102] He then spent three weeks at Muridke, the headquarters of LeT's ostensibly non-violent parent group Jamaat-ul-Dawa situated 30 miles south of Lahore, following a regime of four hours of religious instruction and two hours of sport each day. His original criminal career forgotten, Amir rapidly developed new interests. Seen as a promising recruit, he underwent three further weeks of mixed military and religious instruction in a LeT camp in a village near the town of Mansehra in the North West Frontier province before a series of courses of increasingly specialized instruction in smaller groups. Finally, he found himself back at Muridke with twelve others being taught how to swim. After nine months or more of training, the thirteen young men were briefed on their mission. They were not heading to Kashmir, as many of them had thought. They would be sent direct to Mumbai, India's cosmopolitan, bustling commercial capital, to conduct a spectacular raid which would end in their deaths. After two attempts to cross the sea from Karachi in the late summer and autumn failed, finally the group succeeded in boarding an Indian fishing trawler. They forced the crew (who were later killed) to take them to their destination, which they reached in the evening of November 26. Once ashore, the militants fanned out across the city. Amir – who would be erroneously dubbed Kasab by Indian police and then the press – and one other gunman made their way to the seething Chhatrapati Shivaji railway station, entered the toilets, took their weapons from their backpacks, headed out on the concourse and opened fire.[103]

The attack's aim was to maximize publicity. Their target was civilians. Kasab and his partner killed fifty-three at the railway terminus, mainly evening commuters. Another seven, including a commando, were killed in the Nariman House, a centre for ultra-Orthodox Jews in the city, by another group of gunmen. Ten were killed at the Leopold Café, a hangout for tourists and young locals, when it was randomly sprayed with bullets. One group of militants targeted the five-star Oberoi hotel, where they killed thirty. A second group attacked the famous Taj Palace hotel, yards from the sea and the monumental arch known as the Gateway to India, where they succeeded in holding out against security forces for nearly three days. Witnesses later told of the attackers marching through corridors, restaurants and ballrooms, demanding the identity of guests, holding some hostage, shooting others. Another thirty died there. In all more than 160 civilians were killed in the attack, and more than 300 injured. Kasab survived and was detained. All the other gunmen were shot dead. Two of them came from the town of Dera Ismail Khan in the North West Frontier Province. The rest came from the southern Punjab.[104]

In the aftermath of the attack, with Lashkar-e-Toiba clearly identified as the perpetrators, two urgent questions needed answering. The first was obvious: what was the involvement of the Pakistani security establishment? The second was equally pressing for security services around the world: did the Mumbai attacks, with their range of international targets, signal that Lashkar-e-Toiba, arguably the biggest violent Islamic extremist organization in the world other than Hamas or Hezbollah, had gone global? The answers to both would not become clear for some time and, when they did, would be, as ever, complex and nuanced.

Kasab was a junior figure, a footsoldier and a new recruit, who knew nothing of the background of the plot he had become involved in. Much of the background of the genesis of the attack, arguably the most spectacular of the 9/11 Wars other than the September 11 attacks themselves, was eventually revealed by David Headley, a Pakistani-American member of LeT who was arrested in the USA in 2009 and spoke to Indian investigators while in American custody as part of a plea bargain. Headley's own life-story was the stuff of bad thrillers. Born Daood Gilani, the son of an American woman and a Pakistani civil servant, he had grown up in Pakistan but had spent much of his adult life in Philadelphia. When jailed for heroin trafficking in the late 1990s, Headley had agreed to work for US authorities as an agent, though the relationship had ended by 2000. He had joined LeT, aged forty-two, in 2002 after returning to his native land, seized with enthusiasm for radical Islam and a deep hatred of India.[105] While in US custody, he explained to his Indian questioners how he had spent the first years of his association with LeT frustrated as, despite having successfully completed the various training courses necessary for aspirant combatants, he was never sent across the Line of Control into Indian Kashmir to fight.[106] He was too old, and only a very low level of infiltration was being allowed by the ISI at the time. In late 2005, arrested near Peshawar, Headley mentioned his links to LeT to police, was interviewed by an ISI major and freed. Back at his home in Lahore, he was contacted again by the ISI, interviewed at length about his avowed ambitions to do harm to India or Indian interests by a lieutenant colonel and assigned a handler, a 'Major Iqbal', who sent him back to the USA in the spring of 2006 to change his name and get an Indian visa. On his return, the officer assigned a junior colleague to train Headley in clandestine techniques, and in the autumn of 2006, 'Major Iqbal' handed his new recruit $25,000 and sent him to Mumbai. His job was to survey dozens of different locations ranging from embassies to the offices of nuclear-related government organizations, filming and photographing everything he saw and bringing the material back to Pakistan.[107]

Headley's association with the ISI complemented rather than replaced his activities with LeT. The two were interlinked. From 2006 to 2008, Headley undertook seven more visits to India, including several to Mumbai, on behalf of both the intelligence service and the militant group. After each, the former video store owner would meet both his ISI handler, who continued the training in clandestine techniques, and his LeT associates. On several occasions Headley went as far as to give both the same images and film copied on to two memory sticks. His contacts with 'Major Iqbal' continued up to and beyond the actual attacks in Mumbai, with Headley apprising his handler of last-minute changes in the planning of the operation, in particular of its targets. For Headley, the logic of the ISI in encouraging the attacks was clear. The service was worried that LeT, the Pakistani military's most effective reserve of irregular forces and the one with which it had the closest relationship, might follow the example of other groups and pursue more aggressive agendas closer to the internationalist position of al-Qaeda. 'The ISI was under tremendous pressure to stop any integration of Kashmir-based jihadi organizations with the Taliban-based outfits,' he told his interrogators. Even worse was the prospect that significant elements of the LeT might begin to fuse with the Pakistani Taliban. 'The ISI . . . had no ambiguity in understanding the necessity to strike India. It would serve three purposes: controlling further split in the Kashmir-based outfits, providing them with a sense of achievement and shifting the theatre of violence from the domestic soil of Pakistan to India,' Headley explained.

Another driver for the project to strike India was the internal tension within LeT itself. It was in these dynamics that the answer to the second question posed by the Mumbai attacks – the potential globalization of LeT – was to be found. Like so many other radical groups over previous chapters, LeT had its own problems with indiscipline and ideological dissent. Headley told his questioners of the ongoing tension within LeT, which pitted leaders like founder Hafiz Mohammed Saeed and top military commander Zaki ur Rehman Lakhvi against even more extreme elements within the organization. These latter had grown increasingly numerous as the 9/11 Wars had ground on. Many had split away to go and fight in Afghanistan. Others had stayed within LeT but argued forcibly that the group's historic arrangements with the Pakistani security establishment were no longer justifiable, particularly as the 'jihad' in Kashmir appeared to have been abandoned and Pakistani state policy seemed to be to support Washington. Saeed and Lakhvi appear thus to have agreed to a Mumbai operation, which at its outset was supposed to be limited only to a *fedayeen*-style raid by two or three gunmen on a single hotel in the city, to head off internal dissent. The plot had then taken on a momentum of its own, building up a sufficient head of steam for the plan to largely escape efforts by the senior leadership of LeT to keep it to a scale that would be less politically contentious. Instead, the final weeks saw the number of gunmen increased, the list of targets lengthened and, rather than escape by train or bus to Kashmir and thence to Pakistan, it was decided that the militants were to hold out until they were killed.

The escalation of the plot also appears to have caught out the ISI. For if it is clear that low-level ISI officers knew much about the strike – Headley talks of 'Iqbal' approving the controversial last-minute addition of the Jewish centre to the target list – it is less certain that senior officers were aware of what was being planned in Mumbai. Headley implicated several majors and a colonel and said that the handler of Zaki ur Rehman Lakhvi was a brigadier. But he also said that Lieutenant General Ahmed Shuja Pasha, the director general of the ISI, visited Lakhvi in prison after the attacks 'to try to understand them', implying that the broad assessment of MI6 and other agencies that the upper ranks of the ISI were unaware of the scale of the plan was probably correct.[108] The nature of the relationship between the service and the militant group was such that the ISI had much less control over LeT than it liked to think – if probably more than it ever publicly admitted.[109] The Mumbai attacks were thus, like so many terrorist operations over the previous years, the result of a range of structural and short-term factors among which the demands of a progressively more radicalized international jihadi movement and internal dynamics within a given group were key. The same had been true of the 9/11 attacks themselves. Lashkar-e-Toiba had not yet gone global – but were under significant internal and external pressure to do so.

The final weeks of 2008 thus saw – in a broad arc from the western coast of India to the Afghan–Iranian border – one of the most concentrated periods of violence in any theatre of the 9/11 Wars to date, rivalling even the worst times in Iraq in sheer savage intensity. There was the quotidian violence in Pakistan itself: a suicide bomb in the valley of Swat that killed nine; a second killed six in the Orakzai agency; a huge blast in the congested, narrow lanes of old Peshawar killed thirty-seven; a strike in Buner, even closer to the lowlands and Islamabad, killed even more. Through November, hundreds of radical militants loyal to mullahs close to the Pakistani Taliban – with Fazlullah, the former ski lift operator, among them – stormed through Swat, taking control of what had once been a favoured tourist destination for the Pakistani middle class. The security forces there seemed powerless to stop them, and the militants, calling for land reform, *sharia* law, an end to 'moral corruption' and American interference, surged on to the plains below the hills. They were now only 100 miles from the capital.

In Afghanistan too there was no let-up. Taliban leadership figures had made clear their intention to fight through the winter, and there were major Taliban attacks in Khost, in northern Parwan and in central Ghazni. There was a big ambush in Baghdis in the far north-west, an area hitherto largely free of violence. There was fighting near the

Iranian border, a suicide bomb at the airport of Herat, continued heavy combat in Helmand and a series of low-level strikes, few reported, in and around Kabul.[110] Kandahar and its environs saw dozens of incidents of intimidation and several assassinations.

The toll from the last five weeks of 2008 was staggering: the dead included more than 160 in Mumbai, 27 Western servicemen in Afghanistan, around 60 Pakistani and Afghan soldiers, about 50 Afghan policemen, around 100 or so Afghan non-combatants and at least two or three times that number of Pakistani civilians, some killed by drones, most by suicide bombings.[111] Then there were the casualties among the Afghan Taliban or Pakistani insurgents, estimated to be in the hundreds, and even a few Western volunteers, dead somewhere high in the hills of the FATA or just over the border in Afghanistan. Overall more than 1,000 people had been killed and many more injured.

At the midpoint of this 1,500-mile-long arc of violence was the historic Khyber Pass, leading from Peshawar across the mountains to Afghanistan and eventually on to Jalalabad and the road to Kabul. Through December 2008, the various factions of the Pakistani Taliban launched nightly attacks on NATO convoys carrying supplies across the pass from Karachi to bases like Bagram. Eighty per cent of the supplies of the coalition fighting in Afghanistan were brought in via the Khyber, and the crossing point at Chaman near Quetta. The series of spectacular raids might have had only a minor impact in material terms – though nearly 250 vehicles were destroyed – but the footage of flaming trucks and stores brought home to millions watching in Europe and America just how tough the wars their nations were engaged in were and how 'victory', however defined, was unlikely to come soon. Militants even managed to get hold of a Humvee, which they paraded under a banner saying 'The Caravan of Baitullah', in honour of the Pakistani Taliban's leader, Baitullah Mehsud.[112] Watching the scenes on CNN in his office at the Quai d'Orsay in Paris, Bernard Kouchner, the French foreign minister, turned to an aide and said simply: 'C'est foutu', it's fucked. Many of his counterparts elsewhere were expressing the same sentiments, though usually in slightly more diplomatic language.[113]

# PART SIX

# Endgames: 2009–11

# 15

# The 9/11 Wars: Europe,
# the Middle East, Iraq

## A CHANGE IN THE WHITE HOUSE

On November 4, 2008, Americans had elected, by 52.9 per cent to 45.7 per cent, Barack Hussein Obama, the forty-seven-year-old Democratic Senator for Illinois, as their president. Some argued that the changes that Obama would introduce in the day-to-day American approach to the 9/11 Wars were more of style rather than substance. But though the compromises forced on the Bush administration in the last eighteen months of its tenure as popular support waned and a host of other problems had crowded in had blunted its ideological edge, the arrival of someone of the new president's appearance, origins, views and charisma nonetheless created an obvious break that went beyond merely a shift in tone. At the very least, the departure of Bush meant an inevitable reformulation of the narrative of the conflict for all involved. The senior leadership of al-Qaeda, for example, had been sufficiently concerned to issue a series of pre-emptive statements attacking Obama for being a 'house negro'.[1]

The new president's early speeches did not disappoint those around the world hoping for a clear shift in policy, tone and approach. Obama repeatedly signalled a new realism, a new will to find inclusive multilateral solutions, a desire to enter into, and remain in, conversation with both allies and potential adversaries. Though the rhetoric might sometimes have been vague, it was attractive, occasionally inspirational and managed to sound radically new without challenging the broadly accepted package of values that, domestically at least, were associated with 'being American'. In his acceptance speech, the new president had deftly turned his predecessor's 'you are either with us or against us' into a resounding slogan of righteousness, strength and hope. 'To those who would tear this world down: we will defeat you ... To those who seek peace and security: we support you.'[2]

But Obama's arrival in the White House was not the strategic inflection point in the 9/11 Wars that some had hoped it might be, and the 'Obama effect' was less potent than the al-Qaeda leadership had apparently feared. Opinion polls showed that the accession of the new president provoked a measurable increase in 'confidence in America to do the right thing' in international affairs almost everywhere but, though Obama was certainly more popular than Bush, also revealed that there was little change in the deep ambient anti-Americanism in the Muslim world. The surveys found that, even if the proportion of people trusting US leadership in world affairs rose dramatically in 2009 in Egypt and in Jordan, in most Muslim-majority countries the number of people expressing a favourable view of the USA remained at an appallingly low level.[3] In some places, such as the Palestinian territories, Obama's arrival in the White House seemed to have no effect at all. In others, views of the US actually got worse, dropping to levels not seen since the months around the 2003 invasion of Iraq.[4]

Within forty-eight hours of taking office, Obama announced the appointment of two 'special representatives'. The first was Senator George Mitchell, who was given the job of spearheading a new bid to reinvigorate a Middle East 'peace process' which had been moribund for a decade or more. There was little indicating that Mitchell would meet with any greater success than any of his predecessors, but the gesture, coming with the new president's statements that he wanted to see the expansion of Jewish settlements in the West Bank frozen, was nonetheless welcomed.[5] The second appointment was the veteran diplomat Richard Holbrooke, the architect of the Dayton Agreement, which had ended the conflict in the Balkans fifteen years before. Holbrooke became special representative to Afghanistan and Pakistan, soon abbreviated to 'AfPak'.[6] Obama also signed three executive orders. One ordered that, 'without exception or equivocation', the United States would 'not torture'. The second decreed the closure of the Guantanamo Bay detention camp. The third commissioned a comprehensive review of procedures of holding and trying terrorism suspects 'to best protect our nation and the rule of law', which meant the effective suspension of ongoing tribunals of detainees. That the US Supreme Court had already judged that 'enemy combatants' were protected by the Geneva Conventions and by the United States Constitution, that 'Gitmo' would prove far harder to close than thought and that the prisoner review would lead to far lesser results than originally anticipated did not strip the announcements of their significant symbolic value.[7] If they did little to mitigate the entrenched anti-Americanism around the globe, they did not exacerbate it either. This, in the battered, febrile world left after seven years of the 9/11 Wars, was something of an achievement in itself.

Obama also moved to distance himself from the lecturing of the Islamic world that had been characteristic of the Bush administration. The ambitious 'Freedom Agenda' was set aside. Instead of 'draining the swamp of terrorism' through revolutionary change, the emphasis was placed on peaceful coexistence. In Ankara in April 2009, he spoke of relations between the West and the Muslim world. 'I know the trust that binds us has been strained . . . We will listen carefully . . . and seek common ground,' he said. 'We will be respectful even when we do not agree.'[8] In Cairo in June, four years after Condoleezza Rice's speech there announcing the Bush administration's push for greater democratization in the region, Obama, in an address entitled 'A New Beginning', would speak of his own childhood in Indonesia, the world's most populous Muslim nation, and of hearing the *adhan*, or call to prayer, 'at the break of dawn and at the fall of dusk' and would argue that, though basic human rights were universal, 'no system of government can or should be imposed by one nation on any other'.[9] He flew from Egypt to Germany to visit the Buchenwald concentration camp and then stopped in France, where he explained that his pride in his own country did not 'lessen [his] interest in recognizing the value and wonderful qualities of other countries'. 'We're not always going to be right . . . other people may have good ideas [and] in order for us to work collectively, all parties have to compromise, and that includes us,' the new president said.[10] When asked in a press conference how he would resolve the theoretical conflict between respecting state sovereignty and intervening to defend the universal rights of oppressed people, Obama answered that 'the threshold at which international intervention is appropriate . . . has to be very high'.[11] At the American cemetery above Omaha beach in Normandy on the sixty-fifth anniversary of the D-Day landings, the president, flanked by British Prime Minister Gordon Brown, French President Nicolas Sarkozy and Canadian Prime Minister Stephen

Harper, told his audience that 'we live in a world of competing beliefs and claims about what is true. It is a world of varied religions and cultures and forms of government. In such a world, it is rare for a struggle to emerge that speaks to something universal about humanity.' Carefully avoiding any reference to current conflicts other than to pay tribute to 'the young men and women who carry forward the legacy of sacrifice', Obama made clear that, though committed to the war in Afghanistan, for him the days of the radical, 'muscular' interventionist liberal humanitarianism of Bush and Tony Blair were gone.[12] The term 'War on Terror' was another casualty of Obama's arrival. Instead, the president spoke of 'a battle or a war against some terrorist organizations'.[13]

The challenges facing the new administration were manifold – a grave economic crisis, a vast budget deficit, the Iranian nuclear programme, climate change, continuing problems with America's multiple security services, the deteriorating situation in Afghanistan and Pakistan and many others. Obama's mandate too was much weaker than many overseas believed or wanted to believe. Yet the new president had one huge advantage: not only did he incarnate the hope of the advent of a new and brighter period after the dark and tense pessimism of previous years but he came to power at a moment when, for the first time for many years, it was reasonable to imagine that the optimism that the new president projected was at least in part justified. Through 2008 and into 2009, the indications of the potential for a more positive evolution of the 9/11 Wars that had first become visible in 2006 and 2007 broadened and consolidated. With the bad news pouring out of Afghanistan and Pakistan it was easy to forget what was going on elsewhere. But one of the reasons 'AfPak' could receive so much attention was that, in almost every other theatre previously touched by the 9/11 Wars, there was progress. Any advances were fragile, of course, and there was considerable potential for a sudden reversal, but, though no one even imagined returning to the pre-2001 situation, the news from many of the various fronts was undeniably better than it had been for many years. If the map that had shown the rapid spread in violence out of south-west Asia, across the Middle East and into Europe in one direction and out into the Far East in the other direction between 2001 and 2005 had been redrawn in the spring of 2009, a glance would have shown that the density of incidents had thinned markedly and the extent of the zone of conflict had shrunk. Nowhere did this appear clearer than in Europe.

## THE ATLANTIC WALL

In the autumn of 2008, the Belgian and French volunteers who had complained of being deceived by al-Qaeda propaganda had left the tribal areas and returned to Europe, retracing their steps through Pakistan, Iran and on via Istanbul to their homes in the Moellenbeek area of Brussels and in Vénissieux, a tough immigrant suburb of the French city of Lyon. European security services had been alerted to their return through the interception of emails sent from the FATA to friends and family members back in Europe and were waiting for them. In December 2008, Belgian and French police thus made a series of arrests. In Belgium, newspapers ran headlines warning that the group was planning an attack on the metro. Police and prosecutors argued that the group's claims to have come home because they were disappointed, ill or homesick were simply a poor cover for their re-entry to Europe. The group's lawyers argued that the men were sincere.

The raids, in which one woman and six men were detained, attracted little international interest. Such operations had become wearily familiar over previous years. Nothing about the profile of the suspects was at all out of the ordinary. The men arrested were all young first- or second-generation immigrants who had been drawn into radical activity either through the internet or in person by an experienced activist, in this case a veteran called Moez Garsallaoui, who himself was married to a well-known online female radical polemicist.[14]

Little in the composition or the activities of the group diverged from that seen elsewhere in Europe at the time either. The group was a small network – a half-dozen or so core members, a dozen or so in an outer circle who were less engaged on a day-to-day basis, and then a few dozen more who were tacitly aware of what was going on but not directly involved.[15] According to the European Union's criminal intelligence agency, two-thirds of individuals active in Islamic militancy on the continent belonged to such 'small autonomous cells' rather than any known larger groups.[16] Those arrested in Moellenbeek and Vénissieux, again typically, were ordinary men, neither desperately poor nor particularly wealthy, neither utterly without education nor especially well qualified. Several of them had been involved in petty crime before drifting into radical militancy – once more reflecting broader trends. One had committed more serious offences.[17]

As increasingly was the case elsewhere, the combination of a virtual community sustained by a radical website and a real community of friends had been key in the creation of the Brussels group. The approbation of the community – several of those who went received money to allow them to travel from close relatives fully conscious of the goal of the journey – had also been a crucial factor.[18] Radicalization for the Belgian and French suspects, as for so many others, had been a gradual process involving a series of key contacts with other interested individuals rather than deriving from any inherent personal proclivity to violent militancy. Again this was now seen as fairly standard.

That such conspiracies posed a clear and present threat – 'The answer is not *fatwas* . . . it is boooooooooms,' a web posting by the leader of the Brussels–Lyon network, Garsallaoui, from mid 2008 read – and that they would continue to pose a threat in the future was self-evident. One of the biggest problems for reporters working on terrorism and militancy – as for police and policy-makers – was the difficulty in gauging the real nature of that threat. There was a very natural tendency on the part of security authorities to err on the side of caution. The penalties for not warning political leaders far outweighed the credit to be gained by a more sober assessment of any potential danger. There was an equal logic driving journalists to err on the side of sensation. Yet the cumulative numbers of those involved in such plots in 2008 and into 2009 seemed difficult to tally with the more pessimistic announcements about the extent of radicalization in Europe of even a year or so previously. This was certainly evident in the UK. Though British newspapers, quoting 'security sources', continued to speak of up to 4,000 British citizens trained in terrorist camps, the number of annual arrests on terrorist charges in the UK had averaged 212 each year since 2002. This total included detentions linked to Irish Republican terrorism and other forms of political violence. In 2008, only 174 individuals had been arrested on terrorist charges and 207 people in 2009.[19] Importantly, only a third of those arrested were eventually charged.[20] British intelligence officials spoke of around thirty 'significant' individuals travelling to Pakistan each year.[21] Others travelled to Somalia, they said, but only a 'handful'.[22] This was enough to cause a significant problem but remained far from the vision of hordes of young militants that had once been thought on the brink of unleashing a wave of violence in the UK. MI5 officials contrasted the current sentiment within their own service with

that during the dark days of 2005 and 2006. 'Back [then] it felt genuinely out of control ... we were very worried there would be one
[attack] and then another and another and another,' one told the author.
'Now we feel we've got a pretty good handle on it.'[23] In July 2009, the
official assessment of the level of the threat of terrorist attack on Britain, based since 2003 on the conclusions of the Joint Terrorism Analysis
Centre or JTAC, was lowered from 'severe', highly likely, to 'substantial', a strong possibility, for the first time since the September 11
attacks.[24] As if to underline the difficulty of gauging the threat, it was to
return to its previous level only eight months later. But that it had been
lowered at all was significant.

The situation was similar in continental Europe. The number of
failed, foiled or successful attacks reported by EU member states in
2009 was down a third on 2008, which had itself seen a steep drop
from 2007. The vast bulk of these incidents involved internal separatist
violence within European countries and were not linked to Islamic militancy. The trend was also reflected in the number of arrests for Muslim
extremism in the EU outside Britain. These numbered 110 in 2009, a
decrease of 22 per cent from 2008, of 30 per cent from 2007 and of
more than 50 per cent from 2006, when 257 individuals had been
detained.[25] The number of member states reporting arrests for Islamic
militancy had also dropped from fourteen to ten.[26] Like their British
counterparts, senior European counter-terrorist officials and policy-
makers continued to insist that a threat remained – 'It only takes a few
to get through the net to cause a very big problem,' as Alain Grignard,
the head of the Belgian counter-terrorist police put it in March 2009 –
but the number of radicalized individuals who did manage to evade
counter-terrorist measures appeared extremely small.[27] Throughout
2008, there had been only one partially successful attack in the whole
of Europe attributable to Islamic militancy, that executed by a twenty-
two-year-old, psychologically ill, self-radicalized convert, Nicky Reilly,
who had injured himself badly while trying to detonate a home-made
bomb in the toilet of a shopping mall restaurant in Exeter, in south-west
England. In 2009, there was also only a single operation that came close
to succeeding – again by an apparent lone operator, an Italian who
made an unsuccessful attempt to carry out a suicide bombing on a
Milan military barracks. Six months after the UK dropped its threat
level, the Dutch dropped theirs too. This was the second time Dutch

intelligence services had moderated their estimation of the threat terrorism posed to the Netherlands. In 2007, they had said that 'the situation surrounding the known jihadist networks in the Netherlands can . . . be described as reasonably calm', arguing that 'a [positive] phenomenon that was described [last year] in cautious terms appears to be a trend'.[28] In March 2008, the release of a provocative film by populist anti-Islamic politician Geert Wilders had caused the threat level to be raised once more, but by mid-December 2009, the Dutch authorities were once again convinced that the danger from Islamic terrorism could be better described as 'slight' rather than 'substantial'.[29] In Germany too, there was a new calm – though inevitably punctuated by occasional scares. There were fears, for example, that the rising profile of Berlin's troops in Afghanistan and elections in the autumn of 2009 might provoke an attack. In the end, none occurred. In France senior advisors to Sarkozy said that their main concern was no longer al-Qaeda or its ideology but state-sponsored terrorism, particularly from Iran.[30] This may have been going too far – domestic counter-terrorist officials once again made sure that the sense of threat did not die away completely by making a fresh series of frightening statements – but French security officials privately remained confident of containing the threat from radical Islam both to French interests overseas and within France. 'We did OK before 9/11, we did OK after 9/11 and we are doing OK now,' one DST officer said.[31] No one anywhere in Europe was declaring victory, least of all the security services or the politicians – nor would they have been right to do so given the rapidity with which any stabilization could be reversed. However, for once something appeared to be going at least partly right, rather than very badly wrong.

Exactly what was going right was as difficult to answer as levels of threat were difficult to guage. One factor was certainly the constantly improving competence, capability and reach of security services, the police and all others involved in the counter-terrorist effort. Bolstered with new legislation, funding and understanding, authorities had been able to build on the strategic shifts undertaken in 2006 and 2007 to take the initiative against Islamic militancy. British officials used a convoluted metaphor involving the defensive tactics of Arsenal, the north London football club, in the 1980s to describe how by bringing in local police, social services, even schools and mosques, they were able to divert individuals who they felt were potential threats from becoming real dangers well before they became involved in serious militancy. Headmasters, clerics, community workers and others, MI5 felt, were much better placed to intervene to divert 'individuals of concern' from potential radicalism than the security service. As in the USA, another key development was legal. Earlier in the decade many trials in Britain had collapsed. This was partly due to a failure of prosecutors to understand the phenomenon they were up against – individuals were repeatedly charged with membership of al-Qaeda and were then acquitted for lack of evidence – but also due to a variety of legal loopholes. With many of these now plugged, law-enforcement agencies were able to get those who did become involved in violence locked up much more easily. Conviction rates in trials for terrorism offences in the UK in 2008–9 were 86 per cent.[32] In France, surveillance and contacts within Muslim communities, already extensive, had been rolled out further. In Germany, where strict privacy laws had once contributed to the 9/11 hijackers evading detection, new legislation granted powers of investigation and information-gathering that, coupled with further research into the process of radicalization undertaken by police sociologists, allowed security authorities to believe, like so many of their counterparts and despite public statements, that they had 'the problem largely under control'.[33] At a European level, though officials at the Commission had concerns about an overly 'politically correct' approach, as the EU's counterterrorism coordinator, Gilles de Kerchove, put it, successive measures enhancing cooperation were bearing fruit.[34] Improved transatlantic relations also had an impact. Whereas the New York Police Department's liaison officer in Paris had once been largely ignored by his Parisian counterparts, left in his office to watch the river traffic on the Seine, by mid 2009 he was being invited into key meetings. If he had spoken French he might even have been able to understand what was being said in them.[35]

Another factor was geopolitical. Sentiments in Muslim communities in Europe had obviously been very influenced by what was happening in the Islamic world. The winding-down of the messy and brutal war in Iraq, the American withdrawal from all but a few bases in the country and the departures of Blair and Bush had all undermined the neat lines of the Islam-against-the-West worldview that had been propagated so effectively earlier in the decade. Other issues – global warming, swine flu, the financial crisis – were increasingly forcing the conflict further and further down the news agenda. The war in Afghanistan undoubtedly provoked strong reactions. So too did the Israeli military operations in Gaza in January 2009. But the militant 'single narrative' was increasingly based on events that appeared historical and the actions of individuals who had left the scene.[36] New voices from within Muslim communities in the UK and elsewhere also continued to emerge to counter the extremists with growing confidence.

The later years of the decade had also seen the positive effects of the new scholarship on radical Islam and related questions. Arguments based on ignorant generalizations or stereotypes had progressively became harder to sustain in the face of solid research. One good example was the idea that Muslim hordes would overrun a 'senescent Europe' or constitute a 'fifth column' based in 'mini-Fallujas' to undermine it from within. Successive studies showed that in fact the growth of the Muslim-majority countries of the Middle East and north Africa was slowing rapidly, with the average number of children born per woman dropping from seven in 1960 to three in 2006 or even drifting down to the replacement level of about 2.1 children per woman.[37] The American Rand Corporation concluded that by 2025 the youth bulge problem in the Middle East would begin to ease.[38] A flood of Muslim immigrants thus looked unlikely. As for the Muslim population within Europe, no one doubted that it had grown rapidly in recent decades and, particularly given its relative youth, would continue to expand in years to come. However, demographers again predicted that fertility rates would decline as they had done among almost all other populations which had experienced progressively higher levels of wealth, healthcare access and literacy. There certainly appeared little reason why immigrants should reproduce more in Europe than in their countries of origin.[39] One Dutch study showed that births among Turkish- and Moroccan-born women in the Netherlands had dropped from 3.2 to 1.9 and from 4.9 to 2.9 respectively between 1990 and 2005, and fertility rates for Pakistani and Bangladeshi immigrants to the UK had gone from 9.3 in 1971 to 4.9 in 1996 and finally to under three by 2009.[40] That nominally Muslim populations would reach a size that would have a significant impact culturally and politically was clear, but the reality appeared to be a long way from the inflammatory estimates of those who had seen 'Eurabia' as an inevitable consequence of immigration.[41]

Further contributing to a drop in tension, even if the tabloid press and mainstream right-wing politicians continued to stoke popular fears of being 'overrun' or 'swamped', were the actions taken by European governments. These, by the summer of 2009 almost entirely centre-right, moved swiftly to further restrict immigration from Muslim countries and elsewhere.[42] Along with the clear messaging from almost all states but Britain that Muslim Turkey, with its population of 80 million, was not welcome in the European Union, these often severe measures showed that governments were responsive to the concerns of their population and, whatever the economic arguments or the long-term strategic considerations, would move to restrict immigration if that was what the electorate wanted. This undermined some of the more fantastic projections of the future growth of immigrant communities in European nations, which were based on the premise that no politicians on the continent would or could move to restrict the influx from overseas because of the potential impact on ailing economies desperately in need of manpower to support ageing populations. It was connected to another emerging trend: a shift in the nature of the animosity directed at Europe's various Muslim communities. As the end of the decade approached, the antipathy towards Muslims appeared to be less specific, part of a more generalized resentment directed against immigrants rather than being directly linked to a perceived threat of violence as it had been for several years. In the tight economic times of 2008 and 2009, the individual Western European citizen seemed to be defining his or her 'security' more broadly than he or she had done in the immediate aftermath of the 9/11 attacks. Classic issues such as employment, the cost of social welfare, crime and delinquency – historically associated with immigrants in popular imagination – resurfaced. In Holland, only 1 per cent of people asked in 2009 said they were concerned about terrorism and terrorist attacks, though 13 per cent worried about unemployment and about 'neighbourhood safety'.[43] Alongside the concern about the threat 'Muslims' posed came a recrudescence, especially in eastern Europe, of that old European malaise: anti-Semitism.

Significantly 18 per cent of those questioned in the Dutch poll said they were concerned about 'values'. For alongside this new broader sense of insecurity going well beyond a sense of physical threat came a sharpening of the perception of a 'cultural' threat. Here, unsurprisingly given the history of European relations with Islam, there were many potential flashpoints. Though some claimed otherwise, the reality remained that Muslim communities in Europe, like other faith groups on the continent, were largely much more conservative than the population in general. This, as it had done over previous years, led to repeated clashes on issues such as *burqas* and veils (in France), mosque construction (in Germany), minarets (in Switzerland), segregation and diet (pretty much everywhere). Many such rows were either based in misunderstandings – such as over exactly what '*sharia* law' might mean – or bordered on the absurd – such as a British Muslim cook who claimed financial damages for discrimination on the basis that wearing plastic gloves and using tongs was not enough to protect him from the possibility of being spattered with pig fat while preparing pork sausages – but they were often based in genuinely different visions of what was acceptable social behaviour.[44] Though surveys revealed that local national specificities often had a much greater impact than usually thought – where adultery or pornography were generally accepted, such as in France or Germany respectively, so they were accepted by a higher proportion of local 'Muslims' – overall the views of many who described themselves as Muslims on moral questions remained much closer to those of the American religious right than the largely secular local communities among whom they lived.[45] Importantly, the long-cherished idea that younger people, the children of the immigrants, would prove to be more liberal than their parents was also proving questionable. Indeed, throughout most nations in Europe there were strong indications of a new affirmation of a Muslim religious and cultural identity among 16–24-year-olds which went beyond the simple maintenance of inherited traditions, focusing instead on outward signs of difference rather than on conventions and customs inherited from parents who had been born in Algeria, Pakistan, Turkey or wherever.[46] In many European countries, though only a small minority wore the headscarf or veil, those who did so were usually no longer following an inherited tradition but making a deliberate choice to assert their difference both from the broader community and from their parents.[47] In Holland, though mosque attendance dropped sharply and the gap between 'autochtones' and immigrants in education and the labour market narrowed, more 'people with a non-Western background' chose to move to homes in the same neighbourhoods and avoid the company of 'Westerners'.[48] In France, even as rates of intermarriage or use of French as a first language in the home continued to increase, rates of declared observance of the Ramadan fast and professed abstinence from alcohol climbed steeply too.[49] Though 48 per cent of British Muslims said they never attended a mosque, 78 per cent said their religion was 'very important' to them.[50] As polls in the UK (and elsewhere) also showed that Muslims wanted more integration not less, that Muslim populations tended to admire institutions such as parliament or the courts more than non-Muslim populations, that fewer and fewer would serve the cuisine of their parents to a visitor and that Muslims were much more likely to be part of a local sports club than of a religious association, the only conclusion was that no one tendency was dominant.[51] If integration had progressed more than was often said, it had occurred very unevenly, throwing up powerful reactions and counter currents. Though talking of a single, monolithic 'Islamic identity' or community in Europe was impossible, one strong emerging trend amid the mass of apparently conflicting data was a new affirmation of a strong and conservative cultural and religious identity among Europe's Muslims which posed, as it did in the Middle East and in south Asia and elsewhere, a significant social and political challenge for Western policy-makers.

Whatever future evolutions were likely to be, it was clear by 2009, however, that few of the darker predictions made over previous years had been realized. There had been no mass uprising. The 'European Intifada' that both Abu Musab al-Suri and right-wing commentators had predicted following the 7/7 attacks in London had not taken place. There had still been no significant follow-up to the French riots of 2005 or the cartoons crisis. There were no mini-Fallujas. 'There are six million [French] Muslims. If the community had got really radicalized it would have been pretty obvious,' noted Kamel Bechik, a thirty-five-year-old who ran a Muslim Scout organization in south-west France. At the Marché d'Aligre in Paris's twelfth arrondissement, where wealthy local Parisians go at the weekend to buy fruit and vegetables from largely Tunisian stall holders or beef from halal butchers, Amos, who was sixteen when he first ran errands for his immigrant parents on the market, pointed to his two employees – one from Algeria, the other from Morocco. One was married to a French-born Catholic, he said, the other to 'a black girl'. 'Integration? Politics? Religion? None of that here,' he said. 'We're just trying to earn a living. The only people who get involved in religion are the ones with something on their conscience.' Anis Bouabsa, the baker who supplied the presidential palace with breakfast patisserie, said he would be fasting for Ramadan while still cooking bread for his clients. 'It's my roots, my culture, that's how I grew up,' Bouabsa told the author. 'But I'll still be in the bakery twelve hours a day.'[52]

## THE MAGHREB, THE MASHRIQ

If there was cause to be somewhat more sanguine in Europe, there was equal reason to be more optimistic in much of the Maghreb and the countries of the core Middle East, the Mashriq.[53] The effect of the 9/11 Wars on communities from the eastern edge of the Atlantic to the Arabian Sea had been inevitably much greater than on the nations of Europe. In the latter it had been the relatively small Muslim minorities who were at risk of being been drawn into violent extremism (plus a statistically negligible number of converts). But in the former whole populations could potentially have been radicalized, with tens of millions of people suffering the direct effects of the conflict or, in the case of Iraq, under occupation themselves. But by the summer of 2009, the wave of violence and polarization that had flowed across the region since 2001 and particularly since 2003 seemed to be very much on the ebb. Almost everywhere, Islamic militants affiliated to, or simply inspired by, al-Qaeda or its ideology were on the defensive. The turning-away from radicalism that had begun to manifest itself in 2005, 2006 and 2007 was now well consolidated. A crude measure was the level of support pollsters found for Osama bin Laden. In almost every country from Morocco to Saudi Arabia, the popularity of al-Qaeda and its leader had continued the decline it had begun three or four years earlier or at the very least remained at a relatively low level. Confidence in bin Laden 'to do the right thing in world affairs' was highest in the Palestinian territories – at more than 50 per cent – but more generally lay between the 5 and 25 per cent mark.[54]

One of the best examples of the problems faced by militant groups in the region – and there were many – was the plight of the grandly named al-Qaeda in the Maghreb. AQIM, as it became known, had been formed by the remnants of the Algerian Groupe Salafiste de Prédication et Combat (GSPC) in late 2006, and its existence and new affiliation to the al-Qaeda central leadership announced by Ayman al-Zawahiri in

January 2007. 'We pray to Allah that this [alliance] would be a thorn in the neck of the American and French crusaders and their allies, and an arrow in the heart of the French traitors and apostates,' Zawahiri said, with careful if rather outdated attention to local sentiments towards former colonial overlords. The logic behind the GSPC's decision to finally accept the various invitations of bin Laden and al-Zawahiri after many years of stubborn independence was simple.[55] The GSPC was formed from a faction that had broken away from the defunct Groupe Islamique Armée in the late 1990s as the latter disintegrated. It had, like its parent organization, had trouble gaining any popular support or legitimacy. It had also been hit badly by a series of amnesties from 1999 which had reduced its strength from several thousand to a few hundred. By 2005, the organization was split, with one half effectively using radical Islamic ideology as a cover for running a trafficking and kidnapping racket in the southern deserts and the other half, more ideologically committed, largely confined to the eastern uplands of Algeria with very limited local support and considerable difficulties in escaping the effective, if brutal, security services.[56] 'We saw the merger with al-Qaeda as giving us the breathing space we badly needed,' Abu Umar Abd al-Birr, the former head of the GSPC's media committee, later recalled. 'Faced with the national reconciliation process in Algeria, we'd no choice but to stop fighting. But with the merger we gained new authority in people's eyes: it allowed us to project an image of ourselves as a new group.'[57]

As ever, the credibility, status and resources furnished by an alliance with 'al-Qaeda central' came at a high price. The internationalization of the GSPC's campaign might have been superficially attractive as a propaganda coup which also brought valuable technological and strategic advice but it had no perceptible impact on the broad rejection of violence by Algerians generally, and, though the group now theoretically had a regional reach, genuine links with groups elsewhere in the Maghreb proved very difficult to build. One major obstacle was the simple chauvinism of the GSPC's Algerian leaders, who, after nearly three decades of fighting a local battle against local authorities, had little genuine knowledge of, or interest in, the conflicts in neighbouring countries. They had even less enthusiasm for sharing authority with anyone 'from outside'.[58] Desultory bids to mobilize networks of supporters in Europe, particularly in France, also failed to make much progress. This disappointed the al-Qaeda senior leadership, who had seen the alliance with the GSPC as a way of acquiring a network in Europe that might reinvigorate the campaign there and resolve their growing strategic problems on the continent. Worse for AQIM, the tactics they were encouraged to use by the al-Qaeda senior leadership proved disastrous. Though the dark years of the civil war of the 1990s had seen appalling atrocities, Algeria had never previously seen suicide bombers nor massive bombings with the very visible civilian 'collateral damage' they inevitably caused. Successive attacks on government buildings, the United Nations offices, police stations and a range of other civilian targets between April 2007 and August 2008 killed large numbers of ordinary Algerians, provoked redoubled efforts on the part of Algiers' security services and did nothing to endear the militants to a public that, despite their grievances against the incompetent, avaricious and undemocratic government, was even less keen on violent radicalism and all it entailed than they had been a decade or so earlier.[59] Memories of where such activities led were all too fresh. Even within militant ranks such tactics were deeply controversial and prompted a number of defections. One mid-ranking leader who left the group after the April 2007 bombings in Algiers explained that his decision stemmed from the complaints of his comrades-in-arms about 'carrying out suicide operations, shedding the blood of innocents in public places'. Another, charged with enforcing the application of *sharia* law in one area where the group was fighting, opposed the use of such tactics, because Algeria was not occupied by foreign infidel forces as Iraq and Afghanistan were.[60] Attempts to 'relocalize' the AQIM's agenda by invoking the name of very specific historical figures such as Tariq bin Ziyadh, the Berber general who led Muslim forces in the conquest of Spain in 711, looked merely clumsy.[61] By 2009, though occasional attacks continued, no one could pretend that AQIM were a significant force.[62] For one British security official, the spate of attacks in 2007 and 2008 and the GSPC's alliance with al-Qaeda was the 'dead cat bounce' of Algerian militancy.[63] The comment may have been premature – cats have nine lives after all – but was not entirely unjustified.[64]

The same could be said for many of the other militant groups which had looked to be such a threat four or five years earlier. Egypt had always been, politically and culturally as well as geographically, the keystone in the arch of Arab Muslim-majority states spanning the north African shoreline to west Asia. It had been where many of the new modern revivalist ideas that had emerged in response to Western colonialism in the Islamic world had first been synthesized and articulated in the late nineteenth century and where the first major Islamist movement – the Muslim Brotherhood – had been founded in 1928. Through the later twentieth century too, Egypt had set the ideological tone for much of the region. From the revolution of 1952 and the subsequent rule of Gamal Abdel Nassr and on through the decades of the domination of socialist, nationalist and pan-Arabist ideas, the example of what the Egyptians were doing or thinking had been crucial to developments elsewhere in the Middle East and beyond. So too was the emergence of Islamism as an ideological alternative, an opposition movement and discourse of dissent in the country in the wake of the 1967 and 1973 wars with Israel. The Islamic militant violence of the 1980s and 1990s had played a crucial role in forging the fundamentals for the new global vision and strategy of al-Qaeda and its like. It had been the course of the militancy in Egypt that had revealed so much about the reality of such activism, its strengths and weaknesses, and it was, of course, from Egypt that much of the al-Qaeda senior leadership had come. The country, ruled by President Hosni Mubarak since 1981, was also representative of so many other repressive, incompetent and unyielding governments in the region. Seen historically by Washington as the key to local stability, Egypt had received more than $60 billion of American aid since signing the 1979 peace treaty with Israel. It was on Egypt too that the Bush administration's 'Freedom Agenda' had, for a brief moment, been focused and it was, of course, in Cairo that Condoleezza Rice had spoken of how America had too long preferred stability in the region to democracy in her speech in June 2005.[65]

Egypt was representative of the region economically too. Despite the growth towards the end of the decade due to radical liberal economic measures, food prices had continued to rise rapidly, with inflation reaching 25 per cent in 2007.[66] While new gated communities were constructed with fountains in the desert outside major cities, millions went without running water. Corruption was endemic. Especially for the 29 per cent of the country between fifteen and thirty years old, life remained tough. Crammed into insalubrious, poorly maintained apartments, with a desperate daily struggle for basic services let alone decent employment, the young had very few prospects. Graduates drove taxis or ran shops. The average age for marriage had crept steadily up as the expense incurred and the shortage of homes made even as basic an act as forming a couple and having children extremely difficult. As elsewhere too, particularly among the lower middle class and parts of the working classes, a new social and religious conservatism was more and more evident among a population long known for relative tolerance, moderation and a disdain for purely ritual devotion. One national survey found that 10–29-year-olds claimed to spend an average of forty minutes every day on religious devotions, and by far the most popular ringtone on the now ubiquitous mobile phone was the call to prayer. In one revealing incident the transport minister had to resign after eighteen died in a train crash caused by a signalman who left his post to pray. In 1986, there had been one mosque for every 6,031 Egyptians, according to government statistics. By 2005, there was one mosque for every 745 people – and the population has nearly doubled.[67] As elsewhere too, anti-Americanism in Egypt remained at a historically high level. Nonetheless, none of this translated directly into any backing for renewed Islamic militant violence. After the attacks of 2004, 2005 and 2006 in the Sinai, Egypt had remained relatively untroubled by violent radicalism. Though support for Islamism as a political doctrine remained significant and the radicals' single narrative had been integrated into the fundamental worldview of tens of millions, only a very few became involved in extremism.[68] Undoubtedly the vicious efficiency of the experienced Egyptian security services was a factor, but so too were the trends evident elsewhere in the Middle East and the Maghreb. Support for suicide bombing in Egypt had dropped from around 33 to 8 per cent after the wave of attacks in the middle of the decade before stabilizing at around 15 per cent.[69] When bin Laden and al-Zawahiri attempted to create an 'al-Qaeda in the land of Egypt' towards the end of 2007, they had failed ignominiously. The man chosen to lead the new group, a veteran of the violence of the 1990s who had been based in the FATA since 2001, was unable to convince those few former associates he was able to contact to become involved. The fact that many such approaches took place online did not help. Nor did his death in a drone strike in August 2008.[70]

A similar situation to that in Egypt prevailed in Morocco, where the young Mohammed VI, dubbed 'His Ma-Jet Ski' following reports of playboy antics, was attempting a hugely ambitious infrastructural and social 'great leap forward' all while retaining a grip on power in the face of a similarly rising social and cultural conservatism among, in particular, the lower and newly urbanized middle classes. 'We are in the middle of trying something that lots of people have said is impossible. It is absolutely essential that we make it work ... I don't even want to imagine the consequences if we fail,' Mohammed el'Ghass, the minister for youth, told the author in an interview in his immense office in the capital, Rabat.[71] Walking through the housing estates and commercial streets of towns like Salé, just outside Rabat, where all women wore scarves and maintained strict segregation as they waited for the over-crowded buses, made clear how, as in Pakistan and elsewhere, it was the lower middle classes who were driving the new trend of non-violent moderate or mild Islamist activism coupled with a renewed reassertion of a religious identity. In Morocco too, as in Pakistan, the dynamics were intertwined with cultural issues. The Islamists – such as Abdelwa-hed Motawakil, the secretary general of 'the Union of Faith and Social Charity' – preferred to speak English as an alternative to Arabic when interviewed rather than French, the language of the elite and the former colonial rulers. El'Ghass, like most ministers, preferred the latter.[72] At elections in late 2007, the biggest and most moderate Islamist party had won forty-seven out of 325 seats, coming second only to the main regime-sponsored secular nationalist party. Even this relatively impres-sive result was largely seen as disappointing, and officials of the Justice and Development Party blamed a record low turn-out and rigging. Local and international commentators argued that it was in fact the more radical Islamist groups – such as that led by Motawakil – which had boycotted the poll that were its true beneficiaries.[73] Yet though there had been several further spasms of violence including new suicide bombings, by the end of 2008, it was clear that the fears of a major internal insurrection or of Morocco becoming a launching pad for sys-tematic Islamic militant assault on Europe were very unlikely to be realized.

Close parallels with developments in Morocco and Egypt could be found too in Libya. There, again despite a range of political circum-stances and social and economic conditions very similar to those in neighbouring countries, militants were also very much on the back foot. Networks formed to send volunteers to Iraq and to fight the regime had been repeatedly broken up between 2004 and 2006. In 2007, there had been disturbances and rioting in the poor coastal cities of Benghazi and Darnah. But since then there had been no real sign of militant activity, let along widespread extremism.[74] The leadership of the Libyan Islamic Fighting Group remained split between firebrand radicals who had chosen to remain in Afghanistan or Pakistan after the war of 2001 and an imprisoned local leadership. While the former faction claimed that the LIFG was now part of al-Qaeda and was increasingly visible among the upper ranks of bin Laden's organization, the latter rejected violence entirely, publishing in July 2009 a 417-page document which argued that 'arms are not for use to ... bring about change in Muslim countries'. This was perhaps the most exhaustive scholarly repudiation of jihadi doctrine by former militants yet seen in the 9/11 Wars.[75] There was plenty of resentment and discontent at the rule of Muammar Gaddafi – whispered carefully to the author by waiters, taxi drivers, students, professionals and even archaeologists in Tripoli during celebrations in September 2007 of the thirty-eighth anniversary of the military coup that had brought the Supreme Guide of the Revolution to power – but it was not being channelled into radical Islam.[76]

In Jordan, in Syria and in the Levant too, it was the same story: the peak of Islamic militancy appeared to have passed.[77] In the Lebanon, the most notable incident of violence associated with radical Sunni militancy, the uprising of the Fatah al-Islam in the Nahr al-Bared Palestinian refugee camp of May 2007, had not been repeated. In neighbouring states too, support for the violent extremists had dropped, as elsewhere sublimated to some extent into a new social conservatism and increased support for the more classic political Islamism of the Muslim Brotherhood and its various offshoots.[78] In Jordan, where before the hotel bombings in Amman in November 2005 support for suicide bombing (outside Israel-Palestine) stood at 57 per cent, this figure had declined to just 12 per cent by 2009.[79] One of the most interesting and revealing incidents came in the Gaza Strip in August 2009, when Hamas launched a bloody military operation against one of a number of emerging pro-al-Qaeda groups.[80] The latter were few in number, and their support depended very heavily on local tribal or clan dynamics, but nonetheless Hamas felt it necessary to direct the full force of their security apparatus against them. Twenty-four 'Jund Ansar Allah' fighters were killed when the Ibn Tamiyya mosque in Rafah, the city on the Egyptian border with Gaza, was stormed in perhaps the biggest direct armed confrontation between forces loyal to a local political Islamist organization and Salafi jihadists for many years.[81] Again, if anyone in the region was benefiting from the polarization caused by the previous years' violence it was the Muslim Brotherhood and its offshoots, not the extremists loyal to, or inspired by, bin Laden.

A final example of the failure of al-Qaeda to successfully provoke a conflict or to lever local conditions and tensions in the Middle East was Saudi Arabia. The first signs of the strategic defeat of al-Qaeda in the Arabian peninsula had, as elsewhere, in Europe and much of the Islamic world, been evident by the middle of the decade, as previous chapters described. By the summer of 2009, militancy in Saudi Arabia was still a problem but not one that threatened in any way to destabilize the state. The storm of 2003 to 2004 had apparently been weathered, and as early as April 2007, the Saudi militants' own *Sawt al-Jihad* publication had glumly noted that 'none of the Jihadi fronts were deserted as much as the Jihadi front in the Arabian peninsula.'[82] Successive waves of arrests were announced, but the high numbers involved – 701 terrorist-related detainees in one single sweep, according to a single communiqué of June 2008 – owed more to the authorities' desire to maintain a useful level of anxiety and thus vigilance among the general population and to continue to attract support for the House of al-Saud as the guarantor of local order against the extremists than anything else.[83] Certainly, the jihadi effort in Saudi Arabia had singularly failed to split the religious establishment of the kingdom – indeed it had rather unified clerics behind the regime – or to garner any real popular support. Though cash continued to flow to extremist organizations and charities engaged in activities overseas, polls in December 2007 put the level of Saudi Arabian citizens viewing bin Laden favourably at 15 per cent, one of the lowest levels in the entire region.[84] At the same time a series of effective policies had squeezed the militants' resources. Authorities had progressively filled the many loopholes in the charitable and financial sectors that had enabled the militants to obtain funds, cracked down on the previously extensive illegal arms market and increased border control, making explosives and detonators more difficult to procure. A series of month-long general amnesties, in part inspired by the Algerian example, had also helped thin militant ranks, as did discreet mediation initiatives involving influential clerics with radical credentials. Considerable resources continued to be devoted to a media campaign aimed at bolstering the now broad consensus in the kingdom that the militants were terrorists – a 'misguided sect' as they were called in official media.[85] A further useful measure was the sacking of over a thousand of the more radical imams and the retraining of tens of thousands more.[86]

But anyone searching for signs of a genuine spirit of liberal reform among rulers in Riyadh or among the population more generally would be disappointed. Those governing Saudi Arabia had long recognized that their survival depended to a significant extent on a skilful balancing of the demands of Western interlocutors and the inherent conservatism of most of the people they governed. Changes such as allowing the occasional risqué satire or the creation of an effectively secular national holiday to celebrate the 1932 unification of the country (to the dismay of irritated conservatives, who insisted that Islam forbids anything but religious celebrations) did not signal any great shift, significant though they were in their context. If there had been some changes to textbooks which promoted anti-Semitism and a deeply intolerant worldview, Saudi schoolchildren were nonetheless still taught that it was wrong to say hello to non-Muslims.[87] As the threat from militants internally had subsided and the memory of the 9/11 attacks receded, so the reform process, which had appeared at one time to be picking up some small momentum, slowed.[88] Nor did there appear to be any significant lessening of the efforts made by Saudi religious establishments and private individuals to further the spread of rigorous Salafist Islam, largely at the expense of broader, less dogmatic and more moderate strands of practice, across the Islamic world. Such proselytism was carefully differentiated from the violent ideologies of bin Laden and his kind and had been an integral part of the kingdom's foreign policy – originally to counter the influence of Shia Iran and Communism – since the early 1980s. It had been part of the deal struck by the house of al-Saud with the 'Ikhwan' religious warriors whose swords, guns and faith had brought them to power in the Arabian peninsula. Despite the contradictions inherent in a deeply conservative country bankrolling and directing a programme of religious preaching and teaching that had revolutionary effects, such as changing how tens of millions worshipped across much of the Islamic world, the fundamentals of the grand bargain which underpinned the structure of the kingdom remained unquestioned.

By the summer of 2009, however, the vast proportion of militants in the Arabian peninsula were based in the Yemen, not active in the strategically crucial Saudi Arabia. The growing prominence of the Yemen and to a lesser extent east Africa, where the 'al-Shabab' movement had broken away from the Islamic Courts Union in Somalia to pursue an increasingly radical agenda, was sometimes taken as evidence of the protean indestructibility of contemporary Islamic militancy. Instead, it showed the extent to which, by 2009, radical activism had been marginalized geographically as well as socially, politically and culturally across almost the entire Middle East.[89] Then, of course, there was Iraq.

## IRAQ: AN UGLY PEACE

By around 5 a.m. in Baghdad in the pre-Ramadan weeks of August 2008, the temperature had dipped to a still brutal 33 degrees, and the city began to wake. In the poor working-class Shia areas, small knots of the faithful walked through the rubbish-strewn streets to morning prayers, and the bakers, no longer working with an AK-47 by their sides as had been the case during the worst of the civil war, began to pound their dough and stoke their ovens. As the first rays of sunlight slanted across the city, the taxis began to circulate, and those who had been sleeping on the roofs of their apartments to escape the heat stowed their bedding. Another day was beginning. The lights of the Green Zone, as bright as ever during the night in a city with patchy electricity, faded into the bright early morning.

By 7 a.m. there was heavy traffic on the roads, choked around the barricades, the checkpoints, the gaps in the blast walls, stalled in long lines on the bridges over the Tigris. The queues were growing outside the petrol stations. Children played football on patches of wasteland before the heat and school. On Mutanabi Street, as they had under Saddam, booksellers were laying out their wares, a greater range of publications than anyone could have dreamed of under the dictator. Soon the officials were arriving in the ministries, unlikely to stay much longer than a few hours. One was Abu Mujahed, the insurgent whom the author had interviewed back in 2004 and whose formation of 'resistance cells' to lay mines for American convoys or mortar their bases featured in Chapter 6. Abu Mujahed had not only stayed alive but had kept his job in his ministry through all the upheavals of subsequent years. A year after the invasion, he could no longer afford a chicken for his family's dinner. Now, with a raised salary, he was relatively comfortable. By ten o'clock, he and the office workers and bureaucrats were sipping tea at their desks, and the shops were opening too, shutters clattering up where there were any and awnings pulled down to provide some shade. For an hour or so, there was life in Sadr City, the vast and overcrowded poor Shia suburb in eastern Baghdad and the site of heavy fighting only a few months before, as housewives in black chadors clustered around vegetable sellers haggling over the price of aubergines and tomatoes and toddlers played with makeshift toys in the dust and dirt. By late morning, with the temperature climbing, the streets emptied, the stall-holders and the police and soldiers on the checkpoint fled the blinding white light of midday, the football players disappeared, and the city settled to wait out the long, harsh afternoon.

In the evening, as the sun began to dip, life returned to the streets. The traffic choked once again at the checkpoints. In the upmarket central Karada neighbourhood, where barber Jaffar had reopened his shop after returning to Baghdad after eighteen months in Jordan, the pavements filled with shoppers inspecting windows of shops selling furniture and white goods. Jaffar's own barber shop, newly refurbished, was full. On days after bombings, few chanced his ground-floor salon with its open glass windows, but as there had been a week's calm, business was good. Near by, new cars dropped off wealthy families in front of newly opened restaurants. On Abu Nawas Street by the Tigris, cafés served the traditional grilled fish and beer to groups of men, and couples walked through the nearby park along the riverside. Across the city, a thousand games of football were underway. By late evening, the promenaders, who had grown more numerous as the temperatures dropped, began to thin. A few revellers sought further entertainment. Most went home before the midnight curfew, and for the first four hours of the next day the streets were empty but for the patrols until, finally, at 4 a.m., as the eastern sky began to lighten, the bakers and the faithful once more headed out, and the roof sleepers again rolled up their bedding and set a pot to boil water for tea.

The Iraq of 2009 was not that of 2008 and was profoundly different from that of 2007. Each year had seen a new combination of the kaleidoscope of different elements, internal and external, that determined the overall evolution of the battered country. None of the successive Iraqs were 'very pretty', as one US State Department official who had rotated in and out of Baghdad over the previous thirty-six months commented. 'We are talking degrees of ugliness,' he explained. 'And the degree of ugliness today is a bit less ugly than yesterday.' [90]

For compared to what had gone before, it was difficult to argue that the situation in Iraq had not improved. The country was more fragmented than perhaps it had ever been, split along ethnic, sectarian and political lines, with significant external interference, rampant corruption, patchy rule of law, deep poverty, poor security and high levels of criminal, political and extremist violence but, eighteen months after the first of the American troops that had been deployed for the Surge had begun to pull out, there were few who still predicted the imminent catastrophic collapse of order in the country. Indeed, those looking at Iraq from Washington or London, and there were a diminishing number of them, given the focus on the deteriorating situation in Afghanistan and Pakistan, saw something that was beginning to resemble the 'messy, sloppy status quo' that the then Senator Obama had described back in April 2008 as an acceptable endstate for the US mission there. 'If we had presented the Iraq of today in a Powerpoint five years ago and said this is what you get for a trillion dollars: four thousand dead American servicemen and women and pretty much all our diplomatic capital in the Arab world, the Islamic world and beyond, then I don't suppose anyone would have been particularly impressed,' a State Department official said. 'But we are ... where we are. And where we are is better than where we were.'[91]

If the situation in Iraq in 2009 was undoubtedly better than it had been two or three years previously, it was much more difficult to be sure that any progress would be maintained in the future. Iraq had stepped back from the brink, but quite what happened next was still very unclear. The optimistic scenario saw the country treading a slow, haphazard but steady path towards relative stability and prosperity, gradually resolving the thorny outstanding issues such as the sharing of its immense oil wealth between its various communities, the contested status of the northern city of Kirkuk, its exact relationship with neighbours like Iran, Syria and Saudi Arabia and how to integrate its Sunni minority into a majority Shia state. The pessimistic scenario saw a gradual loss of all the ground made up since 2007, accelerating violence, a resurgent al-Qaeda, a new civil war and worse chaos than ever previously seen. The two divergent paths naturally started from the same point: the precarious fragility of the immediate post-Surge period.

The critical period in consolidating the gains made during the Surge had been the long year from the end of operations in November 2007 through to the provincial elections of January 2009. As discussed in Chapter 11, critical to the success of the Surge had been four major factors: the effective victory of the Shias in the civil war and the resultant redundancy of Muqtada al-Sadr's al-Mahdi Army as well as the organization's internal problems; the 'Awakening' of the Sunni tribes; the continuing structural weaknesses of al-Qaeda in Iraq; and the actions of regional powers. Since the end of the Surge, two of these major trends had definitively progressed in a positive direction, deepening and broadening, contributing enormously to the relative stabilization of the situation. A third, the continued interference in Iraq by its neighbours, did not immediately look likely to send the country back to the cusp of total breakdown. The evolution of the fourth, the retreat of the jihadi militants, was harder to chart.

The effective collapse of the al-Mahdi Army as a fighting and social force had been evident within months of the end of the Surge. Its authority, coherence and legitimacy had already been undermined by indiscipline, criminality and growing interference from Tehran. With the threat in Baghdad from Sunni death squads greatly reduced, the militia's role as protector of Shia communities had disappeared and with it much of its popular support. In a series of rolling offensives ordered by Prime Minister Nouri al-Maliki through the spring of 2008, first Basra and the smaller southern cities and then Sadr City in Baghdad were all retaken by government security forces backed by American airpower and logistics. Fragmented, discredited and with its leader in self-imposed exile in the holy city of Qom in Iran, the al-Mahdi Army was unable to sustain any serious resistance, losing up to 1,000 fighters by May 2008.[92] The force was soon effectively 'stood down', and within weeks its authority had evaporated even in those former strongholds where it had retained a presence. The tens of thousands of young men who had joined al-Sadr's organization over previous years remained in their homes or on the street, but the balance of power had clearly shifted. 'The Iraqi government broke their branches and took down their tree,' Abu Amjad, a civil servant in the northern Baghdad district of Sadr City said.[93] Radical Shia groups, some trained, equipped and directed by elements within the Iranian Revolutionary Guards, continued campaigns of violence and intimidation in much of the south and were still present, if less active, in Baghdad, and al-Sadr, who appeared to be hoping to convert the mass militia he once led into a political and cultural movement with an armed wing along the lines of Lebanon's Hezbollah, still retained the loyalty and even adulation of a significant portion of young, poor, working-class, urban Shia men. 'Moqtada al-Sadr is a great man and a perfect leader, and without him all the Shia in Iraq would have been killed or live their lives oppressed and humiliated, and Iraq would have been destroyed by the occupiers and al-Qaeda,' said Qahtan Ali Hussein, a twenty-four-year-old al-Mahdi Army fighter.[94] But the days of major street battles with American or Iraqi security forces seemed to be definitively over. The Friday prayers and sermons that had once seen frenzied demonstrations of support for the young cleric still drew big crowds but were now quieter affairs. In the areas they had once controlled, the al-Mahdi Army's strictures on Western haircuts, dress and music were no longer enforced or obeyed. Local leaders no longer received their protection money, and the lucrative rackets the Army had run had disintegrated. 'I can buy [cooking] gas for a tenth of what it was, I can listen to what I want to, I don't have to hide my trade either,' said Jaffar, the barber.[95] Marginalized politically, former al-Mahdi Army fighters turned on those marginalized socially, attacking, torturing and killing hundreds of local homosexuals.[96]

A measure of stability, it had been frequently said, would come to Iraq when the Shia had recognized they were the winners and the Sunni minority understood they were the losers in the deposition of Saddam Hussein and the civil conflict that had followed. The Awakening, which had seen the Sunni tribes of Anbar and eventually Baghdad and surrounding provinces join with the Americans against al-Qaeda-affiliated or inspired groups, had been rooted in part in the realization that continuing resistance to either foreign occupying forces or the demographically stronger Shia community was likely to be counterproductive. Through 2008, the forlorn plight of the Sunni fighters who had turned against the religious extremists in Anbar and elsewhere underlined the degree to which the community had lost out in the fighting in 2006 and 2007. Promised jobs in the new Iraqi security forces, the 'Sons of Iraq' found themselves shut out by Iraq's predominantly Shia political leaders and largely abandoned by those they had once fought alongside. The Americans, though they pressed for more of the 130,000-odd fighters they had recruited to end up wearing Iraqi National Army or police uniforms, understood too that the government they protected neither had the will nor the means to incorporate such a large number of men, many of whom had played significant roles in the sectarian violence of previous years, into the new security forces.[97] In Anbar, former 'Sons of Iraq' had found jobs in local police forces, but in Baghdad itself or in provinces like Diyala they were largely left to their own devices, their salaries paid late if at all, their relatives regularly targeted by those they had fought against over previous years. Without their powerful allies in the American military, the Sons of Iraq were vulnerable, and in the twelve months after the Surge, around 550 had been killed.[98] 'We became victims,' Hassan Abdel Karim, who led one Baghdad group, said with disgust.[99] Dyaa Jameil, a thirty-five-year-old member of an Awakening council from the tough Sunni Baghdad neighbourhood of al-Doura, described his and his comrades' future as 'like a dark night without the light of the moon'.[100] That these men, who had been in the vanguard of the insurgency back in 2003 and 2004, appeared to reject any return to armed resistance to the government was an indication of just how weak they judged their own position to be. In the provincial elections of January 2009, Sunnis voted, and even if the turnout in Anbar was only 40 per cent, it was still a vast improvement. Some even voted for al-Maliki, who, though a conservative Shia, had acquired some credibility as a 'national' leader through dismantling the al-Mahdi Army the previous spring. For the first time in any of the polls held since the invasion of 2003, security for the elections, which passed off relatively uneventfully, was provided by local Iraqi forces. Only 191 Iraqis were reported to have died in violence during January, the lowest monthly toll since American and British tanks had crossed the berm from Kuwait just under six years before.[101]

Optimists saw the low casualty figures as evidence that the al-Qaeda threat in Iraq was over. As ever, gauging the potential danger posed by radical Sunni jihadi extremism within Iraq was problematic – as it was more generally. Compared to the darkest days of 2004, 2005 or 2006, when 'al-Qaeda in the Land of the Two Rivers', or al-Qaeda in Iraq (AQI), had posed a genuine strategic threat to Iraq and to the region, the situation in 2009 was undoubtedly much improved. The Islamic State of Iraq (ISI), the successor of AQI, had failed in its core project of establishing a local bridgehead from which to wage a campaign to create a new caliphate in the Middle East.[102] Even within Iraq, the capabilities of the jihadi militants had been much reduced. Though the narrative of global jihad continued to draw some foreign volunteers, the numbers were negligible compared to the earlier period of 2003 to 2006. As in the Middle East more generally, the Islamic militants in Iraq had been geographically marginalized, forced successively out of Anbar and Baghdad, then out of the densely populated semi-agricultural zones around the city where they had once been well implanted, and finally restricted to Nineveh province in the north-west. The extremist groups were scattered and fragmented and had suffered significant casualties; their senior and middle-level operatives had been decimated by the increasingly sophisticated and effective American-trained Iraqi special forces. The use of female suicide bombers, as well as that of the very young and the mentally ill or disabled, reinforced their loss of broad popular legitimacy.

Yet the tenacity of the 'jihadis' nonetheless surprised many observers. The evolution of radical militancy in Iraq had mirrored that in other theatres of the 9/11 Wars. The huge pressure under which the groups had existed for many years had forced radical evolution. Hierarchies had been flattened, capability sacrificed for resilience, mass mobilization based on the appeal of a radical ideology had been replaced by recruitment determined by association, family links, shared tribal or other community connections. Local militants now dominated the various fragmented groups that together constituted the phenomenon of al-Qaeda-style militancy in Iraq.[103] In Mosul, the capital of Nineveh province and a metropolis with a population of 1.8 million, a variety of specific local conditions had been leveraged by the extremists to secure a base.[104] Chief amongst them was the ongoing tension between the newly confident Kurds and the large local Sunni Arab community, which allowed the extremists to fulfil the same role as in the early days in Anbar and Baghdad, posing as protectors of the latter against the former. With limited rule of law in the city, there were few alternatives for Sunnis scared of losing their homes and livelihoods other than to turn to the militant groups. Another factor helping the militants was the city's geographic position astride the trails that led through the desert from the Syrian border. These allowed extremist groups both to receive supplies from over the frontier and, crucially, to build mutually beneficial relationships with local tribes which had long earned their living from smuggling.[105] Avoiding the errors of the 2003 to 2006 period, the extremists cooperated with local sheikhs rather than trying to appropriate their businesses. Finally, as Mosul had been home to a high number of Ba'athist former army officers who themselves had taken up arms against the Americans and the Baghdad government and continued to be responsible for the bulk of attacks on government or American forces in the area, the extremists found willing allies on the ground.[106] The steady ideological convergence between the once aggressively secular Ba'athists and the 'jihadis' also helped smooth relations. And despite successive operations by Iraqi security forces, which the militants tended simply to avoid confronting, and the election of a hardline Sunni chauvinist provincial government and governor, Nineveh province remained 'bandit country' throughout 2008 and 2009. It thus constituted the single most significant base of violent radical activism between Morocco and the Afghan–Iranian border. Western intelligence services judged the threat that this base posed to be 'relatively restricted', pointing out that the militants based there showed little interest in exporting violence overseas. However, as repeated statements by local extremist strategists made clear, the Iraqi extremists' aim was not to wage 'international jihad' immediately but to plunge their country into chaos to allow them to take power, establish an 'Islamic state' and then launch such global operations on a large stage at a later stage, if they were necessary. The al-Qaeda-linked groups demonstrated that they retained significant capabilities despite the pressure on them with a series of massive and technically sophisticated bombs directed at ministries, hotels, embassies and Shia targets through the summer of 2009.

There were other reasons to fear that the more pessimistic scenarios for the future of Iraq might be realized. A close analysis of voting patterns in January's provincial elections also showed that the divisions of Iraqi society remained very deep indeed. Though sectarian parties had suffered major losses at polls – in Baghdad the coalition led by the Shia Islamic Supreme Council of Iraq took just 5.4 per cent of the vote, compared to 39 per cent in 2005 and lost heavily in the Shia religious heartlands of Najaf and Karbala – they had been punished more for their failure to deliver basic governance and services than for their chauvinist rhetoric or their championing of one particular community's interests.[107] Most Iraqis continued to be deeply sectarian in their political and social lives. The taxis that plied Baghdad streets might have given the impression of a bustling, cosmopolitan city, but Shia drivers kept to Shia areas and Shia clients, and their Sunni counterparts did the same. Sect and ethnicity were the primary determinants of political allegiance. The evident nationalism of many Iraqis did not imply any enthusiasm for genuine pluralism.

Nor did the new stability mean a new tolerance or moderation. By 2009, a new social conservatism – a parallel of that elsewhere in the Islamic world and among Muslim communities in Europe – was also evident in Iraq. Few women in Baghdad and none in Basra or in conservative places like Anbar or Diyala ever went unveiled. The degree to which this was enforced or voluntary was very difficult to determine, but those out drinking on Abu Nawas Street, despite the attention they attracted from Western reporters, were a small minority. Those patronizing the new nightclubs were even less representative. 'I do not go to the [cafés on the] banks of the Tigris, I go to mosques,' said Alyaa Ali, a sixty-five-year-old housewife from Shia Shu'laa in north-west Baghdad. Many looked more to their own cultural traditions and a newly assertive religious identity than to values and ideologies that had been tainted by association with occupiers or those who had profited from the invasion and deposition of Saddam. 'To relax I visit the holy shrines in Najaf and Karbala,' said Qahtan Ali Hussein, the al-Mahdi Army fighter. Posters of Shia heroes plastered over streets and government offices, religious music played from police radios, religious flags flying over government buildings and massive attendance at religious festivals gave the impression of a full-scale cultural revival, at least among the country's Shia. In Basra, the number of 'honour killings' almost doubled in the single year of 2008.[108]

So the apparent normality of the daily routine was deceptive. Life for most in Baghdad remained extremely tough. In a city where a bit of bad luck, an illness, an accident, the wrong word spoken in anger to the wrong person was enough to send a household spiralling downwards into poverty, those living in deep deprivation did not constitute a static population but a shifting and mobile one. The rate of inflation – a litre of petrol that once cost 20 dinars was now 500 dinars (about 25p or 35 American cents), a bottle of cooking gas was 20,000 dinars – was enough by itself to strip millions of a decent standard of living. Nearly 80 per cent of households depended on the monthly food ration from the government for their basic needs, but nearly half received the supplies only intermittently. Malnutrition, in a country with vast oil reserves, was rife. Millions who had been forced to flee their homes during the civil war remained in over-crowded temporary accommodation, often without any but the most basic facilities. By 2009, Iraq was generating more than 6,000 megawatts of electricity as against a pre-war maximum of around 4,000, but this still meant a third of households across the country still only had power for three hours or less per day.[109] No electricity meant no refrigeration, no fans and often no water because there was no power for pumps. In rural areas it often meant no irrigation either. For the poorest, a lack of electricity made little difference. Between a quarter and a third of the population were without any access to drinking water whatever, and nearly two-thirds of the population simply dumped untreated solid waste on open land.[110] 'We do not have a sewage system so we discharge our wastewater into a pit beside the house and then into the street once it is full. We do this with our own hands,' Jameela, a fifty-year-old widow from Najaf who sold incense and candles to mourners in a local cemetery to support her mentally disturbed son, told researchers from Oxfam, the British NGO.[111] Healthcare was at best rudimentary. The streets of every city were still full of checkpoints, barricades, barbed wire, blast walls, for, though it had dropped, the overall level of violence was still appallingly high.[112] Iraq was in the paradoxical position of suffering more deaths from terrorist attacks than any other country in the world while no longer being seen as a major theatre of conflict.[113] One worrying trend was that the violence, having dropped to around half of that in 2008 by the late spring of 2009, then stayed at the same level.[114] Ramadan in 2009 brought little celebration. August alone – the holy month started on the 21st – saw between 400 and 500 dead and at least 2,000 injured in more than 40 bombings. In September, the American vice president, Joe Biden, made his second visit to Baghdad in as many months, greeted by insurgents firing mortars and rockets into the Green Zone. A few days earlier, bombs near Mosul had killed dozens in a Kurdish village. Biden pledged that the US would keep to the schedule of ending the US 'combat mission' in Iraq by the end of August 2010 and withdrawing all US forces by the end of 2011. His comments attracted little attention. Many Iraqis had other concerns. 'Life in Baghdad is miserable. It is thirty-nine degrees centigrade and we get electricity one or two hours per day. When we get any water, it is not fit for human consumption. The children get sick,' said Amal Kamel, the twenty-year-old economy and administration student. 'I am not proud of my country.'[115]

# 16

# 'AfPak' 2009–10

## AFGHAN ENDGAME

Captain José Vasquez, the commanding officer of Cherokee Company of the 371st Cavalry Squadron, wiped his mouth with the back of his hand, stowed the bottle of water in his backpack, checked his map, looked up at the dusty road and waved his men forward. To his right ten Americans and twenty soldiers from the Afghan National Army left the trees where they had been resting and rose to their feet and moved out across the empty fields. To his left another similar group, a few moments earlier lying prone beside the bank of an irrigation channel, also moved on. A radio crackled, a soldier swore as he filled his boots with water by slipping into a stream, two crows croaked loudly before flying off, beating heavy wings, black against the blue sky.

Baghdad, where Vasquez had done two tours, had been hotter in every sense of the word, the twenty-nine-year-old from El Paso, Texas, said. The ambushes had involved more attackers, and the temperatures had been higher. 'There were just a whole lot more people wanting to fight you,' he said. 'And we just cooked in the summer.' His unit, now attached to the 10th Mountain Division, had been scheduled to return to the Iraqi capital in January 2009. Just before their deployment, however, the orders had been changed, and instead of patrolling the streets of Sadr City Vasquez and 5,000 others were now spread out over the mountains and plains of Afghanistan's Logar and Wardak provinces. For years international forces had maintained a minimal presence in both, despite their critical location to the south and south-east of Kabul. Vasquez was part of a new belated effort, ordered in the last weeks of the Bush presidency, to change the tide of the war in Afghanistan.

On this last day of a three-day operation, though, there had still been no contact with the insurgents. The American-led force – 116 strong in all, with Mrap semi-armoured anti-IED trucks, planes and drones overhead, the ability to call in artillery bombardments from the main base a dozen miles away, biometric testing kits, road accident hazard signs, an embedded military intelligence unit – had met no one but local farmers, villagers on bicycles, school children and the occasional elder. 'When we come out in force they don't like to play. They are ballsy . . . but not stupid,' Vasquez explained. The reception from local people to the soldiers had been determinedly neutral: desultory *salaams* in response to slightly tired greetings, a nod from a shepherd, a brief conversation with a local mullah. An effusive invitation to tea, politely declined, came from a wealthier local merchant suspected of being part of the support structure for a village's insurgents. 'We know when the bad guys are here because, when they're around, everyone kind of stays away from us,' said Vasquez. Over three days he and his men crossed from neutral to hostile territory and back a hundred times, he added. There was little friendly terrain. 'This side of the creek is OK, they don't like getting involved. On the other side they love getting involved, just not on our side unfortunately. And they have a lot of RPGs.'

Vasquez was, for 2009, the very model of a modern infantry officer. Laconic, calm, experienced and better equipped, fed, based and supported than possibly any fighting soldier for decades, he stopped his men from walking through the overgrown cemetery grounds outside villages, refused to take on Taliban targets when they appeared at the edge of an inhabited compound for fear of civilian casualties despite the gung-ho enthusiasm of his tobacco-chewing rooky lieutenant, tried to convince the Afghan troops that you shouldn't get the people whose houses you were searching to make you tea. In the village of Yusuf Khel, a typical jumble of narrow passages and low mud walls between compounds, Vasquez listened patiently to local elders complain about local police confiscating their mobile phones and motorbikes. Asked what the community needed, the elders conferred and requested grain, a useful compromise between something big like a road or a well which would have caused problems with local insurgents and nothing at all. 'I am looking forward to helping this town and coming back,' Vasquez told them and tapped the fingers of his right hand against his left chest in the traditional sign of respect before turning and walking out of the village to join his men in the fields beyond. 'This tribe extends all the way to behind the mountains,' he said as the whole force moved off again, the sun now dipping towards a horizon of dry hills to the west. 'We've met a few of them. The whole tribe seem to be fence sitters. We'll see. Maybe we can do something for them. Maybe they will start helping us. Who knows?'[1]

In the spring of 2009, there were hundreds of officers like Vasquez across much of eastern and southern Afghanistan, all hiking through villages, all listening to elders, many – if not most – displaying the same mix of awareness and weariness that the veteran twenty-nine-year-old had done. The operations in Iraq's Anbar province and the subsequent success of the Surge in Baghdad, the promotion of key senior officers, the simple learned ground experience of more junior servicemen who had spent years fighting in different theatres coupled with the distribution of the 2006 COIN field manual and the broader public debate it had sparked meant that the new language of counter-insurgency was now being spoken everywhere in Afghanistan. The commanding officer of Vasquez, Colonel David Haight, also fresh from Baghdad, said his aim was 'to separate the people from the enemy'. 'I can become someone's worst enemy in a second, but that is a short-term solution. We need to bring governance, security, sustainability,' he explained. At headquarters in Kabul senior NATO staff officers displayed impressively detailed slides showing the tribal dynamics of Afghanistan, exploring historic urban–rural tensions and explaining their strategy of 'Shape, Clear, Hold, Build'. General David McKiernan, commander of NATO-ISAF since June the previous year, stressed the importance of respecting local cultural traditions, protecting the population, reducing civilian casualties and good driving.[2] 'We have learned a lot over the last few years and need to put that into practice on the ground,' McKiernan told the author, pointing out, with evident professional pique, that General David Petraeus was not the only senior American soldier involved in the evolution of the new COIN strategy and tactics.

The new doctrine required more troops, however. After successive reviews of American strategy in Afghanistan, one ordered in the last months of the Bush administration, another by Obama shortly after taking office, these had flowed in through early 2009. Vasquez had been part of the 12,000 ordered in by Bush in one of his last acts as president. Obama agreed to send another 21,000 after the second review in the late spring. In May 2009 a third review was launched when General Stanley McChrystal, the lean, intense former commander of special forces operations in Iraq, replaced McKiernan. Perhaps predictably, it too recommended a very significant increase in men, money and other resources.

Many of those forces arriving through the first six months of the year had been sent with the specific aim of securing the presidential elections in Afghanistan, scheduled for the late summer. Western strategists had anticipated a variety of potential problems with the polls. These largely revolved around potential insurgent action to disrupt the vote, the assassination of one of the principal candidates or logistic issues. In the end it was the actions of President Karzai himself, the man placed in power by Western forces in 2001 with the Bonn agreement and the favourite to win the polls, which damaged the whole exercise in the most drastic way.[3] Karzai's close supporters organized a massive fraud to avoid their candidate facing a second-round run-off with Abdullah Abdullah, the former foreign minister.[4] Over a quarter of votes, the vast bulk in Karzai's favour, had to be rejected. Each of the three American strategy reviews had stressed the critical importance of having a central Afghan government that had political legitimacy, the lack of which was felt to be undermining the whole Western project in the country.[5] Everyone, generals, politicians, diplomats, aid workers, Obama, had repeatedly insisted through the spring and early summer that successful elections were absolutely necessary to 'reinvigorate the whole project' in Afghanistan. In this, the polls abjectly failed. The massive voter registration drive hailed as such an achievement by Western governments undoubtedly reached large numbers of ordinary Afghans but also allowed somewhere around 5 million fake, duplicate or otherwise fraudulent voting cards into the system. The turnout was, despite official claims to the contrary, lower than in the previous elections even if the vast and systematic cheating made knowing the exact number of those who voted impossible. Violence, despite the deployment of all the new troops sent to secure the vote, was higher than on any other single day since the invasion. The aftermath of the poll brought little cheer either. When Karzai was eventually found to have won 49 per cent of the vote, a percentage point lower than necessary to avoid a run-off, the incumbent president refused to go to a second round and successfully retained power by default when his disgusted rival pulled out of the contest. The president's behaviour might have appeared baffling to angry and frustrated Western interlocutors but was explained relatively easily. In March, Bill Wood, the American ambassador in Kabul, had assured the author that he was certain America would remain deeply committed to Afghanistan for, if perhaps not 'the natural lifespan of the sun', then certainly for the long term. In fact, as Humayun Hamidzada, Karzai's press secretary, pointed out, no state can make even a plausible ten-year pledge unless it is a monarchy or a military dictatorship.[6] Western nations are democracies and respond to public opinion expressed at frequent elections and, as most people prefer their wars short and victorious, long-term overseas commitments win few votes. It was clear that the Western publics were increasingly unhappy about the international effort in Afghanistan. Pledges that the mistakes of the early 1990s would not be repeated and the country would not once more be abandoned by the West and Arab powers as after the war against the Soviets could thus not be trusted. Karzai was not going to sacrifice his personal interest – and that of his family, close associates and allies – to ease the task of foreign backers whose desire to leave the country and its increasingly bloody mountains, deserts and villages was more obvious with every passing day.

For, along with the new doctrines and the new troops, another major development of 2009 was the West's increasingly explicit exasperation with Afghanistan, the Afghans and efforts to stabilize and secure the country. This was true of troops on the ground – 'It would be so much easier for everyone if they would just let us help them,' complained Sergeant Amber Robinson of the 10th Mountain Division in Logar – and of policy-makers and strategists in Western capital cities.[7] In March 2009 42 per cent of respondents to one poll said the United States had made 'a mistake' in sending military forces to Afghanistan, up from 30 per cent in February. One poll in August 2009 showed that a majority of Americans saw the war in Afghanistan as not worth fighting, and just a quarter said more US troops should be sent to the country.[8] In the same month, another survey showed half of Republican congressmen and 70 per cent of Democrats were against any escalation of US commitment to the war in Afghanistan. By September, polls showed even lower levels of support among politicians and the public alike.[9] It was against this background that, after months of debate, Obama finally announced that he had made his decision on McChrystal's recommendations. The general's review, conducted by a mixed group of academics, experts and soldiers, had stressed that the reinforcements earlier in the spring had been too few to make a significant strategic difference, and the president decided to order a further reinforcement of 30,000. Other coalition members reluctantly contributed a further 5,000 over the year, and thus, by the early months of 2010, the NATO-ISAF commander in Afghanistan disposed of around 135,000 troops, seven times as many as eight years before, and with more American troops there than in Iraq for the first time. However, Obama also announced that American forces would start coming home in the summer of 2011. Though the military had asked for a commitment through to 2013, there was no way the new president was going to risk going into mid-term elections or even a campaign for a second term with an escalating war on his hands. 'I'm not doing 10 years,' Obama was reported to have told Defense Secretary Gates and Secretary of State Clinton. 'I'm not doing long-term nation-building. I am not spending a trillion dollars.'[10] Other NATO countries, also responding to public opinion that had long turned sour on the war in Afghanistan, were already imposing dates by when they would withdraw their soldiers.[11] In Paris, the French ministry of defence had appointed an admiral to look at ways of managing local public opinion. 'Selling a retreat is quite difficult,' he admitted.[12] The constant bad news, the growing casualties, the apparent complexity of the conflict, the disaster of the elections, the fact that al-Qaeda had not successfully attacked anywhere outside the Middle East or Maghreb for several years and was based, as far as anyone could tell, not in Afghanistan at all but in neighbouring Pakistan all combined to further undermine any remaining support for the war in the West. Domestic opinion was 'dynamic', of course. American backing for some kind of surge rose temporarily at the end of 2009, and internal UK government polling showed that support in Britain for the war ticked up 9 per cent when it was revealed that Prince Harry, the Queen's grandson, had been fighting in Helmand and rousing footage of the young aristocrat firing heavy weapons at invisible 'Terry Taliban' was released.[13] But the overall trend was evident to all. It was hardly surprising, therefore, that Karzai and his entourage should be sceptical of the repeated US claims of a long-term commitment.

This led to an apparently paradoxical situation: at the exact moment when the Americans, reluctantly followed by leaders such as Britain's Gordon Brown, were escalating the Western commitment to Afghanistan to levels many times greater than ever seen before – the troop increases were accompanied by a 'civilian surge' of advisers, aid workers, technicians, diplomats and others as well as a commensurate boost to development assistance and UN funding – support for the war back home was disappearing. It was in this environment that the final major development in 2009 emerged: a collective recognition on the part of Western strategists and policy-makers that a serious effort needed to be made to negotiate with at least some of the insurgents. This would have been anathema in the first six or seven years of the conflict in Afghanistan, but alarm at the seriousness of the situation in 2008 and the recognition that many of the original aims of the Western project in Afghanistan had become simply unrealizable, had led to the understanding among some analysts and diplomats that, if the West was ever going to extricate itself from Afghanistan, it would be necessary to talk, somehow to the Taliban.

In fact, various different initiatives involving 'reconciliation' had been underway for some time, all aiming in one way or another to convince those insurgents who were felt to be fighting for 'non-ideological' reasons to lay down their arms. At the lowest level, there had been an Afghan government initiative that had aimed to convince simple fighters – the so-called 'Tier Three Taliban' in NATO parlance – to hand in their weapons in return for a small sum and a guarantee of no prosecution. Assessments showed that almost none of the 5,000 or so 'fighters' who had supposedly surrendered under this programme could be reliably identified as insurgents. With its funding exhausted, it was effectively defunct. Then there had been the efforts to engage slightly higher-level Taliban, mainly leaders of groups of between a few score and a couple of hundred fighters. These 'Tier Two Taliban' had been engaged via a range of intermediaries in a variety of local initiatives. These efforts had also met with mixed success. Some had seen some partial progress, but many of the more ambitious attempts at bringing over Tier Two Taliban had gone disastrously awry. One British bid to win the loyalty of an insurgent leader in Helmand had prompted a huge political row between London and Kabul, resulting in the expulsion of the senior EU diplomat used by MI6 as an intermediary.[14] Then there were efforts directed at the senior leadership, the Tier One Taliban. One initiative by the Saudi Arabian royal family saw a group of senior former Taliban figures including Mullah Wakil Muttawakel, the former foreign minister, and Abdul Salaam Zaeef, the former ambassador to Islamabad, as well as several individuals with more direct connections to members of the 'Quetta Shura' invited to Mecca to talk over potential roles for Riyadh in any peace process. This bid to establish contacts and lever the Saudis' religious authority had gone nowhere despite logistic and diplomatic support from the British intelligence services and government.[15]

The spring of 2009 saw efforts at all levels re-energized with talks between representatives of Gulbuddin Hekmatyar and Karzai and a range of other contacts between the government and senior Taliban leaders through figures such as Maulvi Rahmani, the former deputy education minister who was also now living in Kabul. Once shunned, Muttawakel and Rahmani now regularly met a range of diplomats or other representatives of European and Middle Eastern powers as well as, more discreetly, the Americans. At the other end of the scale, commanders like Colonel Haight in Logar were meeting 'shadow councils' made up of 'all kinds of people' including active insurgents and in Helmand the creation of 'leadership councils' sponsored by the British in scores of villages in the south was allowing 'people with broad contacts among the insurgents', in the delicate formulation of one UK diplomat, to enter into dialogue with both the Kabul government and NATO-ISAF forces.[16] But there was still little real progress. William Wood, the US ambassador in Kabul, called on the insurgents to drop their key demand to talk only once foreign troops had left the country. Taliban spokesmen and intermediaries maintained their position that the occupiers must go before any political process could be engaged. The new counter-insurgency manual overseen by Petraeus advised not wasting time on 'extremists' but concentrating on 'groups with goals flexible enough to allow productive negotiations'.[17] But who would negotiate? And about what? And with whom? The idea of 'reconciliation' raised as many questions as it provided potential answers. If any such process was going to work, a significant restructuring of not just the strategy but the entire project of the international community involved in Afghanistan was going to be necessary.

The groundwork for this restructuring had been laid during the spring of 2009, when, hitherto less sceptical than their European allies about achieving 'victory', many in the American security, military and political establishments began to question basic assumptions about what was achievable in Afghanistan. A key moment was reached when senior American officials began talking about 'mitigating' rather than eliminating the Taliban threat. Bob Gates, the American defense secretary, spoke about the folly of trying to create 'Valhalla' in central Asia. The mythical and geographic references might have been a little haphazard, but the sense was clear nonetheless. Wood, the American ambassador in Kabul, spoke of how everyone, including the Americans, had been 'a bit too optimistic' in the early years of the conflict in Afghanistan as regards to what kind of country could be built. 'Certainly not your standard issue Western democracy,' he explained.[18] The new pragmatism Obama outlined in his Cairo speech and elsewhere was one driver. Another was the more generalized lack of confidence that even McChrystal's new strategy might work. 'Success is not unattainable, but I am pessimistic,' Andrew Exum, a former US army officer and veteran of Afghanistan who had been part of the team of outside experts brought in to advise McChrystal, told the author a few weeks after returning from his mission in Afghanistan.[19] Bruce Riedel, the former CIA analyst who had chaired the first Obama review, was more blunt: 'It may be that the patient was dead on arrival.'[20] Even within the White House there were very significant doubts, particularly on the part of Vice President Biden.

Through the summer and autumn of 2009 it thus became very clear that the more ambitious of the goals of the West's mission in the country were being quietly abandoned.[21] To an extent Western governments had been caught out by their own previous rhetoric, having sold a security operation as a humanitarian intervention back in 2002 and subsequently used moral and ethical arguments to bolster public support. Many ordinary people in the US, the UK and elsewhere still believed that troops were in Afghanistan, at least in part, to spread liberal, secular modern values and to protect women from the 'medieval' Taliban. Ditching all the more idealistic rhetoric and returning to a more pragmatic, security-based justification for intervention in Afghanistan was, at the very least, a delicate operation. 'Our objectives are being recalibrated in view of the circumstances,' one senior FCO official admitted privately in October 2009. In July, a month which saw twenty-two

British soldiers killed and ninety-four wounded in Helmand and seventy international troops killed across the country as a whole, the British foreign secretary, David Miliband, called for a 'long-term inclusive political settlement in Afghanistan' to draw away conservative Pashtun nationalists from the Taliban.[22] In the face of criticism from elected representatives in the UK who argued that 'it is fundamental to the rebuilding of Afghanistan that international commitments made by the Government of Afghanistan and by donors on the rights of women are honoured and given greater priority', officials pointed at the American experience in Iraq as an example of what an overly ideological approach could bring.[23] An internal review of priorities at the British aid ministry, DFID, saw 'gender equality somewhat downgraded', a second official admitted.[24] When, in August, McChrystal's review had been submitted to the president, it included, alongside the demand for 40,000 new troops, the recommendation that alternative political vehicles such as moderate Islamist parties be created for Taliban supporters and recommended that 'reconciled' insurgents be removed from the sanctions list established under UN Security Council Resolution 1267 back in 1999. Such a measure had been mentioned by many of the intermediaries such as Muttawakel or Rahmani as something important to senior insurgents and was a significant concession which British intelligence described to the author as 'probably the first step towards genuine dialogue'. By November internal memos within the British Foreign Office – shared with McChrystal's staff – were urging 'a settlement with (most of) the Quetta Shura'. The memos also proposed a *loya jirga* – or national assembly – to be held in Kabul within two years that would work on reforming the Afghan constitution and reformulating the structure laid down by the Bonn agreement of late 2001.[25] People like Sadiqa Mobariz, a Hazaran female member of the Afghan national assembly and thus exactly the sort of person who would suffer from any concessions to the conservatives, repeatedly expressed their fears of betrayal. Western politicians made little effort to allay such concerns. In January 2010, at a major conference in London the West finally declared their collective desire to 'talk to the Taliban' – or at least the 'moderates' among them. Half a billion dollars was pledged to buy off Taliban footsoldiers. A renewed – though less publicized – push to engage Taliban leaders would be made at a strategic level too. When asked in an interview days before the conference if it would be acceptable 'if all this ended with a Taliban government in Kabul committed to a *sharia* caliphate state in Afghanistan', Miliband had said his objection would be to the 'caliphate' element as that would mean an al-Qaeda link. His answer implied that a rigorous religious regime in Kabul would none-theless be tolerated. A few days after the London conference's close, Britain's defence minister told reporters that Western powers were not seeking an 'unconditional surrender' of Taliban insurgents in Afghani-stan because many could form part of a settlement'.[26] His words contrasted with statements by his predecessor, who, just over a year before, had described 'negotiating deals with the Taliban' as 'conceding defeat by another name'.[27] Though the London conference also saw a renewed pledge of support from forty-odd nations to the strategy out-lined in McChrystal's review and sanctioned by Obama a month or so previously, it was obvious that the aim of the campaign of 2010 was not going to be paving the way for 'outright victory' but allowing any even-tual negotiations with the insurgents to take place in a more favourable environment. No one at the conference deviated from the message about leaving behind a 'sustainable, secure' Afghanistan which would no longer pose a threat to the West but no one could conceal their impatience to close the increasingly gruelling Afghan chapter of the multi-volumed encyclopedia of the 9/11 Wars as soon as possible either.

## THE TALIBAN'S VIEW

It is unlikely that any Taliban commander really did tell his interrogator the oft-repeated aphorism 'You have the watches, but we have the time', as often said. After all, most Taliban commanders did have watches – along with, by the end of 2009, an array of sophisticated military equipment that few amongst them had even heard of a few years previ-ously. But the phrase did nonetheless sum up perfectly the point, so evident by the time of the London conference of January 2010, that to win, all insurgents in Afghanistan had to do was avoid losing.

It was still the case that many of the insurgents' problems were internal. Over the previous eighteen months the Taliban leadership in Quetta – those with whom the British FCO had suggested concluding a settlement – had continued to work hard to manage the various chal-lenges thrown up by their successful resurgence. The insurgents were still fragmented and, though the faction led by Jalaluddin Haqqani did now liaise relatively closely with the senior leadership of the Quetta Shura Taliban, there was still almost no coordination with many other groups scattered across the country. '[Gulbuddin] Hekmatyar is a *mujahid* and we respect him but he is independent,' a Taliban spokesman said.[28] Problems of discipline continued despite Mullah Omar's injunctions over the previous eighteen months. The *leyha* or rulebook for the Taliban was repeatedly republished and redistributed by senior leaders in a bid to curtail the more anarchic followers but seemed often to have minimal effect. When the third edition of the 'code of conduct' was released in the late spring 2009 it stated that the use of suicide bombings should be limited to high-value targets and that 'the utmost effort should be made to avoid civilian casualties'.[29] The aim, spokesmen said, was 'to guide faithful fighters in the way of the jihad to best liberate the country with minimum loss'.[30] The use of suicide bombs did drop – down from a peak of 142 in 2007, to 122 in 2008 and to around 90 in 2009 – but the use of IEDs increased, as did the number of political assassinations. The result was that the toll of civilians being killed through the actions of the insurgents continued to climb.[31] The United Nations estimated that more than two-thirds of the 6,000 non-combatants killed and injured in Afghanistan in 2009, the worst year yet for civilian casualties, were caused by the Taliban.[32] Others put the figure as high as 80 per cent.[33] Young commanders remained often difficult to control, and many Taliban 'fellow travellers' continued to ignore efforts by the hierarchy to dictate strategic directives. A wave of executions to impose order and the bureaucratic reshuffles of 2008 and 2009 had had some impact with many more senior, experienced men appointed to senior posts in the 'shadow government' and the more criminal, and often more extreme, elements being weeded out.[34] A range of efforts continued to be made to build or retain broader community support. Some involved a degree of flexibility on the rigorous codes that often alienated locals. So the new appointees frequently turned a blind eye to girls being educated, at least at primary level. Other efforts were more active. In some areas, Taliban commanders enforced limits on expenditure on weddings, a seemingly draconian measure but, in a society where the spiralling cost of marriage was forcing many men into prolonged celibacy, one that was popular, particularly among the young males whose support the Taliban most wanted. A 'commission' of high-ranking Taliban officials was appointed and travelled through various provinces to question local communities about the behaviour of local Taliban commanders.[35] Taliban propaganda operations also continued intensively, with a range of products from traditional night letters through to increasingly sophisticated DVDs or internet video clips which all carefully depicted the movement as primarily local and nationalist. When Mullah Omar rejected the talks that the Saudis, Karzai and various others were hoping to open, he did so categorically, saying 'our *mujahid* people will not accept the negotiations that will add legitimacy to the continuing occupation in their country. Afghanistan is our home, and no one accepts [these] negotiations that'll give others a share of our home and to manage it.' In a long speech devoted 'to the supporters of freedom from the people of Europe and the West in general', Omar stated:

> Your colonist rulers have attacked our country in the name of war against terrorism, and that is to serve a small number of capitalists and suckers of people's blood, in order to gain more wealth. They have built their new colonialist traps and daily they kill our youths, elderly, women and children. And at night they barge into our homes and destroy our green gardens and general property, educational and trade centers, with blind air raids. Pushing away this aggression and defending our country is our legitimate and national right, and we will use our rights to defend with all methods and sacrifices . . . [against your] financial power and your satanic trickery.[36]

Though Western observers, particularly within coalition ranks, and urban, worldly Afghans saw this kind of rhetoric as a mendacious effort to disguise the Taliban's global pan-Islamist agenda by appealing to local sentiment, at least part of the appeal of the insurgents for some continued to stem from the ease with which they could appropriate the mantle of legitimate defenders of the 'Afghan' nation. The bottom line remained that the Taliban were local Muslim men fighting, on the whole, non-Muslim foreigners. As ever the propaganda was backed up with other means of persuasion. 'Spies' continued to be executed, often publicly hanged, and 'collaborators' assassinated with statements issued to justify – and publicize – the murders.[37] The combination of intimidation and 'hearts and minds' campaigns was usually effective in areas where conditions were right.

One problem that did prove insurmountable to the Taliban was the ethnic divide in the country. Despite carefully avoiding any statements that might encourage ethnic or sectarian violence, only a few low-level commanders from non-Pashtun ethnicities ever joined Taliban ranks, and these did so for the kind of micro-political reasons that had historically been so recurrent within the conflicts in Afghanistan. Attempts to push recruitment in the north of the country were successful – but only in Pashtun areas. This imposed a natural limit on the Taliban's expansion and stymied the efforts to depict the movement as a 'national uprising', as Taliban propaganda so consistently sought to do. One obvious question for all involved in the conflict at the end of 2009 and the beginning of 2010 was thus the level of support the Taliban actually had. This was impossible to quantify. The Taliban's 'commission' had been one effort to do so. The coalition and international community relied on other means, more familiar in the West, such as surveys. But pollsters faced huge practical problems, largely as a result of the parlous security situation in two-thirds of the country, and were thus limited to the urban areas, where Taliban support was lowest. Often surveys were carried out by telephone, again favouring urban literate populations. Equally, for obvious reasons, few Afghans would openly confess to supporting insurgents or their ideology. Nonetheless results in January 2010 indicating that 68 per cent of Afghans supported the presence of US forces – down from 71 per cent in 2007 and 78 per cent in 2006 but up from 63 per cent in 2008 – and that 69 per cent saw the Taliban as the main threat to the country – up 10 per cent from the year before – were probably accurate for those communities surveyed.[38]

Much more important than national statistics were support levels in the third of the country where insurgency was raging. This was even harder to gauge. Even the best-informed Western analysts in Afghanistan – specialists who had been in Kabul for decades – admitted that the international community 'had no visibility in the villages'. All they could say was that support for the insurgents in Pashtun conservative areas was 'extremely variable'.[39] It could be very high in one community and much lower on 'the other side of the creek', as Captain Vasquez had found in Logar. As ever in Afghanistan, such support was contingent on local circumstances, dynamics between tribes, the behaviour of individual families and leaders. There was still much fence-sitting. What did appear certain was that the overwhelming emphasis among Western soldiers and policy-makers on the economic roots of the insurgency seemed misplaced. At all levels within NATO and among Western diplomats and policy-makers the idea that the insurgents were fighting for money was dominant. Colonel Haight of Taskforce Spartan had said, 'Give a man a day's wage and a spade and he will put down his Kalashnikov.' Biden, the American vice president, said that 70 per cent of the Taliban had purely financial motives.[40] Miliband and others had repeatedly quoted the old Victorian-era saw that 'you can rent an Afghan, but you can't buy him', arguing that insurgents were 'rented by the Taliban'.[41] But even if such generalizations had been true when they had been coined they were of limited use a century or so later.

A study for the British Department for International Development based on hundreds of interviews with fighters found that a desire for cash was only one of a number of personal reasons which had brought young men into insurgent ranks. Often recruits sought status or a degree of protection. Frequently a desire to gain advantage in an ongoing dispute with another family or relative over land or water was critical. Even these factors themselves inevitably existed in a context defined by structural issues such as the perception of the government as partisan and corrupt. Genuine religious belief played a part too, the study found, though levels of religious knowledge among combatants were low, and their faith was more heavily informed by the new 'single narrative' popularized by radicals over the previous decade than scholarly Islam.[42] Another indication that money was far from a prime motivation for most insurgents was that some at least, though clearly a minority, did have relatively good incomes, sometimes even from jobs within the government administration.[43] People plunged in the everyday social warp and weft of the insurgency also painted a very different picture from that given in NATO briefings. Roshana Wardak, a trained gynaecologist from a major political family in Wardak province who was a popular and effective member of parliament, spoke of how 'there are ten educated ideological Taliban in the entire province and for each there are 100 pro-Taliban [people] who don't like foreign troops and are fighting to defend their religion'. Where she lived at least, she said, 'it is not common for the Taliban to pay'. The member of the national assembly for Ghazni, Daoud Sultanzoy, said the insurgents in his home area included 'one per cent staunch Taliban', some former Hezb-e-Islami commanders who act as 'pivots' in logistics networks, other local small-scale warlords who had lost out to the original Taliban in the 1990s and about 'eight to nine per cent who are just local thugs'. Taliban fighters themselves reacted with predictable but genuine anger to the proposal that they might accept money to stop fighting when asked by reporters, citing faith, principles, patriotism and vengeance for dead family members and comrades.[44] Miliband was an intelligent man who evidently doubted the simplistic formula he was often forced to use. The insurgents were, he explained to one interviewer shortly after a trip to Afghanistan, 'on the whole conservative Pashtun nationalists' who were 'pursuing a local grievance' and who 'need to be inside the political system'. This meant that, if the Taliban rented them, he said, it was 'not easy to rent them back'.[45] Money would not necessarily trump culture and identity.

The Taliban closely monitored Western media and were thus well aware of the various debates about strategy that evolved over the year. NATO's new campaign plan, with its emphasis on 'valley-by-valley' solutions and securing the population, was an undoubted improvement. But in three main areas that McChrystal saw as critical to turning around the situation in Afghanistan – the rapid development of Afghan security forces, the improvement of 'governance' and the reduction of civilian casualties – trends were mixed at best, still firmly negative at worst.

The ramifications of the use of increasing numbers of Afghan troops was an example of the way that the new NATO strategy risked exacerbating the broad structural problems that fuelled the insurgency in Afghanistan – such as the lack of legitimacy of the central government and their allies – in the south and south-east even while achieving certain limited tactical objectives. As in Iraq, the mantra from Western policy-makers and strategists was, even if it was never put in such terms, 'We will stand down as they stand up.' The sooner the Afghan security forces were effective, the sooner international forces could leave. Yet this strategy faced a similar problem as in Iraq: the local security forces both were weak and, to start with at least, lacked ethnic and cultural balance. In Iraq, however, the demographics had meant that the Sunnis had eventually little choice but to join the security forces, albeit as the auxiliaries of the Awakening. But in Afghanistan, with the Pashtuns totalling around 45 per cent, the insurgents often embedded in communities and no equivalent of al-Qaeda in Iraq to turn local populations towards the government or occupation forces as the lesser of two evils, the situation was very different. McChrystal's plan had envisaged doubling the Afghan National Army (ANA), but though the numbers of the

ANA were growing and its patchy fighting capacity slowly improving, many ANA deployments against the insurgents had a variety of potential negative consequences of which most Western commanders appeared unaware. First, the significant ethnic imbalance meant that the soldiers who had been manoeuvring with Vasquez and his men in Logar or were being sent down to Kandahar and Helmand were largely of Tajik or Hazara origin, and thus each further *kandaq*, as battalion-sized units were known, deployed in Pashtun-majority areas risked aggravating a civil war that had been running for several decades and an ethnic power struggle that dated back a century or so.[46] Perhaps worse, a high percentage of those ANA officers who were Pashtun had served with the Moscow-backed Afghan Communist forces against the *mujahideen* in the 1980s.[47] Many senior officers had been part of the hardline and notoriously brutal Khalq faction of the PDPA. Some, such as General Ali Ahmed, who was in charge of the ANA training centre in Kabul, referred both to the Taliban and to those who had fought the Soviets in the 1980s as 'insurgents', or *dushman*, enemy. That he should use the term to describe the Taliban was not surprising but that he should call the *mujahideen* of the earlier period 'enemy' was striking, particularly when the long-serving minister of defence had been one of them.[48] As the impressive briefing slides shown at the ISAF headquarters had made clear, if one of the many ongoing strands of historical conflict in Afghanistan was ethnic, so other strands pitted those who had benefited from Communist rule, often urban, educated communities, against those who had suffered enormously under it, usually rural communities. Taliban commanders might claim that they did not like fighting the ANA because the troops were 'Afghans' and villagers tell reporters that they preferred soldiers recruited from far away to the rapacious locally hired police, but General Ahmed's vocabulary underlined the cultural gulf that rent Afghanistan and fuelled the internal conflict. Overcoming these fundamental fractures was not impossible. Certainly in some parts of the country communities had begun to welcome the ANA. But consolidating such progress needed time and resources – and a legitimate central government.[49]

The second plank of the McChrystal strategy aimed to deal with all the multiple failings of the Afghan state revealed so brutally over the previous years. 'Ultimately, defeating the insurgency will depend upon the government's ability to improve security, deliver effective ...

services and expand development for economic opportunity,' John McConnell, the United States director of national intelligence, had told Senators the previous year and one reason why so much had been pinned on the presidential elections was that there had been so little sign of any rapid improvement of governance or aid and development delivery. The paradox of 'no security without development, no development without security' remained unresolved in much of the country, particularly of course the south. Venal, brutal, still largely untrained and often unpaid police – described by ISAF staff officers as 'the strategic hope' of the international effort in Afghanistan – were still a scourge for many communities.[50] Local people still turned to Taliban courts in much of the country for the speedy resolution of disputes. The official judiciary was corrupt, derided, inefficient and fearful. 'The government asked me to accept a post in Baki Barrak [a remote town], and I think the people would have liked me to be there, but I was too scared,' one Logar judge confessed.[51] The lack of governance inevitably hindered efforts to reduce opium cultivation and combat the vast narcotics industry. Though the opium harvest for 2009 did in fact fall 10 per cent to 6,900 tons, this was more due to external factors such as low opium prices and high wheat prices on the global market than to any developments within Afghanistan. Even if the extent of cultivation registered a steeper decline – to 123,000 hectares, down from a peak of 193,000 hectares in 2007 – the money being generated overall by the drugs industry was still enough to contaminate every part of Afghan public and political life.[52] Sadiqa Mobariz, the Hazara member of the national assembly and a staunch enemy of the Taliban, said she had been sufficiently shocked by the corruption she had seen among senior politicians for all her illusions to be shattered: 'When I saw the parliament and all the new laws back in 2004 and 2005, it was like a dream ... now that has become a nightmare.'[53] She did not plan on standing for re-election. Occasional prosecutions by newly formed special teams of investigators and judges made little difference – not least because those convicted were regularly pardoned by the president. Nor did the new commitment of NATO to target opium factories and facilities and key individual traffickers.[54] The corruption naturally impacted on aid delivery – or at least the willingness of donors to fund assistance programmes. Though the days of shoddily built schools costing half a million dollars or tube wells sunk with no regard for the local water table were largely over, a huge amount of cash continued to be spent by either foreign companies or NGOs independently of the Afghan government. 'How can people respect their own authorities if they see that anything that is worthwhile is built by other people?' asked Mohammed Ehsan Zia, the rural rehabilitation and development minister.[55] 'How can we give them the cash if we can't be sure it isn't going to be stolen?' countered a Western aid official, citing reports that $3 billion in cash, of which a significant portion was embezzled US aid and drugs money, had been openly flown out of Kabul International Airport between 2007 and 2009 to financial safe havens abroad.[56] There were continuing question marks over the integrity of President Hamid Karzai's close entourage, the interior ministry and other key institutions. In October 2009, the then vice president, Ahmad Zia Massoud, was stopped and questioned in Dubai when he flew into the emirate with $52 million in cash. He was no exception. 'Vast amounts of cash come and go from the country on a weekly, monthly and annual basis,' the American ambassador noted in a cable.[57] Grave problems remained with senior local officials. Other cables from the American embassy in Kabul back to Washington accused the governors of two key provinces of 'embezzling public funds, stealing humanitarian assistance, and misappropriating government property'.[58] American suspicions of the president's half-brother's involvement in a range of illicit activities including narcotics were well known.[59] 'You'd think finding a dozen competent ministers and thirty provincial governors would be possible, but apparently it isn't,' said Daoud Sultanzoy, the opposition MP.[60] Nor did it look likely to suddenly become possible in the near future. NATO officers had been repeating for years that the Taliban were not strong, but the state was weak. In the end it did not matter where the relative strength lay. The Taliban simply needed to impede any improvement in governance, and most of their job would be done. As ever in such a conflict, all the insurgents needed to do was to avoid losing and wait for the foreign occupiers to run out of men, money or patience so they could get on with their primary strategic aim of fighting the country's local rulers. 'We are very closely following the EU and US opinion and all assessment shows that people [there] are tired of this war and they will ask Obama to withdraw from Afghanistan,' the Taliban spokesman told the author in October 2009.[61]

The third element of McChrystal's plan was to reduce the number of civilian casualties, clearly a key element of 'protecting the population'.

Western public opinion, particularly as it turned negative, was sensitive to Afghan civilian casualties too. Inevitably given the nature of the coalition and the structure of American forces, the implementation of the new COIN thinking within Afghanistan was uneven, whatever senior officers' orders. Ten minutes after leaving an interview with the commander of NATO-ISAF forces, the author's local taxi was effectively run off the road by an American army Humvee, whose masked top gunner very deliberately added insult to near injury by offering a single erect gloved finger as his own vehicle swung by. If getting soldiers to drive courteously in the capital was hard, ensuring that frontline tactical commanders chose to forgo air power and risk the lives of their own men rather than those of locals was naturally significantly harder.[62] When McChrystal called for a policy of 'courageous restraint' in the use of firepower, he provoked a furious response from many of his own soldiers, who accused their commander of irresponsibly depriving them of the most effective weapons in NATO's arsenal. However, the use of air power and heavy weapons did diminish steadily over 2009 and into the next year – down 60 per cent by the early months of 2010 even if the tension between the short-term objective of 'force protection' and the long-term aim of 'protecting the population' that had dogged military operations for years was as present as ever.[63] Overall the new emphasis on avoiding civilian casualties meant that international troops or their Afghan allies were responsible for significantly fewer Afghan civilians killed or injured during 2009, despite heavier fighting.[64]

There was also the issue of the 'collateral damage' associated with the American special forces teams tasked with picking up 'high-value targets'. Such units, drawn mainly from the 7th Special Forces Group at Fort Bragg, North Carolina, though with some from the British Special Boat Service and other allied elite units, had been responsible for many of the most egregious incidents of civilian casualties over the previous seven years.[65] The units often contained significant numbers of Afghans, and it was the latter who often exacted the highest price from local communities suspected of sheltering senior Taliban figures, though without their international mentors apparently making much effort to restrain them.[66] Concerns about the local fall-out of such operations had been repeatedly raised by commanders on the ground and had led to a short moratorium on such raids in early 2009.[67] However, one lesson that McChrystal had taken away from the special forces operations he had led in Iraq had been that pressuring the enemy's middle-level ranks could pay major dividends, 'squeezing' the entire command and control structure of the insurgents. He therefore sought to increase the 'operational tempo' of his special forces troops three-, four- or five-fold. In this McChrystal was backed by his superior, David Petraeus, who, politic as ever, understood that the higher-value targets 'taken down' were useful to boost the morale of wavering politicians back home and thus bought the military much needed time. Senior officers also argued that such 'surgical' operations meant less need for conventional troops to 'go blundering around the Afghan countryside', and the raids intensified in the second half of 2009.

The first major test for McChrystal, the new NATO strategy and the new troops that had been arriving all through 2009 came in early 2010 at Marjah, a small rural district to the west of Lashkar Gah in the centre of Helmand province. Marjah, which had a population of approximately 100,000, had little inherent strategic importance other than being the westernmost point of a crescent of densely inhabited land running all the way across to the Pakistani border and being the target of the first major NATO-ISAF operation aimed at proving the ability of the newly reinforced Western and local forces to clear a Taliban-run area and then hold it through the creation of a more or less functional local administration.[68] The district of Marjah had already been fought over in 2007 but, though 'won' from the insurgents, had subsequently been infiltrated once again by the Taliban, who had then killed many of those who had cooperated – or collaborated, depending on your point of view – with the Western forces. This time, the local population was told, not only would the area be secured and its inhabitants protected when the operation was over, but Marjah would then see a major development and administrative effort which would maintain the authority of the central government for the foreseeable future. Beyond the local aims, the operation had a broader national and international significance too. Not only would Marjah show how the new McChrystal strategy could work but it would 'shape' the local environment for what was planned to be the main event of the summer: a much more complex campaign for Kandahar which would break the stalemate in Afghanistan and change the course of the war.

The Marjah operation, named 'Moshtarak', or 'Togetherness', to emphasize the unity of effort of Afghan and international forces, turned out to be inconclusive. There were certain predictable problems – artillery and air strikes caused dozens of civilian casualties early on, for example – but the 15,000-strong Western-led force successfully fought its way through the villages for the loss of only thirteen men. An Afghan flag was raised by ANA soldiers over a badly damaged and abandoned marketplace in Marjah district centre on 17 February 2010. Though there had been some resistance, the insurgents had largely avoided a conventional confrontation, leaving behind hundreds of IEDs that continued to kill soldiers and locals for weeks. The operation was rapidly declared over, the main force pulled out and the attempt to establish a competent and responsive government was launched. This – the 'build' phase – met with limited success. The first governor installed turned out to be an incompetent virtual illiterate with a criminal record acquired while a refugee in Germany. The police deployed into Marjah proved as rapacious and brutal as anywhere else. Security forces proved unable to keep the insurgents out, as most of the latter were local men, whereas the ANA soldiers deployed to the district were from hundreds of miles away. Within weeks, the Taliban were back, at least at night. Local communities once more found themselves in the invidious position that had been so often theirs over previous years: trying to negotiate a miserable middle way between the insurgents and the Afghan government and their international allies. Within months, the United Nations had recorded at least 74 civilians killed in Marjah, 29 killed by 'pro-government forces', 32 by insurgents and 13 dying at the hands of 'unknown actors'. Partly as a consequence, few of the 4,000 families who fled the spring fighting returned.[69] In the aftermath of the Marjah operation the Kandahar campaign was postponed to allow 'further shaping' of the strategic environment. In May, the Taliban for their part launched their own offensive, named al-Faath, or 'Conquest', or 'Victory'. All parties involved in the fighting in Afghanistan were very aware that its evolution through the summer would inevitably depend greatly on what was happening across the border, in Pakistan.

## PAKISTAN, 2009–10

In February, as the Marines and their Afghan allies were fighting their way into Marjah, Pakistani intelligence officials had arrested more senior Taliban in a few days than they had done in the previous eight and a half years. Among those picked up in a series of dawn raids was Mullah Abdul Ghani Barader, effectively Mullah Omar's deputy and one of the most capable and respected of the Quetta Shura members.[70] Others included Maulvi Abdul Kabir, the former governor of Jalalabad who had escaped over the Spin Ghar mountains as the Tora Bora battle unfolded more than eight years before, who was picked up from a substantial house in which he had been living for some time on the outskirts of Peshawar.[71] Several, including key advisers of Mullah Omar, were arrested in Karachi. In all, an impressive number of veteran Taliban figures, the arrest of whom had been sought by the West for many years, were detained.[72] The response from Washington and European capitals was effusive. Richard Holbrooke, the special representative, called the arrests 'another high water mark for Pakistani and American collaboration'.[73] Bruce Riedel, who had led the Obama administration's spring 2009 'AfPak' policy review, hailed a 'very major shift in Pakistani behaviour'.[74]

A month later, the Pakistani army announced total victory in the agency of Bajaur, nearly two years after starting operations there. The campaign was described as 'effective' by American officials and projected as further evidence that senior Pakistani officers had finally recognized the urgency of dealing with the internal threat posed by the militants. The previous year – 2009 – had seen a series of new efforts by the Pakistani military to take on the militant havens along the Afghan frontier. A key moment had come when groups allied to the Pakistani Taliban had moved out of the upland areas along the frontier or the various spurs of the Hindu Kush mountains and started to take ground on the fertile lowlands only a couple of hours' drive from Islamabad. After a controversial deal with the militant leaders who had seized the valley of Swat in April 2009 which had granted the extremists the right to impose a version of *sharia* law and had provoked international fury, 52,000 Pakistani troops had spent the summer using relatively innovative tactics including some of the new counter-insurgency doctrines being implemented elsewhere to regain control of the area. Despite the attraction of their project of land reform to some communities, support for the militants in Swat had rapidly dwindled as local elders had been humiliated by young fighters, venerated local religious figures were killed and their bodies desecrated, singing and dancing banned and girls' schools destroyed.[75] In October, three divisions of troops had finally moved into South Waziristan and, by exploiting splits between militant groups and with US drones feeding intelligence to battlefield commanders, were able to force militants out of village strongholds and into remote forest or mountain camps. The same month the Pakistanis had acceded to the longstanding request of the Americans and allowed a very small number of US special forces troops – just over a dozen – to operate in the tribal areas.[76] With the militants still divided by a bitter succession row following the death of Baitullah Mehsud, the leader of the Pakistan Taliban, in a drone strike earlier in the year, it seemed possible that the gains made in the operations over the summer and autumn might for once be consolidated. Certainly, some communities, albeit mainly on the periphery of the tribal areas, appeared willing to take up arms themselves against the militants. Even if their primary motivation was to pursue blood feuds, their stance nonetheless indicated a degree of confidence in the government and the Pakistani military to protect them in at least the near future.[77] Fighting had continued along the length of the tribal belt – though not in the critical North Waziristan – through the winter of 2009–10 and into the spring. 'I couldn't give the Pakistani Army anything but an "A" for how they've conducted their battle so far [in the FATA],' enthused Admiral Mullen, the American chairman of the Joint Chiefs of Staff.[78] Naturally in private senior defence officials and their civilian counterparts were less extravagant in their praise, but, with the progress in the FATA and the arrests of important members of the Taliban high command, it was unsurprising that some began to see grounds for optimism.

However, closer inspection revealed little reason to believe that the Pakistani security establishment had significantly reversed or even moderated its Afghan policy or that the operations in the FATA would lead to the rapid elimination of militancy, either local or international, from the tribal zones. Rather than a 'sea change', the arrests of so many of the Taliban high command in February 2010 could be seen more as the beginning of a new phase in Pakistan's long-term bid to assure its influence in Afghanistan and to roll back that of its regional competitors. The arrests served several purposes at once for the Pakistani security establishment: pleasing Western allies, reminding the obstinately independent-minded Taliban leadership that their well-being depended to a considerable extent on Pakistan's calculation of its interests, and rendering the ISI indispensable once, as looked inevitable, some kind of peace process got underway across the border. Those Taliban arrested were also those who had repeatedly showed themselves to be the most pragmatic. Though reports that the most senior amongst them had indirectly been involved in talks with the Kabul government were denied by all sides, there was evidence that all those detained belonged to a small but influential faction within the Taliban which had come to the conclusion that victory – defined as restoring the Islamic Emirate of Afghanistan that had existed before 2001 – was impossible by military means alone.[79] The detention of these figures, coming immediately after the London conference, where 'reconciliation' with the Taliban had become stated coalition policy in Afghanistan, restored Pakistan's control over political developments and a peace process that had threatened to spin out of their control. Those on the ground in Pakistan remained sanguine about prospects for any breakthrough. As a vast $7.5 billion aid package made its way through Congress, Anne Patterson, the US ambassador in Islamabad, had cabled Washington to stress that 'there is no chance that Pakistan will view enhanced assistance . . . as sufficient compensation for abandoning support to [militant] groups' including the Taliban and Jalaluddin Haqqani's insurgent network.[80]

Equally, the Pakistanis' declaration of victory in the FATA also appeared very premature. There were plenty of signs that any respite would be temporary. Only 600 of an estimated 10,000 militants in South Waziristan were thought to have been killed, and, more importantly, most of the multitude of groups that had sprung up over previous years remained mobilized. Baitullah Mehsud's successor, Hakimullah Mehsud, was first declared dead with '90 per cent certainty' by American officials and then embarrassingly shown to be alive when he surfaced in a video. As in Afghanistan, the 'clear' phase of counter-insurgency operations was proving much simpler than the 'hold' and 'build'. Indeed, the problems of governance posed in southern Afghanistan and those in the FATA had much in common. As outlined in previous chapters, the problems in the FATA were, like those underlying all Islamic radicalism, a complex mesh of international and local factors reaching back decades, if not centuries. They were thus likely to take decades, if not centuries, to unpick, and it seemed unlikely that the Pakistani civilian government or military, both increasingly mired in ongoing internal power struggles, had either the will or the capacity to do so. Simply changing the name of the North West Frontier province to Khyber Pakhtunkhwa, as was done with some fanfare in April 2010, certainly was not likely to make much of a difference. By the late spring of 2010 there were already signs of low-intensity guerrilla-style war against the Pakistani army in the FATA with ambushes, IEDs and other tactics developed and honed in Afghanistan or other theatres of the 9/11 Wars killing an increasing number of soldiers and paramilitaries.[81]

It was also looking increasingly likely that Pakistan might suffer a generalized durable insurgency in areas well beyond the FATA along the lines of the violence that had half-paralysed countries in the Maghreb and beyond in the 1990s. Spring 2009 had seen an appalling surge in violence in Punjab. The Sri Lankan cricket team had been attacked in Lahore, then a police training centre, then a Barelvi mosque. The bombings and *fedayeen*-style assaults, by which a heavily armed squad of fighters attacked well-defended targets in the near certain knowledge that they would be killed, continued through the summer and the autumn.[82] In October, there was an unprecedented assault on the military's general headquarters in Rawalpindi followed by a triple assault on police offices and training centres in Lahore, which killed more than thirty. The attacks continued in the west of the country – over 100 died in a bombing in Peshawar that coincided with the arrival of Hillary Clinton, the American secretary of state, in Pakistan on October 29 – but it was the quickening tempo and growing intensity of violence outside the FATA and its immediate environs which was most striking. In all in 2009, 3,025 people died in terrorist attacks in Pakistan, almost exactly the number of victims of the September 11 attacks. The strikes had continued through the spring of 2010.

As worrying as the level of violence was the identity of those behind the attacks. Investigations revealed the perpetrators of the violence to be part of fragmented, dynamic and ad hoc networks composed of militants from a range of different organizations. The process of internationalization of local Pakistani groups, highlighted earlier, had continued since the death of Bhutto and the terrific violence of 2008. Though many had once been focused exclusively on sectarian strife, Kashmir or fighting in Afghanistan, other groups had become patched into a range of new contacts among the Pakistani Taliban and its offshoots or even al-Qaeda itself.[83] Much of the collaboration between these various elements remained tactical – the Pakistani Taliban had reserves of suicide bombers, the Punjabi groups had safehouses and sanctuaries, for example, so individuals from the two networks frequently joined forces – and was not therefore evidence of any solid linkage. However, they did share a vision of the Pakistani government and security establishment as enemies. The steady ideological convergence between groups and the simultaneous organizational fragmentation of Pakistani radical militant organizations over the course of the 9/11 Wars was a particularly dangerous combination which made effective counter-terrorism extremely difficult. It also revealed – in microcosm – the nature of modern Islamic militancy more generally.

The critical element within both the Algerian and the Egyptian insurgencies of the 1990s and during the previous decade of the 9/11 Wars had been the rejection of extremism by local populations. The good news was that, by the end of 2009 and early 2010, there was some evidence that popular sentiment in Pakistan was finally turning against the militants and their violence. In 2005, about half (52 per cent) of Pakistani Muslims expressed confidence in bin Laden to do the right thing in world affairs; in 2010 only 18 per cent shared this view, and levels of disapproval of suicide bombing – 80 per cent – were the highest in the Islamic world.[84] Even in the Khyber Pakhtunkhwa/North West Frontier province some polls showed that support for bin Laden had fallen dramatically.[85] But the bad news was the levels of support for militants, of all kinds, which still remained. A shift from around one in four having a positive view of the Taliban and al-Qaeda in 2008 to under one in six over the same period still meant tens of millions of people continued to consider Mullah Omar, bin Laden and other extremists as people who were, at the very least, making a positive overall contribution to local regional and world affairs. The issue of public sentiment towards such figures was closely linked to another important question posed by broader social developments in Pakistan: would the new urban middle classes, especially the lower middle classes recently lifted from relative poverty, swing towards a more pro-Western, liberal, secular and democratic position as they expanded or in another direction? Here too there was little ground for optimism. Elsewhere in the Islamic world, the lived experience of radical violence had led to its rejection. However, that rejection had frequently been accompanied by a consolidation of a new social conservatism, an attraction to 'mild' Islamism, a reaffirmation of a non-violent but intolerant Muslim identity and a profound anti-Americanism. There appeared to be little reason to expect any difference in Pakistan.[86] In late spring 2010, according to Pew Research, 85 per cent of Pakistanis favoured the segregation of men and women in the workplace, 83 per cent favoured stoning adulterers, 80 per cent favoured lashing thieves or amputating their hands, and 78 per cent supported the death penalty for apostates. Overall, nine out of ten said it was a good thing that Islam played a big role in the political life of the country and almost two-thirds saw the US as an enemy.[87] A survey of under-thirties found that only a third now believed democracy was the best system of govern-ance, a third preferred *sharia* law, while 7 per cent thought dictatorship was a good idea.[88] A fierce nationalism also continued to strengthen. This manifested itself both internally – 89 per cent of respondents in the Pew Survey said they were Pakistani before being a member of their ethnic group – and externally – an incident in September 2009 that saw US troops crossing the border into South Waziristan from Afghanistan provoked an extraordinary outpouring of rhetoric about infringed sov-ereignty and the right of Pakistan to be 'respected' on the world stage.[89] The intensifying drone strikes continued too to provoke anger, particu-larly as it was widely and wrongly thought that they did not have the sanction of the Pakistani government. Very large numbers of civilians and soldiers continued to believe that Indians or even the US or Israel were running the militants in the FATA and now also in the Punjab to deliberately weaken Pakistan.[90] One American diplomatic cable noted: 'America is viewed with some suspicion by the majority of Pakistan's people and its institutions . . . We are viewed at best as a fickle friend, and at worst as the reason why Pakistan is attacking its own.'[91] Much of the nation's vastly expanded media – considered 'unbiased' by 76 per cent of Pakistanis – continued to peddle half-truths and prejudice. A fairly typical headline in the *Nation*, one of the better local English-language newspapers, revealed that Benazir Bhutto had been assassinated by a special death squad formed by former US Vice President Dick Cheney and headed by General McChrystal.[92] No doubt partly as a result of the slew of sensationalist and poorly sourced reporting, when asked what was the greatest threat to their country, nearly three-quarters of Pakistanis in 2010 identified India, less than a third chose the Taliban and only 3 per cent pointed to al-Qaeda.[93] Inevitably, these kind of sen-timents continued to spill over into the security establishment's strategic vision. So too did the widespread ambivalence towards the militants now active from the FATA to the eastern frontier. In March 2010, Shahbaz Sharif, the brother of opposition leader Nawaz Sharif and chief minister of the Punjab, pleaded with the Taliban to leave the province alone as his administration shared their aim of opposing 'foreign [i.e. American] dictation'.[94] When in May over ninety Muslims from the minority Ahmedi strand, considered heretics by the intolerant and orthodox, were killed in a series of bombings, the attacks went without comment by many of the country's politicians and were only reluctantly criticized by others. The global financial crisis had revealed the structural weaknesses of the Pakistani economy that had been obscured by the boom of the Musharraf years and now imperilled the hard-won advances made by many people. With the economy continuing to deteriorate, in part because of the appalling security situation but also due to a lack of electricity to run factories and agricultural equipment, Zardari's poll ratings plummeted, and the mild Islamo-nationalist rhetoric of Sharif brought him approval levels of up to 89 per cent.[95] A projected crackdown on the militants in the Punjab stalled in the face of a row between the government and the opposition.[96] Politicians even campaigned alongside well-known extremist leaders. This may have been deeply cynical, selfish and even immoral but made good pragmatic political sense given that polls had revealed that Lashkar-e-Toiba, the best known of the local militant groups, were seen favourably by at least a quarter of the national population and by over a third of people in the Punjab.[97] Few other groups had Lashkar-e-Toiba's popular base or connections to the security establishment, but there was no doubt the militants in general retained significant political clout and legitimacy. Though under undoubted pressure, the myriad militant groups existing across the whole of Pakistani soil were showing little significant weakness. The summer promised to be bloody, in Pakistan as in Afghanistan.

## KASHMIR AND A GENERATIONAL STRUGGLE

In the spring of 2010, as the snow melted from the lower slopes of the foothills of the Himalayas and buds began to appear on the apple trees, violence in the Indian part of the long-disputed state of Kashmir, having touched a twenty-year low the year before, began to rise once again.[98] Day after day, young men, often teenagers, took to the streets to hurl stones at ill-trained ill-equipped security forces. The police and para-militaries often countered the stones with bullets.[99] In the narrow streets of the centre of Srinagar, the summer capital of the state, and in small, hardscrabble towns like Sopore or Anantnag, choking tear gas filled the air as the wounded and sometimes the dying were carried away. In the rural areas, moving from house to house, were the armed militants, less numerous than for many years but nonetheless hopeful of exploiting the renewed mobilization that accompanied the street violence to gain recruits among a new generation of Kashmiri youths.

One of longest conflicts involving radical Islam in the world, pre-dating the 9/11 Wars by a decade or more, violence in Kashmir had followed a trajectory familiar from previous pages. After an initial explosion of violence between 1988 and 1991, there had been a steady intensification through the early 1990s. As elsewhere, a clumsy reaction on the part of security services had led to appalling violence, continuing abuses by all sides, a collapsing local economy and terrible suffering among civilians. By the end of the decade, it was clear that the popula-tion was slowly but steadily turning away from militancy. Combined with geopolitical shifts, particularly the post-9/11 pressure on Pakistan to reduce support to Kashmiri militants and to stop Lashkar-e-Toiba and other Pakistan-based groups sending fighters across the Line of Control to attack Indian security forces, this had meant a significant decline in violence from around 2002. By 2010, the local militants of early 1990s were dead or in their forties, married and drinking coffee in newly opened Srinagar cafés. Active fighters, once more than 1,500 strong in 'the Valley', as the principal and most prized part of Kashmir was known, probably numbered no more than around 250.[100] Kashmir had been a sideshow of the 9/11 Wars, caught in their backwash, drawn into the complex of conflicts they constituted, without ever really being a key theatre. Nonetheless, Kashmir indicated many of the qualities of the conflict as a whole – and indicated its possible evolution.

Various short-term factors had sparked the resurgence of violence in Kashmir in the spring of 2010. There was local anger at stalled political processes, possibly a degree of interference from across the border as Pakistan's intelligence services carefully ramped up their involvement and, in particular, the presence of large numbers of frustrated and under-employed youth.[101] These young men – though bored – were not poor. Kashmir is one of the richest parts of India and, though good jobs are rare, no one is starving. Nor were they ill-educated. Almost all were literate, most were articulate, and many had university degrees. The key factor in the violence was instead the age of the teenagers out throwing stones at security forces week after week. For all of them the dark days of the 1990s, when tens of thousands died in militant attacks, in cross-fire, in torture chambers run by the army and the police, were little more than a childhood memory. They were prepared to contemplate a return to violence because they had forgotten what taking up arms had brought and because, they said, they felt the weight of expectations on their generation. 'I grew up listening to stories of the struggle, of the heroes, of the *mujahideen*. Now I am old enough. I do not want to show myself less committed or less brave or less strong than they were before,' said Mehboob Lone, nineteen. The repeated shootings – each death led to a funeral and a demonstration where another youth was killed which thus meant another funeral – had created a momentum that was hard to stop. Mehraan, a twenty-two-year-old shopkeeper and veteran of the protests, said he had started attacking security forces when his cousin was shot dead. Since then, he said, he had wanted two things: *azadi* (freedom) and revenge, or 'blood for blood'. 'These things happen, and nothing is changed, and then they happen again,' he commented and shrugged. He and his friends spent many hours in internet cafés surfing Kashmir protest websites, watching videos of protests shot on mobile phones, on social networking sites or in groups that the police were unable to access. Though few visited radical jihadi sites, those celebrating Palestinian protests or the words and works of the most well-known contemporary Islamic clerics were popular. For feeding the resentment was the same new social conservatism and interest in pan-Islamic identities seen elsewhere. The old, traditional Sufi-influenced strands of Islam in Kashmir had been ceding ground to newer, harsher, more rigorous, more intolerant and more politicized styles for many years. Though a broad rejection of global al-Qaeda-inspired militancy was evident, the hero of the stone throwers was eighty-one-year-old Syed Ali Shah Geelani, a reactionary political Islamist and the most uncompromising of the local leaders.

Through the spring and into the summer of 2010, the demonstrations continued with a steady toll of a death or two every week. Under the hail of broken bricks, the police retreated behind their barbed-wire barricades and the concrete blast walls which had, over the previous years, replaced the ramshackle defences around their bunkers. Though the vast bulk of their activity was still limited to hurling stones, the step to using more lethal arms would clearly not be a difficult one for the young Kashmiri men to take. When interviewed, they all echoed the implicit threats made by their political leaders, saying that they did not want to resort to armed violence, but that the possibility was always there if their demands, inchoate as they might have been, were not met. Officials recognized the rhetoric for what it was but were alarmed nonetheless. 'If there were weapons we'd have ten thousand militants,' one senior police officer said.[102] Intelligence reports described dozens of teenagers known for their involvement in demonstrations going underground to join the militants as the months passed.[103] In one village, as Indian army soldiers searched houses in a bid to catch a fugitive senior militant commander responsible for a series of local shootings, men told the author of the six or eight teenagers who had recently left their homes for the hills where the militants were thought to be based and of the 'informers' who had recently been executed by their neighbours.

No one needed to be reminded what such volunteers could end up doing. In January, a series of suicidal attacks, the first for two years, had shaken Kashmir.[104] They underlined three key lessons of the 9/11 Wars: how one generation can bequeath violence to another, how routes into activism vary and how militancy so often remains very localized indeed. One of the militants who died was Mansoor Ahmed Bhat, a nineteen-year-old house painter. Bhat came from a modest farming family in the small village of Pett Sirr, an hour's drive north of Srinagar and flanked in February by barren wheat fields and acres of orchards. His home lay down a muddy path between barn-like farmhouses. It was hard to imagine the village as lying in 'the epicentre of regional violence', as described by Indian officials. However, over the previous twenty years of the conflict at least two dozen men from Pett Sirr had joined militant groups. Bhat, his parents said, had never indicated any interest in following them, however. 'We are just farmers,' said Ghulam, the dead man's forty-five-year-old father. 'We are never involved in politics. Our only interest has been our livestock and our orchards.'

As ever, it is almost impossible to find any one moment when Bhat, who his parents and friends said was a 'quiet young man' who had left school at thirteen to work in the fields, began the journey that led to his violent death. He had grown up, after all, steeped in the ambient violence. His father believes the critical moment came in the summer of 2008, when Bhat participated in a demonstration during which six people were shot dead by local police. 'That changed him,' Bhat senior said. A few months later, his son told his parents he had got a job in Srinagar as a house painter and disappeared. The months passed, and his worried father reported the teenager missing. 'The police came and raided us and searched everything and told us to call them if we had news,' he said. Another six months went by. On January 3, 2010, his son walked through the door. He stayed a few hours, said little, ate and left again. 'He told us nothing,' Bhat's mother remembered. Four days later, local police rang the family's single mobile phone to say that their son was one of two armed militants who had attacked security forces in the centre of Srinagar with grenades and were now firing at anyone who approached from the upper storeys of a hotel. They asked Ghulam Bhat to call his son on his mobile phone and talk him into surrender, but he refused, fearing some kind of trap. After a twenty-two-hour siege, during which two policemen and a bystander were killed, Mansoor Bhat was shot dead.[105] A month after the attack, in the bare living room of the home in Pett Sirr, a picture of Bhat lay wrapped in a green cloth on a shelf next to the Koran.

# 17

# The End of the First Decade

## AL-QAEDA

On May 1, 2010, as the Marjah operation in Afghanistan was drawing to a close, as fighting continued in the FATA and as militants attacked with ever-greater frequency across swathes of eastern Pakistan, police in Times Square in the centre of New York discovered a large bomb in a Nissan Pathfinder parked on the corner of 45th Street and Seventh Avenue. The man who had prepared the device and placed it there was Faisal Shahzad, a thirty-one-year-old Pakistani who had become an American citizen the year before. The bomb was made of petrol, propane, fireworks and fertilizer and failed to ignite because Shahzad, in an amateurish error typical of many attempted attacks by Islamic militants over the previous ten years, had set the timer wrongly. However, if such an elementary mistake had not been made, the bomb could have killed scores, possibly hundreds of people, injuring many times that number, in the centre of Manhattan.

Though the plot was clearly nowhere near the scale or professionalism of the 9/11 attacks, it was at least very close to one of their main targets and as such was the nearest radical militants had come to repeating the earlier strikes.[1]

Two weeks later, in the UK, a twenty-one-year-old student called Roshonara Choudhry used a kitchen knife to stab a member of parliament, Stephen Timms, who had supported the war in Iraq. Timms survived the attack, and Choudhry was arrested. In early interviews with police she said she had acted entirely alone after viewing scores of hours of lectures by radical American-born Yemen-based cleric Anwar al-Awlaki. 'I told no one. No one else would have understood,' she said.[2]

Newspapers described Choudhry nonetheless as a 'remote-controlled Al Qaeda assassin' who had been 'brainwashed'.[3]

Through the summer of 2010 and into the autumn, a series of scares reminded publics across the world of the threat that Islamic militancy still posed. In July, a plot was uncovered in Norway involving recent immigrants – a Chinese Uighur, an ethnic Uzbek and an Iraqi Kurd.[4] In October came warnings, transmitted to US intelligence by German counterparts, of a series of 'Mumbai-style' attacks in Europe. Then in November came a new scare when a tip-off led security services to parcel bombs sent from the Yemen to Jewish targets in Chicago on cargo planes. Yemen had been in the spotlight since the last week of 2009, when a young Nigerian from an elite family was arrested on a plane flying into Detroit after he tried and failed to detonate explosives sewn into his underwear. It had soon emerged that Umar Faroul Abdultalleb, the would-be bomber, had, after a period in the UK where he joined Islamic societies at London University, started his journey across the world from Sana'a, the Yemeni capital. The exact provenance of the new threat emanating from the Yemen was unclear. Many threads ran back to Anwar al-Awlaki, the extremist cleric.

One element that all these various plots had in common was the tenuous nature of their links to the al-Qaeda hardcore. Faisal Shahzad, the aspirant bomber of Times Square, had been trained and partly funded by the Pakistani Taliban, a group which shared the views of al-Qaeda but was certainly not part of bin Laden's organization, on a winter trip a few months before to his home country. Neither he nor Choudhry, the putative assassin, nor Abdultalleb had ever met anyone from the al-Qaeda hardcore.[5] Even the links of FATA-based Ilyas Kashmiri, the veteran Pakistani now emerging as a major figure in global Islamic militancy and thought to be behind the 'Mumbai-style' attacks plan, to the al-Qaeda hardcore were uncertain. Al-Awlaki's own relationship with bin Laden and al-Zawahiri was subject to debate. The opacity surrounding the origins of the evident threat inevitably fuelled further debate on one question: 'what is al-Qaeda?'

The answer had been simpler back in the immediate aftermath of the 9/11 attacks. Then, analysis was fairly straightforward. Al-Qaeda was the best-known and most significant amid the hundreds of organizations involved in radical Sunni militancy. It comprised three clear elements. There was the hardcore leadership of the group, the network of other entities with formal affiliation to it and the ideology, the uniquely effective mix of modern and ancient historical references, filled out with selective quotations from scriptures and from other Muslim revivalist and reformist thinkers, that comprised the narrative, the language and the doctrines that underpinned the group's particular worldview. Al-Qaeda was certainly not without its challengers, competitors and rivals within the broad movement of radical Islam, but the group had been able to establish a centrality, real and virtual, in the global landscape of radical militancy in the late 1990s which, in the aftermath of the 2001 attacks, was undisputed.

Nearly a decade later, as the successive scares of 2010 revealed, the situation had clearly evolved drastically. In interviews, serving intelligence officers spoke of a 'fragmented, chaotic' picture that was 'immensely difficult' to track. The threat was 'broader' than it had ever been. Quite what the role of Osama bin Laden actually might be remained unclear. With every year that had passed since the 9/11 Wars had begun, the situation had become more complex, even as the threat of catastrophic violence itself had stabilized. By the end of the decade, the old analysis of al-Qaeda comprising a hardcore leadership, a network of affiliates and an ideology evidently needed revision.

## THE HARDCORE, THE NETWORK OF NETWORKS, THE IDEOLOGY IN 2010 AND 2011

In 2010 and into early 2011 the al-Qaeda senior leadership continued to face a number of challenges. The most immediate was the continuing threat to their own personal security. The drone strikes in the FATA were more numerous than ever, and if bin Laden and al-Zawahiri had so far escaped the missiles falling on the tribal areas, many others did not. More than fifty strikes had been ordered by Obama in the first year of his administration, more than had ever been ordered by Bush, and 118 took place in 2010. One high-profile loss in May 2010 had been Mustafa Abu al-Yazid, the senior al-Qaeda militant who had played a key liaison role with local groups and the Afghan Taliban. He was just one of several senior figures and scores of middle-ranking fighters killed by the drones, however.[6] Given that most intelligence suggested that the number of Arabs comprising the main body of al-Qaeda in the FATA did not number more than 300, of whom three-quarters fulfilled relatively minor roles or were 'footsoldiers', these casualties were heavy.[7] The strikes also had an evident impact on the capabilities of the 'al-Qaeda hardcore'. Interrogated militants said that the senior leadership had ordered that no groups of more than ten people remain together for more than ten minutes. Intercepted conversations between militants spoke of the difficulties of planning and meeting. It was obvious too that the systems which had once allowed fresh videos to be uploaded simultaneously on to dozens of servers remained significantly degraded.[8] By late 2010, communications were taking lengthy and circuitous routes to reach mainstream media organizations, and instead of well-produced videos, al-Qaeda was forced to return to using audiotapes.[9]

Beyond the operational environment, the broader strategic problems that had been gathering for the al-Qaeda leadership since the middle years of the decade were becoming acute. Jihadi internet forums often featured comments recognizing that no major attack had successfully been executed by al-Qaeda in the West for many years. The deaths of two senior Iraqi al-Qaeda leaders in a joint operation of American and Iraqi forces near Tikrit in April 2010 provoked an extraordinary outburst of criticism directed at the senior leadership. 'Al-Qaeda's media wing is lying and spreading false information. Everyone is tired of al-Qaeda's stupidity,' argued one user of a known jihadist forum.[10] In the ultra-competitive world of militancy, the risk for bin Laden and al-Zawahiri of being consigned to the role of pioneers whose best work was now behind them grew with every month that passed without a major attack for which they could convincingly claim the credit. In *The Vision*, a long treatise by an apparently experienced and senior militant that was published on the internet in 2010, bin Laden and al-Zawahiri's approach was damned with faint praise as 'useful at a particular time'.[11] The threat to their influence from younger, more credible figures such as the English-speaking al-Awlaki, the cleric who had inspired Choudhry and others, continued to grow. Al-Awlaki had a Facebook page with 4,800 'friends'. Bin Laden, once so quick to master the potential of new communications technology and forms of networking, did not. The contributions of charismatic figures who had recently been inducted into the al-Qaeda senior leadership's ranks such as the Bagram escapee Abu Yahya al-Libi could only go so far in maintaining al-Qaeda's appeal among a generation for whom the 9/11 attacks were ancient history. Superficial gestures like al-Zawahiri appearing in videos without his thick glasses did not help much either. Then there was the ongoing revisionist challenge from within the movement. Some of the criticism was mild. Some was fierce. One frequent theme was the mounting proportion of Muslims to Westerners killed in militant violence, an inevitable result of the increasingly indiscriminate nature of attacks.[12]

This was one reason, of course, for the continuing failure to gain real traction over significant masses of the population. The number of volunteers making their way to the FATA indicated that al-Qaeda still had the power to attract sufficient individuals to sustain its existence for the foreseeable future – the primary task of any clandestine militant outfit – but there was no indication through 2010 that the decline in support amid populations more generally in the Islamic world or in the West was going to be reversed. Attempts to make the al-Qaeda message more 'locally specific' appeared to have little effect.[13] Nor did a sudden interest in new issues such as climate change. 'The number of victims caused by climate change is very big … bigger than the victims of wars,' bin Laden said in a video in October 2010. The al-Qaeda leader even proposed the creation of a new aid organization to help Muslims, an astonishing turnaround for the leader of a group founded with the explicit aim of forgoing social activism in favour of direct action. 'The famine and drought in Africa that we see and the flooding in Pakistan and other parts of the world, with thousands dead along with millions of refugees, that's why people with hearts should move quickly to save their brothers and sisters,' bin Laden told his audience. But the sudden interest in global warming and humanitarianism merely reinforced the impression of an individual whose prime had passed trying, with almost painful artifice, to keep up with the times.[14]

Beyond the hardcore was what the early analysis of al-Qaeda had identified as the 'network of networks', or 'affiliates'. This too had changed hugely over the course of the 9/11 Wars. By 2010, many of those groups once drawn into the mesh of alliances, fealty and shared obligations woven by bin Laden through the 1990s had simply ceased to exist, such as the smaller Kurdistan-based militant factions or the Singapore-based groups which had solicited logistic support from al-Qaeda back in 2000 and 2001. Others had abandoned the fight, such as the Indonesian Jemaa Islamiya. Never more than very tangentially linked to al-Qaeda, the leaders of the latter had decided by the end of the decade, in another example of how local considerations often trump global solidarity, that they should abandon the jihad 'at home'. This, they said, was because conditions in Indonesia no longer justified armed struggle, though they still considered the jihad 'abroad' potentially legitimate.[15] When the veteran Indonesian militant leader Noordin Top was killed in September 2009, his 'al-Qoida of the Malayan Peninsula', named in homage to his hero, Ayman al-Zawahiri, died too.[16] There was no sign that the rapid decline of Al-Qaeda in Saudi Arabia and Al-Qaeda in the Maghreb (AQIM), discussed in Chapter 15, had even slowed, let alone been reversed.

Nor were those groups which had joined the network, at least nominally, much help in restoring al-Qaeda's fortunes. One was al-Shabab, a radical splinter from the Islamic Courts Union movement which had been able to briefly seize power in Somalia before being ejected from Mogadishu by Ethiopian troops in an American-backed offensive in 2006. A senior figure within al-Shabab, Saleh Ali Saleh Nabhan, had suddenly pledged allegiance to bin Laden in September 2008 in a video released to the internet. As had been the case for the Algerians two years previously, the appeal to the al-Qaeda leadership was prompted by a loss of local popularity and legitimacy largely due to al-Shabab's harshness and incompetence.[17] However, again in a parallel with developments elsewhere, the enrolment of al-Shabab as supposed affiliates brought little real benefits for the al-Qaeda hardcore. When, in July 2010, al-Shabab blew up restaurants in Kampala, Uganda, and thus executed their first international attack, they did so following a purely regional strategic logic of threatening a local state on the point of reinforcing its contingent of peacekeepers in Somalia. The attack was not on the orders of al-Qaeda's senior leadership and did not fit particularly with any broader strategic agenda. Indeed, it was criticized as counterproductive by a variety of senior core al-Qaeda figures both publicly on internet forums and privately in communications intercepted by American and other security agencies.[18] By late 2010, the least one could say was that the 'network of networks' was battered and disjointed. In many ways, it had simply ceased to exist.

There was one area, however, where al-Qaeda had achieved undeniable success. What cases like that of Faisal Shahzad and Roshonara

Choudhry showed was that bin Laden and his associates had been able to attain at least one of their major strategic aims: to disseminate the al-Qaeda worldview – the ideology, the third element of the post-2001 analysis – to a huge new audience, even if their own role within global Islamic militancy was now diminished. That worldview, increasingly relayed by stand-alone, independent poles of militant activity such as those constituted by al-Qaeda in the Yemen, by the Pakistani Taliban and increasingly by groups like Lashkar-e-Toiba, was more widespread than ever before. Shahzad told a court that he was a '*mujahid*' acting to defend Muslims against aggression in which all the people in Times Square that night, even children, were complicit. 'I am part of the answer to the US terrorising the Muslim nations,' he said. 'We Muslims are one community. We're not divided.'[19] Roshonara Choudhry had confessed immediately after her arrest, telling police she had stabbed the MP because 'as Muslims we're all brothers and sisters and we should all look out for each other and we shouldn't sit back and do nothing while others suffer. We shouldn't allow the people who oppress us to get away with it and to think that they can do whatever they want to us and we're just gonna lie down and take it.' Choudhry barely spoke at her trial, but after the sentence was passed, a group of men in the public gallery began shouting 'Allahu akbar', 'British go to hell', and 'Curse the judge'.[20]

This phenomenon was particularly clear in the USA. As ever, the number of people actively involved in violent activism was minuscule in comparison with the general population but were nonetheless higher than it had been since 2001.[21] Analysts spoke of signs that American Muslims, long considered immune to the radicalizing effects of the ongoing conflict and extreme ideologies due to their economic and social success in America and their high levels of education and wealthier origins, were finally following European Muslim communities towards a higher relative level of activism, radicalization and alienation. 'Jihadism' attracted a range of odd misfits too, drawn to militancy as to a cult. There were question marks over many of the investigations – not least because the FBI made liberal use of sting operations involving agents provocateurs – but nonetheless it was clear that many of those involved had indeed followed a similar route into radicalism to that of European, especially British, militants. The case of Shahzad, the Times Square bomber, was a classic example of self-radicalization by a deeply troubled individual who found in radical Islam the legitimization and

15. When in late 2005 a Danish newspaper printed cartoons of the Prophet Mohammed, a group of local clerics set out to create outrage and succeeded in provoking protests across the Islamic world. Religious leaders and governments competed in the rush to capitalize on the anger many Muslims felt. Most demonstrations – such as this by Hamas supporters in Gaza – were peaceful. Some were violent. The affair seemed to confirm a clash of civilizations.

16. In autumn 2005, riots broke out in poor urban areas across France. Young men of immigrant origin burned vehicles such as this bus in Toulouse, attacked schools and clashed with police. Though many feared 20 million European Muslims were becoming radicalized, in fact, religion played no part in the disturbances, hinting that the overwhelming pessimism of the fourth year of the 9/11 Wars was perhaps misplaced.

17. This thirty-five-year-old female suicide bomber sent by al-Zarqawi from the Iraqi city of Ramadi failed to detonate her device at a wedding reception in Amman, the capital of Jordan, in November 2005. Her husband and two others did, however, killing fifty-seven. Her brother had been killed by US forces in fighting in Iraq.

18. The Amman attack marked a turning point. Before, support for al-Qaeda and the insurgents in Iraq had been high in Jordan. Afterwards, it plummeted. The demonstrations against terrorism in Amman, such as the candlelit vigil pictured here, showed how it is easier to support global terrorism when the bombs explode elsewhere than when it is familiar places or people that are under attack. From 2006, the fortunes of al-Qaeda began to decline.

19. Tony Blair left office after ten years in power shortly after this visit to Iraq in May 2007. His record as prime minister was dominated by the controversial UK involvement in the 9/11 Wars. Ironically, the moment of his departure saw a relative stabilization in Iraq as US troops mounted a 'Surge' into Baghdad and the surrounding areas.

20. By 2007, blast walls were going up all over Afghanistan. The author took this picture in a factory on the outskirts of Kabul, where scores of labourers worked to meet the demand for the concrete barriers, a distinctive sight of the 9/11 Wars. 'Business is good,' the owner said, sadly.

21. Benazir Bhutto played only a small role in the 9/11 Wars but was a prominent victim. After years in exile she came back to Pakistan in October 2007 and was assassinated three months later. This picture was taken only hours before she was killed. Afghan President Hamid Karzai, on her right, remains alive and controversial.

22. Taj Hotel on fire. In November 2008 a team of Pakistani suicide attackers from the Lashkar-e-Toiba organization attacked hotels and other sites in Mumbai, the Indian commercial capital, killing more than 150 people. Documents later revealed how the group's senior leadership had sanctioned the strike under huge pressure from hardline elements within their ranks – and that at least low-level officials of the ISI, the main Pakistani military intelligence service, knew about it in advance.

23. Western policy towards narcotics in Afghanistan was muddled and poorly resourced. It was soon too late to do much about the burgeoning industry. The same was true of counter-insurgency efforts. Here British troops patrol in Helmand, the drug-ridden southern province.

24. By 2008, Western publics were tired of the war in Afghanistan. Policy-makers saw a massive expansion of local troops as a potential way out. Here, new recruits train at an Afghan National Army camp near Kabul. But such forces depended very heavily on the coalition. In some areas they still gained some local support as the 'least bad' option.

25. In 2008, a new war was added to the complex of conflicts that was the 9/11 Wars, when the Pakistani army pushed into areas along the border with Afghanistan that had fallen under the influence of local militants. The agency of Bajaur, used as an occasional base by al-Qaeda figures and as a rear area by insurgents in Afghanistan, saw fierce fighting. Pakistani troops like these had mixed sentiments about their enemy and the West.

26. This American officer – Captain José Vasquez – was deployed in Logar province in 2009, trying to reclaim the hinterland of Kabul. But progress was slow. The Taliban avoided a straight fight, preferring to outlast not outfight their well-equipped and well-armed enemy. In a week's operations, Vasquez, his men and the author did not glimpse a single insurgent.

27. Protesters in Tahrir Square, Cairo. Through the early months of 2011, crowds of young people, often mobilized through social networking, achieved in weeks what al-Qaeda had been unable to in decades: depose long-term rulers in Egypt and in Tunisia as well as shake others elsewhere. Angry and alienated, they called for democracy in non-violent protests which were a stunning rejection of radical Islam.

28. This image of anti-Mubarak demonstrators praying over an Egyptian flag on February 5 at Tahrir Square is a reminder of three crucial lessons of the 9/11 Wars: the importance of local identity, the enduring strength of the nation state and the depth of a new conservatism and new cultural religious identity which – though not incompatible with democracy – will be hugely influential on politics and society in the Middle East and beyond in coming years.

encouragement for acts that he may well have already been contemplating. There were many others. One was the case of Nidal Hasan, an American army major at the military base of Fort Hood in Texas, who shot thirteen of his colleagues in November 2009. Michael Leiter, director of the US National Counterterrorism Center, described plots disrupted in New York, North Carolina, Arkansas, Alaska, Texas and Illinois during 2010 as 'unrelated operationally but ... indicative of a collective subculture and a common cause that rallies independent extremists to want to attack the Homeland'.[22] A journey to the country of their or their parents' birth was often a key element in the radicalization process of young Americans. By 2010, at least twenty Somali Americans were active in the ranks of al-Shabab, and one, Omar Hammami, had become a local field commander and jihadi internet celebrity.[23] Most recruits showed the same low level of religious knowledge as their European counterparts too. Generational tensions within families also played a role for some.

Above all, it was the widely disseminated extremist worldview popularized by bin Laden but taken forward by al-Awlaki and others that was important. In the summer of 2010, al-Awlaki and al-Qaeda in the Yemen had launched an English-language internet magazine called *Inspire*. This had global penetration. From the Arabian peninsula to the USA to the UK, the range of the extremists' propaganda machine remained impressive, even if the hardcore leadership of the network had met with serious reverses. Mentioned by US officials as a serious threat, downloaded copies of *Inspire* were found by police in the UK conducting searches after the arrests of twelve young Britons of Bangladeshi origin suspected of planning a series of bomb attacks in Britain over Christmas 2010. One article was entitled 'How to make a pipe bomb in the kitchen of your mom'; others included 'What to expect in jihad' and 'Tips for our brothers in the US'.[24] The youngest of those arrested for the 'Christmas terror plot' was nineteen and thus only ten years old at the time of the 9/11 attacks. The youth of such suspects reinforced the sense that, though the hardcore and the network of networks were in some difficulty, the 'al-Qaeda-ist' ideology had created a movement with its own distinctive principles, modes of action and momentum. Beyond the major clusters of the well-known organizations, that movement was composed of individuals or small groups. These latter were too small to have a name, often well below the radar of security services, sometimes patched together by mutual association and often simply autonomous. At its most dispersed, but most widespread, level, this movement was little more than a way of thinking, a way of understanding the world, an identity with its own dress codes, ideas, values, rituals and prescribed behaviour, its own self-sustaining culture. Transmitted through peers, through the media, at schools, colleges, at sports clubs or prayer groups alike, from parents to children, from brothers to sisters, through internet magazines and carefully crafted videos, this movement was resilient and deeply rooted. This was not the 'global Intifada' that al-Suri had hoped for. Nor was it the mass mobilization that al-Qaeda leaders had set out to achieve – even if it assured them sufficient recruits to survive as a clandestine organization for the foreseeable future. But it was something that had not existed a decade before. It was one of the real – and worst – legacies of the 9/11 Wars.

## THE END OF THE FIRST DECADE

If the evolution of al-Qaeda and its affiliates during 2010 and the early part of 2011 continued on broad lines established over previous years, so too did developments in Afghanistan and Pakistan.

In the former, the Taliban continued to have problems. Up to 200 mid-level commanders and operatives were being killed every month by the coalition special forces units and their Afghan auxiliaries in the 'night raids', and, with public support for the insurgents as variable as ever, the movement's leaders were forced to turn to tactics that risked further damage to their popularity. Through 2010 suicide attacks occurred at a rate of about three per week and the use of IEDs nearly doubled.[25] These latter accounted alone for around a third of Afghan civilians killed or wounded over the year.[26] Another sign of weakness was that the insurgents intensified their unpopular and increasingly brutal campaign of assassinations and intimidation, even, in a series of well-publicized incidents, targeting children.[27] Discipline and unity continued to be problems. Many of the older Taliban field commanders were now battle-weary and resentful of the senior leadership secure in Pakistan. Tensions and competition with other insurgent groups – Hekmatyar's fighters or the 'Haqqani network' – were often sharp. The very young commanders replacing the more experienced men killed in the special forces raids often had no memory of the 1990s, no understanding of the original mission of the Taliban and no respect for the hierarchy. Orders given before the 2011 spring offensive once again stressed the twin causes of nation and of Islam. More fragmented than ever, increasingly contaminated by criminal elements, the movement remained a largely local phenomenon, however. Even if many wintered in Pakistan, between 80 and 90 per cent of Taliban captured or killed were found within 12 miles of their home villages.[28]

Yet the reinforced international coalition, now commanded directly by General David Petraeus after McChrystal was sacked for effective insubordination in July, still struggled to achieve a breakthrough. In many areas massive application of resources had undeniably made a difference.[29] In Marjah, a force of 2,000 Marines spending a million dollars a month on development projects, backed by 300 policemen, 700 Afghan National Army soldiers and, controversially, an 800-strong locally raised militia had imposed some kind of order. But there was no way such resources could be committed even across the whole of the south. Kandahar and its surrounding districts appeared more secure, so too was the immediate hinterland of Kabul. But countrywide the violence was as intense as anything seen since 2001. In Wardak and Logar, many of the 'ideological' Taliban had been driven out, but warlordism and criminal violence were rife. In the north, insurgent influence had grown. Afghan security forces were expanding rapidly, with better training and equipment, but governance was still grotesquely flawed. Corruption was worse than ever and, along with simple incompetence, still crippled efforts to deliver basic services. Though officials rightly pointed to millions of children in thousands of new schools and effective vaccination programmes, any improvements in the police or justice system were, at best, incremental. Much of the population continued to prefer the swift and honest Taliban-run courts. Very large quantities of drugs continued to be produced. Pressurized by domestic opinion and failing finances, Western political leaders continued their increasingly desperate search for some kind of relatively dignified exit. Every few months there were new reports of talks with the insurgent leadership. A Quetta-based shopkeeper posing as a senior commander with access to Mullah Omar was paid a large sum of money and flown to Kabul. Other envoys moved back and forth. The most senior figures in the US administration attempted to persuade Pakistan's security services to deliver potential interlocutors all while trying to convince a sceptical American public that withdrawing troops from July 2011 onwards was not an admission of partial defeat and that a total 'transition' to local control in Afghanistan, now scheduled for 2014, did not imply failure. Disagreements within the Obama adminstration and between allies over exactly what might happen if some kind of deal was concluded with the Taliban continued. Would the movement host al-Qaeda as before? Would they act more reasonably than in the 1990s? Was any kind of inclusive political settlement even possible or desirable? But such questions were rapidly becoming academic. The West was on the way out of Afghanistan. It was only a matter of time.[30]

Across the border in Pakistan, broad trends established over the previous years continued too. Catastrophic floods in the summer of 2010 led to a temporary halt in the ongoing violence but had a variety of hugely negative effects well beyond the immediate humanitarian impact. Vast grain stocks were destroyed, livestock wiped out, roads and power lines washed away, and millions made homeless. Not only did the state show itself to be corrupt and incompetent, but many landlords failed to respond to the needs of communities who had worked their fields for generations. The deference and hierarchies already under such strain were further degraded. The floods also accelerated the migration of populations from rural areas to the cities, with millions of refugees from the countryside seeking refuge in the urban centres. In Karachi, the influx altered the ethnic and political balance of the city, provoking violence which killed dozens in October 2010. Elsewhere the population of migrants simply swelled the reservoirs of the rootless, displaced urban working class or lower middle class, the classic constituency for political Islamists. The weak and unstable government of Asif Ali Zardari proved as incapable of managing the natural catastrophe as it was of managing the various man-made disasters affecting Pakistan. Even without the floods, the economy was in very deep trouble, with negative or negligible growth and runaway inflation.

Nor, despite the problems at home, was there any sign of change in the Pakistani security establishment's basic strategic vision or understanding of its nation's interests. Even two years after the Mumbai attacks, only token measures had been taken to find and incarcerate those responsible, for example. Individuals like Hafiz Saeed, the founder and effective leader of Lashkar-e-Toiba, continued to be viewed as potential strategic assets rather than as dangerous liabilities.[31] With every indication being that the Pakistanis' 'spoiling' strategy in Afghanistan was likely to be successful there was little reason for much change there either. The Pakistani security establishment was still committed to making sure they had a de facto right of veto, via their support for Taliban elements, over any political settlement in Afghanistan. There was no major assault by the army into North Waziristan, despite strong American pressure. Militant attacks, often indiscriminate, continued to intensify. In December, forty-five died when a suicide bomber – possibly a woman – detonated a device among a crowd queuing to receive United Nations food aid. In all 2010 saw 2,113 militant, insurgent and sectarian attacks, in which 2,193 people died and nearly 6,000 were injured.[32] In January 2011, Salman Taseer, the moderate and outspoken governor of the Punjab, was shot dead in Islamabad by one of his own bodyguards, who was led away smiling after the murder. Taseer was killed for having vocally supported a Christian woman who had been accused of blasphemy and faced the death sentence. The lack of explicit condemnation by many of Pakistan's political leaders was as striking as the public celebration that accompanied his killing in some places. More than 1,000 lawyers volunteered to defend Taseer's killer for free. Clerics across the country condoned the assassination.[33] A month later, the shooting of two men by an American 'diplomat', in fact a CIA contractor, in Lahore led to a protracted diplomatic row and a new low for relations between Pakistan and the USA. If the summer of 2010 had been bloody, that of 2011 promised to be worse.

Then there was Iraq. Here again the broad trends established in recent years continued. Iraq still teetered between slow but definitive improvement and rapid regression. The bombings of government forces and religious minorities perpetrated by the various networks linked to al-Qaeda, who hoped to restart the sectarian civil war of 2004 to 2007, killed hundreds through the summer of 2010 and intensified as the autumn went on. The daily average of deaths from suicide bombs or gunfire and executions in Iraq through 2010 was 17.34, which maintained the country's position as the most violent place in terms of terrorism in the world.[35] More than 150 people – 89 civilians, 41 police and 21 soldiers – were killed in December 2010 alone.[36] The social conservatism of the Shia working classes and most Sunnis continued to broaden and deepen. There was little sign that the dangerous politicization of the security forces was at all diminished. The economic situation of most people saw little if any amelioration. For much of the year, the political process was paralysed. Elections in March had resulted in an impasse. The more moderate secular and non-sectarian party of Ayad Allawi had won the polls by a slim margin but finally – after ten or more months of negotiations – it was the incumbent, Nouri al-Maliki, who formed a government. The end of the American combat mission in Iraq on August 31, 2010 and the subsequent draw-down of troops was marked by widespread violence which, though anticipated, nonetheless shook many. The Kurds in the north continued to separate themselves economically, culturally and politically from the rest of the country. Major problems such as the future of the contested city of Kirkuk or the partition of the growing oil revenues remained unresolved, potential flashpoints for future strife. In January 2011, Muqtada al-Sadr returned to Iraq from Iran, where he had spent much of the previous four years studying to become an ayatollah. The thirty-seven-year-old cleric, whose representatives had won enough seats in the parliamentary elections to play a deciding role in the subsequent negotiations, spoke first at Najaf, the holy city. He gave thanks to God for the successful transition of his al-Mahdi Army into a political party, pledged support to the government and promised to fight on against 'our joint enemy: America, Israel and Britain'.[37] Both inside and outside Iraq, many watched nervously. 'I am happy that the US leave but they left a destroyed country controlled by bad people,' said Amal Kamel, a twenty-year-old student at a Baghdad college.[38]

Yet anyone who sensed a renewed drift into stagnation in the Middle East as 2010 turned to 2011 was about to be surprised. In early January 2011, food riots in Algeria had rattled the authorities and led to calls to calm – 'Islam is serenity' – from government-backed clerics as the youthful population seethed. The regime had held on, but the disturbances presaged a greater upheaval. First it was the turn of Tunisia, where the self-immolation of an out-of-work graduate who had tried to eke out a living as a fruit and vegetable seller triggered an uprising that led to the deposition of the corrupt and repressive president, Zine el Abidine ben Ali. From Tunisia, with its population of 10 million, the spirit of rebellion spread. Within a week of ben Ali's downfall, crowds had poured onto the streets in Egypt, calling for an end to the thirty-one-year rule of President Hosni Mubarak. After three further weeks of extraordinary scenes, of battles in central Cairo between protestors and pro-Mubarak thugs, a settlement was reached which saw the veteran leader deposed and the army effectively take power pending elections in the autumn. The news immediately sparked demonstrations in Bahrain, Kuwait, Algeria, Yemen, Syria, Morocco and in Colonel Gaddafi's Libya. In the latter the protests, first repressed with the loss of hundreds of lives, turned into a fully fledged revolt as the Libyan leader's extensive security apparatus collapsed across much of the country. With some irony, bulldozers brought in for the use of the scores of overseas companies that had moved into Libya since Gaddafi had opened its economy to foreign investment a decade before were used to attack military bases in and around Benghazi, the eastern port city two hours' drive from the Egyptian border, which soon became the de facto capital of 'Free Libya'. Gaddafi and those security forces which remained loyal hit back, bloodily retaking towns to the west of Tripoli and fighting their way east along the coast towards the rebel strongholds until forced to halt by airstrikes involving French jets and British and American missiles that, this time, were sanctioned by the United Nations Security Council. By the third week of March, the 'Arab Spring' had seen popular pressure achieve in the space of just over two months what decades of Islamic militant activism had been unable to do: unseat two of the hated 'hypocrite, apostate' dictators of the Middle East, destabilize the rule of a third and mobilize hundreds of millions across the entire region. An entirely new political, social, cultural and ideological cycle in the region appeared to be starting.

Yet, though undoubtedly constituting a radical break, these events could only be properly understood and explained by reference to the more general effects and evolution of the 9/11 Wars. Indeed, the events of early 2011 reinforced rather than contradicted a number of key trends and key lessons picked out earlier in this narrative. The first was that violence, revolt and revolution in the Islamic world is not rooted simply in a supposed clash between reactionary societies and 'modernity' in the form of the West; nor do they depend solely on the actions or interventions of Western leaders. No society is fixed, changeless or stuck in a 'medieval time-warp'. One of the reasons many observers were taken by surprise by the events of early 2011 was the perception that places like Egypt, Libya or Bahrain had somehow been bypassed by the major political, cultural, technological developments elsewhere. The Arab world, in the words of one prominent commentator, had been 'insulated from history for the last 50 years'.[39] This, of course, was total rubbish, as misleading as the descriptions of Saudi Arabia as a 'medieval monarchy' or Afghanistan as a 'thirteenth-century country', and further evidence of the stubborn Western tendency to see Muslim-majority societies as backward or timeless that had coloured so much policy-making and analysis with such damaging results for so long.[40] All countries in the Islamic world, as elsewhere in the developing world and beyond, had undergone a series of dynamic, unpredictable and complex internal transitions in recent decades which, if perhaps less than evident to outside observers, were no less profound for all that. Across the Middle East, the decades of political stasis had disguised rapid social evolution.[41] In Egypt, it was the combination of new economic growth – up to 8 per cent in 2007, only slightly less in the following years – with old cronyism, corruption, patronage and increasingly extreme inequality that proved explosive. This came at a time when demographics ensured a very large population of young people, a critical minority of whom had acquired an unprecedented capacity for social and political organization through the use of new social media. The same was true of Libya, where the revolt started in the economically marginalized eastern zones which had not benefited from Gaddafi's tentative steps towards economic liberalization, and whose tribes were less loyal to the regime. In Libya, the technologically savvy Westernized middle class prominent among the protestors in Egypt were less evident. The rebellion there had slightly different roots, a more traditional structure and a more populist tone as a result. Unlike in Tunisia and Egypt, average levels of education had not been rising over previous years, and schoolteachers in the newly liberated port city of Benghazi pointed out the spelling mistakes in the revolutionary slogans daubed on walls to reporters.[42] However, whatever their exact age or background, as protestors spilled out on to streets across the whole region, they ensured that it became increasingly difficult to see the Muslim or Arab world as a reactionary brake on the rest of the planet's steady ride towards a prosperous, stable and peaceful 'modernity'.

The second element seen repeatedly over previous years and reinforced by the events of early 2011 was the contingent nature of the appeal of democracy. As stressed previously, there is nothing in the norms, customs and values of Muslim majority countries that is essentially incompatible with any given political system. In Iraq 'democracy' had been rejected by different communities for a variety of reasons. Chief amongst them was that democracy itself had become associated with an accelerated and damaging process of Westernization, with brutal measures of economic liberalization and with the mismanagement typical of the occupation. In Afghanistan, a similar situation prevailed. There too the word 'democracy' had acquired negative connotations for large numbers of people. Pollsters in 2010 found that for many Afghans 'democracy' did not simply mean elections and parliamentary politics but 'an entire package of Western liberal values, where freedom is equated with an absence of rules, immorality, and secularism'.[43] The same was also true, to an extent, in Pakistan, where a government drawn from a Westernized elite continually risked being seen as distant from authentic national values and was forced to compensate with populist measures and rhetoric, particularly against the USA, as a result. In those theatres that had hitherto been at the heart of the 9/11 Wars, democracy, though in theory nothing more than a neutral system, had become synonymous with an unwelcome process of Westernization. But in Egypt and Libya the context was very different. In Egypt the protests were against a leader who had been backed by the West for longer than most of the protestors had been alive and who was pursuing a liberal economic agenda in line with the recommendations of international institutions such as the World Bank. After surrendering his nuclear weapons programme in 2003, Colonel Gaddafi too had been viewed as an ally and commercial partner by London, Paris and, increasingly, Washington. For the protestors in Cairo and then in Benghazi, democracy thus was seen not as a foreign import alien to local culture and values which had been imposed upon them but the opposite.[44] Democracy was something denied them by their leaders with the complicity of the West. It did not mean Westernization but simply the freedom to chose one's own government. There was therefore no conflict between being a 'campaigner for democracy' and being an Egyptian, a Libyan, and an Arab or a Muslim.

Third, the events in Egypt and elsewhere showed the complex relationship between the growing social and religious conservatism of many Arab and Islamic societies and formal politics. Again, this has also been seen elsewhere, in Pakistan, for example, or in Indonesia. In Egypt, the Muslim Brotherhood played a minor role in the upheaval's early stages though its well-organized activists were important in later phases. In part this was due to the movement's elderly leadership's early tactical miscalculations but it was also because the narrative within which the protests were framed was not a religious one. Yet the *informal* influence of Islamism – of which the fundamental project is the appropriation of the modern state, not its destruction – on the behaviour, culture and worldviews of very large numbers of people over recent decades and particularly during the 9/11 Wars in places such as Egypt, Libya, Algeria and Jordan, as well as in Pakistan, Turkey, Morocco and Indonesia and elsewhere, could not be doubted. So, though surveys had showed that 59 per cent of Egyptians believed that democracy was preferable to any other form of government, the same polls also revealed that 85 per cent also thought that Islam's influence in politics was positive.[45] A crowd of 200,000 turned out to hear Yusuf al-Qaradawi, the conservative Egyptian theologian who had last preached in his homeland thirty years before and who had a decade earlier tried to dissuade the Taliban from destroying the Bamiyan Buddhas, lead Friday prayers in Tahrir Square and speak of an 'unfinished revolution'.[46] Before the courthouse in Benghazi in the second week of March, a reporter noted that, behind those shouting 'Free Libya' and playing Arab pop music over loud-speakers, was another crowd, twenty ranks deep and chanting prayers. 'Re-Islamization' – the wave of conservatism that had spread across the Islamic world through the 9/11 Wars – might not have brought electoral success to the Muslim Brotherhood or other Islamist groups but had meant a different sort of quieter victory. This did not mean that the Egyptian protestors or the Libyan 'revolutionaries' or those risking the wrath of security forces in Syria, Bahrain or elsewhere were not committed democrats or that they did not believe in pluralism. But it did not make them secular either. Their religious culture and identity may have shifted out of the sphere of traditional political activity but was deep and strong nonetheless.

Fourthly, the demonstrations in Cairo and in other Middle Eastern cities and the fighting in Libya also saw a return and a reappropriation of each respective country's flag. This again reinforced trends seen elsewhere and over previous years. A thirty-two-year-old mother of three in the Yemen who had been leading demonstrations against the veteran president, Ali Abdullah Saleh – in power three years longer than even Mubarak had been – told one reporter that there was 'a race between Yemen and Algeria to see who would be next', revealing a sense of national pride that many had discounted as impossible in a region rent by tribalism, kinship ties or religion.[47] The 9/11 Wars had not only made clear, whatever the hyperbole about globalized identities, the sheer parochialism of the worldview of most people but also shown the remarkable resilience of the nation state, despite the obituaries prematurely written in the 1990s. Even militants in Pakistan had chosen to be the 'Pakistani Taliban'. The Afghan Taliban, for their part, went to great lengths to underline their nationalist credentials, which at the very least suggested that their leaders appreciated the resonance such rhetoric had. Only outsiders had ever seriously suggested the break-up of Iraq. Indeed, one of the many reasons al-Qaeda had lost support in 'the land of the two rivers' was that its attempt to appropriate local patriotic sentiment by renaming its affiliates 'the Islamic State of Iraq' had offended local nationalists, including potential allies among other insurgent groups and particularly former Ba'athists. The insults hurled at Tunisian president Ben Ali, Mubarak, Gaddafi, Saleh and others often revolved around the idea of 'treachery'. But those insulted were accused of being a traitor not to their religion, the key element of the Islamic militant discourse, but to the nation. Even protestors in the obviously artificial states of Bahrain or Kuwait, whose historic roots are slender, asserted their patriotic credentials as they demanded reform. Given the choice between the 'flat' globalized pan-Islamism of the extremists, with its almost total lack of local specificity, and 'the nation', the choice of the vast majority was clear. The Muslim Brotherhood, Jamaat Islami and other 'classic' or 'moderate' political Islamists had long recognized this and junked – or at least postponed – the universalizing 'pan-Islamic' project in favour of nationally based political and social activity. The wisdom of this pragmatic strategic choice was amply demonstrated when revolution finally came.

The challenge this new pluralist, democratizing nationalism posed in the spring of 2011 to al-Qaeda's internationalist ideologues and propagandists, coming on top of the evident rejection of their ideas and tactics by so many over previous years, was evident. Neither bin Laden's organization nor local groups, affiliated or otherwise, played even a marginal role in the upheavals that shook Tunisia and Egypt. The end to the rule of President Mubarak had been one of the primary aims in the minds of the founders of al-Qaeda back in the late 1980s, yet it took almost a month before the group made a statement on the most significant popular upheaval in the Arab world for many decades. The delay spoke volumes. The message when it came was tired and irrelevant. One significant component of the dissent sweeping the Middle East was the impatience and frustration felt by the young at being lectured by their elders, whether those elders, supposed to be held in such deference but so often incompetent or self-seeking or both, were eighty-two-year-old presidents, aged generals, kings, establishment scholars or radical ideologues. This appeared to have been entirely lost on the al-Qaeda senior leadership. Dismissing Mubarak as 'the biggest Arab Zionist', fifty-nine-year-old Ayman al-Zawahiri warned that democracy meant 'that sovereignty is subject to the desires of the majority, without committing to any quality, value or creed'.[48] His views on Egypt could not have been more distant from the sentiments expressed by those participating in the unrest and apparently shared by so many others. The senior leadership of al-Qaeda had apparently little to say about events in Libya either, even as once again a Western-led military operation was launched against an Arab, Muslim-majority state. In Tunisia, it had been the spectacular and public suicide of fruit and vegetable seller Mohammed Bouazizi – in which no one else was hurt – that had set off the uprising that overturned the regime of ben Ali. It was almost impossible to imagine an act that would undermine the tactics of al-Qaeda – suicides in which many people, often entirely innocent, were killed or maimed – more effectively. The same could be said for demonstrators in Syria, Bahrain and elsewhere, all of whom were resolutely non-violent. The geographic, organizational, ideological and cultural marginalization of both al-Qaeda in particular and of extremist radical Islam more generally had been increasingly evident for several years. The upheavals that shook the Arab and Islamic worlds in the early spring of 2011 made it blindingly obvious. Throughout them all, bin Laden remained silent.

However, despite so much apparent justification for a rare if relative optimism about the future evolution of state and society in the Middle East, two final elements nonetheless gave pause for thought. The first was uncertainty about the degree to which the young, web-surfing, often highly educated urban-based activists who had led the protests – described by *Time*, *Newsweek* and other major publications as 'the generation that is changing the world' – actually were as representative of their societies as they were portrayed to be in the West. The courage and organizational capabilities of such men and women were undoubted. But the question of how widely people in small towns, in rural areas or in the slums, whether young or old, shared their values and vision of the future still remained to be resolved. The second element that should have tempered the hopes of a shining new future, justifiable though they might have been, was the weight of expectation the events of the spring of 2011 had generated. For the successive uprisings had revealed the depth of the problems – social, political, economic – confronting the region. A quick historical survey showed the extent to which it had always been the young that had brought change, backing successive projects of reform and national revival, in the region's recent history. Each of these projects – secular nationalism, pan-Arab Socialism, Islamism, post-Islamist local violent militancy – had disappointed. It was this series of failures that had made bin Laden's new hybrid blend of religion, politics, tradition and innovation so attractive and had led, in the late 1990s, a small but significant number of young men to set out for the camps of Afghanistan. If, as a new transformative ideology swept the region in early 2011, there was one thing of which all observers could be sure it was that renewed disappointment would cut deep into the fragile fabric of already battered societies and would affect the young, now as expectant and as motivated as ever before, more than anyone. The challenge of meeting these expectations was a very great one.


## THE END OF BIN LADEN

Bin Laden had in fact been working on a new communiqué giving his views on the Arab Spring. Recorded some time in March or April, it would only be released posthumously. On May 2, just after midnight, the fifty-four-year al-Qaeda leader was shot dead by American special forces in the bedroom of a three-storey house set behind high walls in the northern Pakistani garrison town of Abbottabad. By the time the speech was finally uploaded on to an extremist internet forum, its author had been dead for three weeks.

Bin Laden did not die as either he or his followers had hoped. Unarmed at the moment of death, neither he nor the three other men in the house put up any significant resistance. There was no spectacular martyrdom. The seventy-nine Navy SEALs who assaulted the compound came under fire for a few moments at the beginning of the raid, but that was all. The al-Qaeda leader was surrounded not by loyal retainers fighting to the last but by his three wives, his children and grandchildren. Bin Laden's twenty-two-year-old son Khaled was killed with his father. Their bodies were flown out to an aircraft carrier in the Arabian Sea and, after some kind of religious rite had been performed, slid beneath the waves.

The other two men killed in the assault were Pakistani brothers. One of them had inadvertently led the CIA to bin Laden. His name was Arshad Khan, though for many years the agency had only known his *nisbah*, or *nom de guerre*, Abu Ahmad al-Kuwaiti. He had long been of interest, ever since his name had surfaced repeatedly in the interrogations of detainees in the years after 9/11. He was clearly trusted and relatively senior, a veteran associate of the leadership. His exact role, however, was unclear. Major figures such as Khaled Sheikh Mohammed were evasive when questioned about him, encouraging the CIA to focus further resources on tracking him down.

In 2007, the agency discovered that their target was not al-Kuwaiti after all but a man called Mohammed Arshad Khan, who, though he had brought up in the Gulf state, was of Pakistani nationality. Fluent in Arabic, Urdu and Pashto, Khan could communicate with foreign militants and locals in the North West Frontier Province as well as more generally across Pakistan. One reason for the breakthrough was a new understanding, in part gleaned from operations in Iraq, of the nature of militant groups. Instead of working their way up the vertical hierarchy of al-Qaeda, investigators had built up a picture of horizontal networks instead, creating vast maps of the potential connections and functions of target individuals. In 2009, they got a phone number for Arshad Khan. Using new software and communications technology to detect phone calls and emails and then further map the webs of connections between them, the CIA created models of his personal relationships. A year later, Pakistani agents working for the Americans located their target in Peshawar. He was followed to the Abbottabad house, which was put under observation. By April, no positive identification of bin Laden had been achieved, but the tall man who was seen pacing the garden of the home alone for long periods was judged to be the al-Qaeda leader, and a raid went ahead.[49] 'We can say to those families who lost loved ones to al-Qaeda's terror: justice has been done,' Obama told the American nation in a television address hours later. The death should be welcomed by all who believe in peace and dignity, the president said. Whatever the arguments over international law, sovereignty or the manner of bin Laden's killing, it was difficult to argue with either sentiment.[50]

The Navy SEALs collected computers, stacks of documents and scores of hard drives and USB keys from the compound where bin Laden had been living. They left the children, the wives and the bodies of the two brothers. The youngest wife, a twenty-nine-year-old Yemeni who had married bin Laden eleven years earlier, told Pakistani security forces who arrived on the scene after the Americans had left that she and her daughter, ten-year-old Safiya, had lived in the compound for five years.[51] This raised the possibility that bin Laden had been in Abbottabad for half a decade. With hindsight, there was nothing that indicated that this might not have been the case. It appeared that bin Laden, having almost certainly spent years immediately after his flight from Afghanistan either in a major Pakistani city or more likely in the FATA, had indeed decided to trade operational effectiveness for security, probably moving into the Abbottabad safehouse soon after it was completed in 2005. The house had no internet access or telephone lines, and communication, the CIA team examining the material seized there soon found, had relied on a laborious system by which bin Laden would write emails that would then be sent by a courier, usually one of the two brothers, from a distant internet café. He had, however, been kept aware of developments within al-Qaeda and its affiliate groups and of ongoing plans for attacks. A notebook found by the Americans was full of jottings: a calculation of how many US citizens would have to be killed to force Washington to disengage entirely from the Middle East, remarks on the suitability of various candidates for senior positions within the group, comments on which American officials other than the president it was worth targeting and apparent outrage over a suggestion by one contributor to the magazine *Inspire* that a farm machine or tractor be fitted with blades for an attack in America. This, bin Laden tetchily noted, he could not endorse as it would lead to 'indiscriminate killing' and was thus not 'something that reflects what al-Qaeda does'.[52] There were also indications that bin Laden was planning – or perhaps simply dreaming of – a bid to unite all the disparate factions fighting the US-led coalition in Afghanistan into a grand alliance under his leadership. This would have been the al-Qaeda leader's most ambitious attempt to date to appropriate a local struggle for his own global one.[53]

The death of bin Laden naturally raised many questions. What, many asked, was the al-Qaeda leader doing in Abbottabad? With relatively good road links in all directions, including into rugged terrain to the north-west, from where Afghanistan or the militant stronghold of Bajaur would not be too hard to reach, the town had certain advantages. That the safehouse was in a discreet suburb favoured by retired army officers and was close to Pakistan's main military academy clearly posed a risk but also offered freedom from fear of missile attack and the benefits of being genuinely seen as a highly unlikely place for the world's most wanted fugitive to hide. The chief attraction, of course, was, in the often makeshift, make-do world of militancy, that the safehouse already existed, created by Arshad Khan.

Did someone in the Pakistani security establishment know of bin Laden's presence in Abbottabad? Though sympathy for much of what bin Laden stood for was deep in the ISI, in the army and among the population at large, it seems likely that the al-Qaeda leader's ability to hide 'in plain sight' was more evidence of the institutional weakness of the country, the incompetence of senior officers and of systemic failure within the intelligence services than anything more sinister. Though there was plenty of evidence of support for local and regional Islamic extremists by the ISI, there was no solid proof of the agency ever assisting international militants. Indeed, the record of the ISI when it came to operations against such figures was relatively good. In the absence of hard evidence, the ISI, though justifiably criticized for its role in supporting insurgents in Afghanistan and for running, with increasing difficulty, Pakistani militant groups like Lashkar-e-Toiba, was probably not directly implicated in sheltering bin Laden. The fact that, according to references among the data seized in the compound, there were indications that, around a year before he died, bin Laden himself had pondered a possible truce with local Pakistani authorities, along the lines of that which militants in London in the 1990s had thought they had concluded with the British government, reinforces this conclusion.[54]

The question of the complicity – or stunning incompetence – of Pakistan's security establishment naturally had a regional dimension. The death of bin Laden immediately triggered another crisis in Pakistani–American relations, already at a low point. Behind the rhetoric, though, the think-ing in Washington remained that Pakistan was simply 'too big to be allowed fail' and that continuing aid, though perhaps with better focus and criteria, needed to be made available even if patience with the coun-try's security establishment was wearing extremely thin. Demands were made again for the detention or 'rendering' of Mullah Mohammed Omar and several other senior militants, but more in hope than in anticipation of any immediate action. Pakistani public reaction swung between a vociferous assertion of a variety of conspiracy theories, anger at the army, anger at the Americans and anger at bin Laden. A major theme was a diffuse, inchoate but nonetheless real sense of shame.

The real 'game changer', however, was in Afghanistan. With bin Laden gone, not only was Obama (and to some extent key allies such as the UK) presented with an opportunity to accelerate the drawdown of forces there, scheduled to begin in the summer, but the president, with eighteen months to go before an election, now faced even greater diffi-culty in persuading domestic opinion that the long, gruelling and hugely expensive war in Afghanistan still needed to be fought. Less than 100 international militants were believed to be in Afghanistan in the spring of 2011, of whom only 'a handful' were interested in targeting the West.[55] US military expenditure alone there was nearly $10 billion each month. 'Are we moving towards transition? Yes. Are we trying to get out of Afghanistan as fast as we can? Absolutely not. There is no scurry for the exit,' insisted one US official in Kabul.[56] Allies such as the UK earnestly repeated the same sentiments all while trying to accelerate a political settlement by lifting sanctions on former Taliban. But with all Western activity in their country increasingly framed around 2014 – the agreed date by which international combat troops would be gone – such statements inevitably did little to reassure nervous Afghans. Many felt, not unreasonably, that once the soldiers had left aid and attention would disappear too. 'It will be chaos. It will be civil war. Everything we have gained will go,' Fatima Karimi, a twenty-nine-year-old student teacher, told the author as she picnicked with her family by a river on the out-skirts of Kabul a month and a day after bin Laden's death. Despite the spread of chicken, fried potato cakes, salad and melon, the atmosphere was far from festive. The Karimi family were from the Shia religious and Hazara ethnic minorities and had much to lose.[57] Kabul may have been calmer in the spring of 2011, but it was an anxious place.

For al-Qaeda, there was obviously the question of bin Laden's succession. This was never going to be a simple issue. Though al-Zawahiri was clearly the leading candidate to take on the leadership of al-Qaeda, his candidacy was not without controversy. Irascible, argumentative and lacking in charisma, even if his experience was respected, the fifty-nine-year-old Egyptian did not have universal support either within the 'hardcore' or among affiliates. Al-Zawahiri's pragmatism also angered the many middle-ranking militants committed to a purely literal extremist reading of Islamic texts.[58] As an Egyptian, he was less well placed than bin Laden had been as a Saudi to mediate between factions within the group. But the younger leaders like Abu Yahya al-Libi were far from ready to take on any such a high-profile role. Further fragmentation of the group, the networks, even the ideology appeared likely, at least in the short and mid term. Ten days after bin Laden's death a statement from al-Qaeda's al-Fajr online media centre issued a new call to arms. 'Do not consult anyone about killing Americans or destroying their economy,' the statement said. 'We ... incite you to carry out acts of individual terrorism with significant results, which only require basic preparation. We say to every *mujahed* Muslim, if there is an opportunity, do not waste it.' An appeal to the social movement created over previous years, this was the quintessential expression of a strategy of 'leaderless jihad'.

A week later, bin Laden's final public words were broadcast. The dead leader welcomed the Arab Spring and predicted, as he had done so many times before, 'winds of change blowing over the entire Muslim world'. There was little of the sanguinary rhetoric that had marked previous statements and no calls for violent attacks. 'Let the truth ring out,' bin Laden said. 'Remember those that go out with a sword are true believers, those that go fight with their tongue are true believers, and those that fight in their hearts are true believers.' The release of the tape was barely noticed in the Islamic world. Most people were much more interested in the news from Libya, where fighting between rebels and Gaddafi's forces continued amid Western air strikes, or from the Yemen, where President Ali Abdullah Saleh's regime appeared close to falling, or from Syria, where security forces had killed and tortured thousands in violent repression of protestors calling for democratic reform, than in the late bin Laden's familiar exhortations.

Elements of the material seized by the Americans continued to be selectively leaked over the months following the Abbottabad raid. The claim that a stash of pornography had been found appeared a fairly transparent and clumsy effort to blacken the dead al-Qaeda leader's posthumous reputation among current or potential followers. Little emerged to support repeated public assessments by US officials that bin Laden had been deeply involved in the detailed day-to-day running of the group either. One video released by the CIA unequivocally re-inforced the sense of a historical figure whose time had passed. It showed bin Laden, stroking his beard, wrapped in a blanket with a woollen cap on his head, sitting on the floor in a room probably in the Abbottabad compound, watching a television set on a desk beside a blacked-out window. On the screen ran images of a younger man – the viewer him-self in 2002 or 2003 – wearing a combat jacket and walking through wooded hills, then further footage of the al-Qaeda leader firing an AK-47 in around 2000, some pictures of the 9/11 attacks and finally a sequence of fighters on an assault course somewhere amid dusty desert hills. Then the pictures were gone and only a blank screen remained.

# Conclusion: The 9/11 Wars

## THE 9/11 WARS:
## THE GLOBAL AND THE LOCAL

So as the end of the first decade of the 9/11 Wars approached, some of the answers to the questions that the sight of the American forces spread out in the sand, scrub and pitted concrete at Bagram all those years before had become clear.

Certainly the nature of the conflict was now more evident. The qualities established in those early campaigns – at Tora Bora, in the streets of Baghdad as the insurgency in Iraq took hold or in the dust of Majjar al-Kabir, where the six Redcaps were to die, in Abu Ghraib, in the bombings of nightclubs in Bali and consulates in Istanbul – had been consolidated as time had passed. This new war was chaotic and scattered, with few heroes and many villains. It was a conflict where gain and loss had been determined as much by the relative venality or brutality of participants as by courage or resourcefulness. It was a conflict marked by violence to civilians, to prisoners and by an appalling ignorance among many decision-makers of the local conditions, the circumstances and the cultures of other protagonists. It was, at the end of its first ten years as at its beginning, still marked by the extreme diversity of the scores of interwoven wars that it comprised.

These wars existed on multiple levels. At the local level, they were a mass of private battles, fratricidal skirmishes, communal clashes, often sparked by specific incidents of misgovernance or injustice, some pitting village against village, neighbourhood against neighbourhood, tribe against tribe. At the next level, the wars were often about the participation of a particular group in politics at a provincial or national level.

Frequently they involved conflicts about the definition of a certain ethnic or religious group's position within a state. Only at the final level, the biggest in scale, could some of these conflicts be integrated into an overarching cosmic conflict pitting the West and its allies against radical Islam. Each level provided a different prism through which the overall conflict could be seen. Not all were equally valid. Only by glossing over the local specificities of all its component elements could the 9/11 Wars be seen a war between religions, between the secular and the faithful, between the West and the East or between global 'haves' and global 'have-nots'. Such generalizations, with their easy assumptions and seductive simplicity, at best highlighted only one element of the overall conflict, at worst obscured and distorted the nature of the phenomenon they supposedly described.

As their first decade ended, enough of the course of the 9/11 Wars was also now evident to be able to tentatively offer a prediction for what the next years of the conflict might bring. After the stunning violence of their beginning in the autumn of 2001 and the short lull in 2002 and early 2003 the Wars had grown in extent and intensity to a peak in around 2005 and 2006. This was followed by a relative decline that was partially – but not totally – offset by rising levels of localized violence in Pakistan and Afghanistan. The most recent phase of the conflict, still ongoing in the summer of 2011, had seen a fragile stabilization, leaving it finely balanced. Despite a continuing level of violence that was undoubtedly much higher than in the years preceding the 9/11 attacks, there was nothing to indicate an imminent global conflagration as had once been feared. Indeed, the events in the Arab world in early 2011 suggested that such an eventuality was extemely unlikely. The most probable scenario for the coming years of the 9/11 Wars was thus that this delicate equilibrium would be maintained for the foreseeable future with violence and militancy shifting between new nodes of activism and geographic zones according to local circumstances, the emergence of new leaders and the creation of new groups.[1] Generational shifts and heightened expectations after the 'Arab Spring' would be important factors in determining the level of any violence. The ability of local regimes and rulers to defuse demands for reform and of new governments to meet the new hopes for peace, prosperity and, in particular, 'dignity' of hundreds of millions of people would be crucial in determining its location. An important factor too would be the adaptability of al-Qaeda in all its manifestations, following bin Laden's death. But though any renewed militancy would cause problems, it was nonetheless unlikely to pose an existential threat, either to the West or to the Islamic world.

What major factors had determined the course of the 9/11 Wars so far? The answer is the key lesson from the last decade. In the introduction to this work, the importance of the tension between the 'global' and the 'local' was flagged as critical to the evolution of the conflict. This was repeatedly proven over the course of the years. At every level, the resistance offered by the particular to the general was crucial. At the grandest scale, it was the rejection of the globalized ideology of radical Islam propagated by bin Laden and others like him in around 2005 and 2006 by hundreds of millions of Muslims across the Islamic world that marked the major turning point in the conflict. The message of bin Laden, deliberately stripped of local specificity and as disrespectful of local custom or belief as anything emanating from the West, began losing popularity among its primary audience when its local implications became clear. Al-Qaeda's call to arms had had some broad appeal, plugging into deep-felt feelings of humiliation and a defensive narrative that had become widespread over previous decades as well as a range of broader social, demographic and economic factors that in some cases dated back a century or more. This attraction was not diminished – indeed it was often deepened – when the militants married deeds to words, when bombs exploded in distant towns, strikes were launched on distant cities, particularly American ones, or when occupying forces in the heart of the Middle East were attacked. But when the violence came home, it provoked a very different reaction. The sight of blood on one's own streets, the dismembered bodies of one's own compatriots, the grieving parents who could have been one's own – as well as the evident economic and cultural damage done by radical Islamic activism to any society – turned entire populations away from violence. When viewed from up close, the ideas and practices of men like bin Laden were much less appealing than they appeared on the internet or on the evening news, and the impact on established local customs, identities, practices and communities much greater. The result was that both Abu Musab al-Suri's plans for a global uprising, apparently so close to being fulfilled in 2005, and the 'open front' strategy favoured by Abu Musab al-Zarqawi, which once also looked like succeeding, foundered on the stubborn parochialism that characterizes most people's vision of the world most of the time.

It was not just the projects of the militants that were undermined by the resistance of 'the local' to the global. Early on in the 9/11 Wars, Western leaders, in particular President Bush and Prime Minister Tony Blair, had, like the extremists, both understood and projected the conflict as part of a cosmic contest. Their decisions had, in part, been determined by a desire to propagate a series of universal principles. These may have been far more attractive than those of radical Islam but, particularly when they were imposed by force, could be as alienating. The key shift in the first decade of the conflict came when, at the same time as sentiment turned against al-Qaeda in the Islamic world, and in part as a result of this change, Western policy-makers and strategists began to question whether the earlier ideological approach was constructive and whether aggressively seeking generalized solutions based in a broad package of 'liberal democratic' and free-market capitalist ideas were likely to further the interests of the states they led in the conflict they now found themselves engaged in. From 2006 or 2007 onwards, new thinking based on a more careful consideration of the views, ideas, interests and values of the communities that in many ways constituted the battlefield in the 9/11 Wars began to be implemented. In every case – whether it was American soldiers on the ground in tough neighbourhoods of Baghdad, men and women from MI5 fanning out across the UK to be based in police stations, a return to intelligence services relying on human sources not merely telecommunications intercepts – the new tactics implied and brought a deeper understanding of other societies, a better knowledge of 'human terrain', a greater tolerance of difference and encouraged a new pragmatism. At a local level, such as in Iraq, this allowed local circumstances to be exploited to first slow and then reverse a descent into hellish violence. In Afghanistan, though coming too late and after too many errors to make a major difference, it at least mitigated some of the damage previously done. At a global level, the new approach allowed space for the growing antipathy towards violent extremism in the Islamic world to thrive and for the idea of 'democracy' to be divorced in the minds of many from a coercive project of Westernization. It encouraged the calmer atmosphere of the latter years of the decade. Without this shift, it is unlikely the relative stabilization of the threat that al-Qaeda and the movement of contemporary radical Muslim militancy posed could have occurred.

This approach – privileging the micro over the macro, the local over the global – helps us to understand the lessons of the 9/11 Wars as regards the nature and genesis of radical violence. In the search for an answer to the question of why or how 'ordinary men' become 'terrorists', the 9/11 Wars have taught us, once more, that the specific rather than the general is of most use. Early attempts at profiling – constructing general laws to designate masses of population as potentially dangerous – or to find universally relevant 'predictor' factors of militancy failed. In the later years of conflict, the discussion in counter-terrorist circles was instead about the process by which individuals became radicalized. It was no longer about the 'who' but about the 'how', and it focused on the role of friends or brothers or fathers, exposure to the internet, whom an individual happened to meet and when. The earlier approaches were rejected as too blunt to be of much use. The plotting of vertical hierarchies was replaced by the modelling of horizontal networks. Each path to violence was seen as unique and had to be dealt with as such. Extrapolation – 'joining the dots' – was thus replaced by 'granularity' – precise, knowledge-based, case-by-case analysis. Though some patterns could, of course, be discerned – a decline in the educational level of militants in Saudi Arabia from 2005 onwards, the rising proportion of converts in Europe over the decade or the increasing number of Iraqi suicide bombers with family members in prison in 2008 or 2009 – these were only useful for establishing what was going on in any one locality. Comparing the path into violence of, say, Abu Mujahed, the Sunni insurgent the author interviewed at length in Baghdad, and the 7/7 bombers, or of Abit, the Pakistani suicide bomber who failed to detonate his bomb at the last minute, and the drug-dealing 'El Chino' who had played such a key role in the Madrid bombings of 2004, was of limited use. As much as any new laws or powers for the police, it was this realization that enabled security services to feel more confident by 2008 or 2009 than they had done for many years previously. They had learned that the path to violence involves such a broad range of potential factors and situations that any single explanatory theory of why some are attracted to violence – religion, class, deprivation – was bound to fail. There are broad trends that can establish a background. There are short-term factors that may encourage a certain type of behaviour. There are catalysts which can spark a critical change for a specific individual or even a group. But, as in the 9/11 Wars as a whole, there are no global rules.

## WINNERS AND LOSERS

Has the West won the 9/11 Wars? The West has certainly – despite al-Qaeda's various successes over the years – avoided defeat. The power of terrorism resides in its ability to create a sense of fear far in excess of the actual threat posed to an individual. Here what has not happened is as significant as what has happened. Governments have largely protected their citizens, and few inhabitants of Western democracies or indeed Middle or Far Eastern nations today pass their lives genuinely concerned about being harmed in a radical militant attack.[2] In July 2010, President Obama even spoke of how the USA could 'absorb' another 9/11, a statement that would have been inconceivable a few years before.[3] Despite significant damage to civil liberties in both Europe and America, institutional checks and balances appear to have worked on both sides of the Atlantic. In the face of a worrying militarization and 'securitization', other forces have been strong enough to ensure that liberal democratic societies have kept their values more or less intact. The integration of minorities, always a delicate task, is generating significant tensions but is proceeding, albeit unevenly. Even though now facing serious problems of debt, America has been nonetheless able to pay for the grotesque strategic error of the war in Iraq, at a total cost of up to a trillion dollars depending on how it is calculated, and a ten-year conflict in Afghanistan all while financing a huge security industry at home in the midst of one of gravest economic crises for decades. In 2009, American military expenditure was $661 billion, considerably more than double the total of ten years previously and a sizeable enough sum, but still not enough, as bin Laden had hoped, to fundamentally weaken the world's only true superpower.[4] In Europe, supposedly creaking old democracies have reacted with a nimbleness and rapidity that few imagined they still possessed to counter domestic and international threats. In short Western societies and political systems appear likely to digest this latest wave of radical violence as they have digested its predecessors.[5] In 1911, British police reported that leftist and anarchist groups had 'grown in number and size' and were 'hardier than ever, now that the terrifying weapons created by modern science are available to them'. The world was 'threatened by forces which would be able to one day carry out its total destruction,' the police warned. In the event, of course, it was gas, machine guns and artillery followed by disease that killed millions, not terrorism.[6] In the second decade of the 9/11 Wars other gathering threats to the global commonwealth such as climate change will further oblige Islamic radical militants to cede much of the lime-light to those phenomena which genuinely do pose a planetary menace, at least in the absence of a new, equally spectacular cycle of violence.

But if there has been no defeat for the West then there has been no victory either. Over the last ten years, the limits of the ability of the USA and its Western allies to impose their will and vision on parts of the world have been very publicly revealed. Though it is going too far to say that the first decade of the 9/11 Wars saw the moment where the long decline of first Europe and perhaps America was made clear to the world, the conflict certainly reinforced the sense that the tectonic plates of geopolitics are shifting. After its military and diplomatic checks in Iraq and Afghanistan, a chastened Britain may well have to finally renounce its inflated self-image as a power that 'punches above its weight'. The role of NATO in the twenty-first century is unclear. Above all, though the power, soft and hard, cultural and economic, military and political, of the USA and Europe remains immense and often hugely underestimated, it is clear that this will not always be the case. For many decades, the conventional wisdom has been that economic devel-opment around the globe would necessarily render the project of liberal democracy and free-market capitalism more popular. One of the lessons of the 9/11 Wars is that this optimism was misplaced. A sense of national or religious chauvinism appears often to be a corollary of a society get-ting richer rather than its opposite, and the search for dignity and authenticity is often defined as much by opposition to what is seen, rightly or wrongly, as foreign as anything else. In some places, the errors of Western policy-makers over recent years have provoked a reaction which will last a long time. The socially conservative, moderately Islam-ist, and strongly nationalist, narrative that is being consolidated in Muslim countries from Morocco to Malaysia will pose a growing and increasingly coherent challenge to the ability of the USA and European nations to pursue their interests on the global stage for many years to come. This, alongside the increasingly strident voices of China and other emerging nations, means a long period instability and competition is likely before any new *modus vivendi* is reached. American intelligence agencies reported in their quadrennial review in late 2008 that they judged that within a few decades the USA would no longer be able to 'call the shots'. Instead, they predicted, America is likely to face the challenges of a fragmented planet, where conflict over scarce resources is on the rise, poorly contained by 'ramshackle' international institutions.[7] The previous review, published in December 2004, when President Bush had just been re-elected and was preparing his triumphal second inauguration, had foreseen 'continued dominance' for many years to come, considering that most major powers had effectively forsaken the idea of balancing the US.[8] The difference over the intervening years from 2004 to 2008 is thus stark. If these years brought victory, then America and the West more generally cannot afford many more victories like it.

If clear winners in the 9/11 Wars are difficult to find, then the losers are not hard to identify. They are the huge numbers of men, women and children who have found themselves caught in multiple crossfires: the victims of the 9/11 strikes or of the 7/7 and Madrid bombings, of sectarian killings in Baghdad, badly aimed American drone strikes in Pakistan or attacks by teenage suicide bombers on crowds in Afghanistan. They are those executed by Abu Musab al-Zarqawi, those who died sprayed with bullets by US Marines at Haditha, those shot by private contractors careering in overpowered unmarked blacked-out four-wheel-drive vehicles through Baghdad. They are worshippers at Sufi shrines in the Punjab, local reporters trying to record what was happening to their home towns, policemen who happened to be on shift at the wrong time in the wrong place, unsuspecting tourists on summer holidays. They are the refugees who ran out of money and froze to death one by one in an Afghan winter, those many hundreds executed as 'spies' by the Taliban, those gunned down as they waited for trains home at Mumbai's main railway station one autumn evening, those who died in cells in Bagram or elsewhere at the hands of their jailers, the provocative film-maker stabbed on an Amsterdam street, all the victims of this chaotic matrix of multivalent, confused but always lethal wars.

The cumulative total of dead and wounded in this conflict so far is substantial. Any estimates of casualties in such a diverse and complex conflict is necessarily very approximate, but some idea of its human cost can be obtained nonetheless. The military dead are the best documented. Though some may have shown genuine enthusiasm for war or even evidence of sadism,[9] many Western soldiers did not enlist with the primary motive of fighting and killing others. A significant number came from poor towns in the Midwest of America or council estates in the UK and had joined up for a job, for adventure, to pay their way through college, to learn a craft. By the end of November 2010, the total of American soldiers who had died in Operation Iraqi Freedom and its successor, Operation New Dawn, was 4,409, with 31,395 wounded in action.[10] More than 300 servicemen from other nations had been killed too and many more maimed, disabled or psychologically injured for life. In Afghanistan, well over 2,000 soldiers from 48 different countries had been killed in the first nine years of the Afghan conflict. These included 1,300 Americans, 340 Britons, 153 Canadians, 49 Frenchmen and 44 Germans.[11] Military casualties among Western nations – predominantly American – in other theatres of Operation Enduring Freedom from the Sudan to the Seychelles and from Tajikistan to Turkey added another 100 or so. At least 1,500 private contractors died in Iraq alone.[12]

Then there were the casualties sustained by local security forces. Around 12,000 police were killed in Iraq between 2003 and 2010.[13] In Afghanistan, the number of dead policemen since 2002 had exceeded 3,000 by the middle of 2010.[14] Many might have been venal, brutal and corrupt, but almost every dead Afghan policeman left a widow and children in a land where bereavement leads often to destitution. In Pakistan, somewhere between 2,000 and 4,000 policemen have died in bombing or shooting attacks.[15] As for local militaries in the various theatres of conflict, there were up to 8,000 Iraqi combat deaths in the 2003 war, and another 3,000 Iraqi soldiers are thought to have died over the subsequent years.[16] In Afghanistan, Afghan National Army casualties were running at 2,820 in August 2010, while in Pakistan, around 3,000 soldiers have been killed and at least twice as many wounded in the various campaigns internally since 2001.[17] Across the Middle East and further afield in the other theatres that had become part of the 9/11 Wars, local security forces paid a heavy price too. More than 150 Lebanese soldiers were killed fighting against radical 'al-Qaeda-ist' militants in the Nahr al-Bared refugee camp in Lebanon in 2007, for example. There were many others, in Saudi Arabia, in Algeria, in Indonesia. In all, adding these totals together, at least 40,000 or 50,000 soldiers and policemen have so far died in the 9/11 Wars. Casualties among their enemies – the insurgents or the extremists – are clearly harder to establish. Successive Western commanders said that they did not 'do body counts', but most units kept a track of how many casualties they believed they had inflicted, and these totals were often high. At least 20,000 insurgents were probably killed in Iraq, roughly the same number in Pakistan, possibly more in Afghanistan.[18] In all that makes at least 60,000 people, again many with wives and children.

Then, of course, there are those, neither insurgent nor soldier, neither terrorist nor policeman, who were caught in a war in which civilians were not just features of the 'battle space' but very often targets. In 2001, there were the 9/11 attacks themselves, of course, with their near 3,000 dead. In 2002 alone, at least 1,000 people died in attacks organized or inspired by al-Qaeda in Tunisia, Indonesia, Turkey and elsewhere. The casualties from such strikes continued to mount through the middle years of the decade. One study estimates 3,013 dead in around 330 attacks between 2004 and 2008.[19] By the end of the first ten years of the 9/11 Wars, the total of civilians killed in terrorist actions directly linked to the group or affiliated or inspired Islamic militants was almost certainly in excess of 10,000, probably nearer 15,000, possibly up to 20,000. To this total must be added the cost to civilians of the central battles of the 9/11 Wars. In Iraq generally, estimates vary, but a very conservative count puts violent civilian deaths (excluding police) from the eve of the invasion of 2003 to the end of 2010 at between 65,000 and 125,000.[20] They included more than 400 assassinated Iraqi academics and almost 150 journalists killed on assignment.[21] The true number may be many times greater. In Afghanistan, from October 7, 2001, the day when the bombing started, to mid October 2003, between 3,000 and 3,600 civilians were killed just by coalition air strikes.[22] Many more have died in other 'collateral damage' incidents or through the actions of the insurgents. The toll has steadily risen. In 2005, the total was probably around 450 civilian casualties. From 2006 to 2009 between 5,000 and 7,000 civilian deaths were documented, depending on the source. In 2010 alone, 2,777 died, mostly due to insurgent action. Half as many again had already died by mid May 2011. In all, between 14,000 and 17,000 civilians have been killed in Afghanistan, and at least three or four times that number wounded or permanently disabled. In Pakistan, which saw the first deaths outside America of the 9/11 Wars, the number of casualties since that first handful died when police shot into demonstrations in September 2001 are estimated by local authorities and regional analysts at around 9,000 dead and between 10,000 and 15,000 injured.[23] Add these admittedly rough figures from the principal theatres of the Wars together and you reach a total of well over 150,000 civilians killed. In all the approximate overall figure for civilian and military dead of the violence associated with the 9/11 Wars is probably near 250,000. If the injured are included – even at a conservative ratio of one to three – the total number of casualties reaches one million. This may be a sum that is lower than the losses inflicted on combatants and non-combatants during the murderous major conflicts of the twentieth century but still constitutes a very large number of people. Add the bereaved and the displaced,[24] let alone those who have been harmed through the indirect effects of the conflict, the infant mortality or malnutrition rates due to breakdown of basic services, and the scale of the violence that we have witnessed over the last years is clear. The changes in our lives and societies will be commensurate. Some day this conflict – the 9/11 Wars – will be remembered by another name. Most of the dead will not be remembered at all.

## ALI SHAH

At 11 o'clock a cold, hard wind cut across the frozen mud and dry grass of a patch of wasteland hidden by a thick line of gorse and brush behind a lay-by a few hundred metres from the outer perimeter fences of the northern French port of Dunkirk. Among the bushes, a hundred or so young men had built makeshift shelters. It was a week or so since the local police had come by with bulldozers, and the shelters, rebuilt after each such raid, were crowded. Under the wood stripped from nearby trees, plastic sheeting handed out by local campaigners, dustbin bags, salvaged sheets of rusted corrugated iron, blankets and the occasional upturned shopping trolley, groups of young men huddled around fires. Above, gulls circled and shrieked in the grey winter sky.

Kurds and Arabs from Iraq, a handful of Somalians, a smattering of Iranians, a few dozen Afghans, two Syrians, an Algerian and a Pakistani, they came from almost every theatre touched by the 9/11 Wars. Among them was a twenty-four-year-old Hazaran Afghan with a thin beard, worn jeans and a cheap red ski jacket pulled tight over a thin cotton sweater. This was Ali Shah, the young shepherd with a taste for learning English who had escaped from Bamiyan over the mountain trails at night as the Taliban had prepared to destroy the Buddhas all those years before. Ali Shah had eventually made his way to Iran and had watched the news of the 9/11 attacks in a café near the eastern Iranian city of Mashhad, where he worked as a mechanic's assistant. In 2003, after briefly being jailed, he had returned to Afghanistan to find his family in Kabul, where he was hired by an international NGO as a driver. He earned good money until repeated threats from insurgent sympathizers forced him to flee. Having decided to try his luck in Europe, Ali Shah set his sights on the UK. His savings were enough to pay the traffickers. Old friends looked after him on his way through Iran. He had trekked over the Iranian–Turkish frontier, hitchhiked to Istanbul and then paid $3,000 to get to Greece before spending almost all his remaining money – $1,400 – to be brought by boat to Italy. He had taken a train from Milan to Paris, slept in a park for a week near the Gare de l'Est and then taken a train to Calais. Almost picked up by the police there, he had managed to slip away through undergrowth before hitching north to Dunkirk, where he had heard things were better. Now he was stuck again. Every night he tried to get into trucks heading for the UK but without success. He had no money and relied on sympathetic locals for food and firewood. 'I have been travelling for too long. I would like to go home, but the situation in Afghanistan is very bad,' he said and looked towards the lines of trucks parked in the dusk beside the port. 'Hopefully things will be better when I get to the other side. I am now very tired.'[25]

# Notes

## INTRODUCTION

1. Both World Wars, the French Revolutionary and Napoleonic Wars and a host of other major conflicts share it too. The Second World War was much more than a straight fight between democratic states and repressive, fascist ones. It comprised equally significant ideological, economic and cultural contests as innumerable subsidiary conflicts, between states, communities, even families. The Cold War was also far from a simple Manichaean battle between two ideological blocs. Struggles for national liberation, ethnic and tribal wars, social conflict also made up its rich and varied fabric. My thanks to the late Professor Fred Halliday, who kindly shared his thoughts on the multi-dimensionality of this current conflict and sent me a draft of his essay 'Global Jihad, "Long War" and the Crisis of American Power', in Fabio Petito and Elisabetta Brighi, eds., *Il Mediterraneo nelle Relazioni Internazionale: tra Euro-Mediterraneo e Grande Medio Oriente*, Fondazione Laboratorio Mediterraneo, 2007.

## CHAPTER 1: THE BUDDHAS

1. Basic café serving tea and food.
2. Author interview with Ekram Shinwari, VOA reporter who travelled incognito to Bamiyan to film the scene, Kabul, March 2009.
3. Author interview, near Dunkirk, France, December 2009.
4. The split between Shia and Sunni dates back to the earliest generations of the first Muslims and a dispute over the inheritance of the moral and political authority of the Prophet Mohammed which in very general terms pitted those who believed that it should pass down the bloodline of the dead leader, the Shia, against those who believed in a more political and meritocratic choice of successor, the Sunni. Behind this superficially political division, historians have shown, lies a range of cultural, ethnic and tribal differences.
5. The date of the Buddhas' construction has been various estimated between

the third and seventh centuries. In 1989, the art historian Deborah Klimburg-Salter argued a seventh-century date but according to Dr Fred Hiebert, an archaeologist and National Geographic fellow, carbon dating of lumps of wood found in the debris of the destroyed statues reveals a fourth-century date. Holland Cotter, 'Buddhas of Bamiyan: keys to Asian history', *New York Times*, March 3, 2001. Author telephone interview with Dr Fred Hiebert, March 2009.

6. A change which many attributed to the advice of Pakistani military officers.

7. The last Soviet troops left in January 1989.

8. The word Taliban had been used to describe small groups of independent and relatively effective fighters from religious schools who had fought alongside the main groups of '*mujahideen*' in the war against the Soviets. See Abdul Zaeef, *My Life with the Taliban*, Hurst, 2010, for an interesting account. The word 'Taliban' originated in Arabic. Its singular form is *talib*, which means knowledge-seeker. Over time a Dari ending – *alef* (a) and *noon* (n) – was added to create a plural, 'Taliban'.

9. Pakistan has three major intelligence agencies. The Intelligence Bureau (IB) is the main civilian intelligence agency and focuses on domestic intelligence, reporting to the prime minister rather than the minister of the interior. Military Intelligence (MI) compiles reports for the chief of army staff. The Directorate of Inter-Services Intelligence (ISI) draws together the intelligence capabilities of the three military service branches, as well as acting independently of all of them through its clandestine S Department or Branch. The ISI theoretically reports to the prime minister, but in practice has always reported direct to the chief of army staff.

10. Further assistance came from a large number of former members of some of the most extreme factions within the Afghan Communists who had learned to use artillery, armour and planes in Kabul's armed forces in the 1980s, had then gone on to fight for various *mujahideen* factions and were both experienced and proficient. The role of these 'Khalqis', so-called for their allegiance to the hardline Khalq (the People) faction of the Communist People's Democratic Party of Afghanistan, has been often underplayed. For more on the Khalqis, see Thomas Barfield, *Afghanistan: A Political and Cultural History*, Princeton University Press, 2010, pp. 225, 259. Also Barnett R. Rubin, *The Fragmentation of Afghanistan*, Yale University Press, 2002, pp. 82, 105. Many eventually resurfaced in the reconstituted Afghan National Army after 2001.

11. Much of the original leadership of the Taliban were former fighters – often junior commanders – of Mohammed Nabi Mohammedi's Harkat-ul-Inqelabi-ul-Islam party.

12. 'We are seekers of peace and honour in the way of God. Our aim is to secure the peace and honour of our nation and our people,' Mullah Hassan

Rachman, the Taliban governor of Kandahar explained. Rachman, an arch conservative who had lost a leg fighting the Soviets and had the disconcerting habit of placing his artificial limb beside him on a sofa during interviews, did not often travel to Kabul, describing the capital as 'a bad place' from which 'much wrongdoing and vice [had] come that poisoned the country'. Author interviews, Kandahar, August, October 1998. On the Taliban's outreach programme in the mid 1990s see also Seth Jones, *In the Graveyard of Empires*, Norton, 2009, p. 58; Abdul-Kader Sinno, 'Explaining the Taliban's Ability to Mobilize the Pashtuns', in Robert D. Crews and Amin Tarzi, *The Taliban and the Crisis of Afghanistan*, Harvard University Press, 2008.

13. Multiple author interviews with former senior Pakistani officers, Islamabad, Rawalpindi, 2002, 2005, 2008. US Department of State cable, 'Afghanistan: Pakistanis to regulate wheat and fuel trade to gain leverage over Taliban', August 13, 1997. US Embassy Islamabad cable, 'Bad news on Pak Afghan Policy: GOP Support for the Taliban appears to be getting stronger', July 1, 1998, National Security Archives. Some Pakistani paramilitaries appear also to have fought with them on occasion.

14. There is an enormous range in census data. Compare, for example, the CIA factbook of 2000 with the United Nations Afghanistan Information Management Systems estimates of 2003. The Taliban were almost exclusively drawn from Afghanistan's Pashtun tribes, who make up around 45 per cent of the population, though figures are contested. With no census since 1979 and ethnicity a deeply fluid concept, estimates can only be rough. In addition to the Pashtuns and the Hazara, Tajiks and Uzbeks there were around thirty other recognized discrete ethnic or linguistic groups including Aimaq, Pashai, 'Arab' as well as other population groups defined differently, such as Syeds, who claim to be descendants of the Prophet, his family or his immediate entourage.

15. Figures from the World Bank, data bank, accessed January 2011. Unicef lists the literacy rate for 2003–8 at 28 per cent.

16. A controversial veteran of the movement's campaigns across Afghanistan over the previous six years, Dadaullah's excessive violence had already led to his being removed twice from command. Born in a small village in the central province of Oruzgan in 1966, he had grown up in a Pakistani refugee camp, returning to Afghanistan to fight the Soviets during the 1980s before returning in the early 1990s to join the Taliban. On Dadaullah, see Jason Burke, 'Hunt for the Taliban trio intent on destruction', *Observer*, July 9, 2006; Ron Moreau and Sami Yousafzai, 'In the footsteps of Zarqawi', *Newsweek*, July 3, 2006.

17. Author interviews in Bamiyan, March 2002, Kabul 2009. Human Rights Watch, 'Afghanistan: Ethnically-Motivated Abuses Against Civilians', *Human Rights Watch Backgrounder*, October 2001. Human Rights Watch Annual

Report, *Massacres of Hazaras in Afghanistan*, February 1, 2001. Interviews with United Nations specialist, Kabul, 2009. See also Rory Stewart, *The Places in Between*, Picador, 2005, pp. 247, 263, 299 and 302. Author interview with Stewart, Kabul, March 2009. Stewart also gives a colourful account of the shifting allegiances of various commanders. Ahmed Rashid, *Descent into Chaos*, Allen Lane, 2008, p. 299.

18. Author interviews with senior former Taliban ministers, Kabul, March, 2009.

19. Author interview with Dr Said Omara Khan Masoudi, National Museum director, Kabul, March, 2009. Those against destroying the Buddhas included the education minister, Arsala Rahmani, the foreign minister, Mullah Wakil Ahmed Muttawakil, and the culture minister, Qadrutullah Jamal.

20. Men like Mullah Mohammed Hassan Akhund, the governor of Kandahar and one of the most conservative of the Taliban leaders, and the deputy minister of culture, Mullah Nuruddin Turabi.

21. See United Nations Development Programme, *Afghanistan Annual Opium Poppy Survey*, 2001, p. ii for statistics.

22. Author interviews with Rahimullah Yusufzai, BBC, and Ekram Shinwari, VOA (Voice of America), both of whom had met Omar, Kabul and Peshawar, 1999–2001.

23. See US Embassy Islamabad cable, 'Afghanistan: The Taliban's decision-making process and leadership structure', December 31, 1998, confidential, 15 pp., declassified 2009.

24. The last person to bring out the cloak was King Ahmed Shah Durrani in 1768. See Jos L. Gommans, *The Rise of the Indo-Afghan Empire c.1710– 1780*, Brill, 1995, pp. 65–6.

25. Many communities had been alienated by enforced conscription, by bans on popular local customs and by being progressively shut out of decision-making processes. There was armed resistance in the east of Afghanistan against forced conscription in 1999, for example, and small incidents, such as attempts by local Taliban to ban traditional pastimes such as 'egg fights', could spark violence. The Noorzai tribe in the south near Kandahar were only barely kept from outright mass revolt.

26. Author interviews with Wakil Ahmed Muttawakel and Arsala Rahmani, Kabul, March 2009. See also Ron Gutman, *How We Missed the Story*, United States Institute of Peace Press, 2008, pp. 235–9; and Peter Bergen, *The Osama Bin Laden I Know*, Simon and Schuster, 2006, p. 248. Author interview with Vahid Mojdeh, Kabul, August 2008.

27. Finbarr Barry Flood, 'Between Cult and Culture: Bamiyan, Islamic Iconoclasm, and the Museum', *The Art Bulletin*, December 2002.

28. See above and State Department memo, Assistant Secretary of State for South Asian Affairs Karl F. Inderfurth to Secretary of State Madeleine Albright, 'Taliban under pressure', May 1, 2000, confidential, declassified 2009.

29. A good example of the legends created deliberately by Abdul Rahman can be found in the probably fictional or at least exaggerated account of his personal impromptu decapitation of an elderly Herati cleric who had legitimized a rebellion with a *fatwa*, Barfield, *Afghanistan*, p. 146.

30. Gutman, *How We Missed the Story*, pp. 238–40.

31. Author interview with a retired Pakistani military officer present at meeting between Omar and Mahsud Ahmed, ISI chief in Kandahar, Rawalpindi, November 2008. Gutman, *How We Missed the Story*, p. 239. 'Lost Chance', *Time*, August 12, 2002. Steve Coll, *Ghost Wars*, Penguin, 2005, pp. 554–5.

32. Multiple author interviews with senior Taliban ministers, officials, Kabul, Kandahar, 1998–2000. See Jason Burke, *Al-Qaeda: The True Story of Radical Islam*, Penguin, 2004, pp. 116–35, 193–4. Alan Cullison and Andrew Higgins, 'Computer in Kabul holds chilling memos', *Wall Street Journal*, December 31, 2001. A Defense Intelligence Agency cable of October 2, 2001 predicted 'eventually the Taliban and al-Qaeda will wage war with one another . . . Al-Qaeda has not integrated with Afghans in the Taliban.'

33. Author interviews with Mullah Nabi Mohammedi, Kabul 1998, numerous senior Taliban officials, Kabul, Kandahar 1999.

34. Militants from the international groups were warned against any contact with the Afghans. See the testimony of Abdurahman Khadr, broadcast in the PBS Frontline programme *Son of al Qaeda*, April 22, 2004, who said he had been punished for speaking to the Afghans while in a training camp. A copy of al-Qaeda guesthouse regulations included the prohibition on talking to the Afghans who did the cooking and cleaning. Author collection.

35. Excepting those who had participated in a delegation which had travelled to Sugarland, Texas, for consultations with UNOCAL, an American company interested in building a 1,300 km gas pipeline across Afghanistan. See 'Taleban in Texas for talks on gas pipeline', BBC News Online, December 4, 1997. The relative lack of animosity among the Taliban towards the United States was implicitly recognized by a volunteer in one Afghan training camp who asked bin Laden in 2000: 'Has al-Qa'eda under your command pledged [an oath] to the Islamic Imarah in Afghanistan? If so, how do you call for fighting the United States knowing that the Taliban did not hear of it for reasons concerning the security and stability of Afghanistan? We pray to God that He saves the Taliban.' Harmony documents, Harmony Program, West Point, Combating-Terrorism Center, document ID: AFGP-2002-801138.

36. There are many other differences. Wahhabis belong to the Hanbali madhab, one of the most rigorous of the four schools of Sunni Islam, for example, whereas the Deobandis are part of the Hanafi madhab, an entirely different school of Islamic theology. Letters found by the author in Khaldan Camp, November 2001, revealed further animosity between Afghans and their foreign 'guests'. See also Burke, *Al-Qaeda*, pp. 169–71. Bergen, *The Osama Bin Laden I Know*, p. 179. Harmony Documents, document ID: AFGP-2002-602181.

37. The recognition quote is from Abdul Salaam Zaeef, author interview, Islamabad, 2000.

38. Another factor was the Taliban refusal of Pakistani demands to hand over sectarian militants responsible for widespread violence in Pakistan itself who had sought sanctuary across the border.

39. Author interview with Maleeha Lodhi, Pakistan's then ambassador to Washington, March 2009. 'The realization that Pakistan's identification with the Taliban regime was increasingly becoming a diplomatic liability was there in the establishment and not just the civilian part,' Lodhi said. See also Coll, *Ghost Wars*, p. 547. Jason Burke, David Rohde, Tim Judah, Paul Harris and Paul Beaver, 'Al-Qaeda's trail of terror', *Observer*, November 18, 2001.

40. See Burke, *Al-Qaeda*, p. 186; Coll, *Ghost Wars*, pp. 400–402.

41. Michael Keating, 'Dilemmas of Humanitarian Assistance in Afghanistan', in Bill Maley, ed., *Fundamentalism Reborn?*, New York University Press, 1998, p. 136. In the 1980s UN agencies had cooperated with Afghan Communist government programmes for the education of women and a variety of other empowerment projects focused on urban Afghan women. Pankaj Mishra, *Temptations of the West*, Picador, 2006, p. 365.

42. Author interview with Francesc Vendrell, London, February 2009, with Daniel Roggio, UN political adviser, Kabul, March 2009. Pamela Constable, 'Annan appeals to Taliban to spare Buddha statues', *Washington Post*, March 12, 2001. Vendrell himself had met Mullah Omar a year previously.

43. Gutman, *How We Missed the Story*, p. 239. Author interviews in Kabul, March 2009.

44. The cameraman concerned, Tayseer Ayouni of al-Jazeera, claimed in an interview in 2004 that he had filmed secretly. However, given his astonishing images of the destruction and its aftermath, this seems highly unlikely. Author interview with a Taliban official, Islamabad, 2001.

45. Author interviews with locals, officials in Bamiyan, March, 2002.

46. A school of religious thought and practice, rather than a specific group or strand, Salafism is, in literal terms, the emulation of the *salaf*, or the first three generations of Muslims. (Some say the first four generations should be included.) These, followers say, were the only believers to have truly lived according to Allah's instructions to man as communicated via the Prophet Mohammed. Since those early days, the understanding of Allah's message and thus Islamic religious practice and with it social practices too have become corrupted by innovation, *bid'ah*, by the return of the polytheism that pre-dated Islam, *shirq*, and by foreign influences. Only a return, through a rigorous implementation of a literalist and ultra-conservative reading of the Koran, to earlier practices can ensure the return of the just society of the time of the Prophet across the *ummah*, the global community of Muslims. At the centre of Salafism is the concept of *tawhid*, or the unity or oneness of God.

Such views have proved attractive at regular intervals over the centuries. Ibn Tammiya, a key Salafi scholar and a major influence on modern ideologues including bin Laden and others among the al-Qaeda leadership, was writing in the thirteenth century after the fall of Baghdad to the Mongols, an event he blamed on the corruption and lassitude of the ruling Muslim dynasty and their subjects. In the nineteenth century, as Muslim societies and states came off worst in their one-sided battle with an expansionist West, new thinkers resurrected the idea of an Islamic renaissance based on a return to basics. With Salafis divided over how best to respond to the challenge posed by the technological, military and apparent cultural superiority of the invaders, various strands of thought emerged. Some called for a total rejection of all Western innovation and a harsh puritanism, others for its appropriation, a position which evolved towards the political ideology of Islamism, which calls for the appropriation of the modern state apparatus rather than its replacement by a model based on that believed to have been current in seventh-century Arabia and inevitably implies the formation of parties rather than a rigorous adherence to an individual relationship with God. Some thinkers justified violence, others called simply for spiritual renewal. From the Maghreb to the Far East, Salafi movements took hold, perhaps most spectacularly in Saudi Arabia, where Salafi clerics became an integral part of the new state of Saudi Arabia, and in Afghanistan, where the Taliban fused a mythic conception of Pashtun tribal culture with Salafi ideas to produce a revolutionary and potent new local strand.

47. Ahmed Rashid, *Descent into Chaos*, p. 20. Author interview with Nigel Inkster, former deputy head of MI6, London, February 2009.

48. Author interviews with Nigel Inkster, Richard Dearlove, London, February 2009. Richard Dearlove, former head of MI6, response to question at conference, London, February 2009.

49. Material later found by US forces showed, however, that, though he appeared assured and confident on the finished video, he had in fact had been nervous and irritable, and it had taken many attempts to record his statement. See Martyr Tape of Ziad Samir Jarrah, reproduced in Referral Binder – Part I, Ali Hamza Ahmad Suliman al Bahlul, AFGP-2003-001320.

50. Charge sheet, USA vs. Ali al-Bahlul, FBI interrogation of al-Bahlul report statement, July 30–31, 2003. Author collection.

51. Educated at a private school and then at the engineering faculty of Abdel Aziz university, bin Laden had been raised in a strict Wahabi household. Subsequently, like millions of young men across the Muslim world, he had been exposed in the late 1970s to the modern ideas of political Islam that were gaining in strength at the time. Bin Laden did not, as often claimed, head 'straight for Afghanistan' when the Soviets invaded in 1979 but in fact probably first arrived in Peshawar in 1981. He raised funds through his own

network of wealthy contacts and helped with the administration of Abdullah Azzam's 'Office of Services' organization, which raised funds from the Islamic world and Muslim communities in Europe and America to aid the Afghan refugees and wounded *mujahideen* and, to a much lesser extent, recruited volunteers to fight. Azzam's propaganda videos, with their bloody images of civilians wounded in Soviet attacks and exciting footage of ambushes among the scruffy, scrubby hills of eastern Afghanistan, were rudimentary but extremely effective on both wide-eyed teenagers and on the devout, wealthy patrons in the Gulf whom bin Laden solicited for funds. In 1989 bin Laden led a group of international militants at the catastrophic battle of Jalalabad, when, at the bidding of the Pakistani ISI, the squabbling *mujahideen* factions and their Arab auxiliaries incurred massive losses as they attempted to storm the eastern Afghan city.

Further points worth making about the issue of CIA support for bin Laden or others like him include the fact that the CIA were not allowed to enter Afghanistan (an injunction they obeyed), and did not instruct any Arab Afghans, disburse funds to them or supply them directly with equipment. As pointed out in the main text, any US contact with *mujahideen* of any background was indirect, with the Pakistani ISI acting as an intermediary, and the latter trained and supplied only Afghans, and then only from the seven factions that they recognized. Afghan leaders like Gulbuddin Hekmatyar, favoured by the ISI, had no wish or need to share hard-won resources with foreigners. Nor indeed did men like bin Laden, with their own sources of funding, need assistance. The Saudi Arabian government matched US aid to the *mujahideen* dollar for dollar, but these resources too were distributed by the ISI. The only exception was the faction of Abdul Rasul Sayyaf, an Afghan cleric who was very close to Saudi Wahhabi networks and the Saudi intelligence services, who received funds directly. As mentioned in the main text, techniques taught by the ISI on the basis of manuals and instruction from the CIA did bleed into the world of the Arab volunteers – the eleven-volume *Encyclopedia of Jihad* compiled in 1991 by international militants in Peshawar and dedicated to bin Laden and Azzam is based on American instruction manuals – but no direct instruction took place.

As for the other myths, it is worth stressing that the bulk of foreign volunteers arrived in Peshawar after the Soviets had begun withdrawing, and even the military contribution of foreigners who had arrived earlier was negligible. Most were engaged in construction, missionary or humanitarian work. Those who did fight were distributed in tiny groups among the *mujahideen* factions of Hekmatyar and Sayyaf. Rodric Braithwaite argues convincingly in his excellent *Afgantsy: the Russians in Afghanistan 1979–1989*, Profile, 2011, that the impact of the American Stinger surface-to-air missiles distributed from 1986 onwards was minimal too, as the Soviets soon found ways to reduce their losses to previous levels.

52. A useful account of this period to be found in Chapter 2 of Peter Bergen's excellent *The Longest War*, Simon and Schuster, 2011. Also, Bergen, *The Osama Bin Laden I Know*, pp. 80–81. Also in Lawrence Wright, *The Looming Tower*, Allen Lane, 2006, pp. 132–4. Early sources include documents provided to the author by Ron Motley, lead lawyer, 9/11 victims vs. Saudi Arabia, 2003. Also of interest is the US government evidence in USA vs. Enaam Arnout, January 2003, which deals in part with al-Qaeda in the 1990s. See also Burke, *Al-Qaeda*, Chapter 1, 'What Is Al-Qaeda?'. Minutes of the final meeting on August 20, 1988 at which the formation of the group was agreed ends with the line that 'the work of al-Qaeda commenced on September 9, 1988'.

53. Quoted in Rohan Gunaratna, *Inside Al Qae'da*, Hurst, 2002, p. 3.

54. His Saudi citizenship was withdrawn three years later.

55. A multitude of works now exist on this period. See Peter Bergen, *Holy War Inc.*, Touchstone, 2002; Gilles Kepel, *Jihad*, I. B. Tauris, 2002; Wright, *The Looming Tower*; *The 9/11 Commission Report*, W. W. Norton, 2004; and Burke, *Al-Qaeda*.

56. Khaled Sheikh Mohammed jealously guarded his autonomy and consistently refused to swear the *bayat* or oath of allegiance to bin Laden. See *The 9/11 Commission Report*, p. 59. Also: 'Sheikh Mohammed said he attempted to postpone swearing the *bayat* as long as possible to ensure that he remained free to plan operations however he chose,' Substitution for the testimony of Khaled Sheikh Mohammed, United States vs. Moussaoui, July 31, 2006, the United States District Court, Eastern District of Virginia.

57. The first version of the plan envisaged all the planes crashing into their targets except for one, which would land to allow Khaled Sheikh Mohammed himself to give a press conference.

58. Author interview with David Hicks, July 2010.

59. Another senior militant later remembered: 'I was staying at the general guesthouse when a bus arrived from the camp with at least forty-five trainees on board . . . When we asked why they had left the camp they told us that it had been closed down on bin Laden's orders because the date of the martyrdom operation was approaching. Everyone based in the camp was to head to Kandahar or Kabul or dispersed into the mountains to avoid becoming an easy target for any military strike.' Interview with Mohammed al-Tamimi, in Arabic newspaper *al-Hayat*, September 20, 2006, quoted in Camille Tawil, *Brothers in Arms*, Telegram, 2010, p. 182. The general guesthouse he referred to was in Kandahar and used by new arrivals.

60. Both men had travelled from Belgium, where they had been living, to Afghanistan earlier in the year. One had travelled, his wife later said, after seeing footage of bin Laden on the evening news. Like many of those who were enrolled in the 9/11 attack, the pair had been selected for their 'martyrdom mission' by al-Qaeda leaders who regularly visited the camps looking for tal-

ent among the trainees. The killing was a sweetener for the Taliban, who had already made their opposition to any direct attacks on American soil very clear, though bin Laden repeatedly told associates he did not expect the 'cowardly' US to send any soldiers to Afghanistan in retaliation for the coming attack. He cited the use of missiles only following the embassy bombings of 1998 as evidence.

61. A useful account of the assassination can be found in John Lee Anderson, *The Lion's Grave*, Atlantic Books, 2002.

62. Charge sheet, USA vs. Ali al-Bahlul, FBI interrogation reports, author collection. Court testimony of Ali Soufran and Christopher Anglin, FBI agents, USA vs. Ali Hamza al-Bahlul, November 2008.

63. Wright, *The Looming Tower*, p. 358.

64. Ibid. Questions answered by email by David Fratz, al-Bahlul's lawyer, July 2009. Evan Kohlmann, *Inside As-Sahaab: The Story of Ali al-Bahlul and the Evolution of al-Qaida's Propaganda*, Nefa Foundation, 2008.

## CHAPTER 2: 9/11, BEFORE AND AFTER

1. George Bush, *Decision Points*, Virgin, 2010, p. 134.

2. Richard Clarke, *Against All Enemies*, Simon and Schuster, 2004, p. 2. Bob Woodward, *Bush At War*, Simon and Schuster, 2003. *The 9/11 Commission Report*. Alistair Campbell, *The Blair Years*, Hutchinson, 2007, pp. 560–61.

3. Michael Powell, 'In 9/11 Chaos, Giuliani forged a lasting image', *New York Times*, September 21, 2007.

4. Bush, *Decision Points*, p. 144.

5. Campbell, *The Blair Years*, p. 561.

6. Sharon had been elected in February.

7. On October 9, 2001, in Britain's *Mirror* newspaper, David Trimble, the Unionist leader in Northern Ireland, declared that there was no difference between 'Irish and Arab terrorists'. In the run-up to the March presidential elections, President Robert Mugabe labelled his opponents 'terrorists', thus appearing to condone violent attacks by his supporters on his political opponents. 'Amnesty Now', *Amnesty International* magazine, summer 2002.

8. 'Reaction from around the world', *New York Times*, September 12, 2001. 'Attacks draw mixed response in the MidEast', CNN, September 12, 2001. Saddam Hussein afterwards denied approving the terms used by the newsreaders in question. This seems unlikely given the nature of his regime, but possible.

9. 'Islamic world deplores US losses', BBC News Online, September 14, 2001.

10. 'Sheikh Yusuf Al-Qaradawi condemns attacks against civilians: forbidden in Islam', IslamOnline and News Agencies, September 13, 2001.

11. See *America's Image in the World: Findings from the Pew Global Attitudes Project*, March 2007. A problem with gauging pre-9/11 sentiment is the lack of reliable data for the 1990s. Though anecdotally evidence of the attraction of living in the USA is clear, hard data is again difficult to find. Immigration statistics are one indication. US Department of Homeland Security and US Census figures show rising numbers of entrants to the US from Indonesia, Pakistan and Saudi Arabia in the late 1990s.

12. Such conflicted feelings were particularly evident among many Palestinians. Though Yasser Arafat, the Palestinian leader, expressed shock at the attacks, ostentatiously giving blood for the victims, reports of cheering Palestinians in parts of the Occupied Territories and in some Palestinian refugee camps in the Lebanon were genuine, despite internet rumours to the contrary. The real question was not whether 'celebratory gunfire' had echoed in the West Bank city of Nablus but to what extent those who had fired were representative of more general sentiments. A single portrait of bin Laden at a rally by Hamas supporters in Gaza was wrongly taken as evidence of widespread sympathy for al-Qaeda's leader. See 'Bin-Laden poster seen at Gaza rally', Associated Press, September 14, 2001; 'AP protests threats to freelance cameraman who filmed Palestinian rally', Associated Press, September 12, 2001; Joseph Logan, 'Palestinians celebrate attacks with gunfire', Reuters, September 12, 2001; 'Palestinians in Lebanon celebrate anti-US attacks', Agence France-Presse, September 11, 2001.

13. The 4,000 figure appears to have come from a *Jerusalem Post* internet article quoting an Israeli Foreign Ministry statement that 4,000 Israelis were believed to have been 'in the areas of the World Trade Center and the Pentagon at the time of the attacks'. 'The 4,000 Jews rumor: hundreds of Israelis missing in WTC attack', *Jerusalem Post* online, September 12, 2001.

14. Douglas Feith, *War and Decision*, Harper, 2008, p. 93.

15. Brian Whitaker, 'Muslim peoples doubt role of Arabs in September 11', *Guardian*, February 28, 2002. Gallup Poll of the Islamic World, based on interviews of nearly 10,000 residents in nine predominantly Islamic countries, Gallup, February 2002, Washington, DC.

16. ICM/BBC, BBC Poll of British Muslims, *Today*, Radio 4, November 2001.

17. Author interview with Mike Scheuer, CIA, head of Alec Station, August, 2005. See also the useful accounts in Coll, *Ghost Wars*; *The 9/11 Commission Report*; and Wright, *The Looming Tower*. A 1995 National Intelligence Estimate correctly analysed the danger as coming from 'transient groupings of individuals' that lacked 'strong organization but rather are loose affiliations' and operated 'outside traditional circles but have access to a worldwide network of training facilities and safe havens'. Effective and timely action was not taken.

18. Coll, *Ghost Wars*, p. 425.

19. Author interview, September 2008.

20. Department of Defense budget for Financial Year 2000, US DoD news release, February 1, 1999.

21. Lawrence Freedman, *A Choice of Enemies*, Weidenfeld and Nicolson, 2009, p. 370. Author telephone interview with Jack Cloonan, 2008.

22. Author interview with senior former MI6 officer, London, 2003.

23. Gary C. Schroen, *First In*, Ballantine Books, 2005, p. 26.

24. Coll, *Ghost Wars*, p. 493.

25. Ibid., p. 499.

26. See the testimony of Abu Jandal. That a meeting was to be held that bin Laden would chair at the camp was apparently widely known. Also Coll, *Ghost Wars*, p. 410.

27. Author interview with American officials, Riyadh, 2008

28. Author telephone interview with former senior CIA analyst, August 2009. Indian intelligence officials later admitted to the author that there was 'no evidence at all' of bin Laden's presence in Kashmir. The admission came in 2003 at a time of a relative thaw in relations between India and Pakistan.

29. Author interviews with three Middle Eastern intelligence service officials, Islamabad 1999–2000. Coll, *Ghost Wars*, p. 443.

30. Author interview with Michael Scheuer, CIA, head of Alec Station, 2002.

31. Author telephone interview with Art Keller, April 2008.

32. Ibid.

33. There was no station in Kabul. Author interview with British intelligence official, 2010.

34. Author interview, London 2009.

35. The identity of those at Tora Bora is a useful guide. Along with the Saudis, Egyptians and Yemenis who made up the core strength of al-Qaeda were Moroccans and Kuwaitis, Palestinians from Jordan, Syrians, Turks and many central Asian fighters, especially Uzbeks. There were several Chinese Uighur Muslims, a handful of Britons, a large number of Pakistanis and at least three Frenchmen.

36. The number of Egyptians appears to have dropped away during the 1990s, as one would expect given the course of the militancy in Egypt itself. By 2000, one volunteer was posing the question 'What is the reason for not having new Egyptian freedom fighters amongst us?' to bin Laden. Harmony documents, document ID: AFGP-2002-801138.

37. Tim Judah, 'The Taliban Papers', *Survival*, vol. 44, no. 1, spring 2002. The body of evidence produced by the recruits themselves in the form of interviews with journalists or their own published accounts of their experiences, the published biographies of 'martyrs', evidence later found in Afghanistan by intelligence operatives and reporters as well as the imperfect but nonetheless useful testimonies hundreds of them gave to investigators or tribunals while in custody now allows, a decade after 9/11, a relatively accurate picture

to be put together of who they were and how and why they travelled to Afghanistan. In April 2011, the author was able to consult 800 leaked official secret files on every detainee in Guantanamo Bay compiled between 2003 and 2007 to support recommendations for release or continued imprisonment. Each provided detailed biographies of their subject. Among other useful primary sources are the court proceedings and witness statements of Abu Jandal, Ali al-Bahlul, al-Batarfi, who all ended up in Guantanamo Bay, and the testimonies of al-Utaiba, Hossein Kertchou and Jamal al-Fadl during the 2001 trial of the 1998 east African bombings, USA vs. Usama bin Laden, New York Southern District Court, February 2001. Also John Walker Lindh indictment, February 2, 2002, US vs. John Walker Lindh in the US Eastern District Court of Virginia. Material that emerged during investigations of the Millenium Plot is also informative: testimony of Ahmed Ressam, USA vs. Mokhtar Houari, July 3, 2001; testimony of Judge Jean-Louis Brugiere, trial of Ahmed Ressam, Los Angeles, April 2, 2001; USA vs. Abu Doha sealed complaint, US Southern District Court, New York, July 2, 2001. Also related are the interrogation report of Djamal Beghal, author collection; Moroccan Ministry of Justice, interrogation report of Zuhair Hilal Mohammed al-Tubaiti, Casablanca, June 19, 2001, author's collection. Also among the many interviews the author conducted on this topic two of the most useful were with Mohammed Umr al-Madani, Kabul, 2008, and Noman Benotman, formerly of the Libyan Fighting Group, London, 2002, 2003 and 2008. There are now voluminous secondary sources on the training camps in Afghanistan in the 1990s though still relatively little on exactly who made the journey to reach them.

38. See Giles Kepel, *Jihad: The Trail of Political Islam*, I. B. Tauris, 2002; and Olivier Roy, *The Failure of Political Islam*, Harvard University Press, 1998. An additional advantage was that it drew heavily on the language and thought of those strands that had preceded it and thus seemed less alien.

39. Human Rights Watch, *Annual Report*, 2001.

40. See Bergen, *Holy War Inc.*; Bergen, *The Osama Bin Laden I Know*; Wright, *The Looming Tower*; Andy Worthington, *The Guantanamo Files*, Pluto, 2007; Burke, *Al-Qaeda*, pp. 56–72.

41. See Thomas Hegghammer, *Terrorist Recruitment and Radicalization in Saudi Arabia*, Middle East Policy, 2006, p. 44.

42. Ibid., p. 49.

43. A couple sought martyrdom to join a brother already killed in Afghanistan in heaven. See Hegghammer, *Terrorist Recruitment*, p. 49 and note 33 for further sources.

44. Others, such as the French convert Hervé Loiseau, simply followed older or respected charismatic individuals on whom they had developed a certain degree of emotional dependence. Loiseau and another young Frenchman of Algerian origin followed a much more motivated and capable nineteen-year-old called Mourad Benchellali, whose father was a radical cleric whose brother

had tried and failed to fight in Chechnya. Three of his family had spent time in French prisons. Benchellali insisted he had sought 'adventure', enhanced local status and to rival his brother and later published a fairly unapologetic book about his time in Afghanistan. Worthington, *The Guantanamo Files*, p. 63.

45. Sharon Curcio, 'Generational Differences in Waging Jihad', *Military Review*, July–August 2005, pp. 84–8.

46. Notebooks found at Darunta and Khost camps by the author, November 2001.

47. Letters found in New Khaldan camp by the author, November 2001.

48. A very high proportion of accounts from Western recruits refer to sickness. See also Curcio, 'Generational Differences'.

49. Author interview with David Hicks, July 2010.

50. Author interview with cleric and courier 'Haji Anwar', Peshawar, October 2001.

51. By the end of the 1990s, 'America stood out as an object for admiration, envy and blame . . . This created a kind of cultural asymmetry. To us, Afghanistan seemed very far away. To members of al-Qaeda, America seemed very close. In a sense, they were more globalized than we were,' the official American commission of inquiry into 9/11 accurately noted in 2004. *The 9/11 Commission Report*, p. 340. Though unfair to President Clinton and many of the senior counter-terrorist officials in Washington who recognized that fanatical politically or religiously motivated violence would be a growing threat as the world became more interconnected, these words did adequately capture how very few grasped how close the threat had become.

52. Two examples are Abu Qutada and Abu Musab al-Suri, who was perhaps the single most significant militant strategist of the 9/11 Wars.

53. Ruling of Special Immigration Appeals Commission, March 8, 2004. Tawil, *Brothers in Arms*, p. 125. An MI5 officer present at the meeting apparently sensed that Abu Qutada was close to offering to assist investigations into radical activity in the UK.

54. Abu Musab al-Suri, 'A Message to the British and the Europeans, August, 2005', quoted by Tawil, *Brothers in Arms*, p. 126.

55. Brynjar Lia, 'The Al-Qaida Strategist Abu Mus'ab al-Suri: A Profile', Presentation OMS-Seminar, March 15, 2006, Oslo, Norway. Author interviews with Omar Mohammed Bakri Fostok, London, 2000, 2001.

56. He received no reply, however. Tawil, *Brothers in Arms*, p. 125.

57. Author interview with a Special Branch officer, London, 2004.

58. Sums of between £25,000 and £100,000 were regularly seized, larger sums less frequently. One activist at the time told the author how he had given £50,000 to Lashkar-e-Toiba and £50,000 to Chechen groups, proceeds from a range of businesses that he and other activists ran, between 1999 and 2000. Indian intelligence services complained frequently to the British government – and the author – about these activities.

59. Author interview with an MI5 officer, London, 2005.

60. Author interview with an MI6 officer, London, 2009.

61. John Kampfner, *Blair's Wars*, The Free Press, 2003, p. 113.

62. Condoleezza Rice, testimony before 9/11 Commission. Daniel Benjamin and Steven Simon, *Age of Sacred Terror*, Random House, 2002. Clinton officials later insisted they had in fact repeatedly emphasized the threat of terrorism to Bush, Rice and others, and though many of the threat reports which reached senior administration figures were indeed vague or historic and desperately short of actionable details they did collectively speak of an unprecedented level of evident danger.

63. Clarke, *Against All Enemies*, p. 234. Bush, *Decision Points*, pp. 134–5.

64. *The 9/11 Commission*, p. 333. Rice, testimony before 9/11 Commission. The Principals Committee in Bush's White House included Rice, Attorney General John Ashcroft, Defense Secretary Donald Rumsfeld, Secretary of State Colin Powell, Treasury Secretary Paul O'Neill and CIA Director George Tenet, among other senior administration officials.

65. Bush, *Decision Points*, p. 135.

66. Ibid., p. 128.

67. CNN, Text of Bush's address, September 11, 2001.

68. Abizaid was born in California to a Lebanese-American father and an American mother. Though Arab-speaking, he is not Lebanese-born, as sometimes reported. See Jones, *In the Graveyard of Empires*, p. 243.

69. Bush, *Decision Points*, p. 145.

70. Feith, *War and Decision*, pp. 3–11

71. David E. Sanger, 'Ex-occupation aide sees no dent in "Saddamists"', *New York Times*, July 2, 2004. For Dick Cheney 'the situation when President Bush and I came to office' was that 'where terrorists were emboldened by years of being able to strike us with impunity'.

72. Manuel Perez-Rivas, 'Bush vows to rid the world of evil-doers', CNN, September 16, 2001.

73. George W. Bush, 'An Address to a Joint Session of Congress and the American People', September 20, 2001

74. The name was changed after Muslim scholars complained about the religiously charged initial name, 'Infinite Justice'.

75. See Pervez Musharraf, *In the Line of Fire*, pp. 201–4, for a colourful if not entirely reliable account of this episode.

76. *Operation Enduring Freedom: Foreign Pledges of Military and Intelligence Support*, CRS Report for Congress, October 17, 2001. Stephen Tanner, *Afghanistan: A Military History*, Da Capo, 2007, p. 292.

77. Bush, *Decision Points*, p. 191.

78. President George W. Bush, Commencement Address at the United States Naval Academy in Annapolis, Maryland, May 25, 2001. 'We must build forces that draw upon the revolutionary advances in the technology of war that will allow us to keep the peace by redefining war on our terms,' Bush had also said.

79. Thomas Ricks, *Fiasco*, Penguin, 2007. Feith, *War and Decision*, p. 75.

80. Kampfner, *Blair's Wars*, p. 117. One reason the Pentagon was reluctant to accept the myriad offers of aid flowing in was that, quite apart from few having the means to transport their troops to the theatre themselves or supply them once they were there, the forces offered were insufficiently equipped to fight effectively alongside a military as technologically sophisticated as the American army.

81. James F. Dobbins, *After the Taliban*, Potomac Books, 2008, p. 28. Feith, *War and Decision*, p. 51. Donald Rumsfeld, 'A new kind of war', *New York Times*, September 27, 2001.

82. Author telephone interview with Paul Pillar, former deputy director CIA Counter Terrorist Centre, national intelligence officer for the Near East and south Asia, November 2008.

83. Assistant Secretary of State for Intelligence and Research Carl Ford to Secretary of State Colin Powell, 'Pakistan – poll shows strong and growing public support for Taleban', November 7, 2001, National Security Archive. The levels had gone from 38 per cent of people saying they favoured increasing their country's support to the Taliban to 46 per cent and from a third to just over half seeing the Taliban more favourably as the coming war loomed.

84. 'Pakistan protests turn violent', BBC News Online, September 21, 2001.

## CHAPTER 3: WAR IN AFGHANISTAN

1. Claudio Franco, 'The Tehrik-e Taliban Pakistan', in Antonio Giustozzi, ed., *Decoding the New Taliban*, Hurst, 2009, p. 272.

2. An Afghan equivalent of General Cambronne's useless but much admired 'merde' at Waterloo in 1815 or General McAuliffe's 'nuts' at Bastogne during the Battle of the Bulge, 1944, to name but a couple of examples.

3. Musharraf, *In the Line of Fire*, p. 216. See also Zahid Hussein, *General on a Mission*, Newsline, 2001, and *Frontline Pakistan*, Columbia University Press, pp. 41–3.

4. RAND Corproration, Benjamin S. Lambeth, *Air Power against Terror: America's Conduct of Operation Enduring Freedom*, 2005, p. xvi.

5. Author telephone interview with Bob Grenier, CIA station chief Islamabad 2001–2, January 2009. The Taliban commander concerned was Mullah Akhtar Mohammed Osmani. See also George Tenet, *At the Center of the Storm: My Years at the CIA*, HarperCollins, 2007, pp. 182–3.

6. These included Younis Khalis, the cleric and former *mujahideen* commander who was close to bin Laden and the Taliban but remained independent and a power in his own right. He was approached in early November. Author interview with Michael Scheuer, CIA head of Alec Station, 2002.

7. Schroen, *First In*, p. 300. Bob Woodward, 'CIA led way with cash handouts', *Washington Post*, November 18, 2002. Jason Burke, 'Torture, treachery and

spies – covert war in Afghanistan', *Observer*, November 4, 2001. Multiple author interviews, Peshawar, autumn 2001, London, 2009.

8. 'President notifies Congress about troop deployment. U.S. claims air supremacy over Afghanistan', CNN, October 9, 2001.

9. Author telephone interview with Paul Pillar, CIA national intelligence officer for the Middle East 2000–2005, with Bob Grenier, CIA station chief Islamabad 2001–2, January 2009. See also Schroen, *First In*.

10. At sixteen, after a row with his recently appointed Socialist schoolteacher, he had launched an attack on a police station. The capture and torture of one of his associates merely taught him, he later told interviewers, to plan operations properly.

11. See Robert D. Kaplan, *Soldiers of God*, Vintage, 2008, for an excellent account of Haq's life, especially pp. 145–6. Also the useful documentary *Afghan Warrior: The Life and Death of Abdul Haq*, Touch productions for BBC2, 2003.

12. Much of the violence was directed at relatively Westernized schoolteachers sent to provinces from Kabul, such as the one who had been the immediate catalyst for Haq's activism.

13. Kaplan, *Soldiers of God*. Author interviews with former *mujahideen*, BBC film; Afghan journalists who covered the war, Peshawar, 1998–9.

14. Author interview with a former MI6 senior official. Rashid, *Descent into Chaos*, p. 20.

15. 'We are firm on road of jihad', *The Times*, September 25, 2001. Author interview with Haji Din Mohammed Arsala, Peshawar, November 2001. A letter addressed to the Pakistani people called on them to 'rise in defence of Islam' and welcomed the 'martyrdom' of those killed in the recent demonstrations.

16. Author interview with Abdul Haq Arsala, Peshawar, October 2001.

17. Instead Haq was bankrolled by two Afghan-American businessmen.

18. See Burke, 'Torture, treachery and spies'.

19. Author interview with Haji Din Mohammed Arsala, Peshawar, November 2001.

20. R. W. Apple Jr, 'A military quagmire remembered: Afghanistan as Vietnam', *New York Times*, October 31, 2001.

21. Bush, *Decision Points*, pp. 153, 154.

22. Seymour M. Hersh, 'The getaway. Questions surround a secret Pakistani airlift', *New Yorker*, January 28, 2002. Bob Woodward, 'Doubts and debates before victory over the Taliban', *Washington Post*, November 18, 2002. The letters turned out to have been sent by a disaffected American research scientist.

23. Feith, *War and Decision*, p. 78.

24. *United States Special Operations Command History*, 6th edn, 2007, p. 96. Schroen, *First In*, pp. 265–7. Hamid Karzai, *Letter from Kabul*, Wiley, 2006, p. 117.

25. Author interview with Noman Benotman, former Libyan militant, March 2011. See also Quillam Foundation, Camille Tawil, *The Other Face of al-Qaeda*, London, 2010, p. 17.

26. Author interview with Mohammed Ishaq Mir Ali, Nowshera, October 2002.

27. Schroen, *First In*, p. 345. Anthony Davis, 'The Fall of Kabul', *Jane's Defence Weekly*, November 13, 2001.

28. See Karzai's own account in *Letter from Kabul. United States Special Operations Command History*, p. 97.

29. Author interviews with Zaheer Arsala, Kabul August 2008, Abdul Qadir, Hazrat Ali, Jalalabad, November 2001.

30. Jason Burke, 'Mujahideen back to "rob and beat us"', *Observer*, November 18, 2001.

31. Report of interrogation of Saleem Ahmed Saleem Hamden, Guantanamo Bay, Cuba, 062870902.

32. Abdullah al-Shihri, 'Aide to Bin Laden surrenders', Associated Press, July 14, 2004. Bin Laden on Tape: Attacks "Benefited Islam Greatly"', CNN, December 14, 2001.

33. *Tora Bora Revisited: How We Failed to Get Bin Laden and Why It Matters Today: A Report to Members of the Committee on Foreign Relations, United States Senate, 111th Congress first session*, November 30, 2009. p. 5

34. Jagdallak was where the final remnants of a retreating British army had been destroyed by local tribesmen in 1842.

35. Philip Smucker, 'How bin Laden got away: A day-by-day account of how Osama bin Laden eluded the world's most powerful military machine', *Christian Science Monitor*, March 4, 2002.

36. Author interviews with Hazrat Ali, Haji Din Mohammedi, Haji Zaheer Arsala, Jalalabad, October 2002.

37. Author interviews with Zaheer Shah, Hazrat Ali in Jalalabad, October 2002. Memorandum for Commander, US Southern Command, CSRT Input, US9AF–000782DP, Awal Malim Gul, February 15, 2008, secret, author collection. Jasan Burke, 'Guantanamo Bay files rewrite the story of Osama bin Laden's Tora Bora escape', *Guardian*, April 26, 2011.

38. Author interviews with Jan Mohammed and other commanders, Peshawar, June 2002.

39. Rashid, *Descent into Chaos*, pp. 242–3 .

40. John F. Burns, '10-month Afghan mystery: Is bin Laden dead or alive?', *New York Times*, September 30, 2002.

41. 'How Al Qaeda slipped away', *Newsweek*, August 19, 2002.

42. Author interview with Mohammed Shah Shinwari, Hadda, October 2002.

43. Author interview with police chief, Asadabad, Kunar, October 2002. Memorandum for Commander, US Southern Command, CSRT Input, Sabar Lal Melma, US9AF–000801DP, June 5, 2005, secret, author collection.

44. President Musharraf's aides later claimed that at least 300 had been handed

over to the Americans. A variety of activists, such as the lawyer, politicians and cleric Javed Ibrahim Parachar, who was based in Kohat, secured the release of at least 300 more, he told the author in Kohat, July 2005. The total is likely to be around 600.

45. See the testimony of Musab Omar Ali al Mudwani, quoted in Worthington, *The Guantanamo Files*, p. 41. For wives, see testimony of Salem Ahmed Salem. Bahlul was leading a group of two and a half dozen others, largely members of bin Laden's security detail, who swiftly became known as the 'Dirty Thirty' to their captors. Memorandum for Commander, US Southern Command, CSRT Input for Guantanamo Detainee, US9YM-000039DP, Ali Hamza Suleiman al-Bahlul, June 5, 2005, secret, author collection.

46. He had decided to travel after long conversations with a cleric and after viewing videos of 'Kashmir, Bosnia, Chechnya and how the soldiers mistreated the women and the children'. He had hoped to fight in Chechnya or with the Taliban but was not unhappy to find himself in a camp connected to al-Qaeda.

47. Author interview, Kabul, 2008.

48. Interview with Mohammed al-Tamimi, in the Arabic newspaper *al-Hayat*, September 20, 2006, quoted in Tawil, *Brothers in Arms*, p. 183. Ayman al-Batarfi, Summary of Administrative Review Board Proceeding ISN 556, 2006, p. 14. http://www.dod.mil/pubs/foi/detainees/csrt_arb/ARB_Transcript_ 2397-2490.pdf. A Yemeni fighter remembered 'anti-aircraft guns', but these appear to have been Soviet-era manually operated weapons entirely unsuited to defence against contemporary air power. Memoranda for Commander, US Southern Command, CSRT Input, US9AG-000238DP, Nabil Said Hadjarab, January 22, 2007, and US9YM-00054920, Omar Said Adayn, June 2008, secret, author collection.

49. *Tora Bora Revisited*, p. 21.

50. *United States Special Operations Command History*, p. 98.

51. In early December there were only about 1,300 US troops in country.

52. MI6 former senior official, London, February 2009.

53. Bin Laden also ordered his wives not to remarry and his 'women kinsfolk' to avoid cosmetics so as not to resemble the 'whore-ish and mannish females of the West' and warned his sons not to join al-Qaeda and the armed struggle. Al-Majallah, 'Al-Majallah Obtains Bin Laden's Will', October 27, 2002, pp. 22–6, quoted in 'Foreign Broadcast Information Service Report, Compilation of Usama Bin Laden's Statements 1994 to 2004', published 2004. Available at: http://www.fas.org/irp/world/para/ubl-fbis.pdf.

54. According to a declassified version of an official history of US special forces' operations during the Afghan campaign of late 2001, published in 2007, 'All source reporting corroborated his presence on several days from 9–14 December.' The claim was based on accounts of commanders and intelligence officials. *United States Special Operations Command History*, p. 101, 6th edn, March 2008, quoted in *Tora Bora Revisited*, p. 10.

55. A further intercepted message was probably a pre-recorded sermon played to cover the senior leadership's flight. Ilene R. Prusher, 'Two top Al Qaeda leaders spotted', *Christian Science Monitor*, March 26, 2002. Memoranda for Commander, US Southern Command, CSRT Input and Recommendation for Guantanamo Detainee, US9SA-000062DP, US9SU-000054DP, Mohammad Salah Ahmad, November 15, 2007, and AF-0003148, Harun al'Afghani, August 2, 2007, secret, author collection.

56. On NBC's *Meet the Press* on December 2, 2001 Tim Russert, the host of the programme, showed Secretary of Defense Donald Rumsfeld with the artist's rendering of bin Laden's fortress.

> Russert: *The Times* of London did a graphic, which I want to put on the screen for you and our viewers. This is it. This is a fortress. This is a very much a complex, multi-tiered, bedrooms and offices on the top, as you can see, secret exits on the side and on the bottom, cut deep to avoid thermal detection so when our planes fly to try to determine if any human beings are in there, it's built so deeply down and embedded in the mountain and the rock it's hard to detect. And over here, valleys guarded, as you can see, by some Taliban soldiers. A ventilation system to allow people to breathe and to carry on. An arms and ammunition depot. And you can see here the exits leading into it and the entrances large enough to drive trucks and cars and even tanks. And it's own hydroelectric power to help keep lights on, even computer systems and telephone systems. It's a very sophisticated operation.
>
> Rumsfeld: Oh, you bet. This is serious business. And there's not one of those. There are many of those. And they have been used very effectively. And I might add, Afghanistan is not the only country that has gone underground. Any number of countries have gone underground. The tunnelling equipment that exists today is very powerful. It's dual use. It's available across the globe. And people have recognized the advantages of using underground protection for themselves. (http://video.google.com/videoplay?docid=-4697166259112889282#).

57. 'Yemeni doctor describes bloody siege at Tora Bora', Associated Press, September 7, 2007. Memorandum for Commander, US Southern Command, CSRT Input, US9YM-000627DP, Ayman al-Batarfi, April 29, 2008, secret, author collection.

58. Andy McNab, 'SAS hero Andy McNab describes regiment's Al-Qaeda battle', *Daily Mirror*, February 16, 2002, pp. 26–7. In fact, few knew very much about the caves or anything else. Intelligence on the actual defences was minimal, and the vast surveillance resources that would later be used by the America military and, by extension, some of its allies, were not yet available.

59. The number was 300 according to Susan B. Glasser, 'The battle of Tora Bora: secrets, money, mistrust', *Washington Post*, February 10, 2002.

60. 'Dalton Fury' was, unsurprisingly, a pseudonym. Dalton Fury, *Kill Bin Laden*, St Martin's Press, 2008, pp. 277–8.

61. 'How Osama Bin Laden escaped', *Foreign Policy*, December 11, 2009.

62. His body was found by local tribesmen weeks later and buried. A shrine was built over his tomb, which has since become a place of pilgrimage. Djamel Loiseau, 'Itinéraire d'un soldat d'Allah', *France*, 3, April 13, 2007. The story of the Briton who died was cited by the bombers who struck London in 2005 as a key inspiration. Home Office, *Report of the Official Account of the Bombings in London on 7th July 2005*, 2006. p. 19.

63. See Memorandum for Commander, US Southern Command, CSRT Input, US9TS-000510DP, Riyad Nassr Muhammed Atahar, September 15, 2008, secret, author collection.

64. Audio tape, al-Jazeera, 2003, transcript at http://news.bbc.co.uk/2/hi/2751019.stm: 'Complete failure of the international alliance of evil, with all its forces, [to overcome] a small number of *mujahideen* – 300 *mujahideen* hunkered down in trenches spread over an area of one square mile under a temperature of –10 degrees Celsius. The battle resulted in the injury of 6 per cent of personnel – we hope God will accept them as martyrs – and the damage of 2 per cent of the trenches, praise be to God.'

65. Author interview with Mohammed Umr al-Madani, Kabul, August 2008.

66. Smucker, 'How bin Laden got away'.

67. *United States Special Operations Command History*, p. 99.

68. Drew Brown, 'How al Qaeda fighters escaped; Bin Laden told his men to disperse, witness says', *Miami Herald*, October 17, 2002.

69. Author telephone interview with Bob Grenier, January 2009.

70. Author email exchange with Lodhi, February 2011. Author interview with General Orakzai, London, February 2009.

71. Seth Jones, *In the Graveyard of Empires*, p. 101.

72. *Newsweek*, author interviews.

73. Ghanim Abdul Rahman al Harbi, Combat Status Review Tribunal, Summary of Evidence, Guantanamo Bay, 16 August 16, 2004; Administrative Review Board Round 1 Summaries , June 23, 2006. Worthington, *The Guantanamo Files*, pp. 29–30. Interview with local residents, Hadda, Jalalabad, Milawa, November 2001, October 2002. Burns, '10-month Afghan mystery'. Glasser, 'The battle of Tora Bora'.

74. Rory Carroll, 'Biker Mullah's great escape', *Guardian*, January 6, 2002.

75. See 'The Global War on Terrorism: The First 100 Days', p. 11.

76. Bob Woodward, 'The inside story of the CIA's proxy war', *Australian Age*, November 20, 2002.

77. Tenet, *At the Center of the Storm*, p. 255

78. Woodward, 'CIA led way with cash handouts'.

79. The same was the case in the UK. Matthew Engel, 'First British casualties as four SAS men shot', *Guardian*, November 27, 2001. The first US casualty in Afghanistan was Evander E. Andrews, Master Sergeant US Air Force, age thirty-six, from Solon, Maine, on October 10, 2001, according to the *Washington*

*Post*. He was killed in a forklift accident. 'Faces of the Fallen' project, Washington Post Online, accessed July 2010.

80. The airlift took place with the permission of senior Bush administration figures, who appear to have been largely unaware of exactly who was being lifted where. Hersh, 'The getaway'. Douglas Frantz, 'Pakistan ended aid to Taliban only hesitantly', *New York Times*, December 8, 2001. Ahmed Rashid, *Descent into Chaos*, pp. 90–93.

81. Author interview with Haji Saifullah, Gardez, April 2002.

82. Bob Woodward, *Plan of Attack*, Simon and Schuster, 2008, p. 8. Bush, *Decision Points*, p. 234.

83. Judith Miller, 'An Iraqi defector tells of work on at least 20 hidden weapons sites', *New York Times*, December 20, 2001.

## CHAPTER 4: THE CALM BEFORE THE STORM

1. Author telephone interview with Robert Grenier, former CIA station chief Islamabad, January 2009.

2. Author telephone interview with Bruce Riedel, CIA senior analyst and senior director for Near East Affairs on the National Security Council 1997–2002, October 2008.

3. 'When we received intitial reports of al-Qaeda's presence [in South Waziristan] we did not take them very seriously,' said General Musharraf. See *In the Line of Fire*, p. 264.

4. Including one attack involving young Britons.

5. Bush, *Decision Points*, p. 166.

6. Rama Lakshmi, 'Gunmen with explosives attack Indian parliament', *Washington Post*, December 14, 2001. Simon Jeffrey 'The Moscow theatre siege', *Guardian*, October 28, 2002.

7. Carol Eisenberg, 'On religion, faith and rituals', *Newsday*, December 22, 2001. Pew Forum on Religion and Public Life, December 2001. The post-9/11 figure was 59 per cent, up from 45 per cent six months previously.

8. Jason Katz, Victoria Cullen, Connor Buttner and John Pollock, 'American Newspaper Coverage of Islam Post-September 11, 2001: A Community Structure Approach', *Association for Education in Journalism and Mass Communication*, August 8, 2007. The study also discovered that communities with highest levels of education and revenues were not those whose newspapers reflected more positive views of Islam in the aftermath of 9/11. Depictions of Islam became more negative over the years up until 2005.

9. Emily Wax, 'In times of terror, teens talk the talk', *Washington Post*, March 20, 2002.

10. In March 2003 those figures were 64, 50 and 59 per cent respectively. The period saw a predictable crash in views of the US too. See *Pew Global Attitudes*

*2003: Views of a Changing World*, 2003, pp. 19, 46. The number of people giving the United States a positive rating has dropped by 22 points in Turkey and 13 points in Pakistan since 1999. See ibid., p. 4.

11. Ibid., p. 34.

12. 'The 2002 Gallup poll of the Islamic world'. Muslims overwhelmingly cited technology, computers and knowledge when asked what they liked most about the West. Scott Atran, 'Trends in Suicide Terrorism: Sense and Nonsense', paper presented to World Federation of Scientists Permanent Monitoring Panel on Terrorism, Erice, Sicily, August 2004. Mark Tessler, 'Do Islamic Orientations Influence Attitudes toward Democracy in the Arab World? Evidence from Egypt, Jordan, Morocco, and Algeria', *International Journal of Comparative Sociology*, vol. 2 (2002), pp. 229–49. Mark Tessler and Dan Corstange, 'How Should Americans Understand Arab and Muslim Political Attitudes?', *Journal of Social Affairs*, vol. 19 (2002).

13. Author interviews, Jalalabad, October 2002.

14. Author interviews Jalalabad, Gardez, Kabul, May and October 2002.

15. Michael O'Hanlon, 'Staying Power: The U.S. Mission in Afghanistan Beyond 2011', *Foreign Affairs*, September/October 2010.

16. Author interviews, Kabul, 2002–3. Interviews with Ashraf Ghani, former minister of finance, Kabul, January 2007 and August 2008. Author interview with Clare Lockhart, Ministry of Finance adviser, Kabul, January 2007. For the row over the road to Kandahar, see Dobbins, *After the Taliban*.

17. Clare Lockhart, 'Learning from experience', *Slate*, posted November 5, 2008.

18. Radio address by Mrs Bush, Office of the First Lady, November 17, 2001. Kampfner, *Blair's Wars*, p. 123.

19. Images of the execution of a woman convicted of murder in Kabul in November 1999, which the author had witnessed, were repeatedly broadcast and became, despite the relative infrequency of such events, symbolic of the Taliban rule.

20. Afghan women and children relief act of 2001, US Congress, 107th Congress, December 12, 2001, US Government Printing Office, 2001. Public Law 107-81 states: 'the President is authorized, on such terms and conditions as the President may determine, to provide educational and health care assistance for the women and children living in Afghanistan and as refugees in neighboring countries ... In providing assistance under subsection (a), the President shall ensure that such assistance is provided in a manner that protects and promotes the human rights of all people in Afghanistan, utilizing indigenous institutions and nongovernmental organizations, especially women's organizations, to the extent possible ...'

21. But the experience of Afghan women was much more complicated than many in the West expected. When Florence Aubenas, correspondent for the left-wing French newspaper *Libération*, was asked by her editors to report on why such a large majority of Kabul's women had kept their *burqas* she was first told they feared acid attacks. On discovering that there had been no such

incidents reported, she asked again and was told that in fact the women did not want to leave home without the full covering because they had grown used to it. Florence Aubenas, *Grand Reporter: petite conférence sur le journalisme*, Bayard, 2009, p. 12.

22. 'Lauded at pageant, woman condemned by Afghan officials', Associated Press, November 10, 2003. 'Afghan Supreme Court bans beauty pageants', Agence France-Presse, October 30, 2003.

23. The most extreme representatives of this new vision for Afghanistan were to be found among the eclectic collection of visitors who turned up in Kabul, few of whom had shown any previous interest in Afghanistan, through 2002. One was French intellectual Bernard-Henri Lévy, dispatched by President Jacques Chirac to report on what France could provide to assist the reconstruction of Afghanistan. A senior French government bureaucrat told the author in 2009 that Lévy's ten-day expedition and the subsequent publication of his 200-page report used up a significant proportion of the funds the French government had available for Afghanistan at the time. His suggestions included, among other things, 'a year of French cinema', 'the creation of a French cultural centre, to be jointly developed with the intelligentsia of Kabul' and for 'the emergence of a democratic "Afghanitude" (identity)' to combat the rule of the warlords, the creation of a corps 'of black hussars for democracy, who would travel all over the country, in the name of President Karzai, preaching the message of citizenship and fundamental human rights'.

24. Marion and Peter Sluglett, 'The Historiography of Modern Iraq', *American Historical Review*, 1991, pp. 1,412–13. Barfield, *Afghanistan*, p. 339.

25. A good example was the extremely successful Afghan-government-run and World-Bank-funded National Solidarity Programme, which offered grants and loans to village committees for local infrastructure or training projects.

26. Author interview with Malalai Kakar, Kandahar, November 2003.

27. Author interview, Bagram, Afghanistan, May 2003.

28. These are figures for the Department of Defense Base Budget. If what are known as emergency supplementals are included they rise to $316 billion and $345 billion respectively. Figures provided by the Department of Defense, July 2009.

29. Dobbins, *After the Taliban*, p. 140

30. Jones, *In the Graveyard of Empires*, p. 142.

31. Ricks, *Fiasco*, p. 44.

32. Jones, *In the Graveyard of Empires*, p. 119. The figure for Northern Ireland includes both British troops (not technically international) and the Royal Ulster Constabulary. See James T. Quinlivan, 'Burden of Victory: The Painful Arithmetic of Stability Operations', *RAND Review*, vol. 27, no. 2 (summer 2003), pp. 28–9.

33. Bush, *Decision Points*, p. 207. Bob Woodward, *Bush at War*, Simon and Schuster, 2003, pp. 82–3. In fact, both had misread Afghan history and its present. The Soviets in fact had maintained a relatively light footprint, and it

was their lack of an effective counter-insurgency strategy that had been the problem, not the number of their troops.

34. Dobbins, *After the Taliban*, p. 130. Feith says this was not the case but is less convincing.

35. Author interview with Ron Nash, British ambassador in Kabul, 2002–3, July 2009.

36. The warlords and their militias, despite being seen by most Afghans as the principal threat to their security, were often hired by US troops and especially the CIA as their local eyes, ears and often hands as well. They included individuals like Pacha Khan Zadran, who by the spring had taken to mortaring the town of Gardez after being dumped as a client by the Americans. In the important Helmand province, which has a population of over a million and was crucial both as a centre of the opium trade and as a fief of the Taliban, the only foreign soldiers were around sixty American special forces and a couple of hundred regulars who conducted nocturnal raids to pick up suspected 'AQT'.

37. Jason Burke and Peter Beaumont, 'West pays warlords to stay in line', *Observer*, London, July 21, 2002. Jones, *In the Graveyard of Empires*, p. 130. Antonio Guistozzi, *Empires of Mud*, Hurst, 2009, pp. 89–91.

38. Worthington, *The Guantanamo Files*, pp. 19–25. Yusef al-Rabesh, author interview, Riyadh, June 2011.

39. According to an affidavit filed in a US court by his attorney, US soldiers 'blindfolded Mr. Lindh, and took several pictures of Mr. Lindh and themselves with Mr. Lindh. In one, the soldiers scrawled "shithead" across Mr. Lindh's blindfold and posed with him . . . Another told Mr. Lindh that he was "going to hang" for his actions and that after he was dead, the soldiers would sell the photographs and give the money to a Christian organization.' Human Rights Watch, *The Road to Abu Ghraib*, June 2004, p. 20.

40. See David Rose, 'See how MI5 colluded in my torture: Binyam Mohamed claims British agents fed Moroccan torturers their questions', *Daily Mail*, March 8, 2009, for what was happening by spring 2002.

41. Ian Cobain, 'The truth about torture', *Guardian*, July 8, 2009. The British MI6 officers received legal advice that they were not obliged to intervene to prevent abuse.

42. Dana Priest and Barton Gellman, 'U.S. decries abuse but defends interrogations', *Washington Post*, December 26, 2002, Human Rights Watch, *The Road to Abu Ghraib*, p. 23. Freedman, *A Choice of Enemies*, p. 395. Bush signed the directive at a private meeting with Cheney apparently without even sitting down.

43. Douglas Jehl and Andrea Elliott, 'Cuba base sent its interrogators to Iraqi prison', *New York Times*, May 29, 2004.

44. These details come from Chris Mackey and Greg Miller, *The Interrogators: Inside the Secret War against al Qaeda*, Little, Brown and Company, 2004. Also Shafiq Rasul, Asif Iqbal and Rhuhel Ahmed, *Composite Statement:*

*Detention in Afghanistan and Guantanamo Bay*, Centre for Constitutional Rights, New York, July 26, 2004.

45. Worthington, *The Guantanamo Files*, pp. 81–99, 176.
46. With intelligence operatives and guards all searching to 'improve' their methods to meet the huge demands for information, there was an inevitable logic of escalation.
47. Stephen Grey, *Ghost Plane*, Hurst, 2006, pp. 250–56.
48. 'New' in recent times. Waterboarding had been used in the Second World War by Japanese soldiers.
49. See Jane Mayer, *The Dark Side*, Doubleday, 2008. David Rose, 'Tortured reasoning', *Vanity Fair*, December 16, 2008. Mark Mazzetti and Scott Shane, 'Interrogation memos detail harsh tactics by the C.I.A.', *New York Times*, April 21, 2009. Scott Shane, '2 suspects waterboarded 266 times', *New York Times*, April 19, 2009. In May 2008, Glenn Fine, the Department of Justice inspector general, reported that, as he recovered in the hospital from the bullet wounds sustained when he was captured, Abu Zubaydah had cooperated with two FBI agents but was then handed over to the CIA, who, according to Fine, felt they 'needed to diminish his capacity to resist'. Bush discussed Abu Zubaydah's treatment in 2006, saying: 'As his questioning proceeded, it became clear that he had received training on how to resist interrogation. And so the CIA used an alternative set of procedures ... The procedures were tough, and they were safe, and lawful, and necessary.' Even before it had been declared legal in a secret finding by Justice Department lawyers in August, it appears probable that Abu Zubaydah was already being subjected to the practice of waterboarding. The newly hired consultants proved highly inventive. At one point they asked for permission to play on Abu Zubaydah's phobia of stinging insects by introducing a harmless bug into his cell and telling him it was dangerous. Their request provoked extraordinary legal contortions as the CIA tried to get permission from lawyers at the Ministry of Justice, who eventually decided that, though Abu Zubaydah's interrogators could not tell the suspect that the insect was venomous because it was illegal to threaten prisoners with imminent death, they could place Abu Zubaydah in a 'confinement box' with a harmless insect if he was told nothing about it. The CIA proposed using a caterpillar. In the end, the plan was abandoned. Mike Isikoff and Evan Thomas, 'The lawyer and the caterpillar', *Newsweek*, April 18, 2009.
50. Author interview with Haji Ghalib, former police chief of Khogani and Guantanamo detainee, Kabul, August 2008.
51. Worthington, *The Guantanamo Files*, pp. 174, 188–9.
52. Author telephone interview with Omar Deghayes, April 2010.
53. Amnesty International, *Secret Detention in CIA 'Black Sites'*, November 8, 2005. See also Stephen Grey's very useful *Ghost Plane*. Jason Burke, 'Secret world of US jails', *Observer*, June 13, 2004. Stephen Grey, 'United States:

Trade in torture', *Le Monde Diplomatique*, April 2005. Dana Priest, 'CIA holds terror suspects in secret prisons', *Washington Post*, November 2, 2005.

54. 'Ex-CIA contractor guilty of assault', Associated Press, August 16, 2006. 'Two soldiers reprimanded for assaults', *Los Angeles Times*, January 27, 2007.

55. Author interview, London, July 2009. British intelligence officials also visited these facilities, though their superiors claim they did not take part in any mistreatment of suspects. 'We just couldn't imagine that the Americans would be doing this,' said one. 'We simply had no idea it was going on,' Sir John Scarlett, deputy head of MI6 at the time, later claimed. However, a series of legal cases in the UK – such as that of Binyam Mohammed – showed that MI6's sister service MI5 had been at the very least complicit in some abuse. One charge was that the service supplied information with the express aim of helping questioners get more out of suspects who were held in atrocious conditions and often seriously tortured. Nor evidently was MI6 likely to refuse information that it felt was tainted by torture, as Scarlett explained to the author in July 2009, arguing that to do so would be dangerous and counterproductive.

56. Author interview with Haji Rohullah, Kabul, August 2009.

57. Haji Shahzada, Guantanamo Bay, Summary of Evidence, January 12, 2005. See Worthington, *The Guantanamo Files*, p. 250.


## CHAPTER 5: WAR IN IRAQ I:
## THREATS, FALSEHOODS AND DEAD MEN

1. Estimates of the Iraqi dead range from 160,000 to 250,000.

2. See the controversial but useful UNICEF Report, *Situation Analysis of Children and Women in Iraq*, April 30, 1998. Also Jason Burke, *The Road to Kandahar*, Penguin, 2006, Chapter 4, for the author's reporting of the humanitarian situation in Iraq in the late 1990s.

3. There remained a small number of Shia at senior levels in the Ba'ath Party.

4. See the excellent International Crisis Group report, *Iraq Backgrounder: What Lies Beneath*, October 1, 2002 for a useful exploration of some of these themes.

5. Powell went into great detail, speaking of the efforts to acquire centrifuges, the 100 to 500 tons of chemical weapons agent, the mobile launchers. United States Senate Select Committee on Intelligence, *Whether Public Statements Regarding Iraq Where Substantiated by US Government Officials Were Substantiated by Intelligence Information*, June 2008, pp. 3, 17, 25, 30.

6. David Kay, testimony before the US Committee on Armed Services, January 28, 2004. *Comprehensive Report of the Special Advisor to the Director of Central Intelligence on Iraq's WMD, Charles Duelfer*, September 30, 2004. Freedman, *A Choice of Enemies*, p. 424. These statements were examined and subsequently corroborated by the Report of the Commission on the

Intelligence Capabilities of the United States Regarding Weapons of Mass Destruction, presented March 31, 2005.

7. *Comprehensive Report of the Special Advisor to the DCI on Iraq's WMD, Chemical Section*, p. 123.

8. Bush, *Decision Points*, p. 262.

9. Freedman, *A Choice of Enemies*, pp. 412–16.

10. Jonathan S. Landay and Tish Wells, 'Iraqi global misinformation campaign was used to build case for war', Knight Ridder, March 16, 2004.

11. Martin Chulov and Helen Pidd, 'How US was duped by Iraqi fantasist looking to topple Saddam', *Guardian*, February 15, 2010.

12. The full interrogation documents of Saddam Hussein by the FBI in March 2004 are available at www.nsarchive.org. See also Glenn Kessler, 'Hussein pointed to Iranian threat', *Washington Post*, July 2, 2009.

13. Rose, 'Tortured reasoning'.

14. National Intelligence Estimate, *Iraq's Continuing Programs of WMD*, October 1, 2002, pp. 66–8. Jason Burke, 'The missing link', *Guardian*, February 9, 2003. Jeffrey Goldberg, 'The great terror', *New Yorker*, March 25, 2002.

15. Also Jonathan S. Landay, 'Abusive tactics used to seek Iraq-al Qaida link', *McClatchy Newspapers*, April 21, 2009. The Bush administration systematically leaked information from Abu Zubaydah's interrogations. One analyst who worked at the Pentagon told reporter David Rose of *Vanity Fair*: 'I first saw the reports soon after Abu Zubaydah's capture. There was a lot of stuff about the nuts and bolts of al-Qaeda's supposed relationship with the Iraqi Intelligence Service. The intelligence community was lapping this up, and so was the administration, obviously. Abu Zubaydah was saying Iraq and al-Qaeda had an operational relationship. It was everything the administration hoped it would be.'

16. The author learned of this meeting at the time from Saudi and Pakistani security sources but was unable to confirm sufficiently for publication.

17. United States Senate Select Committee on Intelligence, *Whether Public Statements Regarding Iraq Where Substantiated by US Government Officials Were Substantiated by Intelligence Information*, p. 63.

18. John Solomon, 'First declassified Iraq documents released', Associated Press Online, March 16, 2006. Tariq Aziz, the former Iraqi foreign minister, later told interrogators that Saddam 'had only ever expressed negative sentiments about bin Laden'. Robert Burns, 'Iraqi: Saddam "delighted" in terror attacks on US', Associated Press, September 22, 2010.

19. Technically outside the no-fly zone and thus the haven, Mosul and its tradition of Islamism had been and was an important factor.

20. For more see Burke, *Al-Qaeda*, pp. 225–7, which draws on interviews with militants in Kurdish custody and with Kurdish intelligence officers in August 2002 in Suleimaniyah, Iraq, as well as Western intelligence documents, principally the interrogation report of German members of the al-Tawhid group.

21. Bergen, *The Longest War*, pp. 144–5.

22. Subsequently, the bipartisan commission of inquiry set up in November 2002 by Congress and, reluctantly, the president to report on the causes of the 9/11 attacks concluded that there was no evidence of a 'collaborative . . . operational relationship', and a study by the Institute for Defense Analyses, written for the US Joint Forces Command and based on 600,000 documents captured in Iraq after the invasion, found that nothing indicated 'direct coordination and assistance between Saddam Hussein's regime and al-Qaeda'. *The 9/11 Commission Report*, p. 66. Institute for Defense Analyses, 'Iraqi Perspective Project: Saddam and Terrorism', March 20, 2008, at http://www.fas.orga/irp/eprint/iraqi/index.html. See also Congressional Research Service (Kenneth Katzmann), *Report for Congress: Al'Qaeda in Iraq: Assessment and Outside Links*, updated August 15, 2008. In his memoirs, the CIA director at the time, George Tenet, also indicated that the CIA view was that any contacts were simply exploratory rather than collaborative – though he played a close role in the preparation of Powell's United Nations presentation. See Tenet, *At the Center of the Storm*, pp. 341–58. 'Report. No proof of Qaeda–Saddam link', CBS News, September 8, 2006.

23. See the useful discussion in Kampfner, *Blair's Wars*, pp. 264–7. For the flaws in the dossier see Burke, *Al-Qaeda*, pp. 16–17.

24. Briefings citing 'intelligence' given to 'lobby' or political correspondents rather than specialist security reporters had been a favoured method of consolidating support for the invasion of Afghanistan. One of the more egregious examples of this kind of material was the revelation that bin Laden was set to unleash a '£20bn flood of heroin' on the West: Kamal Ahmed, 'The terrorism crisis: No 10 fears £20bn flood of heroin, troops aim to destroy huge stockpile of opium about to be released on to the world market', *Observer*, September 30, 2001.

25. *The 9/11 Commission Report*, p. 170.

26. Human Rights Watch briefing, *Opportunism in the Face of Tragedy*, New York, 2002. Katherine Arms, 'China links separatists to training by al-Qaeda', UPI, June 26, 2002.

27. Burke, *Al-Qaeda*, p. 15. *Herald*, Karachi, May, 2002. Nicholas Wood, 'Macedonian officials suspected of faking terror plot', *New York Times*, May 15, 2004. 'Macedonia faked "militant" raid', BBC News Online, April, 30, 2004. Four security service officers were charged with murder. 'It was a monstrous fabrication to get the attention of the international community,' Interior Ministry spokeswoman Mirjana Kontevska told a news conference.

28. Tariq Panja and Martin Bright, 'Man Utd bomb plot probe ends in farce', *Observer*, May 2, 2004.

29. Burke, *Al-Qaeda*, pp. 14–19, 285. For an example of the media reporting see 'Ricin suspects linked to al-Qaeda', CNN, January 17, 2003.

30. A leak to the *Sun* did the rest. No charges were ever brought. See the excellent investigation by Peter Oborne, 'The Use and Abuse of Terror', in *Playing Politics with Terrorism*, ed. George Kassimeris, Hurst, 2007, pp. 124–5.

31. Hala Jaber, 'Ryanair gunman: I was not going to crash plane', *Sunday Times*, October 13, 2002.

32. José Padilla was eventually convicted of terrorism charges, but the allegation of planning a dirty bomb – leaked to the press and covered extensively – was dropped. For more on the interrogation of Abu Zubaydah see Rose, 'Tortured reasoning'.

33. Chris McGreal, 'The Nevada gambler, al-Qaida, the CIA and the mother of all cons', *Guardian*, December 23, 2009.

34. John Mueller, 'Is There Still a Terrorist Threat? The Myth of the Omnipresent Enemy', *Foreign Affairs*, September–October 2006. Testimony of Robert S. Mueller III, Director, FBI, before the Select Committee on Intelligence of the United States Senate, February 11, 2003.

35. 'The truth is that for reasons that have a lot to do with the U.S. government bureaucracy we settled on one issue that everyone could agree on, which was weapons of mass destruction as the core reason.' *Vanity Fair* Interview with Sam Tannenhaus, May 9, 2003, transcript on http://www.defense.gov/transcripts/transcript.aspx?transcriptid=2594.

36. One influence on Bush and other senior administration figures was Bernard Lewis, the American historian of the Islamic world, who forcefully argued that a lack of Western-style freedoms was the fundamental cause of the Middle East's economic, social and political weaknesses. He made these views to a mass audience in the best-selling '*What Went Wrong': Western Impact and Middle Eastern Response*, Oxford University Press, 2002. See also the article of the same title, *Atlantic Monthly*, January 2002. In his memoir, Bush talks of how 'the Middle East was the centre of a global ideological struggle. On the one side were decent people who wanted to live in dignity and peace. On the other were extremists who sought to impose their radical views through violence and intimidation. They exploited conditions of hopelessness and repression to recruit and spread their ideology. The best way to protect our countries in the long run was to counter their dark vision with a more compelling alternative. That alternative was freedom. Once liberty took root in one society it could spread to others.' *Decision Points*, p. 232.

37. Thomas Powers, 'War and its consequences', *New York Review of Books*, March 27, 2003.

38. Freedman, *A Choice of Enemies*, p. 422.

39. James Fallows, 'Blind into Baghdad', *Atlantic Monthly*, January/February 2004. Feith also explained that Donald Rumsfeld's vision was about 'the need to deal strategically with uncertainty. The inability to predict the future. The limits on our knowledge and the limits on our intelligence.'

40. Robert K. Brigham, *Iraq, Vietnam and the Limits of American Power*, p. 2.

41. See Bush, *Decision Points*, pp. 248–9. This preoccupation with humanitarian issues, it is worth pointing out, was also shared by many anti-war campaigners and international institutions such as the UN.

42. Ricks, *Fiasco*, p. 146. Ricks quotes from an internal American Army War College summary. The war plan designed by General Tommy Franks, stated baldly that 'regime change' was the 'endstate of this mission'.

43. Sixteen months of effort by a full military staff went into planning the war, eight weeks of work by a scratch team into planning for the post-war situation. A Congressional Research Service Report of April 2003 entitled *Iraq: Recent Developments in Humanitarian and Reconstruction Assistance* optimistically states: 'After an initial period of U.S.-led aid activities, existing Iraqi ministries, nongovernmental organizations (NGOs), and international organizations are expected to assume some of the burden.'

44. Freedman, *A Choice of Enemies*, p. 429.

45. Quoted in Fallows, 'Blind into Baghdad'.

46. George Packer, 'Dreaming of democracy', *New York Times*, March 2, 2003.

47. The campaign was expected to take 100 days, according to Lieutenant General Sir Frederick Viggers. 'West put "amateurs" in charge of Iraq occupation, inquiry told', Staff and agencies, guardian.co.uk, December 9, 2009.

48. Ricks, *Fiasco*, p. 118. Gregory Fontenot, E. J. Degen and David Tohn, *On Point: The United States Army in Operation Iraqi Freedom*, Combat Studies Institute Press, 2004.

49. See David Zuccino, *Thunder Run: The Armored Strike to Capture Baghdad*, Atlantic Monthly Press, 2004. Some accounts state that one of the operations killed at least 2,000 Iraqi soldiers. This seems unlikely. However, many residents of areas along the route of the two operations described numerous civilian deaths to the author, often simply caused by ricochets or in the crossfire.

50. See Iraqbodycount.org. Carl Conetta, 'The Wages of War: Iraqi Combatant and Noncombatant Fatalities in the 2003 Conflict', Project on Defense Alternatives Research Monograph 8, October 20, 2003.

51. Kosovo in 1999 may arguably have preceded Iraq in this but in very different circumstances and in a much less dramatic fashion.

52. Again as in Afghanistan, these mechanisms were often less 'traditional' than they seemed to Western observers. The Iraqi tribal system was very different from the days when Iraq was a predominantly rural society in the immediate post-war decades or a prosperous oil-rich emerging Arab state in the 1970s. Equally, there was little that was traditional about the rhetoric of the movement led by the young cleric Muqtada al-Sadr, which, within days of the fall of the regime, was organizing political meetings, taking over mosques and distributing food and other necessities in the vast Shia slum areas to the north of Baghdad.

53. For a useful account of this episode see Patrick Cockburn, *Muqtada al-Sadr, the Shia revival and the Struggle for Iraq*, Simon and Schuster, 2008, pp. 122–4.

54. Polls in the aftermath of the invasion showed George Bush's domestic approval level at over 90 per cent. On May 1, the president had landed in a

navy combat jet on the aircraft carrier the US *Abraham Lincoln* off the coast of California under a banner, the work of the ship's crew, bearing the legend 'mission accomplished'. He acknowledged difficult work ahead. 'The battle in Iraq is one victory in the war on terror that began on September 11th, 2001,' he said.

55. Adopted by a vote of fourteen to zero on May 22, 2003. The measure also had the advantage of freeing up Iraq's frozen oil revenues from the Oil for Food deal. 'In August I thought that it could still get better,' remembered Andy Bearpark, the CPA's British director of operations and deputy later. Author interview, Bath, July 2004.

56. Bing West, *The Strongest Tribe*, Random House, 2005, p. 6.

57. Author interview with Andy Bearpark, CPA director of operations, Bath, July 2004.

58. Bremer later insisted that British officials had been fully briefed before his order was issued. Statement by Ambassador Bremer to Chilcot commission, May 18, 2010, http://www.iraqinquiry.org.uk/background/statement-bremer. aspx.

59. Bush admits as much in his memoirs. The 'psychological impact' of disbanding the army had been underestimated and the de-Baathification went much further than was intended, he writes. *Decision Points*, p. 259.

60. See Toby Dodge, 'The Ideological Roots of Failure: The Application of Kinetic Neo-Liberalism to Iraq', *International Affairs*, vol. 86, no. 6 (November 2010), pp. 1,269–86. Paul Bremer, *My Year in Iraq: The Struggle to Build a Future of Hope*, Simon and Schuster, 2006, p. 39.

61. Author interview with John Wilkes, deputy British ambassador, Baghdad, June 2003.

62. The influence of the post-war measures in Germany on Bremer in particular is evident from his account of his time in Baghdad, *My Year in Iraq*. In fact de-Nazification had been far less severe than de-Baathification was to be.

63. Patrick Cockburn, *The Occupation, War and Resistance in Iraq*, Verso, 2006, p. 71. Ricks, *Fiasco*, pp. 162–3.

64. Rajiv Chandreshekan, *Imperial Life in the Emerald City, Inside Iraq's Green Zone*, Knopf, 2006, pp. 79–80.

65. Quoted in ibid., p. 159

66. At least two years according to Congressional Research Service (Kenneth Katzman), *Report for Congress: Iraq: Elections, Government, and Constitution*, November 20, 2006.

67. 'Rumsfeld rejects "cleric-led" rule', BBC News Online, April 25, 2005.

68. Author interview with Charles Heatley, Baghdad, June 2003.

69. Author interview, Najaf, June 2003.

70. Author interview, Baghdad, March 2003. See also the useful *Meeting the Resistance: A Film by Molly Bingham and Steve Connors*, 2007.

71. Author interviews, Baghdad, May and June 2003.

72. 'Poll shows Iraqis wary about Western-style democracy', VOA News, December 11, 2003.

73. *United Nations Report of the Security in Iraq Accountability Panel (SIAP)*, New York, March 3, 2004, p. 30.

74. See Jason Burke, 'Left to die', *GQ*, August 2004. Multiple author interviews with relatives of the casualties and soldiers involved, UK, February, March 2004.

75. British spokesman Lieutenant Colonel Ronnie McCourt denied any troops had 'molested', i.e. searched, women. 'We are the British army. We just don't do that,' he said. Author interviews, Abu Ala and Basra, June 25 and 26, 2003.

76. The author was shown the agreement in Majjar al-Kabir on June 25, 2003, the day after the deaths of the Redcaps.

77. Draft MoD report, 'On the events in Majjar al-Kabir, June 23 2003', March 2004, author collection.

78. Author telephone interview with Katie, Hamilton-Jewell's girlfriend, March 2004.

79. See, for example, David Blair, 'The Last Stand at Majjar al-Kabir', *Daily Telegraph*, June 26, 2003.

80. Excerpts from Ministry of Defence, Special Investigation Branch, draft report, obtained April, 2004. The investigation found that only two rounds out of one magazine for at least one of the Redcaps' personal weapons had been fired.

81. Author interview with Abbas Bairphy, Majjar al-Kabir, June 2003.

82. Ibid.

83. Ibid.

84. See 'The Lord of the Marshes Takes a Mediating Role in Iraq', *Terrorism Focus*, vol. 3, no. 33, August 23, 2006. Rory Stewart, *Occupational Hazards*, Picador, 2007, is an excellent and colourful account with much useful detail on Abu Hatem and Maysan province more generally.

85. Author interview with Abu Ala villagers, June 2003.

86. Author interview, Whitehall, London, August 2003.

87. See *Guardian* correspondent Rory McCarthy's account of his time in Iraq from 2003 to 2005, *No One Told Us We Are Defeated*, Guardian Books, 2006.

88. Author interview, Baghdad, August 2004.

89. In their first debriefing reports of the battle, the British patrol in Majjar al-Kabir estimated they might have killed up to 200 people and feared the incident might provoke a general insurrection across the region. In fact the local hospital registered five killed and nineteen wounded, who included several women and children and a fifty-year-old ambulance driver hit in the crossfire. Many locals involved, however, are likely to have been treated – or buried – by relatives so the true number is almost certainly much higher. Author interview with Lieutenant Colonel Stuart Tootal, present in Amarah, March 2004, London. Author interviews, Majjar al-Kabir hospital, June 2003.

90. Copy given to the author by Tony Hamilton-Jewell, Simon Hamilton-Jewell's brother, March 2004.

## CHAPTER 6: WAR IN IRAQ II: LOSING IT

1. The tattoo detail is from Bush, *Decision Points*, p. 267.
2. In part, this omission had been forced on the Americans by the refusal of the Turks to allow 15,000 troops across their territory.
3. The best two biographies of Saddam are Alexander and Patrick Cockburn, *Out of the Ashes: The Resurrection of Saddam Hussein*, Harper Perennial, 2000, and Said Aburish, *Saddam Hussein: The Politics of Revenge*, Bloomsbury, 2000.
4. Scott Peterson, 'How Wahhabis fan Iraq insurgency', *Christian Science Monitor*, September 17, 2003.
5. Jason Burke, 'In a land without law or leaders, militant Islam threatens to rule', *Observer*, April 27, 2003.
6. Author interview with senior Iraqi intelligence investigators, Baghdad, May 2004.
7. Nir Rosen, 'Losing it', Asia Times Online, July 15, 2004.
8. Nir Rosen, 'Home rule: letter from Falluja', *New Yorker*, July 4, 2004.
9. Author interview, Falluja, July 2003.
10. The al-Dulaimi had been loyal to Saddam and rewarded handsomely for their support. However, their loyalty was not unconditional. In 1998 Saddam had hanged an army general from Ramadi, and relations had been tense ever since. The al-Dulaimi nonetheless had been strongly present in Saddam's intelligence and security apparatus.
11. Author interview, Ramadi, July 2003.
12. 'U.S. Commander in Iraq says year-long tours are option to combat "guerrilla" war', *New York Times*, July 17, 2003.
13. Hoffman also perceptively argued that in Iraq one saw 'the closest manifestation yet of netwar, the concept of warfare involving flatter, more linear networks rather than the pyramidal hierarchies and command and control systems (no matter how primitive) that have governed traditional insurgent organizations ... [It] involves small groups who communicate, coordinate, and conduct their campaigns in an internetted manner, without a precise central command.' RAND Corporation (Bruce Hoffman), *Insurgency and Counterinsurgency in Iraq*, June 2004. For more on Netwar see John Arquilla, David Ronfeldt and Michele Zanini, 'Networks, Netwar and the Information-Age Terrorism', in RAND Corporation (Ian Lesser et al.) *Countering the New Terrorism*, 1999, p. 47.
14. See the very useful discussion in Scott Atran, *Talking to the Enemy*, Harper-Collins, 2010, pp. 267–8.

15. Jessica Stern, *Terror in the Name of God*, Harper Perennial, 2004, p. 271: resilience is the 'ability of a network to withstand the loss of a node or nodes. To maximise resilience, the network has to maximise redundancy. Functions are not centralised. Capacity – the ability to optimise the scale of the attack – requires coordination, which makes the group less resilient because communication is required. Effectiveness is a function of both capacity and resilience.'

16. Author interviews with American army intelligence officers, Tikrit, May 2004, Baghdad, September 2004. Author interviews with British army intelligence officers, Basra, August 2004. Also with insurgents, Baghdad and Ramadi, April and September 2004. Greg Grant, 'The IED Marketplace', *Defense News*, March 2005. Amatzia Baram, 'Who Are the Insurgents? Sunni Arab Rebels in Iraq, April 2005', special report for the United States Institute of Peace. See also Rory McCarthy, 'For faith and country, insurgents fight on', *Guardian*, December 16, 2004. Other classic operational elements of Abu Mujahed's group would include the way in which they accessed military expertise – partly as a result of the hasty demobilization of the army. The post-invasion period saw a rapid dissemination of such knowledge among the civilian population. Also, though Abu Mujahed did not mention it, the internet aided some groups to learn both about ambush tactics and, crucially, about the media potential of the acts. Abu Mujahed was entirely typical not only of the modern Sunni Iraqi militant but of the reality of such militancy globally.

17. The overall commander of Marine Expeditionary Force One was General James T. Conway.

18. The lynching, as journalist Nir Rosen pointed out, was an Iraqi tradition called *sahel*, a word unique to Iraqi Arabic, which once meant dragging a body down the street with an animal or vehicle, but eventually grew to mean any sort of public killing or lynching. Rosen, 'Losing it'.

19. Author interview with Andrew Rathmell, CPA policy planning office, 2004.

20. Author interview with senior Ministry of Defence official, London, August 2004.

21. Author interviews with Andrew Rathmell, senior CPA officials, London, 2004. Jonathan F. Keiler, 'Who Won the Battle of Fallujah?', *Proceedings, U.S. Naval Institute*, January 2005, p. 59. Sean D. Naylor, '"Paying the price" for pulling out: commanders see a tough fight to retake Fallujah', *Army Times*, October 4, 2004.

22. Abu Anas al-Shami, the diary of Falluja, Arabic al-Fajer media, 2004, author collection. An English translation is reprinted in Loretta Napoleoni, *Insurgent Iraq: Al Zarqawi and the New Generation*, Seven Stories, 2005: see p. 219.

23. The exact number of dead civilians was heavily contested. American military spokesmen insisted that the bulk of the 800 or 900 civilian dead were

insurgents. Doctors in Falluja said that many of those they had treated were neither male nor of combat age. Iraq Body Count, 'No Longer Unknowable: Falluja's April Civilian Toll is 600', October 26, 2004.

24. Ricks, *Fiasco*, p. 342.

25. A 'stunning victory' in the words of a memo written by Nathaniel Jensen, a State Department diplomat attached to the CPA. Ibid., p. 345.

26. Bing West, *The Strongest Tribe*, Random House, 2009, p. 31.

27. Propaganda produced years later by militants in Europe, Afghanistan and Pakistan still mentioned Falluja. In 2009, for example, videos entitled 'Lions of Falluja' were still being posted on the internet by European extremists. To have participated in the fighting at Falluja was seen as particularly praise-worthy. See al-Muderii, Abdul'Aala transcript: 'The Martyr Abu Usama Walid walad al-Hibatt al-Tunisi', As-Sahab Media foundation via the NEFA Foundation, November 30, 2009, p. 1. http://www.nefafoundation.org/mis-cellaneous/nefaWalidTunisi1109.pdf.

28. Ricks, *Fiasco*, pp. 258–9.

29. SIGINT stands for Signals Intelligence. Ibid., p. 194. The latter, for example, gave analysts a false impression of the number of non-Iraqis among the insurgents as the 'internationals', who did not have the personal relationships that locals had, made heavier use of the telephones that the eavesdropping technology picked up.

30. Author interview, Tikrit, May 2004.

31. Philip Gourevitch and Errol Morris, *Standard Operating Procedure*, Picador, 2009, pp. 21–2.

32. Mark Danner, 'US torture: voices from the black sites', *New York Review of Books*, April 9, 2009.

33. Gourevitch and Morris, *Standard Operating Procedure*, pp. 38–9.

34. Mark Danner, 'Abu Ghraib: the hidden story', *New York Review of Books*, October 7, 2004, p. 33. The military intelligence unit that oversaw interroga-tions at the Bagram detention centre, where at least two prisoners' deaths were ruled homicides, was later placed in charge of questioning at Abu Ghraib prison in Iraq. Captain Carolyn A. Wood, who served at Bagram from July 2002 to December 2003, brought to Iraq interrogation procedures developed during service in Afghanistan, according to Congressional testimony. It was apparently Captain Wood who wrote the interrogation rules posted on the wall at Abu Ghraib. Human Rights Watch, *The Road to Abu Ghraib*, pp. 23–4.

35. Thomas E. Ricks, 'In Iraq, military forgot the lessons of Vietnam: Early mis-steps by U.S. left troops unprepared for guerrilla warfare', *Washington Post*, July 26, 2003.

36. Prisoners there later remembered how much more brutal their custodians had become as a result. Author interviews with former prisoners, Kabul, August 2008.

37. Associated Press, 30 April 2004, excerpts from writings of an accused soldier who helped run Baghdad prison.

38. Interrogators in Bagram told investigators that the knowledge that those at the most senior levels of political power in the country had 'denied the Geneva convention' to detainees had influenced their behaviour.

39. Black had unapologetically insisted before Congress that 'after 9/11 ... the gloves had come off' regarding the rules governing the operations conducted by the CIA.

40. Feith, Douglas, *War and Decision*, p. 485.

41. A total of thirty-four members of Taskforce 145, involved in the hunt for al-Qaeda fugitives, were eventually disciplined for mistreating detainees. Five US army rangers were convicted of assault. Mark Bowden, 'The ploy', *The Atlantic*, May 2007. Gourevitch and Morris, *Standard Operating Procedure*, p. 210.

42. Hundreds of complaints by Iraqis eventually made their way into British courts. In addition to the abuses mentioned above, many complained of sexual humiliation by women soldiers, or being held for days in brightly lit cells as small as one metre square. Ian Cobain, 'Servicemen at "UK's Abu Ghraib" may be guilty of war crimes, court hears', *Guardian*, November 8, 2010. 'No public probe into Iraq "abuse"', BBC News Online, November 14, 2009. 'Torture by British soldiers in Iraq was not carried out by "few bad apples ... there was something rotten in the whole barrel"', *Daily Mail*, September 21, 2009. Ian Cobain, 'Iraq deaths in British custody could see military face legal challenges', *Guardian*, July 1, 2010. Very serious allegations of execution and subsequent mutilation of corpses in Maysan province in 2004 have never been fully investigated. British military courts dismissed charges against all defendants except one, who was convicted for inhumane treatment. See *The Aitken Report, An Investigation into Cases of Deliberate Abuse and Unlawful Killing in Iraq in 2003 and 2004*, Crown Publishers, January 25, 2008, for the British army's official response.

43. Low-ranking personnel were, often enthusiastically it is true, frequently only carrying out the instructions of the interrogators, who wanted their subjects 'softened up'. Gourevitch and Morris, *Standard Operating Procedure*, p. 94.

44. Though various individuals have claimed to be the man in the iconic photograph, none have been positively identified. He is believed to be Abdou Hussain Saad Faleh (detainee 18170). An American army spokesman said Faleh was released from American custody in January 2004. Kate Zernike, 'Cited as symbol of Abu Ghraib, man admits he is not in photo', *New York Times*, March 18, 2006.

45. Author interview, Abu Ghraib, May 2004.

46. The rest of the city, on coalition maps, was not secure and thus 'the Red Zone'.

47. See Chandreshekan, *Imperial Life in the Emerald City*, for a vivid and perceptive view of life in the Green Zone. See also George Packer, *The Assassins' Gate: America in Iraq*, Farrar, Straus and Giroux, 2006.

48. Many State Department officials spent only ninety days in the country. Some spent even less. See US Office of the Inspector General Oversight and Review Division, December 2008 report titled *An Investigation of Overtime Payments to FBI and Other Department of Justice Employees Deployed to Iraq and Afghanistan*, p. 18, which suggests ninety-day deployments were standard, but many served much less: 'The FBI trainers generally stayed in Iraq for the duration of the courses (typically a few weeks) rather than for 90 days.'

49. Description based on the author's reporting, 2003–4.

50. Author interview, Bath, July 2004.

51. Author interview, Tikrit, April 2004.

52. Rory McCarthy of the *Guardian* was the reporter.

53. Author interview, June 2004.

54. Author interview, Tikrit, 2004.

55. Author interview with Rory Stewart, Kabul, March 2009.

56. Benon V. Sevan (Executive Director of the Iraq Programme) statement: 'Phasing down and termination of the Programme pursuant to Security Council resolution 1483 (2003)', Office of the Iraq Programme, Oil-for-Food, November 19, 2003.

57. The corruption was only the extension of that spreading throughout Iraqi society – $100 could avoid a delay of twelve days and a lot of queuing for new passports; joining the new Iraqi chamber of commerce cost nothing, except the $250 backhander.

58. *Special Inspector General for Iraqi Reconstruction Quarterly and Semi Annual Report to Congress*, January 30, 2006, pp. 17 and 33.

59. Author interviews, Dr Adel Mirza Ghadban, Baghdad, July 2003. See Jason Burke, 'Iraq: an audit of war', *Observer*, July 6, 2003.

60. George Packer, 'War after the War', *New Yorker*, November 24, 2003.

61. The National Security Strategy of the United States of America, September 2002, Introduction, p. 1. Cited in Dodge, 'The Ideological Roots of Failure'.

62. Twenty-three per cent of Iraqis say that they would like to model their new government after the US; 17.5 per cent would like their model to be Saudi Arabia; 12 per cent say Syria, 7 per cent say Egypt and 37 per cent say 'none of the above'. John Zogby, 'How the poll results on Iraq were manipulated', *Arab News*, October 23, 2003. Only 38 per cent said they thought democracy would work, while discussion groups held by Thomas Melia, director of research at the Institute for the Study of Diplomacy at Georgetown University, in July 2003 revealed a deep unease about indecency and licentiousness that was associated with Western democracies especially during conversation about the role of women, daughters and family. VOA, 'Poll shows Iraqis wary about Western-style democracy', VOA, December 11, 2003.

63. 'We are thinking in terms of one or two years,' Deputy Ambassador John Wilkes told the author.
64. Bush, *Decision Points*, p. 359.
65. The Mahdi is a divinely guided redeemer of Muslims, associated with the 'occulted' or hidden twelfth imam in the Shia tradition but recognized by many Sunnis though not by the most orthodox. The Mahdi's anticipated rule will be just and will see both the religious purity and political power of Islam restored. It will also, in the eschatological tradition, herald the end of time. The Jaysh al-Mahdi should be properly translated as the militia of the messiah rather than the al-Mahdi Army. However, the conventional usage has been preferred here, not least because of the complex theological implications of the word messiah.
66. Ayatollah is a sign of senior rank among the Shia clergy, denoting, among other things. a high degree of scholastic authority and learning.
67. See Fred Halliday, *Two Hours That Shook the World*, Saqi Books, 2002.
68. In 1968, al-Sadr I had created the Dawa party, a clandestine Islamist organization, with a rhetoric and cell structure that drew heavily on that of the Communists and the atheistic, quasi-Fascist Ba'athists who took power in Iraq in the same year. The type of organization had been introduced to the region by the Communist Third International from the 1920s and also through Fascist and Nazi channels before being adopted through the late 1920s and 30s by a range of different currents – Communists in Syria, Egypt and Iraq and the Muslim Brotherhood in Egypt.

   The Leninist model proved its superiority over the politics of notables, which was centred on elite figures and saloon gatherings with no root organization. It overwhelmed the imagination of some young Islamic-minded Najafi lay groups. These young men observed with admiration and awe the appeal of the Marxist utopia and the efficiency of the clandestine communist organization in Najaf which even competed with them in organzing ashura rituals. They were eager to command such powerful instruments of recruitment and mobilization. Young clerics also shared this fascination. (Faleh A. Jabar, *The Shi'ite Movement in Iraq*, Saqi Books, 2003, pp. 78–9)

   The new thinkers even went as far as to claim that it was the duty of clerics, as interpreters of religious law and scholars, to govern too.
69. Around 5,000 were detained and at least 250 were tortured to death.
70. Nicolas Pelham, *A New Muslim Order: The Shia and the Middle East Sectarian Crisis*, I. B. Tauris, 2008, p. 16. Between 1982 and 1985 some Shia communities in the south of Iraq even organized their own resistance to Iran's advance independent of state direction.
71. International Crisis Group, *Iraq's Muqtada Al-Sadr: Spoiler or Stabiliser?*, July 11, 2006, p. 4.

72. Al-Sadr was born on August 12, 1973.

73. Author telephone interview with Hilary Synnott, October 2009.

74. Author interview with David Richmond, Baghdad, March 2004.

75. Author interview, Tikrit, March 2004.

76. The episode is related vividly by Rory Stewart, British diplomat and CPA official at the time, in his *Occupational Hazards*, pp. 391–3.

77. Patrick Cockburn, *Muqtada al-Sadr and the Fall of Iraq*, Faber and Faber, 2008, p. 171.

78. Ibrahim al-Marashi, 'Boycotts, Coalitions and the Threat of Violence: The Run-Up to the January 2005, Iraqi Elections', *The Middle East Review of International Affairs*, January 2005.

79. This was certainly the view of British intelligence specialists in Iraq at the time. Author interview with MI6 official, Kabul, May 2011. See International Crisis Group, *Iran in Iraq*, March 2005, pp. 10–13. Edward T. Pound, 'The Iran Connection', *US News and World Report*, November 22, 2004. A useful analysis can be found in Mark Urban, *Task Force Black*, Little, Brown, 2010, p. 111.

80. This account is largely based on the author's reporting in Najaf during the fighting of August 2004.

81. Interview on al-Arabiya, 13 January 2006. Cockburn, *Muqtada al-Sadr*, p. 205.

82. Sistani had been born in Mashad, Iran.

83. International Crisis Group, *Iraq's Muqtada al-Sadr*, p. 14.

## CHAPTER 7: AL-QAEDA AND THE 9/11 WARS

1. 918 to be precise, according to Iraqbodycount.org. Iraq Body Count's totals, compiled from reliable media reporting, can be considered a guaranteed minimum. The true figures are likely to be higher.

2. See Bernard Lewis, *The Crisis of Islam: Holy War and Unholy Terror*, Random House, 2004, for a useful discussion.

3. *Pew Global Attitudes Project: How Global Publics View: War in Iraq, Democracy, Islam and Governance and Globalization*, June 2003, pp. 3, 46.

4. Throughout this chapter, as in the rest of the book, I refer to Setmariam as al-Suri. The latter is, of course, a nickname, simply meaning the Syrian, and it would be better to use his family name. However, al-Suri, like al-Zarqawi, has entered popular usage, and I have thus followed that custom.

5. It is possible he may subsequently have travelled again, conceivably even to Iraq.

6. Alison Pargeter, *The New Frontiers of Jihad*, I. B. Tauris, 2008, pp. 1–4. Murad Batal Al-shishani, 'Abu Mus'ab al-Suri and the Third Generation of Salafi-Jihadists', August 15, 2005, *Terrorism Monitor*, vol. 3, no. 16, August 15, 2005. The ruling family in Syria is from the minority Allawite sect of Shia Islam though the majority of the Syrian population is Sunni.

7. Abu Musab al-Suri, 'Da'wat al-Muqawama al-Islamiyya al-Alamiyya', pp. 710–11, quoted in Tawil, *Brothers in Arms*, p. 29.

8. Probably the best single work on al-Suri is Brynjar Lia, *Architect of Global Jihad: The Life of Al Qaeda Strategist Abu Mus'ab Al-Suri*, Columbia University Press, 2008.

9. See Paul Cruickshank and Mohammad Hage Ali, 'Abu Musab al-Suri: Architect of the New al-Qaeda', *Studies in Conflict and Terrorism*, 30, 2007, pp. 1–14.

10. Another reason was that al-Suri was also accused of organizing the assassination of two more moderate Algerian Islamists. Pargeter, *The New Frontiers of Jihad*, p. 68. See also Brynjar Lia, 'Abu Mus'ab al-Suri's Critique of Hard Line Salafists in the Jihadist Current', *CTC Sentinel*, vol. 1, no. 1, December 2007, p. 3.

11. Al-Suri was released as he had not actually, under legislation at the time, committed any offence. For quote on the Taliban, see Lia, *The New Frontiers of Jihad*, p. 234.

12. Adam Shatz, 'Laptop jihadi' *London Review of Books*, March 20, 2008. Lia, *Architect of Global Jihad*. Interrogation report of Ahmed al-Sayyid al-Najjar, Egyptian militant by Egyptian investigators, quoted in Tawil, *Brothers in Arms*, p. 156.

13. Quoted in Cruickshank and Hage Ali, 'Abu Musab al-Suri: Architect of the New al-Qaeda'.

14. See 'al-Suri Da'wat al-Muqawama al-Islamiyya al-Alamiyya', 2005, quoted in Devin Springer, James Regens and David Edger, *Islamic Radicalism and Global Jihad*, Georgetown University Press, 2008, p. 176.

15. Bagram airport was referred to as al-Qaeda al-Bagram by Arab fighters in Afghanistan.

16. Burke, *Al-Qaeda*, pp. 1–2.

17. Andrew Black, 'Al-Suri's Adaptation of Fourth Generation Warfare Doctrine', *Terrorism Monitor*, vol. 4, no. 18, September 21, 2006.

18. 'Al-Suri, the Call to Global Resistance', pp. 1,396–7. Quoted Springer et al., *Islamic Radicalism and Global Jihad*, p. 113.

19. Gilles Kepel, *Le Terreur et le martyre: Relever le défi de civilisation*, Flammarion, 2008, p. 138.

20. Quoted in Cruickshank and Hage, 'Abu Musab al-Suri: Architect of the New al-Qaeda'.

21. Springer et al., *Islamic Radicalism and Global Jihad*, p. 72.

22. 'Abu Musa'ab 'al-Suri D'awat al-Muqawama', p. 41, quoted in Tawil, *Brothers in Arms*, p. 186.

23. Such as Christians.

24. The military used the Islamists against the Communists too.

25. See International Crisis Group, *Indonesia Backgrounder: Why Salafism and Terrorism Mostly Don't Mix*, September 13, 2004, pp. 5–6. Also Howard M.

Federspiel, *Islam and Ideology in the Emerging Indonesian State: The Persatuan Islam, 1923 to 1957*, Leiden, 2001, pp. 15, 21–2.

26. Including a period when the Indonesian army had sponsored Muslim anti-Communist gangs.

27. See Burke, *Al-Qaeda*, for more on the camp at Pabbi. Atran, *Talking to the Enemy*, p. 140.

28. Author interviews with Indonesian intelligence officer, Jakarta, October 2002. Memorandum for Commander, US Southern Command, CSRT Input for Guantanamo Detainee, US9ID–010019DP, Riduan Isamuddin, October 30, 2008. Another link was Mohammed Mansour Jabarah, who was allegedly central to a plan to blow up the Australian, Israeli and US embassies in Singapore in 2001. Jabarah, an explosives expert, confessed to playing a role as an intermediary between al-Qaeda and Jemma Islamiya, and as an envoy of Khaled Sheikh Mohammed. He pleaded guilty to acts of terrorism in a 2002 agreement that was kept secret at the time and then began working as an informant for the FBI. New York University Center on Law and Security, Terrorist Trial Report Card 2001–2009, published 2010, p. 45.

29. International Crisis Group, *Terrorism in Indonesia: Noordin's Networks Crisis Group Asia*, May 5, 2006. p. 5.

30. Selma Belaala, 'Slums breed jihad', *Le Monde Diplomatique*, Morocco, November 2004.

31. The marginalization was very clear when the author was visiting the slums in 2007. Even reaching them from the centre of the city was extremely difficult with no public transport serving them and no taxi drivers willing to make the journey. Wasteground and rubbish dumps provided further barriers.

32. Elaine Sciolino, 'Moroccans say Al Qaeda was behind Casablanca bombings', *New York Times*, May 23, 2003. Sebastian Rotella, 'Morocco indicts 6 more suspects in Casablanca blasts', *Los Angeles Times*, May 30, 2003. Author interviews with senior Moroccan government investigators, analyst Mohammed Darif in Casablanca, January 2006, March 2007.

33. *Pew Global Attitudes 2004: A Year after Iraq*, March 16, 2004, p. 1. In Morocco the figure was 66 per cent.

34. The national assembly voted 'no' by 266 to 264. A consequence of this would be that many of the areas in Iraq which were to have been the responsibility of the powerful and highly mechanized 4th Infantry Division in the immediate post-war period were taken on by tired and overstretched troops who had fought their way up from Kuwait.

35. Dilip Hiro, *Inside Central Asia*, Overlook Duckworth, 2009, p. 117. The invasion was one of the very few issues which could unite all Turks, from Islamists to secularist nationalists.

36. Karl Vick, 'Al-Qaeda's hand In Istanbul Plot', *Washington Post*, February 13, 2007. Excerpts of intercepts and interrogation reports, author collection. Details from Turkish government indictment, February 2004. Author collection.

37. Edmund F. McGarrell, Joshua D. Freilich and Steven Chermak, 'Intelligence Led Policing as a Framework for Responding to Terrorism', *Journal of Contemporary Criminal Justice*, vol. 23, no. 2, 2007, pp. 142–58.

38. Atran, *Talking to the Enemy*, p. 199.

39. The Shahada is the profession of faith by a Muslim: 'I bear witness that there is no God but Allah and Mohammed is his prophet.'

40. José Maria Aznar, Spain's conservative prime minister, personally called the editor of Spain's most important newspaper, the left-leaning *El Pais*, to make sure the headlines reflected this interpretation.

41. Atran, *Talking to the Enemy*, p. 181.

42. Scott Atran and Marc Sageman, 'The Great Train Bombing', draft from October 10, 2007, p. 7.

43. 'Madrid bombing probe finds no al-Qaida link', Associated Press, March 9, 2006. Javier Jordan and Robert Wesley, 'The Madrid Attacks: Results of Investigations Two Years Later', *Terrorism Monitor*, vol. 4, no. 5, March 9, 2006. Author interviews with senior Spanish police officers, Madrid, October 2006.

44. NYPD, *Intelligence Report: Radicalization in the West*, 2007, p. 39. Author collection.

45. Atran, *Talking to the Enemy*, p. 179.

46. Ibid., p. 183.

47. Lawrence Wright, 'The terror web: were the Madrid bombings part of a new, far-reaching jihad being plotted on the internet?', *New Yorker*, August 2, 2004. Author interviews, Spanish Centro Nacional de Inteligencia officials, Saudi Arabia, March 2008.

48. Atran, *Talking to the Enemy*, pp. 201–2.

49. Wright, 'The terror web'.

50. See White House press release, January 10, 2006. In a key speech Bush laid out 'the political, security, and economic elements of the strategy for victory in the central front of the War on Terror, what has been achieved, the challenges faced at the start of 2006'.

51. Napoleoni, *Insurgent Iraq*, p. 218.

52. Abu Anas al-Shami diary, author collection.

53. Some sources say he was indeed involved in fighting around Khost in 1990. See Romesh Ratnesar, 'Face of terror: how Abu Mousab al-Zarqawi transformed the Iraq insurgency into a holy war and became America's newest nightmare', *Time*, December 19, 2004 .

54. Author interviews with American intelligence officials, Tikrit and Baghdad, May 2004. Author interviews with former associates, Amman, June 2003. There are many useful accounts of al-Zarqawi's life and works. Cross-referencing between works such as Napoleoni, *Insurgent Iraq* and very different publications such as Gilles Kepel, ed., *Al-Qaida dans le texte*, PUF, 2008, pp. 370–416, allows a coherent and relatively accurate picture to emerge. On the amnesty in Jordan, see Bergen, *The Osama Bin Laden I Know*, p. 353.

55. The timing of al-Zarqawi's arrival in northern Iraq is unclear, but he was not mentioned by anyone in a comprehensive range of interviews the author conducted with militants and Kurdish intelligence officials in the summer of that year.

56. German police intelligence report on al-Tauhid, compiled spring 2003. Author telephone interviews with Afghan and Libyan former activists, in London and in Pakistan, February 2003.

57. Full text of Colin Powell's speech, *Guardian*, February 5, 2003. Powell said: 'What I want to bring to your attention today is the potentially much more sinister nexus between Iraq and the Al Qaida terrorist network, a nexus that combines classic terrorist organizations and modern methods of murder. Iraq today harbors a deadly terrorist network headed by Abu Musab Al-Zarqawi, an associated collaborator of Osama bin Laden and his Al Qaida lieutenants.'

58. He certainly had both legs firmly attached to his body when finally killed in 2006. Nor was there any real evidence of the chemical and biological weapons factory Ansar-ul-Islam were supposed to have established in the enclave north of Halabjah.

59. See Jason Burke, *Al-Qaeda*, pp. 225–7, for further details of Ansar ul Islam. See Linda Robinson, *Masters of Chaos*, Public Affairs, 2005, pp. 296–323, for a detailed account of the operation from the point of view of the American special forces.

60. See Jason Burke, 'Theatre of terror', *Observer*, November 21, 2004.

61. The video was uploaded by a twenty-three-year-old Moroccan-born student living in Britain. David Pallister, 'Three plead guilty to inciting murder on Islamist websites', *Guardian*, July 5, 2007. For the half million reference: Abigail Cutler, 'Web of terror', *The Atlantic*, June 5, 2006.

62. For al-Zarqawi's 'snakes' comment see Anton La Guardia, 'Zarqawi rails against Shia "snakes"', *Telegraph*, June 3, 2006.

63. Thomas Ricks, 'U.S. military conducted a PSYOP program "to magnify the role of the leader of al-Qaeda in Iraq"', *Washington Post*, April 11, 2006. Jonathan Finer, 'Among insurgents in Iraq, few foreigners are found', *Washington Post*, November 17, 2005. It is interesting to speculate what might have happened if the pan-Arabism of previous decades had still been prevalent in the early twenty-first century. Would the American strategy have failed with its subject seen as a pan-Arab hero? Or would al-Zarqawi's excesses have alienated local communities nonetheless?

64. The contemporary understanding of the concept of *takfir* owes much to the writings of Syed Qutb among others.

65. Jean-Charles Brisard, *Zarqawi: The New Face of Al-Qaeda*, Policy Press, 2005, p. 135. Al-Shami told listeners: 'If the infidels take Muslims as protectors and these Muslims refuse to fight, it is permitted to kill these Muslims.'

66. Audio cassette message from al-Shami, July 2004, author collection. Al-Shami authored the 'diary of Falluja'.

67. Author interview, Riyadh, March 2008.

68. Ruben Paz, 'Arab Volunteers Killed in Iraq: An Analysis', *The Project for the Research of Islamist Movements (PRISM)*, vol. 3, no. 1 (March 2005).

69. Smugglers running people usually take the same paths used for smuggling livestock. Cigarettes or similar goods move on trucks.

70. Toby Jones, 'Shifting Sands', *Foreign Affairs*, March/April 2006; Eric Rouleau, 'Trouble in the Kingdom', *Foreign Affairs*, July/August 2002. John C. K. Daly, '"Saudi Black Gold": Will Terrorism Deny the West Its Fix?', *Terrorism Monitor*, vol. 1, no. 7 (May 5, 2005). See also Robert Lacey, *Saudi Arabia Exposed: Inside a Kingdom in Crisis*, Palgrave Macmillan, 2006.

71. In Saudi Arabia, fully 40 per cent of the population was under fifteen in 2006. RAND Corporation (Christopher G. Pernin et al.), *Unfolding the Future of the Long War: Motivations, Prospects, and Implications for the U.S. Army*, 2008, p. 213. Useful works on Saudi Arabia include Mamoun Fandy, *Saudi Arabia and the Politics of Dissent*, Palgrave Macmillan, 2001, and the truly excellent Thomas Hegghammer, *Jihad in Saudi Arabia*, Cambridge University Press, 2010.

72. See Combating Terrorism Center (Brian Fishman), *Al'Qa'ida's Foreign Fighters in Iraq: A First Look at the Sinjar Records*, West Point, December 2007, pp. 12–15, for more detail on groups travelling together from their home towns.

73. It is interesting to note that Syria featured in the Rand Corporation study of possible future evolutions of the 9/11 Wars as a low probability, medium-risk, medium- to long-term potential danger. Pernin et al., *Unfolding*, p. 74.

74. Author interview, Riyadh, Saudi Arabia, March 2008. Al-Fawzan had been released from prison eight weeks previously.

75. Each had a coordinator back home, usually the leader of a mosque or another prominent person who had vouched for him. Abu Thar, arriving on his own, was at first considered suspicious. That was 'until they called my master in the religious school in Yemen', he said.

76. Ghaith Abdul-Ahad, 'Seeking salvation in city of insurgents', *Washington Post*, November 11, 2004.

77. See CTC (Fishman), *Foreign Fighters in Iraq*, p. 27. Also Combating Terrorism Center, *Bombers, Bank Accounts and Bleed Outs: al-Qaida's Role in and out of Iraq*, West Point, July 2008, pp. 9, 57.

78. For a description of al-Shami's death and the reaction of his comrades see the postings 'The Secrets of History: Zarqawi as I Knew Him' on the '7th Century Generation' forum, www.7cgen.com, especially 'A Treatise Written by Shaykh Maysarah al-Gharib'. Al-Shami died on September 24.

79. 'The progress we had hoped to make with Iraqi security forces is not as was expected . . . A large number of police did not stand up when their country called,' General Kimmitt, the chief military spokesman in Iraq, had been forced to admit after the first battle.

80. Ricks, *Fiasco*, p. 399.

81. At least to the time of writing in December 2010. The battle of Shah-e-Kot in

March 2002 in Afghanistan had seen far fewer US troops deployed and a much smaller number of militants.

82. Ghaith Abdul-Ahad, 'We are not here to liberate Iraq, we're here to fight the infidels,' *Guardian*, November 9, 2004.

83. Full transcript of bin Laden's speech, Al Jazeera Archive, Aljazeera.net, November 1, 2004.

84. Ibid.

85. Author interview with Nigel Inkster, deputy director MI6 until 2004, London, February 2009.

86. Author interview with Mahmood Shah, Peshawar, November 2008.

87. Author telephone interview with Grenier, January 2009. Pervez Musharraf wrote: 'When we received initial reports of al-Qaeda's presence [in South Waziristan] we did not take them very seriously.' Musharraf, *In the Line of Fire*, p. 264.

88. On reports of presence in Shakai, see Memorandum for Commander, US Southern Command, CSRT Input for Guantanamo Detainee, US9LY-010017DP, Farraj al-Libby, September 10, 2008, US9AF-003148DP, Harun al-Afghani, August 2, 2007, secret, author collection. A key influence here was Ayman al-Zawahiri, who, with his own practical experience of the difficulties of fighting a militant campaign in Egypt, balanced the tendency of bin Laden, who had always been a propagandist more than a fighter, to tilt towards al-Suri's views. Al-Zawahiri stressed repeatedly that the establishment of a secure haven from which to plan and organize should be one of the priorities of the jihadist movement.

89. The useful term 'inciter-in-chief' comes from Michael Scheuer. Author interview, September 2006.

90. The *dar ul kufr* itself is subdivided into the lands of war, *dar ul harb*, and the lands where a covenant had been concluded between the Muslims who lived there and the infidel authorities which tolerated their presence and to some extent protected them. These latter zones comprised what was known as the *dar ul ahd*. See discussion in Kepel, *Jihad*, p. 197.

## CHAPTER 8: THE 9/11 WARS REACH EUROPE

1. Author interview, Amsterdam, November 2004.

2. Ian Buruma, 'Letter from Amsterdam, final cut: after a filmmaker's murder, the Dutch creed of tolerance has come under siege', *New Yorker*, January 3, 2005.

3. See David Levering Lewis, *God's Crucible: Islam and the Making of Europe 570 to 1215*, Norton, 2008, pp. 160–76. Some argue that Poitiers actually occurred in 733; see J. H. Roy and J. Deviosse, *La Bataille de Poitiers, Octobre 733*, Paris, Gallimard, 1966.

4. In fact, the Ottomans signed a peace treaty with Spain. Equally, as Professor Efraim Karsh, head of Middle East and Mediterranean Studies at King's College, London, pointed out in an editorial in the *New York Times* in February 2010: 'Even during the Crusades, the supposed height of the "clash of civilizations", Christian and Muslim rulers freely collaborated across the religious divide, often finding themselves aligned with members of the rival religion against their co-religionists. While the legendary Saladin himself was busy eradicating the Latin Kingdom of Jerusalem, for example, he was closely aligned with the Byzantine Empire, the foremost representative of Christendom's claim to universalism.' 'Muslims won't play together', *New York Times*, February 28, 2010.

5. The terms above are clearly both ethnic and religious, and the emphasis on which quality is seen as definitive has also evolved.

6. Shakespeare's depiction of the 'Moor', like his depiction of the Jew, tends to be complex, sensitive and often, for the period, sympathetic.

7. Orlando Figes, *Crimea: The Last Crusade*, Allen Lane, 2010.

8. Clearly the Asian subcontinent at the time was home to followers of many faiths, but much of the Indo-Gangetic plains as well as the Indus valley and the uplands to its west were dominated by Islam, and the ruling power over much of the region was Muslim.

9. Jean-Léon Gerome, painting around a time of extreme violence as an uprising led by clerics and tribal chiefs shook Algeria, avoided the new French colony as a setting for mosque paintings for the period of the disturbances, preferring Egypt. Rather than show violence to Westerners, Orientalist art largely showed violence to other 'Orientals', as well of course as the saccharine, the picturesque and often the erotic. Linda Nochlin, *The Politics of Vision: Essays on Nineteenth-Century Art and Society*, Westview Press, 1991, pp. 51–52, 59. See also Linda Nochlin, 'The Imaginary Orient', in Vanessa R. Schwartz and Jeannene M. Przyblyski, eds., *The Nineteenth-Century Visual Culture Reader*, Routledge, 2004, p. 296. Delacroix's earlier canvases had shown vengeful Ottoman hordes massacring Grecian peasants.

10. Salahuddin Malik, *1857 War of Independence or Clash of Civilizations*, Oxford, 2003. pp. 13, 17, 115, 118–19, 140, 148. A British government anxious to shift the burden of blame from their own recent policies in the subcontinent blamed Muslim 'Wahabi' agitators for much of the violence – despite the fact that most of the 'mutineers' were Hindu. Media claims of a global 'Islamist' plot, however, failed to convince a sceptical public. Through the late nineteenth century and into the first half of the twentieth, other perils supplanted or complemented the one that many had once thought 'the Muslims' had constituted. In 1900, *Gunton's Magazine* informed its readers that the Boxer Rebellion in China might prove the 'gravest' that 'Christendom has faced since the Moorish invasion of Europe' and could presage an apocalyptic struggle between 'western civilization and oriental barbarism'. See William

W. Bates, 'Chinese Outrages', *Gunton's Magazine Review of the Month*, p. 113 of archive. For a long period too the fear was of supposedly highly organized networks of anarchists and left-wing political activists. As a British police report from 1911 noted, 'These criminal organizations have grown in number and size. They are hardier than ever, now that the terrifying weapons created by modern science are available to them. The world is today threatened by forces which, once freed from their chains, will be able to one day carry out its total destruction.' According to William Dalrymple, author of *The Last Mughal: The Fall of a Dynasty*, Vintage, 2009, the mutinous Company soldiery was 90 per cent Hindu, though there were regional centres such as Lucknow where the street fighting civilian population was maybe 50 per cent Muslim as well as some cavalry units which were majority Muslim. Personal communication with the author, December 2010.

11. Andrew Wheatcroft, *The Infidels: The Conflict between Christendom and Islam, 638–2002*, Viking, 2003, p. 41. Arab armies at the time were largely composed of footsoldiers with a few cavalry and some camels, not, as in later images, a horde mounted on fine Arab horses. 'The Arabs were poor men, often with little more than a spear as a weapon. They walked ... using less water and food than any animal. Previously they had fought in small groups, but now, marshalled by the leaders of Islam, they numbered hundreds.' Nor incidentally did the early Arab invaders convert by the sword, rather the opposite. There was significant resistance to the conversion of many local populations from the elite who claimed their privilege as both as descendants of the original Arab settlers and as Muslims.

12. See Patrick Porter, *Military Orientalism*, Hurst, 2007, for a useful discussion of the idea of Western or Oriental styles of fighting.

13. Ian Buruma and Avishai Margalit, *Occidentalism*, Penguin Press, 2004.

14. Wheatcroft, *The Infidels*, pp. 190–91, 202.

15. Munqidh quote in Amin Maalouf, *The Crusades through Arab Eyes*, Schocken Books, 1989, p. 39. See also the very useful Carole Hillenbrand, *The Crusades: Islamic Perspectives*, Edinburgh University Press, July 30, 1999.

16. Karen Armstrong, *Holy War: The Crusades and Their Impact on Today's World*, Macmillan, 1998, p. 463.

17. See Malise Ruthven, *A Fury For God: The Islamist Attack on America*, Granta, 2004, for one of the best discussions of Qutb.

18. Porter, *Military Orientalism*, p. 57.

19. Tom Gross, 'The BBC's Augean Stables', *National Review*, February 28, 2005. Sheikh al-Sudais led 15,000 worshippers at prayer at the opening of a six-storey Islamic centre in east London, though he was careful to avoid any anti-Semitic references.

20. See, for example, the Egyptian series *Horseman without a Horse*, a forty-one-part TV melodrama based on the forged *Protocols of the Elders of Zion*.

'Egypt airs "anti-Semitic" series', BBC News Online, November, 7, 2002. Or the Syrian *The Collapse of Legends*, of which the central premise was that there was no archaeological evidence to support the stories of the Old Testament and that the Torah was forged to give the Jews a claim to the Land of Israel. It featured a group of Syrian archaeologists setting out to expose a group of Zionists hoping to plant evidence at a famous archaeological site to give some scientific basis to the forged scriptures. Richard Z. Chesnoff, *Jewish World Review*, December 13, 2002.

21. The author found copies on sale in Kuala Lumpur airport in December 2004.

22. Europe had, of course, its own long and inglorious tradition of anti-Semitism – one that had led to worse violence against the Jews than ever seen in the Islamic world – and the many young British Pakistanis or French Algerians interviewed by the author who spoke of how 'the Jews' were behind the 'war on terror' were unwittingly echoing words which had been banished from acceptable conversation only a few decades previously. See Denis MacShane, *Globalising Hatred: The New Anti-Semitism*, Weidenfeld and Nicolson, 2009, for a provocative and informed survey. For an impressive and profoundly researched history, Robert Wistrich, *A Lethal Obsession: Anti-Semitism from Antiquity to the Global Jihad*, Random House, 2010.

23. Author telephone interview with Christopher Caldwell, July 2009. Caldwell's book, *Reflections on the Revolution in Europe*, Allen Lane, 2009, is often tendentious, relying on the arrangement of carefully selected factoids and subjective readings of data to give what is overall a misleading and alarmist description of the genuine problems of integration and assimilation of 'Muslim' communities in Europe. He is right, however, to argue that little thought was given to the consequences of importing labour in the 1960s and 1970s.

24. 'A large coloured community as a noticeable feature of our social life would weaken the concept of England or Britain to which people of British stock throughout the Commonwealth are attached,' a report of the British Colonial Office observed in 1955. Kenan Malik, *From Fatwa to Jihad*, Atlantic, 2009, p. 43.

25. Some in fact accelerated the influx as communities in the West sought to beat the deadlines imposed by successive waves of legislation. A total of 17,210 Pakistanis came to Britain between 1955 and 1960. In the eighteen months before the Immigration Act of 1962, 50,170 more arrived. See ibid., p. 43.

26. There are various guides to the vexed questions of numbers. One is the excellent and comprehensive Pew Research Center, *Mapping the Global Muslim Population: A Report on the Size and Distribution of the World's Muslim Population*, October 2009, which says, on p. 22, of Europe:

> Europe has about 38 million Muslims, constituting about 5% of its population. European Muslims make up slightly more than 2% of the world's Muslim

population. Readers should bear in mind that estimates of the numbers of Muslims in Europe vary widely because of the difficulty of counting new immigrants. Nevertheless, it is clear that most European Muslims live in eastern and central Europe. The country with the largest Muslim population in Europe is Russia, with more than 16 million Muslims, meaning that more than four-in-ten European Muslims live in Russia. While most Muslims in western Europe are relatively recent immigrants (or children of immigrants) from Turkey, North Africa or South Asia, most of those in Russia, Albania, Kosovo, Bosnia-Herzegovina and Bulgaria belong to populations that are centuries old, meaning that more than six in ten European Muslims are indigenous. Despite the limitations of the underlying data for Europe, it appears that Germany is home to more than 4 million Muslims – almost as many as North and South America combined. This means that Germany has more Muslims than Lebanon (between 2 million and 3 million) and more than any other country in western Europe. This also puts Germany among the top 10 countries with the largest number of Muslims living as a minority population. While France has a slightly higher percentage of Muslims than Germany, this study finds that it has slightly fewer Muslims overall. The United Kingdom is home to fewer than 2 million Muslims, about 3% of its total population.

As if to underline the difficulties of counting, Pew in 2010 revised their figure for UK Muslims upwards, to 2,869,000 Muslims in Britain, around 4.6 per cent of the population. See Pew Research Center, *Muslim Networks and Movements in Western Europe*, September 15, 2010. The European countries with the highest concentration of Muslims are located in eastern and central Europe: Kosovo (90 per cent), Albania (80 per cent), Bosnia-Herzegovina (40 per cent) and the Republic of Macedonia (33 per cent). Greece is about 3 per cent Muslim, while Spain is about 1 per cent Muslim. Italy has one of the smallest populations of Muslims in Europe, with less than 1 per cent of its population being Muslim. See also John Carvel, 'Census shows Muslims' plight', *Guardian*, October 12, 2004. For France see the excellent discussion in the first chapter of Jonathan Laurence and Justin Vaisse, *Intégrer l'Islam, la France et ses Musulmans: enjeux et réussites*, Odile Jacob, 2007, pp. 31–9. Laurence and Vaisse argue for a figure of 5 million. The website of the French Foreign Ministry says 'between four and five million'. The Ministry for the Interior gives the figure 4.5 million. See Haut Conseil à l'intégration, *L'Islam dans la République*, Paris, 2000.

27. By 2004, many of the younger militants suddenly coming to the attention of the authorities were in fact 'third generation'.

28. Less than a half of non-Western immigrants had a salaried job compared to 67 per cent of native Dutch. Figures from The Netherland's Social and Cultural Planning Office (Sociaal en Cultureel Planbureau, SCP), January 2009.

29. Carvel, 'Census shows Muslims' plight'.

30. Employees' religious backgrounds are not registered in German employment statistics. Thus, estimations are based primarily on national origins. Unemployment rates are consistently twice as high for non-Germans, with Turkish nationals appearing to be in the worst situation. In some *Länder*, the unemployment rate among the young Muslim population is estimated to be around 30 per cent. Even when comparing foreigners to Germans without any qualifications, a greater proportion of foreigners (three-quarters) than Germans (one-third) are unemployed. See http://www.euro-islam.info/country-profiles/germany/. Not only are French Muslims more likely to be unemployed than the rest of the population, they also encounter more problems finding long-term and full-time jobs.

31. For France, see Laurence and Vaisse, *Intégrer l'Islam*, pp. 64–5.

32. The Commission on the Future of a Multi-Ethnic Britain, cited Malik, *From Fatwa to Jihad*, p. 62.

33. Author interview, November 2004.

34. Lawrence James, *Warrior Race*, Little, Brown, 2001. There were also questions of Englishness as opposed to Britishness (or Welshness, Irishness and Scottishness), with one poll revealing that immigrants felt happier with a 'British' identity rather than an 'English' one.

35. Maleeha Lodhi, the Pakistani High Commissioner at the time of the 7/7 attacks, and many others saw a difference between 'integration' and 'assimilation'. Lodhi called on Pakistanis in Britain to integrate even if they did not want to assimilate. Author interview, London, July 2005.

36. The violence spilled over on to the streets of Paris, with bombs going off in Metro stations in 1995 and a French airliner hijacked at Algiers in 1994.

37. Malik, *From Fatwa to Jihad*, pp. 123–5.

38. See Martin Bright, *When Progressives Treat with Reactionaries*, Policy Exchange, 2006.

39. In the UK mosques went from 51 in 1979 to 329 six years later. In France in the same period, the rise was fivefold, from 136 to 766. Pargeter, *The New Frontiers of Jihad*, p. 19.

40. Laurence and Vaisse, *Intégrer l'Islam*, p. 281. The responsibility for 90 per cent of anti-Semitic attacks in the 1990s lay with the extreme right; that for 80 per cent of such attacks from 2000 onwards lay with 'Arabo-Muslim' aggressors.

41. 'I was of a generation that did not think of itself as Muslim or Hindi or Sikh or even as Asian but as black,' remembered the British academic and journalist Kenan Malik, explaining that one reason for a growing disaffection with left-wing groups was their focus on the class struggle rather than discrimination. Malik, *From Fatwa to Jihad*, pp. xi, 21.

42. Paul Harris, Martin Bright and Burhan Wazir, 'Five Britons killed in "jihad brigade"', *Observer*, October 28, 2001.

43. Details of April 30, 2003 Tel Aviv suicide bombing, Israeli Ministry of Foreign affairs, press release, June 3, 2003.

44. Shiv Malik, 'Omar Khan Sharif: profile', *New Statesman*, April 24, 2006. Hamas claimed responsibility for the attack.

45. Author interview, Amsterdam, November 2004.

46. Eliza Manningham-Butler, director general of the Security Service, 'Global Terrorism: Are We Meeting the Challenge?', James Smart lecture, City of London Police Headquarters, October 16, 2003.

47. Dominic Casciani, 'MI5 "too stretched " before 7 July', BBC, May 19, 2009. UK Parliament and Intelligence and Security Committee, *Report into the London Terrorist Attacks on 7 July 2005*, HMSO, 2006, p. 33.

48. John Stevens, *News of the World*, March 6, 2005.

49. 'Geheimdienste warnen vor Islamisten-Terror in Deutschland', *Der Spiegel*, November 13, 2004.

50. Beatrice de Graff, 'The Nexus between Salafism and Jihadism in the Netherlands', *CTC Sentinel*, vol. 3, no. 3, March 2010, pp. 17–22.

51. Author interviews with senior Dutch security officials, London, July 2008. See *Paths to Global Jihad: Radicalization and Recruitment. Proceedings from FFI Seminar*, Oslo, March 15, 2006, p. 18.

52. Interestingly, many of Hezb-ut-Tahrir's early members in the UK were former members of extreme left-wing groups such as the Socialist Workers' Party.

53. Author interview with Ed Husain, London, July 2007. See also Ed Husain, *The Islamist: Why I Joined Radical Islam in Britain, What I Saw Inside and Why I Left*, Penguin, 2007.

54. See the useful discussion in Malik, *From Fatwa to Jihad*, p. 45.

55. Anshuman Mondal, 'British Islam after Rushdie', *Prospect*, April 26, 2009.

56. Author interview with Shiraz Maher, London, July 2007.

57. Ibid.

58. Author interview, MI5, London, July 2007.

59. Unedited records of court reporting and transcript of trial at Old Bailey, London. Prosecution statement, April 24, 2007. Convictions in the case were quashed on appeal in 2008.

60. Of the twenty-six Islamic seminaries in Britain in 2006, seventeen are Deobandi.

61. Qadir continued fundraising through 2003 but eventually turned his energy to running a youth club aimed at combating gang violence among British Pakistani teenagers. Author interview with Hanif Qadir, Walthamstow, July 2007.

62. Another example from this period would be Dhiren Barot, a British convert to Islam jailed in 2006 for planning a range of mass-casualty attacks in the UK. Barot fought in Kashmir with Pakistani-based militants at the end of the 1990s before going on to pursue an almost decade-long career in Islamic terrorism.

63. Transcript, complete reporting records, Operation Crevice trial, London, March 2006 to April 2007. Author collection.

64. The ingredient was ammonium nitrate.

65. In 2007 the author compiled a survey of key personal data on over eighty British militants detained between 2001 and 2006. Their average age was twenty-nine when they were arrested. See Jason Burke, 'Omar was a normal British teenager who loved his little brother and Man Utd. So why at 24 did he plan to blow up a nightclub in central London?', *Observer*, January 20, 2008. A later study published in 2010 arrived at a median age of 27.6. Institute for Strategic Dialogue and Jytte Klausen, *Al Qaeda-Affiliated and 'Homegrown' Jihadism in the UK: 1999–2010*, 2010, p. 10. Many studies have been done showing that psychological problems among militant activists, Islamic or otherwise, are no more prevalent than in the general population.

66. Scott Atran, 'Who Becomes a Terrorist Today?', *Perspectives on Terrorism*, vol. 2, no. 5, May 2008.

67. Author interview, Scotland Yard, London, April 2005.

68. 'What was the 9/11 Hamburg cell if not a gang,' said one. Author interview, Walthamstow, August 2006.

69. Ed Husain, *The Islamist*, pp. 32–33.

70. Some accounts, such as that of the excellent Ian Buruma in the *New Yorker* edition of January 3, 2005, entitled 'Final cut', describe Bouyeri, van Gogh's killer, wearing 'a long Middle Eastern-style shirt'. Others, such as an eyewitness quoted in *De Telegraaf* the day after van Gogh's murder, refer to a hooded sweater. These are not are mutually exclusive. He was variously described by witnesses as wearing a hooded sweater, jeans and a long Maghreb-style traditional shirt. In fact, he appears to have been wearing all three.

71. Author interview, Walthamstow, London, July 2007.

72. This account is based on transcripts of the trial of the Crevice conspirators.

73. Junaid Babar testimony, author collection.

74. Author interviews, Thames House, London, July 2007.

75. Crevice transcripts.

76. Al-Iraqi had been a major in the Iraqi army in the 1980s but a member of al-Qaeda 'since the late 1990s', eventually rising to a position on the Shura or council which acted as an advisory body to bin Laden and al-Zawahiri – before the 9/11 attacks. His real name was Nashwan Abdulrazaq Abdulbaqi.

77. Crevice transcripts.

78. Crevice transcripts.

79. Crevice transcripts.

80. Author interview, Suleimaniyah, Iraq, August, 2002

81. Author interviews, Kabul, August 2008, March 2009; Rawalpindi, 2008; Jammu, India, 2003.

## CHAPTER 9: BOMBS, RIOTS AND CARTOONS

1. Karen McVeigh and Alexandra Topping, '7/7 inquest witness saw bombers "celebrate like sports team" before attack', *Guardian*, October 13, 2010.
2. Andrew Malone, 'Tavistock Square: "I watched as the anxious man on the bus kept going into his bag"', *Independent*, July 8, 2005.
3. Author interviews with Scotland Yard senior officers, London, January 2006.
4. Khan was born in Leeds, grew up in Beeston and moved to Dewsbury a few months before the July bombings. Tanweer was born in Bradford but grew up in Beeston. Lindsay took the name Abdullah Shaheed Jamal following his conversion to Islam. He later moved to Aylesbury, Buckinghamshire.
5. Shiv Malik, 'My Brother the bomber', *Prospect*, 135, June 2007.; Sandra Laville and Dipazier Aslam, 'Mentor to the young and vulnerable', *Guardian*, July 14, 2005. UK Parliament and Intelligence Security Committee, *Report into the London Terrorist Attacks July 7 2005*. Melanie Newman, 'Greenwich and Leeds Met given "limited confidence" ratings by QAA', *Times Higher Education Supplement*, October 15, 2009. Khan's wife's family were Deobandi. His own were broadly Barelvi.
6. Leeds Metropolitan University was ranked 85 out of 115 in the 2011 universities league table.
7. Khan had an eight-month-old daughter. His wife was expecting a second. Jonathan Brown, 'Mohammed Sadique Khan: expectant father whose chosen path meant he would never see his baby', *Independent*, July 15, 2007.
8. Jason Burke, 'Secrets of bomber's death tape', *Observer*, September 4, 2005. London bomber: text in full, BBC, September 1, 2005. In fact, the latter has sections missing. Al-Jazeera broadcast the whole version. Text in author collection.
9. Home Office, *Report of the Official Account of the Bombings in London on 7th July 2005*, HMSO, May 11, 2006, p. 19.
10. Richard Norton-Taylor and Riazat Butt, 'Queen is target for al-Qaida, security sources confirm', *Guardian*, November 14, 2005.
11. In February 2004, Khyam had been recorded by MI5 telling Khan, a few months before the latter had set out for a training camp, that 'you'll be with Arab brothers, Chechen brothers. The only thing I will advise you . . . is total obedience to whoever your Emir is . . . whether he is Sunni, Arab, Chechen, Saudi, British . . . I'll tell you up there you can get your head cut off.' See James Brandon, 'Al-Qa'ida's Involvement in Britain's "Homegrown" terrorist plots', *CTC Sentinel*, vol. 2, no. 3, March 2009, p. 10.
12. Esther Addley, '7/7 inquest: "Pandemonium here . . . we have really got to get some control"', *Guardian*, October 11, 2010.
13. British ministers made extraordinary efforts to deny any causative link between the strikes and the war in Iraq, despite the advice of their own secur-

ity services, despite blindingly obvious evidence all around them and despite, exactly a year after the bombings, the release of the videoed testament of Shehzad Tanweer, who explained that 'the non-Muslims of Britain' were being targeted because they had 'openly supported the genocide of over 150,000 innocent Muslims in Falluja'.

14. The two men Ibrahim was travelling with are believed to have died in Afghanistan. 'Police monitored bomb plotters', BBC News Online, January 18, 2007.

15. Evan Kohlmann, 'Abu Musab al-Suri's final "Message to the British and the Europeans"', *Nefa Foundation*, August 2005.

16. Author interview with Pakistani intelligence officials, Riyadh, March 2008. 'Al-Suri has not surfaced anywhere since though may have been "rendered" to Syria.' William Maclean, 'Al Qaeda ideologue in Syrian detention – lawyers', Reuters, June 10, 2009.

17. Text of statement by Mayor Ken Livingstone, *Financial Times*, July 7, 2005.

18. In 2001, 30 per cent of Londoners were born outside England. See Leo Benedictus, 'Every race, colour, nation and religion on earth', *Guardian*, January 21, 2005. For 2006, the figure for Londoners born outside the UK was 32 per cent according to the Greater London Authority's Data Management and Analysis Group report by Laura Spence, February 2008, *A Profile of Londoners by Country of Birth Estimates from the 2006 Annual Population Survey*, p. 1.

19. Obituaries of those who died in the 7/7 bombing, Guardian Online, accessed July 7, 2010.

20. Kenan Malik, 'The Islamophobia Myth', *Prospect*, 107, February 2005.

21. GfK NOP Social Research, *Attitudes to Living in Britain – A Survey of Muslim Opinion*, August 2006.

22. Michael Meacher, 'This war on terrorism is bogus', *Guardian*, September 6, 2003.

23. Oriana Fallacci, *The Rage and the Pride*, Rizzoli, 2002. For sales figures: Jennifer Schuessler, 'Gift books for millionaires', *New York Times*, December, 20, 2010.

24. Bruce Bawer, *While Europe Slept*, Doubleday, 2006. Melanie Phillips, *Londonistan*, Encounter Books, 2006.

25. Address at the opening of courses at the University of Leiden, September 2004.

26. Christopher Caldwell, 'Islamic Europe: When Bernard Lewis speaks', *Weekly Standard*, October 4, 2004.

27. Tony Blankley, 'An Islamist threat like the Nazis', *Washington Times*, September 12, 2005.

28. Robert Leiken, 'Europe's Angry Muslims', *Foreign Affairs*, July/August 2005.

29. Charles Krauthammer, 'What the uprising generation wants,' *Time*, November 13, 2005.

30. Niall Ferguson, 'Eurabia?', *New York Times*, April 4, 2004.

31. See CIA World Factbook 2007 listings for Algeria, Turkey, Tunisia, France. Available online at https://www.cia.gov/library/publications/the-world-factbook/index.html. A series of other commentators dismissed a complex and technical debate among demographers and considerable evidence that reproduction rates among European Muslims are already declining and are likely to decline further in coming years (as they have done both for other European migrant communities and in many Muslim migrants' countries of origin) as European wishful thinking. See Chapter 14 for more.

32. Bat Ye'or, *Eurabia: The Euro-Arab Axis*, Fairleigh Dickinson University Press, 2005.

33. 'Tales from Eurabia', *The Economist*, June 22, 2006.

34. Extracts from the Zawahiri tape, Times Online, August 4, 2005. Al-Zawahiri issued a statement towards the end of 2005 which specifically targeted British Muslims, calling the Queen 'one of the severest threats to Islam' and, in passing, revealing deep cultural ignorance, threatening all those who called themselves 'British citizens, subject to Britain's crusader laws' and who were 'proud of [their] submission . . . to Elizabeth, head of the Church of England'.

35. Author interview with Alain Bauer, criminologist, Paris, March 2008.

36. Exact figures are hard to find. For example, at Aulnay-sous-Bois Ministry of the Interior press officers gave a figure of sixteen vehicles burned whereas the fire brigade recorded 150 separate interventions during a week of rioting. Author interviews, Paris, November 2005.

37. Mucchielli, *Quand les banlieues brûlent*, La Découverte, 2007, p. 20.

38. Many on the French left argued that they were in fact youngsters without previous criminal involvement who were more motivated by rage, hate, despair, alienation and a deep identity crisis than any involvement in narcotics. The arguments over the cause of the riots was in part political theatre, a result of internal French domestic politics, mainly the bitter and personal rivalry between Sarkozy, whose political persona and appeal was based on tough rhetoric on law and order, and his rival for the succession to President Jacques Chirac as leader of the French right, the less populist, urbane Dominique de Villepin, who favoured a more centrist, 'compassionate' conservatism. Uninspired and uninspiring, the French Socialists had little influence on the public conversation.

39. 'Les juges ne confirment pas le portrait des émeutiers dressé par Sarkozy', Agence France-Presse, November 17, 2005.

40. French Government Centre of Strategic Analysis, Report for the Office of the Prime Minister: *Enquêtes sur les violences urbaines: comprendre les émeutes de Novembre 2005, les exemples de Saint-Denis et de Aulnay-sous-Bois*, Paris, 2006.

41. For more see Timothy Garton-Ash, 'Anti-Europeanism in America', *Hoover Digest*, 2, 2003. Also Justin Vaisse, 'American Francophobia Takes a New Turn', *French Politics, Culture and Society*, vol. 21, no. 2, July 2003. The latter

in particular is an excellent discussion of the development of these stereotypes and of their reinforcement from 2003 onwards in the US media and
among US politicians

42. Melanie Philips, 'Why France is burning', *Daily Mail*, November 7, 2005.

43. Mark Steyn, 'Wake up, Europe, you've a war on your hands', *Chicago Sun Times*, November 6, 2005.

44. Reuven Paz, 'The Non-Territorial Islamic States in Europe', paper, Project for the Research of Islamist Movements, Hertzeliya, Israel, November 28, 2005.

45. 'On faisait un peu le Baghdad, quoi' were the exact words of Paolo Savalli, of mixed Moroccan/Italian background, in Bobigny two months after the riots. Author interview, January 2010.

46. One example from the author's own late teenage years was the controversial 1988 hit 'Fuck Tha Police', by American rappers Niggaz With Attitude.

47. Mucchielli, *Quand les banlieues brûlent*, p. 29. See the 2004 report of the National Human Rights Advisory Commission (Commission nationale con-sultative des droits de l'homme, CNCDH).

48. Laurence and Vaisse, *Intégrer l'Islam*, p. 276.

49. Attacks on French Jews numbered 510 in first six months of 2004 as against 593 in the whole of 2003 according to 'Anti-Semitism on rise in Europe', BBC, March 31, 2004.

50. This killing was the first explicitly anti-Semitic murder in France since 1995. The 'gang of barbarians'' own understanding of Islam was cursory to say the least. Charles Bremner, 'Youssouf Fofana jailed for the torture and murder of Ilan Halimi', *The Times*, July 11, 2009, Pascal Ceaux and Jean-Marie Pon-taut, 'Youssouf Fofana: confessions d'un "barbare"', *L'Express*, January 23, 2008.

51. Author interviews, Bobigny, France, December 2005, January 2006.

52. Cecilia Gabizon, 'La Carte des émeutes de novembre 2005 confirme le pro-fond malaise des immigrants africains', *Le Figaro*, October 15, 2007. See also Hugues Lagrange and Marco Oberti, eds., *Emeutes urbaines et protestations*, Les Presses Sciences, 2006.

53. Christophe Cornevin, 'Des troubles nés de l'exclusion, selon les RG', *Le Figaro*, December 8, 2005.

54. Author interview with Olivier Roy, Paris, December 2005. Also Olivier Roy, 'The Nature of the French Riots', SSRC, November 18, 2005. Jean-Marc Sébé, *La Crise des banlieues*, PUF, 2007, p. 74.

55. French Government Centre of Strategic Analysis, *Enquêtes sur les violences urbaines*, pp. 17, 25.

56. Ibid., p. 47.

57. Jean Chichizola, 'Fous d'Allah et voyous font cause commune sur les braquages', *Le Figaro*, January 13, 2006.

58. One report by the RG detailed sixty-eight of 128 French penal institutions 'con-taminated by Islamism'. Jean Chichizola, '175 Islamistes font du proselytisme

en prison', *Le Figaro*, January 13, 2006. One reason for the radicalization activities occurring outside mosques and Islamic centres was the extremely effective surveillance of such locations by French intelligence services. Text of DGSE confidential presentation, Paris, March 2009, author collection.

59. Netherlands Institute for International Relations Clingendael (Edwin Bakker and Teije Hidde Donker), *Jihadi Terrorists in Europe*, The Hague, December 2006.

60. Author interview with DST official, Paris, January 2009. Jean Chichizola, 'L'Ombre de Zarqaoui s'étend jusqu'en France', *Le Figaro*, December 14, 2005. Atmane Tazaghart and Roland Jacquard, 'La France en ligne de mire', *Le Figaro* Magazine, November 5, 2005. Patricia Tourancheau, 'La "Menace majeure" gagne du terrain', *Libération*, July 9, 2005. A series of arrests stopped a few score more. 'Les Djihadistes de banlieue s'apprêtaient à partir en Irak', *Le Figaro*, September 20, 2005.

61. Author interview with DGSE officer, Paris, January 2007. Eric Pelletier and Jean-Marie Pontaut, 'Islamisme, des étudiants sous surveillance', *L'Express*, November 9, 2006. The numbers of genuine militants remained in more or less the same very low relative proportions as regards the rest of the Muslim population as in the UK. Indeed, it is likely they were probably even lower. However, with a steady stream of plots uncovered through 2004 and 2005, senior officials, like those of almost every security service more or less everywhere from Indonesia to California, went on the record repeatedly in the aftermath of the London bombings and on through the rest of the year to say that the question of an attack in France was a matter not of 'if' but of 'when'. 'We face a tide which we cannot hold back. Despite all the international community's efforts they are capable of striking in Bali, in London and pretty much at any time,' said Christophe Chaboud, director of the French government's counter-terrorism coordinating body, Uclat. 'Le Chef de l'antiterrorisme craint "une lame de fond"', VSD, December 28, 2005.

62. Author interview with senior official, DST, Riyadh, April 2008.

63. Ibid. Author interview with Alain Bauer, criminologist and presidential adviser, Observatoire national de la délinquance, Paris, November 2009.

64. Author interview with senior official, DGSE, Paris, June 2008.

65. France's major Muslim authorities – such as the Muslim Brotherhood-dominated Union of French Islamic Organizations (UIOF) – made repeated calls for the rioting to cease but were resolutely ignored. This failure revealed what many had suspected for some time: that the older generation of political Islamist leaders had little connection with the youth of the *banlieues*.

66. Author interview, Paris, September 2005.

67. The term is from Laurence and Vaisse, *Intégrer l'Islam*, p. 54.

68. Beyond the ramparts was for a long period known as *la zone*, a hinterland of vagrancy, poverty, promiscuity and violence from where gangs were said to come to threaten the urban population.

69. I.e. with a monthly revenue of less than €908. Luc Bronner, 'Zones urbaines sensibles: près d'un mineur sur deux connaît la pauvreté', *Le Monde*, December 1, 2009.

70. Laurence and Vaisse, *Intégrer l'Islam*, p. 56.

71. Statistics from the Institut National de statistiques economiques, www.Insee.fr.

72. As shown by the 2007 film *La Classe*.

73. F. Lainé and M. Okba, 'Jeunes de parents immigrés: de l'école au métier', *Travail et Emploi*, 103, 2005, pp. 79–83.

74. Author collection.

75. A brief experiment with '*police de proximité*' was ended in 2002 by the then minister of the interior, Nicolas Sarkozy, who said that officers had better things to do than 'play football'.

76. Though one can push the parallels too far, accompanying French police in the weeks following the violence of September 2005 was reminiscent of similar experiences with coalition forces on patrol in Afghanistan and, particularly, Iraq. There was the same banter and solidarity among those on patrol, the same undercurrent of sullen resentment and mutual misunderstanding of those being patrolled, the same sense of latent violence and intrusion, the same contest to control territory on the ground. In Iraq it was a strategic street, a market, a bit of wasteland, a dark corner of the local station out of sight of CCTV cameras. In Aulnay, Bobigny and elsewhere it was a bus-stop favoured by dealers, the top floors of an apartment block from which one could see the police coming, a petrol station.

77. Jason Burke, 'Voice of the suburbs', *Observer*, April 23, 2006. Author interview with Faiza Guène, Paris, March 2006, April 2008.

78. Jason Burke, 'The baker who joined Elysée elite', *Observer*, March 23, 2008. 'It's all down to hard work. I've never suffered any discrimination,' he said. Author interview with Anis Bouabsa, March 2008.

79. The canonical vision of French history taught in most schools also offered little room for interrogation by those whose parents remembered the reality of the Algerian war of independence from 1954 to 1962.

80. One rapper, a favourite with the rioters, spoke in one lyric about how he hoped to throw a *pavé*, the traditional Parisian paving stone that has been iconic to street demonstrations from the 1830s through to 1968, through the windows of shops on the Champs Elysées. He was widely condemned for this call to arms, which was, whatever his critics said, very much part of French cultural tradition rather than being an attack on it. Similarly, when, during the *émeutes*, the specialist public order forces, the Compagnies de Sécurité Républicaines (CRS), were deployed, many of the rioters appeared delighted to have merited the presence of the famously brutal CRS in their neighbourhoods and chanted the very predictable 'CR . . . SS' familiar to almost every serious breakdown of public order in France since 1968. The real significance of their words – the insulting reference to Hitler's elite military units, concen-

tration camp guards and so on – entirely escaped the rioters – at least those the author spoke to. There may have been some who were more expert in the political and military history of the twentieth century, but they were certainly thin on the ground in Aulnay and Clichy-sous-Bois.

81. Author telephone interview with Flemming Rose, January 2011

82. Malik, *From Fatwa to Jihad*, p. 144.

83. Ibid.

84. Legal charges brought against *Jyllands-Posten* were eventually dismissed at the beginning of January 2006 on the grounds that the publishing of the cartoons did not violate laws on religious or racial discrimination or on blasphemy.

85. Author telephone interview with Rose, January 2011.

86. Pargeter, *The New Frontiers of Jihad*, p. 195.

87. Ibid., p. 191.

88. Christian Makarian, 'Noirs desseins', *L'Express*, February 9, 2006.

89. René Backmann and Henri Guirchon, 'Les dessins de la colère', *Le Nouvel Observateur*, February 9–15, 2006.

90. Angela Stephens, 'Publics in Western countries disapprove of Muhammad cartoons but right to publish widely defended', February 16, 2006, www. worldpublicopinion.org. '"A New Crusade", bin Laden threatens Europe over Muhammad cartoons', *Der Spiegel*, March 20, 2008.

91. Author telephone interview with Rose, January 2011. Anna Badkhen, 'What's behind Muslim cartoon outrage?', *San Francisco Chronicle*, February 11, 2006.

92. Salah Gaham, a caretaker, died of smoke poisoning while trying to extinguish a fire started in a basement. Jean-Jacques Le Chenadec, a retired Peugeot worker, died from head injuries after being reportedly struck by a hooded man in the street after he and a neighbour went to inspect damage to a bin.

93. For Rice's remarks at the American University in Cairo see Congressional Record, *Proceedings and Debates of the 109th Session of Congress*, vol. 151, part 10, p. 14,415.

94. John Esposito and Dalia Mogahed, *Who Speaks for Islam? What a Billion Muslims Really Think*, Gallup Press, 2007, pp. 69–70. Investigative Project on Terrorism, 'Dalia Mogahed: A Muslim George Gallup or Islamist Ideologue?', April 5, 2010.

95. For the head of the UK's MI5, Eliza Manningham-Buller, the Al-Qaeda threat was 'serious [and] growing' and would last at least 'a generation'.

## CHAPTER 10: THE AWAKENING

1. According to some sources, they wore Iraqi special forces uniforms.

2. Author interview with senior Iraqi security official, London, August 2006. Some reports mentioned a second Iraqi involved in the bombing. Edward

Wong, 'Iraqi led bombing of Shiite sites, official says', *New York Times*, June 28, 2006.

3. Post-tour interview with Major Darrel Green, Combat Studies Institute, Fort Leavenworth, February 27, 2007.

4. 'Interview with Maj. Jeremy Lewis', Combat Studies Institute, February 29, 2007, p. 12. Also quoted by Thomas Ricks, *The Gamble*, Penguin, 2009, p. 32.

5. Some of the worst were the blast at the end of August 2003 which had killed ninety-five Shia in Najaf, including Ayatollah Mohammed Baqr al-Hakim, and the series of attacks on Shia mosques during the Ashura holiday in March 2004, which killed nearly 200.

6. Nelson Hernandez and Saad Sarhan, 'Insurgents kill 140 as Iraq clashes escalate', *Washington Post*, January 6, 2010. 'Iraq suicide bomb blasts kill 120', BBC News Online, January 5, 2006.

7. Sam Knight and agencies, 'Bombing of Shia shrine sparks wave of retaliation', *The Times*, February 22, 2006. Jonathan Finer and Bassam Sebti, 'Sectarian violence kills over 100 in Iraq, Shiite–Sunni anger flares following bombing of shrine', *Washington Post*, February 24, 2006. Robert F. Worth, 'Blast at Shiite shrine sets off sectarian fury in Iraq', *New York Times*, February 23, 2006.

8. 'Interview with Lewis', p. 16.

9. Quite where sectarian violence started and criminal violence stopped was often difficult to say. Some sectarian gangs sold the remains of dead victims to bereaved relatives – a macabre form of posthumous ransom.

10. The policy had been outlined in the 'National Strategy for Victory in Iraq' of November 2005.

11. Cockburn, *The Occupation*, 167. In 2005, they totalled 846 dead and 5,944 wounded respectively. The Brookings Institution (Michael E. O'Hanlon and Ian Livingston), *The Iraq Index: Tracking Variables of Reconstruction and Security in Post-Saddam Iraq*, June 30, 2010, pp. 12, 14.

12. David Kilcullen, *The Accidental Guerrilla, Fighting Small Wars in the Midst of a Big One*, Hurst, 2009, p. 124.

13. The number varied by a few thousand. Sharon Otterman, 'Saudi Arabia: withdrawal of US forces', Council of Foreign Relations, Washington, May 2, 2003.

14. Paul von Zielbauer, 'US inquiry hampered by Iraq violence, investigators say', *New York Times*, June 13, 2007, Tim McGirk, 'Collateral damage or civilian massacre in Haditha?', *Time*, March 19, 2006.

15. Thomas E. Ricks, 'In Haditha killings, details came slowly', *Washington Post*, June 4, 2006.

16. West, *The Strongest Tribe*, p. 156.

17. Ricks, *The Gamble*, pp. 7–8.

18. Urban, *Task Force Black*, pp. 94–9.

19. Ibid., p. 106.

20. The coalition gaining the majority of the Sunni overall vote was the Accord

Front, with 16 per cent of the vote and 44 seats. A more radical grouping, the Iraqi Dialogue Front, took 4 per cent and 11 seats. See Toby Dodge, 'The Causes of US Failure in Iraq', *Survival: Global Politics and Strategy*, vol. 49, no. 1 (spring 2007), pp. 85–106.

21. Email exchange with author, December 2005.

22. Department of State, Public Notice 4936, 'Foreign Terrorists and Terrorist Organizations; Designation: Organization in the Land of the Two Rivers', *Federal Register*, December 17, 2004, vol. 69, no. 242.

23. There is also a clear reference to the *tanzim* of the Palestinian al-Aqsa Intifada with their younger more aggressive stance against a senior leadership seen as sedentary and out of touch. The name also, incidentally, shows al-Zarqawi's distance from pure Salafists, who, though they would have agreed with his views that Shia are heretics, would have been against the organization of the faithful into a party or a movement.

24. See Kepel, *Jihad*, pp. 236–53. More radical elements in Bosnia provoked ridicule by trying to argue that Father Christmas was unIslamic.

25. Burke, *Al-Qaeda*, pp. 12, 206.

26. See ibid., pp. 116–35, 213–33.

27. Ian Fisher and Edward Wong, 'Iraq's rebellion develops signs of internal rift', *New York Times*, July 10, 2004. Author interviews with Iraqi militants, Baghdad, September 2004.

28. Dhiya Rassan, 'Patchwork of insurgent groups runs Fallujah', Institute of War and Peace Reporting, September 17, 2004.

29. Karl Vick, 'Insurgent alliance fraying in Fallujah', *Washington Post*, October 13, 2004.

30. Ghaith Abdul-Ahad, 'Seeking salvation in city of insurgents', *Guardian*, November 11, 2004. See Chapter 7.

31. Hannah Allam, 'Fallujah's real boss: Omar the electrician', Knight Ridder *Newspapers*, November 22, 2004.

32. Abdul-Ahad, 'Seeking salvation in city of insurgents'.

33. John Ward Anderson, 'Seven al-Zarqawi insurgents killed in retaliation for Khaldiya slaying', *Washington Post*, March 18, 2005.

34. In a particularly macabre example of the facility with which practices have been communicated from one protagonist in the 9/11 Wars to another, the foreign militants' techniques were borrowed from Shia death squads operating at the time.

35. In 2003, the author interviewed a former torturer from Saddam Hussein's Mukhabarat intelligence service who recounted how he had held babies over boiling water to get their parents to talk.

36. Pelham, *A New Muslim Order*, pp. 197–8. Sunni Arab parties won fifty-five seats in the new parliament (see note 20), up from seventeen in the previous one. In part the division within the insurgent ranks was between 'Salafi jihadi' strands and Islamist strands. There was also a tribal dynamic at play.

37. West, *The Strongest Tribe*, p. 132.

38. Tim McGirk, 'A rebel crack-up?', *Time*, January 22, 2006.

39. The letter from al-Zawahiri to al-Zarqawi is dated July 9, 2005. The contents were released by the US Office of the Director of National Intelligence on October 11, 2005.

40. See, for example, Abu Bakr Naji, *Management of Savagery: The Most Critical Stage Through Which the Ummah Will Pass*, originally published on the internet, 2004, translated into English by William McCants, published by Olin Institute for Strategic Studies, Harvard University, 2006.

41. The letter, written by bin Laden's representative to Algeria, Atiyah Abd al-Rahman, was dated December 12, 2005. See http://ctc.usama.edu/harmony/pdf/CTC-AtiyahLetter.pdf.

42. 'Jordan hotel blasts kill dozens', BBC News Online, November 10, 2005. Conal Urquhart, 'Failed bomb attacker confesses live on air', *Guardian*, November 14, 2005.

43. 'Al-Khalayleh tribe disowns al-Zarqawi', *Jerusalem Post*, November 20, 2005.

44. Nir Rosen, 'Thinking Like a Jihadist: Iraq's Jordanian Connection', *World Policy Journal*, Spring 2006, p. 14.

45. Murad Batal al-Shishani, 'The Amman Bombings: A Blow to the Jihadists?', *Terrorism Focus*, vol. 2, no. 22, November 29, 2005.

46. It had been 57 per cent in 2003. Pew Research Center, *Declining Support for bin Laden and Suicide Bombing*, September 10, 2009. See also Daniel Benjamin, Center for Strategic and International Studies, testimony before the Senate Foreign Relations Committee, June 13, 2006.

47. See Rosen, 'Thinking Like a Jihadist: Iraq's Jordanian Connection'.

48. Jason Burke, Peter Beaumont and Mohammed al-Ubeidy, 'How Jordanians hunted down their hated son', *Observer*, June 11, 2006.

49. On the interrogations see Bowden, 'The ploy'. Author interviews with senior Iraqi security officials, London, September 2009.

50. Interviews with Jordanian intelligence officers, London, June 2006.

51. Pew Research Center, *Global Public Opinion in the Bush Years (2001–2008)*, December 18, 2008.

52. Pew Research Center, *Where Terrorism Finds Support in the Muslim World*, May 2006.

53. Pew Research Center, *Global Public Opinion in the Bush Years*.

54. The blast in Sharm-el-Sheikh killed ninety people, mostly Egyptians. 'Toll climbs in Egyptian attacks', BBC News Online, July 23, 2005.

55. Pew Research Center, *Global Attitudes Toward Islamic Extremism and Terrorism*, August 29, 2007. Data from Pew's Key Indicators Database, accessed January 2, 2011.

56. Jason Burke, 'The Arab backlash the militants didn't expect', *Observer*, June 20, 2004. International Crisis Group, *Can Saudi Arabia Reform Itself?*, July

14, 2004. Poll subject quote from the *Daily Star*, Beirut, Lebanon, June 24, 2004.

57. Esposito and Mogahed, *Who Speaks for Islam?*, p. 73 and passim. Such views appeared to be held regardless of gender or piety, an important nuance missed by many Western commentators. Equally, perceptions of Islam and Muslims among non-Muslims in Europe and America were much more negative after nearly five years of conflict than they had been even in the weeks after September 11. The proportion was higher among 18–24-year-olds and among second-generation immigrants. A Pew poll of Muslim world opinion in 2006 found that majorities in Indonesia, Turkey, Egypt and Jordan said that they do not believe groups of Arabs carried out the September 11, 2001 terrorist attacks. The percentage of Turks expressing disbelief that Arabs carried out the 9/11 attacks has increased from 43 per cent in a 2002 Gallup survey to 59 per cent by 2005. In the UK, 56 per cent of British Muslims said they do not believe Arabs carried out the terror attacks against the US. Only 17 per cent thought they had done.

58. The idea of assembling bombs inside planes had been raised before. This was clearly a serious threat as it circumvented most conventional security procedures. The investigation of the Walthamstow plot led to the banning of fluids in baggage within planes' cabins. Jason Burke, 'Terrorist bid to build bombs in mid-flight', *Observer*, February 8, 2004.

59. 'Meeting with the Representatives of Science: Lecture of the Holy Father', Regensburg, Germany, Libreria Editrice Vaticana, September 12, 2006.

60. West, *The Strongest Tribe*, p. 175.

61. Mushriq Abbas, 'Mutual political and tribal interests coincided with his struggle with al-Qa'ida and al-Maliki: a short and murky journey led Abu Risha to . . . his death', *al-Hayat*, September 16, 2007, cited by Mohammed M. Hafez, 'Al-Qa'ida Losing Ground in Iraq', *CTC Sentinel*, vol. 1, no. 1 (December 2007), p. 7.

62. West, *The Strongest Tribe*, pp. 209, 213–14, 223.

63. US Department of Defense, *Quadrennial Defense Review Report*, February 6, 2006, preface, p. v.

64. Bradley Graham and Josh White, 'Abizaid credited with popularizing the term "long war"', *Washington Post*, February 3, 2006. See also RAND Corporation (Christopher G. Pernin, Brian Nichiporuk, Dale Stahl, Justin Beck, Ricky Radaelli-Sanchez), *Unfolding the Future of the Long War*, 2008, p. 5.

65. Julian E. Barnes, 'National security watch: retiring top soldier warns of "The Long War"', *US News and World Report*, September 29, 2005.

66. William Kristol, 'The Long War: the radical Islamists are on the offensive. Will we defeat them?', *Weekly Standard*, vol. 11, no. 24, June 3, 2006. See also Norman Podhoretz, *World War IV: The Long Struggle against Islamofascism*, Doubleday, 2007.

67. This argument is advanced in an extremely sophisticated form by law professor and historian Philip Bobbitt. See Philip Bobbitt, 'Get ready for the next

long war', *Time*, September 1, 2002. See also, in a very much less intellectually refined form, Tony Blankley, 'An Islamist threat like the Nazis', *Washington Times*, September 12, 2005.

68. 'President discusses global war on terrorism', September 5, 2006. White House press release. National Strategy for Combating Terrorism, September 2006, pp. 5, 11.

69. Bush had said that 'al-Qaeda followed in the path of Fascism, Nazism and totalitarianism', the 'murderous ideologies of the twentieth century'.

70. Kristol, 'The Long War'.

71. *Quadrennial Defense Review*, pp. 9, 21, 22, 36. 'Operational end-states defined in terms of "winning decisively" may be less useful', the review said coyly.

72. *Quadrennial Defense Review*, pp. 10, 11.


CHAPTER 11: THE TURNING

1. There is now a series of detailed and voluminous studies of American operations in Iraq during 2007 and the genesis of the shifts in strategy and tactics they entailed. Two useful accounts of the meeting at Leavenworth can be found in Ricks, *The Gamble*, and Linda Robinson, *Tell Me How This Ends: General David Petraeus and the Search for a Way Out of Iraq*, Public Affairs, 2008. Another useful work is Kimberly Kagan, *The Surge: A Military History*, Encounter Books, 2008.

2. See also Kilcullen, *The Accidental Guerrilla*, p. 119. Author telephone interview with Kilcullen, March 2009.

3. Robinson, *Tell Me How This Ends*, p. 68. Ricks, *The Gamble*, p. 128.

4. Author telephone interview with David Kilcullen, March 2009. Kilcullen proved one of the most original and perceptive analysts despite a relative lack of experience of many of the major theatres of conflict, arguing that the spaces through which contemporary insurgencies were conducted were compound and plural, a complex matrix of the local, the regional and the transnational. He also contributed useful insights such as pointing out how militants tailored their violence to what they wanted to communicate – the message defined the mission – whereas American forces did the opposite, and pointed out too that the term 'foreign fighters', applied to international jihadis, could and should apply to coalition troops as well. To fight insurgencies composed of accidental guerrillas, soldiers should be behaving differently. 'Your role is to provide protection, identify needs, facilitate civil affairs and use improvements in social conditions as leverage to build networks and mobilize the population,' Kilcullen wrote in a widely circulated paper. David Kilcullen, 'Twenty-eight Articles: Fundamentals of Company-level Counter-insurgency', *Military Review*, March 1, 2006.

5. Richard Norton-Taylor and Jamie Wilson, 'US army in Iraq institutionally racist, claims British officer', *Guardian*, January 12, 2006.

6. Nigel Aylwin-Foster, 'Changing the Army for Counter-Insurgency Operations', *Military Review*, December 2005, p. 5.

7. US officers sourly but fairly pointed out that the fact that Aylwin-Foster had been invited to Leavenworth to speak in person was an indication of an open-mindedness that did not necessarily characterize the British military.

8. Montgomery McFate, 'The Military Utility of Understanding Adversary Culture', *Joint Forces Quarterly*, 38, July 2005, pp. 43, 44.

9. *US Army Field Manual 3-24: Counterinsurgency* (December 2006), p. 164.

10. 'Learning Counterinsurgency: Observations from Soldiering in Iraq', *Military Review*, January–February 2006.

11. *US Army Field Manual 3-24*.

12. *The National Security Strategy of the United States of America*, September 2002, Introduction, p. 1.

13. See Dodge, 'The Ideological Roots of Failure'.

14. *US Army Field Manual 3-24*, p. 2.

15. David Galula, *Counter-insurgency Warfare: Theory and Practice*, Frederick Praeger, 2006, p. 20. The work was originally published in 1964.

16. Porter, *Military Orientalism*, p. 6.

17. Iraqi society was invariably described, as it has been along with many others in this book, as 'complex', as if Western societies with their equal number of codes, hierarchies, obligations, norms, laws and values, tribes and castes, were not.

18. The description is from the late Professor Fred Halliday of the London School of Economics. *100 Myths about the Middle East*, Saqi Books, 2005, p. 147. T. E. Lawrence had been read by American soldiers in Iraq since the first days of the intervention. More problematically, the manual and surrounding debate tended to underplay the agency of both individuals and communities, underestimating the dynamism of identity and culture particularly in a conflict situation. Porter, *Military Orientalism*, p. 55. *US Army Field Manual 3-24*, p. 7: 'Lawrence's experiences in the Arab Revolt made him a hero and also provide some insights for today.' Lawrence also once described the Arabs as 'a limited, narrow-minded people, whose inert intellect lay fallow in incurious resignation'.

19. See Derek Gregory, 'The Rush to the Intimate: Counterinsurgency and the Cultural Turn in Late Modern War', *Radical Philosophy*, July/August 2008.

20. Brookings report by Michael E. O'Hanlon and Ian Livingston, *Iraq Index: Tracking Variables of Reconstruction and Security in Post-Saddam Iraq*, December 30, 2010, p. 4.

21. Author email exchange, December 2007.

22. Lieutenant General Raymond Odierno, 'The Surge in Iraq: One Year Later', Heritage lectures, March 13, 2008. Having understood that such relation-

ships were the key to finding the fugitive dictator, Odierno had ordered the construction of a vast map depicting key figures with their interrelationships, social status and last-known locations. Saddam was placed at the centre, not at the top of any hierarchical organogramme. Eventually, patterns had emerged showing that in fact it was not the Ba'ath Party structure that was important but the extensive tribal and family ties between the six main tribes of the Sunni triangle – the Husseins, al-Douris, Hadouthis, Musslits, Hassans and Harimyths – and in particular those between a group of families which had all been linked to Saddam in various unofficial capacities since his youngest days. Tracing key figures in these eventually enabled Saddam to be located. Chris Wilson, 'Searching for Saddam', *Slate*, February 22, 2010. Farnaz Fassihi, 'Charting the capture of Saddam', *Wall Street Journal*, December 23, 2003. Vernon Loeb, 'Clan, family ties called key to army's capture of Hussein', *Washington Post*, December 16, 2003.

23. Bush, *Decision Points*, p. 93.

24. See Congressional Research Service (Amy Belasco), *Report for Congress: Troop Levels in the Afghan and Iraq Wars, FY2001–FY2012: Cost and Other Potential Issues*, July 2, 2009, pp. 9, 39.

25. Michael Duffy, 'The Surge at year one', *Time*, January 31, 2008. The conclusions of the Iraq Study Group led by Jim Baker, secretary of state during the 1991 Gulf War, were radically different.

26. Author interview with a senior American civilian official attached to US military in Baghdad, end 2006, spring 2007. Interview conducted in Afghanistan, March 2009.

27. Including from the veteran members of the bipartisan Iraq Study Group.

28. The exact population at the time was for obvious reasons uncertain. It was 6,554,126 in 2004 before the major sectarian violence according to Gilbert Burnham, Riyadh Lafta, Shannon Doocy and Les Roberts, 'Mortality after the 2003 Invasion of Iraq: A Cross-sectional Cluster Sample Survey', *Lancet*, vol. 368, no. 9,545, October 21, 2006, and 7,145,470 in 2009 according to *The Geographical Location of Baghdad Province*, the Baghdad Governorate, December 13, 2009.

29. Duffy, 'The Surge at year one'.

30. Michael Evans, 'Gated communities will add to Baghdad security', *The Times*, February 10, 2007.

31. John Lee Anderson, 'Inside the Surge', *New Yorker*, November 19, 2007. Bing West, *The Strongest Tribe*, Random House, 2009, p. 300. Kilcullen, *The Accidental Guerrilla*, p. 169.

32. Mohammed Hussein, 'Back from Syria', *New York Times*, May 5, 2008.

33. At twenty-five per day, the 2008 rate for violent civilian deaths was to be equivalent to that existing throughout the first twenty months of post-invasion Iraq, from May 2003 to December 2004, when 15,355 died over 610 days. 'Post-Surge Violence: Its Extent and Nature. What the Detailed

Data Tell Us about Iraq's Civilian Death Toll during 2008 and the Long-term Effect of the "Surge"', iraqbodycount.org, December 28, 2008.

34. Bobby Ghosh, 'The fleeting success of the Surge', *Time*, December 13, 2007. Quoted Freedman, *A Choice of Enemies*, p. 447.

35. Ricks, *Fiasco*, Appendix II.

36. Author interview, Istanbul, March, 2008.

37. Pelham, *A New Muslim Order*, p. 195. Semi-depopulated middle-class neighbourhoods like Adil, where resistance was likely to be less significant than in the tougher working-class neighbourhoods like al-Doura, were targeted first. International Crisis Group, *Iraq's Civil War, the Sadrists and the Surge*, February 7, 2008, p. 2.

38. Ibid., p. 6. For much of 2006, the American high command in Iraq had been largely unaware of the carnage around them. According to Kilcullen, the ongoing civil war only began to be reflected in the American military's daily 'battlefield update' briefings for the commanding general in Iraq from mid July 2006, four and a half months after the blast at Samarra. Kilcullen, *The Accidental Guerrilla*, pp. 121–2. The police were often heavily implicated in the killing but even in the best of cases were so powerless that local people referred to them as *daffana*, or undertakers, because all they were good for was collecting bodies.

39. Sunni gangs made sure that mixed neighbourhoods such as Ghazaliya and Amiriya were thoroughly purged of Shia.

40. See Elisa Cochrane, 'The Fragmentation of the Sadrist Movement', Institute for the Study of War, January 2009, p. 21. International Crisis Group, *Iraq's Civil War, the Sadrists and the Surge*, p. 5.

41. James Hanning, 'Deal with Shia prisoner left Basra at mercy of gangs, colonel admits', *Independent on Sunday*, August 3, 2008.

42. See Cochrane, 'The Fragmentation', p. 7.

43. Sabrina Tavernise, 'A Shiite militia in Baghdad sees its power wane', *New York Times*, July 27, 2008.

44. Urban, *Task Force Black*, pp. 224–5.

45. International Crisis Group, *Iraq's Civil War, the Sadrists and the Surge*, p. 7.

46. Interview, Baghdad, September 2010.

47. Al-Sadr's representatives had withdrawn from government a few months previously and thus were no longer a key element of Prime Minister Nouri al-Maliki's support.

48. See West, *The Strongest Tribe*, pp. 250, 274–5, 301, 318–319, and Ricks, *The Gamble*, p. 22. An ill-judged attempt to take control of the shrine at Karbala, which saw fighting against Iraqi government forces and around fifty worshippers killed and was widely reported on local news, also contributed to further loss of legitimacy. That the government forces were in fact loyal to the rival al-Badr militia did not make a huge difference to the public perception of the events.

49. Odierno quoted by Babak Dehghanpisheh and Larry Kaplow, 'Baghdad's new owners', *Newsweek*, September 10, 2007. Odierno, 'The Surge in Iraq'.

50. David Kilcullen, 'Field Notes on Iraq's Tribal Revolt Against Al-Qa'ida', *CTC Sentinel*, vol. 1, no. 11, October 2008. The 1920 Revolution Brigades split first from their more closely al-Qaeda-affiliated counterparts and then themselves, with one element going on to form Hamas-Iraq, which, though it continued to conduct attacks on coalition and government forces, also made statements opposing sectarian conflict and in favour of a political process.

51. Senior religious figures relayed the change in policy. 'Saudi cleric issues warning over Saudi militants', Reuters, October 1, 2007.

52. Urban, *Task Force Black*, p. 127.

53. Ibid., p. 243.

54. See Kilcullen, *The Accidental Guerrilla*, pp. 136, 167–70. One problem was that the troops stuck to the four- or five-man groups that crewed a vehicle.

55. Presentation to Riyadh meeting and author interview, Riyadh, Saudi Arabia, March 2008.

56. Ibid.

57. Alissa J. Rubin, 'A calmer Iraq: fragile, and possibly fleeting', *New York Times*, December 5, 2007.

58. Martin Fletcher, 'Al-Qaeda leaders admit: "We are in crisis. There is panic and fear"', *The Times*, February 11, 2008.

59. CNN.com transcript of broadcast of Congressional Hearings, April 8, 2008.

60. Interview, Baghdad, November 2010.

61. See Combating Terrorism Center, West Point, *Foreign Fighters in Iraq*, 2007, p. 5. Abu Umar al-Baghdadi, *For the Scum Disappears Like Froth Cast Out*, posted to www.muslim.net on December 4, 2007. At its head was an unknown militant with the resoundingly Iraqi *nisbah* or alias of Abu Umar al-Baghdadi, who American intelligence officials claimed did not actually exist. Dean Yates, 'Senior Qaeda figure in Iraq a myth: U.S. military', Reuters, July 18, 2007. Springer et al., *Islamic Radicalism and Global Jihad*, pp. 119–21.

62. The loss of al-Iraqi was a serious one. He had probably played a key role in a number of other plots in Europe too, including the 7/7 London attacks, acting as the intermediary between the senior al-Qaeda leadership and the Pakistani militant groups who had been the Westerners' first point of contact.

63. Joby Warrick and Robin Wright, 'U.S. teams weaken insurgency in Iraq', *Washington Post*, September 6, 2008.

64. According to American officials. Jim Michaels, 'Foreign fighters leaving Iraq, military says', *USA Today*, March 21, 2008.

65. Records of the Mujahideen Shura Council – the rebranded al-Qaeda in Iraq – seized by American troops in a major operation on a large training and transit camp in Sinjar in the north-west of Iraq showed both how claims that the organization was predominantly 'Iraqi' were false and how numbers of

recruits from overseas remained relatively low with only a few dozen volunteers arriving each month by the end of 2007.

66. Author interview, Riyadh, March 2009. See also Thomas Hegghammer, *Paths to Global Jihad*, report, FFI, 2006, p. 27.

67. Author interview with Otayan al-Turki, Riyadh, March 2009.

68. Author interview with Dr Abdulrahman al-Hadlaq, Riyadh, March 2009. Jason Burke, 'Saudis offer pioneering therapy for ex-jihadists', *Observer*, March 9, 2008. In 2010, figures were released which showed that in fact around one in ten of those undergoing the Saudi rehabilitation programme did eventually become involved once more in extremist activities. The vast bulk of these were former prisoners of Guantanamo Bay.

69. Author interview, Riyadh, March 2009.

70. Author interview, Riyadh, March 2009.

71. International Crisis Group, '*Deradicalization*' *and Indonesian Prisons*, November 19, 2007.

72. Amanda Ripley, 'Reverse radicalism', *Time*, March 13, 2008.

73. Author interview, senior UK counter-terrorism official, London, August 2008.

74. They cited sociologist Quintan Wictorowicz as the best guide to the nature of modern Islamic militancy. Author interviews, London, July 2007.

75. Author interviews, MI5, London, July 2009.

76. Cobain, 'The truth about torture'.

77. Charles Farr, head of OSCT, quoted in Home Affairs Committee, *Project CONTEST: The Government's Counter-terrorism Strategy: Ninth Report of Session 2008–09, House of Commons*, July 7, 2009, p. 29. Author interview with Farr, London, September 2007. PREVENT was part of the UK Counter-Terrorism Strategy known as CONTEST and in place since 2003.

78. One poll in 2006 had found that less than half of British Muslims respected Iqbal Sacranie, the MCB's general secretary (while 69 per cent respected the Queen) and only 12 per cent thought that the MCB represented their political views. NOP/Channel Four poll, 2006, cited Malik, *From Fatwa to Jihad*, p. 129.

79. Richard Kerbaj, 'Government moves to isolate Muslim Council of Britain with cash for mosques', *The Times*, March 30, 2009. See also the useful and controversial pamphlet on the MCB, for which the author wrote an introduction, by British journalist Martin Bright: *When Progressives Treat with Reactionaries*, Policy Exchange, July 2006.

80. James Brandon, 'The UK's Experience in Counter-radicalization', *CTC Sentinel*, April 2008, vol. 1, no. 5.

81. Individuals like Shiraz Maher and Ed Husain, the two former Hezb-ut-Tahrir members quoted in Chapter 8, were joined by others whose jihadi credentials may have been exaggerated. Husain's book, *The Islamist*, became a bestseller. For criticism, see *Final Report of the Communities and Local Government Select Committee Inquiry into Preventing Violent Extremism*, HMSO, March 30, 2010.

82. Author interview, August 2007.

83. www.tajdeed.net.tc on July 8, 2006: 'Al-Sahab for Media Production'. David Pallister, 'Three jailed for engaging in "cyber jihad" for al-Qaida', *Guardian*, July 6, 2007.

84. Dalia Mogahed, *Beyond Multiculturalism vs. Assimilation*, Gallup, 2007, p. 4. The conclusion was based on 500 interviews in London between 29 November 2006 and 18 January 2007.

85. Gallup World Poll 2007.

86. Jason Burke, 'Target Europe', *Observer*, September 9, 2007; Erik Kirschbaum, 'German suspects had deadline for attacks: report', Reuters, September 8, 2007. The German case also threw a light on the continuing role of the tribal areas of Pakistan in many, though by no means all, European investigations. In the case of the German converts, the main suspects were believed to have trained not with al-Qaeda but with the little-known Islamic Jihad Union, an offshoot of the Islamic Movement of Uzbekistan. Converts had already figured significantly in terrorism in Europe, comprising 8 per cent of militants arrested in Europe. The Netherlands Institute of International Relations Clingendael, *Jihadi Terrorists in Europe*, 2006.

87. Some key changes were technical but important, such as the new ability of British financial investigators to use classified information to freeze assets.

88. Author interview, London, spring 2009.

89. From primary and secondary sources including the scores of trials of alleged militants. Legal proceedings did not always kill off some of the more fantastic claims – right-wingers in Spain continued to claim that Basque separatists were responsible for the Madrid attacks even after one of the longest and most exhaustive trials in Europe in recent decades convicted those responsible – but they did provide relatively well-founded evidence that could be deployed to contradict the ubiquitous conspiracy theorists. Diane Cambon, 'L'Aile dure de la droite espagnole defend toujours la théorie de complot', *Le Monde*, February 14, 2007.

90. Dipak Gupta, *Understanding Terrorism and Political Violence*, Routledge, 2008, p. 3. The degree to which the public was well informed can be exaggerated. Even in 2006, counter-terrorist specialists and key Congressmen in America proved unable to explain the difference between Shia and Sunnis. Jeff Stein, 'It's not a trick question', *International Herald Tribune*, October 18, 2006.

91. The ruling was on June 29, 2006, in Hamdan vs. Rumsfeld.

92. *New York University Center on Law and Security, Terrorist Trial Report Card 2001–2009*, published 2010, pp. i–iii, 6–7. Convictions on headline charges of very serious offences were sought – and often denied – and suspects who could have been jailed on lesser charges went free.

93. Ibid., p. v.

94. Author telephone interview with Mudd, June 2010. See Scott Shane and

Lowell Bergman, 'F.B.I. struggling to reinvent itself to fight terror', *New York Times*, October 10, 2006.

95. Robert S. Mueller III, director Federal Bureau of Investigation, Citizens Crime Commission, James Fox Memorial Lecture, New York, April 26, 2006. Author interview with Carl Newns, Foreign Office, London, September 2006. Jason Burke, 'Britain stops talk of "war on terror"', *Observer*, December 10, 2006.

96. Author interview, London, September 2006.

97. Author interview with Jonathan Freeman, London, September 2006.

98. Matthew Lee, '"Jihadist" booted from government lexicon', Associated Press, April 24, 2008.

99. United States Army, *Full Spectrum Operations, Unified Quest 2007*, pamphlet published April 22, 2008, p. 22.

100. 'Few Muslims back suicide bombs', BBC News Online, 25 July 2007. Pew Research Center, *Pew Global Opinions Survey, 2007: A Rising Tide Lifts Mood in the Developing World*, p. 55.

101. Ibid., p. 57.

102. Terror Free Tomorrow poll, 'Saudi Arabians Overwhelmingly Reject Bin Laden, Al Qaeda, Saudi Fighters in Iraq, and Terrorism; Also among Most Pro-American in Muslim World', Washington, December 2007, p. 3.

103. Peter Bergen and Paul Cruickshank, 'The unraveling: the jihadist revolt against bin Laden', *New Republic*, June 11, 2008. Omar Ashour, 'De-Radicalization of Jihad? The Impact of Egyptian Islamist Revisionists on Al-Qaeda', *Perspectives on Terrorism*, vol. 2, no. 5, May 2008.

104. See Mamoun Fandy, *Saudi Arabia and the Politics of Dissent*, Palgrave Macmillan, 2001, for an excellent account of the early activities and ideological development of al-Auda.

105. Bergen and Cruickshank, 'The unraveling'. Sheikh Salman al-Auda, 'Letter to Osama bin Laden', September 14, 2007, www.islamtoday.net. Michael Scheuer, 'Al-Qaeda: Beginning of the End, or Grasping at Straws?', *Terrorism Focus*, vol. 4, no. 32, October 12, 2007.

106. Interview at the Saudi Interior Ministry, March 2008.

107. Transcript of Usama bin Laden Audio Recording produced by the As-Sahab Media Foundation: 'A Message to the Islamic Nation', released May 18, 2008, NEFA Foundation.

108. Author interviews with Western and Afghan intelligence officials, Kabul, August 2008. Amit R. Paley, 'Al-Qaeda in Iraq leader may be in Afghanistan', *Washington Post*, July 31, 2008.

## CHAPTER 12: AFGHANISTAN AGAIN

1. Author interview, Maidan Shar, August 2008.

2. The company was renamed Xe.

3. 'Thanks to our British troops – along with allies from 40 countries – the Taliban have been beaten back.' Des Browne, 'Des Browne's speech to the 2008 Labour Party Conference', September 22, 2008. Transcript, Labour Party website.

4. Author interview, Kabul, August 2008.

5. Author interview with judges, Kabul, August 2008.

6. Author interview with Sherard Cowper-Coles, Kabul, August 2008. A leaked French diplomatic memorandum described Sir Sherard talking privately of the need for an 'enlightened dictatorship'.

7. The plural of *medressa* in Urdu is *madari*. However *medressas* has entered common English-language usage and so is preferred here.

8. Author interview with Rahmani, Kabul, 2009.

9. Author interview with Mullah Taj Mohammed, former Taliban deputy intelligence chief, Jalalabad, Peshawar, June 2002.

10. Karzai's exile was initially ended when he accompanied *mujahideen* leaders into Kabul in 1992 on the fall of the Najibullah regime. However, he remained in Afghanistan for only a short period, being forced once more to leave for Pakistan. His exile was thus only definitively ended in 2001.

11. See International Crisis Group, *The Problem of Pashtun Alienation*, August 5, 2003. Francesc Vendrell, the European Union special representative to Afghanistan and intimately involved in the planning of the conference, recalled that at Bonn 'the Taliban were seen as subhuman'. Author interview with Vendrell, London, February 2009. The title of the US Congress House Committee on International Relations, Subcommittee on International Operations and Human Rights, on 31 October 2001, Washington, DC, gives a fairly good idea of how the Taliban were considered: 'Afghan people vs the Taliban: the struggle for freedom intensifies'. See both Dobbins, *After the Taliban*, and Rashid, *Descent into Chaos*, for more. None of the opening speeches at the Bonn conference were translated into Pashtu but only into Dari, the language of the Tajik minority. One problem at Bonn was the disproportionate political and media attention accorded to a large number of long-term exiles whose understanding of contemporary Afghan politics was limited. Many delegates had not visited their country for several decades. Those who, at the very least, represented what Afghanistan had become over recent years were less welcome. When Abdul Qadir, the anti-Taliban Pashtun warlord, walked out of the conference in protest at the lack of ethnic balance, his gesture was largely dismissed as populist. Political theatre it may well have been, but Qadir's understanding of what might resonate with many of his countrymen was sharp, and his gesture deserved more serious attention.

12. Fourteen per cent in 2005 and 5.3 per cent in 2006.

13. World Bank, *Afghanistan: Statebuilding, Sustaining Growth and Reducing Poverty*, Washington 2005, p. 373.

14. An announced 'Marshall plan' for Afghanistan – the original post-war

version comprised funds totalling between 3 and 7 per cent of American GDP at the time – was nothing of the sort. Dobbins, *After the Taliban*, p. 164.

15. Conor Foley, *The Thin Blue Line*, Verso, 2008, p. 118. See ACBAR, *Falling Short: Aid Effectiveness in Afghanistan*, March 25, 2008. Rashid, *Descent into Chaos*, p. 399. The overall spend including for the military in Afghanistan per month was around a fifth of that in Iraq. Kilcullen, *The Accidental Guerrilla*, p. 43.

16. Very rough back-of-the-envelope arithmetic revealed that this meant under $20 per capita per year since 2002.

17. The coalition presence in Helmand consisted of 130 US special forces, civilians and contractors.

18. In a poll in May 2002, 50 per cent of Afghans in rural areas said they had no contact with Afghan National Police and less than 20 per cent trusted them. The problem was most acute in the south. Jones, *In the Graveyard of Empires*, p. 181. See Sarah Chayes, *The Punishment of Virtue*, Portobello, 2007, for a fascinating if often provocative account of this time in south-east Afghanistan.

19. A special forces team had fought alongside him and organized food supplies for his 800-odd armed followers. *United States Special Operations Command History*, 6th edn, p. 97. The two tribal figures were Mullah Naqib of the Alokozai and Bashir Noorzai.

20. As Ahmed Rashid has pointed out, unlike Northern Alliance warlords, who tended to defy President Karzai's authority, warlords like Sherzai were friends of the government and helped secure the local vote for Karzai in the two Loya Jirgas and the two elections in 2004 and 2005. These embedded, with the enthusiastic endorsement of the international community, his power. See Rashid, *Descent into Chaos*, chapter 'Drugs and Thugs'. Karzai eventually reassigned Sherzai to be governor of Nangahar province in 2005, replacing him with Asadullah Khalid, a family ally. Ahmed Wali Karzai, the president's brother and head of the tribal council in Kandahar, was also suspected of involvement in the drug trade. In 2006, the author obtained a stolen US classified briefing naming him as a key trafficker.

21. A 2006 poll by the US State Department found that more than 50 per cent of Afghans thought Karzai and his administration had failed to combat corruption. Nearly three-quarters of those who admitted supporting the Taliban said there was corruption among the police or the courts, and two-thirds said local government was corrupt. Anecdotal evidence in places like Kandahar indicated much higher levels of discontent.

22. This has escaped many accounts. The Taliban groups were largely non-tribal, an important difference from the heavily tribalized *mujahideen* groups operating in the south-east during the 1980s.

23. Koochi nomadic tribesmen had a disproportionately large presence in the ranks of the Taliban given their numbers. The Koochi are Pashtun.

24. See accounts of Taliban penetration of Helmand and Oruzgan in Giustozzi, ed., *Decoding the New Taliban*, pp. 124 and 157, for two examples. There are many others.

25. Ibid., p. 161.

26. An anecdotal illustration of this was the experience of an Australian special forces officer exploring south of Ghazni in late 2002 who, when he had asked local elders if there were any Taliban in their village, had been directed to an empty house a few yards away from the mulberry tree in its centre. Its owner, head of one of two families who had contested power in the village for decades, had thrown in his lot with the Taliban a few years previously and had thus gained the upper hand. When the Taliban fell, he had been summoned to a village meeting and then left for Pakistan the following day. His rival, a relative, took over as the community's leader. 'So, no, there are no Taliban in the village . . . for the moment,' the Australians were told. Author interview, senior Australian officer, Kabul, March 2009.

27. Author interview, Peshawar, June 2002.

28. Three clerics who opposed the Taliban were killed in June and July of 2003 in Kandahar with another dozen dying over the next two years in the city.

29. See the perceptive analysis in Jones, *In the Graveyard of Empires*, p. 244. Also referring to the Taliban as a social movement is Barfield, *Afghanistan*, p. 261. See Robert D. Crews and Amin Tarzi, *The Taliban and the Crisis of Afghanistan*, Harvard University Press, 2008, p. 243.

30. Author interview, Kandahar, November 2003.

31. See Antonio Giustozzi, *Koran, Kalashnikov and Laptop*, Hurst, 2007, pp. 38–39, 55–6. See Ron Moreau, Sami Yousafzai and Michael Hirsh, 'The rise of Jihadistan', *Newsweek*, October 2, 2006. Multiple author interviews with military or other intelligence officials, British, American, Afghan, in Kabul, Kandahar, London, 2006, 2007. Interviews with local MPs in Afghanistan, July 2006, August 2008, March 2009. Interview with United Nations security experts, July 2006, August 2008.

32. In Oruzgan and in western Zabul.

33. Turn-out for the polls was very high, with up to 60 per cent of the eligible population registering even in Kandahar.

34. Hekmatyar had returned to Afghanistan (probably via Pakistan) after being released from house arrest in Iran in 2002 as relations between Tehran and Washington deteriorated.

35. My estimate is based on interviews with senior NATO officers, Afghan and Western intelligence officials, Taliban spokesmen. For an alternative estimate see Giustozzi, *Koran, Kalashnikov and Laptop*, pp. 35, 68. Also in November 2006, a UN report estimated the number of armed insurgents in Mullah Omar's movement to be around 4,000–5,000. UN Security Council, *Sixth Report of the Analytical Support and Sanctions Monitoring Team Appointed Pursuant to Security Council Resolutions 1526 (2004) and 1617 (2005)*

*Concerning Al-Qaida and the Taliban and Associated Individuals and Entities*, November 7, 2006.

36. Testimony of Lieutenant General David W. Barno, USA (Ret.) before the Committee on Foreign Affairs US House of Representatives, February 15, 2007.

37. Jones, *In the Graveyard of Empires*, p. 205.

38. Ronald Neumann, *The Other War: Winning and Losing in Afghanistan*, Potomac Books, 2009, pp. 39–40.

39. Author interview with Amrullah Saleh, former head of Afghan National Directorate of Intelligence, Kabul, June 2011. In 2005, the Americans had a total of 19,000 troops in the country, with one less infantry battalion than in 2002, with their multinational allies in ISAF maintaining around another 15,000. In October 2003, US troops numbers were about 14,000, and NATO less than 6,000. They had then risen slightly to 16,500. See Jones, *In the Graveyard of Empires*, p. 204.

40. Reid said that the British 'would be perfectly happy to leave in three years and without firing one shot because our job is to protect reconstruction'. 'UK troops "to target terrorists"', BBC, April 24, 2006. See also Rashid, *Descent into Chaos*, pp. 357–8.

41. The US troops on the eastern frontier would remain part of the original Operation Enduring Freedom and therefore commanded direct from CentCom in the USA. Total American troops in Afghanistan were 22,300.

42. Author interview, July 2006.

43. Author interviews with Mark Laity, NATO spokesman, Kabul, July 2006 and February 2008. Author interview with Brigadier General Richard Blanchette, Kabul, 2008.

44. 'Insurgent activity rising in Afghanistan', Associated Press, November 13, 2006.

45. Author interview, Kabul, July 2006.

46. 'Nato hails shift on Afghan combat', BBC News Online, November 29, 2006.

47. Others had once been kept in check by a powerful local commander with strong conservative religious credentials who had backed Karzai before being detained by American forces acting independently. The story of that commander, Haji Rohullah, deserves a chapter in itself. A hardline Salafi commander in Kunar, Rohullah backed the central government after the fall of the Taliban but ended up in Guantanamo Bay. The author met him in Kabul in 2008, shortly after his release. Violence, limited in Kunar until his arrest, increased dramatically afterwards.

48. One problem for commanders in the east was the degree to which their operational environment was influenced by what happened across the border. A truce in 2005 between the Pakistani army and local militants had trebled the number of cross-border attacks almost overnight. French troops east of Kabul tracked groups of fighters crossing over from Pakistan, moving along mountain roads before dropping off the hills and on to their positions. Author interviews,

French officers, Forward Operating Base Tora, Sorobi, March 2009. Author interview, Chris Alexander, deputy head of mission, UNAMA, Kabul, March 2009. The most active insurgent networks along the Afghan side of the frontier were connected to Jalaluddin Haqqani, who was known to have lines of communications to Pakistani intelligence services, and a broader regional agenda clearly informed some of the clashes. So when an Indian construction company won a contract to build a major road close to the border around Khost, one of the largest forces yet seen in the area massed to attack them.

49. United Nations Assistance Mission in Afghanistan, *Internal Security Assessment on Wardak*, June 2008. Author collection.

50. Author interviews with French officers, Forward Operating Base Tora, Sorobi, March 2009. Author interview with Qazi Syed Suleiman, vice governor of Nangahar, Sorobi, March 2009.

51. Tom Coghlan, 'The Taliban in Helmand: An Oral History', in Giustozzi, ed., *Decoding the New Taliban*, p. 122.

52. Author interview with General Chris Brown, Kabul, July 2006.

53. Author interviews, Kabul, August 2008.

54. For the Belfast reference see Patrick Hennessey, *The Junior Officers Reading Club*, Allen Lane, 2009. I was invited to brief the Parachute Regiment, the Royal Green Jackets and 52 Mechanised Brigade HQ before departure.

55. Canadians arriving in Kandahar took care to learn from their US predecessors, touring much of their new territory with the Americans and even fighting alongside them over a period of months. See Coghlan, 'The Taliban in Helmand', pp. 128, 152.

56. Draft of report on 'The situation in Helmand', Ron Nash for FCO, 2007, author collection.

57. See Kilcullen on Kunar, *The Accidental Guerrilla*, pp. 74–107.

58. The British version of the *American Field Manual 3-24*, the counter-insurgency guide published in the US around the time the British troops arrived in Helmand, spoke of British 'best practice' in counter-insurgency and ingrained traditions of 'cultural sensitivity' and pointed to the examples of Malaya and Kenya among others. However, British tactics in Malaya, where the term 'hearts and minds' had been coined, had involved the forcible resettlement of 500,000 people, mass arrests, the death penalty for carrying arms, detention without trial for up to two years, deportations, control of food, censorship, collective punishment in the form of curfews and fines, the hanging of hundreds of prisoners and repeated atrocities in which unarmed civilians or combatants were killed. Means deployed against the Kikuyu or Mau Mau in Kenya included torture, hanging, indiscriminate bombing and toleration of local proxies' use of sadistic violence, dismemberment and killing in custody. Though some of these measures were employed in Afghanistan, most were seen, for obvious and good reasons, as neither feasible, desirable nor appropriate. As for the oft-cited experience of Northern Ireland, the differences between

south Armagh and Helmand fairly comprehensively outweighed any similarities, as soldiers driving the antiquated 'Snatch' Land Rovers through towns like Gereshk or Garmseer frequently pointed out in usually colourful language.

59. Author interview, Kandahar, July 2006.

60. Author interview with Brigadier Ed Butler, Kabul, July 2006.

61. US Naval War College, Damien Mason, *Air Strikes and COIN in Operation Enduring Freedom*, Joint Military Operations Department report, May 3, 2010.

62. Author interviews, Kajaki, January 2007. Giustozzi, *Koran, Kalashnikov and Laptop*, p. 202.

63. In late 2003 in Sangesar, the village that had been home for two decades to Mullah Mohammed Omar himself, villagers had planted opium.

64. United Nations Office on Drugs and Crime (UNODC), *Afghanistan Opium Survey 2006*, September 2006. See Pierre-Arnaud Chouvy, *Opium: Uncovering the Politics of the Poppy*, I. B. Tauris, 2009, for a useful discussion.

65. See also Ahmed Rashid, 'Afghanistan: Taleban's second coming', BBC News Online, June 2, 2006.

66. See also Gretchen Peters, *Seeds of Terror: How Heroin Is Bankrolling the Taliban and Al Qaeda*, Oneworld Publications, 2009, pp. 7–22. Also Giustozzi, ed., *Decoding the New Taliban*.

67. Author interviews with British and American anti-narcotics officials, military intelligence, Kabul, Kandahar, Lashkar Gah, January 2007, August 2008.

68. Author interviews with British officials, Kabul 2007, 2008. Author interview with Christine Orguz, country director Afghanistan, UNODC, Kabul, 2008. Classified/NoForn RC South briefing on Narcotic Trafficking, PowerPoint presentation and documents, May 2005. See also Testimony of Lieutenant General David W. Barno, USA (Ret.) before the Committee on Foreign Affairs, US House of Representatives, February 15, 2007.

69. Author interviews with British government counter-narcotics officials, London, 2008.

70. The British estimates were based on those of the United Nations. See UNODC, *Afghanistan Opium Survey 2007*, September 2007, p. 7.

71. Author interview with Orguz. See also UNODC (Doris Buddenberg and William Byrd), *Afghanistan's Drug Industry, Structure, Functioning Dynamics and Implications for Counter-Narcotics Policy*, 2006.

72. Anthony Loyd, 'Corruption, bribes and trafficking: a cancer that is engulfing Afghanistan', *The Times*, November 24, 2007. See also Elizabeth Rubin, 'In the land of the Taliban', *New York Times*, October 22, 2006.

73. 'The policy of being nice to farmers was a complete failure. The British army position was completely unacceptable. We never had a yelling match and did have some frank discussions but we always went for dinner afterwards,' said Thomas Schweich, former State Department narcotics official, 2006–7, author telephone interview, September 2008. One major argument was over

the use of chemical spraying. Schweich and the American ambassador in Kabul, William Wood, were both fierce proponents of the technique. The Afghans and the Europeans were very much opposed. 'It would have handed the Taliban a huge PR victory and lost the consent of the Afghan people. There were practical issues with low-flying planes – they would have got shot down – and even if it works one year the next year they'll just mix their crops,' said a senior British Foreign Office specialist, author telephone interview, September 2008.

74. Author interview, Helmand, July 2006.

75. Graeme Smith, 'Talking to the Taliban', *Globe and Mail*, March 2008.

76. Author email exchange with Brigadier Andrew McKay, January 2008.

77. Author interview with Chris Alexander, UNAMA, January 2007.

78. Figures from an ISAF briefing, Kabul 2009.

79. Brigadier Andrew McKay told his troops in October 2007: 'I do not want to see a single PowerPoint slide presented to a single visitor that articulates enemy Killed In Action. We may analyse the value of attrition but not as a sign of success.' 'COIN in Helmand, Task Force Operational Design', restricted ISAF brief, October 30, 2007, author collection.

80. In all 103 UK soldiers died in Afghanistan between June 30, 2006 and July 1, 2008. Helmand Province accounted for 60 per cent of the casualties in the country for that time period. There had been 370 coalition fatalities in Afghanistan (hostile and non-hostile) from January 2002 to May 2006. icasualties.org.

81. Over the previous twelve months civilian casualties had risen between 40 and 56 per cent, according to the United Nations. 'Top Afghan policewoman shot dead', BBC News Online, September 28, 2008. Attacks on Afghan government employees in 2008 were 124 per cent higher than in 2007.

82. Stuck on a dusty wasteland without any resources on the outskirts of the city, the refugees' accounts of life in places like Musa Qala and Kajaki were among the most upsetting the author had heard in well over a decade of visiting the country. Millions had had similar experiences. Jason Burke, 'Destitute and confused: bleak future for Afghan refugees caught in the crossfire', *Guardian*, October 3, 2008.

83. 70,000, according to Mohammed Nader Farhad of the UNHCR. Author interview, Kabul, July 2008.

84. Author interview, Kabul, July 2008.

85. Author interview, Maiwand, July 2006.

86. Rahman had no time for Osama bin Laden either. 'He too is a foreigner. He is not an Afghan. We Afghans are strong. We do not need Osama.'

87. Author interviews with General David Richards, ISAF commander, senior ISAF officials, Kabul, January 2007. Officially NATO claimed that 512 insurgents had been killed. Unofficially, senior officers said they thought the number of casualties inflicted was at least 1,000, possibly more.

88. The question of the influence of Iraq on the tactics of the Taliban is an

interesting one. There was evidence of at least some cooperation between insurgents in Iraq and Afghanistan. Militants in Iraq were reported to have provided information and tips over the internet. Members of the Taliban, Hekmatyar's group and others may even have made their way to Anbar, Mosul and elsewhere to experience the fighting in Iraq first hand, at least until the turning of the Sunni tribes made such ventures perilous. Analysts believed that the more effective use of IEDs, suicide bombs and other tactics by the Taliban was at the very least influenced by what was happening in Iraq if not actually taught by Iraqi insurgents arriving in Afghanistan as the failure of the al-Qaeda project in 'the land of the two rivers' became apparent. By 2008, some Taliban units – though very few – did include Arab or other fighters with Iraqi or other experience. There were also reports that the Taliban had acquired new commercial communications gear and field equipment from Iraqi groups as well as tips on camouflage and the use of snipers. The posting of execution videos on the internet by a handful of the most extreme Taliban commanders was also clearly influenced by what had been happening in Iraq. Author interview with Defence Minister Abdur Rahim Wardak, Kabul, January 2007. Jones, *In the Graveyard of Empires*, p. 292. Testimony of Lieutenant General David W. Barno, USA (Ret.) before the Committee on Foreign Affairs, US House of Representatives. Sami Yousafzai and Ron Moreau, 'Afghanistan on the brink: Where do we go from here?' February 15, 2007. 'Taliban gets help, inspiration from Iraq', *Newsweek*, September 26, 2005. Senior militants certainly travelled from Afghanistan to Iraq. One was Omar al-Farooq, who escaped from the prison at Bagram airbase and made his way to Basra, where he was eventually killed.

89. One was Mullah Akhtar Mohammed Osmani, the man who had met Bob Grenier, the CIA Islamabad station chief, in the Serena hotel in Quetta a week or so before the bombing started in 2001. Dadaullah was killed in a British special forces raid in May 2007, probably after his location was given away by rivals within insurgent ranks worried about his growing influence, personal following and extremism. Jason Burke, 'Hunt for "traitors" splits Taliban', *Observer*, May 27, 2007.

90. The estimate is Michael Semple's, the former deputy to the EU special representative to Afghanistan and one of the most knowledgeable experts on the country. Semple spent more time than perhaps any other Westerner meeting Taliban commanders in Helmand. Author telephone interview, August 2009.

91. One was the British journalist James Fergusson, in 2006. See James Fergusson, *A Million Bullets: The Real Story of the British Army in Afghanistan*, Transworld, 2008. The other was Nir Rosen, working for *Rolling Stone*, in Ghazni in August 2008.

92. Even in 2006, a commander known as Mullah Sabir had told one reporter: 'We have about 15,000 men. Forty per cent are not really Taliban, have not graduated from any religious school; they are youngsters who join our

ranks in sympathy [with our cause].' Interview with Mullah Sabir, quoted in 'The new Taliban codex', *Signandsight*, 28 November 2006, quoted in Anne Stenersen, 'The Taliban Insurgency in Afghanistan – Organization, Leadership and Worldview', Norwegian Defence Research Establishment (FFI), February 5, 2010, p. 30.

93. In southern Wardak, a well-known hardliner was replaced as governor by a more moderate figure, to the relief of many locals. Author interview with Roshana Wardak, MP, Kabul, 2008.

94. Copy of 2006 'Laheya', author collection.

95. Author interview with Antonio Giustozzi, London, August 2009.

96. This research was undertaken in a fairly unscientific fashion by the author and two researchers in Afghanistan in August 2008 and in March 2009.

97. Jeremy Page, 'Children and MPs killed in worst Afghan suicide bomb', *The Times*, November 7, 2007. Author interview with Taliban spokesman 'Zabibullah Mujahed', by email. November 2007.

98. See International Crisis Group, *Taliban Propaganda: Winning the War of Words?*, July 24, 2008.

99. In May 2006 it had been attacked by a mob rioting following a traffic accident involving an American convoy.

100. Including the author.

101. According to a cable obtained by WikiLeaks and subsequently made available online, within weeks of the attack, British diplomats were talking to American counterparts of 'a growing body of [intelligence] reporting suggesting . . . that Pakistan's Inter-Services Intelligence Agency (ISI) was possibly involved in the July 7 bombing of the Indian Embassy in Kabul – though likely without the knowledge of the civil elements of the GOP [Government of Pakistan]'. Cable, id: 162707, date: July 18 2008, source: Embassy London, origin: 08LONDON1887.

102. See David Sanger, *The Inheritance: The World Obama Confronts and the Challenges to American Power*, Crown, 2009, p. 250. A United Nations study in 2007 found that more than 70 per cent of suicide bombers in Afghanistan came from across the border. UNAMA (C. Christine Fair), *Suicide Attacks in Afghanistan, 2001–2007*, 2007.

103. The Afghan government was keen to underline the role that they said Pakistan – or at least some Pakistanis – played in the ongoing violence in Afghanistan. Foreign journalists who struggled through the bureaucracy and could call in a few favours could, at least in 2008, get interviews with detainees, in the company of their jailers.

104. Abit had probably been beaten by Afghan interrogators in prison and almost certainly on his arrest. He was equally likely to have edited his story, minimizing his own responsibility and exaggerating his current repentance. But his account was nonetheless largely credible, matching the picture revealed by studies by the United Nations. A second interview with a would-be suicide

bomber in Kabul – that of a destitute, illiterate and clearly mentally unstable shepherd captured near Khost with a suicide bomb strapped to his body – showed how recruiters for extremist networks often target the most marginal elements in society and particularly those who have slipped out of traditional social networks of support and authority. Author interviews, Kabul, August 2008.

## CHAPTER 13: PAKISTAN

1. The population of Pakistan in 2010 was 177 million, according to the CIA Factbook. https://www.cia.gov/library/publications/the-world-factbook/geos/pk.html. For the Pew Research Center, it was 174 million. See Pew Research Center, *Mapping the Global Muslim Population*. The rate of population increase in Pakistan is dropping. It was 3 per cent in 1990, 2.5 per cent in 2000 and 2.2 per cent in 2008, according to Unicef. The USA, with 400 million, Indonesia, with 270 million, and India, with 1.1 billion, cannot be considered primary theatres of conflict like Afghanistan, Iraq, Pakistan or countries such as Saudi Arabia. Secondary theatres would also include European countries and many other Middle Eastern or Maghreb states.

2. United Nations Development Programme, *Human Development Report*, editions of 2008 and 2009. Available at http://hdrstats.undp.org/en/countries/country_fact_sheets/cty_fs_PAK.html.

3. 'The most dangerous nation in the world isn't Iraq. It's Pakistan', *Newsweek*, October 29, 2007.

4. Two excellent recent investigations of these questions include Farzana Shaikh's academic *Making Sense of Pakistan*, Hurst, 2010, and Owen Bennett-Jones, *Pakistan: The Eye of the Storm*, 3rd edn, Yale, 2003.

5. See Anatol Lieven, *Pakistan: A Hard Country*, Allen Lane, 2011, pp. 65–7.

6. These included the infamous Hudood Ordinances, introduced in 1979, which ruled that the evidence of a woman is worth half that of a man. Under these laws a woman who is raped can end up being convicted of adultery or fornication if she is unable to provide four male Muslim witnesses to the crime against her. The sentence, though rarely or never implemented, is death by stoning. Under the same code alcohol is banned and amputation recommended for convicted thieves.

7. An important point is that Maududi was fiercely anti-clerical and Jamaat Islami kept their distance from organizations representing the clergy, whether moderate or extreme. The writings on Maududi and Jamaat Islami are voluminous. See Roy, *The Failure of Political Islam*; Giles Keppel, *Jihad*. Useful points are made by Philip Jenkins, 'Clerical terror: The roots of jihad in India', *The New Republic*, December 24, 2008.

8. On Maududi see also Burke, *Al-Qaeda*, pp. 50–51.

9. Iftikhar Malik, *Pakistan: Democracy, Terror and the Building of a Nation*, New Holland, 2010, p. 35.

10. Bhutto built pragmatic alliances with the Deobandis to bolster a tenuous grip on power.

11. Less well known is the prohibition on foreign aid to Pakistan imposed when the country fell into arrears in servicing its debt to the United States in late 1998.

12. The first major challenge to Musharraf, who seized power with broad popular support though international disapproval, came with the 9/11 attacks. As noted in Chapter 2, after some deliberation, the former commando decided he had to agree to almost all American demands for cooperation. This he did not out of any loyalty to the USA, who after all had imposed heavy sanctions on Pakistan for its pursuit of nuclear weapons technology, but because he decided that it was in the best interests of his country.

13. Statistics from Karachi town hall, secretary to the mayor, author interview, November 2008.

14. Karachi's Pashtun population made it the largest single urban Pashtun community in the world.

15. Fewer than 8 per cent of Pakistanis speak Urdu, the national language, as their mother tongue.

16. The Mohajir Quami Movement was founded in 1984 to represent the interests of the descendants of immigrants from India, the Mohajirs. They later converted themselves into the Muttahida Quami Movement and supposedly abandoned both guns and ethnic politics. Their leader, Altaf Hussein, lives in Edgware, London.

17. Though in fact the Bhuttos were not actually among the first-rank families of really major landowners with serious historic heritage.

18. And including a Briton, Omar Saeed Sheikh. Pearl appears to have been first abducted by local militants led by Sheikh, before being passed to a group led by Khaled Sheikh Mohammad.

19. International Crisis Group, *Pakistan: Karachi's Madrasas and Violent Extremism*, March 29, 2007. The report refers to 1,000 schools and 200,000 students, though these figures are contested. All statistics dealing with *medressas* are highly controversial. For example, between March 2002 and July 2002, figures for *medressa* enrolment cited in the *Washington Post* tripled from 500,000 to 1.5 million. The ICG report put the total of Pakistani children of primary-school age in *medressas* at 33 per cent. This was later adjusted downwards to 3.3 per cent when a calculation error was pointed out. However, the orignal estimate or similar estimates were quoted in President Bush's remarks on June 24, 2003, President Musharraf's remarks on November 20, 2003, Colin Powell's on March 11, 2004, Hillary Clinton's on February 24, 2004 and the 9/11 Commission Report. See Tahir Andrabi, Jishnu Das, Asim Ijaz Khwaja and Tristan Zajonc, 'Religious School Enrollment

in Pakistan: A Look at the Data', John F. Kennedy School of Government Working Paper Series, 2005, p. iii.

20. One of these was the attack on French naval technicians in 2002. This was attributed to al-Qaeda or local militants at the time and is still listed as such in many accounts. However, press reports in France in 2010, and a French parliamentary inquiry, found that the strike was probably linked to corruption surrounding a major naval deal between France and Pakistan and the non-payment of bribes. See Guillaume Dasquié, 'Le Rapport Karachi divise les deputés', *Libération*, May 13, 2010; Mathieu Delahousse, 'Karachi: la mission parlementaire sur la piste des commissions', *Le Figaro*, May 13, 2010.

21. According to the city's mayor, Kamal Mustafa. Author interview, Karachi, November 2008.

22. See William Dalrymple, 'On the long road to freedom, finally', *Tehelka Magazine*, March 8, 2008, for statistics.

23. With a total of 1.8 million registered vehicles on the road in 2008. According to Wajid Ali Khan, Deputy Inspector General Traffic Police Karachi, in a presentation at Urban Resource Centre, Karachi, April 16, 2008.

24. Dalrymple, 'On the long road to freedom, finally'.

25. Author interview with Ijaz Shafi Gilani, Islamabad, December 2008.

26. The first nuclear-related sanctions had been imposed in 1990 and reinforced after Pakistani nuclear tests in 1998. In 2001, the remittances totalled a little more than $1 billion. From 2002 to 2006, Pakistan received around $4 billion in remittances. By 2009, despite the economic crisis, the total had reached $7 billion.

27. Dilawar Hussain, 'High per capita income not a sign of prosperity', *Dawn*, May 10, 2009.

28. Property prices went up by up to 1,000 per cent, and rents doubled or tripled. Adnan Adil, 'Pakistan's post-9/11 economic boom', BBC News, September 21, 2006.

29. David Rohde, 'Pakistani middle class, beneficiary of Musharraf, begins to question rule', *New York Times*, November 25, 2007. In 2005, international retail industry experts had estimated that the coming years would see the expansion of the upper and upper-middle class, to say nothing of the much more numerous lower middle classes, to around 17 million. Jawaid Abdul Ghani, 'Constituting a Grocery Market Worth $1.7bn. Consolidation in Pakistan's Retail Sector', *Asian Journal of Management Cases*, vol. 2, no. 2, 2005, pp. 137–61.

30. CIA Factbook, 2010. The United Nations estimate is 36 per cent. See United Nations Population Fund, *Life in the City*, June 2007, p. 3. Sher Baz Khan, 'Pakistan most urban country in S. Asia', *Dawn*, October 11, 2004.

31. Department for International Development (Dr Emma Hooper and Agha Imran Hamid), *Scoping Study on Social Exclusion in Pakistan: A Summary of Findings*, October 2003, p. 30.

32. In 2003, the country had fewer than 3 million cellphone users; in 2008 there were almost 50 million.

33. I.e. one who can read a newspaper and write a simple letter, in any language. Figures from Unicef, http://www.unicef.org/infobycountry/pakistan_pakistan_statistics.html, and UNESCO (Munir Ahmed Choudhry), *Where and Who Are the World's Illiterates?*, April 2005. Some other estimates are lower, particularly for recent years.

34. When Makhdoom Shahabuddin, Benazir Bhuttos's former finance minister and hereditary owner of thousands of hectares of land a few hours' drive north of the Jatoi's estates, had told the author in 1998 that he was unable to state with any certainty the scale of his property nor the number of 'his people', his ignorance was unfeigned, and the possessive pronoun was entirely justified. The sight of villagers kneeling to touch Makhdoom's feet in respect was nonetheless a reminder that all such change was relative.

35. Author interviews with Jatoi, Sindh, October 2007.

36. http://www.bahawalpur.gov.pk/area.htm. Official website for population figures. Accessed August 2010.

37. Author interview with MI6 official, London, November 2007.

38. Pakistani officers armed and organized militia from the local Jamaat Islami, the political Islamist party, and turned them, with bloody consequences, against intellectuals, politicians and pro-independence activists.

39. There were occasional unsubstantiated reports of some kind of Pakistani assistance to Baluchi rebels in the south-eastern corner of Iran too.

40. HUM deputy chief Maulana Fazlur Rehman Khalil was one of the signatories to bin Laden's 1998 *fatwa* declaring it a Muslim duty to kill Americans and Jews. There was a steady stream of recruits from the UK going to fight in Kashmir. Of the thousands who did so, only a handful returned to the UK and went on to become involved in further militancy.

41. The author saw HUM fighters on the frontline and spoke to the trainers in mountain skills who had been responsible for coaching them on how to survive at altitude.

42. Author interviews, Peshawar, October 2001. JeM had been set up by one of three militant leaders freed following the hijacking of an Indian airlines jet in 1999.

43. Events in Iraq and Afghanistan helped too, as they had done elsewhere, providing examples of resistance to the otherwise all-powerful America and the Jews.

44. LeT's parent body was allowed to change its name to Jamaat-ul-Dawa and to remain operative.

45. In one of those classic examples of how geopolitical forces interact with microfactors on the ground, the Punjab had become a centre of appalling Sunni versus Shia sectarian violence. This was in part also a legacy of British rule, as colonial administrators had effectively created – or at the very least

maintained and co-opted – a class of predominantly Shia landowners. The vast bulk of poor immigrants arriving in the Punjab after Partition were Sunnis. In the 1980s, firebrand clerics and politicians looking to undermine the Shia landowners' wealth and hold on to political power began working to exploit the longstanding resentments this generated, backed by Zia. The sectarian groups, such as the Sipa e Sahaba Pakistan (SSP), that resulted were backed, indirectly, both by the Pakistani security services and, as Tehran began subsidizing Shia self-protection groups, by a Saudi Arabian government fearful of the Shia renaissance sparked by the 1979 Iranian Revolution. A bloodbath ensued. Khalid Ahmed, 'Fundamental Flaws', in *On the Abyss*, HarperCollins (India), 2000, p. 94. Owen Bennett-Jones, *Pakistan: Eye of the Storm*, Yale University Press, 2003, p. 22. Amir Mir, 'Faith that kills', *Newsline*, October 1998, 'The Jihad within', *Newsline*, May 2002. Also Burke, *Al-Qaeda*, Chapter 7.

46. Mohammed Sidique Khan and Shehzad Tanweer were in Pakistan for about eleven weeks from November 2004 to January 2005. They visited Karachi, Lahore and Faisalabad together, and Tanweer visited his family village Chak-477 (called Chhotian Kota by the *Independent* newspaper), then Manshera in North West Frontier province.

47. Investigations into Rauf quickly led to the Dar-ul-Uloom Medina *medressa* in Bahawalpur, a major religious school down a back street near the relatively upmarket area where the Briton had been living since arriving in the town four years before. Rauf had married into the family of Massod Azhar, the cleric who led Jaish-e-Mohammed. The Dar-ul-Uloom Medina *medressa*, founded by Azhar's father-in-law, was widely considered to be a base for the group. Author interview with former Pakistani Interior Minister Aftab Sherpao, with ISI official, with MI6 official, Islamabad, November 2007. Despite repeated requests for extradition by the British, Rauf remained in custody in Pakistan and eventually escaped in mysterious circumstances in December 2007. He was killed, apparently, in November 2008, by a missile fired from an unmanned drone in the tribal areas on the Afghan frontier. The exact fate of Rauf remains unclear. Sir John Scarlett, director-general of MI6, told the author in the summer of 2009 that his service 'simply did not know' if Rauf was dead.

48. Donald Rumsfeld, 'Rumsfeld's war-on-terror memo', *USA Today*, October 22, 2003.

49. JUI in Pakistan split from its parent Indian body. Its political involvement dates from the early 1970s. Author interview, Bahawalpur, November 2008. In fact JUI's foundation pre-dated the creation of Pakistan by two years.

50. Author interview with Maulana Abdul Aziz Ghani, Islamabad, July 2005.

51. Maulana Sohaib, who ran the complex, denied any direct links with Jaish-e-Mohammed or that any students from the school 'went for jihad'.

52. Such as John Walker Lindh, a number of Australians, the 7/7 bombers, Rauf and many others. On Lindh see Burke, *Al-Qaeda*, pp. 195–6. On Australians,

*Radicalization in the West: The Homegrown Threat*, The New York City Police Department, 2007, p. 51. Presentation by Australian Secret Intelligence Service analysts, Riyadh, March 2008.

53. Author interview with Bahawalpur police chief, November 2007.

54. Around 40 per cent of students in public and private schools came from the poorest categories of society and only 43 per cent of *medressa* students. Andrabi et al., 'Religious School Enrollment'.

55. See Christine Fair, 'Militant Recruitment in Pakistan', *Asia Policy*, July 2007, p. 115, table 1.

56. Andrabi et al., 'Religious School Enrollment'. See also Fair, 'Militant Enrollment'.

57. See ibid., table III.

58. Nikhil Raymond Puri, 'The Pakistani Madrassah and Terrorism: Made and Unmade Conclusions from the Literature', *Perspectives on Terrorism*, vol. 4, no. 4, October 2010, p. 53.

59. See Abbas, *Probing the Jihadi Mindset*.

60. RAND Corporation (C. Christine Fair), *Who Are Pakistan's Militants and Their Families?*, January 1, 2008, p. 60. Puri, 'The Pakistani Madrassah and Terrorism', p. 53.

61. This was in part due to the numbers of individuals educated in religious schools reaching adulthood but could equally be attributed to decades of state propaganda on Kashmir and to the generalized increased sense of religious solidarity so marked in much of the Islamic world since the early years of the decade.

62. Author interview with Dr Omar Farooq Zain Alizai, Multan, December 2007.

63. CIA factbook, updated in 2010. https://www.cia.gov/library/publications/the-world-factbook/fields/2177.html.

64. From Terror Free Tomorrow/New American Foundation, Results of a New Nationwide Public Opinion Survey of Pakistan, 2007.

65. Gilani Poll conducted by Gallup Pakistan, August 2009.

66. C. Christine Fair and Seth Jones, 'Pakistan's War Within', *Survival*, December 2009–January 2010, p. 181. Only 4 per cent saw the spread of American culture favourably. Gilani Poll conducted by Gallup Pakistan, August 2009.

67. Zar Nageen, 'Naming a baby in Pakistan', *Daily Times*, July 9, 2007.

68. '78% Males Mostly Wear Shalwar Kameez, 22% Wear Trousers': Gilani poll, Gallup Pakistan, Islamabad, August 27, 2010.

69. Mohammed Hanif, 'The power of the pulpit', *Newsline*, January 2009.

70. Author interview with Ershad Mahmud, columnist, Islamabad, October 2007.

71. Serious efforts at rapprochement between Ms Bhutto and General Musharraf had been underway since 2004. Bhutto met a series of different representatives to discuss her return. General Ashfaq Kayani, then the director-general of the ISI, led an initial round of discussions. The negotiations had begun in

earnest, however, when Musharraf telephoned Bhutto while she was visiting New York in August 2006. By early autumn, following at least two direct interventions by Secretary of State Condoleezza Rice, the outline of a deal had emerged. Bhutto and Musharraf met secretly on January 24, 2007 in Abu Dhabi and again six months later in Abu Dhabi. Multiple author interviews with PPP officials, Islamabad, Karachi, November 2008. See also Steve Coll, 'Time bomb, the death of Benazir Bhutto and the unravelling of Pakistan', *New Yorker*, January 28, 2008. See also *Report of the United Nations Commission of Inquiry into the Facts and Circumstances of the Assassination of Former Pakistani Prime Minister Mohtarma Benazir Bhutto*, April 15, 2010. Bhutto herself joked to the author about the long telephone conversations she had with President Musharraf, saying that he called her Benazir and she called him 'Mushy'.

72. Zaffar Abbas, 'The emerging contours of PPP-govt deal', *Dawn*, April 21, 2007. Author telephone interviews with Bhutto, September 2007, and in Islamabad, December 2007. See also *Report of the United Nations Commission of Inquiry into the Facts and Circumstances of the Assassination of Former Pakistani Prime Minister Mohtarma Benazir Bhutto*, p. 59, and on 'deep' ISI involvement, p. 60.

73. Between September 2006 and September 2007, Musharraf's approval rating plummeted from 63 per cent to 21 per cent. International Republican Institute (IRI), *Pakistan Public Opinion Survey*, January 19–29, 2008.

74. Author telephone interview, October 2007.

75. Owais Mughal, 'Peshawar–Islamabad Motorway M1 is now open for traffic', Pakistaniat.com. November 11, 2007.

76. This account is based on the author's own reporting, Islamabad and Nowshera, December 2007.

77. Author telephone interview with Bhutto, in Dubai, September 2007.

78. The author conducted three lengthy telephone interviews with Bhutto in June, August and September 2007.

79. The scientific analysis of the suicide bomber's remains by a Scotland Yard team established that he was a teenage male, no more than sixteen years old. According to the Punjab police's investigations, he was called Bilal aka Saeed and from South Waziristan. British High Commission, *Scotland Yard Report into Assassination of Benazir Bhutto*, February 8, 2008, executive summary. *Report of the United Nations Commission of Inquiry*, pp. 41, 60.

80. Amir Mir, *The Bhutto Murder Trail: From Waziristan to GHQ*, Tranquebar, 2010, p. 7.

81. *Report of the United Nations Commission of Inquiry*, pp. 3, 28. *Scotland Yard Report*, p. 3.

82. *Report of the United Nations Commission of Inquiry*, pp. 3, 28. *Scotland Yard Report*, p. 3.

83. Kayani was helped by the new ubiquity of cheap mobile phones, which

meant that TV stations could put a locally hired volunteer correspondent in almost every polling station who gave an impromptu count, obtained from the local returning officers, within minutes of the booths closing thus rendering ballot-box stuffing much harder.

84. Author interview with Qazi Hussein Ahmed, Lahore, February 2008.

85. His consistently hawkish position on Kashmir and acts such as the decision in 1998 to respond in kind to India's 1998 nuclear tests reinforced nationalist credentials too which had been subsequently polished by a stream of anti-Western outbursts and an ambivalent position on cooperation with America on counter-terrorism operations if he ever returned to power.

86. A number of Sharif's family and entourage were involved with the Tabligh Jamaat, a Deobandi-inspired mass organization based on preaching by example which, though non-violent itself, has been an entry point to violent radicalism for a significant number of militants.

87. The reports were difficult to reconcile with reports that in July 1999 Sharif offered to allow US troops to try to kill bin Laden from Pakistani territory apparently to give Washington a stake in the survival of his government. See Bennett-Jones, *Pakistan: Eye of the Storm*, p. 40.

88. Author interview, Islamabad, October 2007.

89. Jason Burke, 'The Guardian profile: Asif Ali Zardari', *Guardian*, September 5, 2008.

## CHAPTER 14: ANOTHER COUNTRY: FATA

1. The writings of Henty, Kipling, Churchill and other, less-talented, authors are full of depictions of the Pashtun border tribes as warlike, brave, stoic and honourable and tell us more about the values of the British Victorians than about the Pashtuns. See Mukulika Banerjee, *The Pathan Unarmed*, Oxford University Press, 2001.

2. Quoted in Sana Haroon, *Frontier of Faith*, Hurst, 2007, p. 89.

3. Ibid., pp. 95–8.

4. Ibid., p. 57. The religious police in Saudi Arabia go by the same name.

5. Albeit one that allowed, through the extraordinary powers granted to the political agent who ran each of the seven FATA for the authorities of the Raj and then of independent Pakistan, the zone to be governed according to their interests rather than those of the locals.

6. Significant funding from Saudi Arabia was part of the effort to extend the reach of Gulf strands of rigorous conservative Sunni Islam to counter the expansion of Shia influence in the wake of the 1979 Iranian Revolution.

7. The contrast they made between their supposed rural, Pashtun religious rectitude and the lack of faith of the urbanized communities and elites of Pakistan would have been entirely familiar to their grandfathers and great grandfathers.

8. Author interview, Khyber Pass, Afghanistan, November 2001.

9. Ahmed was on a visit largely aimed at convincing American counterparts and policy-makers that their view of the Taliban was overly harsh.

10. After all only eighteen months before Musharraf had publicly stated: 'The Taliban cannot be alienated by Pakistan. We have a national security interest there.' Rashid, *Descent into Chaos*, p. 28.

11. Ibid., pp. 50–51.

12. Both Bhutto and her interior minister, Naseerullah Babar, hoped too to open trade routes from Pakistan to central Asia, another constant theme of Pakistani diplomacy and strategic thinking over previous decades and a further reason for the continual insistence on having a favourable government in Kabul. One reason was also internal – the Deobandi Jamaat Ulema Islami party were crucial allies of Bhutto's government – and another was the personal proclivities of the Pashtun Naseerullah Babar. Babar claimed, slightly hyperbolically, to be the 'father of the Taliban'. Author interview, Islamabad, 1998.

13. Author interview with Maleeha Lodhi, London, February 2008.

14. Musharraf, *In the Line of Fire*, p. 237: 'We have earned bounties totalling millions of dollars'.

15. Rashid, *Descent into Chaos*, p. 241.

16. See Mohammed Yousaf and Mark Adkin, *The Bear Trap*, Casemate, 2001.

17. Author interview, Kandahar, November 2003.

18. Author interviews, Peshawar, October 2002, February 2008. Joshua T. White, *Pakistan's Islamist Frontier*, Center on Faith and International Affairs, 2008. 'Government helped MMA leaders' contest elections', *Daily Times*, November 8, 2002. The MMA alliance of conservative religious parties which came to power in the North West Frontier province and, in coalition, in Baluchistan in elections in 2002 benefited from support from the state, which recognized that the Islamists could serve as a useful proxy by which the Musharraf government could marginalize its chief political rivals in the Frontier (the PPP, PML-N and the secular Pashtun nationalist Awami Nationalist Party). The Pakistani military prevented all three parties from campaigning. The religious alliance took 48 of 99 provincial assembly seats, and 29 of 35 national assembly seats from the Frontier.

19. Declan Walsh, 'Across the border from Britain's troops, Taliban rises again', *Guardian*, May 27, 2006. Also Rashid, *Descent into Chaos*, p. 250.

20. Author interview with Maulana Rahat Hussain, Peshawar, October 2007. Not only did the new government of the two provinces embark on a project of radical Islamization, thus creating an atmosphere that encouraged further extremism, but it also proved itself to be predictably incompetent in the management of the provinces' complex social problems.

21. Author telephone interview with Robert Grenier, former Islamabad CIA station chief, January 2009. Author telephone interview with Philip Mudd, former CIA and FBI senior official, June 2010.

22. Author telephone interview with senior serving CIA official, June 2010.

23. Author interviews with intelligence officials, London, Kabul, Islamabad, 2007, 2008.

24. A joint United Nations and European Union paper spoke of 'the wide-ranging nature of ISI involvement'. Jones, *In the Graveyard of Empires*, p. 267. Jason Burke, 'Guantánamo Bay files: Pakistan's ISI spy service listed as terrorist group', *Guardian*, April 25, 2011.

25. Officers echoed the statements of President Karzai and said publicly that the Taliban leadership was coordinating its campaign from Quetta. Declan Walsh, 'Pakistan sheltering Taliban, says British officer', *Guardian*, May 19, 2006. Author interviews with British officers, Helmand, January, 2007, General David Richards, Kabul, February 2007.

26. Author interview with US defence official, Islamabad, October 2007.

27. Author interview, Islamabad, November 2007.

28. Author interview, Riyadh, March 2008.

29. Author interview, London, August 2009.

30. Hearing of the United States Senate select committee on intelligence, Annual Worldwide Threat Assessment, February 5, 2008, Michael McConnell, director of national intelligence, witness testimony.

31. Sanger, *The Inheritance*, p. 248.

32. Mark Mazzetti and Erik Schmitt, 'Pakistanis aided attack in Kabul, U.S. officials say', *New York Times*, August 1, 2008.

33. Burke, 'Pakistan's ISI spy service listed'. Guantanamo Bay Threat Indicator Matrix, September 2007, author collection.

34. Author interview, London, May 2009.

35. In the conversation, intercepted by the ISI and purported to be between Baitullah Mehsud, addressed as Emir Sahib, and an associate, addressed as Maulvi Sahib, the two speakers congratulate each other on an event which, Pakistani government officials claimed on the day after the killing, was the assassination of Benazir Bhutto. The ISI told UN investigators that they already had the voice signature of Baitullah Mehsud and were in a position to identify his voice on the intercept. They also said that they were already monitoring Mehsud's communications, which is how they recorded the conversation. In the English translation of the intercept, the man identified as Mehsud asks his interlocutor: 'Who were they?' The reply comes: 'There were Saeed, the second was Badarwala Bilal and Ikramullah was also there.' Mehsud then asked: 'The three did it?' The cleric he was talking too – 'Maulvi sahib' simply being an honorific for a middle-ranking Deobandi scholar – replied: 'Ikramullah and Bilal did it.' The conversation did not mention Bhutto by name. *Report of the United Nations Commission of Inquiry*, p. 42.

36. Grave concerns remained over the huge shortfalls in the security provision made by the local police and by Musharraf's government for Bhutto but at least two external inquiries, one by Scotland Yard and the other by the United

Nations, found no evidence of active collusion in the killing on the part of the authorities. The general conclusion was that the authorities' role in Bhutto's death was determined by incompetence rather than conspiracy. though it was clear that no one was particularly interested in making a huge effort to protect the controversial former prime minister outside her own entourage. There does, however, appear to have been a genuine attempt to impede investigations by local police following the killing.

37. Either Broomikhel or Zarai Khel of the branch of the Shabikhel subtribe. Mehsud was actually born in Kotka Nor Baz Dawood Shah district near Bannu, according to Azam Tariq, 'The Life of Baitullah Mahsood', published in Urdu-language *Hiteen Magazine*, translation and publication by Global Islamic Media Front, autumn 2010, author collection. This is corroborated by reliable Pakistani sources. See Rahumullah Yusufzai, 'Hidden hand', *Newsline*, February 2008; and Imtiaz Ali, 'Commander of the faithful', *Foreign Policy Magazine*, July 9, 2009.

38. Tariq, 'The Life of Baitullah Mahsood'. The author claims Mehsud matriculated from Bannu City School.

39. Ibid.

40. Author interviews, Peshawar and Islamabad, February 2008.

41. Author interviews with local journalists from Khyber Agency, Peshawar, February, 2008. Author interview with Khalid Aziz, former political secretary NWFP, November 2008. Rahumullah Yusufzai, *The News*, May 22, 2008.

42. Imtiaz Ali, 'The Taliban's versatile spokesman: A profile of Muslim Khan', *CTC Sentinel*, February 2009, vol. 2, no. 2. pp. 6–8. Author interview with aide to Muslim Khan, Karachi, January 2008. Imtiaz Gul, *The Most Dangerous Place: Pakistan's Lawless Frontier*, Penguin, 2010, p. 246.

43. Hakimullah Mehsud, effectively Baitullah Mehsud's deputy, was a member of the Eshangai subtribe, a branch with little prestige, who had never completed his education, either religious or secular, before going off to fight for the Taliban in the mid 1990s and returning in 2001 or 2002. In Waziristan, where war had been a way of making a living for centuries, the money militants could earn, in addition to the valuable weapons and ammunition that could be seized, was much better than that paid to the paramilitary frontier corps or the police, who received 7–8,000 Rs or 6–7,000 Rs respectively per month. A militant could easily earn half as much again. A literate tribesman could earn up to ten times more, as such people were needed to keep basic accounts, stocks of ammunition and so on. For a good example of how the TTP linked into criminal gangs see Tariq Saeed Birmani, 'Riversides may be housing some militants', *Dawn*, October 13, 2009, about the situation in Dera Ghazi Khan adjacent to the FATA.

44. Author interview with Khalid Aziz, former secretary NWFP, November 2008. When peasants had rebelled in Charsadda district next to Mohmand in the 1970s, one of their chief demands had been land reform. See also Jane

Perlez and Pir Zubair Shah, 'The Taliban's latest tactic: Class warfare; inroads are being made in Pakistan by playing poor against wealthy', *New York Times*, April 17, 2009. See Owen Bennett-Jones, 'Pakistan inequality fuelling Taliban support', BBC, May 2010.

45. The fact that the Mahmund, with their greater links to the world outside the high valleys of birch trees and terraced sandy fields of the high frontier, were the most extreme of local factions was not in a sense surprising. The situation in the FATA was inevitably affected by the evolution of the 9/11 Wars more generally and it was those most exposed to the various effects of the conflict, particularly the broad currents of polarization and radicalization that had become so evident from 2003 onwards, who were most likely to end up on the frontline.

46. Four hundred according to Gul, *The Most Dangerous Place*, p. xiv.

47. Between 2003 and 2008, 1,200 Pakistani soldiers were killed, along with more than 6,000 tribesmen. The sums that could be earned from sheltering the foreign militants was made clear when Baitullah Mehsud and other militants concluded a 'peace agreement' with the Pakistani authorities, again after inflicting heavy casualties on the Pakistani army, in 2004. Mehsud and others were paid hundreds of thousands of dollars to compensate them for the money they would have received from al-Qaeda. International Crisis Group, *Appeasing the Militants*, December 11, 2006, p. 17. The rents paid by militants were as high as 60,000 Rs per month. (Though exchange rates in the period were variable and thus make an accurate conversion difficult, the sums work out at around $1,000/£500 in the summer of 2008.) As foreigners would not be allowed to take residences in the centre of villages, this rent was for relatively cheap properties on the margins of settlements. Author interview with Khalid Aziz, former secretary NWFP, November 2008. Further funds were sourced through kidnaps of government officials, extortion and, on one occasion in mid 2007, an entire unit of 280 paramilitary troops.

48. Fair and Jones, 'Pakistan's War Within', p. 172. In one survey of tribesmen in 2008, 80 per cent of respondents said that the local tribal *jirgas* frequently provided justice. Community Appraisal and Motivation Programme, Islamabad, *Understanding FATA: Attitudes towards Governance, Religion and Society in Pakistan's FATA*, xxvii, pp. 62–8.

49. In one day – June 25, 2008 – ten schools were burned in Swat. Gul, *The Most Dangerous Place*, p. 113. A total of twelve boys' and seventeen girls' schools had been burned down by the various TTP factions between January and May 2008, and dozens of teachers killed. Mohammed Amir Rana, 'The Taliban Consolidate Control in Pakistan's Tribal Regions', *CTC Sentinel*, June 2008, vol. 1, no. 7, p. 8. Author phone interview with Ibrahim Paracha, Kohat politician and cleric, February 2008.

50. On *sharia*, Community Appraisal and Motivation Programme, *Understanding FATA*, p. xvii. Author interview with Shafi Rullah Wazir, political agent,

Bajaur, November 2008. Mushtaq Yusufzai and Hasbanullah Khan, 'Salarzai Lashkar kills militant in Bajaur to avenge elders killings', *The News*, August 27, 2008.

51. On interpreters see Shuja Nawaz, 'The Pakistan Army and Its Role in FATA', *CTC Sentinel*, vol. 1, no. 1, January 2009, p. 20.

52. Gul, *The Most Dangerous Place*, p. 22.

53. Fair and Jones, 'Pakistan's War Within', p. 175.

54. The first occasion was in January 2006.

55. Jason Burke and Imtiaz Gul, 'The drone, the CIA and a botched attempt to kill bin Laden's deputy', *Observer*, January 15, 2006.

56. Testimony of Hicham Beyayo to Belgian police, statements on April 2, 2009, May 6, 2009, May 15, 2009, Brussels. Author collection.

57. Testimony of Walid Othmani to French interrogators, January 30, 2009, document M.20-2-9, p. 43. Author collection.

58. 'The dark pursuit of truth', *The Economist*, August 1, 2009.

59. Nigel Inkster, deputy director of MI6 to 2006, said he knew of no strong lead-up to his departure from the service. Author interview, December 2008. In June 2010, Leon Panetta, director of the CIA, said that there had been very little new information in recent years. Paul Cruickshank, 'New information emerges on post-9/11 hunt for bin Laden', CNN.com, September 13, 2010. Other British security officials admitted in 2009 that they still had no 'solid information' on a location since 2001. Also Rory McCarthy, 'The inside story of the hunt for Bin Laden', *Guardian*, August 23, 2003.

60. Author telephone interview with Bob Grenier, former CIA station chief Islamabad, 2009.

61. Author interview with Ron Nash, London, April 2009.

62. Keller said Pakistan had a poor reputation too as a workplace. Even Afghanistan was seen as a better posting. Author telephone interview, December 2008.

63. Author telephone interview, December 2008.

64. Bin Laden and al-Zawahiri had spent much less time in the FATA than often thought, having passed much of the 1980s in Peshawar and the late 1990s in Afghanistan itself.

65. New American Foundation / Terror Free Tomorrow, *Results of a New Nationwide Public Opinion Survey of Pakistan*, August 2007.

66. Interrogation testimony of Bryant Neal Vinas, March 10 and 11, 2009, New York, dossier of Hicham Beyayo. United States of America vs. Bryant Neal Vinas. Indictment, United States District Court, Eastern District of New York, November 14, 2008.

67. See Burke, 'Target Europe'. Author telephone interview with MI6 officials, September 2007.

68. Vinas testimony.

69. Othmani and Beyayo testimony.

70. USA vs. Abdur Rehman Hashim Syed, 'Criminal Complaint', Northern District of Illinois, 2009.

71. 'Sabine am Orde, un gamin de la Sarre perdu au Waziristan', *Die Tageszeitung*, republished *Le Courrier International*, May 20, 2010.

72. Othmani testimony.

73. Paul Cruickshank, 'Enlisting Terror: Al-Qaeda's Recruitment Challenges', in *Al-Qaeda's Senior Leadership*, Jane's Strategic Advisory Services, November 2009, p. 14.

74. Not all, however. Cüneyt Ciftci, a twenty-nine-year-old German of Turkish origin born near Munich in 1979, who on March 3, 2008 died in a huge explosion, having driven a delivery truck loaded with several tons of explosives up to barracks in Khost. The blast killed five, including two American soldiers and Ciftci himself.

75. Author interview with Western intelligence official, Kabul, August 2008. See also Ron Moreau and Sami Yusufzai, 'The Taliban in their own words', *Newsweek*, September 26, 2009.

76. Author interviews, MI6, London, April 2009.

77. Guido Steinberg, the German expert, has usefully emphasized how al-Yazid's opposition to the 9/11 attacks helped bolster his credibility among Taliban figures who saw the strikes not merely as counterproductive but as extremely destructive. See Guido Steinberg, Towards Collective Leadership: The Role of Egyptians in Al-Qaeda', in *Al-Qaeda's Senior Leadership*, p. 9.

78. Tariq, 'The Life of Baitullah Mahsood'.

79. Sanger, *The Inheritance*, p. 234.

80. Author interviews, Pakistani and American officials, Islamabad, November 2009.

81. Beyayo and Othmani testimony.

82. Vinas testimony. Author collection.

83. Dexter Filkins, 'Right at the edge', *New York Times*, September 5, 2008.

84. 'Bin Laden in Palestinian call', BBC News Online, March 21, 2008.

85. Jarret Brachman, 'The Next Osama', *Foreign Policy*, September 10, 2009. Jarret Brachman, 'Retaining Relevance: Assessing Al-Qaeda's Generational Evolution', in *Al-Qaeda's Senior Leadership*. Jarret Brachman, 'Abu Yahya's Six Easy Steps for Defeating al-Qaeda', *Perspectives on Terrorism*, vol. 1, no. 5 (December 2007). Michael Scheuer, 'Abu Yahya al-Libi: Al-Qaeda's Theological Enforcer – Part 1', *Terrorism Monitor*, vol. 4, no. 25 (July 31, 2007).

86. 'Al-Qaeda deputy pens book justifying armed struggle', Associated Press, March 3, 2008.

87. Some estimates were higher, up to 300,000. Zahed Hussein, 'The turning point', *Newsline*, October 2008.

88. Account based on author's reporting, December 2008.

89. The attacks included two against the ISI, two against the army headquarters

in Rawalpindi, one aimed at the air force in Sargodha and one directed at the base of the Pakistani special forces. This total does not include almost 500 security forces and civilians killed in armed clashes. Total Pakistani casualties in 2007, including the number of injured security forces and civilians, exceeded the cumulative total of all the years between 2001 and 2006 and overall the year was to see more than 2,000 terrorist, insurgent and sectarian attacks. Hassan Abbas, 'A Profile of Tehrik-i-Taliban Pakistan', *CTC Sentinel*, vol. 1, no. 2 (January 2008). Hearing of the United States Senate select committee on intelligence, Annual worldwide threat assessment, February 5, 2008, Michael McConnell, director of national intelligence, witness testimony. Pakistan Institute for Peace Studies, *Pakistan Security Report, 2008*, 2009, p. 3.

90. According to Rehman Malik, Pakistan's interior minister, the country's civilian leadership had been scheduled to dine at the hotel but had changed location at the last minute. 'Pakistan leaders' "narrow escape"', BBC news, September 22, 2008.

91. 'They are savages, beasts,' Makhdoom Shahabuddin, the planning minister, told the author after one viewing.

92. Including more than sixty men killed.

93. Author interview, Bajaur, Peshawar, November 2008.

94. Author interview with Colonel Nauman Saeed, Bajaur, November 2008.

95. Author interview, Islamabad, November 2008.

96. National Investigation Agency, Interrogation report of David Headley, June 2010, pp. 7, 9. Author collection.

97. Private soldiers and NCOs for Pakistan's army have long been recruited from rural villages, often through family connections to existing servicemen or a traditional relationship between a particular community and a given unit. This tradition has continued, though efforts to bring down the high proportion recruited from the northern Punjab have led to an increase in numbers from other provinces, largely unchanged for sixty years.

98. Shuja Nawaz, *Crossed Swords*, Oxford University Press, 2008, p. 571. See also Ayesha Siddiqa,, *Military Inc.*, Oxford University Press, Pakistan, 2007, pp. 213–16; Malik, *Pakistan*, p. 118.

99. Nawaz, *Crossed Swords*, p. 572.

100. See C. Christine Fair and Shuja Nawaz, 'The Changing Pakistan Army Officer Corps', *Journal of Strategic Studies*, forthcoming, pp. 26–7. Overall in 1998, 28 per cent of the Pakistani population was urban.

101. Nawaz, *Crossed Swords*, p. 571. Repeated bouts of military rule in which officers serve in government offices as managers and administrators has brought thousands of middle- and senior-ranking servicemen into prolonged contact with the workings and worldview of the Pakistan's bureaucracy, which is itself perhaps the single most important factor in moderate political Islamism in the country. Musharraf inducted at least 3,500 officers into bur-

eaucratic posts, for example. Siddiqa, *Military Inc.*, p. 211. A further factor was that, though the historic dominance of the officer corps by the Punjab had been mitigated slightly by efforts to increase the representation of other ethnicities within the forces, in 2005, 60 per cent still came from Pakistan's biggest, richest, best-educated – and most Islamist – province. Interestingly, the proportion of officers from the NWFP had increased from 10 per cent in 1971 to 22 per cent in 2005.

102. Statement of Mohammed Ajmal Amir Qasab, November 2008, author collection.

103. Ibid. Pranab Dhal Samantha, 'GPS records, CD transcript boost India's case', *The Indian Express*, July 6, 2010. Jason Burke, 'Mumbai: behind the attacks lies a story of youth twisted by hate', *Observer*, November 30, 2008. For name confusion see Prabeen Swami, 'Terrorist's name lost in transliteration', *The Hindu*, December 6, 2008. Kasab is the name of the gunman's caste, mispelt by Indian policemen who needed a surname for their paperwork.

104. Its spokesmen had been happy to meet the author in a five-star Lahore hotel in March 2008.

105. Possibly initially as an informer for the Drugs Enforcement Agency. Headley had been convicted of heroin smuggling in 1998 and cooperated to reduce his sentence.

106. National Investigation Agency, Government of India, Interrogation Report of David Headley, June 2010, p. 89. Author collection.

107. When in America, a US-based LeT member had assisted Headley and, days after returning to Pakistan after completing his first surveillance mission, Headley met with senior LeT associates and discussed potential targets in India.

108. Interrogation Report of David Headley, pp. 1–5, 39, 44, 63, 66–9, 79, 84. See indictments: USA vs. Abdur Rehman Hashim Syed, 'Criminal Complaint', Northern District of Illinois, 2009; USA vs. David Headley, 'Criminal Complaint', Northern District of Illinois, 2009. Author collection.

109. What was clear, however, was the confluence in thinking and worldview between men like 'Major Iqbal' and his immediate superiors and people like Headley, Zaki ur Rehman Lakhvi and others. When Headley reported to his handler that the Jewish Nariman House had been added to the target list, 'Major Iqbal' was very pleased. This did not mean that he was a violent extremist, simply that he shared the anti-Semitic and anti-Zionist worldview of the LeT militants and all those many millions across the Islamic world who saw attacks on Israeli, and by extension Jewish, targets as entirely justified.

110. 'Suicide bomber hits foreign forces in Afghanistan', Reuters, December 26, 2008. The British Ministry of Defence announced eight soldiers killed in Helmand in the first two weeks of December alone. Michael Evans and

Alexi Mostrous, 'Three Royal Marines killed in Afghanistan by boy with wheelbarrow bomb', *The Times*, December 13, 2008.

111. Dexter Filkins, 'Afghan civilian deaths rose 40 percent in 2008', *New York Times*, February 17, 2009. United Nations Assistance Mission in Afghanistan figures, obtained March 2009, Kabul. Ismail Sameem, 'Taliban kill 20 police in Afghanistan', Reuters, January 1, 2009.

112. Riaz Khan, 'Militants seize convoy for US-led forces', Associated Press, November 11, 2008. Rahimullah Yusufzai, 'No to Nato', *Newsline*, December 2008. For Caravan reference, see Tariq, 'The Life of Baitullah Mahsood'.

113. Author interview with a senior French diplomat, Paris, February 2009.

## CHAPTER 15: THE 9/11 WARS: EUROPE, THE MIDDLE EAST, IRAQ

1. 'Let the American people prepare to continue to reap what has been planted by the heads of the White House in the coming years and decades,' bin Laden said. 'Double blast against Obama shows strain on Qaeda', Reuters, June 3, 2009.

2. Full text of Obama victory speech, BBC, November 5, 2008.

3. Those with a favourable view of the US in Jordan rose from 19 per cent to 25 per cent and in Egypt from 22 per cent to 27 per cent. Pew Research Center, *Pew Global Attitudes Survey: Confidence in Obama Lifts U.S. Image Around the World*, July 23, 2009.' Pew Research Center, *Pew Global Attitudes Survey: Muslim Disappointment: Obama More Popular Abroad than at Home, Global Image of US Continues to Benefit*, June 17, 2010. The new American president was popular in Indonesia, where he spent several years as a child, where 71 per cent of Indonesians voiced confidence in him, and among Nigerian Muslims (81 per cent), Israeli Arabs (69 per cent) and Lebanese Sunnis (65 per cent).

4. The favourability rating of the US in the spring of 2009 in Turkey was 14 per cent, lower than shortly before the Iraq war of 2003. In Pakistan those expressing a favourable view of the US actually dropped from 19 per cent before Obama's election to 16 per cent afterwards. Pew Research Center, *Confidence in Obama*, p. 5. There many, predictably and depressingly, suspected a conspiracy. One senior journalist, looking out on the crowded streets from the window of the newsroom of the country's biggest satellite TV news channel on the day of Obama's victory, told the author that he could not believe that 'a black' could make it to such a powerful position in America without the help of the Jews or the CIA. 'Blacks just aren't intelligent enough. And Americans are too racist,' he explained.

5. The request was as ever coupled with a reassurance that the security of Israel was paramount. Obama's ratings were particularly high among Israeli Arabs (69 per cent), according to one poll. Pew Global Attitudes Project, *Little Enthusiasm for Many Muslim Leaders*, February 4, 2010.

6. Holbrooke refused the title 'envoy' on the basis that it meant 'you're sent to do things'. George Packer, 'The Last Mission', *New Yorker*, September 28, 2009.

7. Obama had said in June 2007: 'To build a better, freer world, we must first behave in ways that reflect the decency and aspirations of the American people. This means ending the practices of shipping away prisoners in the dead of night to be tortured in far-off countries, of detaining thousands without charge or trial, of maintaining a network of secret prisons to jail people beyond the reach of the law.' Barack Obama, 'Renewing American Leadership', *Foreign Affairs*, July–August 2007.

8. He had signalled his more pragmatic approach, different both from the Clinton administration's belief in the inevitable benefits of globalization and the more ideological approach of Bush, in the repeated Congressional hearings on Iraq over the previous fifteen months. David Miliband, 'Stay with Obama on Muslims', *International Herald Tribune*, November 6, 2010.

9. Remarks by the President, June 4, 2009, The White House. 'A New Beginning', Cairo University.

10. News conference by President Obama, Palais de la Musique et des Congrès, Strasbourg, France, April 4, 2009.

11. Michael Scherer, 'The five pillars of Obama's foreign policy', *Time*, July 13, 2009.

12. Jason Burke, 'We must never forget the lessons learned from D-Day, says Obama', *Observer*, June 7, 2009.

13. CNN, interview with Anderson Cooper, February 3, 2010. Cited in Bergen, *The Longest War*, Simon and Schuster, 2011, p. 303.

14. Garsallaoui, who had accompanied those arrested to Pakistan, had left them soon after their arrival there and had subsequently remained in the FATA. His wife, who had posted a picture of her husband firing a rocket-propelled grenade on her website, was also detained. Consultation du dossier de Mr Hicham Beyayo, Testimony of Walid Othmani to French interrogators, January 30, 2009; both author collection. Author interviews, Christophe Marchand, lawyer for Hicham Beyayo, Alain Grignard, head of Belgian counter-terrorism police, Brussels, February 2009. Gilbert Dupont, 'Les Six du réseau kamikaze', *La Dernière Heure*, December 13, 2008. Belgium had seen other plots over previous years. The two men who had killed Ahmed Shah Massood forty-eight hours before the 9/11 attacks had come from Belgium, passing through London to collect the credentials which ensured their access to the Northern Alliance leader. There had been the female suicide bomber – one of the first of the 9/11 Wars – who with her Moroccan-born husband had driven to Iraq in their family car.

15. French nationals Bassam Ayachi and Raphael Gendron were remanded in custody and charged with terrorism offences after Italian authorities established their ties to an extremist network operating in France and Belgium. Bruce Crumley, 'Europe pieces together terrorism puzzle', *Time*, May 12, 2009.

16. Europol, *TE-SAT 2009 – EU Terrorism Situation and Trend Report*, April 2009. The British government's published counter-terrorist policy argued that al-Qaeda as an organization had fragmented, leading to a greater role for self-starting groups.

17. Cécilia Gabizon, 'A Vénissieux, terre d'expansion de la burqa', *Le Figaro*, July 1, 2009.

18. Hicham Beyayo, the supposed suicide bomber, had grown up on the Place Alphonse Lemmens in Anderlecht with seven siblings and Moroccan parents who had arrived in Belgium in 1966. Beyayo and two of his brothers had a history of involvement in theft, handling stolen goods and assault.

19. Ben Leapman, '4,000 in UK trained at terror camps', *Sunday Telegraph*, April 19, 2008. Home Office Statistical Bulletin, quarterly update to December 2009, June 2010, p. 5.

20. Alan Travis, 'Two-thirds of UK terror suspects released without charge', *Guardian*, May 13, 2009.

21. One good indication of when the conventional threat was considered to be less worrying was a renewed emphasis on unconventional attacks involving radioactive 'dirty' bombs, makeshift chemical weapons or similar. Briefings of journalists by politicians and security officials about the terrorist threat to the UK in early 2009 frequently stressed the potential consequences of such an attack.

22. Four British men in their early twenties, known as the Nairobi Four, were arrested in Kenya in January 2007, after allegedly fighting in the Somali civil war, and an unnamed twenty-one-year-old university student from Ealing, west London, was reported to have blown himself up at a checkpoint in Somalia in February 2009.

23. Author interview, London, August 2009.

24. Alan Travis, 'Britain downgrades al-Qaida terror attack alert level', *Guardian*, July 20, 2009.

25. Europol, *TE-Sat 2010 – EU Terrorism Situation and Trend Report*, 2010, p. 12; Europol, *EU Terrorism Situation and Trend Report*, 2009, p. 17.

26. Thomas Renard, 'Europol Report Describes Afghanistan-Pakistan Connection to Trends in European Terrorism', *Terrorism Monitor*, vol. 7, no. 12, May 8, 2009.

27. Grignard, author interview, Brussels, March 2009.

28. National Coordinator for Counterterrorism, *National Terrorist Threat Assessment No. 8*, April 25, 2007, p. 3.

29. The Netherlands National Coordinator for Counterterrorism, *Sixth Progress Report on Counterterrorism*, The Hague, June 4, 2007. The Netherlands National Coordinator for Counterterrorism, 'Threat level for the Netherlands once again to "substantial"', press release, March 6, 2008, The Netherlands National Coordinator for Counterterrorism 'The level of the terrorist threat against the Netherlands has been lowered', press release, December 15, 2009.

30. Author interview, Dr Alain Bauer, Paris, July 2009.

31. Author interview, Paris, July 2009.

32. Institute for Strategic Dialogue (Jytte Klausen), *Al Qaeda-Affiliated and 'Homegrown' Jihadism in the UK: 1999–2010*, September 2010, p. 8.

33. Author interviews, Berlin, September, 2009.

34. Author interview with Gilles de Kerchove, counter-terrorism coordinator for the European Union, Brussels, September 2008. Jason Burke, 'Don't be soft on Islam, says EU terror chief', *Observer*, September 28, 2008.

35. Author interview, NYPD representative in Paris, Paris, September 2006, September 2008.

36. Operation Cast Lead sparked both outrage and a spate of anti-Semitic attacks. Overall around 270 cases of anti-Jewish racist violence were reported in the UK in 2009, according to figures compiled by the Community Security Trust (CST), the body that monitors anti-Jewish racism, with most blamed on anti-Israeli sentiment in reaction to hostilities in Gaza. Attacks recorded during the first Palestinian Intifida of the late 1980s averaged sixteen a month. Mark Townsend, 'Rise in anti-Semitic attacks "the worst recorded in Britain in decades"', *Observer*, February 8, 2010. Altogether, there were 113 anti-Semitic incidents in France during the month following the December 27 launching of Operation Cast Lead against Hamas in Gaza, including twenty-two attacks against private individuals and five attempts to burn down synagogues. Bernard Edinger, 'Tense ties in France', *The Jerusalem Report*, March 2, 2009, Paris. In the June elections to the European Parliament, Geert Wilders' Dutch Party for Freedom in the Netherlands won 17 per cent of the national vote. The anti-immigrant British National Party, which warned of the 'creeping Islamification' of British society, won its first two seats. In Austria the right-wing Freedom Party almost doubled its share of the vote, at 13 per cent. 'The first Islamic invasion of Europe was stopped at [the battle of] Poitiers in 732. The second was halted at the gates of Vienna in 1683. Now we have to stop the current stealth invasion,' argued Wilders.

37. Replacement level was reached in Iran, Lebanon, Tunisia, and Turkey. While the average age at first marriage for women was between eighteen and twenty-one in most countries in the region in the 1970s, it was between twenty-two and twenty-five by the late 1990s. North African countries saw an especially steep increase in marriage age. In Libya, the average rose from age nineteen to age twenty-nine between the mid 1970 and late 1990s. The average marriage was above age twenty-five in all the north African countries except for Egypt, where it was just twenty-two in 1998. Farzaneh Roudi-Fahimi and Mary Mederios Kent, 'Challenges and Opportunities – The Population of the Middle East and North Africa', *Population Bulletin*, vol. 62, no. 2, 2007.

38. Pernin et al., *Unfolding the Future of the Long War*, p. 213.

39. Author interview with Carl Haub, senior demographer, Population Reference Bureau, Washington, July 2009.

40. William Underhill, 'Why fears of a Muslim takeover are all wrong', *Newsweek*, July 10, 2009. Eric Kaufmann, 'Europe's Return to the Faith', *Prospect*, 2010, p. 57.

41. Another study predicted the nominally Muslim population in countries such as Switzerland and Austria – which already had very substantial Muslim populations – might reach between 9 and 15 per cent by 2030 and between 10 and 20 per cent by 2050. Ibid., p.58.

42. Olivier Schmitt, 'Sécurité en Europe, la France compte parmi les pays les plus durs', *Le Monde*, August 19, 2010. President Nicolas Sarkozy of France was a particularly good example of a mainstream politician whose language, particularly during the presidential campaign of 2007, had veered close to that of the extreme right. In one rally in Metz, the author heard Sarkozy speak of how the France he dreamed of was one 'where no sheep were slaughtered in a bathtub', a common accusation against the French Muslim Arab or Berber immigrant community. A telephone survey of twenty mayors in areas with major immigrant populations conducted by the author revealed that no such incident had occurred for a decade at least.

43. 'Few fear terrorist attack in the Netherlands', Press release, November 26, 2009, National Coordinator for Counterterrorism, The Netherlands.

44. Justin Davenport, 'Muslim chef sues "insensitive" Met over pork sausages', *Evening Standard*, May 11, 2009.

45. *The Gallup Coexist Index 2009: A Global Study of Interfaith Relations*, May 2009. Author telephone interview with Magali Rheault, Gallup researcher, July 2009. One depressing example of this was the prevalence of conspiracy theories. If significant numbers of French Muslims doubted the official accounts of 9/11, so did 11 per cent of their non-Muslim compatriots. NOP found that 36 per cent of British Muslims thought that Princess Diana was murdered in 1997 to stop her marrying a Muslim and 17 per cent thought the Holocaust was 'exaggerated' (the view of most Holocaust deniers). An ICM poll published in the UK's *Jewish Chronicle* in 2004 found that 14 per ccent of people in the UK more generally thought that the scale of the Holocaust had been exaggerated and 27 per cent of the general public told NOP in 2003 that Princess Diana had been murdered. 'Six years after her death, a quarter of Britons say Diana was murdered: poll', AFP, August 31, 2003.

46. See, for example, 'Ramadan: jeûne pour 70% de Musulmans', AFP, August 20, 2009, citing IFOP poll of 1,300 interviewees. Cécilia Gabizon, 'Les Contrastes de l'intégration à la française', *Le Figaro*, October 15, 2009.

47. In Germany, for example, the number of women who *always* wore a headscarf dropped; the proportion of those who *sometimes* wore a headscarf rose among second-generation immigrants. Survey: Muslim life in Germany, Federal Minister of the Interior, June 2009, pp. 6–7.

48. 'More Dutch Muslims are skipping the mosque', *NRC Handelsblad*, July 29, 2009. Annual Report on Integration, Netherlands Government Bureau of

Statistics, press release, 16 December 2008. Author interview with Professor Jan Latten, director Netherlands Government Bureau of Statistics, January 2009. Jason Burke, 'Holland's first immigrant mayor is hailed as "Obama on the Maas"', *Observer*, January 11, 2009.

49. Cécilia Gabizon, 'Le ramadan séduit de plus en plus les jeunes', *Le Figaro*, August 21, 2009.

50. Malik, *From Fatwa to Jihad*, pp. 12–13

51. Cecile Calla, 'Les Musulmans d'Allemagne seraient assez bien integrés', *Le Monde*, June 27, 2009.

52. Author interviews, Paris, August 2009.

53. The Arabic terms the Maghreb and the Mashriq have been in use since the seventh or eighth century CE and broadly indicate 'the region west', i.e. the north African coast, and 'the region east', i.e. the land west of modern Iran and south of present-day Turkey including, by some definitions, the Arabian peninsula. Theoretically Egypt is part of the Mashriq, as is, according to the *Encyclopedia Britannica*, the Sudan. In reality Egypt floats between the two. The use of both terms here is, in part, meant to underline quite how Eurocentric the Western term 'the Middle East' is.

54. Pew Global Attitudes Project, *Declining Support for bin Laden and Suicide Bombing*, September 10, 2009.

55. An invitation had been extended to successive Algerian groups but rejected systematically since the early 1990s.

56. The failure of the GSPC, as previously mentioned, had been widely noted as an object lesson in how not to execute a jihad by radical Islamic strategists such as al-Suri and Abu Bakr Naji. For more on the latter, see Jarret Brachman and William McCants, 'Stealing al'Qaida's Playbook', *Studies in Conflicts and Terrorism*, May 2006. Also, Devin Springer, James Regens and David Edger, *Islamic Radicalism and Global Jihad*, Georgetown University Press, 2008, pp. 23–5, 46–7, 49, 173. For more on Algerian militancy see Burke, *Al-Qaeda*; Kepel, *Jihad*; John Philips and Martin Evans, *Algeria: Anger of the Dispossessed*, Yale University Press, 2008. See also Jean-Pierre Filiu, 'The Local and Global Jihad of al-Qa'ida in the Islamic Maghrib', *Middle East Journal*, vol. 63, no. 2, spring 2009. One of the most notable figures to accept amnesty was Hassan Khattab, the former chief and one of the founders of the GSPC. 'Hassan Hattab, un ex-chef sanguinaire dans la peau d'un "réconciliateur"', *El Watan*, February 11, 2009.

57. Tawil, *Brothers in Arms*, p. 203. Tawil, a London-based correspondent for *al-Hayat*, is probably the best reporter and analyst working on Islamic militancy in the Maghreb. He interviewed al-Birr in Algeria in March 2009.

58. See Jean-Pierre Filiu, 'Al'Qa'ida in the Islamic Maghreb', *CTC Sentinel*, vol. 3, no. 4, April 2010, p. 14.

59. Tawil, *The Other Face of al-Qaeda*, pp. 42–3.

60. The first militant also complained about 'setting up fake checkpoints to rob

Muslims of their money and abducting and terrorizing innocents in order to receive money', Springer et al., *Islamic Radicalism*, pp. 177–8.

61. AQIM appealed direct to Algeria's Berbers, 'our brothers, the free kabylie, the descendants of Tariq bin Ziyadh ... to stand against "the traitorous rulers"'. Andrew Black, 'Al-Qaida Operations in Kabylie Mountains Alienating Algeria's Berbers', *Jamestown Terrorism Focus*, vol. 5, no. 16, April 23, 2008.

62. 'Cinq gardes communaux sauvagement assassinés', Liberté, June 23, 2009.

63. Author interview, London, June 2009.

64. A largely independent semi-criminal faction was based in the far desert south.

65. The secretary of state had even, despite the ongoing close cooperation between the notoriously brutal Egyptian intelligence services and their American counter-terrorist counterparts, singled out Egypt for criticism over human rights abuses. In response to the criticism, Mubarak made a number of small cosmetic changes then proceeded to make sure he won 87 per cent of votes cast at the 2005 presidential elections. The new pragmatism forced on the Bush administration in Iraq was rapidly communicated to the White House's general approach to the region. By 2007 and 2008, there was little pressure for serious reform. What did remain of the 'Freedom Agenda' by the time Obama took power in Washington was, however, the liberalizing economic element. This had seen taxes cut, tariffs removed and foreign direct investment courted. Egypt was dubbed with the slightly unlikely title of 'world's top reformer' in 2007 by the World Bank, then under Paul Wolfowitz, the long-standing advocate of democratization, neoliberal economics, the invasion of Iraq and the man who as deputy defense secretary had been one of those most blamed for the failures that had followed the 'liberation' of 2003. The Egyptian economy had started growing rapidly towards the end of the decade. After averaging about 4 per cent through the 1990s, economic growth reached 8 per cent in 2007. John R. Bradley, *Inside Egypt*, Palgrave Macmillan, 2008, p. 167. Isobel Coleman, 'Egypt's Uphill Economic Struggles', The Council on Foreign Relations, February 2011.

66. Bradley, *Inside Egypt*, p. 40.

67. Michael Slackman, 'Stifled, Egypt's young turn to Islamic fervor', *New York Times*, February 17, 2008. 'Saving faith: Islam seems to be fading as a revolutionary force', *The Economist* Special report on Egypt, July 17, 2010, p. 14.

68. At legislatives of December 2005 the Muslim Brotherhood had won 88 seats, or 20 per cent, becoming the most successful opposition bloc despite well-documented fraud and heavy-handed security interference.

69. Pew Research Center, *Declining Support for bin Laden and Suicide Bombing*, September 10, 2009.

70. For a detailed account of post-9/11 militancy in Egypt see Tawil, *The Other Face of al-Qaeda*, pp. 32–6. Author telephone interview with Noman Benotman, March 2011.

71. Author interview, Rabat, March 2007.

72. Author interview, Saleh, March 2007.

73. Roula Khalaf, 'Forgotten flowering', *Financial Times*, December 11, 2008.

74. The most common hometowns listed in the Sinjar Records for overseas volunteers arriving to fight in Iraq were Mecca, Saudi Arabia (43), Benghazi, Libya (21), and Casablanca, Morocco (17). Other Libyan coastal towns also supplied a disproportionately high number of volunteers, especially Darnah, a working-class town of 80,000, from where an astonishing 53 fighters listed in the Sinjar records came. CTC (Brian Fishman) *Bombers, Bank Accounts and Bleed Outs: Al'Qaeda's Road in and out of Iraq*, 2008, pp. 38–9. Both Darnah and Benghazi have long been associated with Islamic militancy in Libya, known in particular for a brutally suppressed uprising in the mid 1990s.

75. Alison Pargeter, 'LIFG Revisions Unlikely to Reduce Jihadist violence', *CTC Sentinel*, October 2009, vol. 2, no. 10. Paul Cruickshank, 'LIFG Revisions Posing Critical Challenge to al'Qaida', *CTC Sentinel*, December 2009, vol. 2, no. 12. Tawil, *Brothers in Arms*, pp. 196-7. Author interview with Noman Benotman, London, 2008.

76. Jason Burke, 'Westerners flocking to dig into Gaddafi's deep pockets', *Observer*, September 2, 2007. Gaddafi had publicly admitted a chemical and nuclear weapons programme six days after Saddam Hussein's capture in 2003.

77. See Nir Rosen, *Aftermath: Following the Bloodshed of America's Wars in the Muslim World*, Nation Books, June 2009, for a fuller account. Bilal y Saab and Magnus Ranstorp, 'Securing Lebanon from the Threat of Salafist Jihadism', *Studies in Conflict and Terrorism*, vol. 30, no.10, 2007. Bilal y Saab, 'The Failure of Salafi-Jihadi Insurgent Movements in the Levant', *CTC Sentinel*, September 2009, vol. 2, no. 9, p. 15.

78. In Jordan another counter-attack against al-Qaeda's theological arguments was launched by a senior cleric and former stalwart of armed international Islamic extremism called Abu Mohammad al-Maqdisi. See Murad Batal al-Shishani, 'Jihad Ideologue Abu Mohammad al-Maqdisi Challenges Jordan's Neo-Zarqawists', *Terrorism Monitor*, vol. 7, no. 20, July 9, 2009. Michael Slackman, 'Generation faithful: Jordanian students rebel, embracing Conservative Islam', *New York Times*, December 24, 2008; Lina Sinjab, 'Syrian Islamic revival has woman's touch', BBC News, November 28, 2009.

79. Pew Research Center, *Confidence in Obama*, pp. 83–6.

80. For a good overview see Benedetta Berti, 'Salafi-Jihadi Activism in Gaza: Mapping the Threat', *CTC Sentinel*, May 2010, vol. 3, no. 5, pp. 5–7.

81. Nidal al-Mughrabi, 'Pro-Qaeda group declares "Islamic emirate" in Gaza', Reuters, August 14, 2009. See also on Beverly Milton-Edwards and Stephen Farrell, *Hamas*, Polity Press, 2010. These clashes contributed to the growing sense that the ideological battle between the inheritors of various strands of conservative, revivalist Islamic thought that had preceded the 9/11 Wars by many decades – indeed in some significant ways had provoked the conflict –

was resurfacing. See Jean-Pierre Filiu, 'The Brotherhood vs. Al-Qaeda: A Moment of Truth?', Hudson Institute, 2009, for a useful discussion.

82. Michael Knights, 'The Current State of al'Qaida in Saudi Arabia', CTC *Sentinel*, September 2008, vol. 1, no. 10, p. 7.

83. Ibid.

84. Kenneth Ballen, 'Bin Laden's soft support', *Washington Monthly*, May 2008.

85. Hegghammer, *Jihad in Saudi Arabia*, pp. 19–20, 49.

86. Magdi Abdlehadi, 'Saudis to retrain 40,000 clerics', BBC, March 20, 2008.

87. On textbooks see *Update: Saudi Arabia's Curriculum of Intolerance*, Hudson Institute Center for Religious Freedom, 2008.

88. 'Reform in Saudi Arabia: At a snail's pace', *The Economist*, October 2, 2010.

89. Two Guantanamo returnees who had been through the deradicalization programme but had nonetheless resumed violent activism surfaced in the Yemen in January 2009.

90. Author interview, March 2009.

91. Ibid. The exact number at the time was 4,238 American servicemen killed.

92. The militia is estimated to have lost up to a 1,000 fighters in the battles.

93. Sabrina Tavernise, 'A Shiite militia in Baghdad sees its power wane', *New York Times*, July 27, 2008.

94. Interview, November 2010.

95. Author telephone interview, August 2008.

96. Afif Sarhan and Jason Burke, 'How Islamist gangs use internet to track, torture and kill Iraqi gays', *Observer*, September 13, 2009.

97. Martin Chulov, 'They turned the tide for America. Now, as withdrawal nears, sons of Iraq pay the price', *Guardian*, May 14, 2010.

98. Compared to 1,287 regular police. Iraq Body Count, 'Post-Surge violence, its extent and nature', December 28, 2008. http://www.iraqbodycount.org/analysis/numbers/surge-2008/.

99. Rosen, *Aftermath*, p. 542.

100. Interview, Baghdad, November 2010.

101. 'At least 27 die in Iraq as bombs, shootings shatter lull', AFP, February 11, 2009.

102. AQIP had theoretically ceased to exist in 2006. The very declaration of the ISI had angered many of the more nationalist fighters, who carried out the vast proportion of attacks on government and American forces, presuming as it did overall command of 'resistance efforts' and the right to decide the future of the country. See Mohammed M. Hafez, 'Al-Qa'ida Losing Ground in Iraq', *CTC Sentinel*, December 2007, vol. 1, no. 1, p. 7.

103. A significant predictor of involvement in radical 'jihadi' militancy in Iraq in 2009, according to network analysis carried out by American intelligence specialists, was the previous or current involvement of a family member. Many of the female suicide bombers were widows of dead militants. A dozen bombers came from a single village in Diyala province, one of the few

remaining strongholds of the extremists. See Martin Chulov, 'Innocent grandmother – or suicide bombing mastermind?', *Guardian*, June 11, 2009. Another predictor was a recent jail sentence. With the state's prison system now in Iraqi hands, many of the hardened al-Qaeda militant leaders held by the Americans had been released, often quickly returning to violence, recruiting family members and friends to fight alongside them.

104. Nineveh was heavily affected by Saddam's Arabization strategy, which had seen hundreds of thousands of local Kurds driven from their homes, which were then given to Arabs from the south, particularly military families loyal to Saddam. These latter clearly stood to lose much if sufficient calm returned for either the Kurds to make claims to land beyond the current limits of the three provinces they controlled or the central Baghdad government to decide to implement laws that called for measures to reverse Arabization.

105. In Anbar a few years earlier the attempts by radical Islamists from outside the province or indeed the country to seize control of lucrative local trafficking networks had been one of the key drivers behind the turning of the local sheikhs towards the Americans. Andrea Plebani, 'Ninawa Province: Al'Qaida's Remaining Stronghold', *CTC Sentinel*, vol. 1, no. 1, January 2010, p. 20.

106. Ibid., p. 21.

107. In Najaf and Karbala the ISCI score was 14.8 per cent and 6.4 per cent, down from 45 per cent and 35 per cent in 2005. See Joost Hilterman, 'Iraq on the edge', *New York Review of Books*, November 19, 2009, for a useful analysis.

108. Afif Sarham, 'Hitmen charge $100 a victim as Basra honour killings rise', *Observer*, November 30, 2008.

109. Baghdad received power only for twelve to fourteen hours. NYT, Op-Chart, June 18, 2009. 'Iraq: key figures since the war began', Associated Press, January 2, 2009. Oxfam International, *In Her Own Words: Iraqi Women Talk about Their Greatest Challenges*, March 2009, p. 5.

110. In comparison with pre-war Iraq this was an improvement. Before the war, 12.9 million people had potable water and 6.2 million had sanitation. On October 2, 2008, 20.9 million people had potable water and 11.3 million people had sanitation. 'Iraq: key figures since the war began', Associated Press. Martin Chulov, 'Iraq withdrawal: Amid heat and broken promises, only the ice man cometh', *Guardian*, August 30, 2010.

111. Oxfam International, *In Her Own Words*, p. 10.

112. As ever, compared to what had gone before there was improvement. But though many lauded the fact that 'only' twenty-five civilians a day were dying on average through 2008 in Iraq, fewer pointed out that the rate had been roughly equivalent to that of the first twenty months of post-invasion Iraq from May 2003 to December 2004. Iraq Body Count, 'Post-Surge violence: its extent and nature', December 28, 2008. http://www.iraqbodycount.org/analysis/numbers/surge-2008/.

113. Ibid.
114. In all in 2009 there were 706 explosions causing 2,972 deaths. Iraq Body Count, 'Civilian deaths from violence in 2009', December 31, 2009. http://www.iraqbodycount.org/analysis/numbers/2009/.
115. Interview, Baghdad, November 2010.

## CHAPTER 16: 'AFPAK' 2009–10

1. This passage is based on the author's reporting during a week spent with the 10th Mountain Division in March 2009.
2. Author interview with David McKiernan, Kabul, March 2009. Author interviews and briefings with senior NATO-ISAF officers, Kabul, March 2009.
3. Participation levels were however much lower than in 2005, and there was still considerable violence even if it did not reach the intensity some had feared.
4. The bulk of which occurred in the insecure southern Pashtun heartlands. Abdullah Abdullah, though of mixed Tajik and Pashtun background, broadly represented the northern, Panjshiri, Dari-speaking and urban constituency. Karzai had rallied an unsavoury array of backers comprising many of Afghanistan's most notorious warlords and powerbrokers but even with their support appears to have been unsure of outright victory. Whether or not the president himself was aware of the fraud is unclear.
5. For a useful account of the review process see Bergen, *The Longest War*, pp. 539–45.
6. Author interview, Kabul, March 2009.
7. Author interview, Logar, Afghanistan, March 2009.
8. 'Poll: More view Afghan war as mistake', *USA Today*, March 16, 2009. Jennifer Agiesta and Jon Cohen, 'Public opinion in U.S. turns against Afghan war', *Washington Post*, August 20, 2009. Paul Steinhauser, 'Poll: Support for Afghan war at all-time low', CNN, September 15, 2009.
9. George Packer, 'The last mission', *New Yorker*, September 28, 2009.
10. Steve Luxenberg, 'Bob Woodward book details Obama battles with advisers over exit plan for Afghan war', *Washington Post*, September 22, 2010.
11. The Dutch were to be out by the summer of 2010 and the Canadians by 2011, for example.
12. Author interview with Admiral de Tarly, Paris, October 2008.
13. 'In U.S., more support for increasing troops in Afghanistan', Gallup, November 25, 2009. The Ministry of Defence released footage of the young man, third in line to the throne, blasting away at insurgents – 'Terry Taliban' – on a heavy machine gun. Author interview with senior Whitehall official, London, February 2009.
14. A major political row in Helmand in 2007 saw the expulsion from Kabul of two foreign envoys, an Irish EU official, Michael Semple, and another Irishman, for 'illicit meetings with the Taliban'. Author telephone interview, Michael

Semple, October 2008. On assessments of success of reintegration programmes see Michael Semple, *Endgames: Reconciliation in Afghanistan*, United States Institute of Peace, September 2009, p. 55, cited in Thomas Ruttig, *The Battle For Afghanistan*, New America Foundation, May 2011. Author interviews with NATO, Afghan officials, Kabul, August 2008, March 2009.

15. Jason Burke, 'Secret Taliban peace talks', *Observer*, September 28, 2008; author interviews with Muttawakel, Rahmani, Zaeef, Kabul, March, 2009. One reason was that perhaps the biggest contribution the Saudis could make was granting a respectable and safe asylum to senior figures who did decide to come in from the cold. None, however, appeared keen to take them up on the offer.

16. Author interviews, Kabul, March 2009.

17. Author interviews with Wood, Taliban spokesmen, senior US officers, Kabul and Logar, March 2009. *US Army Field Manual 3-24*, pp. 1–15.

18. Gates actually said: 'If we set ourselves the objective of creating some sort of central Asian Valhalla over there, we will lose, because nobody in the world has that kind of time, patience and money.' Ann Scott Tyson, 'Gates predicts "slog" in Afghanistan', *Washington Post*, January 28, 2009.

19. Author telephone interview with Andrew Exum, August 2009.

20. Author telephone interview with Bruce Riedel, August 2009.

21. As early as March 2009, Nick Williams, McKiernan's senior political adviser, had told the author that the Taliban's ability to fight through the previous winter had 'provoked . . . a major reassessment of what is feasible in Afghanistan'.

22. On casualties, 'British injury toll in Afghanistan revealed', Sky News, August 17, 2009 and UK Ministry of Defence website http://www.mod.uk/DefenceInternet/FactSheets/OperationsFactsheets/OperationsInAfghanistanBritishFatalities.htm.

23. From House of Commons International Development Committee report 2008, Paragraph 19. Author interviews, London, 2009.

24. Author interview with DFID official, August 2009.

25. Gordon Corera, 'UK backs Taliban reintegration', BBC News, November 13, 2009. Author interviews with British diplomats, Kabul, August 2008, March 2009.

26. Dave Graham, 'No Taliban "unconditional surrender" sought – Britain', Reuters, February 6, 2010.

27. John Hutton, Remembrance Day speech, November 11, 2008, published text.

28. Author interview by email with Taliban spokesman, October 2009.

29. Stenersen, *The Taliban Insurgency in Afghanistan*, p. 26.

30. The move indicated that the faction within the Taliban senior command which had opposed their use had won the argument. 'Code of Conduct, the Taliban', May 9, 2009, posted in Pashto on the Shahmat website on August 6, 2009.

31. See Hekmat Karzai, 'Suicide Terrorism: The Case of Afghanistan', *Security*

*and Terrorism,* March 2007, p. 36; and data for Centre for Conflict and Peace Studies (CAPS), Kabul. Author interviews with Hekmat Karzai, Paris, Kabul, 2009.

32. UNAMA, *Afghanistan Annual Report on Protection of Civilians in Armed Conflict, 2009,* December 31, 2009. pp. 7–8. Over 1,000 were killed directly by suicide attacks or IEDs.

33. Anthony H. Cordesman, 'The Afghan War: The Campaign in the Spring of 2010', Centre for Strategic and International Studies, May 24, 2010.

34. Author interview, MI6, Kabul, March 2009.

35. See Thomas Ruttig, *The Other Side: Dimensions of the Afghan Insurgency,* The Afghan Analysts Network, July 2009.

36. Taliban Leader Mullah Omar, 'In Celebration of Eid al-Adha', NEFA Foundation, November 25, 2009.

37. UNAMA, *Afghanistan Annual Report on Protection of Civilians in Armed Conflict, 2009,* pp. 12–13.

38. 'Afghan people "losing confidence"', BBC, February 9, 2009. The Afghan Centre for Social and Opinion Research in Kabul carried out the fieldwork, via face-to-face interviews with 1,534 Afghans in all of the country's thirty-four provinces between December 30, 2008 and January 12, 2009. The poll was commissioned by the BBC, ABC News of America and ARD of Germany. 'Afghans more optimistic for future, survey shows', BBC, January 11, 2010. This second survey was also conducted by the Afghan Center for Socio-Economic and Opinion Research (ACSOR). Interviews were conducted in person, in Dari or Pashto, among a random national sample of 1,534 Afghan adults December 11–23, 2009.

39. Author interview, United Nations official, Kabul, March 2009.

40. 'Biden cites mounting problems in Afghanistan, but says war "far from lost"', Radio Free Europe, March 10, 2009.

41. Marr interview with David Miliband.

42. Sarah Ladbury, Testing Hypotheses on Radicalisation in Afghanistan, for Department for International Development, August 14, 2009. The study also made the very useful point that much of the process of 'radicalization' occurred after the individual had come into contact with or become integrated with a group of Taliban or insurgent circles.

43. Kate Clark, 'Afghanistan's "weekend jihadis"', *The World Tonight,* Radio Four, September 11, 2009.

44. Ron Moreau and Sami Yousafzai, 'Turning the Taliban', *Newsweek,* February 22, 2010.

45. Marr interview with David Miliband.

46. 'We have very few Pashtuns,' admitted General Ali Ahmed, the commanding officer of Camp Alamo, to the author in March 2009. Each *kandaq* should have been composed according to the ethnicity of the whole country, so with

between 40 or 45 per cent Pashtuns. Instead, the proportion was around 10 per cent, and most of those were from the north and east, not the south. The output data were based on those sent from the Afghan recruiting centres, where scant attention was paid to ethnic balance given the pressure to create new units. The Western officers were incapable of telling the difference between ethnic groups. When asked to produce a recruit from Helmand, those running the training camp brought forward a handful of disconsolate Helmandi Hazaras, one of the most persecuted local communities, for whom life as a soldier was better than that in Lashkar Gah, whatever the risks to their family.

47. General Ali Ahmed had joined the army in 1982 and had thus fought for the Communist regime against the *mujahideen*. So too had the officers leading the detachment in Logar with Captain Vasquez.

48. This was Abdul Rahim Wardak.

49. Author interviews, Camp Alamo, March 2009.

50. Author interview, ISAF headquarters, Kabul, March 2009.

51. Author interview, Wakil Safir Rahman, Kabul, March 2009.

52. UNODC, *Afghan Opium Survey 2009*, 2 September 2009, pp. 3–5.

53. Author interview, Kabul, March 2009.

54. James Risen, 'U.S. to hunt down Afghan drug lords tied to Taliban', *New York Times*, August 10, 2009. 'NATO to attack Afghan opium labs', BBC News, October 10, 2008.

55. Author interview with Mohammed Ehsan Zia, Kabul, March 2009.

56. Matthew Rosenberg, 'Corruption suspected in airlift of billions in cash from Kabul', *Wall Street Journal*, June 25, 2010.

57. The cable adds: 'Many other notable private individuals and public officials maintain assets (primarily property) outside Afghanistan, suggesting these individuals are extracting as much wealth as possible while conditions permit.'

58. Jonathan Steele and Jon Boone, 'Afghan vice-president landed in Dubai with $52m in cash', WikiLeaks, December 2, 2010.

59. Jonathan Steele, 'US convinced Karzai half-brother is corrupt, WikiLeaks cables say', *Guardian*, December 2, 2010.

60. Author interview, Kabul, March 2009.

61. Author interview by email, October 2009.

62. Units continued searches of homes, often using dogs, seen as unclean in Afghanistan and many Islamic nations.

63. Insurgents knew this, and there was some evidence that they exploited it deliberately by drawing fire into areas where civilians were sheltering.

64. UNAMA, *Afghanistan Annual Report on Protection of Civilians in Armed Conflict, 2009*, December 31, 2009, pp. 16–19.

65. Most were grouped into 'Taskforce 373'. Scores, possibly hundreds, of such events, often occurring in remote locations and systematically downplayed or denied by coalition spokesmen, had gone unreported. Some were revealed by

WikiLeaks in August 2010. They included one incident in June 2007 in which seven Afghan National Police were killed. In another, in October 2007, an internal log listed casualties as follows: twelve US wounded, two teenage girls and a ten-year-old boy wounded, one girl killed, one woman killed, four civilian men killed, one donkey killed, one dog killed, several chickens killed, no enemy killed, no enemy wounded, no enemy detained. Nick Davies, 'Afghanistan war logs: Task Force 373 – special forces hunting top Taliban', *Guardian*, July 25, 2010. The leaked logs showed how coalition public statements had systematically been economical with the truth, if not downright misleading.

66. Up to 3,000 Afghans served with American special forces units, according to some estimates.

67. Author interview with McKiernan, March 2009, Kabul.

68. The higher estimates were those of American commanders.

69. UNAMA, *Mid Year Report on Protection of Civilians in Armed Conflict 2010*, Kabul, August 10, 2010, p. 15.

70. Barader had taken over following the arrest of Mullah Obaidullah in early 2007.

71. Thomas Ruttig, 'The Taliban Arrest Wave in Pakistan: Reasserting Strategic Depth', *CTC Sentinel*, vol. 3, no. 3, March 2010, p. 5.

72. Munir Ahmad, 'Pakistani officials: nearly 15 top Taliban held', Associated Press, February 25, 2010.

73. Chris Allbritton, 'Holbrooke hails Pakistan–U.S. collaboration on Taliban', Reuters, February 18, 2010.

74. Author telephone interview, February 2010.

75. Lieven, *A Hard Country*, pp. 470, 474.

76. Declan Walsh, 'WikiLeaks cables: US special forces working inside Pakistan', *Guardian*, November 30, 2010.

77. Declan Walsh, 'The village that stood up to the Taliban', *Guardian*, February 5, 2010.

78. 'Admiral Mullen praises Pakistan army's war plan', CBS, December 16, 2009.

79. Ruttig, 'The Taliban Arrest Wave', p. 6.

80. Other cables referred to the relationship between Pakistan and the USA being 'transactional in nature' and 'based on mutual mistrust' and expressed deep concerns over the security of Pakistani nuclear fuel, potential 'soft coups' by the army, the collapsing economy, a lack of governance in much of the country and the deep anti-Americanism. 'US embassy cables: "Reviewing our Afghanistan-Pakistan strategy"', *Guardian*. November 30, 2010. 'US embassy cables: Relationship with Pakistan based on "mutual distrust", says US', *Guardian*, December 1, 2010. 'US embassy cables: Despite massive US aid, anti-Americanism rampant in Pakistan', *Guardian*, November 30, 2010.

81. Jane Perlez and Eric Schmitt, 'Pakistan army finds Taliban tough to root out', *New York Times*, July 5, 2010.

82. *Fedayeen* tactics are typical of Kashmir. The theological difference between actively seeking death – a suicide attack - and partaking in an attack which implies a very high chance of dying is important.

83. The career of 'Dr Usman', the only survivor among the attackers on the army general headquarters in October 2009, gives a clue. Usman was a former army medical corps officer who, after leaving the military, became involved with a series of extremist groups around his hometown of Kahuta in central Punjab. Having risen up through the ranks of the Bahawalpur-based Jaish-e-Mohammed, he fled to the FATA like so many such militants, where he linked up with Pakistani Taliban groups and with Ilyas Kashmiri, the veteran Pakistani with close links to al-Qaeda. 'Dr Usman's desperate last act', *Daily Times*, October 13, 2009.

84. Pew Global Attitudes, *Pew Global Attitudes: Overview: Concern about Extremist Threat Slips in Pakistan*, July 29, 2010, p. 11.

85. From 70 per cent in 2007 to single digits at the end of 2008, according to TerrorFreeTomorrow polls. Kenneth Ballen, 'Bin Laden's Soft Support', *Washington Monthly*, May 2008.

86. Especially given the collapse of the boom that had benefited so many in the Pakistani lower middle class.

87. Pew Research Center, *Overview: Pakistani Public Opinion*, August 13, 2009.

88. British Council report, *Pakistan: the Next Generation*, November 2009.

89. Gul, *The Most Dangerous Place*, pp. xvi–xvii.

90. Forty per cent blamed the fighting in Waziristan on America. Military Action in Waziristan: Opinion Poll, Gilani Poll/GallupPakistan, Islamabad, November 3, 2009.

91. 'US embassy cables: Despite massive US aid, anti-Americanism rampant in Pakistan', *Guardian*, November 30, 2010.

92. Aryn Baker, 'Casualty of war', *Time*, June 1, 2009.

93. Pew Research Center, *Overview: Concern about Extremist Threat Slips in Pakistan*, p. 3.

94. 'Into the heartland', *The Economist*, June 5, 2010.

95. Pew Research Center, *Overview: Concern about Extremist Threat Slips in Pakistan*.

96. Arif Jamal, 'Half-hearted security operations in Punjab do little to restrain Taliban', *Jamestown Terrorism Monitor*, vol. 8, no. 31, August 5, 2010.

97. Pew Research Center, *Overview: Concern about Extremist Threat Slips in Pakistan*, p. 10. Support for all extremist groups, including al-Qaeda and the Taliban, was strongest in the Punjab. While 27 per cent in the Punjab offered a favourable opinion of al-Qaeda and 22 per cent expressed a favourable view of the Taliban, support for these groups was only in the single digits in Sindh, NWFP (renamed Khyber Pakhtunkhwa) and Baluchistan.

98. South Asia Terrorism Portal, New Delhi. In 2008, 69 civilians and 90 members of the security forces were killed in terrorism-related violence in Jammu

and Kashmir. There were 49 explosions using improvised devices or land mines or hand-grenades in which 29 persons were killed. There were no incidents of suicide or suicidal (*fedayeen*) terrorism. In 2009, 55 civilians and 78 members of the security forces were killed. There were only 7 explosions, in which 11 civilians were killed. There were no incidents of suicide or suicidal terrorism during 2009 either.

99. The demonstrations were inspired directly by those in Palestine, down to the *keffiyehs* which the participants tied around their faces, in the same way that the first round of demonstrations in Kashmir, those that had sparked the first wave of the insurgency in the disputed state back in the late 1980s, had been inspired by the mass movements against Communist rule in eastern Europe.

100. Author interviews with senior police, Jammu, and Kashmir police officials, Srinagar, Sopore and Baramullah, Kashmir, February and June 2010.

101. Sixty-two per cent of the population are aged under thirty, and youth unemployment is 50 per cent.

102. Author interview, Srinagar, June 2010.

103. Muzamil Jaleel, 'Alarm bells: Stone-pelters join militant ranks', *Indian Express*, November 25, 2010.

104. One operation had seen a nineteen-year-old blow himself up in a strike against an army convoy on a road near Sopore, in the heart of wealthy apple-growing country and an area with a local tradition of political dissidence, Islamism and insurgency. The son of a radical preacher removed from his post as village cleric by the authorities, he had been raised in a harsh and politicized environment. Sent to a *medressa* in the western Indian state of Gujrat for his education at the age of sixteen, he had ended up in Pakistan, almost certainly recruited by Lashkar-e-Toiba, before finally returning to his village only weeks before committing his final, suicidal attack only a few miles from his home. 'As a Muslim I am happy. As a father I am sad,' his father said as he received visitors come to congratulate him on the martyrdom of his child.

105. Jason Burke, 'Kashmir: young militants take pot shots at fragile peace process', *Observer*, February 24, 2010. Author interview, Pett Sirr, February 2010. 'Two terrorists killed as Srinagar gunbattle ends', Press Trust of India, January 7, 2010.

## CHAPTER 17: THE END OF THE FIRST DECADE

1. Shahawar Matin Siraj was found guilty of participating in a conspiracy to attack the Herald Square subway station in 2004, three days before the Republican national convention was to begin at Madison Square Garden.

2. 'Roshonara Choudhry: police interview extracts', *Guardian*, November 3, 2010.

3. Tom Rawstorne, 'The remote-controlled Al Qaeda assassin: how brilliant student was brainwashed into stabbing MP', *Daily Mail*, November 6, 2010.

4. Petter Nesser and Brynjar Lia, 'Lessons Learned from the July 2010 Norwegian Terrorist Plot', *CTC Sentinel*, vol. 3, no. 8, August 2010.

5. He may have been in touch with Anwar al-Awlaki but had never been near Pakistan.

6. Another was Ahmed Mohammed Hamed Ali, al-Qaeda's chief of military operations in Afghanistan and a veteran militant indicted for his role in the 1998 bombings of American embassies in East Africa.

7. A total of nearly 600 militants were killed, according to one estimate, indicating that new militants replacing the dead were being killed too. Greg Miller, 'Increased U.S. drone strikes in Pakistan killing few high-ranking militants', *Washington Post*, February 20, 2011. David E Sanger and Mark Mazzetti, 'New estimate of strength of Al Qaeda is offered', *New York Times*, June 30, 2010. The fact that senior al-Qaeda figures began to move to Pakistani cities and towns indicated how effective the drone strikes were.

8. A nine-month break in communications from bin Laden had been ended only in March 2009. Seth Jones, *In the Graveyard of Empires*, p. 291.

9. An audiotape was released in January and another at the end of September.

10. Abdul Hameed Bakier, 'Internet Jihadists React to the Deaths of al-Qaeda Leaders in Iraq', *CTC Sentinel*, May 2010, vol. 3, no. 5, p. 14.

11. Abu Jihad al-Shami, *The Vision*, published summer 2010. The author's *nom de guerre* indicates he is either from or has fought in Jordan or Iraq.

12. According to a study published in 2009, outside of the war zones of Afghanistan and Iraq, 99 per cent of al-Qaeda's victims in 2007 and 96 per cent in 2008 were non-Western. Combating Terrorism Centre, *Deadly Vanguards: A Study of al'Qaida's Violence against Muslims*, December 2009, p. 10.

13. An example would be when, in July 2009, 200 people were killed in riots between Han Chinese and local Uighurs in Xinjiang. This led al-Qaeda to issue its first direct threat against China, framing the recent events in the classic narrative. Abu Yahya al-Libi described the 'massacre' as 'not being carried out by criminal Crusaders or evil Jews who have committed crimes against our nation [but] by Buddhist nationalists and communists'. Three months later, al-Libi was claiming 'China is working to destroy the Muslim identity and culture of ethnic Uighurs in Xinjiang and pursuing policies to 'sever the link between the people and their history'. Chris Zambelis, 'Uighur Dissent and Militancy in China's Xinjiang Province', *CTC Sentinel*, vol. 3, no. 1, January 2010. James Rupert, 'Al-Qaeda vows holy war on China over Uighurs' plight, *Bloomberg*, October 8, 2009.

14. Bin Laden carefully clarified that 'the majority of those states have signed the Kyoto Protocol and agreed to curb the emission of harmful gases', except, under President George Bush, the United States. David Usborne, 'Bin Laden goes green to exploit Pakistan flood aid frustration', *Independent*, October 2,

2010. 'Bin Laden criticizes Pakistan relief, urges climate action', Reuters, October 1, 2010.

15. See the author's chapter in John Esposito, ed., *Oxford Handbook of Islam and Politics*, Harvard University Press, to be published end 2011.

16. Ibid. Author telephone interview with Sidney Jones, April 2010. The even more localized 'al-Qaeda in Aceh' disappeared too. In the Philippines too the Abu Sayyaf Group, which had also been drawn tangentially into the broader al-Qaeda network in the late 1990s, moved sharply away from international involvement and, emasculated by a relatively successful American-supported counter-insurgency campaign, returned to kidnapping and banditry. Deep problems remained, with ethnic and religious resentment of the central government still deep, but the threat from a once potent militant group was residual. 'Peace in our time, maybe', *The Economist*, August 9, 2008. Zachary Abuza, 'The Philippines Chips Away at the Abu Sayyaf Group's strength', *CTC Sentinel*, vol. 3, no. 4, April 2010. See also Eliza Griswold, *The Tenth Parallel*, Allen Lane, 2010.

17. As Nir Rosen, the journalist and analyst, points out, a major motivation for al-Shabab declaring al-Qaeda allegiance was attracting funding from al-Qaeda's Arab donors, in the same way that al-Qaeda's local enemies use the discourse of counter-terrorism to win backing from the West. Nir Rosen, 'Somalia's al-Shabab, a global or local movement?' *Time*, August 20, 2010.

18. Author interviews with British and American officials, Delhi, September and November, 2010.

19. Lorraine Adams with Ayesha Nasir, 'Inside the mind of the Times Square bomber', *Observer*, September 19, 2010.

20. Vikram Dodd, 'Roshonara Choudhry jailed for life over MP attack', *Guardian*, November 3, 2010.

21. Richard Esposito and Pierre Thomas, 'Terror attacks against US at all-time high', ABC News, May 26, 2010.

22. Michael Leiter, Director of National Counterterrorism Center, 'Statement for Record, Senate Homeland Security and Government Affairs Committee, Nine Years after 9/11: Confronting the Terrorist Threat to the Homeland', September 22, 2010.

23. Andrea Elliott, 'The jihadist next door', *New York Times*, June 22, 2010. Frank Cilluffo, Jeffrey Cozens and Magnus Ranstorp, 'Foreign Fighters: Trends, Trajectories and Conflict Zones', Homeland Security Policy Institute, George Washington University, 2010, p. 24. Leiter, *Statement*.

24. Paul Lewis, '"Christmas terror plot" suspects are remanded in custody', *Guardian*, December 27, 2010.

25. Complex suicide attacks were recorded at roughly two per month, higher than the average of one complex attack per month during 2009. UNAMA, *Report of the Secretary-General Pursuant to Paragraph 40 of Resolution 1917 (2010)(S/2010/318)*, June 2010.

26. UNAMA, *The Situation in Afghanistan and Its Implications for International Peace and Security*, (S/2010/463), September 2010.

27. See UNAMA, *Mid Year Report on Protection of Civilians in Armed Conflict 2010*, Kabul, August 2010. UNAMA, *Afghan Civilian Casualties Rise 31 Per Cent in First Six Months of* 2010, August 10, 2010. In a new grim twist these now included public executions of children.

28. Laheya and 2011 Spring Offensive statement, author collection. Author interview with US military intelligence officer, Kabul, May 2011.

29. US Department of Defense, *Report on Progress Toward Security and Stability in Afghanistan*, November 2010, pp. 7–8. 'ISAF and Afghan National Security Forces gradually are pushing insurgents to the edges of secured population areas in a number of important locations … Progress across the country remains uneven, with modest gains in security, governance, and development in operational priority areas.'

29. Yaroslav Trofimov, 'U.N. maps show Afghan security worsens', *Wall Street Journal*, December 26, 2010.

30. Multiple author interviews with US, Afghan and British officials and military officers, Kabul, May 2011.

31. Author interviews, Srinagar, Delhi, April, June 2010. By late spring 2010, there was even evidence of increased infiltration of militants into Kashmir, Indian security officials claimed.

32. Asra Nomani and Barbara Feinman Todd, 'Land of the Scot-free', *Newsweek*, February 7, 2011.

33. Carlotta Gall, 'Pakistan faces a divide of age on Muslim law', *New York Times*, January 11, 2011. Aatish Taseer, 'The killer of my father, Salman Taseer, was showered with rose petals by fanatics. How could they do this?', *Daily Telegraph*, January 11, 2011. 'Has Pakistan passed the tipping point of religious extremism?', BBC News Online, January 7, 2011. Eventually some political leaders did move to condemn the killing. The Punjab Assembly, including religious parties sitting, unanimously passed a resolution against the murder, praising the late governor's political and social achievements. Hussain Kashif, 'PA passes resolution condemning Taseer's assassination', *Daily Times*, January 11, 2011.

35. According to Iraq Body Count, the UK-based organization.

36. 'Total 2010 Iraq death toll tops 2009: government', AFP, January 1, 2011.

37. Aaron C. Davis, 'Sadr foments resistance by Iraqis', *New York Times*, January 9, 2011.

38. Interview, Baghdad, November 2010.

39. Thomas Friedman, 'The things we do for oil', *International Herald Tribune*, February 23, 2011.

40. Tom Coghlan, 'Afghans accuse Defence Secretary Liam Fox of racism and disrespect', *The Times*, May 24, 2010.

41. The parliamentary election in November and December saw the ruling National Democratic Party take nearly 95 per cent of the 221 seats available

in the first round. A second round took place amid clumsy fraud and without the participation of the Muslim Brotherhood, the main opposition, and indicated clearly that Mubarak, eighty-two, had no intention of relinquishing power other than, perhaps, passing it to his carefully groomed son Gamal

42. 'Building a new Libya', *The Economist*, February 26, 2011.

43. Andrew Lebovich, 'Afghan perspectives on democracy', *Foreign Policy*, February 9, 2011, citing research by the Afghanistan Research and Evaluation Unit from 2008.

44. The same was true in Algeria. Since 2001, President Abdelaziz Bouteflika had been embraced as a partner in the Global War on Terror by Washington.

45. Only 6 per cent less than in Indonesia and 17 per cent more than in Pakistan. Pew Research Center, *Democracy and Islam*, January 31, 2011.

46. Dan Murphy, 'Egypt revolution unfinished, Qaradawi tells Tahrir masses', *Christian Science Monitor*, February 18, 2011.

47. Bobby Ghosh, 'Rage, rap, and revolution', *Time*, February 28, 2011.

48. 'Al-Qaeda message on Egypt, belatedly', MSNBC, February 18, 2011.

49. See Memorandum for Commander, US Southern Command, CSRT Input for Guantanamo Detainee, US9SA-000063DP, Muhammad Mani Ahmad Al Shalan Al Qahtani, October 30, 2008, secret, author collection. Michael Isikoff, 'How profile of bin Laden courier led CIA to its target', NBC News, May 5, 2011; Mark Mazzetti, Helene Cooper and Peter Baker, 'Clues gradually led to the location of Qaeda chief', *New York Times*, May 2, 2011.

50. Remarks by the President on Osama bin Laden, May 2, 2011, Office of the Press Secretary, White House.

51. Author telephone interview with senior ISI official, May 2011.

52. Sebastian Rotella, 'New details in the bin Laden documents: portrait of a fugitive micro-manager', *Propublica*, May 12, 2011.

53. Author telephone interview with officials in New York, Pakistan, May 2011. Author interviews, US and British officials, Kabul, May 2011.

54. Mark Mazzetti, 'Signs that bin Laden weighed seeking Pakistani protection', *New York Times*, May 26, 2011.

55. Author interviews with American and British intelligence officials, Kabul, June 2011.

56. Ibid.

57. Ibid.

58. Quilliam Foundation, *The Coming Struggle within al-Qaeda*, London, 10 May 2011.

## CONCLUSION: THE 9/11 WARS

1. By 2010, support for suicide bombing in many countries of the Islamic world, after declining so dramatically in the middle years of the decade, began to

edge up again. Often the change was slight. In Egypt it went from 13 per cent believing suicide bombing was sometimes or often justified in 2008 to 15 per cent in 2009 and then to 20 per cent in 2010. In Pakistan, the levels went from 5 to 8 per cent, still a fraction of the 33 per cent recorded in 2003. In Jordan it went from 12 to 20 per cent between 2009 and 2010. In 2005, it had been 57 per cent. Pew Global Attitudes Key Indicators Database, accessed January 2, 2011.

2. Measured in the number of attacks, the volume of terrorism in the 1970s was far higher than between September 12, 2001 and the end of 2009, with between 60 and 70 strikes per year. Between 1970 and 1978, 72 people died in terrorist incidents in the US. Rand Corporation (Brian Michael Jenkins), *Would-be Warriors*, 2010, pp. 8–9.

3. Steve Luxenberg, 'Bob Woodward book details Obama battles with advisers over exit plan for Afghan war', *Washington Post*, September 22, 2010.

4. Elisabeth Bumiller, 'The staggering cost of American conflicts', *International Herald Tribune*, July 26, 2010. The Stockholm International Peace Research Institute Military Expenditure Database, http://milexdata.sipri.org/result.php4, accessed April 2011.

5. In 2011, for the second consecutive year, President Obama made no reference to bin Laden in his State of the Union address.

6. Walter Laqueur, *Terrorism*, Little, Brown, 1977.

7. National Intelligence Council, *Global Trends 2025: A Transformed World*, November 2008.

8. National Intelligence Council, *Mapping the Global Future, Report of the National Intelligence Council's 2020 Project*, December 2004.

9. Such as the five American servicemen prosecuted late 2010 for premeditated murders of Afghan civilians.

10. icasualties.org, accessed October 9, 2010.

11. 'Names of the dead', *New York Times*, October 8, 2010. Congressional Research Service (Susan G. Cheeser), *Afghanistan Casualties, Miltiary Forces and Civilians*, October 28, 2010, p. 2. Department of Defense statistics, accessed November 19, 2010.

12. In Iraq at least 468 have been killed, according to icasualties.org, accessed December 2010. Some estimates are three or four times this total. See Steve Fainaru, *Big Boys' Rules: America's Mercenaries Fighting in Iraq*, Da Capo Press, 2008.

13. Congressional Research Service, *Iraqi Casualties: US Military Forces and Iraqi Civilians, Police and Security Forces*, October 7, 2010, p. 9. Report to Congress, *Measuring Security and Stability in Iraq*, June 2010, p. 29. This total includes 2,700 previously unreported deaths of Iraqi police and other Iraqi security forces killed after capture revealed by WikiLeaks and calculated by Iraq Body Count. More than 600 died in 2010, considerably more than in 2009, even if both totals paled into insignificance compared with the

2,065 who had died in 2007, the year of the Surge. 'Death for Iraqis jumps', *Beyond Babylon*, Latimes.com, July 2007.

14. Brookings Institution, *Afghanistan Index: Tracing Variables of Reconstruction and Security in post 9/11 Afghanistan*, October 19, 2010, p. 14.

15. Around 500 died in 2010. See the series of reports by the Pakistan Institute of Peace Studies.

16. Conetta, 'The Wages of War', p. 23.

17. Press release, Inter Services Public Relations, ISPR, February 18, 2010. Author telephone interviews, ISPR, November 2010.

18. David Leigh, 'Iraq war logs reveal 15,000 previously unlisted civilian deaths', *Guardian*, October 22, 2010. The logs put insurgent fatalities at 23,984. See PIPS Pakistan Security Report (October 2010), November 10, 2010, and others.

19. Combating Terrorism Center, *Deadly Vanguards: A Study of al'Qa'ida's Violence against Muslims*, December 2009, p. 7.

20. 'Iraq war logs: What the numbers reveal', October 23, 2010. http://www.iraqbodycount.org/analysis/numbers/warlogs/.

21. 'Iraq: Key figures since the war began', Associated Press, January 2, 2009.

22. Project on Defense Alternatives (Carl Conetta), *Operation Enduring Freedom: Why a Higher Rate of Civilian Bombing Casualties*, January 18, 2002. Project on Defense Alternatives (Carl Conetta), *Strange Victory: A Critical Appraisal of Operation Enduring Freedom and the Afghanistan War*, January 30, 2002. Afghan casualties database, http://www.guardian.co.uk/news/datablog/2010/aug/10/afghanistan-civilian-casualties-statistics#data.

23. 'Global war on terror claims 30,000 Pakistani casualties', ISPR release, Islamabad, *The Economic Time*s, February 19, 2010. According to the South Asia Terrorism Portal, 9,230 civilians were killed as a result of the insurgency from 2003 to December 5, 2010.

24. There are an estimated 2 million Iraqis who have left their homeland. Around 5 million refugees returned to Afghanistan after the fall of the Taliban, but at least 2 million are now thought to have left, and the country now has an estimated 240,000 internally displaced. Figures from the International Displacement Monitoring Centre at www.internal-displacement.org based on data from the UNHCR, June 2010.

25. Author interview, Dunkirk, December 2009.

# Select Bibliography

To keep this bibliography manageable, except for a handful of extremely useful texts, only works containing material referenced directly over preceding pages have been included. Several books exist in multiple translations. Again to save space, only the edition consulted has been listed.

## BOOKS

Sohail Abbas, *Probing the Jihadi Mindset*, National Book Foundation, Islamabad, 2007.

Said Aburish, *Saddam Hussein: The Politics of Revenge*, Bloomsbury, 2000.

Zachary Abuza, *Militant Islam in Southeast Asia, Crucible of Terror*, Lynne Reiner, 2003.

Khalid Ahmed, 'Fundamental Flaws', in *On the Abyss*, HarperCollins (India), 2000.

M. J. Akbar, *The Shade of Swords: Jihad and the Conflict Between Islam and Christianity*, Routledge, 2002.

    *Tinderbox: The Past and Future of Pakistan*, HarperCollins (India), 2010.

Ali Allawi, *The Occupation of Iraq: Winning the War, Losing the Peace*, Yale University Press, 2008.

Charles Allen, *God's Terrorists: The Wahhabi Cult and the Hidden Roots of Modern Jihad*, Little, Brown, 2006.

John Lee Anderson, *The Lion's Grave*, Atlantic Books, 2002.

Arthur Arberry (trans.), *The Quran*, Oxford University Press, 1964; first publ. Allen and Unwin, 1955.

Karen Armstrong, Holy War: *The Crusades and Their Impact on Today's World*, Macmillan, 1998.

    *Islam: A Short History*, Phoenix; 2001.

    *Mohammed: Prophet for Our Time*, Harper Perennial, 2007.

Reza Aslam, *How to Win a Cosmic War: God, Globalization, and the End of the War on Terror*, Random House, 2009.

Scott Atran, *Talking to the Enemy, Faith, Brotherhood and the (Un)making of Terrorists*, HarperCollins, 2010.

Florence Aubenas, *Grand Reporter: petite conférence sur le journalisme*, Bayard, Paris, 2009.

Mukulika Banerjee, *The Pathan Unarmed: Opposition and Memory in the Northwest Frontier*, Oxford University Press (India), 2001.

Thomas Barfield, *Afghanistan: A Political and Cultural History*, Princeton University Press, 2010.

Bruce Bawer, *While Europe Slept*, Doubleday, 2006.

Mourad Benchellali, *Voyage vers l'enfer*, Robert Laffont, 2006.

Daniel Benjamin and Steven Simon, *Age of Sacred Terror: Radical Islam's War against America*, Random House, 2002.

Owen Bennett-Jones, *Pakistan: Eye of the Storm*, 3rd edn, Yale University Press, 2003.

Peter Bergen, *The Osama Bin Laden I Know: An Oral History of Al-Qaeda's Leader*, Simon & Schuster, 2006.

> *Holy War Inc.: Inside the Secret World of Osama bin Laden*, Touchstone, 2002.

> *The Longest War: The Enduring Conflict Between America and al'Qaeda*, Simon and Schuster, 2011.

Gary Berntsen, *Jawbreaker: The Attack on Bin Laden and Al Qaeda*, Crown, 2005.

Benazir Bhutto, *Reconciliation: Islam, Democracy and the West*, Harper, 2008.

John R. Bradley, *Inside Egypt*, Palgrave Macmillan, 2008.

Rodric Braithwaite, *Afgansty: The Russians in Afghanistan 1979–1989*, Profile, 2011.

Paul Bremer, *My Year in Iraq: The Struggle to Build a Future of Hope*, Simon and Schuster, 2006.

Robert K. Brigham, *Iraq, Vietnam and the Limits of American Power*, PublicAffairs, 2008.

Martin Bright, *When Progressives Treat with Reactionaries*, Policy Exchange, 2006.

Jean-Charles Brisard, *Zarqawi: The New Face of Al-Qaeda*, Policy Press, 2005.

Jason Burke, *Al-Qaeda: The True Story of Radical Islam*, Penguin, 2003.

*The Road to Kandahar: Travels through Conflict in the Islamic World*, Penguin, 2006.

Ian Buruma, *Murder in Amsterdam, The Death of Theo Van Gogh and the Limits of Tolerance*, Atlantic Books, London, 2006.

Ian Buruma and Avishai Margalit, *Occidentalism: The West in the Eyes of Its Enemies*, Penguin Press, 2004.

George W. Bush, *Decision Points*, Virgin, 2010.

Christopher Caldwell, *Reflections on the Revolution in Europe*, Allen Lane, 2009.

Alistair Campbell, *The Blair Years*, Hutchinson, 2007.

Rajiv Chandreshekan, *Imperial Life in the Emerald City: Inside Iraq's Green Zone*, Knopf, 2006.

Sarah Chayes, *The Punishment of Virtue: Walking the Frontline of the War on Terror with a Woman Who Has Made It Her Home*, Portobello Books, 2007.

Pierre-Arnaud Chouvy, *Opium: Uncovering the Politics of the Poppy*, I. B. Tauris, 2009.

Richard Clarke, *Against All Enemies*, Simon and Schuster, 2004.

Alexander and Patrick Cockburn, *Out of the Ashes: The Resurrection of Saddam Hussein*, Harper Perennial, 2000.

Patrick Cockburn, *Muqtada al-Sadr and the Fall of Iraq*, Faber and Faber, 2008.
*Muqtada al-Sadr, the Shia Revival and the Struggle for Iraq*, Simon and Schuster, 2008.

*The Occupation: War and Resistance in Iraq*, Verso, London 2006.

Stephen Cohen, *The Idea of Pakistan*, Brookings, 2005.

Stephen Coll, *Ghost Wars: The Secret History of the CIA, Afghanistan, and Bin Laden, from the Soviet Invasion to September 10, 2001*, Penguin, 2005.

Rik Coolsaet, ed., *Jihadi Terrorism and the Radicalisation Challenge in Europe*, Ashgate, 2008.

Gordon Corera, *Shopping for Bombs: Nuclear Proliferation, Global Insecurity and the Rise and Fall of the AQ Khan Network*, Oxford University Press, 2006.

Robert D. Crews and Amin Tarzi, eds. *The Taliban and the Crisis of Afghanistan*, Harvard University Press, 2008.

William Dalrymple, *The Last Mughal: The Fall of a Dynasty, Delhi, 1857*, Bloomsbury, 2009.

Mark Danner, *Torture and Truth: America, Abu Ghraib and the War on Terrorism*, The New York Review of Books, 2004.

James F. Dobbins, *After the Taliban*, Potomac Books, 2008.

Toby Dodge, *Inventing Iraq: The Failure of Nation Building and a History Denied*, Columbia University Press, 2003.

John Esposito and Dalia Mogahed, *Who Speaks for Islam? What a Billion Muslims Really Think*, Gallup Press, 2007.

Martin Evans and John Phillips, *Algeria: Anger of the Dispossessed*, Yale University Press, 2008.

Steve Fainaru, *Big Boys' Rules: America's Mercenaries Fighting in Iraq*, Da Capo Press, 2008.

Oriana Fallacci, *The Rage and the Pride*, English edition, Rizzoli, 2002.

Mamoun Fandy, *Saudi Arabia and the Politics of Dissent*, Palgrave Macmillan, 2001.

Howard M. Federspiel, *Islam and Ideology in the Emerging Indonesian State: The Persatuan Islam 1923 to 1957*, Brill, 2001.

Douglas Feith, *War and Decision*, Harper, 2008.

James Fergusson, *A Million Bullets: The Real Story of the British Army in Afghanistan*, Transworld, 2008.

Orlando Figes, *Crimea: The Last Crusade*, Allen Lane, 2010.

Jean-Pierre Filiu, *L'Apocalypse dans l'Islam*, Fayard, 2008.

   *Les Frontières du jihad*, Fayard, 2006.

   *Les Neuf vies d'Al-Qaïda*, Fayard, 2009.

Dexter Filkins, *The Forever War: Dispatches From the War on Terror*, Vintage, 2009.

Alain Finkielkraut, *Qu'est-ce que la France?* Stock, 2007.

Conor Foley, *The Thin Blue Line: How Humanitarianism Went to War*, Verso, 2008.

Gregory Fontenot, E. J. Degen and David Tohn, *On Point: The United States Army in Operation Iraqi Freedom*, Combat Studies Institute Press, 2004.

Lawrence Freedman, *A Choice of Enemies: America Confronts the Middle East*, Weidenfeld and Nicolson, 2009.

Dalton Fury, *Kill Bin Laden: A Delta Force Commander's Account of the Hunt for the World's Most Wanted Man*, St Martin's Press, 2008.

David Galula, *Counter-insurgency Warfare: Theory and Practice*, Frederick Praeger, 2006.

Diego Gambetta, ed., *Making Sense of Suicide Missions*, Oxford University Press, 2005.

David Gardner, *Last Chance: The Middle East in the Balance*, I. B. Tauris, 2009.

Fawaz Gerges, *The Far Enemy: Why Jihad Went Global*, Cambridge University Press, 2005.

Antonio Giustozzi, ed., *Decoding the New Taliban, Insights from the Afghan Field*, Hurst, 2009.

   *Empires of Mud: Wars and Warlords in Afghanistan*, Hurst, 2009.

   *Kalashnikov, Koran and Laptop: The Neo-Taliban Insurgency in Afghanistan 2002–2007*, Hurst, 2007.

Bernard Godard and Sylvie Taussig, *Les Musulmans en France*, Editions Robert Laffont, 2007.

Jos L. Gommans, *The Rise of the Indo-Afghan Empire c.1710–1780*, Brill, 1995.

Philip Gourevitch and Errol Morris, *Standard Operating Procedure*, Picador, 2009.

Stephen Grey, *Ghost Plane: The Untold Story of the CIA's Secret Rendition Programme*, C. Hurst & Co, 2006.

   *Operation Snakebite: The Explosive True Story of an Afghan Desert Siege*, Penguin, 2010.

Eliza Griswold, *The Tenth Parallel: Dispatches from the Faultline Between Christianity and Islam*, Allen Lane, 2010.

Imtiaz Gul, *The Most Dangerous Place: Pakistan's Lawless Frontier*, Penguin, 2010.

Rohan Gunaratna, *Inside Al Qae'da*, Hurst, 2002.

Dipak Gupta, *Understanding Terrorism and Political Violence*, Routledge, 2008.

Ron Gutman, *How We Missed the Story: Osama Bin Laden, the Taliban and the Hijacking of Afghanistan*, United States Institute of Peace Press, 2008.

Mary Habeck, *Knowing the Enemy*, Yale, 2006.

Fred Halliday, 'Global Jihad, "Long War" and the Crisis of American Power', in Fabio Petito and Elisabetta Brighi, eds., *Il Mediterraneo nelle Relazioni Internazionale: tra Euro-Mediterraneo e Grande Medio Oriente*, Fondazione Laboratorio Mediterraneo, 2007.

> *100 Myths about the Middle East*, Saqi Books, 2005.
>
> *Two Hours that Shook the World*, Saqi Books, 2002.

David Hicks, *Guantanamo: My Journey*, William Heinemann, 2010.

Sana Haroon, *Frontier of Faith: Islam in the Indo-Afghan Borderland*, Hurst, 2007.

Thomas Hegghammer, *Jihad in Saudi Arabia: Violence and Pan-Islamism Since 1979*, Cambridge University Press, 2010.

Patrick Hennessey, *The Junior Officers' Reading Club*, Allen Lane, 2009.

Carole Hillenbrand, *The Crusades: Islamic Perspectives*, Edinburgh University Press, 1999.

Dilip Hiro, *Inside Central Asia*, Overlook Duckworth, 2009.

Bruce Hoffman, *Inside Terrorism*, 2nd rev. edn, Columbia University Press, 2006.

James F. Hoge Jr and Gideon Rose eds., *How Did This Happen? Terrorism and the New War*, PublicAffairs, 2001.

Ed Husain, *The Islamist: Why I Joined Radical Islam in Britain, What I Saw Inside and Why I Left*, 2007.

Zahid Hussain, *Frontline Pakistan*, Columbia University Press, 2007.

Faleh A. Jabar, *The Shi'ite Movement in Iraq*, Saqi Books, 2003.

Christophe Jaffrelot and Laurent Gayer, eds., *Armed Militias of South Asia*, Hurst, 2009.

Lawrence James, *Warrior Race: A History of the British at War*, Little, Brown, 2001.

Seth Jones, *In the Graveyard of Empires: America's War in Afghanistan*, Norton, 2009.

Kimberly Kagan, *The Surge: A Military History*, Encounter Books, 2008.

John Kampfner, *Blair's Wars*, The Free Press, 2003.

Robert D. Kaplan, *Soldiers of God: With Islamic Warriors in Afghanistan and Pakistan*, Vintage, 2008.

Hamid Karzai, *Letter from Kabul*, Wiley, 2006.

George Kassimeris, ed., *Playing Politics with Terrorism*, Hurst, 2007.

Gilles Kepel, *Al-Qaida dans le texte: écrits d'Oussama ben Laden, Abdallah Azzam, Ayman al-Zawahiri et Abou Moussab al-Zarqawi*, PUF, 2008.

> *Fitna: Guerre au cœur de l'Islam*, Paris, Gallimard, 2004,
>
> *Jihad: The Trail of Political Islam*, I. B. Tauris, 2002.
>
> *Terreur et martyre: relever le défi de civilisation*, Flammarion, 2008.

Nichola Khan, *Mohajir Militancy in Pakistan. Violence and Transformation in the Karachi Conflict*, Routledge, 2010.

Farhad Khosrokhavar, *L'Islam dans les prisons*, Balland, 2004.

David Kilcullen, *The Accidental Guerrilla: Fighting Small Wars in the Midst of a Big One*, Hurst, 2009.

Robert Lacey, *Saudi Arabia Exposed: Inside a Kingdom in Crisis*, Palgrave Macmillan, 2006.

Hugues Lagrange and Marco Oberti, eds., *Emeutes urbaines et protestations*, Les Presses de Sciences Po, 2006.

Walter Laqueur, *Terrorism*, Little, Brown, 1977.

Jonathan Laurence and Justin Vaisse, *Intégrer l'Islam, la France et ses Musulmans: enjeux et réussites*, Odile Jacob, 2007.

Bruce Lawrence, ed., *Messages to the World: The Statements of Osama Bin Laden*, Verso, 2005.

Robert Leiken, *Europe's Angry Muslims*, Oxford University Press, 2009.

David Levering Lewis, *God's Crucible: Islam and the Making of Europe 570 to 1215*, Norton, 2008.

Bernard Lewis, *The Crisis of Islam: Holy War and Unholy Terror*, Random House, 2004.

    *'What Went Wrong': Western Impact and Middle Eastern Response*, Oxford University Press, 2002.

Brynjar Lia, *Architect of Global Jihad: The Life of Al Qaeda Strategist Abu Mus'ab Al-Suri*, Columbia University Press, 2008.

Anatol Lieven, *Pakistan: A Hard Country*, Allen Lane, 2011.

Amin Maalouf, *The Crusades Through Arab Eyes*, Schocken Books, 1989.

Chris Mackey and Greg Miller, *The Interrogators: Inside the Secret War Against al Qaeda*, Little, Brown, 2004.

Denis MacShane, *Globalising Hatred: The New Anti-Semitism*, Weidenfeld and Nicolson, 2009.

Bill Maley, ed., *Fundamentalism Reborn? Afghanistan and the Taliban*, New York University Press, 1998.

Iftikhar Malik, *Pakistan: Democracy, Terror and the Building of a Nation*, New Holland, 2010.

Kenan Malik, *From Fatwa to Jihad*, Atlantic, 2009.

Salahuddin Malik, *1857: War of Independence or Clash of Civilizations*, Oxford University Press, 2008.

Jane Mayer, *The Dark Side: The Inside Story of How the War on Terror Turned into a War on American Ideals*, Doubleday, 2008.

Rory McCarthy, *'Nobody Told Us We Are Defeated'*, Guardian Books, 2005.

David McDowall, *A Modern History of the Kurds*, I. B. Tauris, 2004.

Barbara Daly Metcalf, *Islamic Revival in British India: Deoband, 1860–1900*, Oxford University Press, 2004.

William Milam, *Bangladesh and Pakistan*, Hurst, 2010.

Beverley Milton-Edwards and Stephen Farrell, *Hamas*, Polity Press, 2010.

Amir Mir, *The Bhutto Murder Trail: From Waziristan to GHQ*, Tranquebar, 2010.

Pankaj Mishra, *Temptations of the West*, Picador, 2006.

Laurent Mucchielli, *Quand les banlieues brûlent . . .* , La Découverte, 2007.

Pervez Musharaf, *In the Line of Fire*, Free Press, 2006.

Abu Bakr Naji, *Management of Savagery: The Most Critical Stage Through Which the Ummah Will Pass*, trans. William McCants, Olin Institute for Strategic Studies, Harvard University, 2006.

Loretta Napoleoni, *Insurgent Iraq: Al Zarqawi and the New Generation*, Seven Stories, 2005.

Vali Nasr, *The Shia Revival: How Conflicts within Islam Will Shape the Future*, W. W. Norton, 2007.

Shuja Nawaz, *Crossed Swords*, Oxford University Press, 2008.

Ronald Neumann, *The Other War: Winning and Losing in Afghanistan*, Potomac Books, 2009.

Linda Nochlin, *The Politics of Vision: Essays on Nineteenth-century Art and Society*, Westview Press, 1991.

Vincenzo Oliveti, *Terror's Source*, Amadeus Books, 2002.

George Packer, *The Assassins' Gate: America in Iraq*, Farrar, Straus and Giroux, 2006.

Alison Pargeter, *The Muslim Brotherhood: The Burden of Tradition*, Saqi, 2010.
    *The New Frontiers of Jihad: Radical Islam in Europe*, I. B. Tauris, 2008.

Nicolas Pelham, *A New Muslim Order: The Shia and the Middle East Sectarian Crisis*, I. B. Tauris, 2008.

Gretchen Peters, *Seeds of Terror: How Heroin is Bankrolling the Taliban and Al Qaeda*, Oneworld, 2009.

Melanie Phillips, *Londonistan*, Encounter Books, 2006.

Norman Podhoretz, *World War IV: The Long Struggle against Islamofascism*, Doubleday, 2007.

Patrick Porter, *Military Orientalism: Eastern War through Western Eyes*, Hurst, 2007.

Madawi al-Rasheed, *A History of Saudi Arabia*, Cambridge University Press, 2002.

Ahmed Rashid, *Descent into Chaos: How the War against Islamic Extremism Is Being Lost in Pakistan, Afghanistan and Central Asia*, Allen Lane, 2008.
    *Taliban: The Power of Militant Islam in Afghanistan and Beyond*, I. B. Tauris, 2010.

Thomas Ricks, *Fiasco: The American Military Adventure in Iraq, 2003 to 2005*, Penguin, 2007.
    *The Gamble: General David Petraeus and the American Military Adventure in Iraq, 2006–2008*, Penguin, 2009.

Bruce Riedel, *The Search for Al Qaeda: Its Leadership, Ideology, and Future*, Brookings Institute, 2010.

Linda Robinson, *Masters of Chaos: The Secret History of the Special Forces*, PublicAffairs, 2005.

    *Tell Me How This Ends: General David Petraeus and the Search for a Way Out of Iraq*, PublicAffairs, September 2008.

Nir Rosen, *Aftermath: Following the Bloodshed of America's Wars in the Muslim World*, Nation Books, 2009.

J. H. Roy and J. Deviosse, *La Bataille de Poitiers*, Octobre 733, Gallimard, 1966

Olivier Roy, *Globalized Islam: The Search for a New Ummah*, Columbia; 2004.

    *The Failure of Political Islam*, Harvard University Press, 1998.

    *Islam and Resistance in Afghanistan*, Cambridge University Press, 1990.

    *Politics and Chaos in the Middle East*, Columbia, 2008.

Barnett R. Rubin, *The Fragmentation of Afghanistan*, Yale University Press, 2002.

Bruce K. Rutherford, *Egypt after Mubarak*, Princeton University Press, 2008.

Malise Ruthven, *Fundamentalism: The Search For Meaning*, Oxford University Press, 2004.

    *A Fury For God: The Islamist Attack on America*, rev. edn, Granta, 2004.

David Sanger, *The Inheritance: The World Obama Confronts and the Challenges to American Power*, Crown, 2009.

Marc Sageman, *Leaderless Jihad*, University of Pennsylvania Press, 2008.

    *Understanding Terror Networks*, University of Pennsylvania Press, 2004.

Nizar Sassi, *Prisonnier 325, Camp Delta : De Vénissieux à Guantanamo*, Editions Denoël, 2006.

Victoria Schofield, *Afghan Frontier: At the Crossroads of Conflict*, I. B. Tauris, 2010.

    *Kashmir in Conflict: India, Pakistan and the Undending War*, I. B. Tauris, 2010.

Gary Schroen, *First In: An Insider's Account of How the CIA Spearheaded the War on Terror in Afghanistan*, Ballantine Books, 2005.

Vanessa R. Schwartz and Jeannene M. Przyblyski, eds., *The Nineteenth-century Visual Culture Reader*, Routledge, 2004.

Farzana Shaikh, *Making Sense of Pakistan*, Hurst, 2010.

Ayesha Siddiqa, *Military Inc.*, Oxford University Press (Pakistan), 2007.

Philip Smucker, *Al Qaeda's Great Escape*, Potomac Books, 2004.

Devin Springer, James Regens, David Edger, *Islamic Radicalism and Global Jihad*, Georgetown University Press, 2008.

Jean-Marc Stébé, *La Crise des banlieues*, PUF, 2007.

Jessica Stern, *Terror in the Name of God*, Harper Perennial, 2004.

Rory Stewart, *Occupational Hazards: My Time Governing in Iraq*, Picador, 2007.

    *The Places in Between*, Picador, 2005.

Hilary Synnott, *Bad Days in Basra*, I. B. Tauris, 2008.

See Seng Tan, Kumar Ramakrishna, eds., *After Bali: The Threat of Terrorism in Southeast Asia*, Institute of Defence and Strategic Studies, Singapore, 2003.

Stephen Tanner, *Afghanistan: A Military History*, Da Capo, 2007.

Camille Tawil, *Brothers in Arms*, Telegram, 2010.

George Tenet, *At the Center of the Storm: My Years at the CIA*, HarperCollins, 2007.

Charles Tripp, *A History of Iraq*, Cambridge University Press, 2007.

Yaroslav Trofimov, *The Siege of Mecca: The 1979 Uprising at Islam's Holiest Shrine*, Doubleday, 2007.

Patrick Tyler, *A World of Trouble: America and the Middle East*, Portobello Books, 2009.

*United States Special Operations Command History*, 6th edn, 2008.

Mark Urban, *Task Force Black*, Little, Brown, 2010.

Bing West, *No True Glory: A Frontline Account of the Battle for Fallujah*, 2005.
 *The Strongest Tribe*, Random House, 2009.

Andrew Wheatcroft, *The Infidels: The Conflict Between Christendom and Islam 638–2002*, Viking, 2003.

Joshua T. White, *Pakistan's Islamist Frontier: Islamic Politics and U.S. Policy in Pakistan's North-West Frontier*, Center on Faith and International Affairs, 2008.

Quintan Wiktorowicz, *Radical Islam Rising. Muslim Extremism in the West*, Rowman and Littlefield, 2005.

Robert Wistrich, *A Lethal Obsession: Anti-Semitism from Antiquity to the Global Jihad*, Random House, 2010.

Bob Woodward, *Bush at War*, Simon and Schuster, 2003.
 *Obama's Wars*, Simon and Schuster, 2010.
 *Plan of Attack*, Simon and Schuster, 2008.

Andy Worthington, *The Guantanamo Files: The Stories of the 774 Detainees in America's Illegal Prison*, Pluto, 2007.

Lawrence Wright, *The Looming Tower*, Allen Lane, 2006.

Bat Ye'or, *Eurabia: The Euro-Arab Axis*, Fairleigh Dickinson University Press, 2005.

Mohammad Yousaf and Mark Adkin, *The Bear Trap: The Defeat of a Superpower*, Casemate, 2001.

Abdul Salam Zaeef, *My Life with the Taliban*, Hurst, 2010.

Ahmad Muaffaq Zaidan, *The 'Afghan Arabs': Media at Jihad*, PFI Islamabad, 1999.

Montasser al-Zayyat, *The Road to al-Qaeda*, Pluto Press, 2003.

Malika Zeghal, *Les Islamistes marocains: le défi à la monarchie*, La Découverte, 2005.

Lawrence Ziring, *Pakistan in the Twentieth Century: A Political History*, Oxford University Press, 1997.

David Zuccino, *Thunder Run: The Armored Strike to Capture Baghdad*, Atlantic Monthly Press, 2004.

## OFFICIAL DOCUMENTS

### UK

*The Aitken Report, An Investigation into Cases of Deliberate Abuse and Unlawful Killing in Iraq in 2003 and 2004*, Crown Publishers, January 25, 2008.

British High Commission, Islamabad, Pakistan, *Scotland Yard Report Into Assassination of Benazir Bhutto*, February 8, 2008.

Department for International Development (Dr Emma Hooper, Agha Imran Hamid), *Scoping Study on Social Exclusion in Pakistan: A Summary of Findings*, October 2003.

(Sarah Ladbury), *Testing Hypotheses on Radicalisation in Afghanistan*, August 14, 2009.

*Final Report of the Communities and Local Government Select Committee Inquiry into Preventing Violent Extremism*, HMSO, March 30, 2010.

Greater London Authority's Data Management and Analysis Group (Laura Spence), *A Profile of Londoners by Country of Birth: Estimates from the 2006 Annual Population Survey*, February 2008.

Home Affairs Committee, *Project CONTEST: The Government's Counterterrorism Strategy: Ninth Report of Session 2008–09*, July 7, 2009.

Home Office, *Report of the Official Account of the Bombings in London on 7th July 2005*, May 11, 2006.

Parliamentary Intelligence Security Committee, *Report into the London Terrorist Attacks on 7 July 2005*, HMSO, May 2006.

### USA

Central Intelligence Agency, *Comprehensive Report of the Special Advisor to the Director of Central Intelligence on Iraq's WMD, Charles Duelfer*, September 30, 2004.

Congressional Record, *Proceedings and Debates of the 109th Session of Congress*, vol. 151, part 10.

Congressional Research Service (Susan G. Cheeser), *Afghanistan Casualties: Military Forces and Civilians*, October 28, 2010.

(Hannah Fischer), *Iraqi Casualties: US Military Forces and Iraqi Civilians, Police and Security Forces*, October 7, 2010.

(Kenneth Katzman), *Report for Congress: Al'Qaeda in Iraq: Assessment and Outside Links*, updated August 15, 2008.

*Report for Congress: Operation Enduring Freedom: Foreign Pledges of Military and Intelligence Support*, October 17, 2001.

*Report for Congress, Iraq: Elections, Government, and Constitution*, November 20, 2006.

(Amy Belasco), *Report for Congress: Troop Levels in the Afghan and Iraq Wars, FY2001–FY2012: Cost and Other Potential Issues*, July 2, 2009.

Department of State cable, 'Afghanistan: Pakistanis to regulate wheat and fuel trade to gain leverage over Taliban', August 13 1997, National Security Archive.

Department of State memo, 'Taliban under pressure', Assistant Secretary of State for South Asian Affairs Karl F. Inderfurth to Secretary of State Madeleine Albright, May 1, 2000, confidential, declassified 2009.

Department of State public notice 4936, 'Foreign Terrorists and Terrorist Organizations; Designation: Organization in the Land of the Two Rivers', *Federal Register*: vol. 69, no. 242, December 17, 2004.

Foreign Broadcast Information Service, *Compilation of Usama Bin Laden's Statements 1994 to 2004*, 2004.

Institute for Defense Analyses, *Iraqi Perspective Project: Saddam and Terrorism*, March 20, 2008.

National Intelligence Council, *Global Trends 2025: A Transformed World*, November 2008.

    *Mapping the Global Future: Report of the National Intelligence Council's 2020 Project*, December 2004.

National Security Council, *National Strategy for Victory in Iraq*, November 2005.

*The National Security Strategy of the United States of America*, White House, September 2002.

New York Police Department, *Intelligence Report: Radicalization in the West*, 2007.

The 9/11 Commission, *Final Report of the National Commission on Terrorist Attacks Upon the United States of America*, W. W. Norton, July 22, 2004.

Report to Congress, *Measuring Security and Stability in Iraq*, June 2010.

*Report of the Commission on the Intelligence Capabilities of the United States Regarding Weapons of Mass Destruction*, March 31, 2005.

Special Inspector General for Iraqi Reconstruction, *Quarterly and Semi Annual Report to Congress*, January 30, 2006.

*Tora Bora Revisited: How We Failed to get Bin Laden and Why It Matters Today; Report to Members of the Committee on Foreign Relations, United States Senate, 111th Congress, First Session*, November 30, 2009.

United States Army, *Full Spectrum Operations: Unified Quest 2007*, A United States Army Training and Doctrine Command (TRADOC) pamphlet, April 22, 2008.

United States Senate Select Committee on Intelligence, *Whether Public Statements Regarding Iraq Were Substantiated by US Government Officials Were Substantiated by Intelligence Information*, June 2008.

US Department of Defense, *Quadrennial Defense Review Report*, February 6, 2006.

*Report on Progress Toward Security and Stability in Afghanistan*, November 2010.

US Department of Justice press release, 'Najibullah Zazi pleads guilty to conspiracy to use explosives against persons or property in US, conspiracy to murder abroad, and providing material support to al'Qaeda', February 22, 2010.

US Embassy Islamabad cable, 'Afghanistan: The Taliban's decision-making process and leadership structure', December 31, 1998, confidential, declassified 2009.

'Bad news on Pak Afghan Policy: GOP support for the Taliban appears to be getting stronger', July 1, 1998, National Security Archives.

US Naval War College, Damien Mason, *Air Strikes and COIN in Operation Enduring Freedom*, Joint Military Operations Department report, May 3, 2010.

US Office of the Inspector General, Oversight and Review Division, *An Investigation of Overtime Payments to FBI and Other Department of Justice Employees Deployed to Iraq and Afghanistan*, December 2008.

White House, National Intelligence Estimate, *Iraq's Continuing Programs of WMD*, October 1, 2002.

press release, 'President discusses Global War on Terrorism, national strategy for combating terrorism', September 5, 2006.

## Europe

Europol, *TE-SAT 2009 – EU Terrorism Situation and Trend Report*, April 2009.
*TE-SAT 2010 – EU Terrorism Situation and Trend Report*, 2010

French Government Centre of Strategic Analysis, Report for the Office of the Prime Minister, *Enquêtes sur les violences urbaines: comprendre les émeutes de Novembre 2005, les exemples de Saint-Denis et de Aulnay-sous-Bois*, Paris, 2006.

Government Bureau of Statistics, *Annual Report on Integration*, The Hague, The Netherlands, December 16, 2008.

National Coordinator for Counterterrorism, *National Terrorist Threat Assessment No. 8*, The Hague, The Netherlands, April 25, 2007.

## Non-governmental Organizations

ACBAR, *Falling Short: Aid Effectiveness in Afghanistan*, March 25, 2008.
Amnesty International, *Secret Detention in CIA 'Black Sites*, November 8, 2005.
Brookings Institution, *Afghanistan Index: Tracing Variables of Reconstruction and Security in Post 9-11 Afghanistan*, October 19, 2010.

(Michael E. O'Hanlon and Ian Livingston), *The Iraq Index: Tracking Vari-*

*ables of Reconstruction and Security in Post-Saddam Iraq*, June 30, 2010; December 30, 2010.

CEIS Paris (Selma Belaala), *Les Facteurs de création ou de modification des processus de radicalisation violente, chez les jeunes en particulier*, 2008.

Center for Strategic and International Studies (Anthony H. Cordesman), *The Afghan War: The Campaign in the Spring of 2010*, Washington, May 24, 2010.

Center on Faith and International Affairs (Joshua T. White), *Pakistan's Islamist Frontier*, Arlington, 2008.

Centre for Conflict and Peace Studies (CAPS), *Suicide Terrorism: The Case of Afghanistan, Security & Terrorism*, Kabul, March 2007.

Combating Terrorism Center (Brian Fishman), *Al-Qa'ida's Foreign Fighters in Iraq: A First Look at the Sinjar Records*, West Point, December 2007.

  *Bombers, Bank Accounts and Bleedouts: Al-Qa'ida's Role in and out of Iraq*, West Point, July 2008.

  *Deadly Vanguards: A Study of Al-Qa'ida's Violence against Muslims*, December 2009.

Community Appraisal and Motivation Programme, Islamabad, *Understanding FATA: Attitudes towards Governance, Religion and Society in Pakistan's FATA*, 2008.

GfK NOP Social Research, *Attitudes to Living in Britain – A Survey of Muslim Opinion*, August 2006.

Hudson Institute, Center for Religious Freedom, *Saudi Arabia's Curriculum of Intolerance*, Washington, 2008.

Human Rights Watch, 'Afghanistan: Ethnically-Motivated Abuses against Civilians', *Human Rights Watch Backgrounder*, October 2001.

  *Annual Report*, 2001.

  *Massacres of Hazaras in Afghanistan*, February 1, 2001.

  'Opportunism in the Face of Tragedy', 2002.

  *The Road to Abu Ghraib*, June 8, 2004.

Gallup, *Gallup Poll of the Islamic World*, Washington, February 2002.

The Gallup Coexist Index 2009, *A Global Study of Interfaith Relations*, May 2009.

Institute for Strategic Dialogue (Jytte Klausen), *Al Qaeda-Affiliated and 'Homegrown' Jihadism in the UK: 1999–2010*, September 2010.

Institute for the Study of War (Carl Forsberg), *Taliban's Campaign for Kandahar*, Washington, December 2009.

  (Elisa Cochrane), *The Fragmentation of the Sadrist Movement*, January 2009.

International Crisis Group, *Appeasing the Militants*, December 11, 2006.

  *Can Saudi Arabia Reform Itself?*, July 14, 2004.

  'Deradicalization' and Indonesian Prisons, November 19, 2007.

  *La France face à ses Musalmans: émeutes, jihadisme et dépolitisation*, March 9, 2006.

*Indonesia Backgrounder: Why Salafism and Terrorism Mostly Don't Mix*, September 13, 2004.

*In Their Own Words: Reading the Iraqi Insurgency*, February 15, 2006.

*Iran in Iraq*, March 2005.

*Iraq Backgrounder: What Lies Beneath*, October 1, 2002.

*Iraq – Provincial Elections* 2009.

*Iraq's Civil War, the Sadrists and the Surge*, February 7, 2008.

*Iraq's Muqtada Al-Sadr: Spoiler or Stabiliser?*, July 11, 2006.

*'Deradicalisation' and Indonesian Prisons*, November 19, 2007.

*Pakistan – The Military and the Medressas Militancy*, 2009.

*The Problem of Pashtun Alienation*, August 5,2003.

*Taliban Propaganda: Winning the War of Words?*, July 24, 2008.

*Terrorism in Indonesia: Noordin's Networks*, May 5, 2006.

*Where Is Iraq Heading? Lessons from Basra*, June 25, 2007.

International Republican Institute (IRI), *Pakistan Public Opinion Survey*, Washington, January 19–29, 2008.

National Human Rights Advisory Center (Centre Nationale Consultative de Droites de l'Homme, CNCDH, France), *Report*, 2004.

The Netherlands Institute of International Relations Clingendael (Edwin Bakker and Teije Hidde Donker), *Jihadi Terrorists in Europe*, The Hague, December 2006.

New America Foundation (Thomas Ruttig), *The Battle for Afghanistan*, May 2011.

New America Foundation/Terror Free Tomorrow poll, *Results of a New Nationwide Public Opinion Survey of Pakistan*, 2007.

    *Saudi Arabians Overwhelmingly Reject Bin Laden, Al Qaeda, Saudi Fighters in Iraq, and Terrorism*, Washington, December 2007.

New York University Center on Law and Security, *Terrorist Trial Report Card 2001–2009*, 2010.

Norwegian Defence Research Establishment (Anne Sternersen), *The Taliban Insurgency in Afghanistan – Organization, Leadership and Worldview*, February 5, 2010.

Oxfam International, *In Her Own Words: Iraqi Women Talk about Their Greatest Challenges*, March 2009.

Pakistan Institute for Peace Studies, *Pakistan Security Report*, 2008, Islamabad, 2009.

Pew Research Center, Washington, *America's Image in the World: Findings from the Pew Global Attitudes Project*, March 2007.

    *Declining Support for bin Laden and Suicide Bombing*, September 10, 2009.

    *Democracy and Islam*, January 31, 2011.

    *Global Attitudes Toward Islamic Extremism and Terrorism*, August 29, 2007.

*Global Public Opinion in the Bush Years (2001–2008)*, December 18, 2008.

*How Global Publics View: War in Iraq, Democracy, Islam and Governance and Globalization*, June 2003.

*Little Enthusiasm for Many Muslim Leaders*, February 4, 2010.

*Mapping the Global Muslim Population: A Report on the Size and Distribution of the World's Muslim Population*, October 2009.

*Muslim Networks and Movements in Western Europe*, September 15, 2010.

*Overview: Pakistani Public Opinion*, August 13, 2009.

*Pew Global Attitudes: Overview: Concern about Extremist Threat Slips in Pakistan*, July 29, 2010.

*Pew Global Attitudes 2003: Views of a Changing World*, June 3, 2003.

*Pew Global Attitudes 2004: A Year After Iraq War*, March 16, 2004.

*Pew Global Attitudes Survey: Confidence in Obama Lifts U.S. Image Around the World*, July 23, 2009

*Pew Global Attitudes Survey: Muslim Disappointment: Obama More Popular Abroad than at Home, Global Image of US Continues to Benefit*, June 17, 2010.

*Pew Global Opinions Survey 2007: Global Unease with Major World Powers*, June 26, 2007.

*Pew Global Opinions Survey, 2007: A Rising Tide Lifts Mood in the Developing World*, July 24, 2007.

*Where Terrorism Finds Support in the Muslim World*, May 2006.

Project on Defense Alternatives (Carl Conetta), *Operation Enduring Freedom: Why a Higher Rate of Civilian Bombing Casualties*, January 18, 2002.

RAND Corporation (Benjamin S. Lambeth), *Air Power against Terror: America's Conduct of Operation Enduring Freedom*, 2005.

(Ian Lesser et al.), *Countering the New Terrorism*, 1999.

(Bruce Hoffman), *Insurgency and Counterinsurgency in Iraq*, June 2004.

(Brian Michael Jenkins), *Would-be Warriors*, 2010.

Quillam Foundation, *The Coming Struggle within Al-Qaeda*, London, May 2011

(Camille Tawil), *The Other Face of al-Qaeda*, London, November 2010.

United States Institute for Peace (Amatzia Baran), *Who Are the Insurgents? Sunni Arab Rebels in Iraq*, May 2005.

## International/Multilateral Organizations

*Report of the United Nations Commission of Inquiry into the Facts and Circumstances of the Assassination of Former Pakistani Prime Minister Mohtarma Benazir Bhutto*, New York, April 15, 2010.

World Bank, *Afghanistan: Statebuilding, Sustaining Growth and Reducing Poverty*, Washington, 2005.

UNESCO, Pakistan (Munir Ahmed Choudhry), *Where and Who Are the World's Illiterates?*, April 2005.

UNICEF, *Situation Analysis of Children and Women in Iraq*, April 30, 1998.

United Nations Assistance Mission in Afghanistan (UNAMA), *Afghan Civilian Casualties Rise 31 Per Cent in First Six Months of 2010*, August 10, 2010.

  *Afghanistan Annual Report on Protection of Civilians in Armed Conflict, 2009*, 31 December 2009.

  *Internal Security Assessment on Wardak*, June 2008.

  *Mid Year Report on Protection of Civilians in Armed Conflict 2010*, Kabul, August 10, 2010.

  *Report to the Secretary General*, June 2010.

  *The Situation in Afghanistan and Its Implications for International Peace and Security (S/2010/463)*, September 2010.

  (C. Christine Fair), *Suicide Attacks in Afghanistan, 2001–2007*, 2007.

United Nations Development Programme, *Afghanistan Annual Opium Poppy Survey*, 2001.

  *Human Development Report*, New York, 2008.

  *Human Development Report*, New York, 2009.

United Nations Office on Drugs and Crime (Doris Buddenberg and William Byrd), *Afghanistan's Drug Industry, Structure, Functioning Dynamics and Implications for Counter-Narcotics Policy* , 2006.

  *Afghanistan Opium Survey 2006*, September 2006.

  *Afghanistan Opium Survey 2007*, September 2007.

United Nations Population Fund, *Life in the City*, June 2007.

*United Nations Report of the Security in Iraq Accountability Panel (SIAP)*, New York, March 3, 2004.

UN Security Council, *Sixth Report of the Analytical Support and Sanctions Monitoring Team Appointed Pursuant to Security Council Resolutions 1526 (2004) and 1617 (2005) Concerning Al-Qaida and the Taliban and Associated Individuals and Entities*, November 7, 2006.

## Legal/Secret Investigative Documents

Ayman al-Batarfi, summary of administrative review board proceeding, Guantanamo Bay, November 28, 2006.

Ghanim Abdul Rahman al-Harbi, Combat Status Review Tribunal, summary of evidence, Guantanamo Bay, 16 August 2004.

Interrogation testimony of Bryant Neal Vinas, March 10–11, 2009, New York, dossier of Hicham Beyayo.

Memoranda for Commander, United States Southern Command, Combatant Status Review Tribunal Input for Guantanamo Detainees:

US9YM-000549. Omar Said Adayn, June 20, 2008.

US9AF-003148DP, Harun al-Afghani, August 2, 2007.

US9YM-000039DP, Ali Hamza Suleiman al-Bahlul, June 5, 2005.

US9YM-000627DP, Ayman Saeed Abdullah al-Batarfi, April 29, 2008, secret.

US9AF-000782DP, Awal Malim Gul, February 15, 2008.

US9AG-000238DP, Nabil Said Hadjarab, January 22, 2007.

US9ID-010019DP, Hambali, October 30, 2008.

US9LY-010017DP, Farraj al-Libby, September 10, 2008.

US9AF-000801DP, Saber Lal Melma, June 5, 2005.

US9AF-000798DP, Mullah Haji Rohullah, June 17, 2005.

US9KU-010024DP, Khaled Sheikh Mohammed, December 8, 2006.

National Investigation Agency, Government of India, Interrogation Report of David Headley, June 2010.

Shafiq Rasul, Asif Iqbal and Rhuhel Ahmed, Composite statement: Detention in Afghanistan and Guantanamo Bay, Centre for Constitutional Rights, New York, July 26, 2004.

Haji Shahzada, Guantanamo Bay, Summary of Evidence, CS Review Tribunals, Guantanamo Bay, January 12, 2005.

Statement of Mohammed Ajmal Amir Qasab to Indian police, November 2008.

Substitution for the testimony of Khaled Sheikh Mohammed. United States vs Moussaoui, July 31, 2006.

Testimony of Hicham Beyayo to Belgian police, statements on 2.4.2009, 6.5.2009, 15.5.2009, Brussels. Author collection.

Testimony of Judge Jean-Louis Brugiere, trial of Ahmed Ressam, Los Angeles, 2 April 2001.

Testimony of Robert S. Mueller, III, Director, FBI, Before the Select Committee on Intelligence of the United States Senate February 11, 2003.

Testimony of Walid Othmani to French interrogators, 30 January 2009, document M.20-2-9, p. 43. Author collection.

Testimony of Ahmed Ressam, USA vs. Mokhtar Houari, July 3, 2001.

Testimony of Ali Soufran and Christopher Anglin, FBI agents, USA vs. Ali Hamza al-Bahlul, November 2008.

USA vs. Ali al-Bahlul, FBI interrogation of al-Bahlul, report statement, 30 July 2003.

USA vs. Ali al-Bahlul, Martyr Tape of Ziad Samir Jarrah, reproduced in Referral Binder: Part I, September 2004.

USA vs. Abu Doha sealed complaint, US Southern District Court, New York, July 2, 2001.

USA vs. David Headley, 'Criminal Complaint', Northern District of Illinois, 2009. Author collection.

USA vs. Abdur Rehman Hashim Syed, 'Criminal Complaint', Northern District of Illinois, 2009.

USA vs. Usama bin Laden, New York Southern District Court, February 2001.

USA vs. Bryant Neal Vinas, Indictment, District Court, Eastern District of New York, November 14, 2008.

USA vs. Najibullah Zazi, Eastern District of New York, indictment, September 21, 2009.

## Statements by Officials

Ambassador Bremer, Statement to the Chilcot Commission, May 18, 2010.

Michael Leiter, Director of National Counterterrorism Center, Statement for Record, Senate Homeland Security and Government Affairs Committee, 'Nine Years After 9/11, Confronting the Terrorist Threat to the Homeland', September 22, 2010.

Eliza Manningham-Buller, Director General of the Security Service, 'Global Terrorism: Are We Meeting the Challenge?', James Smart Lecture, City of London Police Headquarters, October 16, 2003.

Robert S. Mueller, III, Director Federal Bureau of Investigation, Citizens Crime Commission, James Fox Memorial Lecture, New York, April 26, 2006.

Lt. Gen. Raymond Odierno, 'The Surge in Iraq: One Year Later', Heritage lectures (the Heritage Foundation), March 13, 2008.

Benon V. Sevan, Executive Director of the Iraq Programme, Statement, 'Phasing Down and Termination of the Programme Pursuant to Security Council Resolution 1483 (2003)', Office of the Iraq Programme, Oil-for-Food. November 19, 2003.

Testimony of Lieutenant General David W. Barno, USA (Ret.), before the Committee on Foreign Affairs, US House of Representatives, 'Afghanistan on the Brink: Where Do We Go from Here?', February 15, 2007.

Testimony of Daniel Benjamin, Center for Strategic and International Studies, before the Senate Foreign Relations Committee, June 13, 2006.

Testimony of David Kay before the US committee on Armed Services, January 28, 2004.

Testimony of Michael McConnell, director of national intelligence, Hearing of the United States Senate Select Committee on Intelligence, Annual Worldwide Threat Assessment, February 5, 2008.

### SPECIALIST ARTICLES

Zachary Abuza, 'The Philippines Chips Away at the Abu Sayyaf Group's Strength', *CTC Sentinel*, vol. 3, no. 4, April 2010.

Imtiaz Ali, 'The Taliban's Versatile Spokesman: A Profile of Muslim Khan', *CTC Sentinel*, vol. 2, no. 2, February 2009.

'Commander of the Faithful', *Foreign Policy Magazine*, 9 July 2009.

Tahir Andrabi, Jishnu Das, Asim Ijaz Khwaja and Tristan Zajonc, 'Religious School Enrollment in Pakistan: A Look at the Data', John F. Kennedy School of Government Working Paper Series, 2005.

Omar Ashour, 'De-Radicalization of Jihad? The Impact of Egyptian Islamist Revisionists on Al-Qaeda', *Perspectives on Terrorism*, vol. 2, no. 5, May 2008.

Nigel Aylwin-Foster, 'Changing the Army for Counterinsurgency Operations', *Military Review*, November–December 2005.

Scott Atran, 'Trends in Suicide Terrorism: Sense and Nonsense', presented to World Federation of Scientists Permanent Monitoring Panel on Terrorism, Erice, Sicily, August 2004.

'Who Becomes a Terrorist Today?', *Perspectives on Terrorism*, vol. 2, no. 5, May 2008.

Abdul Hameed Bakier, 'Internet Jihadists React to the Deaths of al-Qa'eda Leaders in Iraq', *CTC sentinel*, vol. 3, no. 5, May 2010.

William W. Bates, 'Chinese Outrages', *Gunton's Magazine*, 1900.

Pope Benedict XVI, 'Meeting with the Representatives of Science', Lecture of the Holy Father, Regensburg, Germany, Libreria Editrice Vaticana, September 12, 2006.

Peter Bergen and Swati Pandy, 'The Medressa Scapegoat', *Washington Quarterly*, Spring 2006.

Benedetta Berti, 'Salafi-Jihadi Activism in Gaza: Mapping the Threat', *CTC Sentinel*, vol. 3, no. 5, May 2010.

Andrew Black, 'Al-Qaida Operations in Kabylie Mountains Alienating Algeria's Berbers', *Jamestown Terrorism Focus*, vol. 5, no. 16, April 23, 2008.

'Al-Suri's Adaptation of Fourth Generation Warfare Doctrine', *Terrorism Monitor*, vol. 4, no. 18, September 21, 2006.

Laila Bokhari, Thomas Hegghammer, Brynjar Lia, Petter Nesser and Truls H. Tonnessen, 'Paths to Global Jihad: Radicalisation and Recruitment', *Proceedings from FFI Seminar*, Oslo, March 15, 2006.

Jarret Brachman, 'Abu Yahya's Six Easy Steps for Defeating al-Qaeda', *Perspectives on Terrorism*, vol. 1, no. 5, December 2007.

'The Next Osama', *Foreign Policy*, September 10, 2009.

'Retaining Relevance: Assessing Al-Qaeda's Generational Evolution', *Al-Qaeda's Senior Leadership*, Jane's Strategic Advisory Services, no. 28, November 2009.

Jarret Brachman and William McCants, 'Stealing Al'Qaida's Playbook', *Studies in Conflicts and Terrorism*, May 2006.

James Brandon, 'Al'Qaida's Involvement in Britain's "Homegrown" Terrorist Plots', *CTC Sentinel*, vol. 2, no. 3, March 2009.

'The UK's Experience in Counter-radicalization', *CTC Sentinel*, vol. 1, no. 5, April 2008.

Gilbert Burnham, Riyadh Lafta, Shannon Doocy and Les Roberts, 'Mortality after the 2003 Invasion of Iraq: A Cross-sectional Cluster Sample Survey', *Lancet*, vol. 368, no. 9,545, October 21, 2006.

Frank Cilluffo, Jeffrey Cozens and Magnus Ranstorp, 'Foreign Fighters: Trends, Trajectories and Conflict Zones', Homeland Security Policy Institute, George Washington University, 2010.

Isobel Coleman, 'Egypt's Uphill Economic Struggles', Council on Foreign Relations, February 2, 2011.

Carl Conetta, 'The Wages of War: Iraqi Combatant and Noncombatant Fatalities in the 2003 Conflict', Project on Defense Alternatives Monograph no. 8, October 20, 2003.

Anthony H. Cordesman, 'The Afghan War: The Campaign in the Spring of 2010', Center for Strategic and International Studies, May 24, 2010.

Paul Cruickshank, 'Enlisting Terror: Al-Qaeda's Recruitment Challenges', *Al'Qaeda's Senior Leadership*, Jane's Strategic Advisory Services, November 2009.

   'LIFG Revisions Posing Critical Challenge to Al'Qaida', *CTC Sentinel*, vol. 2, no. 12, December 2009.

Paul Cruickshank and Mohammad Hage Ali, 'Abu Musab al-Suri: Architect of the New al-Qaeda', *Studies in Conflict and Terrorism*, vol. 30, 2007.

Sharon Curcio, 'Generational Differences in Waging Jihad', *Military Review*, July–August 2005.

John C. K. Daly, '"Saudi Black Gold": Will Terrorism Deny the West Its Fix?' *Terrorism Monitor*, vol. 1, no. 7, May 5, 2005.

Anthony Davis, 'The Fall of Kabul', *Jane's Defence Weekly*, November 13, 2001.

Beatrice de Graff, 'The Nexus between Salafism and Jihadism in the Netherlands', *CTC Sentinel*, vol. 3, no. 3, March 2010.

Toby Dodge, 'The Causes of US Failure in Iraq', *Survival: Global Politics and Strategy*, vol. 49, no. 1, Spring 2007.

   'The Ideological Roots of Failure: The Application of Kinetic Neo-liberalism to Iraq', *International Affairs*, vol. 86, no. 6, 2010.

Alexander Evans, 'Understanding Medressas', *Foreign Affairs*, vol. 85, no. 1, January–February 2006.

C. Christine Fair, 'Militant Recruitment in Pakistan', *Asia Policy*, no. 4, July 2007.
   'Who Are Pakistan's Militants and Their Families?' *Terrorism and Political Violence*, vol. 20, no. 1, January 2008.

C. Christine Fair and Seth Jones, 'Pakistan's War Within', *Survival: Global Politics and Strategy*, vol. 51, no. 6, December 2009–January 2010.

C. Christine Fair and Shuja Nawaz, 'The Changing Pakistan Army Officer Corps', *Journal of Strategic Studies*, forthcoming.

Marion Farouk-Sluglett and Peter Sluglett, 'The Historiography of Modern Iraq', *American Historical Review*, vol. 96, 1991.

Jean-Pierre Filiu, 'Al-Qa'ida in the Islamic Maghreb', *CTC Sentinel*, vol. 3, no. 4, April 2010.

   'The Brotherhood vs. Al-Qaeda: A Moment of Truth?', Hudson Institute, November 12, 2009.

'The Local and Global Jihad of al-Qa'ida in the Islamic Maghrib', *Middle East Journal*, vol. 63, no. 2, 2009.

Finbarr Barry Flood, 'Between Cult and Culture: Bamiyan, Islamic Iconoclasm, and the Museum', *Art Bulletin*, December 2002.

Timothy Garton-Ash, 'Anti-Europeanism in America', *Hoover Digest*, no. 2, 2003.

Jawaid Abdul Ghani, 'Consolidation in Pakistan's Retail Sector', *Asian Journal of Management Cases*, vol. 2, no. 2, 2005.

Greg Grant, 'The IED Marketplace', *Defense News*, March 2005.

Derek Gregory, 'The Rush to the Intimate: Counterinsurgency and the Cultural Turn in Late Modern War', *Radical Philosophy*, July/August 2008.

Mohammed M. Hafez, 'Al'Qaida Losing Ground in Iraq', *CTC Sentinel*, vol. 1, no. 1, December 2007.

Thomas Hegghammer, 'Terrorist Recruitment and Radicalisation in Saudi Arabia', *Middle East Policy*, vol. 13, no. 4, Winter 2006.

Marc W. Herold, 'A Dossier on Civilian Victims of United States' Aerial Bombing of Afghanistan: A Comprehensive Accounting', unpublished manuscript, December 2001.

Arif Jamal, 'Half-hearted Security Operations in Punjab Do Little to Restrain Taliban', *Terrorism Monitor*, vol. 8, no. 31, August 5, 2010.

Toby Jones, 'Shifting Sands', *Foreign Affairs*, March/April 2006.

Javier Jordan and Robert Wesley, 'The Madrid Attacks: Results of Investigations Two Years Later', *Terrorism Monitor*, vol. 4, no. 5, March 9, 2006.

Tim Judah, 'The Taliban Papers', *Survival: Global Politics and Strategy*, vol. 44, no. 1, Spring 2002.

Hekmat Karzai, 'Suicide Terrorism: The Case of Afghanistan', *Security and Terrorism*, no. 5, March 2007.

Jason Katz, Victoria Cullen, Connor Buttner and John Pollock, 'American Newspaper Coverage of Islam Post-September 11, 2001: A Community Structure Approach', *Association for Education in Journalism and Mass Communication*, August 8, 2007.

Jonathan F. Keiler, 'Who Won the Battle of Fallujah?', *Proceedings of the U.S. Naval Institute*, January 2005.

Lydia Khalil, 'The Lord of the Marshes Takes a Mediating Role in Iraq', *Terrorism Focus*, vol. 3, no. 33, August 2006.

David Kilcullen, 'Field Notes on Iraq's Tribal Revolt Against Al-Qa'ida', *CTC Sentinel*, vol. 1, no. 11, October 2008.

'Twenty-Eight Articles: Fundamentals of Company-level Counterinsurgency', *Military Review*, March 1, 2006.

Michael Knights, 'The Current State of al-Qa'ida in Saudi Arabia', *CTC Sentinel*, vol. 1, no. 10, September 2008.

Evan Kohlmann, 'Abu Musab al-Suri's Final "Message to the British and the Europeans"', NEFA Foundation, August 2005.

'Inside As-Sahaab, the Story of Ali al-Bahlul and the Evolution of al-Qaida's Propaganda', NEFA Foundation, December 2008.

F. Lainé and M. Okba, 'Jeunes de parents immigrés: de l'école au métier', *Travail et Emploi*, vol. 103, 2005.

Andrew Lebovich, 'Afghan Perspectives on Democracy', *Foreign Policy*, February 9, 2011.

Robert Leiken, 'Europe's Angry Muslims', *Foreign Affairs*, July/August 2005.

Brynjar Lia, 'Abu Mus'ab al-Suri's critique of Hard Line Salafists in the Jihadist Current', *CTC Sentinel*, vol. 1, no. 1, December 2007.

'The Al-Qaida Strategist Abu Mus'ab al-Suri: A Profile', unpublished paper presented at OMS Seminar (Oslo Militære Samfund), Oslo, March 15, 2006.

Montgomery McFate, 'The Military Utility of Understanding Adversary Culture', *Joint Forces Quarterly*, no. 38, July 2005.

Edmund F. McGarrell, Joshua D. Freilich and Steven Chermak, 'Intelligence Led Policing as a Framework for Responding to Terrorism', *Journal of Contemporary Criminal Justice*, vol. 23, no. 2, 2007.

Kenan Malik, 'The Islamophobia Myth', *Prospect*, 107, February 2005.

Ibrahim al-Marashi, 'Boycotts, Coalitions and the Threat of Violence: The Run-up to the January 2005 Iraqi Elections', *The Middle East Review of International Affairs*, January 2005.

Dalia Mogahed, 'Beyond Multiculturalism vs. Assimilation', Gallup, 2007.

Philip Mudd, 'Evaluating the Al'Qaida Threat to the US Homeland', *CTC Sentinel*, vol. 3, no. 8, August 2010.

John Mueller, 'Is There Still a Terrorist Threat? The Myth of the Omnipresent Enemy', *Foreign Affairs*, September–October 2006.

Shuja Nawaz, 'The Pakistan Army and Its Role in FATA', *CTC Sentinel*, vol. 1, no. 1, January 2009.

Petter Nesser and Brynjar Lia, 'Lessons Learned from the July 2010 Norwegian Terrorist Plot', *CTC Sentinel*, vol. 3, no. 8, August 2010.

Barack Obama, 'Renewing American Leadership', *Foreign Affairs*, July–August 2007.

Michael O'Hanlon, 'Staying Power: The U.S. Mission in Afghanistan Beyond 2011', *Foreign Affairs*, September–October 2010.

Sharon Otterman, 'Saudi Arabia: Withdrawal of US forces', Council on Foreign Relations, Washington, May 2, 2003.

Alison Pargeter, 'LIFG Revisions Unlikely to Reduce Jihadist Violence', *CTC Sentinel*, vol. 2, no. 10, October 2009.

Reuven Paz, 'Arab Volunteers Killed in Iraq: An Analysis', *The Project for the Research of Islamist Movements (PRISM)*, vol. 3, no. 1, March 2005.

'The Non-Territorial Islamic States in Europe', *The Project for the Research of Islamist Movements*, (*PRISM*), November 28, 2005.

David H. Petraeus, 'Learning Counterinsurgency: Observations from Soldiering in Iraq', *Military Review*, January–February 2006.

Andrea Plebani, 'Ninawa Province: Al-Qa'ida's Remaining Stronghold', *CTC Sentinel*, vol. 3, no. 1, January 2010.

Nikhil Raymond Puri, 'The Pakistani Madrassah and Terrorism: Made and Unmade: Conclusions from the Literature', *Perspectives on Terrorism*, vol. 4, no. 4, October 2010.

James T. Quinlivan, 'Burden of Victory: The Painful Arithmetic of Stability Operations', *RAND Review*, vol. 27, No. 2 (Summer 2003), pp. 28–29.

Mohammad Amir Rana, 'The Taliban Consolidate Control in Pakistan's Tribal Regions', *CTC Sentinel*, vol. 1, no. 7, June 2008.

Dhiya Rassan, 'Patchwork of Insurgent Groups Runs Fallujah', *Institute of War and Peace Reporting*, September 17, 2004.

Thomas Renard, 'Europol Report Describes Afghanistan–Pakistan Connection to Trends in European Terrorism', *Terrorism Monitor*, vol. 7, no. 12, May 8, 2009.

Nir Rosen, 'Thinking Like a Jihadist: Iraq's Jordanian Connection', *World Policy Journal*, Spring 2006.

Farzaneh Roudi-Fahimi and Mary Mederios Kent, 'Challenges and Opportunities – The Population of the Middle East and North Africa', *Population Bulletin*, vol. 62, no. 2, 2007.

Eric Rouleau, 'Trouble in the Kingdom', *Foreign Affairs*, July–August 2002.

Olivier Roy, 'The Nature of the French Riots', SSRC (Social Science Research Council), November 18, 2005.

Thomas Ruttig, 'The Other Side: Dimensions of the Afghan Insurgency', *Afghan Analysts Network*, July 2009.

 'The Taliban Arrest Wave in Pakistan: Reasserting Strategic Depth', *CTC Sentinel*, vol. 3, no. 3, March 2010.

Bilal y Saab, 'The Failure of Salafi-Jihadi Insurgent Movements in the Levant', *CTC Sentinel*, vol. 2, no. 9, September 2009.

Bilal y Saab and Magnus Ranstorp, 'Securing Lebanon from the Threat of Salafist Jihadism', *Studies in Conflict and Terrorism*, vol. 30, no. 10, 2007.

Michael Scheuer, 'Abu Yahya al-Libi: Al-Qaeda's Theological Enforcer – Part 1', *Terrorism Focus*, vol. 4, no. 25, July 31, 2007.

 'Al-Qaeda: Beginning of the End, or Grasping at Straws?' *Terrorism Focus*, vol. 4, no. 32, October 12, 2007

Murad Batal al-Shishani, 'Abu Mus'ab al'Suri and the Third Generation of Salafi-Jihadists', *Terrorism Monitor*, vol. 3, no. 16, August 15, 2005.

 'Jihad Ideologue Abu Muhammad al-Maqdisi Challenges Jordan's Neo-Zarqawists', *Terrorism Monitor*, vol. 7, no. 20, July 9, 2009.

Murad Batal al-Shishani, 'The Amman Bombings: A Blow to the Jihadists?', *Terrorism Focus*, vol. 2, no. 22, November 29, 2005.

Guido Steinberg, 'Towards Collective Leadership – The Role of Egyptians in Al-Qaeda', in *Al-Qaeda's Senior Leadership*, Jane's Strategic Advisory Services, November 2009.

Azam Tariq, 'The Life of Baitullah Mahsood', Global Islamic Media Front, Autumn 2010.

Mark Tessler, 'Do Islamic Orientations Influence Attitudes toward Democracy in the Arab World? Evidence from Egypt, Jordan, Morocco, and Algeria', *International Journal of Comparative Sociology*, vol. 43, October 2002.

Mark Tessler and Dan Corstange, 'How Should Americans Understand Arab and Muslim Political Attitudes', *Journal of Social Affairs*, vol. 19, 2002.

Justin Vaïsse, 'American Francophobia Takes a New Turn', *French Politics, Culture and Society*, vol. 21, no. 2, July 2003.

Chris Zambelis, 'Uighur Dissent and Militancy in China's Xinjiang Province', *CTC Sentinel*, vol. 3, no. 1, January 2010.


## GENERAL MEDIA ARTICLES AND REPORTS

Mushriq Abbas, 'Mutual political and tribal interests coincided with his struggle with al-Qa'ida and al-Maliki: a short and murky journey led Abu Risha to . . . his death', *al'Hayat*, September 16, 2007.

Zaffar Abbas, 'The emerging contours of PPP-govt deal', *Dawn*, April 21, 2007.

Magdi Abdlehadi, 'Saudis to retrain 40,000 clerics', BBC News, March 20, 2008.

Ghaith Abdul-Ahad, 'Seeking salvation in city of insurgents', *Guardian*, November 11, 2004.

    'Seeking salvation in city of insurgents', *Washington Post*, November 11, 2004.

    'We are not here to liberate Iraq, we're here to fight the infidels', *Guardian*, November 9, 2005.

Lorraine Adams with Ayesha Nasir, 'Inside the mind of the Times Square bomber', *Observer*, September 19, 2010.

Esther Addley, '7/7 inquest, pandemonium here', *Guardian*, October 11, 2010.

Adnan Adil, 'Pakistan's post-9/11 economic boom', BBC News, September 21, 2006.

AFX News Limited, 'US to reduce troop numbers in Afghanistan soon – US spokesman', December 26, 2005.

Agence France-Presse, 'Afghan Supreme Court bans beauty pageants', October 30, 2003.

    'At least 27 die in Iraq as bombs, shootings shatter lull', February 11, 2009.

    'Les juges ne confirment pas le portrait des émeutiers dressé par Sarkozy', November 17, 2005.

    'Palestinians in Lebanon celebrate anti-US Attacks', September 11, 2001.

Jennifer Agiesta and Jon Cohen, 'Public opinion in U.S. turns against Afghan war', *Washington Post*, August 20, 2009.

Munir Ahmad, 'Pakistani officials, nearly 15 top Taliban held', Associated Press, February 25, 2010.

Kamal Ahmed, 'The terrorism crisis, no. 10 fears £20bn flood of heroin, troops aim to destroy huge stockpile of opium about to be released on to the world market', *Observer*, September 30, 2001.

Hannah Allam, 'Fallujah's real boss, Omar the electrician', Knight Ridder Newspapers , November 22, 2004.

Chris Allbritton, 'Holbrooke hails Pakistan–U.S. collaboration on Taliban', Reuters, February 18, 2010.

John Lee Anderson, 'Inside the surge', *New Yorker*, November 19, 2007.

John Ward Anderson, 'Seven al-Zarqawi insurgents killed in retaliation for Khaldiya slaying', *Washington Post*, March 18, 2005.

R. W. Apple Jr, 'A military quagmire remembered, Afghanistan as Vietnam', *New York Times*, October 31, 2001.

Associated Press, 'Al-Qaeda deputy pens book justifying armed struggle', March 3, 2008.

> 'AP protests threats to freelance cameraman who filmed Palestinian rally', September 12, 2001.
>
> 'Bin-Laden poster seen at Gaza rally', September 14, 2001.
>
> 'Ex-CIA contractor guilty of assault', August 16, 2006.
>
> 'Insurgent activity rising in Afghanistan', November 13, 2006.
>
> 'Iraq, key figures since the war began', January 2, 2009.
>
> 'Lauded at pageant, woman condemned by Afghan officials', November 10, 2003.
>
> 'Madrid bombing probe finds no al-Qaida link', March 9, 2006.
>
> 'Yemeni doctor describes bloody siege at Tora Bora', September 7, 2007.

Anna Badkhen, 'What's behind Muslim cartoon outrage?', *San Francisco Chronicle*, February 11, 2006.

Aryn Baker, 'Casualty of war', *Time*, June 1, 2009.

Scott Baldauf, 'Afghanistan's new Jihad targets poppy production', *Christian Science Monitor*, May 16, 2005.

Kenneth Ballen, 'Bin Laden's soft support', *Washington Monthly*, May 2008.

Julian E. Barnes, 'National security watch, retiring top soldier warns of "The Long War"', *US News and World Report*, September 29, 2005.

René Backmann and Henri Guirchon, 'Les dessins de la colère', *Le Nouvel Observateur*, February 9–15, 2006.

BBC News Online, 'Afghan people "losing confidence"', February 9, 2009.

> 'Afghans more optimistic for future, survey shows', January 11, 2010.
>
> 'Anti-Semitism on rise in Europe', March 31, 2004.
>
> 'Bin Laden in Palestinian call', March 21, 2008.
>
> 'Egypt airs "anti-Semitic" series', November 7, 2002.
>
> 'Few Muslims back suicide bombs', July 25, 2007.
>
> 'Has Pakistan passed the tipping point of religious extremism?', January 7, 2011.
>
> 'Iraq suicide bomb blasts kill 120', January 5, 2006.
>
> 'Islamic world deplores US losses', September 14, 2001.

'Jordan hotel blasts kill dozens', November 10, 2005.

'Macedonia faked "militant raid"', April 30, 2004.

'Nato hails shift on Afghan combat', November 29, 2006.

'Nato to attack Afghan opium labs', October 10, 2008.

'No public probe into Iraq "abuse"', November 14, 2009.

'Pakistan leaders' "narrow escape"', September 22, 2008.

'Pakistan protests turn violent', September 21, 2001.

'Police monitored "bomb plotters"', January 18, 2007.

'Rumsfeld rejects "cleric-led" rule', April 25, 2005.

'Taleban in Texas for talks on gas pipeline', December 4, 1997.

'Toll climbs in Egyptian attacks', July 23, 2005.

'Top Afghan policewoman shot dead', September 28, 2008.

Transcript of Andrew Marr interview with David Miliband, January 24, 2010.

'UK troops "to target terrorists"', April 24, 2006.

Selma Belaala, 'Morocco, slums breed Jihad', *Le Monde Diplomatique*, November 2004.

Leo Benedictus, 'Every race, colour, nation and religion on earth', *Guardian*, January 21, 2005.

Owen Bennett-Jones, 'Pakistan inequality fuelling Taliban support', BBC News Online, May 13, 2010.

Peter Bergen and Paul Cruickshank, 'The unraveling, the Jihadist revolt against bin Laden', *New Republic*, June 11, 2008.

David Blair, 'The last stand at Majar al-Kabir', *Daily Telegraph*, June 26, 2003.

Tony Blankley, 'An Islamist threat like the Nazis', *Washington Times*, September 12, 2005.

Philip Bobbitt, 'Get ready for the next long war', *Time*, September 1, 2002.

Mark Bowden, 'The ploy', *Atlantic*, May 2007.

Charles Bremner, 'Youssouf Fofana jailed for the torture and murder of Ilan Halimi', *The Times*, July 11, 2009.

Luc Bronner, 'Zones urbaines sensibles, près d'un mineur sur deux connaît la pauvreté', *Le Monde*, December 1, 2009.

Drew Brown, 'How al Qaeda fighters escaped, Bin Laden told his men to disperse, witness says', *The Miami Herald*, October 17, 2002.

Jonathan Brown, 'Mohammed Sadique Khan, expectant father whose chosen path meant he would never see his baby', *Independent*, July 15, 2007.

Elisabeth Bumiller, 'The staggering cost of American conflicts', *International Herald Tribune*, July 26, 2010.

Jason Burke, 'The baker who joined Elysée elite', *Observer*, March 23, 2008.

'Britain stops talk of "war on terror"', *Observer*, December 10, 2006.

'The Arab backlash the militants didn't expect', *Observer*, June 20, 2004.

'Destitute and confused, bleak future for Afghan refugees caught in the crossfire', *Guardian*, October 3, 2008.

'Don't be soft on Islam, says EU terror chief', *Observer*, September 28, 2008.

'Guantánamo Bay files: Pakistan's ISI spy service listed as terrorist group', *Guardian*, April 25, 2011.

'Guantánamo Bay files rewrite the story of Osama bin Laden's Tora Bora escape', *Guardian*, April 26, 2011.

'The Guardian profile, Asif Ali Zardari', *Guardian*, September 5, 2008.

'Holland 's first immigrant mayor is hailed as "Obama on the Maas"', *Observer*, January 11, 2009.

'Hunt for the Taliban trio intent on destruction', *Observer*, July 9, 2006.

'Hunt for "traitors" splits Taliban', *Observer*, May 27, 2007.

'In a land without law or leaders, militant Islam threatens to rule', *Observer*, April 27, 2003.

'Iraq, an audit of war', *Observer*, July 6, 2003.

'Kashmir, young militants take pot shots at fragile peace process', *Observer*, February 24, 2010.

'Left to die', *GQ*, August 2004.

'The missing link', *Guardian*, February 9, 2003.

'Mujahideen back to "rob and beat us"', *Observer*, November 18, 2001.

'Mumbai, behind the attacks lies a story of youth twisted by hate', *Observer*, November 30, 2008.

'Omar was a normal British teenager who loved his little brother and Man Utd. So why at 24 did he plan to blow up a nightclub in central London?', *Observer*, January 20, 2008.

'Revealed, secret Taliban peace bid', *Observer*, September 28, 2008.

'Saudis offer pioneering therapy for ex-Jihadists', *Observer*, March 9, 2008.

'Secrets of bomber's death tape', *Observer*, September 4, 2005.

'Secret Taliban peace talks', *Observer*, September 28, 2008.

'Secret world of US jails', *Observer*, June 13, 2004.

'Target Europe', *Observer*, September 9, 2007.

'Terrorist bid to build bombs in mid-flight', *Observer*, February 8, 2004.

'Theatre of terror', *Observer*, November 21, 2004.

'Torture, treachery and spies – covert war in Afghanistan', *Observer*, November 4, 2001.

'Voice of the suburbs', *Observer*, April 23, 2006.

'"We must never forget the lessons learned from D-Day", says Obama', *Observer*, June 7, 2009.

'Westerners flocking to dig into Gaddafi's deep pockets', *Observer*, September 2, 2007.

Jason Burke and Peter Beaumont, 'West pays warlords to stay in line', *Observer*, July 21, 2002.

Jason Burke, Peter Beaumont and Mohammed al-Ubeidy, 'How Jordanians hunted down their hated son', *Observer*, June 11, 2006.

Jason Burke and Imtiaz Gul, 'The drone, the CIA and a botched attempt to kill bin Laden's deputy', *Observer*, January 15, 2006.

Jason Burke, David Rohde, Tim Judah, Paul Harris and Paul Beaver, 'Al-Qaeda's trail of terror', *Observer*, November 18, 2001.

John F. Burns, '10-month Afghan mystery, is bin Laden dead or alive?' *New York Times*, September 30, 2002.

Robert Burns, 'Iraqi, Saddam "delighted" in terror attacks on US', Associated Press, September 22, 2010.

Ian Buruma, 'Letter from Amsterdam, final cut, after a filmmaker's murder, the Dutch creed of tolerance has come under siege', *New Yorker*, January 3, 2005.

Daren Butler, 'Al Qaeda says short of food, arms in Afghanistan', Reuters, June 11, 2009.

Christopher Caldwell, 'Islamic Europe, when Bernard Lewis speaks', *Weekly Standard*, vol. 10, no. 4, October 4, 2004.

Cecile Calla, 'Les Musulmans d'Allemagne seraient assez bien integrés', *Le Monde*, June 27, 2009.

Diane Cambon, 'L'aile dure de la droite espagnole defend toujours la theorie de complot', *Le Monde*, February 14, 2007.

Rory Carroll, 'Biker mullah's great escape', *Guardian*, January 6, 2002.

John Carvel, 'Census shows Muslims' plight', *Guardian*, October 12, 2004.

Dominic Casciani, 'MI5 "too stretched" before 7 July', BBC News Online, May 19, 2009.

CBS news, 'Report. No proof of Qaeda–Saddam link', September 8, 2006.

'Ricin suspects Linked to al Qaeda', January 17, 2003.

Pascal Ceaux and Jean-Marie Pontaut, 'Youssouf Fofana, Confessions d'un "barbare"', *L'Express*, January 23, 2008.

Richard Z. Chesnoff, *Jewish World Review*, December 13, 2002.

Jean Chichizola, 'Fous d'Allah et voyous font cause commune sur les braquages', *Le Figaro*, January 13, 2006.

'L'ombre de Zarqaoui s'étend jusqu'en France', *Le Figaro*, December 14, 2005.

'175 Islamistes font du proselytisme en prison', *Le Figaro*, January 13, 2006.

Françoise Chipaux, 'Un Pakistanais de retour de Guantanamo', *Le Monde*, November 9, 2002.

Roshonara Choudhry, 'Police interview extracts', *Guardian*, November 3, 2010.

Martin Chulov, 'Bin Laden on tape, attacks "benefited Islam greatly"', December 14, 2001.

'Innocent grandmother – or suicide bombing mastermind?' *Guardian*, June 11, 2009.

'Iraq withdrawal, amid heat and broken promises, only the ice man cometh', *Guardian*, August 30, 2010.

'President notifies Congress about troop deployment. U.S. claims air supremacy over Afghanistan', *Guardian*, October 9, 2001.

'They turned the tide for America', *Guardian*, May 14, 2010.

CNN, 'Attacks draw mixed response in the Middle East', September 12, 2001.

Ian Cobain, 'Iraq deaths in British custody could see military face legal challenges', *Guardian*, July 1, 2010.

'Servicemen at "UK's Abu Ghraib" may be guilty of war crimes, court hears', *Guardian*, November 8, 2010.

'The truth about torture', *Guardian*, July 8, 2009.

Tom Coghlan, 'Afghans accuse Defence Secretary Liam Fox of racism and disrespect', *The Times*, May 24, 2010.

Steve Coll, 'Time bomb, the death of Benazir Bhutto and the unravelling of Pakistan, *New Yorker*, January 28, 2008.

Jean-Marie Colombani, 'Nous sommes tous Américains', *Le Monde*, September 13, 2001.

Pamela Constable, 'Annan appeals to Taliban to spare Buddha statues', *Washington Post*, March 12, 2001.

Gordon Corera, 'UK "backs Taliban reintegration"', BBC News, November 13, 2009.

Christophe Cornevin, 'Des troubles nés de l'exclusion, selon les RG', *Le Figaro*, December 8, 2005.

Holland Cotter, 'Buddhas of Bamiyan, keys to Asian history', *New York Times*, March 3, 2001.

Paul Cruickshank, 'New information emerges on post-9/11 hunt for bin Laden', CNN, September 13, 2010.

Bruce Crumley, 'Europe pieces together terrorism puzzle', *Time*, May 12, 2009.

Alan Cullison and Andrew Higgins, 'Computer in Kabul holds chilling memos', *Wall Street Journal*, December 31, 2001.

Abigail Cutler, 'Web of terror', *Atlantic*, June 5, 2006.

*Daily Mail*, 'Torture by British soldiers in Iraq was not carried out by "few bad apples . . . there was something rotten in the whole barrel"', September 21, 2009.

William Dalrymple, 'On the long road to freedom, finally', *Tehelka Magazine*, March 8, 2008.

Justin Davenport, 'Muslim chef sues "insensitive" Met over pork sausages', *Evening Standard*, May 11, 2009.

Aaron C. Davis, 'Sadr foments resistance by Iraqis', *New York Times*, January 9, 2011.

Mark Danner, 'Abu Ghraib, the hidden story', *New York Review of Books*, October 7, 2004.

'US Torture, voices from the black sites', *New York Review of Books*, April 9, 2009.

Guillaume Dasquié, 'Le rapport Karachi divise les deputés', *Libération*, May 13, 2010.

Babak Dehghanpisheh and Larry Kaplow, 'Baghdad's new owners', *Newsweek*, September 10, 2007.

Mathieu Delahousse, 'Karachi, la mission parlementaire sur la piste des commissions', *Le Figaro*, May 13, 2010.

Vikram Dodd and Alexandra Topping, 'Roshonara Choudhry jailed for life over MP attack', *Guardian*, November 3, 2010.

Michael Duffy, 'The surge at year one', *Time*, January 31, 2008.

Gilbert Dupont, 'Les six du réseau kamikaze', *La Dernière Heure*, December 13, 2008.

*Economic Times*, 'Global war on terror claims 30,000 Pakistani casualties', February 19, 2010.

*The Economist*, 'Briefing, Afghanistan, more than a one man problem', June 26, 2010.

    'Building a New Libya', February 26, 2011.

    'The dark pursuit of truth', August 1, 2009.

    'Into the heartland', June 5, 2010.

    'Peace in our time, maybe', August 9, 2008.

    'Reform in Saudi Arabia, at a Snail's Pace', October 2, 2010.

    'Saving faith, Islam seems to be fading as a revolutionary force', Special Report on Egypt, July 17, 2010.

    'Tales from Eurabia', June 22, 2006.

Bernard Edinger, 'Tense ties in France', *Jerusalem Report*, March 2, 2009.

Carol Eisenberg, 'On religion, faith and rituals', *Newsday*, December 22, 2001.

Andrea Elliott, 'The Jihadist next door', *New York Times*, June 22, 2010.

Matthew Engel, 'First British casualties as four SAS men shot', *Guardian*, November 27, 2001.

Richard Esposito and Pierre Thomas, 'Terror attacks against U.S. at all-time high', *ABC News*, May 26, 2010.

Michael Evans, 'Gated communities will add to Baghdad security', *The Times*, February 10, 2007.

Michael Evans and Alexi Mostrous, 'Three royal marines killed in Afghanistan by boy with wheelbarrow bomb', *The Times*, December 13, 2008.

James Fallows, 'Blind into Baghdad', *Atlantic*, January–February 2004.

Farnaz Fassihi, 'Charting the capture of Saddam', *Wall Street Journal*, December 23, 2003.

Niall Ferguson, 'Eurabia?', *New York Times*, April 4, 2004.

*Le Figaro*, 'Les djihadistes de banlieue s'apprêtaient à partir en Irak', September 20, 2005.

Dexter Filkins, 'Afghan civilian deaths rose 40 percent in 2008', *New York Times*, February 17, 2009.

    'Right at the edge', *New York Times*, September 5, 2008.

Jonathan Finer, 'Among insurgents in Iraq, few foreigners are found', *Washington Post*, November 17, 2005.

Jonathan Finer and Bassam Sebti, 'Sectarian violence kills over 100 in Iraq, Shiite–Sunni anger flares following bombing of shrine', *Washington Post*, February 24, 2006.

Ian Fisher and Edward Wong, 'Iraq's rebellion develops signs of internal rift', *New York Times*, July 10, 2004.

Martin Fletcher, 'Al-Qaeda leaders admit, "We are in crisis. There is panic and fear"', *The Times*, February 11, 2008.

*Foreign Policy*, 'How Osama bin Laden escaped', December 11, 2009.

Douglas Frantz, 'Pakistan ended aid to Taliban only hesitantly', *New York Times*, December 8, 2001.

Thomas Friedman, 'The things we do for oil', *International Herald Tribune*, February 23, 2011.

Cécilia Gabizon, 'À Vénissieux, terre d'expansion de la burqa', *Le Figaro*, July 1, 2009.

'La carte des émeutes de Novembre 2005 confirme la profonde malaise des immigrants africains', *Le Figaro*, October 15, 2007.

'Les contrastes de l'intégration à la Française', *Le Figaro*, October 15, 2009.

'Le ramadan séduit de plus en plus les jeunes', *Le Figaro*, August 21, 2009.

Carlotta Gall, 'Pakistan faces a divide of age on Muslim law', *New York Times*, January 11, 2011.

Bobby Ghosh, 'The fleeting success of the surge', *Time*, December 13, 2007.

'Rage, rap, and revolution', *Time*, February 28, 2011.

Susan B. Glasser, 'The battle of Tora Bora, secrets, money, mistrust', *Washington Post*, February 10, 2002.

Jeffrey Goldberg, 'The great terror', *New Yorker*, March 25, 2002.

Bradley Graham and Josh White, 'Abizaid credited with popularizing the term "Long War"', *Washington Post*, February 3, 2006.

Dave Graham, 'No Taliban "unconditional surrender" sought-Britain', Reuters, February 6, 2010.

Stephen Grey, 'United States, trade in torture', *Le Monde Diplomatique*, April 2005.

Tom Gross, 'The BBC's Augean stables', *National Review*, February 28, 2005.

*Guardian*, 'Full text of Colin Powell's speech', February 5, 2003.

'US embassy cables: Despite massive US aid, anti-Americanism rampant in Pakistan', November 30, 2010.

'US embassy cables: Relationship with Pakistan based on 'mutual distrust', says US', December 1, 2010.

'US embassy cables: "Reviewing our Afghanistan-Pakistan strategy"', November 30, 2010.

'West put "amateurs" in charge of Iraq occupation, inquiry told', December 9, 2009.

Guardian Online, 'Tributes to those who died in July 7 2005 attack on London'.

Mohammed Hanif, 'The power of the pulpit', *Newsline*, January 31, 2009.

James Hanning, 'Deal with Shia prisoner left Basra at mercy of gangs, colonel admits', *Independent on Sunday*, August 3, 2008.

Paul Harris, Martin Bright and Burhan Wazir, 'Five Britons killed in "Jihad Brigade"', *Observer*, October 28, 2001.

Nelson Hernandez and Saad Sarhan, 'Insurgents kill 140 as Iraq clashes escalate', *Washington Post*, January 6, 2010.

Seymour M. Hersh, 'The getaway. Questions surround a secret Pakistani airlift', *New Yorker*, January 28, 2002.

Joost Hilterman, 'Iraq on the edge', *New York Review of Books*, November 19, 2009.

Dilawar Hussain, 'High per capita income not a sign of prosperity', *Dawn*, May 10, 2009.

Zahid Hussain, 'General on a Mission', *Newsline*, July 2001.

Mohammed Hussein, 'Back from Syria', *New York Times*, May 5, 2008.

Michael Isikoff, 'How profile of bin Laden courier led CIA to its target', NBC News, May 5, 2011.

Mike Isikoff and Evan Thomas, 'The lawyer and the caterpillar', *Newsweek*, April 18, 2009.

Hala Jaber, 'Ryanair gunman, I was not going to crash plane', *Sunday Times*, October 13, 2002.

Muzamil Jaleel, 'Alarm bells: stone-pelters join militant ranks', *Indian Express*, November 25, 2010.

Simon Jeffrey, 'The Moscow theatre siege', *Guardian*, October 28, 2002.

Douglas Jehl and Andrea Elliott, 'Cuba base sent its interrogators to Iraqi prison', *New York Times*, May 29, 2004.

*Jerusalem Post*, 'Al-Khalayleh tribe disowns al-Zarqawi', November 20, 2005.

Jerusalem Post Online, 'The 4,000 Jews rumor, hundreds of Israelis missing in WTC attack', September 12, 2001.

Glen Johnson, 'Bush fails quiz on foreign affairs', Associated Press, November 4, 1999.

Efraim Karsh, 'Muslims won't play together', *New York Times*, February 28, 2010.

Hussain Kashif, 'PA passes resolution condemning Taseer's assassination', *Daily Times*, January 11, 2011.

Eric Kaufmann, 'Europe's return to the faith', *Prospect*, March 2010.

Richard Kerbaj, 'Government moves to isolate Muslim Council of Britain with cash for mosques', *The Times*, March 30, 2009.

Glenn Kessler, 'Hussein pointed to Iranian threat', *Washington Post*, July 2, 2009.

Roula Khalaf, 'Forgotten flowering', *Financial Times*, December 11, 2008.

Riaz Khan, 'Militants seize convoy for US-led forces', Associated Press, November 11, 2008.

Sher Baz Khan, 'Pakistan most urban country in South Asia', *Daily Dawn*, October 11, 2004.

Erik Kirschbaum, 'German suspects had deadline for attacks', Reuters, September 8, 2007.

Sam Knight and agencies, 'Bombing of Shia shrine sparks wave of retaliation', *The Times*, February 22, 2006.

Charles Krauthammer, 'What the uprising generation wants', *Time*, November 13, 2005.

William Kristol, 'The Long War, the radical Islamists are on the offensive. Will we defeat them?', *Weekly Standard*, vol. 11, no. 24, June 3, 2006.

Anton La Guardia, 'Zarqawi rails against Shia "snakes"', *Daily Telegraph*, June 3, 2006.

Rama Lakshmi, 'Gunmen with explosives attack Indian parliament', *Washington Post*, December 14, 2001.

Jonathan S. Landay, 'Abusive tactics used to seek Iraq-al Qaida link', McClatchy Newspapers, April 21, 2009.

Jonathan S. Landay and Tish Wells, 'Iraqi global misinformation campaign was used to build case for war', Knight Ridder, March 16, 2004.

Sandra Laville and Dipazier Aslam, 'Mentor to the young and vulnerable', *Guardian*, July 14, 2005.

Ben Leapman, '4,000 in UK trained at terror camps', *Sunday Telegraph*, April 19, 2008.

Matthew Lee, '"Jihadist" booted from government lexicon', Associated Press, April 24, 2008.

David Leigh, 'Iraq war logs reveal 15,000 previously unlisted civilian deaths', *Guardian*, October 22, 2010.

Bernard Lewis, '"What went wrong?", Western impact and Middle Eastern response', *Atlantic*, January 2002.

Paul Lewis, '"Christmas terror plot" suspects are remanded in custody', *Guardian*, December 27, 2010.

Ken Livingstone, 'Text of statement by Mayor Ken Livingstone', *Financial Times*, July 7, 2005.

Clare Lockhart, 'Learning from experience', *Slate*, November 5, 2008.

Vernon Loeb, 'Clan, family ties called key to army's capture of Hussein', *Washington Post*, December 16, 2003.

Joseph Logan, 'Palestinians celebrate attacks with gunfire', Reuters, September 12, 2001.

Djamel Loiseau, 'Itinéraire d'un soldat d'Allah', *France*, April 13, 2007.

Anthony Loyd, 'Corruption, bribes and trafficking, a cancer that is engulfing Afghanistan', *The Times*, November 24, 2007.

Steve Luxenberg, 'Bob Woodward book details Obama battles with advisers over exit plan for Afghan war', *Washington Post*, September 22, 2010.

Rory McCarthy, 'Collateral damage or civilian massacre in Haditha?', *Time*, March 19, 2006.

'For faith and country, insurgents fight on', *Guardian*, December 16, 2004.

'The inside story of the hunt for Bin Laden', *Guardian*, August 23, 2003.

Tim McGirk, 'Collateral damage or civilian massacre in Haditha?', *Time*, March 19, 2006.

'A rebel crack-up?', *Time*, January 22, 2006.

Chris McGreal, 'The Nevada gambler, al-Qaida, the CIA and the mother of all cons', *Guardian*, December 23, 2009.

Andy McNab, 'SAS hero Andy McNab describes regiment's al Qaeda battle', *Daily Mirror*, February 16, 2002.

William Maclean, 'Al Qaeda ideologue in Syrian detention – lawyers', Reuters, June 10, 2009.

Karen McVeigh and Alexandra Topping, '7/7 inquest witness saw bombers "celebrate like sports team" before attack', *Guardian*, October 13, 2010.

Christian Makarian, 'Noirs desseins', *L'Express*, February 9, 2006.

Andrew Malone, 'Tavistock Square, "I watched as the anxious man on the bus kept going into his bag"', *Independent*, July 8, 2005.

Kenan Malik, 'The Islamophobia myth', *Prospect*, February 2005.

Shiv Malik, 'My brother the bomber', *Prospect*, June 30, 2007.

'Omar Khan Sharif, profile', *New Statesman* , April 24, 2006.

Mark Mazzetti, 'Signs that bin Laden weighed seeking seeking Pakistani protection', *New York Times*, May 26, 2011.

Mark Mazzetti, Helene Cooper and Peter Baker, 'Clues gradually led to the location of Qaeda chief', *New York Times*, May 2, 2011.

Mark Mazzetti and Erik Schmitt, 'Pakistanis aided attack in Kabul, U.S. officials say', *New York Times*, August 1, 2008.

Mark Mazzetti and Scott Shane, 'Interrogation memos detail harsh tactics by the C.I.A.', *New York Times*, April 21, 2009.

Michael Meacher, 'This war on terrorism is bogus', *Guardian*, September 6, 2003.

Jim Michaels, 'Foreign fighters leaving Iraq, military says', *USA Today*, March 21, 2008.

David Miliband, 'Stay with Obama on Muslims', *International Herald Tribune*, November 6, 2010.

Greg Miller, 'Increased U.S. drone strikes in Pakistan killing few high-ranking militants', *Washington Post*, February 20, 2011.

Judith Miller, 'An Iraqi defector tells of work on at least 20 hidden weapons sites', *New York Times*, December 20, 2001.

Amir Mir, 'Faith that kills', *Newsline*, October 1998.

Anshuman Mondal, 'British Islam after Rushdie', *Prospect*, April 26, 2009.

Ron Moreau and Sami Yousafzai, 'In the footsteps of Zarqawi', *Newsweek*, July 3, 2006.

'Turning the Taliban', *Newsweek*, February 22, 2010.

Ron Moreau, Sami Yousafzai and Michael Hirsh, 'The rise of Jihadistan', *Newsweek*, October 2, 2006.

MSNBC, 'Al-Qaeda message on Egypt, belatedly', February 18, 2011.

Owais Mughal, 'Peshawar–Islamabad motorway M1 is now open for traffic', Pakistaniat.com, November 11, 2007.

Nidal al-Mughrabi, 'Pro-Qaeda group declares "Islamic emirate" in Gaza', *Reuters*, August 14, 2009.

Dan Murphy, 'Egypt revolution unfinished, Qaradawi tells Tahrir masses', *Christian Science Monitor*, February 18, 2011.

Zar Nageen, 'Naming a baby in Pakistan', *Daily Times*, July 9, 2007.

Sean D. Naylor, '"Paying the price" for pulling out, commanders see a tough fight to retake Fallujah," *Army Times*, October 4, 2004.

Melanie Newman, 'Greenwich and Leeds Met given "limited confidence" ratings by QAA', *The Times Higher Education Supplement*, October 15, 2009.

*Newsweek*, 'The most dangerous nation in the world isn't Iraq. It's Pakistan', October 29, 2007.

*New York Times*, 'Names of the dead', October 8, 2010.

'Reaction from around the world', September 12, 2001.

Asra Nomani and Barbara Feinman Todd, 'Land of the Scot-free', *Newsweek*, February 7, 2011.

Richard Norton-Taylor and Riazat Butt, 'Queen is Target for al-Qaida, security sources confirm', *Guardian*, November 14, 2005.

Richard Norton-Taylor and Jamie Wilson, 'US army in Iraq institutionally racist, claims British officer', *Guardian*, January 12, 2006.

George Packer, 'Dreaming of democracy', *New York Times*, March 2, 2003.

'The last mission', *New Yorker*, September 28, 2009.

'War after the war', *New Yorker*, November 24, 2003.

Jeremy Page, 'Children and MPs killed in worst Afghan suicide bomb', *The Times*, November 7, 2007.

*El Pais*, 'Entrevista con la Esposa de Jamal Ahmidan, El Chino, Jefe Operativo del "Commando" del 11-M', March 8, 2006.

Amit R. Paley, 'Al-Qaeda in Iraq leader may be in Afghanistan', *Washington Post*, July 31, 2008.

David Pallister, 'Three jailed for engaging in "cyber jihad" for al-Qaida', *Guardian*, July 6, 2007.

'Three plead guilty to inciting murder on Islamist websites', *Guardian*, July 5, 2007.

Tariq Panja and Martin Bright, 'Man Utd bomb plot probe ends in farce', *Observer*, May 2, 2004.

Eric Pelletier and Jean-Marie Pontaut, 'Islamisme, des étudiants sous surveillance', *L'Express*, November 9, 2006.

Manuel Perez-Rivas, 'Bush vows to rid the world of "evil-doers"', CNN, September 16, 2001.

Jane Perlez and Eric Schmitt, 'Pakistan army finds Taliban tough to root out', *New York Times*, July 5, 2010.

Jane Perlez and Pir Zubair Shah, 'The Taliban's latest tactic, class warfare', *New York Times*, April 17, 2009.

Scott Peterson, 'How Wahhabis fan Iraq insurgency', *Christian Science Monitor*, September 17, 2003.

Melanie Philips, 'Why France is burning', *Daily Mail*, November 7, 2005.

Edward T. Pound, 'The Iran connection', *US News and World Report*, November 22, 2004.

Michael Powell, 'In 9/11 chaos, Giuliani forged a lasting image', *New York Times*, September 21, 2007.

Thomas Powers, 'War and its consequences', *New York Review of Books*, March 27, 2003.

Press Trust of India, 'Two terrorists killed as Srinagar gunbattle ends', January 7, 2010.

Dana Priest, 'CIA holds terror suspects in secret prisons', *Washington Post*, November 2, 2005.

Dana Priest and Barton Gellman, 'U.S. decries abuse but defends interrogations', *Washington Post*, December 26, 2002.

Ilene R. Prusher, 'Two top al Qaeda leaders spotted', *Christian Science Monitor*, March 26, 2002.

Ahmed Rashid, 'Afghanistan, Taleban's second coming', BBC News Online, June 2, 2006.

William K. Rashbaum and Karen Zraick, 'Government says al Qaeda ordered N.Y. plot', *New York Times*, April 23, 2010.

Romesh Ratnesar, 'Face of terror, how Abu Mousab al-Zarqawi transformed the Iraq insurgency into a Holy War and became America's newest nightmare', *Time*, December 19, 2004.

Reuters, 'Bin Laden criticizes Pakistan relief, urges climate action', October 1, 2010.
'Double blast against Obama shows strain on Qaeda', June 3, 2009.
'Senior religious figures relayed the change in policy. Saudi cleric issues warning over Saudi militants', October 1, 2007.
'Suicide bomber hits foreign forces in Afghanistan', December 26, 2008.
'Taliban kill 20 police in Afghanistan', January 1, 2009.

Thomas E. Ricks, 'In Haditha killings, details came slowly', *Washington Post*, 4 June 2006.
'In Iraq, military forgot the lessons of Vietnam, early missteps by U.S. left troops unprepared for guerrilla warfare', *Washington Post*, July 26, 2003.
'Military plays up role of Zarqawi', *Washington Post*, April 11, 2006.
'U.S. military conducted a PSYOP program "to magnify the role of the leader of al-Qaeda in Iraq"', *Washington Post*, April 11, 2006.

Amanda Ripley, 'Reverse Radicalism', *Time*, March 13, 2008.

James Risen, 'U.S. to hunt down Afghan drug lords tied to Taliban', *New York Times*, August 10, 2009.

David Rohde, 'Pakistani middle class, beneficiary of Musharraf, begins to question rule', *New York Times*, November 25, 2007.

David Rose, 'How MI5 colluded in my torture: Binyam Mohamed claims British agents fed Moroccan torturers their questions', *Daily Mail*, March 8, 2009.
'Tortured reasoning', *Vanity Fair*, December 16, 2008.

Nir Rosen, 'Home rule, letter from Falluja', *New Yorker*, July 5, 2004.
'Inside the Iraqi resistance, part 1, losing it', *Asia Times*, July 15, 2004.

'Somalia's al-Shabab, a global or local movement?', *Time*, August 20, 2010.

Matthew Rosenberg, 'Corruption suspected in airlift of billions in cash from Kabul', *Wall Street Journal*, June 25, 2010.

Sebastian Rotella, 'Morocco indicts 6 more suspects in Casablanca blasts', *Los Angeles Times*, May 30, 2003.

'New details in bin Laden documents: portrait of a fugitive micro-manager', *Propublica*, May 12, 2011.

Alissa J. Rubin, 'A calmer Iraq, fragile, and possibly fleeting', *New York Times*, December 5, 2007.

Elizabeth Rubin, 'In the land of the Taliban', *New York Times*, October 22, 2006.

Donald Rumsfeld, 'A new kind of war', *New York Times*, September 27, 2001.

'Rumsfeld's war-on-terror memo', *USA Today*, October 22, 2003.

James Rupert, 'Al-Qaeda vows holy war on China over Uighurs' plight', *Bloomberg*, October 8, 2009.

Kevin Sack, 'Army reprimands soldiers for assaults', *Los Angeles Times*, January 27, 2007.

Pranab Dhal Samanta, 'GPS records, CD transcript boost India's case', *Indian Express*, July 6, 2010.

David E. Sanger, 'Ex-occupation aide sees no dent in "Saddamists"', *New York Times*, July 2, 2004.

David E. Sanger and Mark Mazzetti, 'New estimate of strength of al Qaeda is offered', *New York Times*, June 30, 2010.

Afif Sarhan, 'Hitmen charge $100 a victim as Basra honour killings rise', *Observer*, November 30, 2008.

Afif Sarhan and Jason Burke, 'How Islamist gangs use internet to track, torture and kill Iraqi gays', *Observer*, September 13, 2009.

Michael Scherer, 'The five pillars of Obama's foreign policy', *Time*, July 13, 2009.

Olivier Schmitt, 'Sécurité, en Europe, la France compète parmi les pays les plus durs', *Le Monde*, August 19, 2010.

Jennifer Schuessler, 'Gift books for millionaires', *New York Times*, December 20, 2010.

Elaine Sciolino, 'Moroccans say al Qaeda was behind Casablanca bombings', *New York Times*, May 23, 2003.

Ann Scott Tyson, 'Gates predicts "slog" in Afghanistan', *Washington Post*, January 28, 2009.

Scott Shane and Lowell Bergman, 'F.B.I. struggling to reinvent itself to fight terror', *New York Times*, October 10, 2006.

Scott Shane, '2 suspects waterboarded 266 times', *New York Times*, April 19, 2009.

Thom Shanker, 'After the war, military commander in Iraq says yearlong tours are option to combat "guerrilla" war', *New York Times*, July 17, 2003.

Adam Shatz, 'Laptop jihadi', *London Review of Books*, March 20, 2008.

Abdullah al-Shihri, 'Aide to bin Laden surrenders', *Associated Press*, July 14, 2004.

Lina Sinjab, 'Syrian Islamic revival has woman's touch', BBC News, November 28, 2009.

Michael Slackman, 'Generation faithful, Jordanian students rebel, embracing conservative Islam', *New York Times*, December 24, 2008.

'Stifled, Egypt's young turn to Islamic fervor', *New York Times*, February 17, 2008.

Graeme Smith, 'Talking to the Taliban', *Globe and Mail*, March 2008.

Philip Smucker, 'How bin Laden got away, a day-by-day account of how Osama bin Laden eluded the world's most powerful military machine', *Christian Science Monitor*, March 4, 2002.

John Solomon, 'First declassified Iraq documents released', Associated Press Online, March 16, 2006.

*Der Spiegel*, 'Geheimdienste warnen vor Islamisten-Terror in Deutschland', November 13, 2004.

Spiegel Online, '"A new crusade", bin Laden threatens Europe over Muhammad cartoons', March 20, 2008.

Jonathan Steele and Jon Boone, 'WikiLeaks, Afghan vice-president "landed in Dubai with $52m in cash"', *Guardian*, December 2, 2010.

Jeff Stein, 'It's not a trick question', *International Herald Tribune*, October 18, 2006.

Paul Steinhauser, 'Poll, support for Afghan war at all-time low', CNN, September 15, 2009.

Angela Stephens, 'Publics in Western countries disapprove of Muhammad cartoons but right to publish widely defended', www.worldpublicopinion.org, February 16, 2006.

Mark Steyn, 'Wake up, Europe, you've a war on your hands', *Chicago Sun Times*, November 6, 2005.

Praveen Swami, 'Terrorist's name lost in transliteration', *The Hindu*, December 6, 2008.

Sam Tannenhaus, 'Interview with Paul Wolfowitz', *Vanity Fair*, May 9, 2003. Transcript at http,//www.defense.gov/transcripts/transcript.aspx?transcriptid=2594.

Aatish Taseer, 'The killer of my father, Salman Taseer, was showered with rose petals by fanatics. How could they do this?' *Daily Telegraph*, January 11, 2011.

Sabrina Tavernise, 'A Shiite militia in Baghdad sees its power wane', *New York Times*, July 27, 2008.

Atmane Tazaghart and Roland Jacquard, 'La France en ligne de mire', *Le Figaro*, November 5, 2005.

*Time*, 'Lost chance', August 12, 2002.

*The Times*, 'We are firm on road of jihad', September 25, 2001,

The Times Online, 'Extracts from the Zawahiri tape Al'Zawahiri', August 4, 2005.

Patricia Tourancheau, 'La "menace majeure" gagne du terrain', *Libération*, July 9, 2005.

Mark Townsend, 'Rise in anti-Semitic attacks "the worst recorded in Britain in decades"', *Observer*, February 8, 2010.

Alan Travis, 'Britain downgrades al-Qaida terror attack alert level', *Guardian*, July 20, 2009.

    'Two-thirds of UK terror suspects released without charge', *Guardian*, May 13, 2009.

Yaroslav Trofimov, 'U.N. maps show Afghan security worsens', *Wall Street Journal*, December 26, 2010.

William Underhill, 'Why fears of a Muslim takeover are all wrong', *Newsweek*, July 10, 2009.

Conal Urquhart, 'Failed bomb attacker confesses live on air', *Guardian*, November 14, 2005.

*USA Today*, 'Poll, more view Afghan war as "mistake"', March 16, 2009.

David Usborne, 'Bin Laden goes green to exploit Pakistan flood aid frustration', *Independent*, October 2, 2010.

Karl Vick, 'Al-Qaeda's hand in Istanbul plot', *Washington Post*, February 13, 2007.

    'Insurgent alliance fraying in Fallujah', *Washington Post*, October 13, 2004.

VOA (Voice of America) News, 'Poll shows Iraqis wary about Western-style democracy', December 11, 2003.

Paul von Zielbauer, 'US inquiry hampered by Iraq violence, investigators say', *New York Times*, June 13, 2007.

VSD (France), 'Le Chef de l'antiterrorisme craint "une lame de fond"', December 28, 2005.

Declan Walsh, 'Pakistan sheltering Taliban, says British officer', *Guardian*, May 19, 2006.

    'Taliban rises again', *Guardian*, May 27, 2006.

    'The village that stood up to the Taliban', *Guardian*, February 5, 2010.

    'WikiLeaks cables, US special forces working inside Pakistan', *Guardian*, November 30, 2010.

Joby Warrick and Robin Wright, 'U.S. teams weaken insurgency in Iraq', *Washington Post*, September 6, 2008.

Washington Post Online, Faces of the Fallen Project.

Emily Wax, 'In times of terror, teens talk the talk', *Washington Post*, March 20, 2002.

Brian Whitaker, 'Muslim peoples doubt role of Arabs in September 11', *Guardian*, February 28, 2002.

Chris Wilson, 'Searching for Saddam', *Slate*, February 22, 2010.

Edward Wong, 'Iraqi led bombing of Shiite sites, official says', *New York Times*, June 28, 2006.

Nicholas Wood, 'Macedonian officials suspected of faking terror plot', *New York Times*, 15 May 2004.

Bob Woodward, 'CIA led way with cash handouts', *Washington Post*, November 18, 2002.

'Doubts and debates before victory over the Taliban', *Washington Post*, November 18, 2002.

'The inside story of the CIA's proxy war', *Australian Age*, November 20, 2002.

Robert F. Worth, 'Blast at Shiite shrine sets off sectarian fury in Iraq', *New York Times*, February 23, 2006.

Lawrence Wright, 'The terror web, were the Madrid bombings part of a new, far-reaching Jihad being plotted on the internet?', *New Yorker*, August 2, 2004.

Dean Yates, 'Senior Qaeda figure in Iraq a myth, U.S. military', Reuters, July 18, 2007.

Sami Yousafzai, Babak Dehghanpisheh, Rod Nordland, 'How al Qaeda slipped away', *Newsweek*, August 19, 2002.

Sami Yousafzai and Urs Gehriger, 'The new Taliban codex', signandsight.com, November 28, 2006.

Sami Yousafzai and Ron Moreau, 'Taliban gets help, inspiration from Iraq', *Newsweek*, September 26, 2005.

Rahimullah Yusufzai, 'Hidden hand', *Newsline*, February 9, 2008.

Mushtaq Yusufzai and Hasbanullah Khan, 'Salarzai Lashkar kills militant in Bajaur to avenge elders killings', *The News*, August 27, 2008.

Ayman al-Zawahiri, 'Nine years after the start of the crusader campaign', *As Sahab*, September 15, 2010. English translation, available at: http://world analysis.net/modules/news/article.php?storyid=1476.

Kate Zernike, 'Cited as symbol of Abu Ghraib, man admits he is not in photo', *New York Times*, March 18, 2006.

John Zogby, 'How the poll results on Iraq were manipulated', *Arab News*, October 23, 2003.

# *Index*

In Arabic names the definite article (al-), used as a prefix, is ignored in the ordering of entries.

ALLEN LANE
*an imprint of*
PENGUIN BOOKS

## Recently Published

Callum Roberts, *Ocean of Life*

Orlando Figes, *Just Send Me Word: A True Story of Love and Survival in the Gulag*

Leonard Mlodinow, *Subliminal: The Revolution of the New Unconscious and What it Teaches Us about Ourselves*

John Romer, *A History of Ancient Egypt: From the First Farmers to the Great Pyramid*

Ruchir Sharma, *Breakout Nations: In Search of the Next Economic Miracle*

Michael J. Sandel, *What Money Can't Buy: The Moral Limits of Markets*

Dominic Sandbrook, *Seasons in the Sun: The Battle for Britain, 1974-1979*

Tariq Ramadan, *The Arab Awakening: Islam and the New Middle East*

Jonathan Haidt, *The Righteous Mind: Why Good People are Divided by Politics and Religion*

Ahmed Rashid, *Pakistan on the Brink: The Future of Pakistan, Afghanistan and the West*

Tim Weiner, *Enemies: A History of the FBI*

Mark Pagel, *Wired for Culture: The Natural History of Human Cooperation*

George Dyson, *Turing's Cathedral: The Origins of the Digital Universe*

Cullen Murphy, *God's Jury: The Inquisition and the Making of the Modern World*

Richard Sennett, *Together: The Rituals, Pleasures and Politics of Co-operation*

Faramerz Dabhoiwala, *The Origins of Sex: A History of the First Sexual Revolution*

Roy F. Baumeister and John Tierney, *Willpower: Rediscovering Our Greatest Strength*

Jesse J. Prinz, *Beyond Human Nature: How Culture and Experience Shape Our Lives*

Robert Holland, *Blue-Water Empire: The British in the Mediterranean since 1800*

Jodi Kantor, *The Obamas: A Mission, A Marriage*

Philip Coggan, *Paper Promises: Money, Debt and the New World Order*

Charles Nicholl, *Traces Remain: Essays and Explorations*

Daniel Kahneman, *Thinking, Fast and Slow*

Hunter S. Thompson, *Fear and Loathing at Rolling Stone: The Essential Writing of Hunter S. Thompson*

Duncan Campbell-Smith, *Masters of the Post: The Authorized History of the Royal Mail*

Colin McEvedy, *Cities of the Classical World: An Atlas and Gazetteer of 120 Centres of Ancient Civilization*

Heike B. Görtemaker, *Eva Braun: Life with Hitler*

Brian Cox and Jeff Forshaw, *The Quantum Universe: Everything that Can Happen Does Happen*

Nathan D. Wolfe, *The Viral Storm: The Dawn of a New Pandemic Age*

Norman Davies, *Vanished Kingdoms: The History of Half-Forgotten Europe*

Michael Lewis, *Boomerang: The Meltdown Tour*

Steven Pinker, *The Better Angels of Our Nature: The Decline of Violence in History and Its Causes*

Robert Trivers, *Deceit and Self-Deception: Fooling Yourself the Better to Fool Others*

Thomas Penn, *Winter King: The Dawn of Tudor England*

Daniel Yergin, *The Quest: Energy, Security and the Remaking of the Modern World*

Michael Moore, *Here Comes Trouble: Stories from My Life*

Ali Soufan, *The Black Banners: Inside the Hunt for Al Qaeda*

Jason Burke, *The 9/11 Wars*

Timothy D. Wilson, *Redirect: The Surprising New Science of Psychological Change*

Ian Kershaw, *The End: Hitler's Germany, 1944-45*

T M Devine, *To the Ends of the Earth: Scotland's Global Diaspora, 1750-2010*

Catherine Hakim, *Honey Money: The Power of Erotic Capital*

Douglas Edwards, *I'm Feeling Lucky: The Confessions of Google Employee Number 59*

John Bradshaw, *In Defence of Dogs*

Chris Stringer, *The Origin of Our Species*

Lila Azam Zanganeh, *The Enchanter: Nabokov and Happiness*

David Stevenson, *With Our Backs to the Wall: Victory and Defeat in 1918*

Evelyn Juers, *House of Exile: War, Love and Literature, from Berlin to Los Angeles*

Henry Kissinger, *On China*

Michio Kaku, *Physics of the Future: How Science Will Shape Human Destiny and Our Daily Lives by the Year 2100*

David Abulafia, *The Great Sea: A Human History of the Mediterranean*

John Gribbin, *The Reason Why: The Miracle of Life on Earth*

Anatol Lieven, *Pakistan: A Hard Country*

William Cohen, *Money and Power: How Goldman Sachs Came to Rule the World*

Joshua Foer, *Moonwalking with Einstein: The Art and Science of Remembering Everything*

Simon Baron-Cohen, *Zero Degrees of Empathy: A New Theory of Human Cruelty*

Manning Marable, *Malcolm X: A Life of Reinvention*

David Deutsch, *The Beginning of Infinity: Explanations that Transform the World*

David Edgerton, *Britain's War Machine: Weapons, Resources and Experts in the Second World War*